Nora Pleßke
The Intelligible Met

Lettre

Nora Pleßke (Dr. phil.) teaches English studies at the University of Passau. Her research interests include London literature, material culture, mentality, spatial and postcolonial theory.

Nora Pleßke

The Intelligible Metropolis

Urban Mentality in Contemporary London Novels

[transcript]

Also doctoral thesis University of Passau 2012.

Bibliographic information published by the Deutsche Nationalbibliothek
The Deutsche Nationalbibliothek lists this publication in the Deutsche Nationalbibliografie; detailed bibliographic data are available in the Internet at http://dnb.d-nb.de

Cover concept: Kordula Röckenhaus, Bielefeld
Cover illustration: cw-design / photocase.com
Proofread & typeset: Nora Pleßke
Print: Majuskel Medienproduktion GmbH, Wetzlar
Print-ISBN 978-3-8376-2672-8
PDF-ISBN 978-3-8394-2672-2

This London City, with all its houses, palaces, steam-engines, cathedrals, and huge immeasurable traffic and tumult, what is it but a Thought, but millions of Thoughts made into One;—a huge immeasurable Spirit of a THOUGHT, embodied in brick, in iron, smoke, dust, Palaces, Parliaments, Hackney Coaches, Katherine Docks, and the rest of it! Not a brick was made but some man had to *think* of the making of that brick.

Thomas Carlyle, "The Hero as a Man of Letters"

Contents

1 Introduction

1.1 SETTING THE THEME: INTELLIGIBILITY AND LEGIBILITY

An array of British writers have commented on the illimitable, inexhaustible, multifarious, ineffable character of London and thereby emphasised the uneasy impression that the metropolis[1] is unintelligible and illegible, which ultimately leads to the disorientation of the urbanite or the loss of the Self. Initially, the quest for urban intelligibility and legibility is born of the desire to make sense of the urban experience, to re-establish spaces of everyday life and regenerate identity. Early discourses on knowing London, a space seemingly defying any logic and described by Charles Dickens as an "unintelligible mess" (1998: 237), were hence either preoccupied with gathering "intelligence" (Sicher 2003: 5, 43) on the actual living conditions of urbanites or stressed intellectualisation as a dominant response to the city. However, far more than intellectual conception, sensual perception makes it possible to establish orientation in the urban realm and constitutes a vital force in the construction of identity. In this respect, reading becomes a metaphor for perception as a process which orders and stabilises urban experience in a meaningful way.

Legibility of urban space has been an ongoing concern in Urban Studies (e.g. cf. Lynch 1977: 9; Sharpe & Wallock 1987: 16-17; Balshaw & Kennedy 2000: 1; Amin & Thrift 2002: 7; Sieverts 2003: 52). The legibility of the encoded cityscape stresses how images condition urbanites' responses to the city and play an important part in shaping their understanding of the metropolis. Therefore, New Urban Geographers, in regard to the semiotic notion of culture in which the text functions as a *pars pro toto* for all cultural representation, consider the sign system of the city as text which can be decoded and read (e.g. cf. Duncan 1990; King 1996). The legible metropolis thus denotes the way Londoners perceive and give meaning to their city. What is more, however, the notion that the perceived city must be interpreted emphasises that "[l]ike a literary text [it] has as many interpretations as it has readers" (Sharpe & Wallock 1987: 17). In this sense,

1 | In the following the terms metropolis, city, and the urban will be used almost interchangeably.

the city becomes inseparable from its representations. Hence, the urban must be seen as "'*trans-discursive*'" (Shields 1996: 234) in the sense of being produced and producing its own texture of representations – material, social and mental forms and practices. Because of London's illimitable dimensions, the metropolis must also be imagined.

Aesthetic literature on the metropolis provides selective representations of the city: it creates metaphors to encompass its vast nature, maps narratives that describe urban experience, offers myths that help to locate the Self, and consequently re-imagines collective urban identities. Fiction shapes our understanding of the city while simultaneously generating an idiosyncratic knowledge on the urban. Because literature offers a most fundamental tool for making us understand the world, Sebastian Groes (2011: 16) emphasises the need for the city novel as writers become "interpreters and translators of the various, often conflicting discourses the city offers [...]." It is thus not the vastness of megapolitan structures alone that renders the urban illegible and ultimately unintelligible, but as Sharpe & Wallock (1987: 27) stress, if "the city recedes in contemporary urban fiction, its deracinated inhabitants lose their ability to interpret themselves or the world around them." The London novel makes the metropolis intelligible, legible, imaginable, and ultimately also "inimitable" (Wolfreys 2004: 236).

Often, Charles Dickens is cited as **the** novelist of London, not only because most of London fiction is indebted to the author, but because he invented our conception of London by providing a "controlling language through which the city can be read" (Balshaw & Kennedy 2000: 12). In his effort to write faithful to the condition of London, Dickens' descriptions of the city, for example in *Bleak House* (1853), not only chart the physical cityscape and encompass the chance encounters of its social relations, but expose London's mental framework – the forms of thought, world views, memories, psychologies, emotions, etc. Consequently, the city is inseparable from its representations because they resonate with processes between the material and mental spaces of the metropolis as well as depict urban nonconscious structures of thinking (cf. Sharpe & Wallock 1987: 6; Balshaw & Kennedy 2000: 3, 6). In "Cities of Mind, Urban Words" Ihab Hassan (1981: 95) characterises the metropolis and its fictions as an "inscape of mind". Correspondingly, Jerry White (2003: 1) argues:

> London has been peopled as much in the mind as in its streets. No city has been written about more. Nowhere else have novelists more frequently chosen to plot narratives, set characters and explore circumstances. [...]. Perhaps, indeed, London and Londoners can be most truly realized in fiction.

This vital dialectic relation between urban literary and city life is further commented on by Jaye and Watts (1981a: ix): "The literature of the city yields experiences that become integral parts of our lives through time; we seek to revisit, discover, locate, avoid, or create those imaginative impressions and journeys anew." Through reading, an image of the city moulds itself onto the mind of its inhabitants. Thereby the metropolis constitutes an internalised landscape equipped with a certain metropolitan sensibility – a particular frame of mind.

Due to the cultural contrast between city and country as two "fundamental ways of life" (Ray. Williams 1985: 1), the metropolis has not only generated a new ontological model opposed to the country, but has also developed generic cultural practices and specific forms of thinking. Moreover, the "axioms of the metropolitan mind" (Mumford 1997: 258) as a particular "mode of feeling, thinking, acting" (*ibid.*: 263) – and I add 'imagining' – are particular to every single metropolis. Thus, London not only constitutes a geographical region (city) but also presents a specific way of life (urbanity) with its idiosyncratic norms, values, and mental dispositions. Due to the metropolis' particularities – be it its social, historical or topographical nature, or images of its cultural memory – Londoners can be differentiated from inhabitants of other metropolises, by local-specific mental dispositions – or London mentality.

This study on *The Intelligible Metropolis* sets out to investigate urban-generic mental dispositions and attempts to identify urban-specific structures of mentality in contemporary London fiction. It construes how the physical, social and mental urban realm is constructed and shows characteristic ways of thinking, feeling, imagining, and acting. The purpose of the study is to demonstrate that it is the tool of mentality which offers orientation in order to manoeuvre the postmodern urban realm and enables urbanites to gain a common understanding of the metropolis. For the decoding of mental structures, this exposition develops a model of transference regarding urban mentality which can also be employed in the context of contemporary metropolises worldwide. Starting from the hypothesis that London is narratively known, I analyse mental dispositions as represented in twenty London novels published during the Blair era (1997-2007). Beyond the selected corpus, this study presents a thoroughly researched bibliography of recent fiction set in London. With its focus on the regional mentality of metropolitan London, the argumentation particularly takes into account theories of space and spatial semantics against the background of the Spatial Turn and supplements methodological approaches of mentalities with a spatio-narratological analysis. Overall, the objective of *The Intelligible Metropolis* is two-fold: first, I argue that Mentality Studies of literary sources, cultural practices and beyond under the preliminaries of the Spatial Turn offer a particular fruitful approach within Cultural Studies. Second, it is my contention that the concept of mentality presents a missing link within Urban Studies which helps to enhance the understanding of postmodern urban cultures. Insofar, the present study wishes to promote the concept of mentality ("mental turn") as a new interdisciplinary and synergic paradigm of urban experience especially within Urban and Cultural Studies.

The main constituent of Cultural Studies[2] has been the assumption and analysis of cultural difference. Cultural Studies strives to reconstruct culture as a system of interdependent variables by clarifying cultural difference in habits in correspondence to socio-political, economic and cultural structures. According to Jürgen Kamm (1996: 96), Cultural Studies endeavours to acquire "*cultural meta-knowledge*", thus to perceive the lifeworld from the standpoint of the Other and consequently to unravel another society's knowledge. Insofar, Mentality and Cultural Studies are closely connected through their common "hypothesis of [...] alterity" (Bonheim 1994: 2) as they both try to make contact with otherness. Striving for an understanding of the foreign mental world of different people, mentality and cultural studies either concentrate on the different attitudes and values of social collectives or historical epochs and/or geographical regions. Second, one of the main objectives of Cultural and Mentality Studies alike is to reconstruct the

2 | Cultural Studies is understood with Raymond Williams (1984: 63) as a "study of relationships between elements in a whole way of life".

mental dimension of a culture. These significant "standardisations of thinking" (Hansen 2003: 88) are commonly known by the term mentality (cf. Kamm 1994: 37; Kamm 1996: 96; Kamm 2007: 37).

Etymologically, 'mentality' derives from the Latin term *mens* meaning mind, spirit, psyche (cf. *Online Etymology Dictionary*). The *New English Dictionary on Historical Principles* (Anon. 1908: 342) characterises mentality as "nature of the mind or mental action", while today it is defined as a "[m]ental character or disposition" (Anon. 1989: 612) by *The Oxford English Dictionary*, "mode of thought" (*Merriam Webster Online*) or "characteristic way of thinking" (*Oxford Dictionary Online*). The latter is also implied when mentality is used as popular colloquialism or fashionable buzzword. The *Google* hit list for mentality registers results in which way of thinking denotes specific attitudes and values (e.g. siege mentality) that can be of economic (e.g. throwaway mentality), political (e.g. liberal mentality), and social nature (e.g. herd mentality) or refer to a particular habit (e.g. contraceptive mentality). Moreover, these phenomena can be encompassed by a certain philosophy of life which is often connected to a specific space (e.g. ghetto mentality) or region (e.g. Eastern mentality). Often the term is used to identify the way of thinking or thought characteristic of a specific group of people (e.g. peasant mentality) which can be narrowed down to the perceived religious character trait (e.g. Jewish mentality) or gender marker (e.g. male mentality). In this colloquial sense, mentality is used, often pejoratively, in reference to common knowledge.

Under the assumption that every culture has its particular philosophy of life, mentality is today a widely used concept in both popular and academic works which analyse the otherness of thinking as a cultural phenomenon. Hutton (1981: 237) goes so far as to argue that mentality has developed into "a code name for what used to be called culture". This is particularly apparent in the abundance of Cultural/Mentality Studies which concern questions of national character and constructions of national identity.[3] Here the term mentality points towards a national stereotype or collective ('flat') character such as under assessment by cultural xenology (cf. Vester 1996: 11, 113). Bernd Lenz (2002: 52) argues that "[t]he analysis of mentalities should [...] focus on discursive structures, social and cultural aspects, processes of identity formation, auto- and heterostereotypes." In his article he explicates that "Britain's mentality has been moulded [...] by insular experience" (*ibid.*: 51) and that the consequent 'insular mentality' constitutes an integral part of a British national identity. Jürgen Kamm and Gerold Sedlmayr (2007: 7) pay heed to the idea of 'insular mentalities' as a "pertinent collective way of thinking that stresses a belief in the country's strength, superiority and steadfastness".[4]

---

3 | See for example Ake Daun's exemplary study on *Swedish Mentality* (1996) or for the German mentality see Bernhard Nuss (1993), *Das Faust-Syndrom. Ein Versuch über die Mentalität des Deutschen.* Lately, the interest concerning mentality has seen a revival due to the need of understanding different cultural work ethics such is the objective of international management, cross-cultural management and intercultural communication. See for example Jürgen Beneke (1992), *Kultur, Mentalität, Nationale Identität*; Guntram Danne (1996), *Die Rolle von Mentalität und arbeitsbezogenen Wertstrukturen in Transformationsgesellschaften*; Christoph Barmeyer (2000), *Mentalitätsunterschiede und Marktchancen im Frankreichgeschäft.*

4 | Other structures of British mentality refer to traditionalism, pragmatism, freedom, and economy, but also national pride, humour, and the British Empire. For more see Wilhelm Di-

Although London is the capital of the United Kingdom, it has always been argued that the British *mater polis* is neither typically British nor typically English (cf. Kamm & Lenz 2004: 58). Due to its leading role as both national capital and global city[5], London as metropolis[6] has formed a genuine character which stands apart from the national identity traditionally located in the country.[7] This particular distance between Britain and London, according to the historian Jerry White (2008: xii), has "never been wider than at the end of the twentieth century." As the setting of significant socio-political and cultural events, the experience of urban life in London – physically, socially, and mentally – has undergone a dramatic transformation around the millennium.

1.2 'New' London (1997-2007)

Writing on London in the beginning of the 1990s most authors seem to share a pessimistic view on the metropolis' recent decline.[8] In his social history of London first published in 1994, Roy Porter (2000: 1) stresses the crisis, deterioration, and disintegration of the contemporary city and detects "a new pessimism, a new anxiety" (*ibid.*: 470). The social, economic, cultural and environmental maladies suffered by the city

---

belius (1923), *England*; Richard Weight (2002), *Patriots. National Identity in Britain 1940-2000*; Kate Fox (2004), *Watching the English. The Hidden Rules of English Behaviour*; Julian Baggini (2008), *Welcome to Everytown. A Journey into the English Mind.*

5 | Especially see Jonathan Schneer (1999), *London 1900. The Imperial Metropolis*; John Eade (2000), *Placing London. From Imperial Capital to Global City*; Saskia Sassen (1991), *The Global City. New York, London, Tokyo*. For a comparison of London's status to other metropolitan areas see Arjen van Susteren, ed. (2005), *Metropolitan World Atlas.*

6 | For London the term metropolis was first used in 1830, at a time when the city counted more than one million citizens (cf. Hertel 1997: 24). In the beginning of the twentieth century, population had grown to over eight million making London the largest metropolis in the world (cf. White 2008: xvii; Black 2009: 370). After the Second World War, Greater London's population declined gradually to around 6.8 million during the 1980s. Since the mid-1990s population figures have risen steadily again and today Greater London houses 8.3 million inhabitants (2012). In 2000 London had a similar population to 1914, but was geographically twice as large (cf. Phillips 2006: 2). While for some scholars, the urban sprawl of postmodern London presents a megalopolis (e.g. cf. Teske 1999: 27; Deny 2009: 49) this study refutes the notion of the city as dominated by an urban agglomeration with satellite cities in regard to London and consequently further employs the term metropolis, its leading role apparent in the etymological origin as the 'mother city'. For more on London's topography see for example Keith Hoggart, & David Green, eds. (1991), *London. A New Metropolitan Geography.*

7 | See for example the historian of mentalities Fernand Braudel (1958: 737) who claims: "Vivez à Londres une année, et vous connaîtrez fort mal l'Angleterre."

8 | For more see Patrick Wright (1991), *A Journey through Ruins. The Last Days of London*; Andy Thornley (1992), *The Crisis of London*; Iain Sinclair (1997), *Lights Out for the Territory*; Peter Hitchens (1999), *The Abolition of Britain. The British Cultural Revolution from Lady Chatterley to Tony Blair.*

on a colossal scale (cf. Inwood 1998: 937) and the accompanying urban structures of feeling during the 1990s, for example, finds vivid expression in Patrick Keiller's doom-laden film *London* (1994). However, only one year later the American author Bill Bryson (1995: 33) wonders why "Londoners fail to see that they live in the most wonderful city in the world" and subsequently enthuses over London's multiple attractions:

It is [...] far more beautiful and interesting than Paris and more lively than anywhere but New York – and even New York can't touch it in lots of important ways. It has more history, finer parks, a livelier and more varied press, better theatres, more numerous orchestras and museums, leafier squares, safer streets, and more courteous inhabitants than any other large city in the world. (*Ibid.*: 34)

This eulogy of London was taken up by *Newsweek* in 1996 rediscovering London as "The Coolest City in the World" (White 2008: 350). McLeod (2004b: 160) argues that "the optimistic tone of the article points to an important and predominant way of thinking about London's fortunes in the 1990s which had become prevalent by the decade's end." The earlier *fin-de-siècle* mood was replaced by a new "millennial optimism" (*ibid.*) as the decade was closing. The city seemed to have taken on a renewed self-confidence, energy and resolve. In his seminal biography of London, Peter Ackroyd (2001: 777) therefore contends: "If London were a living thing, we would say that all of its optimism and confidence have returned. It has again become 'the capital of all capitals' in every cultural and social sense. The world flocks to it and once more it has become a youthful city."

Although Britain's economic recovery following the recession of the early 1990s was already initiated in the decade before, the landslide election of Tony Blair's New Labour government[9] on 1 May 1997 in general serves as the historio-political event that particularly symbolises the threshold between pessimism and the "*New Dawn*" (Tönnies 2006: 120) of revived optimism. It not only marked the end of eighteen years of Conservative rule, but specifically terminated the debate on the great decline and created a new sense of euphoria, excitement and expectation at this change of government (cf. Kavanagh 2007: 3). Blair pushed the ideological notion of change and renewal by consciously employing media marketing strategies and rhetoric. Merle Tönnies (2006: 119) shows how

9 | Tony Blair was the longest serving Labour Prime Minster winning three general elections in a row (1997, 2001, 2005) until handing over his post to Gordon Brown in 2007. Mediating between Old Left and New Right he reconciled free market conservatism and state socialism under the new coinage of Third Way politics. For more see Tony Blair (1997), *New Britain. My Vision of a Young Country* and Tony Blair (1998), *The Third Way. New Politics for the New Century*. And although the era Blair does not feature as the cutting edge of political transformation, critics overwhelmingly agree that Blair's silent revolution changed Britain for the better: more economically competitive, more socially just, and more tolerant (cf. Kavanagh 2007: 5). For more on Blairite politics see Mark Perryman, ed. (1996), *The Blair Agenda*; Brian Brivati (2007), *The End of Decline. Blair and Brown in Power*; Anthony Seldon, ed. (2007), *Blair's Britian. 1997-2007*; Terrence Casey, ed. (2009), *The Blair Legacy. Politics, Policy, Governance, and Foreign Affairs.*

New Labour spin doctors built a "web of positive connotations" encompassing ideas and images of modernisation, development, innovation, originality and newness, for example in slogans such as "New Labour" and "New Britain" (cf. Kamm & Lenz 2006: 10-13).

In the centre of Blair's first term especially stood the re-branding of London as the showpiece of "Cool Britannia" to a 'New' and 'Sexy' London in which to enter the third millennium (cf. Wolfreys 1998: 201; Chilton 2007: 17; Black 2009: 395).[10] As one of the first initiatives a strategic authority for London, the Greater London Authority (GLA), was re-established in 1999 and one year later "Red" Ken Livingstone became its first directly elected mayor.

The most visible transformation of the metropolis was, however, the facelift of London's cityscape through architectural development, cultural reclamation and reinvention of the image of London that was to lead to the metropolis' reincarnation and make a "Spectacle of London" (Levenson 2002: 225). The millennium was marked by extensive funding by the National Lottery in order to construct London as a "pleasure nexus" (White 2008: xvii). The epitome of this development was the Millennium Dome (1999) in Greenwich, which was to host the millennial celebrations and has become a monument of world-aspiring 'Cool Britannia'. Overshadowed in its first years by miscalculations and mismanagement, the Dome reinvented itself as the O2 Arena in 2005 and has since become a major performance venue (cf. Levenson 2002: 227; Kamm & Lenz 2006: 19). Similarly, the Docklands developments, particularly that of Canary Wharf (2003), and the interconnected transportation projects such as the extension of the Jubilee Line (1999) or the Docklands Light Railway (2005, 2009) were controversial. But while White (2008: xv) criticises the Docklands' "non-London feel", the area has developed into a thriving new centre for the financial and media sector.

Most particularly, the advent of the new millennium has prompted a rush of new cultural developments along the South Bank, bringing attention to the rejuvenated riverside "so that the Thames is once again a cherished and spectacular highway through one of the great cities of the world." (J. Richardson 2001: 5) The old Bankside Power Station was converted and now houses the Tate Modern Gallery (2000). It is connected by the pedestrian Millennium Bridge (2000) to St Paul's on the opposite side of the river. Upriver is the British Airways London Eye (2000), at 135 metres the world's largest revolving passenger wheel. The newly erected City Hall (2002) is surrounded by the *More London* development reaching towards the building sites around London Bridge Borough. The Lloyd's Building (1986) now merely constitutes a forerunner of the architectural Postmodernism taking hold on the historical City from the 1990s which emphasises metropolitan identity and urban "spectatorial visibility" (Levenson 2002: 231).[11]

---

10 | It seems as if the spin doctors of New Labour had actually responded to the visions of contemporary urbanism as proposed by Sharon Zukin in her *The Cultures of Cities* first published in 1995. Therein she argues that urban street style cycled through the mass media of MTV or fashion magazines are divorced from their social context and "become images of cool" (Zukin 1997: 9), while the high visibility of stars and other members of the culture industries "underlines the 'sexy' quality of culture as a mother of economic growth." (*Ibid.*: 13)

11 | Newly built or converted institutions further include MI5's Thames House (1994) or MI6's SIS building (1994), the Eurostar International Terminal at Waterloo (1994) since moved to St Pancras (2007), Somerset House (1997), the British Library (1997), the Royal Opera House

The changing skyline of London during the Blair era and the ongoing projects suggest that the metropolis is more and more turning into a vertical city of skyscrapers.[12] The third line of development is that the manifold building projects since the early 1990s have charted a certain shift towards East London. These found partial completion with the regeneration of the area in the course of the XXX Olympics in 2012 (accepted 2005).

Levenson (2002: 231; emphasis N.P.) contends that "[a]s London tries to imagine a new millennial future, it holds to a vision of the total metropolis, the splendid, but also the **intelligible**, city – a fit site for a liveable community." With Tony Blair's decision to alter national identity, multiculturalism and race relations became a central concern in his project of rebranding Britishness. In this respect, McLeod (2004a: 230) argues that "at the beginning of a new century London was emerging from its long diasporic history with new possibilities of social and cultural transformation". Half of the current net immigration of the United Kingdom flows to London (cf. Black 2009: 370). By 2001, forty-five percent of ethnic minorities lived in London, where they made up twenty-nine per cent of all residents (cf. *National Statistics*; Cuevas 2008a: 61). It is estimated that 300 languages are spoken throughout the city which is inhabited by about thirty communities, the largest groups of which are Indian, Polish, Irish, Bangladeshi and Nigerian. Particular Brick Lane in London's East End has regained prominence as a centre of multiculturalism and "London's Curry Capital" (Black 2009: 386).[13] But the eastern neighbourhoods of Tower Hamlets (Spitalfields, Banglatown) and Hackney are also London's deprived neighbourhoods, while the City of London and Richmond upon Thames remain Britain's most affluent local authorities.

Besides London's renewed role as national, global and cosmopolitan centre, the metropolis between 1997 and 2007 was also the setting of major historical events that moved the world. The widespread public mourning for the 'People's Princess' "provide[d] an object lesson in this idea that it is in the audience watching events that shared identity is created." (Crang 1998: 166) Otherwise, the concomitant nervous break-down of a whole nation and the silence, grief and bitterness that encompassed London in days

(2000), the Great Court at the British Museum (2000). The latest buildings making an impression on the London skyline are the City Point (2000), HSBC Tower (2001), Barclays Tower (2004), and Swiss Re Tower (2004) popular known as the "gherkin" on account of its startling form. For more on London's millennial architecture see Samantha Hardingham (1996), *London. A Guide to Recent Architecture*; Ken Powell (2010), *21st-Century London. The New Architecture*.

12 | Projects that were planned since 2000, but construction only began after 2007 include Strata SE1 (The Razor and locally nicknamed as Isengard), Bishopsgate Tower (The Heron Tower, informally also referred to as the Pinnacle) and The Shard (completed in 2012). With 306 metres The Shard is currently the highest building throughout the EU.

13 | For more on London's recent developments as a nexus of international migration see for example Anthony D. King (1990), *Global Cities. Post-Imperialism and the Internationalization of London*; Susan S. Fainstein, ed. (1992), *Divided Cities. New York & London in the Contemporary World*; Jane Jacobs (1996), *Edge of Empire. Postcolonialism and the City*; Susan Okokon (1998), *Black Londoners. 1880-1990*; Mike Phillips (2001), *London Crossings. A Biography of Black Britain*; Geoff Dench, Kate Gavron & Michael Young (2006), *The New East End. Kinship, Race and Conflict*.

after Lady Di's death must be seen as part of London's structure of feeling that subcutaneously persisted under the new veneer of the city beyond the millennium, despite an overall optimism.

Significantly, as the only immediate reaction in London to the terrorist attacks on New York's World Trade Centre, the tower at the heart of Canary Wharf, One Canada Square, was evacuated. But the globalised urban terrors engendered by 9/11 had one major effect on the London public: in response to the widespread public anxiety about terrorism, the government decided to install the "Ring of Steel" – a network of closed circuit television cameras (CCTV) mounted on the eight official entry gates that control access to the City. At the latest when Britain alongside with the United States went to war in Iraq in 2003 and even 750,000 protesters in London could not change the course of history, the metropolis became number one of Europe's terror targets. On 7 July 2005 home-grown terrorists detonated a number of suicide bombs on three London Underground trains and a bus on Tavistock Square that injured 700 people and killed 56.

The incident proved a major setback for multicultural Britain and the postcolonial cosmopolis because it led to a resurgence of faithism and Islamophobia in the city where eight per cent of the population are Muslim. Also the latest student demonstrations (2010) and riots (2011) are violent signs of how the millennial optimism has not lasted (cf. McLeod 2005: 39) and the feeling of uncertainty has entered a new phase of gloom, particularly with the financial crisis (2008) and the consequent rise in unemployment and return-migration (cf. Black 2009: 406-407). In the period under analysis, London was hailed as "Manhattan-on-Thames" (*ibid.*: 395) and decried as "Reykjavik-on-Thames" (*ibid.*: 399), was seen as a most successful multicultural metropolis and described as "Londonistan" (*ibid.*: 395) after the terrorist attacks. Despite this ebbing of 'Cool Britannia', a fall in self-confidence and recurrent bleak future prospects for London, the city's latest chronicler, the historian Jeremy Black (*ibid.*: 399), ends his book on the note that London "muddles on" because "[t]he vibrancy, the life and the buzz are all still there." (*Ibid.*: 416)

Indeed, it is topical for London's history that extraordinarily destructive periods, for example the Great Plague (1665) and the Great Fire (1666) as well as the Blitz (1940-1941), have always been followed by phases of reconstruction and inventive rebirth.[14] This notion of London as being caught in a cycle of creation and decline was already captured in John Dryden's allegorical poem "Annus Mirabilis" (1667), in which he envisions London's rise like a phoenix from its ashes. This London trope has persisted until the metropolis of the third millennium. Due to London's process of self-transformation, the city, for Julian Wolfreys (2004: 21), needs to be "understood as *becoming* constantly". That the metropolis is predominantly a process of urban crisis and urban renaissance is not only to be seen in spatial and social, but particularly in mental terms (cf. Teske 1999: 37). Consequently, the concept of (urban) mentality pays heed to both mental persistancies and transformations. In this sense, we might understand the Blair era (1997-2007) as a threshold not only between two millennia but also between two world orders (that of the Cold War's closure and the rise of a new age of international terrorism), and a change

14 | The earliest history of London is John Stow (1598), *Stow's Survey of London*. For recent histories of the metropolis particularly see Inwood (1998), J. Richardson (2001), White (2008), Black (2009).

of urban realities constituting an encompassing "time-space compression" (Harvey 1990: 306).

Kamm and Lenz (2006: 16) argue that New Labour's 1997 landslide victory was possible mainly because the party was particularly able to place its political agenda of change and newness within the more general mood of cultural renewal. The numbers show that the creative industries grew constantly especially during Blair's first term in office (cf. Löw, Steets & Stoetzer 2008: 136; Black 2009: 387-388). Because representations and cultural agents were central to Blairite Britain, but also to the urban renaissance of London, this particularly opens the approach to transformations of urban mentality and its literary poetics (cf. Tönnies 2003: 8; Kamm & Lenz 2006: 15).

Metropolitan London has always had a strong hold on the literary imagination. Nevertheless, critics have argued that after the grand London novels of the Victorian era and the first thirty years of the twentieth century, the city has been marginalised in English literature, while American metropolises have stayed at the heart of its fiction (cf. Breuner: 1991 17, 195). But even though there might not have been the one great London novel, at least since the 1980s the metropolis has seen the "fetishization of [...] the London writer." (Gibson 2003: 292). Especially since the 1990s it is fair to say that English urban fiction has experienced a "London Revival" (Coverley 2005: 134). Critics suspect that the reason for this enhanced status of London-based novels and its subsequent steady increase of publications lies in the re-branding of the city in the course of the 'Cool Britannia' campaign (cf. Coverley 2005: 134; Cuevas 2008a: 12). And while literature during Thatcherism, such as Martin Amis' *Money* (1984), Margaret Drabble's *The Radiant Way* (1987), Peter Ackroyd's *Hawksmoor* (1985), Ian McEwan's *The Child in Time* (1987) or Iain Sinclair's *Downriver* (1991) presented London as a capital under strain, towards the millennium urban fiction proved remarkably optimistic (cf. McLeod 2004b: 162, 188; Black 2009: 386-387).

1.3 Selecting the Literary Corpus

The literary corpus of twenty contemporary London novels was selected under the provision of the following criteria: (1) the novels must be wholly or substantially set in London; (2) the texts must have been published between 1997-2007; (3) the temporal setting must lie in the 1990s and 2000s or the near future; (4) they should be city novels in the narrow sense, conveying a picture of urban life, atmosphere, or character; (5) this includes urban genre novels that are considered London fiction by convention; (6) the novel should thematically, stylistically, and narratologically centre on representations of urban mentality; (7) the selected corpus of twenty works should guarantee a certain heterogeneity; (8) the texts chosen should reveal recurrences of bordering practices, chronotopic construction, and metaphoricity.

(1) The novel's main setting had to be London, and for the contemporary aspect (2) I chose a publishing date of the novels between 1997 and 2007 according to the specific cultural-political period described above. My research of London novels was based on extensive search in London and Oxford bookshops, British and German library catalogues, online search at *Amazon.co.uk* and the *Fantastic Fiction* website. Without claiming to be exhaustive, the chronological list of "London Novels (1997-2007)" in the

appendix encompasses 403 titles and provides an apt picture of the production of London fiction during the decade under analysis. With an average of forty novels published every year, the output, in correspondence to London's verve around the millennium, reaches its height with fifty novels published in the year 2000 alone.[15] My choice regarding the year of publication thus excludes authors who dominated British urban fiction during the 1980s and early 1990s, particularly Iain Sinclair and Peter Ackroyd. While the former has of late rather concentrated on non-fiction writing, the latter's *The Plato Papers* (1999), *The Clerkenwell Tales* (2003) and *The Lambs of London* (2004) are exempted from the corpus under analysis, because they are not set within the timeframe stipulated by the third selection principle.

(3) In order to convey connections between London at the turn of the century and its fictional representations, the novels had to be set in the 1990s or the near future. This criterion narrowed the selection of novels down to approximately 200. Unfortunately, this also exempted a large amount of recent bestselling historical novels on the city, for example, those written by Sarah Waters and Lee Jackson. Other important London fiction published between 1997 and 2007 thereby necessarily disregarded is Alan Hollinghurst's exploration of (gay) London during Thatcherism in *The Line of Beauty* (2004) or postcolonial novels such as Andrea Levy's *Small Island* (2004) depicting other eras of the (post)imperial metropolis.

(4) However, not all fiction set in London is to be defined as London novel in the narrow sense. According to Blanche Housman Gelfant's (1954: 6) definition the difference between a city novel and a local colour novel lies in the active part which is prescribed to the city where it becomes more than a mere setting and urban life is presented as an organic whole. The city in the novel acts as a "*physical place*", an "*atmosphere*" and as a "*total way of life*" (*ibid.*: 4), hence its physical topography makes an impression upon the mind, affects emotions and the frame of mind and notably moulds characters and their destinies. Consequently, the genre of the city novel for Gelfant (*ibid.*: 1-10) has to fulfil three main criteria: (1) the main setting is the city, (2) characters and plot are defined by the city and (3) the formal elements (style, plot, tone, theme, structure) convey a particular attitude towards the city.

Furthermore, Gelfant (*ibid.*: 11) distinguishes three forms of the city novel: the "portrait", the "synoptic" and the "ecological" study. The portrait novel follows a certain

---

15 | By comparison, Michael Breuner (1991) merely charts ninety novels about London published between 1896 and 1985. A similar number per year is only reached by the New York novel at the height of the great depression. For more see Robert Nelson Burrows (1959), *The Image of Urban Life as Reflected in the New York City Novel. 1920-1930.* Moira Burgess' bibliography on *The Glasgow Novel, 1870-1970* (1972) encompasses about 190 titles. Wolfram Motz' analysis of the construction of identity in the Scottish novel during the conservative rule between 1979 and 1997 offers an alphabetical bibliography of about 730 titles. For more see Wolfram Motz (2000), *Die Konstruktion von Identität im schottischen Roman während der Ära des britischen Konservatismus 1979-1997.* The latest and largest bibliography in regard to genre to my knowledge is Ansgar Nünning's two-volume genre-study on British historical fiction and historiographical metafiction since the 1950s which includes about 250 works. For more see Ansgar Nünning (1995), *Von historischer Fiktion zu historiographischer Metafiktion Teil I: Theorie, Typologie und Poetik des historischen Romans.*

protagonist in the city and depicts the change of character, as the urban environment impresses its meanings, values and manners on the figure's mind, such as in a novel of development (*ibid.*: 11-12). Hassan (1981: 107) goes as far as to argue that fiction and the urban have been complementary since the rise of the *Bildungsroman*. From the perspective of an analysis of mentalities, these novels chart an individual's acculturation to the urban way of life and through conformation or repudiation reveal the mental mould that determines the modern city man. Moreover, the newcomer to the city leads a certain threshold existence in the metropolis and thereby reveals the boundaries of thinking. In the synoptic novel, the city itself is a protagonist representing the complex patterns and dynamics of the city and its impact on modern sensibility (cf. Gelfant 1954: 14). In her definition of urban literature Diane Wolfe Levy (1978: 66) finds that great city novels which "depict the realities of city life [...] are all primarily novels of character, of experience *in* the city rather than experience *of* the city." In order to show the metropolitan way of life, atmosphere and social relations in unison, the synoptic novel by contrast adheres to a strong urban symbolism as a means of condensation and the focus on innovative linguistic and formal representations of the urban then often takes precedence over character (cf. *ibid.*). While the synoptic is a comprehensive type encompassing the whole city, the ecological novel is a partial type which focuses on a spatial unit of the city, such as a neighbourhood or a single apartment house. The interest lies in the relationships and manners of the social group depicted. With this sociological point of view the "ecological novel can reveal city life as it exists for the native city dweller" (Gelfant 1954: 13). Paying attention to the particular use of language by the characters, this type of city novel directly makes a statement on the state of mind and hence "allows for a comprehensive portrayal of how urban people think, act, and feel." (*Ibid.*)

Consequently in the city novel, the urban not only serves as a background setting but becomes the dominant prospect in the theme, structure, or style of writing, stressing that the city needs to constitute an irreducible element – thematically and structurally – of the text (e.g. cf. Hoffmann 1978: 396; Klotz 1987: 10; Breuner 1991: 9; Mahler 1999: 12; Coverley 2005: 9-12; Cuevas 2008a: 14). This active participation of the urban in structuring the narrative casts a "shift from 'narrated cities' to 'urban narratives'" (Tygstrup cit. in Tinkler-Villani 2005a: xii). Accordingly, paradigmatic city novels that are narratologically connected to the metropolis must be considered, in Wolfgang Hallet's (2009: 84) terms, "*fictions of space*" in the sense that they also devise new forms of spatial constitution or problematise the arbitrariness of spatial constructions. The semantisation as well as the depiction of consciousness is predominantly formed by spatial relations. Hallet (*ibid.*: 108) defines fictions of space as narratives in which: (a) space is the focus of the story, (b) processes of consciousness are imitated by spatial semiotics, (c) intradiegetic and extradiegetic commentaries are explicitly directed towards the issue of space, (d) the fictionalisation of space is connected to individual and cultural constructions of space and reveals this constructive moment.

(5) While these definitions can be a helpful orientation within literary analysis, the London novel is not entirely limited to the 'genre' of the city novel as defined above (cf. Klotz 1987: 10; Hertel 1997: 19). Strictly following such categories of differentiating 'London writing' from a 'writing about London' would lead to a neglect of urban fictions which are considered London novels by 'convention' (cf. Coverley 2005; Pleßke 2006: 56-60). This includes, for example, nineteenth-century city novels of social critique (i.e.

Arthur Morrison's *The Child of the Jago*) which had their revival in the political engagement with the effects of Thatcherism or in contemporary neo-realist ecological novels by first- and second-generation immigrants (cf. Coverley 2005: 14-15; Cuevas 2008b: 385). In regard to the latter also postcolonial writing can be said to have developed into a sub-genre of the London novel, from Sam Selvon's *The Lonely Londoners* (1956) telling about the experiences of early migrants to the post-war city to visions of the multicultural metropolis in Zadie Smith's *White Teeth* (2000). Besides these, especially genre fiction has originated idiosyncratic London novels: Urban science fiction evolves H.G. Wells' *The Time Machine* (1895) offering alternative images of future Londons beyond everyday experiences. Optimistic and pessimistic projections of the city are fictionally created in utopias and dystopias, for example in George Orwell's *1984* (1949), and combine political critique of London with a belief in the city's brighter future (cf. Hoffmann 1978: 398; Coverley 2005: 16). The detective novel can count as the urban narrative form *par excellence* because the genre which became popular with Arthur Conan Doyle's Sherlock Holmes stories (1887-1927) is particularly suited to London's labyrinthine system of streets. Conversely, occult writing, particularly towards the end of the nineteenth-century, such as Robert Louis Stevenson's prominent *The Strange Case of Dr Jekyll and Mr Hyde* (1886), brings to the fore urbanites' psychological state while the Gothic or London noir revival since the early 1990s has produced manifold examples of that urban sub-genre (cf. Coverley 2005: 18, 26). Moreover, Wachinger (1999: 299-300) stresses that in the postmodern city novel these various sub-genres merge into a new hybrid genre of the London novel charting urbanity indirectly in a hidden dimension of its texture.

I therefore argue that urban London genre fiction proves extremely fruitful for an analysis of mentality, also because, according to Highmore (2005: 114), genre fiction is able to register the ordinary "in its distracted gaze on the urban everyday and its adjustments within the genre". Science, horror, fantasy and utopian fictions open the world of the unfamiliar and depict the nonconscious conflicts in certainties to make the seemingly inarticulate both legible and intelligible. Rosemary Jackson (1981: 4) comments that the fantastic "traces the unsaid and the unseen of culture: that which has been silenced, made invisible, covered over and made 'absent'" thereafter "making visible the un-seen, of articulating the un-said." (*Ibid.*: 48) In this sense, genre fiction in general traces the limits of a culture's epistemological and ontological frame (cf. *ibid.*: 23). The transgression of these mental boundaries implies the breach of standardisations of thinking. This aspect is particularly relevant for an analysis of urban mentality, as "[t]he city suggests a creative disorder, an instructive confusion, an interpolating space in which the imagination carries you in every direction, even towards the previously unthought." (Chambers 1996: 189) However, in my selection I left out mystery and detective series (e.g. Barry Maitland's Kathy and Brock or Anny Perry's William Monk and Thomas Pitt novels) as well as designated children's novels and youth fiction (e.g. China Miéville's *Un Lun Dun*).

(6) From that vantage point I am inclined to agree with Coverley (2005: 11): the definition of what constitutes London writing in a sense remains a subjective choice dominated by the topic of the interpretation. Here, in choosing the titles for analysis I specifically scrutinised works that emphasise the idiosyncrasy of London, its whole way of life in general and its physical, social and mental spaces in particular as representing a particular urban frame of mind. I was mainly interested in contemporary London fic-

tion that shows a certain connection between urbanity and literature, hence novels that translate the urban experience in both its aesthetic concept and dominant theme. The choice of novels thereby focussed on the selection of texts which exposed concrete ways of thinking. Moreover, I particularly took into account my findings of an urban-generic and urban-specific mentality. Already Gelfant (1954: 24) argues that because the actualities of city life shape a novelist's vision of the urban, the theories of urbanism offered by modern sociology help in understanding the character of the city novel. Insofar, the selection of the literary corpus under analysis was oriented on notions of how strongly the texts conveyed urban-generic ambivalences and urban-specific factors of influence in regard to a construction of a metropolitan mindset. About 100 works fulfilled all the criteria mentioned so far, eighty of which were critically read and underwent a basic analysis; they therefore also inform my knowledge on recurrent themes.

(7) To further narrow the choice of primary literature to twenty London novels I applied the criterion of heterogeneity: the selected corpus should be heterogeneous and represent a wide spectrum of London prose that narratively conveys diverging – social, temporal, and topographical – perspectives of the metropolis in order to avoid one-sided views on mentality. This parameter made me choose from male as well as female authors to avoid a specific gender-related gaze, applying the same to the generational aspect of the authors. As a further principle of selection the twenty novels were compiled from bestseller, marginal, popular, highly aesthetic, and debut writing. This meant that I wanted to include paradigmatic or canonical contemporary London novels (e.g. *Saturday*, *Brick Lane*, *Millennium People*), but also pay tribute to famous authors whose city novels have not been critically perceived (e.g. Brooke-Rose, Hornby). Moreover, I considered the debut novels of authors who have since become famous in their own right (e.g. Williams, Lott). Importantly, following the notion that "[m]ost great writers have been by birth or adoption, city men" (Brogan 1977: 148), I disregarded the place of birth or nationality of the authors discussed (i.e. Canadian Geoff Ryman). Another aspect was to include all forms of the city novel mentioned by Gelfant – portrait, synoptic and ecological – and to draw texts from various London sub-genres. And finally, (8) as a last principle of selection, I looked for particular recurrences regarding certain mental structures strongly conveyed within the single texts and throughout the chosen corpus (see "Primary Literature").

1.4 The Present State of Research

Due to the notion of London's illimitability it is self-evident that the state of research concerning London literature is abundant. Since Perry H. Boynton's *London in English Literature* published in 1913, thus long before Virginia Woolf's or T.S. Eliot's imaginaries of the modern city, research on literary London has been extensive reaching from epochal and genre-specific to comparative and interdisciplinary studies [16] These provide

16 | For example see Jeanne Gabriel Clark (1957), *London in English Literature, 1880-1955*; Max Byrd (1978), *London Transformed. Images of the City in the Eighteenth Century*; Gail Kern Paster (1985), *The Idea of the City in the Age of Shakespeare*; Ralph Hanna (2005),

a good base for the understanding of certain trends and disruptions in the aesthetisation of the city. A majority of studies has been concerned with specific authors[17], with the emphasis certainly on Charles Dickens[18]. A significant book on contemporary authors is Alex Murray's *Recalling London. Literature and History in the Work of Peter Ackroyd and Iain Sinclair* (2007). London writing by Peter Ackroyd, Iain Sinclair together with Martin Amis, Michael Moorcock, Will Self or women authors such as Maureen Duffy as well as Penelope Lively has received much attention and is by now covered by extensive research. The most relevant collections that encompass various perspectives on twentieth and twenty-first century literary representations of London are Pamela Gilbert's *Imagined Londons* (2002), Susana Onega and John Stotesbury's *London in Literature. Visionary Mappings of the Metropolis* (2002), Lawrence Phillips' *The Swarming Streets. Twentieth-Century Literary Representations of London* (2004) as well as Vanessa Guignery & François Gallix's *(Re-)Mapping London. Visions of the Metropolis in the Contemporary Novel in English* (2008). Besides these, the plethora of literary anthologies and literary guides on London not only proves the city's illimitable writerly inspiration, but these recent publications are further evidence of the important place the study of London literature has gained in the last decades.[19]

London Literature 1300-1380. For a recent analysis of London poetry consult Peter Barry (2000), *Contemporary British Poetry and the City*. Recent publications on the Gothic and London see Lawrence Phillips and Anne Witchard, eds. (2010), *London Gothic: Place, Space and the Gothic Imagination* or Sara Wasson (2010), *Urban Gothic of the Second World War. Dark London*. Comparative studies are particularly found in feminist studies on the city. See for example Squier (1984), Sizemore (1984), Weigel (1988, 1995), Parsons (2000). For interdisciplinary examples see Lawrence Manley (1995), *Literature and Culture in Early Modern London*; Cynthia Wall (1998), *The Literary and Cultural Spaces of Restoration London*; Nicholas Freeman (2007), *Conceiving the City. London, Literature, and Art 1870-1914*.

17 | Recent examples are Sara Haslam, ed. (2005), *Ford Madox Ford and the City* or Jean Moorcroft Wilson (2000), *Virginia Woolf's London*.

18 | An exemplary recent study on Dickens is presented by Sicher (2003), but in all the main collections on the city and representation encompass at least one article on Dickens' London, i.e. in the books edited by Sharpe & Leonard Wallock (1987), Balshaw & Kennedy (2000), Tinkler-Villani (2005).

19 | Paul Bailey's paradigmatic *Oxford Book of London* (1995) charts literary London from the twelfth-century monk William Fitzstephen to Angela Carter. Other examples are A.N. Wilson's *The Faber Book of London* (1996); Barnaby Rogerson, ed. (2004), *London. A Collection of Poetry of Place*; Anna Adams' *London in Poetry and Prose* (2005), Silvia Mergenthal (2006), *Poetischer London-Führer*, and Heather Reyes' *city–lit London* (2009). The latter also encompasses contemporary novels such as Xiaolu Guo's *A Concise Chinese-English Dictionary for Lovers* (2007) and Joseph O'Neill's *Netherland* (2008) and verse by Grace Nichols or Benjamin Zephaniah. London short story collections include Maria Lexton, ed. (1993), *The Time Out Book of London Short Stories*; Maxim Jakubowski, ed. (1994), *London Noir*; Oscar Zarate, ed. (1996), *It's Dark in London. Graphic Short Stories*. Also see literary guides to London, such as Peter Vansittart (1992), *London. A Literary Companion*; Ed Glinert (2000), *The Literary Guide to London*; Anna Quindlen (2004), *Imagined London. A Tour of the World's Greatest Fictional*

A general overview of London literature is provided by Nick Rennison's *Guide to London Writing* (1999) which reaches from examples by John Skelton (1460) to those of Nicholas Royle and Geoff Nicholson (1997). Instead, Merlin Coverley (2005) thematically sketches thirty essential London novels temporally closing with Anthony Frewin's *London Blues* (1997) and Nicholas Royle's *The Director's Cut* (2000). A long-awaited contribution which again marks the current prominence of London writing is the recent *Cambridge Companion to the Literature of London* (2011) edited by Lawrence Manley. This collection unifies experts on literary London, such as Cynthia Wall, William Sharp, Peter Barry, John Ball, John McLeod and James Donald, who offer contributions on medieval urban literature to twenty-first century images in poetry, drama, prose, visual culture and film. Only the probably most productive contemporary researcher on the city, Julian Wolfreys, who has published three volumes on *Writing London* (1998, 2004, 2007), is not listed. Despite this, the book is not only interdisciplinary but cutting-edge in regard to the spatial theories employed for analysis. A very current chapter on twenty-first century city fiction is offered by John McLeod (2011) who particularly takes into account Zadie Smith's *White Teeth* (2000) and Ian McEwan's *Saturday* (2007).

Instead, earlier studies on the contemporary British city novel, such as Michael Breuner's *"Hunger for Place"* (1991), Bernd-Peter Lange's *Die Großstadt in der britischen Gegenwartsliteratur* (1995) or Lawrence Phillips' *London Narratives* (2006) do not expand into the revival era of city fiction during the 1990s. By contrast, Sebastian Groes' current *The Making of London* (2011) charts the work of major London authors as early as the 1970s, but the book also echoes his innovative findings from earlier articles on the latest city novels by McEwan and Ballard (cf. Groes 2008, 2009). Unfortunately, the single chapters are arranged according to particular London authors and thus the analysis, while offering significant insights into particular novels and the transformation of the writers' works, is less informative as concerns topical similarities or stylistic tendencies. Another useful base for this book is offered by Doris Teske's (1999) discursive analysis of different textual constructions of the twentieth-century metropolis in urban theory, city essays and urban fiction (1980s & 1990s). Teske (1999: 1, 196) particularly pays attention to their similarities in devising connections between space and identity and the subjective imagery. The study is also interesting because she is able to prove the longevity of collective constructions of urban reality (*ibid.*: 194). Hence, while the approach to include the theories of Urban Studies in the analysis of London fiction is not a new one, *The Intelligible Metropolis* can build on the interconnection of Urban and Literary Studies devised in Teske not only in regard to the urban renaissance but also the Spatial Turn.

Despite the latter, few studies consciously employ spatial theories in the analysis of contemporary London novels. Based on a Lotmanian approach to spatial semantics, Dagmar Dreyer (2006) looks at the topographical and socio-cultural as well as symbolic

---

City; Eveline Kilian (2008), *London. Eine literarische Entdeckungsreise*; Graham Norton, Janet Street-Porter & Dan Cruickshank, eds. (2010), *London Walks. 30 Walks by London Writers Volume 1*; Robert Elms, Robert Appleby & Bonnie Greer, eds. (2011), *London Walks. 25 Walks by London Writers Volume 2*. Brief anthologies published by Reclam include Adolf Barth (1988), *London Poems*; Tobias Döring (2003), *London Underground. Poems and Prose about the Tube*; Adolf Barth (2003), *London Stories*.

images in two synoptic and four postcolonial London novels published during the 1990s and Martina Deny's (2009) book negotiates urban constructions of identity and postmodern tendencies of fragmentation referring to canonical novels from 1985 to 2003. In difference to Dreyer's study this present publication expands on the notion of the geographical and social cityscape, while in contrast to Deny's analysis it concentrates on mentality rather than means of identity construction and thereby shows that a particular frame of mind assists in countering the dominant perceptions of loss and disorientation in the postmodern metropolis. Furthermore, although this analysis displays overlapping elements with respect to the analysis of Geoff Nicholson's *London Bleeding* (1997) and Monica Ali's *Brick Lane* (2003) no major study to this date expands its main corpus of London novels beyond the millennium's threshold. While Ali's, McEwan's and Ballard's novels are well documented in single essays, *The Intelligible Metropolis* still offers first-time or in-depth analyses on so far largely neglected texts, such as *The Matter of the Heart, Tunnel Vision, Corpsing, A Long Way Down, The Red Men* and *South of the River*.

In her study on literary perception of urban reality within the context of spatial, socio-topographic and narrative perspectives in London novels between Naturalism and Modernism, Kirsten Hertel (1997: 16) exemplifies three major threads in the scholarly research concerning English urban fiction: (1) the psychological-archetypical approach about the psychology of characters and symbolism of the city, (2) the aesthetical-thematic one about the relation between the city described and the narrative techniques applied, (3) and the socio-historical one concerning the interrelations between society, city, and novel. Within the socio-historical approach, the strongest culturally related analytical works concerning literary London have been those concerning the postcolonial metropolis, most importantly by John Ball (2004), John McLeod (2004a, 2004b, 2005, 2007, 2011) and Susanne Cuevas (2008a, 2008b).[20] In *Babylon or Golden City*, Cuevas deals with eight Black and Asian novels in a time frame between 1996 and 2003, which presents a useful basis for the fictions of migration analysed in this monograph. Otherwise, many studies that relate to migrant, diaspora, multicultural, postcolonial, or Black and Asian British literature since the 1990s (i.e. Sommer 2001; Reichl 2002) also refer to London fiction, where incidentally most of these texts are set.[21] Tellingly, the proceedings of the 2000 *Anglistentag* in Berlin included a single section on "London: Multiculturalism and the Metropolis".

The fact that London literature has gained in interest for literary and academic writers is additionally emphasised by the establishment of *The Literary London Journal* in 2003, which publishes reviews and interdisciplinary representations, and the founding of *The Literary London Society* in 2011. Furthermore, an increasing number of conferences con-

20 | For other examples see Joseph McLaughlin (2000), *Writing the Urban Jungle. Reading Empire in London from Doyle to Eliot*; Sukhdev Sandhu (2003), *London Calling. How Black and Asian Writers Imagined a City*; Annette Müller (2007), *London as a Literary Region. The Portrayal of the Metropolis in Contemporary Postcolonial British Fiction.*

21 | Also see Susheila Nasta (2002), *Home Truths. Fictions of the South Asian Diaspora in Britain*; James Procter (2003), *Dwelling Places. Postwar Black British Writing*; Mark Stein (2004), *Black British Literature. Novels of Transformation*; Jan Rupp (2010), *Genre and Cultural Memory in Black British Literature.*

cern the literary metropolis, while London Literature/Studies are now well-established courses at British universities. Thanks to the Cultural/Spatial/Urban Turn also cultural theorists have become increasingly interested in representations of the city particularly in connection with architecture, art, film and of course literature. Therefore, this study has also profited from works which present innovative interdisciplinary approaches on the urban by combining research of space, culture, literature, film, and other media (e.g. Brooker 2002).

Moreover, this growing scholarly interest in the city is not only to be seen in the light of the millennial optimism and the large output of primary sources since the 1990s, but must also be considered against the background of the Spatial Turn and the revival spatial fiction in general or British spaces in particular. For instance, David James' *Contemporary British Fiction and the Artistry of Space* (2008) introduces issues of space and place in literature by paying specific attention to the new relations between spatial description and the aesthetics of readerly engagement by charting major topographical sites in recent British fiction. James (2008: 168) argues that "[a]n emerging body of novelists are taking responsibility for creating a *poiesis* of space that can re-envision the landscape of everyday life, receptive to the social and historical forces under which new habitats are forged." And therein again urban visions play a pivotal role (cf. *ibid.*: 68-95), as "the city itself presents a more familiar but no less complex scenery upon which to focus a survey of space in contemporary fiction." (*Ibid.*: 33)

However, while Haubrichs (1982: 1) delineates three major tendencies on the research of the literary metropolis, namely (1) the changing images of the city, (2) the functions of literature in the city and (3) mentality as represented in texts, I gather that few scholars have attempted to systematically concentrate on urban mentality. By contrast this present study particularly engages with the concept by taking into account both the recent research on urbanity and fictions of space implemented by the Spatial Turn. To this day the concept of narrative space has remained quite vague also because, as James (2008: 26-27) elucidates, landscape descriptions are employed as narrative innovations, the poetics of space necessarily remain in flux. Whereas James exceptionally employs Joseph Frank's idea of "Spatial Form", but also literary theories by Georg Lukács and Michel de Certeau, this treatise inquires into recent publications in narratology, such as Ansgar and Vera Nünning's (2002) collection on new approaches on narratology or that of *Narratology in the Age of Cross-disciplinary Narrative Research* (2009) edited by Sandra Heinen and Roy Sommer. Katrin Dennerlein (2009) presents a useful overview of spatial narratology based on an understanding of space as absolute, and therefore the essays in Wolfgang Hallet and Birgit Neumann's (2009) important collection on Literary Studies and the Spatial Turn prove more applicable to the analysis of urban spatialities as represented in city novels. This argumentation also takes into account the notion of literary topographies as devised by Hillis Miller (1995) and variously developed by Hartmut Böhme (2005); it especially expands on the concepts and tools for spatial narratology as offered by the seminal works of Yuri Lotman (1973, 2001), Mikhail Bakhtin (1998, 1968), Gerhard Hoffmann (1978), Gaston Bachelard (1994) and Michel de Certeau (1988). These are necessarily adapted not only in regard to the spatial relevance of the city, but additionally assessed with reference to the studies of mentalities. All in all, this analysis methodologically builds on the confluence of qualitative and quantitative studies of the history of mentalities, Cultural Studies and Literary Studies as portrayed by scholars of British culture and literature like Ursula Peters (1985), Friederike Meyer (1989), Jürgen Kamm (1994, 1996), Herbert Grabes (1996, 2004), Ansgar (2004a, 2004c) and Vera Nünning (2001, 2004).

Since the 1990s, the history of mentalities has certainly developed into an integral part of Cultural Studies. As was shown above, mentality as a complex phenomenon of culture can mostly be found in research which is not primarily ascribed to the studies of mentality. In British Cultural Studies the correlation between mentalities and Cultural Studies mainly exists within research concerning British historical epochs or national identity. For example, historical British mindsets are an important part of Jürgen Kramer's *Britain and Ireland. A Concise History* (2007), while *Thinking Northern. Textures of Identity in the North of England* (2007) edited by Christoph Ehland presents a regional study concerning British mentalities. But whereas the main title *Thinking Northern* suggests the mental side of culture, the subtitle puts the concept on a level with identity. And although Kramer (2002: 39) chooses the heading "Cultures and Mentalities" in his presentation of the book project, the monograph renames the chapter "Cultures and Ideologies" (Kramer 2007: 139, 157). Also for Lenz (2002: 54) the aforementioned 'insular mentality' ultimately constitutes an ideological construct. In the context of Cultural and Literary Studies, a pre-defined mentality such as insular mentality, 'empire mentality', or the 'mentality of sensibility' has more often served as an instrument to decipher the meanings of the culturally coded texts and explore discursive practices, but has seldom been a direct result of mentality study (c e.g. Kamm & Sedlmayr 2007; A. Nünning 2004a, 2004c; V. Nünning 2001, 2004).

Insofar, this book strives to systematise the theory of mentalities and reassess the concept through drawing on studies by the historians Peter Burke (1990, 1991, 1992, 1997) and Patrick Hutton (1981, 1988, 2002), two pre-eminent representatives of the English-speaking scientific community who generally focus on socio-historical, socio-psychological and anthropological questions of mentalities (cf. Spode 1990: 41-45).[22] However, the most fruitful research concerning mentality is evidently offered by historians of mentality such as the founding father of the *Annales* School Lucien Febvre (2003a, 2003b) and later representatives Fernand Braudel (1958, 1976, 1988), Georges Duby (1961, 1985), Robert Mandrou (1972), Michel Vovelle (1982), Jacques Le Goff (1985, 1986, 1990), Roger Chartier (1988, 1991) and Philippe Ariès (1988, 1991). There exists an array of useful articles by medievalists who scrutinise the main elements of the concept of mentalities (cf. Reichardt 1978; Tellenbach 1982; Schulze 1985; Graus 1987; Spode 1990; Dinzelbacher 1993; Kortüm 1996; Kuhlemann 1996), yet unfortunately, although they offer clarifying systematisations, these adepts lose track of significant assumptions for contemporary Mentality Studies in the context of Cultural Studies. For a systematisation of the theory of mentality, I will mainly draw on articles by the historian Volker Sellin (1985, 1987) as well as refer to the scholars who have written in this tradition within Cultural and Literary Studies, particularly Jürgen Kamm (1994, 1996, 2007, 2010).

But despite the focus on the city from the perspective of Cultural and Literary Studies scholars have obviously neglected the potential of Mentality Studies. As Berking and

22 | For the reception of the histories of mentalities in Britain particularly see Burke (1990: 96-98).

Löw (2008a: 11) explicate, the Cultural Turn has formulated questions in regard to the confluence of cultural and material urban structures, aspects of collective memory, local structures of feeling, urban habitus, city biography and urban mental atmosphere, these have remained largely unanswered. Research concerning urban mentality chiefly exists by historians as brief articles regarding the city of antiquity, the middle ages, and modernity (e.g. cf. Schulz 1980; Darnton 1984; Oesterle 1988; Rossiaud 1990; Barceló 1995; Mohrmann 1996; Schilling 2003). They either diachronically or synchronically chart the *conditio humana* of urban denizens against the background of urban development as part of the history of civilisation. However, these studies while exposing certain lines of tradition in regard to urban life do not draw a coherent image of concrete structures of urban mentality. Most of the systematic work on urban-generic ways of thinking has been conducted by modern urban sociology, such as the seminal works by Georg Simmel (1971, 1992) or Louis Wirth (1967, 1969) and Robert Park (1928, 1931, 1967) of the Chicago School. A reassessment of these texts is deeply interesting because from the point of view of the Spatial Turn their theories offer novel and surprising insights not only, but especially for Mentality Studies. To further delineate a notion of urban mentality, this analysis draws on neo-Marxist scholars of the city, for example Henri Lefebvre (1991, 1996, 2003, 2004), Manuel Castells (1979, 1989), David Harvey (1973, 1985, 1990) as well as postmodern urbanologists such as Edward Soja (1998, 2000, 2001, 2006), Marc Augé (1988, 1995, 1997), Guy Debord (1955, 1994), Jean Baudrillard (1997, 2000) and Celeste Olalquiaga (1992).

For an understanding of urbanism as a whole way of life, especially Lewis Mumford's anthropological *The Culture of Cities* originally published 1938 serves as a guidance updated to the contemporary metropolis by Anton C. Zijderveld's *A Theory of Urbanity* (1998) and Simon Parker's *Urban Theory and the Urban Experience* (2004). These are complemented by cultural analyses of Postmodernism, geography, and the city (e.g. cf. Chambers 1990, 1996; Featherstone 1991, 1996; Robins 1993, 1998; Jarvis 1998). For an understanding of urban-generic mentality, this work mainly draws on the general notion of a sociology of urban life (cf. Fischer 1984; Karp, Stone & Yoels 1991; Löw 2001, 2008; Häussermann & Siebel 2004; Schroer 2006) and the specific findings of important sociologists, such as Richard Sennett (1977, 1994, 2000) and Lyn Lofland (1973, 1998). The notion of urban idiosyncrasy and urban-specific mentality is based on Helmuth Berking and Martina Löw's concept of the "Eigenlogik der Städte" (2008a), while the idea of factors that influence the metropolitan character is predominantly informed by texts from New Cultural Geographers and urban semioticians (cf. Lynch 1977; Gottdiener 2005; Sharpe & Wallock 1987; Daniels and Cosgrove 1989; King 1996; Zukin 1997; Amin and Thrift 2002; Highmore 2005; Degen 2008).

As the present state of research shows, Cultural Studies have largely concentrated on mentality as a synonym for national character or identity. Cultural historians have emphasised the mental structures of the past. While urban sociologists were interested in the urban way of life and urban mindset, many scholars ignored the potential literature has for an analysis of urban mentality. Although the recent cultural analysis of London certainly proposes urban-specific mental structures it is not the central focus of their analysis. Literary Studies have often relied on pre-defined mentalities to support their literary-historical analysis or inform their discursive studies. Literary Studies of London novels in the last decades have been immersed in questions of metaphor, history and identity without penetrating the structures behind, namely the urban way of thinking that these themes reveal. Consequently, an analysis of contemporary fiction regarding a specific mentality has not been published yet. While, according to cultural semioticians, novels are extremely useful for the extrapolation of an urban-specific mentality, none of the works mentioned is primarily concerned with a London mentality as represented in contemporary city novels.

1.5 Structure and Approach

This present study consists of eight chapters and two parts. The first part (chapters 2-5) sets the theoretical as well as the methodological scene for the subsequent analysis of London novels in the second part (chapters 6-9).

On the basis of the history of mentalities, chapter 2 first develops a definition of mentalities as historical and contemporary social constructions of reality particularly by referring to sociological and cultural understandings of the term (2.1.2). The further delineation of the concept's categories is seen as indispensible in order to be able to differentiate mentality from notions of culture, ideology, identity, or habitus. Hence, a third step (2.1.3) devises mentality as both agency and structure: as an organon mentality has the function of organisation, orientation, relief of strain, alignment, regulation, integration. Mental structures understood as a rhizome of dispositions of thinking, imagining, feeling and acting are incorporated by ways of socialisation and acculturation. Through the assumption that mentalities are mainly defined by four parameters of the habitat, namely collectivity, time, space and collective space-time compressions (as their confluence in cultural dynamics), the second sub-chapter thoroughly elaborates on these determinants (2.2). Of particular importance is the spatial component, which due to contemporary post-positivist notions of space must be considered as relative and relational, dynamic and fluid, as well as culturally produced and productive. Moreover, with regard to the Spatial Turn the spatial manageability of daily life by mentality is shown to expand beyond the physical understanding of spatiality to social and mental conceptions of space. Henceforth, mentality can be defined as a rhizomatic organon of dispositional orientation functioning by ways of nonconsicous axiomatic sets of thought, emotion, imaginary and behaviour which are determined by collectivity, time, space and compression. In summary, "The Concept of Mentality" (2.3) therefore offers a catalogue of eleven characteristics for framing the concept in allusion to Kamm's (1994) ten-point list on intercultural meta-knowledge.

From the vantage point that the twentieth century must be regarded as the urban age, chapter 3 reassesses various "Theories of Urbanity" for notions of inner urbanisation (3.1). Because the history of mentalities does not offer a sufficient analysis of urban mentality, this study largely builds on the findings of modern urban sociology and those of contemporary (cultural) urbanologists. On the basis of Georg Simmel's "Die Großstädte und das Geistesleben" (1903) and "Exkurs über den Fremden" (1907), urban mentality in its functions of orientation and relief of strain can be interpreted as a protective mechanism against the overload effect exerted by the metropolis' multiple stimuli (3.2.1). Expanding on this early example of the Spatial Turn *avant la lettre*, the urban ecology of the Chicago School (3.2.3), most importantly Robert Park and Louis

Wirth, also conceptualises theories of urbanism as a way of life. Of special interest for urban mentality this writing identifies the notion of moral regions, the inbetweenness of the marginal man, social disassociation and anomie, role-play and schizophrenia. The analysis of assumptions by the New Urban Political Economy (3.2.3), especially Henri Lefebvre, Manuel Castells and David Harvey, brings into perspective the transformations of urban life in the post-Fordist and globalised metropolis of the late twentieth century. Their findings are important for an understanding of tendencies such as spatial fluidity, social disfragmentation, globalised economies, cultural symbolism, as influencing postmodern urbanity (3.2.4). The exploration of the postmodern city, mainly in reference to Edward Soja's discursive analysis of the Postmetropolis, exposes particular physical, social and mental consequences of ambivalent trends, such as the architectural voids or palimpsestic memories, urban non-places or *lieux de mémoire*, postmodern overload of violence or psychasthenia, which notably take their toll on the mental life of the contemporary metropolis.

From the preliminary categories of mentalities and theories of inner urbanisation, chapter 4 develops "The Concept of Urban Mentality" and devises an urban-generic and urban-specific model for the analysis of the mental side of city culture in order to be able to differentiate a general urban mentality from London-specific mental dispositions. By reference to the new approach to cities of "Eigenlogik der Städte" (Berking & Löw 2008a) it is illustrated that contemporary cities are still identifiable as entities with a particular culture and that each city is defined by its distinctive way of life. Hence, the first section (4.1) takes into consideration the macro-level of an urban-generic mentality and regards the particularity of urbanism as construed by eight ambivalences: city and country, public and private, sociability and anomie, heterogeneity and homogeneity, familiarity and strangeness, community and individualism, indifference and involvement, apathy and vigilance. Insofar, this study takes the city's "unresolvable ambivalence" (Fiedler 1981: 115) as a preliminary for the analysis of urban mentality. The second section (4.2) identifies a cluster of eight factors of influence that determine the particularity in between these polarities on the meso-level of an urban-specific mentality in order to differentiate the mindscape of *The Unique City* (Rasmussen 1937) from that of other cities. The idiosyncrasy of a regional metropolitan mentality specified by culture, imaginary, image, text, narrative, atmosphere, emotion and identity is delineated particularly from the theories of the New Urban Geographers on representation. Finally, these theoretical findings are summarised in a model of urban-generic mentality and one of urban-specific mentality for the 'N-Metropolis' (4.3).

The overall methodological approach to mentality described in chapter 5.1 lies on the interface of the history of mentalities, Cultural Studies, and Literary Studies. Following Kamm's (1996) proposition that particularly the instruments offered by Literary Studies, such as narratology, assist in the analysis of mentalities, this book proposes that texts (in the wider sense), aesthetic literature, but notably narratives and novels present viable sources for the examination of mental structures. Moreover, narrative fiction is of special interest due to the affinity between the city and the novel as described by Volker Klotz. The general narratological prototype approach is adjusted to the focus on spatiality and spatial fiction in the second sub-chapter "A Spatio-Narratological Analysis of Mentalities" (5.2) in order to provide specific tools for the later analysis of the 'spatial mentality' of London. For the delineation of literary topographies I particularly rely on boundaries as devised by Yuri Lotman's idea of spatial semantisation (5.2.2), chronotopes defined as particular space-time relations by Mikhail Bakhtin (5.2.3), and metaphors as narrative elements of great importance for the analysis of both mentality and urban fiction (5.2.4).

Against the background knowledge provided by these four chapters, the second part sets out to analyse twenty contemporary London novels for their representation of urban-generic and London-specific structures of mentality. The spectrum covered by the textual analysis gradually moves from a focus on the topology of the city, to social relations in the contemporary metropolis to the spaces of the urban individual and its psychology. To make apparent the shifting level of discussion, the eight analytical sections are subdivided by three larger chapters: "Cityscape", "Socioscape" and "Idioscape". The suffix 'scape' allows to scrutinise the cultural production and representation of the city in regard to the physical image of London as a whole, its social relations and spatialities, as well as the personal, corporeal and mental spaces of the urban Self, while simultaneously taking into account the fluid and irregular shapes of London's signifying culturescape (cf. Soja 2001: 210). With reference to Gelfant, the choice of texts in the single chapters then largely pays heed to the sub-genres of the city novel: "Cityscape" concentrates on the symbolic value of London's character corresponding to the synoptic novel, while "Socioscape" in its interest on social interactions between an array of urban characters mainly takes into account ecological novels and "Idioscape" with its focus on the spatialities of the urban Self is particularly fruitful when based on portrait studies or novels of development and their depictions of identity formation. However, as a study of mentalities involves a multi-level process of reading and interpretation that strives to decipher recurrent structures of thinking, imagining, feeling and acting, the thematically structured analysis must necessarily refrain from too strictly devised classifications. While particular focus will be on the paradigmatic novels by Ali, McEwan and Nicholson, but also the lesser known texts by Brooke-Rose and Miéville, longer analyses moreover concern Ballard, de Abaitua, Gee, Royle, and Ryman.

Chapter 6 reads the cityscape from the perspective of four dominant representations in contemporary London novels to decipher their underlying mental dispositions. "Public and Private" (6.1) builds on an intrinsic urban-generic ambivalence to explore the significance of topographical but initially also topological (b)ordering practices in the postmodern metropolitan realm. The separate analysis of four major city novels, namely Ian McEwan's *Saturday* (2005), Maggie Gee's *The White Family* (2000), Monica Ali's *Brick Lane* (2003), and Christine Brooke Rose's *Next* (1998) especially exposes structures of feeling that are oriented towards the privatisation of urban life. This must initially be read as a defence mechanism against the penetration of privacy by the public (i.e. habits, language, media, city imagery), while conversely the atomisation of urban society leads to an intensive search for intimacy in the semi-public spaces of urban anonymity.

While this sub-chapter basically takes into view the whole cityscape and its internally shifting boundaries of the public and the private, "Underground London" (6.2) only refers to the partial spatialities of the subterranean city. Drawing on five novels predominantly set beneath the metropolitan surface, China Miéville's *King Rat* (1998), Geoff Ryman's *253* (1998), Tobias Hill's *Underground* (1999), Keith Lowe's *Tunnel Vision* (2001) and Conrad Williams' *London Revenant* (2004), the analysis elaborates on London's underground not only as a major topos, but as particular trope in contemporary urban fiction. In regard to different sections with a thematic focus on the physical, social, and mental implications of the underground, throughout the novels the uncanny features as a dominant motif which resembles the urban-generic ambivalence of familiarity/strangeness between the known and the unknown or Self and Other.

Also the following sub-chapter enters the discussion of *The Intelligible Metropolis* here with regard to altered forms of spatial conception and perception of postmodern London by examining the dynamics of the contemporary cityscape. "Navigating the Flux" (6.3) explores Geoff Nicholson's *Bleeding London* (1997), Christine Brooke Rose's *Next* (1998), China Miéville's *King Rat* (1998) and Ian McEwan's *Saturday* (2005) for their respective forms of urban orientation: mapping, touring, sensing and apprehending. While the first two build on de Certeau's panoramic and street-level focalisation as the difference between reading the abstract city and writing urban everyday life, the latter novels envisage the opposites of somatic/emotional and literary/intellectual navigation. Taken as a whole, the four city novels show an emphasis on the textual knowledge of London.

Insofar, the palimpsest, taken into consideration in sub-chapter 6.4, is of particular interest because the city trope is able to represent the interaction between city, text, and mentality. In "The Palimpsestuous City", I argue that the city as palimpsest constitutes London's contemporary master metaphor and therefore a dominant structure of thinking. Under the lead analysis of Geoff Nicholson's text another seven city novels, amongst them Jane Stevenson's *London Bridges* (2000), Nicholas Royle's *The Matter of the Heart* (1997), and Matthew de Abaitua's *The Red Men* (2007), not only prove the dominance of the trope, but also show the thematic transmutability of the concept. Interpretations of the historical, psychogeographical, socio-cultural, intertextual, and hypertextual palimpsest underline London's idiosyncrasy and urban-specific mentality incorporated in the personification of typical urban figures.

In reference to urban sociologists, chapter 7 "Socioscape" analyses the culture of the city with respect to human interrelations in the urban realm. "Urban Sociability" (7.1) particularly engages with the urban-generic ambivalence of community and individualism, sociability and anomie. The first two sections analyse three ecological novels, namely Tim Lott's *White City Blue* (1999), Nick Hornby's *A Long Way Down* (2005) and Blake Morrison's *South of the River* (2007), for networks of urban interrelations in various forms of primary and secondary relations on the one hand (7.1.1) and phases of isolation, loneliness and individualism on the other (7.1.2). On a second level, J.G. Ballard's *Millennium People* (2003) and its depiction of postmodern London on the verge of anomie (7.1.3) is compared to Monica Ali's vision of a new transcultural sociability in *Brick Lane* (7.1.4). Therein, the city's social life is shown to adhere to a relational fluidity that emphasises Londoners' mental flexibility.

The second sub-chapter "London Metropolarities" (7.2) takes into view the multiple axes of urban hegemonies and inequalities. Thematically arranged according to stratifications such as class (7.2.1), gender (7.2.2) and ethnicity (7.2.3), the single sections compare representations of familiarity and strangeness. The eight novels under analysis, besides others also Patrick Neate's *City of Tiny Lights* (2005) and Gautam Malkani's *Londonstani* (2006), bring to the fore the crisis of the middle-class, male, white citizen who is traditionally seen as the urbanite *per se*. Whereas modern sociology often regards other forms of identity as deviant, the last section, "The Urban Pariah" (7.2.4) not only emphasises a third tendency of twenty-first century representations of London (e.g.

cf. McLeod 2011) which brings into focus the contemporary metropolitan underclass, but as I shall argue, the novels envisage the 'deviant' as best equipped to navigate the contemporary city.

Chapter 8 "Idioscape" explores the spaces of the Self, particular those of identity and psychology. "The City and the Citizen" (8.1) first concentrates on the relation between the individual and the urban. Besides texts analysed in previous chapters, this section additionally takes into consideration Toby Litt's London novel *Corpsing* (2000). The first sub-section (8.1.1) focuses on constructions of identity and exposes performativity and role-play as dominant forms of self-fashioning which strongly influence the mental life of contemporary urbanites, for example in regard to schizophrenia. From the spatial perspective on the city's organism and the urbanites' corporeality, the next aspect puts emphasis on the bodyscape (8.1.2) and draws on Olalquiaga's notion of postmodern psychasthenia to show that anthropomorphic conceptions of the contemporary city are anything but obsolete. Similarly, the mindscape (8.1.3) represented in the texts echoes the possibility of the city's intelligibility. All three aspects hint towards an analogy of the metropolis with the urban Self where this mutual referentiality creates certain hypertrophic mental structures.

The final analytical sub-chapter on "The Urban State of Mind" (8.2) turns the analysis of contemporary London novels to the depths of the urban psyche and uncovers a dominance of structures of feeling based on terror. Taking its vantage point in the ambivalent attitude towards London as expressed in the 'attraction of repulsion', the first section particularly concentrates on the profusion of criminality in city novels (8.2.1). The urban *conditio humana* as dominated by uncertainty and fear becomes especially pronounced in the analysis of "The Spectres of Terror" (8.2.2). This section first continues on the motif of the uncanny and exposes the visions of disasters in the London Tube already before the actual terrorist attacks of 7/7 as a London-specific form of expectancy fear. The direct reactions of post-9/11 London literature similarly uncover this sense of unease under the veneer of the city's alleged coolness. With the last aspect under analysis the argumentation moves to London's "Millennial Apocalyptic Visions" (8.2.3), which contextualise metropolitan mental structures of terror in the continuous circle of the city's death and resurrection.

The conclusion (9) first comments on trends in contemporary representations of London and then sums up the eight structures of mentality identified in the course of the analysis, underlining significant aspects yielded as a result of the literary examination of contemporary London novels. Moreover, it offers a chart which maps London-specific mentality in the model of urban-generic ambivalences. The concluding remarks ponder on the possibility of introducing the approach of mentality as a new paradigm for a more inclusive and interdisciplinary study of the urban which helps rendering the metropolis truly *intellegible* – namely in a synergetic response of urban intelligibility and legibility.

Theory and Methodology

2 Theories and Categories of Mentality

2.1 The Definition of Mentality

2.1.1 The History of Mentalities

The term mentality is verifiable for the first time within the English philosophic discourse of the seventeenth century,[1] where it denotes a collective colouring of inner life, a particular way of thinking, and structures of feeling in regard to a nation or a certain group of people (cf. Le Goff 1985: 171; Sellin 1985: 556). Nineteenth-century French adapts the term,[2] and it becomes a key word in political discussions concerning the Dreyfus Affair (cf. Tellenbach 1982: 385; Spode 1990: 29). In reference, Marcel Proust little later employs mentality in his multi-volume novel *A la recherche du temps perdu* (1913-1927) to describe a specific *état d'esprit* .[3] The term is introduced to French academic discourse by Lucien Lévy-Bruhl's *La mentalité primitive* (1922); the ethnologist makes use of mentality to distinguish between primitive and pre-logical thinking on the one hand and civilised logical thinking on the other hand.[4] By the First World War, mentality

1 | Sellin (1985: 556) pinpoints the date at 1691.

2 | In 1842, a French etymological dictionary describes mentality as an English word (cf. Spode 1990: 29). Instead, Duby (1961: 940) sees the origin of French applications of the term in a philosophical text from 1877.

3 | From the perspective of the archivist Saniette "il y a un mot nouveau pour exprimer un tel genre d'esprit [...]. On dit <mentalité>. Cela signifie exactement la même chose, mais au moins personne ne sait ce qu'on veut dire. C'est le fin du fin et, comme on dit, le <dernier cri>. [...] Mentalité me plait. Il y a comme cela les mots nouveaux qu'on lance." (Proust 1945: 72-73) Probably due to his cultural conceptualisation of mentality and its relevance to Proust's psychological preoccupations, theorists often refer to *A la recherche du temps perdu*. From that stance the cycle of novels could well be termed a meta-text for the concept of mental dispositions.

4 | Lévy-Bruhl for the first time applies the term mentality in the publication "Les fonctions mentales dans les sociétés inférieurs" (1910). In later works he refutes the distinction between "Mentalität der Primitiven" versus "unsere geistige Haltung" (Lévy-Bruhl 1956: 6, 24). In Eng-is firmly established in French historical terminology: the investigation of mentalities develops into an independent form of historiography. This "mentality-movement" (Bonheim 1994: 3) is largely identified with the work of the French *Annales* School[5], whose paradigms of the so-called *histoire des mentalités*[6] promote the academic spread of the concept and the popularity of the term mentality.[7]

The *Annales* deduce the concept of *attitudes mentales* from the sociology of Emile Durkheim, for whom mentalities define a certain way of thinking (cf. Spode 1990: 29-30).[8] According to Durkheim the *conscience collective*, a common consciousness[9] of

---

land the term is used as early as 1913 in a critique of Durkheim by the anthropologist Bronislaw Malinowski, who studies the mentality of Australian Aboriginal families (cf. Burke 1997: 174). And in 1919, the Austrian-American political scientist Joseph Schumpeter chooses to define the mindset of businessmen – "Mentalität der kapitalistischen Lebensform" from a certain 'Diogenes mentality' (cf. Sellin 1985: 556).

5 | The name of the group derives from the journal *Annales d'Histoire Économique et Sociale* founded in 1929 by Lucien Febvre, an historian of the early modern period, and the medievalist Marc Bloch. From 1946 to 1993 it is published under the title *Annales. Economies – Sociétés – Civilisations* and is renamed *Annales. Histoire, Sciences Sociales* in 1994. Representatives of the second generation *Annales* are Fernand Braudel, Jacques Le Geoff, Georges Duby, Pierre Chaunu, Alphonse Dupront, and Emmanuel Le Roy Ladurie. The third generation rises in the early 1970s with Philippe Ariès, Michel Vovelle, and Robert Mandrou, whose approach to mentality *au troisième niveau* puts the focus on culture as the main object of interest. For more information on the *Annales* see Burke (1990).

6 | Other terms used by the *Annales* besides *histoire des mentalités* are *psychologie historique* or *histoire sociale des idées* and *histoire socioculturelle* (cf. Chartier 1988: 11).

7 | Spode (1990: 27-30) shows that an ethnological and comparative history of mentalities already exists *avant la lettre*. He claims that the *Annales* School's focus, like the structure and change of mental and psychological collective phenomena, is a central issue in studies by Edward B. Tylor, Georges Lefebvre, Norbert Elias or Georg Simmel and around 1900 becomes characterised by an interdisciplinary debate between sociologists, anthropologists, historians, and psychologists.

8 | Gebhardt & Kamphausen (1994: 14) argue that Durkheim introduced the term to scientific discourse prior to Lévy-Bruhl, because he employs a concept of mentalities to analyse primitive cultures or to explain the German mentality of war since *De la division du travail social* (1893).

9 | The problem is that consciousness is normally constituted by intentionality, as consciousness can only be the consciousness of something defined. But due to the notion that mentality is unreflective, definitions rendered mentalities to phenomena of a collective 'unconscious'. The *Annales*' notion of a 'collective unconscious' – in opposition to Jung's concept of the archetype as product of the collective unconscious, or the Freudian psychohistory of a personal unconscious, the *id* – describes mentalities as products of culture. "The collective unconscious is a reservoir of tacit understanding on which people draw their everyday lives. It is the 'common sense' of living tradition. Conscious understanding, by contrast, concerns open discourse about public issues. It is the stuff of law, literature and political, and has long been the primary subject matter of history. On the transitional boundary between the two, he [Ariès] located a 'hidden

shared beliefs and moral attitudes, is the basic constituent of a group (cf. Chartier 1988: 17). To decipher this collective mind (*âme collective*) Durkheim's collective psychology delineates *"faits de mentalités"* (*ibid.*: 14).

In opposition to anachronistic readings of mental structures, the *Annales* historically adapt this idea and consequently understand mentality as collective attitudes of a specific epoch. In his article "Une vue d'ensemble: histoire et psychologie" (1938) Lucien Febvre connects the sociological problem of collective consciousness to the historical transformation of consciousness (cf. Sellin 1985: 562-563). Febvre's notion of a historical psychology hence emphasises the temporal determinancy of mental mechanisms, the character of attitudes, and the consequent habits (*ibid.*: 563). Ariès (1988: 402) in regard to Febvre recounts: "Certaines choses étaient donc concevables, acceptables, à une certaine époque, dans une certaine culture, et elles cessaient de l'être à une autre époque et dans une autre culture." Within this context of the history of mentalities the first priority is to uncover the mental (i.e. cognitive, emotional and psychic) dispositions of a particular historical society and decipher "the attitudes of ordinary people toward everyday life" (Hutton 1981: 237).[10] Due to this "interest in deep structures" (*ibid.*: 240) and the everyday of historical reality, the *Annales* initiate a reorientation towards a *nouvelle histoire*.[11]

---

consciousness' (conscience opaque), a realm of knowledge to which only particular groups were privy and that served as a basis for their solidarity and social identity." (Hutton 2002: 2) Therefore, Ariès (1988: 188) terms mentalities "l'inconscient collective" (collective nonconscious). Consequently, I will in the following speak of mentalities as nonconscious phenomena.

10 | The most relevant studies of the *Annales* concern historical events (e.g. the Plague, French Revolution), single regions (e.g. the Mediterranean, the Netherlands), a specific way of life (e.g. class mentality), social groups (e.g. urban elites), institutions (e.g. Spanish Inquisition), and specific dispositions of behaviour (e.g. concerning hunger, epidemics, mortality) (cf. Hutton 1981: 243; Sellin 1987: 107-108, 115-116). The thematic interest of the French history of mentalities includes (1) the vital sphere and collective attitudes towards life (e.g. age, childhood, sexuality, family, sickness, death), (2) attitudes concerning society and social behaviour (e.g. criminality, sociability, economics, agriculture, technology, law, taxes, nutrition, education, religion); (3) mythic, ritual, and religious habits and belief systems (e.g. festivals, rituals, myths, sorcery, witchcraft, religious practices); (4) cosmology in spatial and temporal experiences. An encompassing history of mentalities is offered by Peter Dinzelsbacher's collection *Europäische Mentalitätsgeschichte* (1993). For an overview on research of the history of mentalities see Hervé (1996).

11 | One of the main achievements of the *Annales* historiography is to overcome the claim of historism as the only 'true' history (e.g. as pursued by Leopold von Ranke). According to them the complexities of everyday life are strongly reduced in the history of ideas. Ariès (1988: 170) argues "opposée en bloc à l'histoire politique" and therefore, refuses politics as foundation of historical study and denies the concentration on great individuals such as kings and revolutionaries or the meta-narratives of unending and long-term series of events such as wars or revolutions (cf. *ibid.*). Because it implies a distanciation to the traditional systematisation of history into economic, social, political, and cultural history, this new historiography opens history for an anthropological dimension (cf. Sellin 1985: 562). In general this defines the common man and his mentality as the main object of interest.

In their ambition to write an encompassing history of private lives, this new historiography also constitutes a *histoire totale* rendering interdisciplinarity a prerequisite for its analyses (cf. *ibid.*: 237). Themes and issues explored in the history of mentalities define it as a multi-layered approach which creates a web of constellations including subjects of cultural history and the history of civilisations, social and intellectual history or the history of ideas without being synonymous with either of those.[12]

Scholars see an especially close connection between the history of mentalities and historical anthropology because the *Annales* strive to grasp the culture of an age in the collective mental habits of people (*ibid.*: 243). The rather wide notion of culture within the histories of mentalities initiated interesting new approaches for New Historicism, discourse theory or cultural anthropology. Because of its anthropological and interdisciplinary referentials as well as its interest in the socio-historical alterity of everyday practices, the history of mentalities also constitutes a very interesting and useful approach for Cultural Studies.

Having created new fields of interest in regard to questions of culture, Kortüm (1996: 10) claims that the original history of mentalities has long been dead as an independent discipline. Because of its interdisciplinarity and multifarious orientations we are indeed inclined to question whether the history of mentalities still provides a unified field of study (cf. Hutton 1981: 243-244; Le Goff 1985: 166). While for Traian Stoianovich (1976) the French historical method defines a specific paradigm, for Peter Burke (1990: 107) the history of mentalities rather presents "a cluster of paradigms". In the eyes of Hagen Schulze (1985: 258) the interest in mentality-related subjects is only a scientific branch and Frank-Michael Kuhlemann (1996: 182, 211) classifies it as an aspect of cultural history. Hasso Spode (1990: 10-11) even goes as far as to call the history of mentalities a mere perspective and theme. According to Volker Sellin (1985: 595), mentality presents an approach to grapple with complex subjects. This present analysis not only considers mentality a major object of research and the concept of mentality as a suitable approach within the larger context of Cultural Studies, but hopes to promote 'Mentality Studies'[13] as a genuine interdisciplinary field of study.

Even though mentality presents one of the most successful key terms in historiography, the historians of mentalities largely provide a methodological or discursive agenda and do not offer a unified concept or theory of mentalities.[14] Gurevich (1983: 177) claims that "the school resolutely declares itself to be against theory". The "theoretical

---

12 | Intellectual history, for example, denotes the history of the great ideas and the social zeitgeist rather than the history of the common man. The main difference is, as shown above, that history of mentalities is not focused on the master narratives or the high-culture aspects of leading intellectuals. Yet, according to Chartier (1988: 11-12), intellectual history encompasses all ways of thinking as it combines the history of ideas as well as the history of mentalities. Dinzelbacher (1993: XXVII) shows that intellectual history and the history of ideas can function as ancillary sciences for the history of mentalities, which necessarily encompasses aspects concerned with ideology.

13 | In the first edition Norman Simms (1982: 3) claims that the publication of *Mentalities. An Interdisciplinary Journal* is as an attempt to promote the discipline of Mentality Studies.

14 | For an extensive study of theoretical works concerning mentality see the two volume study by Klaus Neumann (2000), *Das Fremde verstehen - Grundlagen einer kulturanthropologi-*

inexactitude" (*ibid.*: 178) is enhanced due to the immateriality of mentality, the complexity of its subject matter and source material, as well as its applicability to a variety of its disparate fields of study and the consequent transformation of terminology. For Le Goff (1985: 166) the vagueness of the term is its primary attraction because it offers the concept flexibility and adaptability.[15] It is argued that an approximate agreement on the historical category suffices, as long as a precise description is given in relation to the subject matter (cf. Sellin 1985: 559). Consequently, whenever the term is defined, it is never in a very systematic form but rather a framing of the subject matter, a list of synonyms or a temporary inventory of its significations, a metaphorical description or a definition *ex negativo* (cf. e.g. Reichardt 1978: 131-132; Schulze 1985: 259-261). Without a generally valid definition, mentality randomly denotes, for example, "états d'âme", "esprit humain", "attitudes mentales", "la pensée commune", "structures mentales", "façon de sentir", "la sensibilité", "psychologie sociale", "psychologie collective", "attitude psychologique", "habitudes", "coutumes et les manières de vivre", "la manière générale de penser ", "idées et croyances" (Duby 1961: 937-966). Hence, the concept of mentality becomes rather blurred, an impression which is enhanced by the translation of *mentalités* back to English and German that causes additional confusion as well as by the arising discrepancy between the scientific notion of mentality and the day-to-day usage of the word (cf. Sellin 1985: 558-560; Chartier 1988: 11; Burke 1990: 97).

Jöckel (1987: 146) therefore points out how badly a systematic definition of mentality is needed, and there have been various attempts to delineate the most prevailing characteristics of the concept (e.g. cf. Reichardt 1978; Sellin 1985; Graus 1987; Kamm 1994; Burke 1997; Kortüm 1996; Kuhlemann 1996; Hervé 1996). Lenz (2002: 51) argues that "[t]he **term** 'mentality' hardly needs any discussion today since, due to the rise of the histories of mentalities, it is well established now" (emphasis N.P.). Instead, Kuhlemann (1996: 182) stresses that the **concept** of mentalities still lacks in differentiation[16] and a main problem lies in delineating mentality from other concepts such as culture, identity, ideology, and habitus.

In the following I will systematise the concept of mentality to make it applicable for Cultural Studies in general and for an analysis of urban mentality in particular. I will first define mentality according to the concept's appropriation by the sociologist Volker Sellin (1985, 1987). While this offers the most basic ideas for the construction of mentalities, I will secondly employ the classification of mentality in functional and substantial

---

schen Exegese. Untersuchungen zu paradigmatischen mentalitätsgeschichtlichen, ethnologischen und soziologischen Zugangswegen zu fremden Sinnwelten.

15 | For more detailed information see Reichardt (1978: 131-132), Schulze (1985: 259-261), Sellin (1985: 559-560), Graus (1987: 10-11). Even Dinzelbacher (1993: XIII) acknowledges that every article in his collection on a European history of mentality defines and approaches mentality differently.

16 | Because mentalities do not offer an obvious causal relation between social and cultural factors, they are often compared with a vague mental atmosphere (cf. Kuhlemann: 201), for example in terms of "atmosphère mentale", "rythmes de vie" (Duby 1961: 948, 952). Graus (1987: 16) calls mentalities a "tone" of thinking and behaviour. Interestingly, Sellin (1985: 560) argues that confusion about the terminology exists especially within the German context.

aspects as made by Dinzelbacher (1993) and Kuhlemann (1996). This will help to understand mentality as organon and rhizome wrought by dispositions of thinking, feeling, imagining, and acting.

2.1.2 Historical and Contemporary Social Constructions of Reality

Volker Sellin reappropriates the concept for sociology and aims at offering a consistent terminology of mentality.[17] He sees the relevance of mentality-related questions for social history and emphasises the relation between the approaches of the history of mentality and anthropology in their common concern with the change of socio-cultural conditions and the accompanying alteration in habits of the mind. Because anthropological sociology does not only define mentality as a collective nonconscious, but also as collectively shared habits of the everyday, this approach achieves to connect the mental with the social aspects of mentality, namely thinking and attitudes with behaviour and habits (cf. Sellin 1985: 574; Schulze 1985: 266; Gebhardt & Kamphausen 1994: 16).

In recurrence to Edmund Husserl, Sellin (1985: 573-582) combines the phenomenological sociology of Alfred Schütz and Peter L. Berger and Thomas Luckmann's sociology of knowledge with the cultural sociology of Theodor Geiger.[18] Sellin (*ibid.*: 573-574) begins by exemplifying the connection between mentality and "lifeworld": in accord with Husserl, lifeworld denotes the world 'as lived' prior to reflective representations and analysis (cf. *ibid.*). On the one hand, the lifeworld influences people's experiences and thereby collective mental attitudes are formed in relation to their respective habitat, while on the other hand, the world is necessarily perceived in the light of one's mental disposition. Hence, in functioning as mediators between the mental and external world, mentalities describe the process of dialectical transmission between people and their lifeworld (cf. *ibid.*: 575; Beeck 1989: 5; Gebhardt & Kamphausen 1994: 17; Kamm 1996: 89; Kuhlemann 1996: 202-203).

Because mentalities constitute a common pre-theoretical knowledge of the everyday, Sellin (1985: 579), in reference to Berger/Luckmann, understands the history of mentalities as a historical sociology of knowledge. The assumption is that collectives interacting in a social system, for example by ways of communication, form mental conceptions that become habituated over time. Mentalities thereby denote a model of reality as known (*ibid.*: 589-590; cf. Schulze 1985: 266; Kamm 1996: 88). In that sense, mentalities can be defined as specific historical and contemporary social constructions of reality (cf. Kamm 1996: 88).

17 | Scholars following this or a similar conceptualisation of mentality are Schulze (1985); Beeck (1989), Gebhardt & Kamphausen (1994), Kamm (1994, 1996, 2004), and Kuhlemann (1996). For other conceptualisations of mentality see Alex Mucchilli (1985), *Les Mentalités*.

18 | See Edmund Husserl (1936), *Die Krisis der europäischern Wissenschaften. Eine Einleitung in die transzendentale Phänomenlogie*; Alfred Schütz (1932), *Der sinnhafte Aufbau der sozialen Welt. Eine Einleitung in die verstehende Soziologie*; Peter Berger & Thomas Luckmann (1966), *The Social Construction of Reality*; Theodor Geiger (1967), *Die soziale Schichtung des deutschen Volkes. Soziographischer Versuch auf statistischer Grundlage* first published 1932.

By structuring reality, the collective nonconscious knowledge of mentalities serves as an overall function of orientation (*ibid.*: 580). Hutton argues (1981: 241): "In their coherence, prevailing conceptions of the world provide fixed points of orientation against which original ideas must be measured." Furthermore, mentalities describe instinctively knowing the means that are most appropriate to archive certain objectives (cf. Sellin 1985: 578; Gebhardt & Kamphausen 1994: 19). According to Alfred Schütz, behaviour constitutes a conscious act to change the status quo and satisfy basic needs or interests (final motif), while the pre-positioned unreflected causal motif derives from a condition experienced as deficient (cf. Schulze 1985: 248; Kamm 1996: 91; Kamm 2010: 161-162). The concrete conjunction between causal and final motif readily made available by mental structures thereby also contributes to a relief of strain on the consciousness (cf. Sellin 1985: 580). As a principle of order – or structure – mentality is thus not essentially part of nature or a concept *prima causa*, but a socially and culturally constructed entity (cf. Kamm 1996: 87). Without the standardised relations of *stimuli* and *responses* provided by mentalities, social behaviour would be impossible (*ibid.*).

This emphasises how mentalities define the boundaries of thinking (cf. Sellin 1985: 598). When transgressing these borderlines or rules of orientation, reality will be perceived as unfathomable, unthinkable, unimaginable or even impossible; instead, if the scope is too narrow and the borders impenetrable, thinking regresses to fanatism (cf. Graus 1987: 16-17).[19] These bracketing mental axioms function as an apparatus of self-censorship (*ibid.*: 16). A specific mindset therefore always includes normative assumptions which can be verbalised in particular dictums (cf. Sellin 1985: 569; Schulze 1985: 259-260; Beeck 1989: 27). Rather than expressing definite causes of behaviour, however, mentalities define a horizon of possibilities, framed in dispositions (cf. Sellin: 588-589); with various points of reference, mentalities present options or tendencies that pose a scope for acting (cf. Gebhardt & Kamphausen 1994: 19; Kamm 1996: 91; Kuhlemann 1996: 191). In this way, mentalities are the sum of nonconscious possibilities in a collective that organise everyday interaction by means of conditional orientation in a specific frame manifested in rules, etiquettes, rituals, informal laws and norms, which further restrict alternative behaviour.

From this, we can also delineate the main difference between mentality and ideology.[20] Although mentalities have similar functions to ideologies in the sense that they

19 | Le Goff (1985: 172) argues that "[m]entalities seem to be most clearly revealed in irrational and abnormal behaviour." In that respect, acknowledged deviant behaviour can lay bare mental dispositions.

20 | Duby (1985: 152) and Hervé (1996: 6) see Althusser's definition of ideologies as rendering mentalities synonymous with ideologies. Harvey (1973: 18) reveals that Marx regards ideology as an "*unaware* expression of the underlying ideas and beliefs which attach to a particular social situation, in contrast to the *aware* and critical exposition of ideas in their social context which is frequently called ideology in the west." Instead for Burke (1997: 175) Raymond Williams' concept of "cultural hegemony" as an alternative for ideology is closer to the history of mentalities. According to Burke (1992: 92), the study of mentalities stresses "collective attitudes rather than individual ones; [...] unspoken assumptions rather than explicit theories [or] common sense [...]; [...] structures of belief systems [...]." For other explanations of the relation between ideology and mentality see Vovelle (1982). In a way the difference between ideologies offer orientation or present a form of social control through habitualisation, the two terms are not synonymous. Their nonconscious, pre-theoretical, dispositional character is one main constituent of mentalities; dispositions represent unquestioned certainties which are quasi naturally accepted (cf. e.g. Sellin 1985: 561, 584). Mentalities are unreflective interpretations of reality, whereas ideologies are particular conscious and arbitrary constructions (*ibid.*: 575); the general function of mentalities is the transmission of unquestioned certainties, that of ideology to consciously construct specific meaning (*ibid.*: 584). While mentalities cannot directly be mediated by their subjects, ideologies are precisely formulated (*ibid.*: 581).

Sellin (1985: 582-586) explores the difference between the two concepts in reference to Theodor Geiger (1967: 78), who opposes mentality and ideology metaphorically as skin and cloth. Insofar, mentalities as the skin are internal dispositions that form the subjective collective consciousness and state of mind of first order; as a philosophy of life or 'atmosphere' mentalities are formless and necessarily in flux. In contrast, ideologies are the strictly designed fabric of doctrines and theories, formulated in objective ideas of a second order, a cemented 'stratosphere' (cf. *ibid.*: 77-78).

Geiger (1967: 78) acknowledges, however, that under the cloth of doctrines and ideologies various mentalities can be found, and one type of mentality can be variously adapted in diverging ideologies. Successful ideologies as well as their collective habits express unconscious structures of mentality, and ideologies, once formed and accepted, can evolve to or be integrated into structures of mentality (cf. Sellin 1985: 585-586). Because of this qualitative transformability, Kuhlemann (1996: 190-191) advocates the inclusion of ideologies within the analysis of mentalities, claiming that ideologies as well as theories and ideas often form important vantage points to define and name a particular structure of mentality.

2.1.3 Mentality as Organon and Rhizome

In his remarks on mentality Geiger (1967: 78) already differentiates between thought as a result of thinking and the way or style of thinking. Mentalities as the social construction of reality and collective nonconscious dispositions of thinking both, as shown above, describe the primary translational relation between people and their lifeworld as well as the appropriate structures of internalised nonconscious certainties. Mentality is both a mode of thought as well as a mental framework (cf. Burke 1990: 100). Most conceptualisations of mentalities have delineated this difference between mentalities as agency and structure. For example, Dinzelbacher (1993: XXII-XXIII) differentiates "*Denkweise*" as the style of thinking from "*Denkinhalt*" or the content of thoughts. Kuhlemann (1996: 183-184) specifically builds on that notion of the concept's functional and substantial character. I therefore differentiate mentality as agency and structure as organon and rhizome.

---

and mentalities supports the difference between the history of mentalities and the history of ideas as diverging conceptual approaches.

Firstly, mentalities can be understood as **organon** (Greek: *tool*).[21] The functional characteristics[22] of mentalities lie within the process of translating between a group of people and their given habitat (cf. Kuhlemann 1996: 187): constructing reality by ways of nonconscious thinking, mentalities are transmitters[23] between mental structures and material reality. According to Dinzelbacher (1993: XXII-XXIII), mentality presupposes a way of thinking as either causal, associative, inductive, abstract, deductive, or visual and therefore also resembles an instrument of selection which defines a constant point of view to make sense of the world. Febvre (2003b: 141) calls this "*outillage mental*", or mental equipment, which regularises mental activity and sets conceptual limits upon the mental frame.[24] Interpreting the model of mentality as organon of perception, interaction, acculturation, mediation, and memorisation, we can extract various functions of mentalities, some of which have already been delineated before. These functions include self-organisation and orientation through maxims or grammars of behaviour which regulate perception, experience and behaviour, as well as the inclusive function of integration in a specific socio-historical lifeworld (cf. Kuhlemann 1996: 186). Mental dispositions also have the function to align inner life with social realities by continual transformation of its certainties. Mentality as organon therefore serves the main functions of organisation, orientation, relief of strain, alignment, regulation, and integration.

Secondly, mentality can be understood as **rhizome**.[25] The structure of mentalities is defined by interconnections and ruptures between often juxtaposing collective non-

21 | Aristotle's *Organon* defines logic as the tool of science. Francis Bacon's *Novum Organum* (1620) constitutes a revolution of thinking, in which the philosophy of rationality takes over the Aristotelian tradition of perception. Bertolt Brecht's (1949) "Kleines Organon für das Theater" elaborates on the new 'logic' of epic theatre. Karl Bühler (1965) conceptualises "Das Organonmodell der Sprache" in recurrence of Platon's definitions of language as organon or tool of communication. Roman Jakobson's "Closing Statements: Linguistics and Poetics" (1960) expands Bühler's model to six basic function of verbal communication. In reference to these examples, an organon can be considered a toolbox for specific (cognitive) approaches.

22 | In his article "Les fonctions mentales dans les sociétés inférieurs" (1910) Lévy-Bruhl points out the functional parts of mentalities, especially those of memory. For Graus (1987: 16), mentalities are foremost mechanisms. Gurevich (1983: 194) defines mentality as a "prism" (in the sense of a specific tool) through which all stimuli pass, receive a specific illumination, and after their transformation into facts of consciousness become part of behaviour.

23 | Mentality as "Transmissionsriemen" (Kuhlemann 1996:187). Also for Lotman (2001: 143) "the elementary act of thinking is translation."

24 | For example by ways of "aesthetic images, linguistic codes, expressive gestures, religious rituals, social customs" (Hutton 1981: 238) but also "vocabulary, syntax, commonplaces, conceptions of space and time" (Le Goff 1985: 174).

25 | In the philosophy of Gilles Deleuze and Félix Guattari, the rhizome constitutes an image of thought that copes with multiplicities. The first chapter of *A Thousand Plateaus. Capitalism and Schizophrenia* (1980) exemplifies how the rhizome as a mode of knowledge resists duality, chronology, or hierarchy. It is characterised by connection and heterogeneity, multiplicity, a signifying rupture, cartography and decalcomania (cf. Deleuze & Guattari 1998: 5-13), whereby the idea of inbetweenness, fluidity, relationality, and metamorphosis is positioned in the centre

conscious dispositions. We can conceptualise the structure of these multiple spectra of thinking in analogy to the multiplicities, strata, segmentarities, and lines of the rhizome (cf. Deleuze & Guattari 1998: 3-25). Mentality as rhizome pays heed to the connectivity of a heterogeneous array of non-hierarchical dimensions pointing to the interconnections and correlation (roots) between single elements (nodes) of mentality. This substantial part of mentalities refers to the material content, specific cultural patterns of thought, and their overall structure (cf. Kuhlemann 1996: 187). The contents are standardised and stereotypical mindsets which hypostatise in maxims, thoughts, emotions, habits, attitudes, convictions, ideas, or even ideologies (cf. Dinzelbacher 1993: X, XXIV; Kuhlemann 1996: 186). Because mentality seems to be constructed of various micro-elements that inform each other or communicate with each other, mentality cannot be defined by only a few attributes (cf. Dinzelbacher 1993: XVIII). In this sense, structures of mentality can rather be seen as textures (cf. Kuhlemann 1996: 187).

The conception of mentalities as organon and rhizome helps to summarise mentalities as a complex network of beliefs, attitudes, ideologies, world-views, affects, discourses, memories, illusions, etc. which simultaneously influence and are determined by its functional characteristics of translation such as modes of thinking. Consequently, the concept's descriptions oscillate between poles of idea and habit, thinking and feeling, consciousness and nonconscious, norms and images. According to Friederike Meyer (1989: 86), its "attractiveness [...] has probably been enhanced by the fact that the concept conflated the cognitive and emotional aspects of behaviour and with them the various factors which govern behaviour [...]." While many conceptualisations foreground the interrelation of thinking with habits, conducting a word field analysis in texts by the historians of mentality Georges Duby (1961) and Phillip Ariès (1988) shows that mentalities comprise structures of thought, the imaginary, emotion, as well as behaviour and functions of thinking, imagining, feeling, and acting.[26]

The furthermost initials of mentalities appear to denote perceptual processes of **thinking** and the construction of structures of **thought**. For Kamm (2010: 158) in reference to Hansen (2003: 88) mentalities are known as standardisations of thinking. Also the approach to conceptualise mentalities as socio-historical constructions of reality is conducted through foregrounding cognitive ways of thinking; it focuses on the pre-theoretical or stock knowledge as the "conceptions of the world" (Hutton 1981: 254).

Besides thought processes that determine our view of the world, another structure of mentalities and way of perception is the process of **imagining** and the **imaginary**. Michel Vovelle (1982: 18) prefers Robert Mandrou's (1972: 42) definition of mental-

---

of their concept of knowledge (cf. *ibid.*: 25). Especially useful are the devices on the spatial structure of the rhizome as connected to the map, the city, and the brain (*ibid.*: 12, 15).

26 | For example: "attitudes mentales", "la pensée commune", "structures mentales", "façon de sentir", "la sensibilité", "psychologie sociale", "psychologie collective", "habitudes", "coutumes et les manières de vivre", attitude psychologique", "idées et croyances" (Duby 1961: 937-960), "genre d'esprit", "façons de penser", "manières de penser", "les modes de penser", "d'émotions", "les modes de sentir", "des visions du mondes", "l'imaginaire", "l'expression littéraire et l'imaginaire collectif", "mémoire collective profonde", "la conduite des hommes", "attitudes" (Ariès 1988: 168-169, 188).

ities as "visions du monde" that combine world views with subjective images, and he strongly stresses the constructedness of reality. Because the knowledge of the world equals a specific structure of meaning, the process of encoding and symbolisation entails the imagination, dreams, visions as well as their representations in oral folklore, fiction or visual images (cf. Burke 1997: 182). In that respect, the term mentality has been combined with that of "collective imagination" (*ibid.*: 165) or the "imaginary" (Le Goff 1990: 7).[27] Le Goff (1986: 10) even goes so far as to argue that the significance of the imaginary has become prevalent to decode structures of meaning concerning the everyday: "*On passe d'une histoire des mentalités à une histoire de l'imaginaire.*" For Le Goff (1990: 7, 12), there are no thoughts without images and representations serve the mental transmission of the perceived reality. Hence, the study of mentalities is also an analysis of the "part played by human imagination in the evolution of human societies" (Duby 1985: 165). Furthermore, we detect a close connection between the history of mentalities and memory. The intellectual historian Patrick Hutton (1988: 311, 314-315) includes memory as an element in the deep structures of the imagination because it "reconstructs [the past] as a coherent imaginative pattern."[28] Collective memories are not only of interest for the histories of mentalities but have developed into one of the most prominent issues in Cultural Studies. Memories belong to the cognitive processes of thinking or imagining and are closely connected to emotions.

Consequently, mentality also encompasses structures of **emotions**[29] and dispositions of **feeling**. Vester (1990: 444) argues: "Gerade im Mentalitätsbegriff schwingen unverkennbar nicht nur ‚kalte' Kognitionen, sondern auch ‚heiße' Emotionen als Komponenten des Begriffsinhaltes mit." Returning to the origins of the history of mentalities, the concept, as shown before, is first employed in correlation with psychology[30] where mentality denotes the collective nonconscious psychological *conditio humana* of a specific historical period. Especially for the historians of mentality Lucien Febvre and Robert Mandrou, sensibilities and emotions shape the contours of human thought and behaviour

---

27 | For example: "*imaginaire*", "*représentation de l'imaginaires collectives*", "*représentations collectives mentales*", "*illusions collectives*" (Burke 1990: 113, 115 ; Burke 1992: 93). Already Lévy-Bruhl (1956: 7) connects the mentality of primitive cultures with a specific collective imagery. For more on the imaginary also see Duby (1985), Kortüm (1996).

28 | "Memory [...] lends coherence to collective understanding by clarifying the structure of cultural traditions.[. . .] memory colonizes the past by obliging it to conform to present conceptual schemes." (Hutton 1988: 314) According to Ariès, the connection between history and memory is that history emerges out of memory, transcends it in scope and abstraction but is still grounded in this "private realm of history" (*ibid.*: 319-320). Also see Jacques Le Goff (1992) *History and Memory*; Jacques Le Goff & Pierre Nora, eds. (1985), *Constructing the Past. Essays in Historical Methodology.*

29 | Raymond Williams (1984: 64-65) speaks of "structures of feeling" when defining the intangible and mental aspect of cultural change particularly expressed in representations. For more on emotions, mentality and identity see Vester (1990: 441-445).

30 | For psychologists, mentality is often simply a synonym for character or personality (cf. Reichardt 1978: 133). Mandrou (1972: 43) explains the difference between psychoanalysis on an individual basis and the socio-historical psychology of a collective.

(cf. Sellin 1985: 565-566; Chartier 1988: 20; Spode 1990: 36). According to Mandrou (1972: 41-42), it is a major objective of history to reconstitute the sensibilities of a society, such as emotions of hope, solidarity, anxiety, or hostility apparent in collective world-views, but also mass paranoia and cultural schizophrenia. Psycho-historical changes then indicate a transformation of mentalities (cf. Hutton 1981: 247-248; Vester 1990: 445). Consequently, psychological dispositions of an epoch strongly determine perception and behaviour.[31]

In that respect, mentalities moreover constitute structures of **acting** and specific dispositions of **behaviour**. As shown before, the concept of mentality is seen somewhere between cognition and habit. In reference to Clifford Geertz' cultural anthropology, Sellin (1985: 577) defines the history of mentalities as a history of meaning or a history of behavioural patterns. Geertz understands cultural habits as an acted document and human behaviour as symbolic action (cf. *ibid.*: 572-574). Because actions are themselves a form for constructing reality, any kind of behaviour carries implicit meanings of a specific mentality (*ibid.*: 578).[32] In other words, as the lifeworld is represented in habitualised structures of meaning, any act, whether pragmatic or symbolic, characterises the permanent transmission between the habitat and mentality. Mentality can thus be analysed as collective attitudes and certainties materialised in all forms of everyday behaviour like habits, deeds, attitudes, declarations, etc. without simply resembling the sum of these expressions (cf. Graus 1987: 15-16). Because people's everyday practices are subject to certain conventions and the majority of manners, customs, and habits are culturally standardised, some highly ritualised practices do not mirror a current mentality but one from the past (cf. Sellin 1985: 571; Gebhardt & Kamphausen 1994: 20).

In regard to the dispositions of behaviour, mentality often conflates with habitus, although the concepts can be differentiated. For Alheit (2005: 40) mentality represents a macro-, habitus a micro-climate.[33] According to Pierre Bourdieu (1979: 169), habitus constitutes a "Handlungs-, Wahrnehmungs- und Denkmatrix", a matrix of (class-)specific structures of perception, thought and action, normally lasting acquired schemes, which generate and regulate behaviour (cf. Alheit 2005: 40). In that sense, habitus also forms common knowledge that serves as an apparatus of orientation and self-control for human behaviour. Habitus, however, especially allows for an analysis of social differ-

31 | One only needs to think of the *fin-de-siècle* mood at the turn of the nineteenth century as an emotional disposition which greatly influenced attitudes at that time, or the great fear during the French Revolution and the great terror during Robespierrian France that impacted on the behaviour of citizens.

32 | "Alle Aktivitäten sind zugleich Deutungen, Deutungen umgekehrt Aktivitäten." (Beeck 1989: 5)

33 | Alheit (2005) synonymously employs habitus for mentality in reference to Norbert Elias' *The Civilizing Process* (1939). For Elias (1994c), national habitus basically stands for mentality as rules of behaviour once enforced by an elite are imposed by the human psyche. According to Elias, these rules of behaviour such as table manners, sexual etiquette, attitudes towards bodily functions, use of language, etc. have become more disciplined and constrained since the Middle Ages. In this respect the history of mentalities becomes part of a history of civilisation (Elias 1994a). For more see Hutton (1981: 274-249) and Vester (1996: 39-48).

ences or social milieus. It defines the social position according to idiosyncratic lifestyles, which are determined by diverging combinations of 'cultural capital' (Bourdieu 1982: 179, 279); hence lifestyle, albeit in rather materialistic ways, resonates attitudes, values, and world-views. Bourdieu (*ibid.*: 668) calls the base of unquestioned and self-evident beliefs "doxa", which are comparable to dispositions of acting.[34] Thus, habitus, as a physical manifestation of mental structures (cf. Vester 1990: 441), ascribes a certain aspect of mentality, while complex mental structures cannot be defined by habitus alone.

The concept of habitus, however, brings us closer to an understanding of the internalisation of mentalities. People live in and form their habitat but they are also defined by this socio-cultural environment and the experience of everyday life by ways of socialisation and enculturation. Bourdieu (*ibid.*: 277, 730) writes about the embodiment of habitus, by which he means that habitus is acquired through socialisation, internalised and subsequently handed down to following generations. This learned 'character' becomes internalised as mentality. As was shown above, Theodor Geiger stresses the embodiment of mentality. Therefore, we can speak with Bourdieu of the incorporation of mentalities (cf. Alheit 2005: 25). In the sense that the lifeworld is impressed onto people's minds by ways of socialisation, enculturation, and processes of communication, the following chapter deals with the main determinants of mentality: collective, time, space, and compression.

2.2 Determinants of Mentality

Mental dispositions are substantially specified in their relation to a particular habitat and therefore mental structures cannot be seen independent from social, historical, geographical, and cultural realities.[35] According to Kantian *a priori* categories time and space are the two dimensions which frame people's experience.[36] As basic categories of human existence, space and time then not only constitute the most basic referentials of culture but also form the main determinants of collective nonconscious dispositions of thinking, imagining, feeling, and acting. In this sense, mental structures unfold in

34 | As internalised dispositions that produce cultural practices, habitus is close to Febvre's notion of mental equipment. Mentalities as maxims or rules are equally connected to habitus. Other related concepts are, for example, the theory of cultural grammar and Geert Hofstede's dimensions of culture. For more on the connection between mentality, habitus and lifestyle see Kamm (2010). As an exemplary study see Heinz Schilling (2003), *Kleinbürger. Mentalität und Lebensstil.*

35 | Vester's (1996: 116) model explicitly marks the significance of socio-historical realities as the cause for differentiations between mentalities, while Dinzelbacher (1993: XVIII) shows how mentalities also affect the socio-political frame.

36 | "Wenn ich a priori sagen kann: alle äußeren Erscheinungen sind im Raume, und nach den Verhältnissen des Raumes a priori bestimmt, so kann ich aus dem Prinzip des inneren Sinnes ganz allgemein sagen: alle Erscheinungen überhaupt, d.h. alle Gegenstände der Sinne, sind in der Zeit und stehen notwendigerweise in Verhältnissen der Zeit." (Kant cit. in Reichel 1987: 1) See Emanuel Kant (1971), *Kritik der reinen Vernunft* (Engl: *The Critique of Pure Reason*).

a spatially, temporarily and socially marked sphere of experience defining mentalities "d'espace, de temps, de masse" (Duby 1961: 948). In the following I will delineate collectivity, time and space in their determination of mentality in general and their definition of collective, temporal, and spatial mentality in particular. The fourth determinant pays heed to their interdependence and the consequent dynamic of collective space-time-compressions which unfolds as cultural change.

2.2.1 Collectivity and Collective Mentality

The most important preliminary of mentalities is that they are significant collective phenomena. For Durkheim (1933: 38-39) collective consciousness comprehends "the totality of beliefs and sentiments common to average members of the same society". Mentality thereafter becomes defined as a collective nonconscious or socio-temporal construction of reality, which both suggest that mental structures are produced within the bounds of a specific collectivity and thus only become effective collectively.

For Duby (1961: 940), the main prerogative of the history of mentalities is to "observer les mouvements collectifs". Collectives of major interest to the historians of mentalities are peoples and nations; collectives can be based on a common ground in language, class, profession, gender, age, and locale. Because social history is mainly concerned with the mentality of social groups – "les individus d'un même ensemble social" (Duby 1961: 944) – this has created an unseverable link between mentality and milieu (cf. Le Goff 1985: 174).[37] Nevertheless, this relation not only applies to social milieus but also to "milieux géographiques" (Duby 1961: 944).[38] The size of these milieus might vary from a city region to a whole nation state. In this analysis, metropolitan London is considered the significant spatial milieu whose population constitutes geographical collectivity.

Regarding collectivity as a determinant of mentality, one major problem is to differentiate social and collective phenomena from those generated by independently thinking and acting individuals. The question is whether, for example, a certain practice is the action of an individual or an expression of collective habitus. The adage is that mentalities override individual differences and emphasise the immanent commonalities between people. According to Le Goff (1985: 167), "[t]he mentality of any one historical individual, however important, is precisely what that individual shares with other men of his time." Already Durkheim (1933: 38-39) points out that the collective conscious "is an entirely different thing from particular consciences, although it can only be realized

37 | Proust's *Recherche* is also a representation of the mentality of the French aristocracy before and after the First World War from the perspective of an outsider. The narrator, Marcel, is the son of a bourgeois family gaining access to the upper class and aristocratic circles.

38 | Schilling (2003) analyses small bourgeois mentality which is not only connected with a specific social and professional milieu, but this collective can specifically be located in small towns. He identifies authority, closeness, conformity, force, kitsch, smugness, thriftiness and rational order as the main constituents of the social group of businessmen, craftsmen and employees living in small towns, an urban type which is characterised by family, profession, security, chauvinism, etc. (cf. Schilling 2003: 7-9, 81-83).

through them". Regarding mentality, this means that dispositions of thinking, imagining, feeling and acting become effective through the single members of the collective. In other words, the structures of socio-temporal constructions of reality are functionally related to the individual (cf. Kamm 1996: 89). Because the individual is the agent of mentality and nonconscious mental structures are always part of a collective, it does not make sense to create an artificial antagonism between individual and collective (cf. Graus 1987: 13).

Klaus Hansen (2009: 27) defines 'collective' as a partial common ground of its individual members, whereby collectivity is outlined by people's similarities. Thus, collectivity is not delineated by an assemblage of similarities but rather foregrounds commonality on the basis of shared characteristics.[39] Mentality stresses these common denominators of thinking, imagining, feeling, and acting, without which collectivity would be impossible: "Ohne gemeinsames Denken, Fühlen und Meinen sind soziale Gruppen undenkbar." (Jöckel 1987: 148) In this way, mentality and individuality do not oppose each other; rather, mentality is a collective phenomenon the individual unconsciously has in common with a particular collective. Hence mentalities do not contradict or downplay individual variations and neither do they imply a heightened degree of conformity (cf. Beeck 1989: 22-23).

Collectivity as determinant of mentality easily leads to an assumption of homogeneity or the proclamation of one-dimensional collective mentalities (cf. Graus 1987: 14; Burke 1990: 94; Hansen 2009: 81-108). The notion of homogeneous 'mass' thinking, imagining, feeling and acting is certainly inapt. Just as social homogeneity does not exist even in a small village, let alone a metropolis, people of the same habitat do not constitute a homogeneous whole as regards their agency of behaviour or mental dispositions. Beeck (1989: 7) contends that the differentiation of realities since modernity has produced various spectra of mentalities. Although there are certain 'points of reference' important for the collective as a whole, these structures do not constitute a consistent unit that applies to all members of a collective without exception.

Graus (1987: 20) argues, however, that the objective of Mentality Studies does not lie in pre-defining heterogeneity and then simply proving difference in thinking as well. The aim is rather to start with a largely homogeneous group and analyse the strata of mentalities within.[40] In this context, Hansen (2009: 99) positively rates the contemporary use of mentality in the plural (mentalities, dispositions, attitudes) in order to emphasise the often opposing components of a way of thinking. He especially acknowledges the presentation of both 'insular mentality' and 'empire mentality' by Kamm & Lenz (2004) as different aspects of British mentalities (cf. Hansen 2009: 99-100).[41]

---

39 | Berg (1990: 233-234) defines the common denominators of individual and collective created by solidarity, belonging, common roots, descent as well as shared interest and a philosophy of life regarding common worldviews, ideology, religion, political convictions, values and norms.

40 | Nevertheless, Graus (1987: 23) notes that a synchronic comparison between differing groups is definitely helpful for the analysis.

41 | Lately the term 'insular mentality' has been transformed to *Insular Mentalities* (Kamm & Sedlmayr 2007). According to Kamm & Sedlmayr (2007: 8), the plural is to stress "that any mentality is a dynamic construct, a discursive effect, negotiated on various levels of a society."

Due to the "simultaneous coexistence of several mentalities" (Le Goff 1985: 175) in one collective, it consequently appears highly problematic to speak of **the** mentality. As was shown before, mentality itself forms a rather complex rhizomatic structure whose single components juxtapose and whose contents contradict one another. Nevertheless, these opposing elements still share defining features in relation to a specific and common habitat. The focus of this analysis concerning the collective determinant is the metropolitan population. As argued above, a collective unit of a group of people, such as the city's denizens, would not work without a common mentality despite the fact that this group of people is extremely diverse. Consequently, in the following, I will stick to the use of the term in the singular regarding urban or London mentality, although I do recognise that this is made up by various conflicting and ambivalent mental structures.

Probably due to their common interconnection with collectivity, mentality and identity are often used interchangeably.[42] As was shown before, this especially holds true for the colloquial use of mentality, where the term simply denotes the inner characteristics or mental side of a specific group identity. Although identity and mentality are empirically similar elements of culture, the two concepts cannot be considered synonymous (cf. Gebhardt & Kamphausen 1994: 19; Vester 1996: 10).

Social-constructivist notions pertain that identity is formed by means of socialisation and acculturation within a certain collective, while purely constructivist conceptualisations assume that identity is constituted by self-reflexive processes. Hence, the individual by locating itself within various collectives attains different traits of characters or a "patchwork-identity" (Berg 1990: 222). Regarding identity, one can really speak of a basic collective identity wherein other personal identities might coexist (cf. Vester 1996: 122). Because identity stresses an explicit identification with others (*ibid.*: 10), group identity advocates the inclusion within a set of dispositions and habits (cf. Berg 1990: 229).

In contrast, mentality stresses nonconscious dispositions of thinking, imagining, feeling, and acting. Mentality is thus not as easily objectified as the characteristics are deeply connected and its structures cannot be consciously altered (cf. Vester 1996: 11). Moreover, mentality rather points towards the substantial formation of a collective than the self-definition of an individual by ways of a collective identity. In this sense, mentality represents an underlying agency for the formation of a group identity which implies that a unifying mentality is the pre-disposition for a shared collective identity (cf. Berg 1990: 231). Consequently, there is a dialectical process between mentality and identity

---

This approach is especially useful for assessing the transformation of a pre-defined mentality. A change of a specific mental structure as apparent in discursive practices is close to Foucault's understanding of mentality. For more on the connection between Foucault and the historians of mentalities see Hutton (1981: 251-257).

42 | For details see the collection edited by Hahn (1990), especially the essays by Gerhard Winter or Oliver Häußler. The following argument builds on Berg's (1990) and Vester's (1990) essays published in this volume as well as Vester's *Kollektive Identitäten und Mentalitäten* (1996). Although Vester (1996) acknowledges the difference between the concept of mentality and that of identity, he still uses identity and mentality interchangeably in his analysis. For more on the theoretical nexus between collective, mentality and national identity see Hansen (2009).

formation: a common mental attitude furthers the identification with other people, while we can discern collective mentalities from individual preferences for a specific group identity (*ibid.*: 221). Due to mentalities' function of integration, identity is constructed through mental belonging.

This indicates that a basic homogeneity, i.e. a collective mentality, has a unifying effect for a largely heterogeneous urban population. Concerning the social lifeworld of metropolitan collectivity, I propose that urban mentality functions as a significant tool in forming an urban "landscaped citizenship" (Newland 2008: 22) or in the construction of London identity.

2.2.2 Time and Temporal Mentality

As an *a priori* of human experience, time is the second determinant of mentality. The study of mentalities strives to unravel the socio-temporal constructions of reality or decipher the mentality of a specific historical or contemporary period. The adage is that the temporal make-up of the lifeworld determines historio-specific mentalities, something which has popularly been conceived as "zeitgeist". Insofar, Ariès (1988: 188) defines the phenomenon as "commun à toute une société à un certain moment". For him, the history of mentalities is involved in the exploration of historical alterity and he argues: "[l]'histoire des mentalités est donc plutôt celle des mentalités d'autrefois, des mentalités non actuelles." (*Ibid.*: 185) Already Darnton (1984: 4) rejects "the comfortable assumption that Europeans thought and felt two centuries ago just as we do today [...]." Rather "[w]e constantly need to be shaken out of a false sense of familiarity with the past [...]." (*Ibid.*) Consequently, the main questions of the history of mentality concern periods where people and atmosphere appear drastically different from today, especially the Middle Ages, the Early Modern Age or Pre-revolutionary Era.[43] In that respect the emphasis for historians of mentalities lies with epochal differences of mentality. Duby (1961: 939), for example, contends that "coutumes et les manières de vivre, attitude psychologique des hommes n'était peut-être pas restée semblables à toutes les époques". The study of historical epochs not only stresses the relative permanence of mental structures, but in comparison with each other the different mentalities of these periods outline the transformations of dispositions of thinking, imagining, feeling and thinking. This brings to the fore major temporal characteristics of mentalities, namely those of persistence and transformation.

---

43 | See Jacques Le Goff (1960) *Au moyen age*; Jacques Le Goff (1991), *Pour un autre Moyen Age*; Peter Dinzelbacher is editor of the six-volume series *Kultur und Mentalität* (2002-2007) on the Early Middle Ages, High Middle Ages, Late Middle Ages, Early Modern Period, Antiquity and Baroque Era. Others: Ernst Werner (1983), *Stadt- und Geistesleben im Hochmittelalter*; Rolf Sprandel (1972), *Mentalitäten und Systeme. Neue Zugänge zur mittelalterlichen Geschichte*; Sabine Tanz (1993), *Mentalität und Gesellschaft im Mittelalter;* Hans-Henning Kortüm (1996), *Menschen und Mentalitäten: Einführung in die Vorstellungswelten des Mittelalters*; Jan Rüdiger (2001), *Aristokraten und Poeten. Die Grammatik einer Mentalität im tolosanischen Hochmittelalter.* Later analysis expanded to the French Ancien Régime and the French Revolution as well as to the Industrial Revolution and the nineteenth century.

According to Fernand Braudel (1958: 727-731), historical time features three discontinuous strata of time – *longue durée, conjuncture, temps bref* – each of which corresponds to a distinct aspect of historical reality.[44] On these various layers of historical time, historians of mentalities base their assumptions of inertia and mobility in regard to mental structures. For the first generation of historians of mentalities, long duration constitutes the key phenomenon of mental structures, an assumption cemented by Braudel (*ibid.*: 725-753). It is assumed that mentalities are characterised by a high degree of constancy, because they are rooted within the deepest layers of the collective unconscious (cf. *ibid.*: 733). Moreover, this theory of persistence is supported by the notion that "[o]nly by scanning long periods of time could change in the Western mentality be measured" (Hutton 1981: 255) because longer periods of time are able to chart dis/continuities and hence lay bare the slow adaptations or gradual transformations of "new conceptual schemes" (*ibid.*: 255). Consequently, the temporal evolvement of mentalities is characterised by inertia. Due to this 'constancy-axiom' (cf. Spode 1990: 12-13), the history of mentalities has also been interpreted as the most immobile aspect of social history. For Braudel (1958: 731), "les cadres menteaux [...] sont prisons de longue durée". The problem of mentalities as prisons of long duration is the implication of a static milieu (cf. Gebhardt & Kamphausen 1994: 19-20) and the absence of historical movement which paradoxically promotes an ahistorical model of archetypical structures of thought.

The history of mentalities, however, still supposes that societies are subject to change and takes the transformation of mentalities as prime assumption. Michel Vovelle's (1982: 222) concept of a "histoire du mouvement" rejects both the "histoire des résistances" (*ibid.*: 217) as well as the fixation of collective mentalities. For him a social and political change within society necessarily corresponds with a slow and continuous change of mentality. Mentalities inhibit the function of orientation; if these dispositions do not apply anymore to the lifeworld a change in attitude becomes necessary and new structures have to be integrated into the current social constructions of reality. In this exposition, the particular dynamics of mentalities are therefore understood as persistence and transformation.

Due to an alteration between inertia and movement as well as the various layers of historical time, I propose that the concept of mentality can be defined as one of multitemporal dynamics. Braudel's model of historical time initially argues against a simple chronology of history; instead the composite rhythms of long duration, conjunctures, and events promote a "pluralité du temps social" (Braudel 1958: 726). Various strata exert

44 | Long duration (e.g. century) – "l'histoire de longue, même de très longue durée" (Braudel 1958: 727) – reveals the enduring character of phenomena such as geography and climate. This seemingly motionless history, of people in relation to the surrounding milieu, is a history of slow changes, structural long-term modifications and recurrences which, owing to their seemingly flawless adaptations, are often hard to detect (cf. *ibid.*: 731). Medium term (e.g. decade) or the history of slow rhythms – "conjoncture" (*ibid.*: 730) – refers to the social history of groups and mainly reveals modifications in systems such as economic cycles. Micro-history (e.g. brief period) – "temps bref, à l'individu, à l'événement" (*ibid.*: 727) – denotes the history of individuals and those of events (cf. *ibid.*: 728); it is the history of short instances, such as fires, catastrophes, crimes that make the daily news.

different temporal influences – political outsets change rather quickly, society normally transforms slowly and geographical transformations are sometimes barely perceptible. Due to this diachronic assemblage of geographical, social and individual time, mentalities are bound up in the complex dynamics of the respective habitat. Being part of the *longue durée*, social value systems proceed at a different pace, creating a divergence between reality and mentality (cf. Duby 1985: 152). A change of mentality, however, also always takes place in mid-term, so that intergenerational conflicts can be seen mainly as conflicts of mentalities (cf. Sellin 1987: 103, 106). Moreover, the transformation of "mental horizons of an age" (Hutton 1981: 241) can be proved within only a couple of years due to political disruptions or enforced ideologies. Examples of an encompassing social change that alters mental structures in a short time are the Industrial Revolution but also, for example, the Great Plague, the Blitz or single events like the Great Fire or 9/11. Thus, movements of change in mentalities can be of various stability, rhythm, speed, and periodisation.

Seen in this light of various rhythms and pace of transformation, mentalities are complex structures with different temporal layers which can be of contemporary character but might also feature as residual yet persistent components from the past.[45] In Braudel's (1958: 735) words: "Chaque 'actualité' rassemble des mouvements d'origine, de rythme différent : le temps d'aujourd'hui date à la fois d'hier, d'avant-hier, de jadis." Examining mentalities means not to over-emphasise change or neglect stability of mental structures, but to be aware of both continuities and discontinuities (cf. Le Goff 1985: 170; Kortüm 1996: 26). According to Dinzelbacher (1993: XXV), a study of mentalities must first lay bare the various temporal strata, for example by ways of diachronic or synchronic comparisons, in order to identify elements of stability or change.

This study takes the political era Blair as a vantage point for the temporal determination of an epochal contemporary London mentality. The period between 1997 and 2007 is not only influenced by its mid-term characteristics but also wrought by the long-term dynamics of the post-war period and the city's legacy as the former centre of the British Empire. Moreover, this transitional decade has seen a major disruption due to 9/11 and London itself was a setting for major short-term events, such as Princess Diana's funeral or the terrorist attacks in 2005, which have notably impacted Londoners' *conditio humana*.

2.2.3 Space and Spatial Mentality

In accordance with Kant's *a priori*, space is a central element of any ontological and existential dimension and thereby lies at the basis of all world-views. A general "*sense of space*" (Thrift 2008: 395) constitutes "a-whereness" (*ibid.*: 406) which indicates that position and context are vital to any construction of knowledge.[46] Hence, space is the third determinant of mentality. This chapter first engages with the historian of mentalities'

---

45 | Foucault therefore opposes the idea of unifying one culture or one epoch under a single mentality (cf. Jöckel 1987: 155).

46 | According to the Aristotelian tradition, which casts space as a mental category by which objects are named and classified, thinking itself entails a geographical dimension as thoughts are

concentration on regional mentalities and the conceptualisation of space as a main determinant of mentalities by Lucien Febvre and Fernand Braudel. Both can be considered examples of a spatial turn *avant la lettre*. Therefore, I will secondly discuss the propositions of contemporary notions of space as relative and relational and thirdly assess the implications of postmodern concepts of space for the construction of contemporary mentalities.

Fernand Braudel did not only alter the notion of time in historical discourse, but also that of space by exploring the relation between collectives and space or history and geography. Braudel's *La Méditerranée et le monde méditerranéen à l'époque de Philippe II* (1949) is an example of an "approach in historical research, in which problems of natural and social space are considered as important as problems of pluralities of time rhythms." (Gurevich 1983: 173; cf. Braudel 1958: 753) As was shown above, Braudel (1958: 727, 731-732) regards geography and topography as barely perceptible phenomena of long duration which are nevertheless powerful in shaping the human condition.[47] Critics who therein see space as a backdrop and an anthropological constant (e.g. cf. Weigel 2002: 160-161), or read a resurgence of geographical determinism (e.g. cf. Piltz 2008: 85), neglect, however, that Braudel considers long duration as a key element of the history of mentalities. Consequently, geography and space are a major focus of the temporal dynamics oscillating between persistence and transformation and are thus a main indicator of the change of mentalities. Initially, Braudel's concentration on the geographical aspect of mentalities also marks the advent of a great new orientation of the *Annales* concerning "aires culturelles" (Piltz 2008: 86) or regional mentalities.

At least since the 1960s, historians of mentality are intensively engaged in research concerning a "histoire régional culturelle" (Ariès 1988: 183) which is concerned with human geography of a specific cultural-historical space. The history of mentalities is interested in spatial differences of mental structures, trying to decipher the unique characteristics of a region's consciousness (cf. *ibid.*). Gebhardt and Kamphausen (1994: 25) even argue that mentalities are at the core always regional mentalities set in a specific socio-cultural environment. Because individuals are embedded in a particular social, historical, and geographical milieu, they assume, in expanding the lifeworld-model, that mental structures are especially formed by impressions people receive from their spatial surroundings.

Even earlier than Braudel, Lucien Febvre's *A Geographical Introduction to History* (1919), in which he calls for an interdisciplinary human geography connecting history, geography and sociology, explores the relations between man and environment, stressing

---

assembled similar to a landscape (cf. Reichert 1996a: 4; Bachmann-Medick 2006: 303). For further remarks on spatial thinking see Reichert (1996a, 1996b).

47 | "L'exemple le plus accessible semble encore celui de la contrainte géographique. L'homme est prisonnier, des siècles durant, de climats, de végétations, de populations animales, de cultures, d'un équilibre lentement construit, dont il ne peut s'écarter sans risquer de remettre tout en cause. Voyez la place de transhumane dans la vie montagnarde, la permanence de certains secteurs de vie maritime, enracinés en tels points privilégiés des articulations littorales, voyez la durable implantation des villes, la persistance des routes et des trafics, la fixité surprenante du cadre géographique des civilisations." (Braudel 1958: 731-732)

that it is a question of active "reciprocal adaptation" (Febvre 2003a: 87; cf. 1; 20; 361-362). Thereby, Febvre (*ibid.*: 2, 12, 38, 358) firstly refutes the notion of geographical determinism so prominent at the time, and secondly he severely criticises the conception of the spatial fix by introducing the idea of spatial dynamics.[48] He argues: "There is no a priori impossibility that the nature of soil and climate have an influence even on the character of nations, on their way of thought [...] or moral tendencies". (*Ibid.*: 34) And further: by "systematic habits [...] stamping their mark on minds" (*ibid.*: 368) a certain environment can impresses itself on physical and psychical man contributing to the "collective outlook of man and their myths and legends" (*ibid.*: 33). Thus, as with contemporary notions of human geography, even for the first generation of historians of mentalities it is not space or geography as such that determines mental structures, but rather the ascribed semantics of space, such as inclusion, exclusion, suppression or encouragement of a certain behaviour (cf. Schroer 2006: 177-178). In that way, spatial lifeworld and the constructed images of space conduct a strong influence on the development and formation of human character, consciousness, and mentality.

As was shown above, a major interest of a study of mentalities lies within a geographical milieu. This stresses the collective determinant of mentalities here by way of a common regional attachment and the development or formation of a regional mentality or even identity.[49] Schilling (2003: 83) defines the manageability of space as a prereq-

---

48 | The determinist thesis records that geographical frames constitute man and his activities. Besides genetic explanations, geographical arguments have been the most important ones concerning 'natural' determinants of a national character. In the evolutionary ideas of Darwin, the Social Darwinism of Spencer, and especially Ratzel's anthropo-political geography, Febvre (2003a: 13-18) detects geography as the "powers of the soil" exerting strong influences on the "genius of peoples". For example, Febvre (*ibid.*: 67) considers Emile Boutmy's explanation of English collective physiognomy on grounds of the soil as collective ethnology and not geography: "It was as though England, for instance, a country without a navy up to the sixteenth century [...], and a country without manufacturers until the end of the eighteenth century, had none the less been from its origin down to our own times the wonderful island of iron and coal, isolated in the midst of the ocean, whose virtues and praises are so often sung." (*ibid.*: 12) Against this geographical determinism Febvre (*ibid.*: 8, 19) sets the geographical possibilism of Vidal de la Blache. Febvre (*ibid.*: 87) states that it is more than probable that soil and climate influence the distribution of men or facilitate concentration, but there are only geographical possibilities which frame various types of human adaptation. The essential cause is human activity, as man forms the land according to his interests. "There is no human group, no human society, without a territorial basis." (*Ibid.*: 38) Febvre's (*ibid.*: 39-40, 47) examples include the totemic rather than terrestrial bonds of Aborigines in Central Australia or immigrants who take their spatially related structures with them. Soja (1998: 37) describes the myth behind environmental determinism as the idea of a spatial fix which indicates that spatial dynamics are non-existent and that space is always the passive background or context – "a world of passivity and measurement rather than action and meaning." For more on spatial determinism and voluntarism see Schroer (2008: 137).

49 | See, for example, Gisela Tschudin (1990), *Schweizer Käser im Zarenreich. Zur Mentalität und Wirtschaft ausgewanderter Bauernsöhne und Bauerntöchter*; Anselm Zurfluh (1994), *Uri, Modell einer traditionellen Welt? Eine ethno-geschichtliche Studie über die Urner Mentalität 17.-20. Jahrhundert*; Martin Bachmann (1999), *Holländische Mentalität - Moderne Men-*

uisite of spatial identity. Referring to the theory of mentalities developed in this book, **a common mental manageability of space** is prevalent for the formation of identity. This construction of spatial identities is possible on the basis of national, regional, or locale-specific mentalities.[50] Spatial mentality in general can then be defined in terms of spatial scale, from geographical macro-spaces of the nation to regional meso-space to local micro- or even corporeal nano-spaces. In this analysis, the urban meso-space of urban idiosyncrasy is considered the main spatial determinant of London mentality (see chapter 4).

The regional historiography of the French *Annales* School has rightly been mentioned as a major instance of the spatial turn *avant la lettre* (cf. Soja 1998: 38; Soja 2008: 18; Weigel 2002: 160; Bachmann-Medick 2006: 312; Piltz 2008: 82). Not only are the historians of mentality the first to deny time a specific privilege, the first to argue against environmental determination, but also the first to call for an interdisciplinary human geography connecting history, geography, sociology and thereby a general spatial approach in the social sciences. In this respect, with their conceptualisation of mentality they initiate the movement from *Zeitgeist* to *Raumgeist*.[51]

In a much quoted passage originally dated from 1967, the philosopher and historian of ideas Michel Foucault (1986: 22) suggests that with the epoch of Postmodernity space rather than time emerges as the centre of critical analysis:

> We are in the epoch of simultaneity: we are in the epoch of juxtaposition, the epoch of the near and the far, of the side-by-side, of the dispersed. We are at the moment, I believe, when our experience of the world is less that of a long life developing through time than that of a network that connects points and intersects with its own skein. One could perhaps say that certain ideological conflicts animating present-day polemics oppose the pious descendents of time and the determined inhabitants of space.

---

talität? Untersuchungen zum Bürgertum der Provinz Holland im 17. Jahrhundert; Katrin Stech (2002), *Nachbarschaftliche Mentalität im bayerisch-tschechischen Grenzraum.* For more also see Gebhardt & Kamphausen (1994).

50 | In accordance with the postmodern spatial dynamics and the resurgence of local cultures, the notion of regional mentalities is a matter of particular interest. Spatial theory and Cultural Studies have noticed the importance of spatial mentality and included this concept in their research. Also, operational approaches concerning spatial formation of mentalities by ways of regional marketing are common nowadays. New Labour's marketing approach of 'Cool Britannia' and 'New London' can be interpreted as pursuing a transformation of metropolitan mentality.

51 | I allude here to Soja's (2008) article on the Spatial Turn "Vom 'Zeitgeist' zum 'Raumgeist'. New Twists on the Spatial Turn". Soja (2008b: 245-249) traces the subordination of spatial hermeneutics in social theory back to Modernism and Western Marxism. He argues that the process of despatialisation and academic peripheralisation of space during Modernism results in an "ontological distortion of Western social thought" (Soja 2008a: 19) which again leads to disruptions of empirical analysis in regard to the categories of time and space. Therefore, he sees the world-view of the last 150 years as dominated by a historical lens furthering 'spatial blindness' (cf. Soja 2008b: 243).

The 'Spatial Turn' has defined this renaissance of space in cultural and social theory at the latest since Edward Soja's *Postmodern Geographies* (1989).[52] It initially describes the abandonment of time as the main focus for "a view in which geography is not relegated to an afterthought of social relations, but is intimately involved in their construction" (Warf & Arias 2008a: 1). Thereby, the Spatial Turn allows for new analytical approaches concerning "human subjectivity, everyday life, and the multiple dimensions of identity" (*ibid.*: 4).[53] In this respect, the assumptions of concepts of the Spatial Turn also widen the scope for Mentality Studies.

In general, the Spatial Turn describes a new discourse including a critical understanding of spatial concepts as well as a redefinition of the term 'space' employed in a wide interdisciplinary context.[54] According to Bachmann-Medick (2006: 289, 291, 304), space in relation to the Spatial Turn is (1) the central category of analysis, (2) the principle of construction of social behaviour, (3) the main dimension of materiality and experience, and (4) a major strategy of representation. New socio-spatial phenomena, contemporary concepts, and metaphoric vocabulary include, for example, terms of cultural area, historical location, *lieux de mémoire*, non-place, virtual space, contested space, mental maps, place, location, borderlands, marginality, deterritorialisation, etc.

Although as *a priori* the "ontological importance of space is general and not specific to the recent period" (Massey 1998: 223), the Spatial Turn has been variously described as a 'rebirth' of space as well as a 'revolution' in the construction of space, the categorical 're-conception' of spatial components as well as an epochal and transdisciplinary 'shift in paradigm' (cf. Bachmann-Medick 2006: 287; Döring & Thielemann 2008a: 8, 13; Warf & Arias 2008a: 1).[55] The turn towards spatial thinking in critical theory has certainly

---

52 | For Soja (1998: 3, 8; Soja 2008: 249-250) the origin of the Spatial Turn lies in the 1960s; his chosen pioneers of a new postmodern geography are Michel Foucault, Fredric Jameson, Anthony Giddens, David Harvey, Henri Lefebvre and Jane Jacobs.

53 | For more on the Spatial Turn see the collections edited by Döring & Thielemann (2008) or Warf & Arias (2008).

54 | Warf & Arias (2008a: 2) even go so far as to argue that "space is a vehicle for examining what it means to be interdisciplinary or multidisciplinary". Within Cultural Studies issues of territoriality, insider and outsider, uneven developments, centre-margin structures are of main interest; concepts of space are explored with an emphasis on questions concerning cultural differences of spatial perception and the influence of space regarding identity formations. For a survey of influential trends of the Spatial Turn in English Literary and Cultural Studies see Gilbert (2008: 102).

55 | In *Postmodern Geographies* Soja (1998: 11) still sees "no hegemonic shift" but a mere need to privilege the spatial over the historical in order to recreate equilibrium between space and time. However, today, he not only considers the Spatial Turn a "still advancing and potentially epochal paradigm shift" (Soja 2008a: 12) but a real master turn (Soja 2008b: 242-243). Insofar Soja (*ibid.*: 243) also severely criticises Bachmann-Medick's (2006) conception of the Cultural Turn as encompassing seven smaller turns – linguistic, interpretative, performative, rhetorical, literary, postcolonial, translational pictorial/iconic turn. However, in contrast to the paradigm shift as described by Thomas Kuhn, the holistic scientific inquiry has not changed towards the spatial (cf. Frank 2009: 57). For more see Thomas Kuhn (1967) *The Structure of Scientific*

influenced the understanding of space within the contemporary epoch, whereby this shift in social thought reflects a transformation in the economy, politics and culture of the contemporary world. And although "actually lived experience may not have induced such a logical prioritisation" (Soja 1998: 31), the metaphorical use of 'turn' emphasises this historical phenomenon of enhanced spatialised thinking and indicates that space is not only a new object of analysis but defines the current focal medium of perception (cf. Döring & Thielemann 2008a: 12; Frank 2009: 54-55).

This analysis assumes the recently heightened awareness of spatialities. From the perspective of a theory of mentalities, it is dedicated to the new definitions of space as well as postmodern spatial concepts. I employ the concept of spatial mentality in the sense of a spatially determined collective consciousness as well as a space-related or spatially focused human condition. In the following I will tie these preliminaries of the Spatial Turn in with the notion of a spatial determinant of mental structures and thus offer an approach that goes beyond the traditional idea of regional mentalities.

Scholars, like the historians of mentality, have long sought to overcome the initial separation between society and space, collectivity and spatiality, or sociology and geography.[56] In *La production de l'espace* (1974), Henri Lefebvre introduces the idea of space as socially produced: "*(Social) space is a (social) product.*" (Lefebvre 1991: 26) The notion that all social relations are spatial just as spatial relations are social becomes an aphorism especially perpetuated by neo-Marxist geographers and urban sociologists. The general critique is that space is considered as either a container or a blank page waiting to be filled by social constructions, which could imply that the physical is a pure reflection of social dynamics and consciousness. Against the one-sided formulations that spatial forms are manifestations of social processes, Lefebvre's key notion of an interdependency between social and spatial relations helped to develop a socio-spatial dialectic explaining how both, spatial arrangement and social organisation, are space-forming and space-contingent. Analogically and in accordance with constructivist ideas, one can therefore claim that space is similarly culturally constructive (agency) and culturally constructed (structure) (cf. e.g. Soja 1998: 7). Concerning the cultural construction of space, we can, in general, distinguish between:

- Physical Space: material conditions or mapable spatialities,
- Social Space: social relations, negotiations, or interactions,
- Mental Space: representations or thoughts about space.

Accordingly, Lefebvre (1991: 104) further differentiates between three forms of social spatialisation: "thought and discourse *in* space [...], thought and discourse *about* space [...], and thought *adequate to the understanding* of space". Spatial practice describes the perceived social constructions of the everyday, representations of space de-

---

Revolutions. The application of Thomas Kuhn's concept of the shift of paradigm is further highly controversial due to the plurality of paradigms within Postmodernism without a coherent world view of the scientific community (cf. *ibid.*: 54-55).

56 | See for example approaches by sociologists such as Emile Durkheim, Georg Simmel, Alfred Schütz, Henri Lefebvre, Pierre Bourdieu, and Richard Sennett. For detailed information see Löw (2001) and Schroer (2006).

notes conceived technocratic discourses, and spaces of representation are the lived discourses about space (cf. *ibid.*: 38-39).[57] This epistemological spatial triad is defined by dialectical relations. The idea of the different layers superimposing, influencing and repressing each other stresses how material spatial forms do not only express social relations of production but also re-produce them by determining physical and mental space (*ibid.*: 39).

With respect to mentality this implies that social constructions of reality are constituted by the interplay of physical, mental, and social space, while spatial mentality encompasses all three socio-spatial constructions in the form spatial thinking, imagining, feeling, and acting. Consequently, space must be considered the major determinant of mentality in function and content because it influences both dispositions and structures of thinking, imagining, feeling, and acting, while in turn mentality defines perceived, conceived, and lived space. Furthermore, the recognition of space as medium and outcome of socio-cultural processes emphasises the conception of space as relational. In opposition to a notion of absolute space as an independent matter[58], relative space stresses the relationship between objects in space as constituting a certain subjectiveness of spatial perception, while relational space contains the idea of spatialities constructed in the links between these objects, e.g. as produced in processes of thinking, imagining, etc. (cf. e.g. Löw, Steets & Stoetzer 2008: 9).

From this we can discern two major processes of constructing (physical, social, and mental) space: spacing and (b)ordering. First, people spatially arrange aspects for orien-

---

57 | (1) Spatial Practice encompasses perceived, experienced and used space and refers to the physical and material spatial flows and practices. By way of multiple activities that form space, location is produced and reproduced ensuring continuity and cohesion, competence and performance. Everyday life and daily routine determine spatial nonconscious habits or spatial habitus. Spatial practice or perceived space (*espace perçu*) is the medium and outcome of human activity, behaviour, experience (cf. Lefebvre 1991: 38). (2) Representations of Space describe the relation of production and the order of space as conceptualised by planners, architects, and governments in models. This conceived space (*espace conçu*) dominates space in society by ways of a specific logic and the ideological content of signs or significations, codes and abstract theories. It entails both academic knowledge and common-sense thinking (*ibid.*: 38-39). (3) Spaces of Representation describe a fully lived space (*espace vécu*) of sensation, imagination, emotions and meanings, which are incorporated into the way people live day by day. It is the space of the social imaginary, a reflexive discourse of space which often presupposes possible spatial structures. This representational space of symbolic and artistic productions uses metaphors to evoke the symbolic and mythical, whereby new spatial practices and their dialectical relations are mentally envisioned (*ibid.*: 39). For more see Soja's (1998) reading of Lefebvre.

58 | A container space or enclosed territory impresses itself upon the included physical-material contents. It is known as the absolute or abstract and geometrical space of mathematics which is characterised as fixed, dead, superficially material, and undialectical. It can be expressed in the three-dimensional extension of the Euclidean system of coordinates and later refined in Cartesian geometry. Some critics have argued that human perception of the Euclidean three-dimensional space is an anthropological constant whereas others have seen the concept as part of culture-specific linguistic patterns.

tation in their habitat according to specific spatial perceptions.[59] "*Spacing*", according to Martina Löw (2001: 158-161), describes the social operations and the relational ordering of things in space, forming specific spatial structures. Second, a major aspect of the social construction of reality is mapping the world not only by creating connections or areas, but also borders. For Jon Anderson (2010: 44), "*(b)ordering*" promises ontological security due to reduced complexity. Conceptional boundaries, which structure space, are formed by (1) the categorisation in spatial scales (e.g. body, community, city, nation), (2) spatial dichotomies (e.g. city/country, centre/periphery, public/private), and (3) spatial metaphors (e.g. of segregation, marginality, distance).

As these spatial structures show, spatial practices implicate power-relations; because as tools of spatial arrangement categorisation, organisation, and semantisation of space are effective devices of exerting power over social systems and individual people, both spacing and (b)ordering become irrevocably connected to structures of power. Spatial manifestations of hegemonic social relations of class[60], gender[61], and race[62] are ex-

59 | Relational space as "Raum als (An)Ordung" (Löw 2001: 131). These processes of spatial constitution by active placing and organisational positioning include the construction and building of spaces which always happens in relation to other positions. Löw (*ibid.*: 159-160) argues that space is only created by the relational order of things through the process of spacing and the synthetic process of perception, imagination and memory, of creating one element of space. For more on social spacing see Derek Gregory, ed. (1985), *Social Relations and Spatial Structures*.

60 | Class-specific perception is always selectively structured by the habitus and as recursively reproduced in action. However, social structures of class are not only inscribed into the body but also in the physical space such as houses, neighbourhoods, or urban areas (cf. Löw 2001: 174-176; Schroer 2006: 88-102). For Doreen Massey (1998: 20) the spatial organisation of society or the "spatial division of labour" is reified in geographical inequality expressed in specific economic spaces and spaces of class structure: "geography of social structure is a geography of class *relations*" (*ibid.*: 22). An example concerning London would be the alignment of industry, class, and milieu in the East End which is marked as predominantly working class since the nineteenth century. Newland (2008) argues that the construction of the East End as lower class was defining for the whole national hegemonic class structure of Great Britain. For more see Nigel Thrift & Peter Williams, eds. (1987), *Class and Space. The Making of Urban Society*.

61 | Within her feminist approach of *Space, Place and Gender*, Doreen Massey (1998) focuses on the "power-geometries of space" regarding the genderness of all spatial concepts and developments. "Geography matters to the construction of gender, and the fact of geographical variations in gender relations, for instance, is a significant element in the production and reproduction of both imaginative geographies and uneven development." (*Ibid.*: 2) In *Feminism and Geography: The Limits of Geographical Knowledge* Gillian Rose (1993: 5) argues that the male (Self) need of a female Other constructs binary oppositions (cf. *ibid.*: 67, 74-75) which are indeterminably gendered, and suggest specific hegemonic spatial structures. For more on gender and space also see the publications by Linda McDowell.

62 | Postcolonial Studies assess hegemonic relations concerning questions of territory, land, location and migration in order to understand how space is employed in the construction of race, ethnicity or nation. Examples range from Apartheid in South Africa and the land rights

plored in order to determine how spatial power structures influence cultural imaginations, knowledge systems, and contemporary mentalities.[63] Consequently, hegemonic spatialities also serve as major cultural geographies for an analysis of the social organisation of a metropolitan habitat because the "(b)ordering practices of the dominant cultures" (J. Anderson 2010: 117) reveal underlying dispositions of thinking, imagining, feeling, and acting.

In other words, while space is always represented in relation to cultural codes embedded in social power-structures, particular socio-cultural constructions, e.g. class, gender and race, are likewise tied up with specific "ways of thinking about space" (Massey 1998: 2). Due to this 'socio-cultural construction of reality' the habitat is experienced through cultural codes creating spatial images which then re-constitute thinking. Spaces must thus be recognised as sites of ongoing struggles over meaning and value because various ideas, forms, and images are geographically negotiated or interchangeably spaced along socially constructed boundaries, delineating cultural dynamic experiences such as transgressions, negotiations, migrations and superimpositions. As Schroer (2008: 141-142) argues, it is not the qualities of the space *per se* that matter, but the values and attributes connected with space. In that respect, mentalities are best described as spatialised certainties, knowledge that has been metaphorically turned into images of spatial construction.

From the perspective of cultural geographers "'culture' *is* spatial" (D. Mitchell 2000: 63). The overall assertion is "that space is a social construction relevant to the understanding of the different histories of human subjects and to the production of cultural phenomena." (Warf & Arias 2008a: 1) Because spatial thinking is a culturally bound dimension, through various forms of spatial constructiveness and construction by ways of social relations, rituals, memories, emotions etc. the mentality of people living in the country is notably different from those living in the city. Cultural areas, more than the historian of mentalities' geographical regions, serve as structure and medium, unifying physical, social, and mental spatialisations which are co-constitutive in a triad of cultural habitus and practices, culture-specific ideas as well as the imaginary, such as myths or other narratives. As space is not only a cultural but also temporally bound dimension, socio-spatial relations vary over time. In gaining or losing importance, the relation to the spatial habitat alters, and brings to the fore the dynamics of persistence and transformation of spatial mentalities. Consequently, spatial constructions represent a major indicator of either synchronic or diachronic differences in mentality. The following part will investigate the characteristics of contemporary space and its most prevalent spatial concepts.

---

issue of Australian Aborigines, to the contested spaces of London's Brick Lane. In this respect, Weigel (2002: 156-157) criticises that Cultural Studies are often reduced to an ethnographic cultural theory dominated by topographic concepts. For more on "The Place of Ethnicity" see Jon Anderson (2010: 104-118).

63 | For more on the intersection between space, knowledge and power see the works by Foucault or Jeremy Crampton & Stuart Eldon, eds. (2007), *Space, Power, and Knowledge: Foucault and Geography.*

The Spatial Turn characterises Postmodernism[64] as an era of space. In *Postmodernism, or, the Cultural Logic of Late Capitalism* Fredric Jameson (1991: 154), similarly to Foucault, interprets the Spatial Turn as marking the differences between Modernism and Postmodernism. Referring to Raymond Williams' notion of a "structure of feeling", which Jameson (*ibid.*: xiv) understands as "new forms of practice and social and mental habits" in the context of novel modes of economic production[65], he argues that habitus and mentality were completely modified during the 1960s by a "profound collective self-transformation" (*ibid.*) and with "a reshuffling of canonical feelings and values" (*ibid.*).[66] Hence, Postmodernism constitutes a new spatio-temporal condition which marks the shift to new structures of thinking, imagining, feeling, and acting.

One can discern three main characteristics of Postmodernism that are of pivotal importance to the structures of mentality in the contemporary era of little narratives, dissemination, and uncertainty. (1) The postmodern is conventionally defined by the death of all meta- or master narratives. This "antifoundationalism" defines the "end of ideologies" (*ibid.*: xii) as Postmodernism's major "culture-ideology" (Jameson 1999: 46). This means that, due to the condemnation of meta-narratives as totalising, the newly discovered *petites histoires* rather emphasise power relations between smaller systems of knowledge. (2) The emphasis on little narratives is also created by processes of enhanced fragmentation. Harvey (1990: 9) suggests that "[f]ragmentation, indeterminacy, and intense distrust of all universal and 'totalizing' discourses [...] are the hallmark of postmodernist thought." Processes of dissemination, fragmentation, dispersal highlight pluralism and privilege heterogeneity or *différance*. (3) Due to the deconstruction of grand narratives and the various processes of dispersal, Postmodernism is also characterised by a "volatility and ephemerality of ideas and ideologies [as well as] values

---

64 | Postmodernism is both a periodising concept denoting the new era since the 1960s, with the 'post' indicating an after as well as a new style that is a reaction or even revolt against or opposed to dominant Modernism (e.g. cf. Jameson 1999: 1-3). Sometimes the distinction is made between Postmodernity as denoting the period and Postmodernism the precipitation of this new social reality in criticism, literature, art, culture, aestheticism.

65 | Although, Jameson (1991: xiv-xv) argues that this new consciousness is a product of "a continuous reciprocal interaction and feedback loop" between culture and economy, he later refers the alteration of social and psychic conditions back to the relentless commodification and hedonistic culture of late capitalism (cf. Jameson 1999: 1-54).

66 | "Culturally, however, the precondition is to be found [...] in the enormous social and psychological transformations of the 1960s, which swept so much of tradition away on the level of *mentalités*. Thus the economic preparation of Postmodernism or late capitalism began in the 1950s, after the wartime shortages of consumer goods and spare parts had been made up for, and new products and new technologies (not least those of the media) could be pioneered. On the other hand, the psychic *habitus* of the new age demands the absolute break, strengthened by a generational rupture, achieved more properly in the 1960s [...]." (Jameson 1991: xx) For a similar argumentation see Harvey (1990) and Soja (1998) or Jean-François Lyotard (1979), *The Postmodern Condition*. For more on Modernism/Postmodernism also see Brooker (1992: 4) who tries to draw "the map of a certain cultural mentality" which defines the changed "human character" of Postmodernism.

and practices" (*ibid.*: 285). All in all, these developments seem to "denote a deep and widespread loss of logical and ontological certainty" (Brooker 1992: 12).

These characteristics form idiosyncratic structures of feelings which express and carry important implications for the "postmodern and its spatialisms" (Jameson 1991: 156). For Jameson, these new qualities of space can be grasped in the concept of 'hyperspace'. The postmodern emphasis on events, happenings, and spectacles (Debord) on the one hand and the perpetuation of images in pastiche, virtuality, and simulation (Baudrillard) on the other hand creates an elevation of reality to hyperreality. Jameson (1999: 15) sees the spatial equivalent to the hyperreal in the depthlessness of postmodern architecture and explains the "spatial mutation" of the postmodern buildings. According to Jameson (*ibid.*: 11-16), hyperspace is a utopian space characterised by a new spatial language of spectacle and excitement, but also mechanical movement, a novel phenomenon of the hyper-crowd, featuring a return of the repressed or placeless dis-association. Most notably, in his identification of hyperspace he detects a paradoxical juxtaposition between density and emptiness.

In that respect, hyperspace can serve as an example of the supposed implosion, annihilation or abolition of space (e.g. cf. Schroer 2006: 162-163). The trend of rendering space irrelevant seems to be indicated by postmodern temporariness, instantaneity and transience, as well as translocality, dislocation, and the dissolution of national or territorial frontiers. Paradoxically, due to the collapse of spatial boundaries "we become much more sensitized to what the world's spaces contain." (Harvey 1990: 293-294) Ironically, then, just as the death of space or end of geography is announced, the ongoing facts of globalisation, such as international migration, media and communication especially, seem to render a spatial perspective necessary (cf. Warf & Arias 2008a: 5). Postmodernism moreover sees a transformation of the meaning of space, the birth of new kinds of spaces, and a diversification of spatial relations.[67]

The growing fragmentation as a characteristic of Postmodernism becomes apparent in physical, social and mental constructions of postmodern space as plural, heterogeneous, hybrid, coexisting, synchronic, and fluid.[68] Space has been rendered more flexible and due to post-positivist modes of understanding is devised as negotiation rather than only an *a priori* given constituent (cf. Warf 2008: 69). The concept of container space does, however, retain its validity; Schroer (2006: 175-180, 207-215) shows that in order to counter hybridity and uncertainty, absolute space with clear distinctions between inside and outside, Self and Other, private and public, or body and mind, has gained new attractiveness.[69] Hence, the recent epoch sees the establishment of new power containers

67 | Places and spatialities of everyday-life return in form of metaphors in the new media, especially virtual spaces of the internet: cyberspace, chat-room, homepage, portal, window, global village, digital city. For more see Schroer (2006: 252-275) and Löw, Steets & Stoetzer (2008: 78-92).

68 | For example, flows of people, technology, financial information, media images, ideologies, world views.

69 | Schroer (2006: 207-208) argues that despite the opening of the national space due to globalisation and new transport and communication, systems for organising fixed political spaces are reterritorialised, e.g. Fortress Europe, aggressive localism, and private spaces of security.

and a simultaneous (re)construction of hegemonic physical, social and mental spatialities. The following will shed some light on significant postmodern spaces constructed within this juxtaposition of heterogeneity and homogeneity and their implications for spatial mentality.

Firstly, this paradoxical dialectic can be grasped in the hybrid concept of "glocalisation", which unifies processes of globalisation as well as localisation (cf. Jameson 1999: 46; Featherstone 1996: 175).[70] On the one hand, the contemporary phenomenon of globalisation, under the slogan "McDonaldisation", furthers trends of homogenisation, displacement, and implosion of space erasing the local. In contrast, Lefebvre (1991: 86) argues that "[n]o space disappears in the course of growth and development: the *world-wide does not abolish the local*." Instead, the process of globalisation also brings about a familiarisation with the greater diversity of local cultures (cf. Featherstone 1996: 176), insofar as globalisation is manifested differently in various locales, which in turn leads to a sensitivity of local differences. The end of master-narratives has put an emphasis on the knowledge within particular places as well as the construction of imagined (regional) communities or "interpretative communities" (Harvey 1990: 46, 47) by ways of local spatial "commemorative rituals" (Featherstone 1996: 180) or "localized resistance" (Harvey 1990: 47). Regarding spatial mentality, the influence of the global stresses local idiosyncrasy in the dialectics of de-spatialisation and re-spatialisation.

Secondly, according to Jameson (1999: 36), postmodern thought as the "logic of difference or differentiation" is widely concerned with cultural otherness (cf. *ibid.*: 159). Relating to this phenomenon, Edward Soja (2000: 5) establishes a strategy of "thirding-as-Othering", a "critical thirding", by which "the original binary choice is not dismissed entirely but is subjected to a creative process of *restructuring* that draws selectively and strategically from the two opposing categories to open new alternatives." In that respect, 'thirdspace' must be considered the general concept that informs postmodern spatial thinking because it incorporates the heterogeneity as well as the resistance towards the opposed homogeneous structures. Moreover, for Soja (*ibid.*), thirdspace as mental space is a general term for the paradox of the shifting, the dialogic and dialectical, the inbetween of centre and periphery and the "possibility of a both/ and also logic". Thirdspace is a place on the edge characterised by contradictions and ambiguities (cf. *ibid.*: 97). In Soja's (*ibid.*: 1-2) opinion, thirdspace offers the most interesting ways of contemporary thinking about spatiality, such as place, location, locality, landscape, environment, home, city, region, territory, and geography. Accordingly, contemporary spatial practices contest and postmodern geographies question socio-political hegemonies, their congruent spatialities and the binary conceptions of space, creating new imagined spatialities concerning, for example, gender and class or ethnicity and race (cf. *ibid.*: 13).

With regard to gender, Gillian Rose (1993: 78) shows that a transformation of "men–tality"[71] of the man/woman hegemony cannot be perused by a simple inversion of opposites of the "misogynist stereotyping of women" (*ibid.*: 82), but has to challenge

---

70 | The term Glocalisation was originally coined by Eric Swyngedouw in 1992.

71 | Analogically, see allusions to "his-story" as the notion that history has been written mainly by men denying the suppressed stories of women. Instead, "herstory" recognises history from a feminist viewpoint.

the dualisms and displace them with diversity and transdifference. Massey's (1998: 21) concept of the "[p]ower-geometries of time-space", for example, recognises both the dynamics of space as a social construction and what is more its "power-filled nature" and therefore the paradoxical nature of postmodern space.

> The point I want to make is that space and place, spaces and places, and our senses of them (and such related things as our degrees of mobility) are gendered through and through. Moreover they are gendered in a myriad different ways, which vary between culture over time. And this gendering of space and place both reflects *and has effects back on* the ways in which gender is constructed and understood in societies in which we live. (*Ibid.*: 186)

In that respect, Massey (*ibid.*: 188) illustrates how constructions of gender relations may vary over space, and that spatial constructions have to be differentiated according to "local gender cultures". Furthermore, not only does she highlight the regional differences of gender constructs, but also emphasises how ideas about femininity and masculinity become contested and change over time.

Regarding race, ethnicity, or even national identity, processes of globalisation, decolonisation and transnational migration construct new socio-cultural spaces (diasporic, multicultural, transcultural) which – far from the dichotomy of receiving and home country – are complex structures of interconnections and perpetual border crossing. In *The Location of Culture*, Homi Bhabha (1994: 1-2) develops his concept of "Third Space", which constitutes an inbetween space of contestation, translation, negotiation, and collaboration that challenges notions of culture as homogenising. In a postcolonial context, the displacement of native communities, postcolonial migration, exile, refugeedom, and the creation of a cultural and political diaspora fashion new topographies and re-map spaces (cf. *ibid.*: 5). This constitutes neither the reproduction of home nor the assimilation but the construction of new "cultural hybridities" (*ibid.*: 2).[72] While "bridging the home and the world" (*ibid.*: 4), they produce "other spaces of subaltern signification" (*ibid.*: 11) beyond an "assumed or imposed hierarchy" (*ibid.*: 164). Bhabha's (*ibid.*: 2, 13) thirdspace concept thus questions the Orientalist binary divisions of black/white, male/female, native/foreign, private/public, high/low, etc. and their spatially opposed experiences.

Similarly, transculturation is also an intrinsic phenomenon of Mary Pratt's (1992: 4) concept of the "contact zone" which are "social spaces where disparate cultures meet, clash and grapple with each other, often in highly asymmetrical relations of domination and subordination – like colonialism, slavery, or their aftermaths as they are lived out across the globe today." It is a social space constituting the co-presence of people who were geographically or historically separated and who have now become involved with each other, a place including situations of inequality and conflict but also a site of inventive interactions (cf. *ibid.*: 6-7). The contact zone thus emphasises the intercommunication of collectives and the "forms of knowledge and expression that interact

---

72 | Bhabha (1994: 3) argues against the notion of cultural diversity displaying a binary logic of identity construction and instead offers the notion of cultural difference or *différance* (Derrida) emphasising a difference within or transdifference.

or intersect" (*ibid.*: 5). In this sense, the contact perspective describes a social space where various mentalities engage with one another and start to merge into mutual knowing and understanding.

This thirdspace figures as a site for the transformation of mentalities and liminal spaces in the form of spaces of translation and negotiation therefore do not only play a pivotal role for Postcolonial Studies but offer a possibility for the study of mentalities to engage in questions concerning contestations of socio-temporal constructions of reality. Finally, and most importantly, Michel Foucault's (1984: 24) concept of "heterotopia" also encompasses ideas of the thirdspace as a cultural phenomenon and mental space of otherness that feature multi-layered power geometries by acting as a "counter-site[...] [...] in which the real sites [...] are simultaneously represented, contested, and inverted". Featuring endless spaces that are juxtaposed and superimposed (cf. *ibid.*: 25), the heterotopia is a space of heterogeneity and difference *per se*. These postmodern spatialities and their dynamics play a pivotal role in assessing the spatial determinant of urban mentality in general and contemporary London mentality in particular.

2.2.4 Collective Space-Time Compressions

In order to grasp the dynamics of cultural change and the dynamics of the respective mental structures, I propose a fourth determinant of mentalities: collective space-time compression. This compression can be understood as a new quality developed within the dialectics between the determinants of collectivity, time, and space. To mark the importance of postmodern space, both as a focal point of this analysis and as a main constituent for contemporary mentality, I inverse David Harvey's (1990: 201) notion of "time-space compression" to that of space-time compression.

In *The Condition of Postmodernity*, Harvey (*ibid.*: 240-244) charts cultural change by drawing a "history of [...] waves of time-space compression" from the Middle Ages to the Renaissance, to Modernism and finally to Postmodernism. Harvey (*ibid.*: 239) shows that "shifts in systems of representation, cultural forms, and philosophical sentiment" are accompanied by spatial and temporal disruptions. He especially stresses that a change in spatial and temporal experiences indicates a change in social relations, and that the change in social production transforms the meaning of time and space (cf. *ibid.*: 204, 240, 247). This "sense of time-space transformation" (*ibid.*: 208) emphasises that "[t]here is an omnipresent danger that our mental maps will not match current realities." (*Ibid.*: 305) Thus, time-space compression is a signal for a transformation in the construction of reality, and instances of time-space compression become a major indicator of the transformation of mentalities.

Harvey (*ibid.*: 283-284) suggests that the postmodern condition is "an intense phase of time-space compression that has had a disorienting and disruptive impact" on contemporary culture due to "a new set of experiences of space and time". During Modernism the opposition between Being and Becoming describes the tension between a sense of time and the sense of space (cf. *ibid.*: 283)[73] as well as a mode of thinking which is

---

73 | For the whole argumentation see Harvey (1990: 260-270). Also, Lefebvre (1991: 25) identifies the peak of a transformation to modernist ideologies and habitus, which is essentially a

dominated by the prominent leitmotif of the "annihilation of space through time" (*ibid.*: 205). This includes accompanying alterations concerning the space body, consciousness, and psyche. In contrast, postmodern critical analysis tends to "privilege the spatialisation of time (Being) over the annihilation of space by time (Becoming)" (*ibid.*: 273).[74]

Hence as presaged by Foucault, simultaneity, synchrony and juxtaposition rule during Postmodernism. This implies, however, that the Spatial Turn with its resurgent interest in space and Postmodernism as "spatialization of time" (*ibid.*: 205) or "the spatialization of the temporal" (Jameson 1991: 156) does not simply lead to an anti-history or a substitution of the spatial for the historical.[75] Postmodern theories instead see the spatial and the temporal as irreversibly interconnected and promote the inseparability and co-constitution of the two dimensions as space-time (cf. e.g. Massey 1998: 269; Soja 1998: 147).

As discussed before, the historians of mentalities, especially Febvre and Braudel, advocate this ontological parity of space and time. Accordingly, Edward Soja vouches for a more balanced spatial/geographical and temporal/historical imagination. What he has in mind is to "spatialize the historical narrative, to attach to *durée* an enduring critical human geography." (Soja 1998: 1) The imperative of postmodern human geography, from Soja's (*ibid.*: 11) point of view, is to explore and find ways to align time and space, history and geography as well as the diachronic and synchronic. A contemporary analysis therefore has to involve explicitly geographical and historical configurations (cf. *ibid.*: 23). For Frank (2009: 75), this distinctively chronotopic perception might as well imply a "*spatio-temporal turn*". The double perspective of spatial and temporal determination is an intrinsic part of any study of mentalities that focuses on the spatial dynamics or temporal stability of mental structures. Due to the determinant of collective space-time compression, this present study sees postmodern spatial dynamics as undermining the temporal stability of mental structures.

Last but not least, we shall not forget the social emplacement in the postmodern historical and geographical context and its consequent dynamism. Soja (2000: 71-73) exemplifies that the ontological trialectics of "Historicality, Sociality and Spatiality" constructs a similar trialectics in the fields of knowledge of history, geography, society. "As we approach the *fin de siècle*, there is a growing awareness of the simultaneity and interwoven complexity of the social, the historical, and the spatial, their inseparability and interdependence." (*Ibid.*: 3) Thus, as people are caught up in all three, Soja maintains,

---

new mentality, in a disruption of spatial concepts. Equally, for Jameson (1991: 10-11), Postmodernism is rather wrought by a crisis of old conceptions of space. For the aspect of Modernism as a response to a crisis in the experience of space and time, see Stephen Kern (1983), *The Culture of Time and Space, 1880-1980.*

74 | Harvey (1990: 207) describes this notion as the permanence of Being over the transitoriness of Becoming. Being is considered the spatialisation of time, whereas Becoming denotes the annihilation of space by time (cf. *ibid.*: 273). See Gilbert (2008: 104) for a critique of Harvey's concept of time as Becoming and space as Being.

75 | Lefebvre (1991: 96, 130, 241) criticises the separation of space and time and shows how time is inscribed and contained in space while time contains spatial elements: "space implies time and vice versa." (*Ibid.*: 116)

theory should rest on the same triad – temporal-historical, spatial-geographical, social-sociological. In this sense, the determinants of collective (social), time (history), and space (geography), as well as compression (their dialectics) are a timely application in accordance with contemporary theories.

In conclusion, this analysis considers the social, temporal, and geographical determinants of London between 1997-2007 as being caught up in the dynamics of cultural change marked by the new political climate, the long-term economic tendencies of post-Fordism, the anxieties of the *fin-de-millénium* or the new age of terrorism heralding what has been named Post-Postmodernism. Hence, the decade can be characterised as a true threshold of collective experiences of space-time compression.

2.3 The Concept of Mentality

This first chapter has systematised the phenomena of mentalities to make an explicit theory of mentality applicable for cultural analysis. Let me briefly summarise the main assumptions in allusion to Kamm's (1994, 1996, 2010) systematic catalogue of framing mentality:

1. Mentalities are collective nonconscious phenomena.
2. Mentalities are historical (diachronic) and contemporary (synchronic) social constructions of reality formed in a dialectical relation between people and their habitat and incorporated by ways of socialisation and acculturation.
3. Mentalities are always dispositional in nature and thus merely possibilities for actual habits.
4. Mentalities constitute an organon which serves the functions of organisation, orientation, relief of strain, alignment, regulation, and integration.
5. Mentalities are a rhizome containing heterogeneous, non-hierarchical mental dispositions.
6. Mentalities encompass structures of thinking, imagining, feeling, and acting which are likewise dispositional for thought, imaginary, emotions, and behaviour.
7. Mentalities are specifically determined by collectivity, time, space, and collective space-time compression.
8. Mentalities are collective phenomena dependent on the social milieu. Although functionally related to the individual, they stabilise social groups without being synonymous with identity.
9. Mentalities are considered epochal phenomena which are determined by historical or contemporary reality. As dynamic structures, mentalities are liable to persistence and transformation.
10. Mentalities are considered regional phenomena determined by the geographical setting. According to post-positivist notions of space, mentalities are pre-ordained not only by physical but also social and mental spatial constructions.
11. Mentalities are caught up in the combined dynamics of collective space-time compression, which emphasises the mutability of mental structures according to cultural change.

For a study of mentalities, framing the concept helps delineate mental structures in general as dispositions of thinking, imagining, feeling, and acting, the contents of which are specified by determinants of collectivity, time, space, and compression. The four determinants emphasise that structures of mentality have various social, temporal, and spatial depths of dimension: there are specific group mentalities, as well as mental structures of different temporal or spatial scale. Moreover, there are various and often opposing strata of mental dispositions concerning stability, intensity, and coherence. Due to the heterogeneous character of mentalities, scholars often prefer to speak of several mentalities instead of one single determinant mentality.

The conceptualisation of mentality as an organon as well as substantial character of mentality formed by a dynamic rhizome of specific elemental nodal structures helps, however, to perceive a specific mentality as the relation of components. The most dominant component lending its name to the mentality is again to be interpreted as fundamental to the construction of reality in this particular lifeworld. These prevalent structures of mentality are consequently situated at the heart of a concentric model of mentality and can be differentiated from peripheral or residual contents of mentality (cf. Dinzelbacher 1993: XXXI; Kuhlemann 1996: 196). Gebhardt and Kamphausen (1994: 25-26) identify a specific mentality as a concentric structure: at the core lie the local and regional mentalities of the direct habitat, which can be differentiated according to class or milieu. Around this core lie the over-regional and national elements to which political and cultural determinants are elemental. According to Kuhlemann (1996: 193), the complex mental phenomena can further be differentiated into total, macro-, and particular mentalities. Total mentality comprises a mentality shared by all contemporaries, in the sense of a historical period mentality. Macro-mentalities entail national or religious differences of a mentality in a specific epoch, whereas particular or micro-mentalities encompass local characteristics (*ibid.*). He also interprets these strata of mentalities as forming a model of concentric but permeable circles, implying that particular mentalities are either subsumed under a core or macro-mentality or re-configured due to their conflicting elements (*ibid.*: 194-195). Mental paradigms of a dominant mental structure, which belong to micro-mentalities, can develop into macro-mentalities (*ibid.*: 197). Because the dominant features of a lifeworld determine the specific structure of mentality, the synchronic or diachronic analysis of mentality in a first step has to identify and in a second step has to emphasise outstanding priorities or focal points of thinking, feeling, imagining, and acting (*ibid.*: 196-197). In that respect, analysing London mentality will involve the delineation of various elementary mental structures.

This publication offers a socially, temporally and spatially bounded analysis of mental dispositions, with the objective of defining the contemporary (1997-2009) London "frame of mind" (Kamm & Sedlmayr 2007: 10). With London mentality as the central focus of this work, the emphasis – in accordance with the regional studies of mentalities and the Spatial Turn – is on urban character and thus always concerned with the specifics of the metropolitan lifeworld as the supposed main fix point of orientation for London denizens. The centre of attention is therefore not so much a local collectivity of London (ethnically, socially), nor on a certain temporal mental phenomenon during the Blair era; rather, the spatial determinant of the city is taken to be the dominant constituent. Consequently, this treatise truly explores London "mind**scapes**" (Kamm & Sedlmayr 2007: 12; emphasis N.P.).

3 Theories of Urbanity

According to the historian of mentalities Jacques Le Goff (1985: 173-174), certain local systems, such as cities, are of particular importance in the evolution of mentalities. The twentieth century, when city life and its conditions became the norm, was "the age of urbanization" (Blij 1982: 353). Due to the contemporary urban-centred human condition and the urban-focussed spatiality of the postmodern experience, this book on London mentality defines the urban as core mentality.

By the year 1900, the urban world population had risen to nine per cent, exploding to thirty per cent by the 1950s. Today, nearly every second human being lives in urban areas (cf. Parker 2004: 1; Prakash 2008: 3). The UK already reached full-stretch urbanisation in the middle of the nineteenth century, and its current urban population constitutes about ninety per cent (cf. P. Jackson 1989: 100; Parker 2004: 113). For Soja (2006: xviii), the "new urban age" is not just statistics, but understanding the contemporary world means to a large extent understanding cities. This includes the call "for seeing all societies, social relations, sociality itself, as not just spatial but inherently and generatively *urban*." (*Ibid.*: xvii) This "urban turn" (Prakash 2008: 2) in scholarship since the 1980s, which includes research on cultural areas, economic spaces, postmodern geographies and literary landscapes, exhibits the growing interest in urban spatialities.

The historians of mentalities have not developed a specific theory of urban mentality, nor any coherent concept of the city and its mental dispositions; studies on the consequences of urbanisation in regard to mentality are therefore quite scarce.[1] Although the city and the urban condition are elemental to certain analyses (e.g. cf. Oesterle 1988; Mohrmann 1996), most of these works particularly assess city life in specific historical urban decades, for instance, the ancient polis and political consciousness (cf. Barceló 1995), the medieval merchant city and Italian city-state elites (cf. Schulz 1980; Rossiaud 1990), or the rise of the bourgeoisie and the modern metropolis (cf. Schilling 2003). Synchronic comparisons concern the mental difference between city and country, while diachronic analyses focus on mental transformation of a particular city. Thematically, these studies identify urban life as defined by the historical evolution of the city, changes in urban sociability, and psychological trends such as emancipation, freedom, or intellectuality.

---

1 | For more mentality studies on the urban see Hervé (1996).

For the purpose of a coherent study on an urban-based mentality, the development of a theory of urban mentality is one of the main objectives of this analysis. In the following I will generate a theoretical approach to urban mental dispositions by making use of selected theories of urbanity. The focus of this chapter specifically lies first on identifying sociological and spatial theories of the city that can be critically adopted for a theory of mentality, and second on dissecting single aspects of an urban *conditio humana* from the extrapolated models of urbanity, which can, in a third step, be systematically applied to an analysis of urban mentality. In this context, I will focus on the relations between the physical urban environment or the city as habitat on the one hand, and the urban structures of thinking, imagining, feeling, and acting on the other hand. I will discuss theories of urbanity, urbanisation, and urban history in order to offer an insight into the transformation of urban mentality over time, and stress the most relevant themes regarding urbanity used as a guideline for the following chapter. The second sub-chapter will deal extensively with the theories of metropolitan life by Georg Simmel as well as the urban sociology of the Chicago School. Not only did their research lay the foundations of urban theory as such, but the idea of urbanity as a way of life also developed into a central subject that can be a useful approach to contemporary urban mentality. Moreover I will make use of concepts by the New Urban Political Economy devised from the example of the post-Fordist metropolis. Lastly, postmodern urban theories, especially those by geographers of the L.A. School, but also those of cultural critics, will be analysed for conceptions on contemporary urban mentality.

3.1 City and Urbanity

3.1.1 Definition of the City

The study of the city has been pursued through a variety of viewpoints, methods and concepts – geographically, demographically, historically, sociologically, economically[2], politically[3], and culturally[4]. Although urban patterns can be classified by these approaches,

---

2 | Braudel (1988: 501) argues that "every town, wherever it may be, must primarily be a market. Without a market, a town is inconceivable." In contrast to Lewis Mumford's (1938) *The Culture of Cities,* Jane Jacobs shows in *The Economy of Cities* (1969) that all forces for economic growth and development emerge from urbanism.

3 | Originally the name 'city' was given to a settlement that attained a certain degree of economic and political autonomy. For Soja (1998: 153-154) the city presents an administrative centre of political power whereby the "fundamental specificity of the urban [...] arises from the conjunction of nodality, space and power."

4 | Lindner (2004: 386) argues that there are three form of urban culture: (1) The culture of the city (*Kultur der Stadt*) encompasses emphatic urbanity which is often seen as the emancipatory way of life of the European bourgeois population; (2) cultures of the city (*Kulturen der Stadt*) denotes metropolitan heterogeneity of lifestyles of social or ethnic groups as well as subcultures and new types of personality and profession; (3) city culture (*Kultur einer Stadt*) denotes the identity and style of a city.

the essence of the urban is never just one of those characteristics, but is made up of their complexity (cf. Lefebvre 2003: 115-116). For Lefebvre (1991: 101), the essential aspect of the urban phenomenon therefore lies in its centrality: "To say 'urban space' is to say centre and centrality, and it does not matter whether these are actual or merely possible, saturated, broken up or under fire, for we are speaking here of a dialectical centrality." In other words, the urban is defined by spatial and cultural juxtapositions, superimposures, accumulations as well simultaneous aggregations and dispersions (cf. Lefebvre 2003: 116). This notion of synchrony and juxtaposition and the accompanying features of accidental separation and paradoxical opposition – in my terminology configured as urban-generic ambivalences (see chapter 4.1) – have furthered the interest in the city with regards to spatial theories. Hence, the contemporary urban age is not only one defined by geographical size and demographics, but also one of significant character due to its intrinsic concern with space.

In 1938, Louis Wirth (1969: 148) was the first to condense the generic meaning of the city in a minimalist definition: "For sociological purposes a city may be defined as a relatively large, dense, and permanent settlement of socially heterogeneous individuals." The urban can be distinguished by aggregation[5] and dense concentration of population and plurality; based on these elements a theory of urbanism for the city in all epochs and cultures is to be made applicable (cf. *ibid.*: 147-149). More importantly, according to Wirth, the provincials of size, density, and heterogeneity are also constituent for the urbanites' experience and perception of the city. The city does not only form a "conglomeration of buildings, streets, and people", but for the urban sociologist "the city is a set of practices, of common habits, sentiments and traditions which have grown up through several generations of life and are characteristic of a typical cultural unit." (*Ibid.*: 169) In other words, the inhabitants of the designated area must also display a distinct way of life to qualify as a city. With reference to the lifeworld model, this study agrees with the assumption that the essential form of the city has an influence on the culture of its denizens and thereby on their mentality. The urban is not only a space but a state of mind.

3.1.2 Urbanity as the Metropolitan Way of Life

The urban can be distinguished in form and content: while the 'city' denotes a physical phenomenon and a specific spatiality, 'urbanity' refers to the qualitative beyond the mere morphological, structural and quantitative dimensions of the city; hence the cultural phenomena of its distinctive way of life.[6] As a metropolitan way of life, urbanity

---

5 | This definition of the city has long been accepted and its notion of an "urban aggregate" (Brogan 1977: 147) is still of value today, see for example Lefebvre who states (2003: 117): "What does the city create? Nothing. It centralizes creation. And yet it creates everything."

6 | Rossiaud (1990: 165) explicates that originally urbanity "designate[d] an art of living proper to the urban world" and was used more in the context of polite manners and civility distinct from rusticity. Today urbanism and urbanity are employed synonymously. With Zijderveld (1998: 21), I prefer urbanity over urbanism as *–ism* refers to morally inspired ideologies, while the ending of *–ity* like in identity emphasises the cultural dimensions and symbolic infrastructure

encompasses distinct cultural practices such as buildings, artefacts, and products as well as social lifestyles, values, norms and symbolic meanings. First, urbanity as "the art of living in cities" (Parker 2004: 7) presents an urban-generic behaviour. Second, the "*symbolic infrastructure* of the city" (Zijderveld 1998: 20) is essential to urbanity depending on shared social meaning and knowledge. Third, "*Being Urban*" (Karp, Stone & Yoels 1991) also entails a *conditio humana* or socio-psychological state specific to the city. Fourth, urbanity is founded on "a set of mental attitudes" (Rossiaud 1990: 165).[7] Consequently, urbanity includes a dynamic rhizome of mental structures including thinking, feeling, imagining, and acting particular to the city.

The ontology of the city induces the construction of an urban-generic or metropolitan mentality. Following Gottfried Korff (1985: 344-346), I describe the adaptation of denizens' 'inner life' to the urban habitat as 'inner urbanisation', which denotes the incorporation of an urban *outillage mental* and the formation of urban mental structures. Korff (*ibid.*: 355) argues that 'outer urbanisation', the growth of the city or the return of urban denizens to the country, also creates an inner urbanisation of rural mentalities. It is therefore necessary to assess the dialectic between inner and outer urbanisation as well as to differentiate between spatial and cultural urbanisation.

The common adage is that spatial urbanisation (*Verstädterung*) preconditions cultural urbanisation (*Urbanisierung*) and thereby also inner urbanisation.[8] Mumford (1997: 296) notes that due to modern urbanisation, urbanity "once present only in an urban *point*, is now available throughout a whole region" and Harvey (1973: 231) interprets "[c]ontemporary global metropolitanism" as imposing itself on a worldwide scale. Although urbanity as a way of life might still primarily be located in the city, its value system appears not to be generic to the urban realm any more. The double process of urbanisation thus leads critics to assume that the city as built form and urbanism as a way of life, once having been dialectically intertwined, have to be considered separately from each other today. Because the city seems possible without urbanity and vice versa, the individual person displaying urban values does not necessarily need to be a resident of the city, while the city dweller might not manifest patterns of urban thinking.

---

of a certain concept. "The symbolic infrastructure of a city is its urban culture, its urbanity." (*Ibid.*: 20)

7 | According to Zijderveld (1998: 39, 32), this is what Thomas Mann means when writing on the "spiritual form of life" concerning Lübeck, namely the "state of mind of these Hanseatic burghers". For more see Thomas Mann (1926), *Lübeck als geistige Lebensform.*

8 | While the German language differentiates between *Urbanisierung* and *Verstädterung*, English specifically distinguishes between (1) urbanisation as the diffusion of the system of values, attitudes and behaviour or urbanity and (2) urbanisation as a spatial concentration of population in terms of limited dimension or density (cf. Castells 1979: 9). Urbanisation with respect to concentration and population refers to the quantitative aspect of the city; its spatial impact denotes the morphological transformation of the city or explosion of territorial size as well as the accompanying effect of population growth and dispersal. This usage of urbanisation describes the urban as form – its site, location, situation, size, function, centrality, and relation to the periphery. The second meaning of urbanisation refers to the urban as content – its urban way of life.

I contend that this notion of culture first being urban and secondly being urbanised (cf. Martindale 1984: 19) is mainly due to neglecting changes of inner urbanisation in their spatial relation to the city as habitat. In other words, in recent conceptions the city loses its idiosyncrasy as a spatial **and** cultural entity; either the urban is put on the same level as (1) civilisation, (2) modernity, (3) society and (4) nation, or (5) urbanity is confined to the spatio-temporal particularity of the European city. By implication, I will briefly delineate these concepts from an understanding of urbanity in this book and thereby "[detangle] that which is peculiar to the evolution of the city from that which is characteristic of the culture as a whole." (Handlin & Burchard 1977a: vi)

The city is seen as the "natural habitat of civilized man" (Park 1967: 2), with urbanity – in opposition to rusticity – denoting an "urbane culture" (Mumford 1997: 284) as a refinement in manners (e.g. civility, honesty, order, courtesy).[9] Therefore, the civil urban subject *per se* has always been connected to cultured mannerism, intellectuality, humanism, and learning. This assumption also links urban citizenship to the communitarian ideals of the Greek city-state or the urbane standards in the burgher-city. Since modernity, the connection between city and citizenship has forged simultaneity between the urban, the burgher, or the bourgeoisie. In contrast, this text understands the burgher and bourgeois state of mind as socio-specific mentalities with an emphasis on a distinct collective in the geographical milieu of the city. Moreover, since Oswald Spengler's *Der Untergang des Abendlandes* (1918; Engl. *The Decline of the West*) there have been numerous books on the correlation between city development and the rise and fall of civilizations, so that today the history of the city has become almost interchangeable with the history of civilisation.[10] This book does not deny the relationship between the city and civilisations; yet the analysis focuses on the generic and specific cultural aspects of a city, which do not necessarily belong to an overall 'urban civilising mission' while repeatedly adapting to economic and political transformations originating from other urban centres. In this sense, the connection between city and civilisation emphasises the temporal aspect of mentality on a meta-level because the history of civilisation explains the progress of high-culture, while an urban mentality serves as a guideline concerning persistence and transformation of an everyday urban way of life.

For most urbanologists the city is also the seat of modernity, while conversely the privileged figure of modernity is the modern metropolis.[11] It combines processes such

---

9 | "The acquisition of a code of behaviour", as Rossiaud (1990: 173) argues, "was nowhere more valuable than the city." In the following I will distinguish urbane from urban.

10 | The cradle and nursery of civilization is located in the various world culture hearths such as Mesopotamia, Central and South America, Egypt, India, and China; its first cities laying the foundations for later human civilisations. According to Schorske (1977: 97-99), Voltaire saw London representing the new Athens of modern Europe, furthering the dynamics of civilisation with industry and pleasure. The city as workshop and locus of civilisation becomes the epitome of civilisation in particular when a specific urban centre grows into the prestige symbol of a certain culture.

11 | Braudel (1988: 511) calls cities "outposts of modernity"; for Prakash (2008: 1) they present "the principle landscapes of modernity". Already for Simmel the modern metropolis constitutes the seat of modernity and for Park the city is the central phenomenon encompassing modern forms of life (see chapter 3.2.1). Consequently, the city described by Simmel and the

as urbanisation and industrialisation, whose structural transformations again alter human experiences, attitudes, and consciousness – for example by fostering the development of secular individualism, managerial rationalism, and a new primarily functional-relational solidarity. Now that modernisation and modernity have become global phenomena, urbanity has become synonymous with a modern way of life. From the perspective of mentality as temporally specific, modern urbanity experiencing an absorption on a global scale is further transformed during Postmodernism, and its intrinsic structures of feeling are now connected to the characteristics of post-Fordist metropolis.

The metropolis, moreover, serves as a *pars pro toto* for society. For example, Max Weber's "Die Stadt" (1921) constructs the city as the cause of all societal developments and social transformation. Later sociological research largely follows this assumption and degrades the metropolis to a mere projection of society.[12] Because the city presents the prototype of any new society, recent processes originating in the city seem to have initiated the complete "*urbanization of society*" (Wirth 1969: 143). While the city has become the universal base for a way of life, all social phenomena are at the same time urban phenomena and urbanism has become **the** general social form. Postmodern society must certainly be considered urban as its ways of life are thoroughly fashioned by metropolitan centres. In the case of contemporary London, city and urbanity are both products of socio-political processes such as Globalisation, Postcolonialism, Postmodernism, and Blairism. Yet the metropolis also implies the particularisation of these developments in a variegated and centralised environment where necessary adaptations and combinations will delineate urbanity from society. As the discussion of collective mentalities has shown, micro-structures of the community need to be distinguished from those of the meso-level of the city or from the macro-structures of society. Consequently, when analysing mental dispositions of metropolitan London, I do not intend to synchronise London urbanity with Britishness either.

In this regard, I also emphasise the need for differentiation between the city and the nation. Because national populations seem to be completely urbanized, the national way of life or culture might appear to be urban as well. In consequence, this assumption has decreased the relevance of urban and raised the importance of national identity.[13]

---

scholars of the Chicago School is not only connected to a specific style of the modern city, but also to modernity as specifically urban.

12 | As the site of social production and civilisatory progress, the city is seen as a "social emergent" by Mumford (1997: 6). Considered the essence of society concerning a culture's aspirations, achievements, and failures, the Chicago School rendered the city partly into a laboratory or mirror of societal processes, a place to locate modernisation, Postmodernity, or globalisation. According to Häussermann and Siebel (2004: 100), the metropolis thereby ceases to be the subject of social change but becomes the stage on which problems and conflicts of society can be observed. For more also see Löw (2008: 24, 32) and Berking & Löw (2008a: 7-8).

13 | The adage is that citizenship is shaped by national rather than urban allegiance. Braudel (1988: 526) emphasises that the developments of the modern metropolis coincide with the formation of nation states. Although the city offers a national stage for the modern state, it becomes increasingly subjugated under the nation (cf. *ibid.*: 528), which leads to the assumption that the dichotomy between city and state replaces the traditional ambivalence of city and country. Contemporary world cities seem to share more of a universal experience than they do with their own

The city by definition presents a distinctly relational object standing in opposition to the conceptualisation of the nation state as absolute. In reference to Braudel, sociologists like Berking (2008: 19) and Löw (2008: 133-134) show that nation state and city are two completely different spatial organisations: while the territory of the state follows the principle of annexation (*Anschluss*), the metropolis confers to one of inclusion (*Einschluss*); whereas the nation needs boundaries to enhance homogeneity within, the other includes the border between Self and Other to enhance density and heterogeneity instead. Thus, the national way of life necessarily follows a different principle than the metropolitan one.

Moreover, the general assumption of urbanity as the culture of an intrinsically European city[14] cannot hold for the definition of an urban-generic mentality. For example, Zijderveld (1998: 17, 26) specifically considers urbanity a Western phenomenon and a way of life that is exclusively linked to the bourgeois European city of the nineteenth century.[15] He defines urbanity as predominantly constituted by a conjunction of economic culture and a civic culture: as a specimen of the market, urbanity is connected to the Capitalist bourgeoisie, Puritanism, trade capitalism, and the merchant city, while the *oikos* points to the political dimension including the citizenship of burghers, a bourgeois style of life, and class distinction (cf. *ibid.*: 11-13). In consequence, he vouches for a historical and sociological distinction of cities with or exempt of urban culture (*ibid.*: 26). For Zijderveld (*ibid.*: 12, 20) postmodern cities, conurbations, megalopolises lack symbolic infrastructures or are without common sentiments and therefore devoid of any trace of urbanity.[16] This interpretation of urbanity is mainly an idealised historical dimension and does not describe an urban whole way of life. Instead, it draws a normative image defined by the emancipatory condition of a political citizen. In that sense, I strongly reject the suggestion of urbanity as the way of life of the European city; in my mind this approach describes a very specific type of urban mentality, which is only applicable to a very small range of time and space. The transformation of mentalities proves that

national regions. In a way, metropolitan centres emancipate from their territorial connection to the nation state, emphasising their very own city culture as being distinct not only from other urban centres but also from national identity. Saskia Sassen has therefore proposed a United Cities Organisation (cf. Parker 2004: 166).

14 | For an exemplary classification and definition of the European City see Löw, Steets & Stoetzer (2008: 94-95).

15 | Due to this conceptualisation of urbanity, Zijderveld (1998: 12, 34) excludes the ancient cities of China, the Euphrates region, Mexico, Peru as well as historical and contemporary "bazaar cities", which, according to him, are both without *oikos* and collectivity and thus do not produce any kind of urban culture that can be defined as urbanity. From his stance, urbanity is in origin and nature a singular Western-European phenomenon and on that ground he defies any critique of cultural imperialism (cf. *ibid.*: 17).

16 | The quintessential postmodern 'bazaar city' Dubai, with its simulacrum-like cityscape, is largely segregated and strongly separated into classes, while over ninety percent of its citizens are foreigners. Thus, at first sight the city seems devoid of any coherent urbanity, but the specificity of its urban life and the creation of specific historicised landmarks become part of the way of life in this idiosyncratic community of strangers.

notions and contents of what constitutes urban mentality are prone to change and cannot be pinned to an ideal.

In sum, contemporary urbanity neither equals a general civilisation, modernisation, society nor nation, because urban mentality is neither a milieu-mentality nor a meta-mentality. Furthermore, it adapts to the context of its spatial and temporal environment and cannot be preserved in one single spatio-temporal specific manifestation of the city. Wirth's definition of urbanity as a specifically spatial form of community originally aims at the definition of urbanism as specific as opposed to a general way of life. Moreover, according to Häussermann & Siebel (2004: 76), the theory of a propinquity of lifestyle and space is widely accepted today. In that respect, the city and urbanity are not to be separated when we consider urbanity as a spatially specific mentality.

3.1.3 Metamorphosis of the City and Transformation of Urbanity

The double process of urbanisation does not indicate a split between city and urbanity; rather it stresses that urbanity always describes a temporally specific urban way of life. The natural history of the city[17] makes apparent its spatial metamorphosis as well as the transformation of urbanity, emphasising the relationality of structure and content, habitat and mentality. According to the theory of mentality, drafted in the previous chapter, inner urbanisation can be defined as spatial mentality which due to alignment transforms with the metamorphosis of the city. Urban-generic mental dispositions in correspondence to the concept of mentality as a phenomenon of long duration need to be seen in the evolutionary socio-historical developments of the city. The "*geohistory of cityspace*" (Soja 2001: 3) – a general periodisation of the city in history and urban development, such as (1) the origins of the city in Mesopotamia 7,000 years ago, (2) the ancient (Greek, Etruscan, Roman) city, (3) the medieval city of Italy, Germany and Flanders, (4) the modern city emerging from an increase in metropolitan agglomeration, industrialisation, and societal urbanisation, (5) the crisis of the post-Fordist and renaissance of the postmodern city – proves the transformation in urban thinking, feeling, imagining, acting (e.g. cf. Blij 1982: 343-345; Braudel 1988: 515-520; Mumford 1997: 223-231; Soja 2001: 110-116; Lefebvre 2003: 8-15). These spatial-historical metamorphoses of the city are hence accompanied by specific constructions of the urban and urban culture.

Urban historians, especially historians of mentality, see urbanity as wrought by contradictions that describe a set of mental attitudes distinct from rusticity and thus a specific relation between city and country (e.g. cf. Oesterle 1988: 69, 76; Barceló 1995: 51-63; Rossiaud 1990: 154-159, 172-173; Mohrmann 1996: 268-275) Within the city, urbanol-

---

17 | The most influential chronology of the city has certainly been Max Weber's (1921) "Die Stadt", which traces the evolutionary development of the modern city back to its origins in antique society. While he follows the transition from the ancient society to feudalism and to capitalism, the focus of the city's idiosyncrasy lies mainly in its economic character with a high degree of political and administrative autonomy. For more on the history of cities see Gideon Sjoberg (1960) *The Preindustrial City*; Lewis Mumford (1961), *The City in History*; Scott Greer (1962), *The Emerging City: Myth and Reality*; Leonardo Benevolo (1975) *Storia della Città* (Engl. *The History of the City*).

ogists distinguish certain relations between private and public spheres of life. Urbanity moreover includes a significant form of sociability and collectivity. This collective is itself constituted by a specific combination of social hierarchies, whether socioeconomic class, or race, gender, and ethnicity. Urbanity also encompasses a configuration of cosmopolitan culture, in the sense that strangers or migrants are excluded, included, and absorbed into urban culture. In that respect, an urban way of life brings about forms of individuality. The attitudes of humanism or rationalism put an emphasis on a specifically urban psychology. Finally, yet importantly, urbanites express a certain pride in their city which influences their urban as well as personal identity.

While every historical phase has created its own paradigmatic city (i.e. Babylon, Athens, Venice, London, Los Angeles), Lewis Mumford in *The Culture of Cities* (1938) argues that each city additionally incorporates urban-generic stages of development. Following Patrick Geddes, Mumford (1997: 283-292) conceptualises a "Cycle of Growth and Decay" which describes how the urban life cycle encompasses six stages: Eopolis, Polis, Metropolis, Megalopolis, Tyrannopolis, and Nekropolis. In its sixth and final stage, the city becomes "a tomb" (ibid.: 292), "[w]ar and famine and disease rack both city and countryside" (*ibid.*: 291) and "life [is] turned into a meaningless pillar of salt." (*Ibid.*: 292) Nevertheless, all stages feature possibilities for urban renewal (cf. *ibid.*: 294-295). Hence, the urban is able to eliminate and survive its decline and in this sense, on the site of the "ex-city" the "post-city" (Prakash 2008: 5) might grow.

The combination of historical and organic metamorphoses of the city charts the specific cultural-historic stabilities, similarities, mutations, reversals, novelties of urban culture. With the transformation of urban qualities, ways of perception and mental dispositions necessarily need to be adapted. Although the metamorphosis of the city and the transformation of urbanity renders it comparatively easy to detect transformations of mentality, the rapid change of metropolitan realities makes it difficult to apply the notion of mental structures in the long term. Rossiaud (1990: 141) points out that in addition to the urbanite as a historical-social category, most denizens are migrants to the city and are thus only acculturated there. Because of the relative stability of the urban due to its transitivity, an analysis of urban mentality has to take into account two time-spans – brief and long – represented by the dynamics of persistence and transformation. In regard to the historical notions of an urban way of life mentioned above and under the premise of metropolitan metamorphosis, the following section focuses on concrete theoretical approaches to urbanity.

3.2 Urban Theoretical Approaches to Mentalities

Towards the end of the nineteenth century all tendencies to analyse the modern big-city lifeworld are united within urban sociology, a new international academic discipline that takes the implications of a modern urban mentality into consideration. From the beginning, the creation of a new urban order is analytically linked to the notion of urbanity as a whole way of life because it is the objective of urban sociologists to define and analyse the changes in metropolitan existence. Next to the literary reception of the urban space of experience[18], a sociological interest in the actualities of city experience, originates in England, initiated by philanthropic and practical investigators.[19] Even more than their English predecessors, the members of the so-called German School are concerned with the social, cultural, and psychological consequences of life in the modern metropolis.[20] Georg Simmel especially theorises about the impact of the urban environment upon patterns of human consciousness. Considering him as the founder of an approach to inner urbanisation, this study interprets Simmel's sociological conceptions of urban life as paradigmatic for a theory of urban mentality.

3.2.1 Georg Simmel's Sociology of Modern Urbanity

Georg Simmel[21] is profoundly concerned with modern metropolitan life, focussing largely on the social relations in the city as well as on the psychological transitions related to transport, employment, and cultural institutions. Although Simmel's sociology of the urban realm is related to the modern metropolis, his ramifications are still timely and particularly useful for a theory of urban mentality due to the following reasons: first, Simmel's descriptions of everyday life and its cultural manifestations make him an excellent match for interpretations within the whole context of Cultural Studies (cf. Frisby 2006: 8-9).[22] Second, his writings on social space have gained new promi-

---

18 | Sociological realist (documentary) novels are for example Arthur Morrison (1896), *The Child of the Jago*; George Gissing (1889), *The Nether World*; the utopian romance *News from Nowhere* (1890) by William Morris; or ethnographies such as Jack London (1905), *The People of the Abyss*.

19 | For example: Friedrich Engels (1845), *The Conditions of the Working Class in England in 1844*; Henry Mayhew (1851), *London Labour and the London Poor*; Charles Booth (1886-1903) *Life and Labour of the People in London*; William Booth (1890), *Darkest England and the Way Out*. Especially Charles Booth's clustering and cartography of the urban poor is influential for sociological research.

20 | While British Urban Studies continue on the Fabian trajectory of social investigation and the London School of Economics largely produces empirical studies without developing specific theoretical ideas on the city, the centre of urban theory moves first to Germany and then to the Chicago School of Sociology. Robert Park was a student of Simmel and brought his ideas to America, where he integrated them into the theory of the Chicago School. Lately Richard Sennett and Saskia Sassen have revived an interest in London as an urban paradigm, concentrating on issues of the metropolis as global or postcolonial city.

21 | Georg Simmel is known as a sociologist and has been identified a cultural theorist, although he is most of all a philosopher (cf. Kaern 1990: 75; Weinstein & Weinstein 1993: 101; Frisby 2006: 2). For more see David Frisby's major work on Simmel *Sociological Impressionism* (1981) or Michael Kaern, Bernard S. Phillips & Robert S. Cohen, eds. (1990), *Georg Simmel and Contemporary Sociology*.

22 | Frisby's and Featherstone's *Simmel on Culture. Selected Writings* (2006) encompasses various essays and excerpts of Simmel's cultural studies. For more also see Frisby (2001).

nence due to the Spatial Turn.[23] Third, Weinstein & Weinstein (1993: 54) read Simmel as "an anticipator of postmodernism, presenting a thought contemporaneous to postmodernism's." Last but not least, Simmel is considered a phemenologist whose theories are close to the perception of the sociology of knowledge[24] (cf. Kaern 1990: 75; Weinstein & Weinstein 1993: 55, 58; Frisby 2006: 11). This makes it specifically appropriate to apply his ideas to a definition of urban mentality.

Simmel's main contribution to the discourse of the modern metropolis is his seminal essay "Die Großstädte und das Geistesleben" (1903).[25] For Simmel (1971: 324-334) the city necessarily constitutes a social space; the metropolis is the main site of money culture and modernity as well as the centre of cosmopolitanism. As the title of his essay already suggests, Simmel aims to elucidate the influences of the metropolis upon the mentality of its inhabitants. Due to his understanding of 'inner life', Simmel's analysis of metropolitan mentality includes the city's influence on sensibility, temperament, social psychology, life-style, social character, urban personality as well as personal identity (cf. Weinstein & Weinstein 1993: 53). His perspective on the inner life encompasses not

---

23 | For Simmel the formal foundations of sociation lie in the spatio-temporal location constructed by people (cf. Frisby 2006: 10). Thus, Simmel's theory of space is very close to contemporary spatial theories in the sense that he sees spatial constellations as having consequences for the social, whereas social actions also generate spatial structures. Simmel's spatial theory is therefore different from the spatial determinism of the political geography and anthropology of his time, but is to be situated between spatial determinism and social constructionism (*ibid.*: 11). Looking at Simmel's oeuvre, there are various texts that are concerned with the study of the sociology of space: *Soziologie. Untersuchungen über die Formen der Vergesellschaftung* (1908) and its chapter on "Der Raum und die räumlichen Ordnungen der Gesellschaft" includes excursi regarding the "Exkurs über die Soziologie der Sinne" (Engl. "Sociology of the Sense"), "Die Soziologie der Grenze" (Engl. "The Sociology of the Boundary"), as well as "Exkurs über den Fremden" (Engl. "The Stranger") which are necessarily concerned with spatial configurations. Moreover his essay "Brücke und Tür" (1909) (Engl. "Bridge and Door") plays a pivotal role for the analysis of urban spaces. Most notably, there is Simmel's "Soziologie des Raumes" (1903) (Engl. "Sociology of Space"), "Über räumliche Projektionen socialer Formen" (1903) (Engl. "On Spatial Projections of Social Forms"), and last but not least his analysis of the psychological impact of the urban space in "Die Großstädte und das Geistesleben" (1903) (Engl. "Metropolis and Mental Life"). For more on Simmelian theories of space see Löw (2001: 58-63), Schroer (2006: 60-81), and Löw, Steets & Stoetzer (2008: 30-31).

24 | Michael Kaern's essay "The World as Human Construction" in *Simmel and Contemporary Sociology* (1990) argues that the constructionist viewpoint and his philosophy of the "as-if" firmly places Simmel in phemenological and constructionist sociology such as represented by Berger & Luckmann.

25 | Louis Wirth (1967: 219) describes it as "the most important article on the city from the sociological standpoint". It is variously noted that the lack of understanding of Simmel's work is in large part due to the difficulties of translation (cf. Kaern 1990: 84; Nedelmann 1990: 225; Frisby 2001: 65). In the following I will quote from the second English translation of "The Metropolis and Mental Life" by Edward A. Shils (1971). My understanding of the essay is, however, also informed by the German original.

only the mind, but also addresses affects, preferences, moods, and feelings with which knowledge is acquired and the world constructed (cf. Kaern 1990: 76, 90). His essay must therefore be considered essential for any exploration of urban mental dispositions.

Simmel's "cognitive paradigm" (*ibid.*: 97) is close to the definition of mentality as the historical and contemporary social construction of reality and acknowledges the main function of mentality as a reference point for orientation in our everyday world (cf. *ibid.*: 80-82). According to Simmel, the city dweller is confronted with specific metropolitan features that enforce a particular pattern of responses and mentally affect the denizens. This "[r]eciprocal [o]rientation" (*ibid.*: 83) between "external culture" and "bodily existence" (Simmel 1971: 324) presupposes that mentality is determined by material life and aligned to the habitat.[26] As the metamorphosing metropolis conditions the mental response to it, the form of inner life experiences a transformation.

Simmel's main assumption is that the sheer quantity of seemingly disconnected stimuli in the modern metropolis leads to overstimulation. For Simmel (1971: 325) the metropolis insofar constitutes the most fruitful place in the development of mental overexposure, standing in stark contrast to the "more habitual, more smoothly flowing rhythm of the sensory-mental phase of small town and rural existence." The "overload effect" (Milgram 1970: 1462)[27] in the metropolitan psychology significantly distinguishes city from rural life and must be seen as the most prominent dimension of urbanity. According to Simmel (1971: 325), "[t]he psychological foundation, upon which the metropolitan individuality is erected, is the intensification of emotional life due to the swift and continuous shift of external and internal stimuli."[28] Because of the rapid shift of the metropolitan sensory and the consequent "intensified strain on his nerves" (Nedelmann 1990: 231) the urbanite can easily become oversatiated and overwhelmed, which renders him unable to respond. This overload effect on the one hand presupposes superficiality and enhances

---

26 | "In more technical terms of modern sociology one could say that Simmel treats the city as the independent, and the 'inwardness' of the citizens as the dependent variable." (Nedelmann 1990: 226) To grasp the dialectic between outside and inside, how people translate their interpretation of the world in mental reactions, Simmel uses the concept of *Wechselwirkung* (interaction): "as receivers they integrate the effects of the social products they have created themselves into their mental life." (*Ibid.*: 227). "Interaction refers to processes of externalization and objectification of social activity; experience refers to processes of internalization, that is, processes in which individuals integrate the effects of the objective social structure into their personality. When Simmel investigates the metropolis under the perspective of its 'inwardness' he asks how individuals internalize the stimuli they receive from the metropolis. He looks at individuals from the exterior (or outside) when he asks how they by interacting create the social product which is the metropolis." (*Ibid.*)

27 | In his essay "The Experience of Living in Cities" (1970) Stanley Milgram takes up Simmel's idea and develops it into a theory of overload. In the following I will apply the term for Simmel's notion of oversaturation.

28 | Concerning the dominance of the senses in the experience of the city, especially that of the eye and the optical specialties of the urban realm see Simmel's "Soziologie der Sinne" (1908).

objectivity, indifference, impersonal nature, and on the other hand suppresses subjectivity as well as sociality.

The three main characteristics of an urban mentality are (1) intellectuality, (2) blasé attitude, and (3) reserve, all of which serve as organon of relief of a strain on the consciousness derived from the sensory and emotional overload of the city. According to Simmel (1971: 327) these "characteristic mental tendencies" of the city figure as adaptive mechanisms in regard to the metropolitan urban-generic diversity of stimuli. They also serve as a protective defence against the psychic disintegration of being overwhelmed (cf. *ibid.*: 326).

In correspondence to the calculating mentality of the money economy, metropolitan overload encourages the intellectualisation of life.[29] The dialectic between metropolitan existence and mature money economy creates "economic egoism" (*ibid.*: 327) and a certain "matter-of-fact attitude" (*ibid.*: 326). Accordingly, money economy is closely related to the domination of reason and the intellect: because of the city's size and its contrasting physical and social stimuli, individuals are not able to respond to all features and need to develop intellectual awareness, a critical acumen, a rational stance – or vigilance (*ibid.*).[30] The "blasé outlook" (*ibid.*: 328) describes a psychological phenomenon, which according to Simmel is endemic to money culture and especially pronounced in the city as the place of great money turnover. Money as a levelling device neutralises the sense of uniqueness (*ibid.*: 326); not seeing any difference in the value of things first gives rise to a "cynical mentality" (Nedelmann 1990: 229). In contrast, the blasé person has totally lost the feeling for value differences (cf. Simmel 1971: 329). This urban-generic experience is defined by an homogeneity, flatness and greyness (cf. *ibid.*: 330), an indifference rendering the blasé person somewhat unconcerned, bored, but also worldly. Most remarkably, this blunting of discrimination hollows out the incomparability of individuality and therefore "drag[s] the personality downward into a feeling of its own valuelessness" (*ibid.*). According to Simmel (*ibid.*: 331), another aspect of urban mentality that influences social behaviour and interaction is the mental attitude of reserve. Primarily, reserve means distance towards other urbanites. This psychological condition is due to the mistrust against the tentative elements of urban life. Its consequence upon the inner life is again indifference, which can eventually lead to suspicion, slight aversion, mutual strangeness, repulsion, or even hostility and hatred (cf. *ibid.*).

Besides these adaptive and protective mechanisms, Simmel also scrutinises urban social and individual life for the psychological influences of sociation, cosmopolitanism, individuality, and autonomy. Simmel (*ibid.*: 328) comments that an agglomeration of people in the city necessarily results in different forms of sociation. The metropolis is wrought by the money economy and thus widens the gap between objective and personal spirit, which leads to an "atrophy of individual culture through the hyperthrophy of objective culture" (*ibid.*: 338). The weight of objective culture consequently suppresses

---

29 | Simmel (1971: 325) argues that the location of reason is on the upper layers of consciousness and so the most adaptable of all inner forces.

30 | According to Frisby (2006: 17), this central idea derives from Simmel's (1900) *Philosophie des Geldes* (Engl. *The Philosophy of Money*) where he identifies greed, avarice, extravagance, indifference, blasé, and impersonality as central elements of a psychology of money.

all subjective notions. Additionally, the intellectualisation of the urbanite strengthens relations based on rational calculability, consequently furthering the loss of emotional bonding. Thus, the metropolis enhances superficiality and renders urban social contacts utterly impersonal. On the other hand, Simmel (*ibid.*: 332) argues that indifference, apparent in intellectualisation, blasé mentality and reserve, is a necessary prerequisite for the city's social life; what at first glance seems like dissociation is in fact one of the most elementary forms of urban socialisation and sociation. Understood as both integration and disintegration, the mental functions of distanciation serve as instruments of 'negative integration' (cf. Häussermann & Siebel 2004: 40; Kaern 1990: 84-85).

Thus, Simmel's enquiry into metropolitan inner life also helps understand urban interactions and social relations. He specifically defines the city as a construct of interaction between antagonistic social circles (cf. Simmel 1971: 332). For Frisby (2001: 74), this approach generally allows an interpretation of the cognitive zoning of the metropolis according to class or milieu. It has repeatedly been remarked that Simmel's essay omits direct comments on the stratifications of the urban experience, such as social class, gender, ethnicity, and other power structures (cf. *ibid.*: 73-75).[31] Nevertheless, he is occupied with tolerance towards the Other in the city, since urban cosmopolitanism fosters a greater social tolerance for non-regional, unconventional or strange behaviour, such as that of subcultures, and offers a greater freedom for action (cf. Simmel 1971: 334).

General heterogeneity of the metropolis, diversity of social circles, and cosmopolitanism create a tolerant atmosphere towards the stranger, the alien, and the unknown. The metropolis with its overload of stimuli, its complexity and diversity of phenomena as well as the accelerated mobility of denizens, heightens the possibility of coming into contact with the Other (cf. Frisby 2001: 82). This permanent urban confrontation with the Other lies at the centre of Simmel's "Exkurs über den Fremden" (1907). In the excursus, Simmel (1992: 765-766) identifies the spatial existence of the stranger as one of proximity and distance: simultaneously being part of the same spatial ground and an outsider, the stranger is a synthesis of both spatial markers. Due to this interrelation and the stranger's inherent mobility as a wanderer between antagonistic circles, he is characterised as objective, indifferent, and yet engaged with his lifeworld (cf. *ibid.*: 766-767).

In respect of urban society being dominated by objective and endangering individual culture, Simmel also considers the influence of metropolitan emotional reserve and blasé mentality on the Self, meaning the development of individuality in an urban environment. According to Simmel (1971: 336-338), the complexity of the depersonalised city life makes it nearly impossible for the denizen to maintain his personality, also because the objective culture of the metropolis suppresses personal interests and incomparabilities. The individual is devoid of emotional response and idealism, further alienated and characterised by mistrust or coldness. This loss of the urban individual is emphasised firstly by being a mere "single cog" (*ibid.*: 337; German original: "Staubkorn" – speck of dust) within the overwhelming universe of the metropolis and secondly by being internally divided. One of the personal responses to the hypertrophy of objective culture is therefore a retreat to the interior, such as experiences of impersonality, anonymity,

31 | Frisby (2001: 75-76) points out that articles on the gendered dimension of culture, e.g. prostitution and the women's movement, show that Simmel interprets the objective culture of the city as dominated by men.

deprivation, loss of the Self, and a sense of loneliness (cf. *ibid.*: 334) – modern neurasthenia. Thus blasé, reserve, indifference as well as anonymity, distance and loneliness are important prerequisites of individuality that guarantee personal freedom, independence, autonomy, and emancipation endemic to the metropolis (*ibid.*: 332-334). For the "development of individuality within the framework of city life" (*ibid.*: 331-332) the simultaneous forming of personal identity and individual autonomy is crucial.

The complexity and density of the metropolis asks for an analogous response in the need to distinguish oneself from other urbanites, while its levelling effect stimulates people's anxiety about their individuality.

> This leads ultimately to the strangest eccentricities, to specifically metropolitan extravagances of self-distanciation, of caprice, of fastidiousness, the meaning of which is no longer to be found in the content of such activity itself but rather in its being a form of 'being different' – of making oneself noticeable. (*Ibid.*: 336)

The metropolis as a social space is then the site where people feel like extremely personal beings, and their ambivalent desire to be part and yet different from others results in "the narrower type of intellectual individuation of mental qualities" (*ibid.*). In the struggle for social recognition of individuality, urban mentality of intellect, blasé and reserve offers the denizens visible forms of distanciation and self-preservation: "the individual gains a freedom of movement far beyond the first jealous delimitation, and gains also a peculiarity and individuality [. . .]." (*Ibid.*: 332) Moreover, because of the spatial, quantitative, and qualitative growth of groups' inner unity is less stringent, the individual gains freedom. For Simmel (*ibid.*: 334) "the citizen of the metropolis is 'free' in contrast with the trivialities and prejudices which bind the small town person." Personal freedom, however, also means to follow one's inner nature and find one's own space. Due to the complexity and heterogeneity of the metropolis, "the individual's horizon is enlarged" (*ibid.*); this in connection with freedom leads to the emancipation and autonomy of the urbanite.

To summarise: for Simmel the city is the site of money economy, Modernism, and cosmopolitanism, which forms urban life in the ambivalent configuration of personal and objective culture. According to his thinking, the urban condition presents an idiosyncratic social psychology. The city has the ambivalent cardinal effect of promoting intellectuality, distance, competition, individuality and liberty, but also impersonality, loneliness, restlessness and anxiety. Through multiplicity and complexity of stimuli, the urban environment constantly engenders the danger of overload against which the inhabitants of the city create protective and adaptive mechanisms – intellect, blasé and reserve. Nevertheless, Simmel acknowledges that the complexity of the modern metropolis does not allow for consistent structures of personality, but that its various stimuli can give rise to opposing mental responses. Simmel interprets these characteristics as possibilities and thereby underlines how the dispositional nature of urban mentality can materialise in various forms of behaviour. Such are the ambivalences of city life, interpreted by Simmel: atrophy versus hypertrophy, disintegration versus integration, protection versus adaptation, apathy versus vigilance.

3.2.2 The Chicago School of Urban Sociology

In the second and third decades of the twentieth century, the Chicago School of Urban Sociology specified the relationship between the city's physical structures and urban ways of life. With Chicago as urban paradigm, its scholars were interested in the internal character of the city, such as socio-spatial functions and relations of its parts. Soja (2001: 93) sees the Chicago School as the first successful attempt to develop an "explicitly spatial theorization of the city" by recovering space as a social element concerning the city[32] and therefore as another instance of the Spatial Turn *avant la lettre* besides the *Annales*. Both, moreover, share an interest in socio-spatial consequences on structures of thinking, imagining, feeling, and acting.

The Chicago School summarises its common approach in *The City* (1925) as encompassing three major topics: (1) the city as a constellation of spatially localised social worlds, (2) the simultaneous transformation of institutions, and (3) the construction of urban-generic mentalities and habits (cf. Lindner 1990: 108). Robert Park (1967: 1) already outlines the formidable presence of an urban mentality in "The City: Suggestions for the Investigation of Human Behaviour in the Urban Environment" (1915) :

> The city is, rather, a state of mind, a body of customs and traditions, and of the organized attitudes and sentiments that inhere in these customs and are transmitted with this tradition. The city is not, in other words, merely a physical mechanism and an artificial construction. It is involved in the vital process of the people who compose it; it is a product of nature, and particularly of human nature.

In that respect, Park's meditations on the social texture of the modern metropolis carry important implications for a theory of urban mentality. In the following I will assess the particular assumptions regarding the metropolitan state of mind by Park and Wirth, whereby the latter subsumes "[t]he mentality of city life" under "Human Nature and City Life" (Wirth 1967: 164), thus emphasising the connection between ecological characteristics of the city and social psychology of urbanites.

According to his notion of human ecology, Robert Park (1967: 44) assumes that the psychological and moral conditions of the city are reflected in physical structures or spatial practices just as urban materiality shapes the experiences, temptations and suppressions of urbanites.[33] Changes in the urban fabric are "accompanied by corresponding

---

32 | Urban sociology is seen as a special form of spatial theory as it combines the social phenomena and processes of the urban realm with the spatial-physical structures of the metropolis. Due to their ecological approach, the Chicago School is often criticised for their notion of absolute space and the causal importance of spatial factors on social phenomena. Thus other than Simmel they are reproached for largely neglecting the social production of space.

33 | For Robert Park the city constitutes a geographical, ecological and economic unit. The metropolis is foremost the natural human habitation of civilized man, which comprises an own cultural area "characterized by its own peculiar cultural type" (1967: 1-2). In his article "Human Ecology" (1936), Park relates the city, its mobility, cultural attitudes, and social behaviour to biology and the metabolism of the human body. For more on Park's urban sociology see Lindner

changes in the habits, sentiments, and character of the urban population." (*Ibid.*: 23) Park (*ibid.*: 10-11) is especially interested in the inner order of the metropolis with its separate zones or community cultures.[34] Cultural districts or homogeneous urban communities with corresponding natural geographic boundaries or cultural-specific characteristics are the direct outcome of an ecological process, namely the alignment of physical and socio-cultural factors. Human ecology discusses the relation between people and territory or inhabitant and habitat, by considering the territorial organisation of the urban population and the rootedness of specific communities in their neighbourhoods. Due to ecological relations, the city's natural areas are characterised by their idiosyncratic physical structure, culture, and lifestyle; because the ecology and the state of mind of those regions intertwine, the city also consists of various "moral regions" (*ibid.*: 44).

For Park (*ibid.*: 40), physical segregation induces moral distance, which renders "the city a mosaic of little worlds which touch but do not interpenetrate". This moral distance "makes it possible for individuals to pass quickly and easily from one moral milieu to another, and encourages the fascinating but dangerous experiment of living at the same time in several different contiguous, but otherwise widely separated worlds." (*Ibid.*: 40-41) On the one hand, enhancing the superficiality of urbanites, it bears the danger of disintegration; on the other hand moral distance also stresses the possibility of greater autonomy and an adventurous character.

Park (*ibid.*: 40) especially concentrates on the aspect of distanciation as behavioural pattern: the physical proximity of the urban population is one of social and mental distance. Besides, the modern city as the site of commerce and division of labour compels urbanites to specialise in a profession according to this vocation (*ibid.*: 12-13, 17, 19). This rationality is directly expressed in the physical separation of house and work and thus in different moral regions of reproduction and production. Moreover, the division of labour explains how urbanites live in fragmented social relations to each other, whereby the city as a puzzle of separate worlds also promotes isolation (*ibid.*: 26). Metropolitan isolationism is generally caused by the metropolitan "substitution of indirect, 'secondary', for direct, face-to-face, 'primary' relations in the associations of individuals in the community." (*Ibid.*: 23) This transformation affects both social forms of communication as well as personal social contacts.[35] Insofar, vice and crime are specific indicators of the dissolution of local attachment and weakening of inhibitions of the primary group

(1990). For examples of Chicago School on human ecology and the moral order of the city see Nels Anderson (1923), *The Hobo: The Sociology of the Homeless Man*; Louis Wirth (1928), *The Ghetto*.

34 | As an example, Park (1967: 10-11) chooses East London, which he describes as a city of a single class within a city, which is in turn segregated by racial, cultural and professional differences. Peter Jackson (1989: 61) adopts this example of the mosaic of social areas to communities, which develop their own argot, or subcultural vocabulary, such as the 1980s phenomenon of the Sloane Rangers coming from the particular neighbourhood of Sloan Square, Kensington, characterised not only by specific dress and consumptive behaviour, but specifically speech. According to Jackson, they have long been replaced by the Yuppy image locally based in the London Docklands.

35 | For Park (1967: 39), functions formerly supplied by village gossip are taken over by the newspaper industry and advertising: "The absence of this [personal information] in the city

under the influence of city life (*ibid.*: 25). Thus, the development of secondary relations first and foremost constitutes a main example of urban crisis (*ibid.*: 27). For Park (*ibid.*: 22-24), this crisis is furthermore expressed in urbanites' essential rootlessness, segregation, perpetual agitation, amorality, breaking of the moral order, and advance of urban deviance. In order to retain some kind of social equilibrium, social control or even violent force become necessary (*ibid.*: 31), which notably impacts on metropolitan freedom of behaviour and expression tolerated in the city. Yet Park (*ibid.*: 41) claims in particular that

> [t]he attraction of the metropolis is due in part, however, to the fact that in the long run every individual finds somewhere among the varied manifestations of city life the sort of environment in which he expands and feels at ease; finds in short, the moral climate in which his peculiar nature obtains the stimulations that bring his innate dispositions to full and free expression.

Although his depiction of city life and urban mentality are influenced by the notion of urban crisis rather than by Simmel's presentation of urban ambivalences, Park (*ibid.*: 12; 40-41) at least acknowledges the urban individual's mobility and greater freedom.

Similar to Simmel, Park (*ibid.*: 40) also assumes that "[g]reat cities have always been the melting-pots of races and of cultures. Out of the vivid and subtle interactions of which they have been the centres, there have come the newer breeds and the newer social types." In "Human Migration and the Marginal Man" he initially describes a transformation of mentality of the receiving culture due to the dynamism of migration, integration, adjustment, and hybridisation (1928: 883-885): the impact of migration breaks with the former social order and preordains a transformation in culture, such as changes in customs and habits, but also in temperament, physique, or even personality. Mobility releases the migrant from the constraints of traditional modes of behaviour and thought and thus secularises formerly sacred social relations (*ibid.*: 887-888).[36] Freed from former inhibitions, the character of the individual migrant necessarily changes: either he becomes emancipated and enlightened or the transformation manifests itself in negative psychological effects like aggressive self-assertion or overexpression of individuality (*ibid.*). Until the former is followed by reintegration and release into a new social order, the immigrant finds himself in a period of transition, when old habits are discarded and new ones still to be formed: "It is inevitably a period of inner turmoil and intense self-consciousness." (*Ibid.*: 893) For Park (*ibid.*: 888), the emancipated migrant is rather a cosmopolitan defined by detachment and objectivity. As a potential wanderer, he is neither bound by conventions in the former home nor the receiving country and hence a

---

is what, in large part, makes the city what it is." See also Park's article on "Urbanization as Measured by Newspaper Circulation" (1929).

36 | Migration for Park (1928: 886) denotes a definite change of residences and break with home ties. Therein also lies the difference to gypsies, hobos, and other pariah people whose relation with the receiving society is symbiotic rather than social. They tend to be unsettled and mobile yet retain their culture, while being isolated at the same time (cf. Park 1928: 887; Park 1931: 535).

stranger to both worlds – the marginal man (cf. *ibid.*: 888, 893).[37] Nevertheless, striving to live in two places and two cultures the marginal man develops an unstable character, a sensitive mind and spiritual distress wrought with restlessness and disillusionment (*ibid.*: 881, 890-893).

This psychological state of uncertainty also concerns the significant urban type of "racial hybrids" (Park 1931: 534) or people of multi-ethnic background. Similarly, to the marginal man, the mixed-race individual develops a personality type split between two cultures, defined as enterprising, restless, ambitious, sensitive, objective and tolerant, but also serious, aggressive, self-conscious or even egocentric (*ibid.*: 544-549). The additional problem for the hybrid man is that the "conflict of color is embodied" (*ibid.*: 534), visually marking him as Other and rendering cultural integration more difficult. Because it is in the mind of the marginal man that the turmoil of opposing cultures manifests itself, the constructive processes of inner urbanisation may best be studied there.

Another highly significant article of modern urban sociology related to a theory of urban mentality is Louis Wirth's "Urbanism as a Way of Life" (1938). This "*Magna Carta* of American urban sociology" (Häussermann & Siebel 2004: 89) not only offers the paradigmatic definition of the city but also develops a theory of the effects of the urban on collective behaviour and personality. Urbanism as a characteristic mode of life can empirically be approached from three angles: (1) physical structure and ecological order, (2) social structure, (3) attitudes and ideas, collective behaviour (cf. Wirth 1969: 158-159). In general, for Wirth (*ibid.*: 160), there exists a reciprocal interrelation between the size of population, the density of settlement, the heterogeneity of social groups and the way of life of urbanites. In that sense, urban mentality can be read as a direct outcome of size, density, and heterogeneity (cf. *ibid.*: 161-162): the relatively large size of the urban realm and its population creates impersonal, superficial, transitory, and segmental social contacts. Density enhances the effect of size and supports differentiation, specialisation as well as socio-spatial segregation. Heterogeneity and diversity further segregation, the loosening of community ties, and disorientation, which culminates in a general anomie. While Wirth's (*ibid.*: 162) analysis of social life and collective behaviour concentrates on heterogeneity and social anomie, the focus on the individual emphasises the urbanites' segmental roles and schizoid character.

The substitution of secondary for primary contacts is considered the main feature of modern mode of urban life. This includes a weakening of kinship bonds, a decline in the social significance of families, the disappearance of the neighbourhood as well as the undermining of traditional social solidarity. In the view of the ineffectiveness of kinship ties, according to Wirth (*ibid.*: 163), "fictional kinship groups" are created, which render the mutual interrelations between urbanites more complicated, fragile or volatile. This depersonalisation of human association gives rise to loneliness also because "[a] major characteristic of the urban-dweller is his dissimilarity from his fellows"

---

37 | For Park (1928: 892), the emancipated Jew presents the typical marginal man, a cosmopolite, a stranger, and a man of the city. For the Jew as the urbanite *par excellence* see Julia Brauch, Anne Lipphard & Alexander Nocke, eds. (2008), *Jewish Topographies. Visions of Space, Traditions of Place*, particularly Joachim Schlör's "Jews and the Big City. Explorations on an Urban State of Mind" in the same collection of essays.

(*ibid.*: 159). Wirth (*ibid.*: 153) points out that the individual might gain a certain degree of freedom, being independent from close ties, but that he loses a sense of morale and participation. A large population invariably results in the segregation of urbanites; a large number of people also prompts an increase of individual variation, thus creating heterogeneity within the urban population (cf. *ibid.*: 159). Urban heterogeneity and diversity further segregation in social power hierarchies or social stratifications. The density and proximity of physical contacts render social contacts distant, which is expressed through communication, indifference, tolerance, and sharp contrasts (*ibid.*: 160). Wirth (*ibid.*: 153) extensively draws attention to Durkheim's notion of anomie, which due to the break-down of norms engenders urban social problems and personality disorders including social distance, crime, riots, delinquencies, deviance and social pathology on the one hand, while enforcing formal control mechanisms on the other hand.

On the level of the individual, the urban factors of size, density, and heterogeneity foster role segmentation and a schizoid urban character:

> The multiplication of persons in a state of interaction under conditions which make their contact as full personalities impossible produces that segmentalization of human relationships which has sometimes been seized upon by students of the mental life of cities as an explanation for the 'schizoid' character of urban personality. (*Ibid.*: 152)

As size and variation give rise to spatial segregation of a mosaic of social worlds, personal social life becomes compartmentalised (cf. *ibid.*: 151). The transition between tangential or intersecting groups can be rather abrupt and the compartmentalisation of role-playing promises an effective urban existence (cf. *ibid.*: 155). While "urbanites meet one another in highly segmental roles" (*ibid.*: 152) the character of social relationships is changed. Juxtaposing one's divergent personalities and lifestyles produces a relativistic and tolerant stance to differences (cf. *ibid.*: 155). By ways of that heightened mobility and tolerance society can become more integrated and finally result in the levelling of social, ethnic or other social differences (*ibid.*: 156). Psychological features of an urban personality, however, also encompass anonymity, superficiality, transitory character, and lack of commitment (*ibid.*: 157). In its extreme form, schizophrenia and loss of identity express themselves in urban phenomena like personal disorganisation, corruption, mental breakdown or suicide (*ibid.*: 162).

To summarize notable assumptions on urban mentality made by Chicago School members: Park's analysis of urban behaviour is adaptable to the theory of urban mentality which explores the impact of fragmentation of the urban world on social relations and an urban state of mind. Defining the city as melting-pot of cultures which is 'home' to cosmopolitan as well as to marginal existences conveys instances of a transformation of mentality, and therefore mental dispositions related to the new urban environment. Following Park, urban mentality is characterised by specialisation and rationalisation, distanciation and secondary relations, urban deviance and behavioural freedom, as well as strangeness and vigilance. Even more so, Wirth concentrates on the consequences of ecological determinants on urban culture and mentality. According to him, mental dispositions oscillate between hybridity and anomie, vigilant role-play and apathic schizophrenia.

3.2.3 New Urban Political Economy and City Culture

The transformation of cities throughout the urban crisis of the 1960s[38] stimulates a paradigmatic shift in urban theory initiated by Henri Lefevbre, strongly pursued by Manuel Castells and adapted by the early David Harvey. This 'School' of Urban Political Economy strives to understand the dynamics of the industrial capitalist city by connecting all problems of the post-war metropolis, such as suburbanisation, automobile-based consumer culture, metropolitan political fragmentation, decline of the inner city, segregation and ghettoisation, to a neo-Marxist framework of the urban (cf. Soja 2001: 98). The assumption is that the capitalist mode of production determines a capitalist way of life, and inequalities of the city are formed by the power structures of the capitalist society (cf. Häussermann & Siebel 2004: 112-126). Because the spatial differentiation in the Fordist-Keynesian city is superseded by social classifications, it is not the city which is held responsible for social fractions, but merely capitalist modes of production. Insofar, the city is less generator, subject, and initiator of social change, but filter, object, and stage of social processes. Centrally, neo-Marxist urban sociologists replace the Chicago School's conception of an urban way of life by one of the urban as a unit of reproduction and sphere of collective consumption. From this point of view, urban theory is not to be based on the core ambivalence between city and country as such, but on the opposition of production and consumption. This also implies that reproduction, just like leisure, physical regeneration, and education, are spatially organised in the capitalist urban realm. This economic determinism consequently drafts an ontology of the city as an "arena of consumption", a "landscape of leisure" and "sites for new festivals" (Crang 1998: 128). Although members of the New Urban Sociology first oppose the notion of urbanity, their analysis of an urban process as the interaction between urban structure and urban economy and politics – urban planning, urban renewal, urban social movements, local power, and collective consumption – can nevertheless induce interesting perspectives on the city and urban mentality.

For example, Henri Lefebvre's (1991: 89) philosophy and epistemology of space, which considers the dialectics between physical, social, and mental space, also involves the problematic of everyday life in the urban sphere. As a left-wing version of the Chicago School (cf. Soja 2008a: 33) his writings on cities offer a new approach to the urban and on urban mentality.[39] In reference to his theory of social space as producing and produced, for Lefebvre (1996: 100) the "*specificity* of the city" entails a particular relation with society as a whole; the urban metamorphoses according to changes in society, but the metropolis also induces transformations. Thus, the city resembles a projection of society characterised by temporal and spatial discontinuities between urban formations and social relations (cf. *ibid.*: 104-109).

---

38 I The urban crisis of the 1960s is marked by deconcentration, decentralisation, depopulation, decay, de-industrialisation, poverty, racial discrimination, unemployment, administrative expansion, destruction of urban villages and a decline of the traditional urban community.

39 I Lefebvre's writings on the city include: *Le droit à la ville* (1968), *Du rural à l'urbaine* (1970), *La révolution urbaine* (1970), *La ville et l'urbaine* (1970), *La pensée Marxiste et la ville* (1972).

Ultimately, his interdisciplinary urbanism is the link between the problems of modernist urbanity with the 1960s urban crisis on the one hand and contemporary postmodern theories of the city on the other, especially in regard to the urbanisation of society and the differentiation of the urban. In *The Urban Revolution* (1970), Lefebvre (2003: 14-15, 34, 113) identifies the 1960s as a "critical zone" in which the qualitative urban transformation has become a global phenomenon and a homogenising force. Hence, he asserts that today "[s]ociety has been completely urbanized." (*Ibid.*: 1) Lefebvre (*ibid.*: 8-18) argues, concerning the three stages of historical urbanism – political, merchant, and industrial city – that the transformation can be interpreted as a change from a rural to an industrial and finally urban society; urbanisation thus supersedes industrialisation as a global dynamic of capitalism (cf. *ibid.*: 2). The transition of this urban process begins to manifest itself in morphological and sociological structures of the post-Fordist urban fabric: network, differential space, and police centrality (*ibid.*: 120-125).

The other dominant trend during this phase of urbanisation is the internal differentiation process – that is: as the industrial society homogenises, the urban society differentiates (Lefebvre 2003: 37). According to Lefebvre (*ibid.*: 119), the urban is "a place of encounter, assembly, simultaneity" which creates the specificity of the urban situations "according to their differences." (*Ibid.*: 117) One can distinguish three dimensions of the urban phenomenon: the surface area of social relations, the terrain of social relations, and urban practices concerning space (*ibid.*: 86-87). "[T]he city as *the ensemble of differences between cities*" (Lefebvre 1996: 109) also refers to the particularities, urban patterns and the ways of living in the city, in no way contradicting Lefebvre's first assumption of the city as "a *projection of society on the ground*" (*ibid.*). While urban space can be differentiated in isotopes, utopias, and heterotopias (cf. *ibid.*: 113), the city is not only a habitat but entails habitation, namely the rhythms, spatio-temporal organisation and culture of the city (*ibid.*: 112-113). In accordance with his spatial theory, urban practice needs to be understood in connection with the mental and cultural particularities (cf. Lefebvre 2003: 5, 33). Lefebvre's notion of urban homogenisation and heterogenisation as well as the city's particularities in semiotic and rhythmic idiosyncrasy play a pivotal role for drafting a theory of urban-generic and urban-specific mentalities (see chapter 4.2.6.).

Conversely, Manuel Castells' *The Urban Question* (1979) criticises both Lefebvre and the Chicago School for causally linking the ecological form of the city with a specific cultural content. Exempting Wirth's definition of the city, Castells condemns the concept of urban culture as a way of life and the accompanying culturalist values as "anti-urban prejudices" (*ibid.*: 78). According to Castells (*ibid.*: 108), "although spatial forms may accentuate or deflect certain systems of behavior, they have no independent effect, and consequently, there is no systematic link between different urban contexts and ways of life". Thus, a relation between habitat and mode of behaviour or context and lifestyle does not exist (cf. *ibid.*: 97, 111). Rather, he develops a sociological theory of urbanisation which considers the urban system a social structure within a specific spatial and economic unit, functioning as a political apparatus and thus defined by production and consumption as well as symbolic or ideological aspects (*ibid.*: 235-238). Castells' notions are therefore to be read as a neo-Marxist obliteration of the meso-space of the city, either emphasising transformations of society or local contestations, but never urban culture – and thus proliferating the absence of urbanity and urban mentality. Despite rejecting Lefebvre's cultural notions in detail, Castells (*ibid.*: 86-87) nevertheless adapts and expands his overall assumption of the recent socio-urban revolution and the notion of socio-temporal dynamics within the post-Fordist metropolis especially in his later publication *The Informational City* (1989). Castells' ideas on (1) the space of flows of the Informational City and (2) the disruptions of the Dual City are useful for a cultural approach to the postmodern city concerning urban mentality.

According to Castells the new information technologies have a far-reaching impact on society in the sense that they further the rise of the "Informational City" (1989: 6), where "life is transformed into abstraction, cities into shadows" (Castells cit. in Gregory 1998: 55). For Castells (1989: 126) the production and use of new technologies as well as the centralisation and decentralisation of service industries in informational societies constitute a "space of flows". The spatial organisation of global information activities furthers indirect contacts and the construction of spatially discontinuous areas, urban places being superseded by space as a result (cf. *ibid.*: 169). "While organizations are located in places, and their components are place-dependent, the organizational logic is place-less, being fundamentally dependent of the space of flows that characterises information networks." (*Ibid.*: 169-170) This process is accompanied by a growing independence of the organisational and societal logic (cf. *ibid.*: 170). Due to the metropolitan dominance of the service economy and its information networks, cities merely serve as nodes within these rhizomatic structures (*ibid.*: 167-168). Consequently, the Informational City creates a specific urbanity determined by collective space-time compression, be it through the spatial liberation of the individual, the alienation of social life through commodification or the anonymity of suburbia (cf. *ibid.*: 1).

A second trend of the urban space of flows is identified by Castells (*ibid.*: 204-205) as the development of the Dual City which is "manifested in the spatial coexistence of a large sector of professional and managerial middle-class with a growing urban underclass". The post-Fordist metropolis becomes a "shared space within which the contradictory spheres of the local society are constantly trying to differentiate their territories." (*Ibid.*: 217) This new socio-spatial configuration of the urban is based on the transformation of occupational structures and on the polarisation and segmentation of the labour force (*ibid.*: 172). The Dual City "represents an urban social structure that exists on the basis of interaction between opposite and equally dynamic poles [...] whose developmental logic polarizes society, segments social groups, isolates cultures, segregates the use of a shared space." (*Ibid.*: 218) Related to the development of the information economy, this reformulation of a classical juxtaposition between rich and poor to new forms of urban dualism refers to the polarising effects of exclusion as well as to the contradictory and differentiated dynamics of growth and decline.

> The dual city [...] epitomizes the contradictory development of the new informational economy, and the conflictual appropriation of the inner city by social groups who share the same space while being worlds apart in terms of lifestyle and structural position in society. (*Ibid.*: 224-225)

In sum, Castells (1979: 102, 110) denies a link between a specific space and a particular culture; his Dual City constitutes a dislocation of value. This basically implies that the city does not raise a generic mentality. The urban structure only figures specific residential milieus due to the social projection on space because the distribution of housing produces social differentiation, specific urban landscapes, and segregation (cf. *ibid*: 169). Nevertheless, by this concentration of certain social characteristics in space, a link between ecological site and cultural specificity, an internal homogeneity of values, might exist: the population of a residential milieu is linked by a similar socio-economic status, and their common environmental surroundings might strengthen that connection (*ibid.*: 104-108). On the micro-level, even Castells (1989: 350) therefore recognises the need for territorially defined societies to preserve their identities, which can result, for example, in instances of political localism. In regard to urban-generic mentalities, the Informational City emphasises the need not to think of the city and its spaces as isolated, while the Dual City stresses the implications of localised differentiation. Hence, with Castells' conceptualisation of the post-Fordist city a study of urban mentality can focus on the dynamics of de- and re-territorialisation within the metropolis.

Contrary to Castells, David Harvey (1973: 231) follows Lefebvre's use of Marxist methods to interpret the capitalist city as formed by "surplus value" and "founded upon exploitation" (*ibid.*: 314). According to Harvey (*ibid.*: 231-233), structures that comprise the industrial society and continue to dominate urbanism render the city's role dependent on its social, economic, technological and institutional possibilities, a process which entails both external as well as internal differentiation. Consequently, there exists a definitive relationship between urbanism as a social form, the built form of the city, and the dominant mode of production, which implicates that owing to the dominant mode of production, division of labour and economic hierarchies ultimately determine the urban way of life by mediation of space (cf. *ibid.*: 203). Based on a theory of social space, Harvey (*ibid.*: 27) achieves to unite the social determinism of the Chicago School with the economic determinism of the Political Economy within a new conception of urban culture. For a study of mentalities, his ramifications on urban symbolism and on urban mental geographies in particular help fathom the socio-spatial dynamics of urban mental dispositions.

For Harvey (*ibid.*: 30), the city as spatial form can be understood as "the perceptual realm of spatial experience". He distinguishes between (1) biologically determined "*organic space*" which refers to instinctive spatial behaviour, (2) "*perceptual space*" as the spatial experience by optical, tactual, acoustic, and kinesthetic senses, as well as (3) "*symbolic space*", the experience of space through the interpretation of symbolic representations (*ibid.*: 28). "Social space, therefore, is made up of a complex of individual feelings and images about and reactions towards the spatial symbolism which surrounds that individual." (*Ibid.*: 34) Consequently, the spatial form of the city and its spatial symbolism, for example in architecture, play a major role in affecting human spatial behaviour and spatial thinking (cf. *ibid.*: 32). In order to understand space, Harvey (*ibid.*: 34) argues that research must consider the "significant relationships" of people and space and observe people's behaviour as reaction to their spatial environment. In order to assess the significance of space, one has to examine the behavioural dispositions, for instance evaluate the mediation of the cognitive state (cf. *ibid.*: 33). For this assessment of behavioural dispositions and spatial mentality, "[w]e can sample the mental state of the individual or of a group of individuals and discover their attitudes towards and their perceptions of the space which surrounds them." (*Ibid.*) Harvey (*ibid.*: 36) recognises that the mental image is variable between collectives and over time, and that spatial experience and mentality are therefore prone to transformations. Consequently, the common image of city reveals the mental map of the metropolis or urban mentality (for more see chapter 4.2).

As shown before, Harvey's notion of time-space compression can be interpreted as a transformation of mentalities. In *Consciousness and the Urban Experience* (1985) he offers the dialectics of time-space-money as influencing and forming the urban process in particular configurations of the urban condition or consciousness. Thus, "urbanization of consciousness" (Harvey 1985: 250) which necessarily "has to be understood in relation to the urbanization of the capital" (*ibid.* 252) entails that an increasing urbanisation makes the urban the primary level that individuals experience. In other words, like Lefebvre and Castells, Harvey too argues that urban mentality is the general state of mind of capitalism. However, he acknowledges that this process of alternations in urban consciousness is amenable to "continuous restructuring punctuated by periodic revolutions." (*Ibid.*: 262) In other words: "The geographies of the mind have to adapt to a welter of new experiences." (*Ibid.*: 200) His notion that "[t]he urban condition imprints its own qualities of consciousness [...]" (*ibid.*: 253) obviously adapts Simmel and Wirth's approach to the urban condition.[40] At the same time, his Marxist perspective methodologically revises

> how the consciousness produced through the particular patterning of relations between individualism, class, community, state and family affects the paths and qualities of capitalist urbanization that in turn feed back to alter the patterning of relations that underlie the urbanization of consciousness. (*Ibid.*: 253)

Although he severely criticises that the determinist explanation of ecological and economic presuppositions only reflect "surface appearances" and do "little to elucidate inner meaning and connection" (*ibid.*: 263) of the "[c]urious kinds of consciousness [that] arise out of the confusions of [the urban] experience" (*ibid.*: 251), he readjusts the focalisation of urban analysis to one of inner urbanisation, not only determined by spatial, temporal, socio-economic, and political aspects, but by dispositions of the imaginary. In conceptualising urban space as wrought by common images which relate to ideology, values, and consciousness, his analysis of the city can therefore be interpreted as a re-

40 | Firstly, in reference to Simmel, Harvey (1985: 4) interprets the money economy as a major characteristic of modernity, just like individualism, liberty, freedom, and equality. He further argues that the urban way of life necessarily reflects the conditions of metropolitan money culture, such as reserve, distance, intellect, and loneliness (cf. *ibid.*: 4-5). Moreover, he adapts Simmel's notion of urban relations as coordinated by rationality and punctuality (*ibid.*: 9). Secondly, for the analysis of temporal urban dispositions, he directly refers to Le Goff, showing that social relations implicate new urban-based time-rhythms apparent in evolving mental structures as well as material expression (*ibid.*: 7). Thirdly, Harvey (*ibid.*: 13) recognises a domination of space through private property and an appropriation of space by social purposes. Instead of a meeting place, the urban realm becomes a structured place of separation (cf. *ibid.*: 14). The perpetual reshaping of the geographical landscape of the city, through processes of suburbanization, deindustrialisation, restructuring, gentrification, urban renewal is seen as a struggle, either by violence or social control, over private space, territorial rights (*ibid.*: 29, 33).

lief from the monolithic notion of New Urban Economy to an approach based on the interdependencies and interpenetrations of economy, society, and culture. Thereby, the study of urbanity becomes again one of **a whole way of life**. Moreover, he achieves to relate the mere political changes of the post-Fordist city back to the cultural changes of Postmodernism. When the urban becomes a social space of reproduction, distraction, spectacle and display, the money economy leads to the alienation of the individual, and family life is characterised by an increasing privatisation and insulation (cf. *ibid.*: 254-258). The urbanisation of consciousness, according to Harvey (*ibid.*: 276), "threatens a transition to barbarism in the midst of a rhetoric of self-realisation." In this respect he predicts a new quality of social anomie. All in all, the findings of Lefebvre, Castells, and Harvey on the economic variable open interesting perspectives in regard to the socio-spatial dynamism of the post-Fordist metropolis which are employed by contemporary urbanologists to decipher postmodern urbanity.

3.2.4 The Contemporary City and Postmodern Urbanity

The aforementioned approaches to the city are proof of a further turning point in the urban metamorphoses to the new urban era of Postmodernism. Postmodern urban spaces, urbanity, and mentality are specifically influenced by processes of globalisation, mobility, spectacle, and hyperreality. While modern cities are associated with the 1960s crisis of urbanity, the postmodern city returns to difference and particularity. It constitutes, as Robins (1993: 303-304) argues, "the antithesis of modernist abstraction and anomie", by revitalising "urban culture and sensibilities". A critical 'post-modern' approach to urbanism is necessarily based on the paradigmatic research of the Chicago School, but contemporary urban theories also entail specific links with geopolitical economy.

The most influential studies of contemporary urban theory can be appointed to the emergence of the Los Angeles School of urban studies[41] which considers L.A. the post-modern city *par excellence* and the superseding prototype[42] of a new kind of urbanism for the late twentieth and early twenty-first century (cf. Zijderveld 1998: 130-134; Soja 2001: 159). Their contemporary urban theory strives to unite the polycentric, polyglot

---

41 | Allen Scott and Edward Soja's (1996) *The City. Los Angeles and Urban Theory at the End of the Twentieth Century* is a contemporary answer to the Chicago School's paradigmatic publication *The City* (1925). It emphasises the tremendous amount of attention paid to the study of Los Angeles by urban theorists, cultural critics and social commentators alike that relate to urban issues considerably diverging from the Fordist metropolis as an object of the Chicago School.

42 | While Paris was the paradigmatic city of the nineteenth century, and Chicago became the experimental hothouse of twentieth-century urbanism, Los Angeles, as the prime example of the late modern city, pre-shadows urban life in the twenty-first century. According to Soja (2001: 159), Los Angeles as the primary urban laboratory of the twenty-first century, characterised by cultural heterogeneity, is in need of a kind of urban analysis which is open to this diversity of post-Fordist/postmodern metropolis. Consequently, he argues that Los Angeles is one of the most informative "paradigms of twentieth-century urban-industrial development and popular consciousness" (*ibid.*: 248).

and polycultural characteristics of the postmodern metropolis to a global understanding of contemporary urban life and postmetropolitan transition (cf. Soja 2001: xvii). Soja (*ibid.*: xiv, 4) sees the most important work of the Los Angeles School in its commitment to a geographical perspective on the production of knowledge. He also argues that the transdisciplinary interest in the urban "*spatiality of human life*" (*ibid.*: 6-7) offers new insights into geographies of bodies, collective performative interactions, and of constructions of the Self in connection to the formation of the contemporary postmodern metropolis. A critical postmodern approach to urbanity also takes postmodern social theory, postmodern feminism, postcolonialism, postmarxism, Cultural Studies, and poststructuralism into consideration. Accordingly, the following assessment on postmodern urban mentality will not only draw on theories of the city by contemporary urban geographers, especially Edward Soja, but also by anthropologists like Marc Augé, cultural theorists like Celeste Olalquiaga as well as poststructuralists like Guy Debord and Jean Baudrillard.

Edward Soja's *Postmetropolis. Critical Studies of Cities and Regions* (2000) analyses both postmodern urbanism and the postmodern metropolis. While spatiality has long been synonymous with the urban for Soja (2001: 7), in his explorations of the Postmetropolis he highlights the "*spatial specificity of urbanism*".[43] Urban spatial specificity refers to the particular configurations of social relations, built forms, and human activity in a city and its geographical sphere of influence. Hence, Soja (*ibid.*: 13) defines the metropolis as a spatial form and spatially specific context for processes of social formation. He thereby pays tribute to the meso-level of urbanity, instead of relegating urban processes to the meta-level of society and economy, or imprisoning urban life in the micro-level of urban milieus. In his study on the Postmetropolis, Soja emplaces the differentiations of the postmodern city in new processes of urbanisation defined as Flexcity, Cosmopolis, Exopolis, Polarcity, Carceral City, and Simcity.[44] In the following, I will

43 | In his approach to the city, Soja (2001: xvi, 9) explicitly refers to Lefebvre embracing the conceptualisation of the relations between spatiality, society and history. Moreover, he adapts Lefebvre's trialectical approach to space for the city looking at the perceived space of materialised spatial practices, the conceived space of conceptional imagery and mental maps, as well as lived space concerning the simultaneously real-and-imagined (cf. *ibid.*: 11). It actively arises from the social production of cityscape as a distinctive material and symbolic context or habitat for human life (*ibid*: 8). Thus, the urban spatiality consists of the relatively fixed urban form, such as the built environment and physical structures. Secondly, it comprises the mappable patterns of cultural identity or class differences as well as "the whole range of individual and collective attributes, relations, thoughts, and practices of urban inhabitants." (*Ibid.*) Thirdly, the urban spatial specificity also lies in its more dynamic and processual character such as the formation of cityspace and the social construction of urbanism (cf. *ibid.*). Together these aspects contribute to the "historically evolving *specific geography* of cityspace" (*ibid.*). Especially synekistic agglomeration constitutes the spatial specificity of urbanism, which develops into a social and historical force (*ibid.*: 13).

44 | The postmodern metropolis, depending on the emphasis on a specific phenomenon, has, for example, been identified as Space of Flows (Castells), *Zwischenstadt* (Sieverts), Telepolis (Rötzer), Zone (Lyotard), *Non-Lieux* (Augé), Ghost Town (Baudrillard). *Postmetropolis* is concerned with delineating the main kinds of restructuring that define the contemporary ur-

briefly present these and investigate their possible approaches with postmodern urban mentality.

Flexcity is a synonym for the post-Fordist industrial metropolis or the according restructuring of the geopolitical economy of urbanism as industrial. The evolving Postmetropolis is characterised as a region of production, regeneration and transactional linkages that influence contemporary urban life (cf. *ibid.*: 156-157). For example, Soja (*ibid.:* 157) notes the polarisation of the urban labour market as a primary expression of the division of labour. In its centre lies the production, classification, circulation and consumption of postmodern cultural goods with additional new market-oriented consumer occupations (e.g. media and advertising) (cf. Featherstone 1991: 5, 35). The urban existence is adapted to the processes of the Flexcity, e.g. public spaces are altered to cater for the needs of consumption.

Cosmopolis describes the globalisation of cityspace as well as the globalised cityregion. Research on a hierarchy of world or global cities (i.e. Friedmann 1986; Sassen 1994) has shown that metropolitan regions competing globally on a political, economic, and cultural scale actually signal the resurrection of the city-state (cf. *ibid.*: 207-208). The Postmetropolis is also the site for the construction of transnational identities and the concomitant formation of spaces attuned to the diversity of a global geography, such as spaces of differences, hybridity, thirdspace, and contact zones (*ibid.*: 232).[45] Thus, the use of the term cosmopolis encompasses both the globalised and the culturally heterogeneous city (cf. *ibid.*: 229). In connection with a theory of postmodern urban mentality we can consider cosmopolis as "a construction site of the mind [...] in which there is genuine connection with, and respect and space for, the cultural Other" (Sandercock cit. in Soja 2001: 230).

Exopolis stands for the restructuring of urban form to that of the megacity or a post-urban structure. The urban agglomerations of megalopolises encompass discontinuous, fragmented and polycentric spatialities with an enormous yet widely scattered population (*ibid.*: 235). In fact, the city is defined through the city without, the outer or edge city and an urbanisation of the suburbs (*ibid.*: 238). The actual postmodern cityspace revolves around spaces of consumption, such as shopping malls, office-centred developments, as well as specific entertainment zones (*ibid.*: 243, 247). On the one hand, the growth of the outer cities newly characterises the metropolis, whereas on the other hand, it also indicates the death of the city because the Exopolis is a "city-without-cityness" (Soja 2000: 19). These changes in spatial organisation of the Postmetropolis and the according modifications of the urban condition are important for the analysis of urban mentality in the sense that the deconcentration of urban space not only leads to a dissemination of

---

ban process from these various concepts of the postmodern city. For representative texts of the respective discourses see Soja (2001).

45 | Due to the effects of globalisation and following Arjun Appadurei's five landscapes of urban globalisation, one can distinguish ethnoscapes of transnational citizenship, techno- and mediascapes of the internet and news agencies, financescapes of economic interactions as well as international division of labour, and last but not least the expansion of a transnational urban imagery and representation in ideoscapes (cf. Soja 2001: 190; 210-211).

former city centres but also furthers the fragmentation of the urban subject (cf. Soja 2001: 234; Deny 2009: 64).

The Fractal City indicates the restructuring of the social mosaic towards polarisation. Soja (2001: 265) argues that "*inherent in the new urbanization processes has been an intensification of socio-economic inequalities*". The fragmentation of the urban becomes apparent in social segregation and cultural differentiation as well as increased privatism and homogenisation of ghettoes, ethnic neighbourhoods, gated communities, or the urban fringe. This division, however, is not as class-conventional as Manuel Castells' Dual City but more fractured in its social geometry (cf. *ibid.*). Urban space is thus constituted by homogeneous as well as heterogeneous geographies, diversified by structures of communities, class, race, sexuality, religion, age and other social relations (*ibid.*: 265-295). This stresses that urban life consists of the clash and meeting of opposites and that the inner turmoil of the Fractal City has an influence on the socio-psychological state of its denizens or their mentality.

The Carceral City describes a new regime of urbanisation as an intensification of social and spatial control. Soja (*ibid.*: 298-299) borrows the notion of the island-like fortress-city from Michel Foucault and Mike Davis, describing a postmetropolitan landscape filled by protected and fortified spaces or enclosures that barricade individuals and communities against real and imagined dangers. Examples for the Carceral City are social warfare, the destruction of public space, the policing of space by a security-obsessed architecture and surveillance, gated communities and insular lifestyles (*ibid.*: 298-322). An exercise of the "ecology of fear" (*ibid.*: 155) in the Postmetropolis influences the psychological dispositions of its inhabitants.

Simcity finally describes the restructuring of the urban image to one of simulation and hyperreality. For Soja (*ibid.*: 147), the Postmetropolis is foremost a metaphysical reality where the real and imagined commingle. The confusion and final fusion of the imagined and the real, the copy and the original, calls on Baudrillard's notion of simulation, simulacrum and hyperreality (cf. *ibid.*: 325). According to Soja (*ibid.*: 324), the focus on urban imagery reconstructs the contemporary lifeworld, affects everyday life in the metropolis and thus "creat[es] new ways of thinking and acting in the urban milieu". Furthermore, it has a severe impact on the city-centred consciousness, which he explores with the help of Olalquiga's concept of psychasthenia (see chapter 3.2.3).

These notions of the Postmetropolis – flexible, cosmopolitan, ex, fractal, carceral, simulated – help to explore its spatial, social, and mental aspects which offer new qualities regarding structures of a postmodern urban mentality. Since the urban renaissance in the 1980s, the postmodern cityscape has seen substantial material changes, including reconstruction, re-shaping and renewal of the urban fabric. The re-invention of the importance of the spatial practices has also placed a new emphasis on the construction of the built environments, which are not just the backdrop to an urban way of life, but constitute a major element in the urban experience and have been recognised as crucial in forging new structures of feeling (cf. Harvey 1990: 66-67). Significant transformations lie in the palimpsestic or depthless postmodern architecture, the urban memoryscapes on the one hand and the spread of non-places on the other hand as well as the establishment of a general urban liminality.

Postmodern urban theory acknowledges the importance of architecture and deliberately fuses deconstructionist theory with postmodern architectural practices (*ibid.*: 97).

While the modern city is planned and credited with the destruction of the traditional city and its neighbourhood culture, Postmodernism cultivates a palimpsestic idea of urban designs that cater for personalised spaces, monumentalism, and spectacalty (*ibid.*: 66).[46] For Harvey (*ibid.*: 98), these new architectural practices can be summed up as "fiction, fragmentation, collage, and eclecticism" on the one hand, and a "sense of ephemerality and chaos" on the other. The "remarkable eclecticism" (*ibid.*: 66) of the postmodern city seems to enhance chaotic and anomic experiences. At the same time, it creates a sense of ordered complexity, weaving together dynamism, social interaction, and intricacy – ways of expressing postmodern diversity (cf. *ibid.*: 73, 75). Harvey (*ibid.*: 88) sees the quality of postmodern buildings, for example London's Lloyd's building or the Bonaventure Hotel in L.A., as breaking with the notion of interior and exterior to create a sense of "contrived depthlessness". Conversely, critics detect therein a postmodern fascination with surfaces, since the plethora of ornamental facades conceals underlying meaning (cf. *ibid.*: 77; Featherstone 1991: 100).

According to Postmodernism's preoccupation with history, however, the surface appearance is broken to achieve some seemingly greater depths in the recuperation of historic embellishment, ornamentation, and decoration. Due to the overabundance of history, historical continuity and occupation with collective remembrance, memory, either in the form of *lieux de mémoire* (Nora 1984-1992) or as *Erinnerungsräume* (Assmann 1999), has become spatialised in postmodern urban cartographies. This impulse to preserve the past is always intertwined with the need to safeguard a specific sense of the Self, be it in individual or collective identity. In that respect, architecture and urban planning nowadays are informed by a newfound respect for place and tradition, even (re)creating places of memory in order to produce communities, rehabilitate the historically metamorphosed urban landscape, and cater to the enthusiasm for locality (cf. Harvey 1990: 82). Moreover, the reconstruction of historical places also supplies the Postmetropolis with its own heritage industry (*ibid.*: 85-87). Historical quotations thus achieve a certain dramatisation of urban spaces, resulting in major attraction of the city and duly intensifying inter-urban competition (*ibid.*: 92-93). The historical image thereby becomes instrumentalised for urban self-fashioning.

The French anthropologist Marc Augé develops a theory of non-places which negates the idea of culture localised in time and space and can therefore count as counter-concept to Pierre Nora's *lieux de memoire*; "a non-place is a space from which we can neither read identities nor relations, nor history." (Augé 1997: 13) Augé's (1995: 78) hypothesis is "that supermodernity produces non-places" such as commercial centres, supermarkets, retail outlets, airports, motorways, parking lots, hotel chains, holiday clubs, hospitals, refugee camps, shantytowns, cable and wireless networks.[47] The concept of

---

46 | For more see Harvey (1990: 66-98) and Jameson (1999: 10) or Chris Jencks (1984), *The Language of Postmodern Architecture*; Jane Jacobs (1961), *The Death and Life of Great American Cities* as well as the writings of Paul Virilio.

47 | Augé (1995: 29-31, 40-41) sees Postmodernity or Supermodernity as an "excess of time" and events, "spatial overabundance" as well as an excessive individualisation. These three instances of excess involve concrete physical transformations, most notably the movement of people, urban concentrations as the multiplication of what he terms non-places (cf. *ibid.*: 34).

non-place thus designates spaces constructed for certain means – transport, transit, commerce, leisure (cf. *ibid.*: 94). Whereas places designate individual identities, non-places in turn create shared identities of their 'users' – namely passengers or customers (cf. *ibid.*: 101).[48] For Augé (*ibid.*: 94), the social basis of the urban is therefore rather defined by "solitary contractuality". Due to the ephermerality, loss of identity and contingency of the non-place transit spaces the individual is overcome by notions of powerlessness, solitariness and existential outsider-feeling (cf. *ibid.*: 78). Yet the anonymity of the non-place offers the individual the freedom of being "relieved of his usual determinants" (*ibid.*: 103). The non-places of transition and their spatial anonymity are the new home of the passing stranger (cf. *ibid.*: 106). Thereby the sense of solitude and anonymity can also lead to the "passive joys of identity-loss, and the more active pleasure of role-playing." (*Ibid.*: 103) However, the postmodern urban subject is alienated and without the thin line between place and non-place "there can be only terror or madness." (Augé 1997: 24) In that sense, the postmodern urban mentality of non-places can be considered one of enhanced anomie but with the new qualitative notion of transitoriness.

Devoid of any history and depleted of the possibility for social relations or identity formation, the postmodern metropolis is characterised by an increasingly pervasive placelessness. In that respect, Rötzer (2000: 29) comments that the Postmetropolis at the turn of the twenty-first-century presents the threshold of a non-place existence. Although Augé's non-places are not limited to the transit spaces of the city, they largely tend to be located on the edge of the city; postmodern spaces of transition and non-places are literally no-man's land between city and country. Stressing technological networks between cities, Guggenberger (2000: 44-57) speaks of "Teleopolis", an urbanity created by a strictly placeless existence, a way of life within segments of TV programmes between the living room and the world which turns the urbanite into a kind of vagabond. For Chambers (1990: 53), the traditional city represents a geographical, economic, political and social unit, whereas the postmodern "metro-network" features a transformation of the urban into a mere place of transit of "intersections, stations, junction", a "twilight region". Lyotard (2000: 121-122) considers the inbetween "Zone" a ghost town and emphasises how the "*Urbs*" has become an encompassing "*Orbs*" with neither inside nor outside. These various forms of placeless postmetropolitan non-existence exponentiate the alienation and the disorientation of the postmodern Self.

In the essay "Die Stadt und der Haß" (2000) Jean Baudrillard interprets indifference and omnipresent but diffuse emotional deviance, especially hate, as an outcome of the universal process of spatial concentration and simultaneous emptiness (cf. Deny 2009: 68-69), disintegration and disorganisation leading to a parasitical satellite existence (cf.

48 | In respect of this publication, we might ask whose mentality non-places eventually address. For example *Westfield* shopping centre in Shepherd's Bush: for the London shopper in general it might present one of those typical consumer non-places mentioned by Augé because there is nothing that relates to their identity or mental structures as probably the same shops (Topshop, Zara, Mango, HMV) would on Oxford Street. However, Australian Londoners actually prefer shopping in their homegrown mall which offers them a feeling of a one-day trip home: ice-cream parlours and boutiques only to be found Down Under can be enjoyed there alongside the plethora of globalised merchandise. Thus, *Westfield* shopping mall is not only a definite working place for its London employees, but also a place of identification for the Australian diaspora.

Baudrillard 2000: 132). Baudrillard (*ibid.*: 131-132) sees the suburbs and satellite cities as ghost towns and poles of emptiness inhabited by "ghost people". He identifies the postmodern city as a functional and anonymous aggregation of people, whose 'critical mass' leads to an acceleration and intensification of all urban processes which then results in indifference, confusion, and finally self-destruction (cf. *ibid.*: 134). Moreover, all positive emotions are inversed and simplified to basic vital chains of instinctive reactions: attraction to repulsion, disgust and finally hate (*ibid.*: 135). Positive notions of the urban like multiculturalism, cosmopolitanism and tolerance provoke and turn into criminality, racism, indifference and a blast of hate as virtual violence and terrorism (*ibid.* 136-137). Emotionally deviant phenomena associated with psychological disorders such as resentment, self-hate and hate ineluctably belong to the mental dispositions of the hyperreality of the postmodern metropolis (*ibid.*: 138-140). Especially through the anomic urban staging of hate, the urbanite as debased Other expresses feelings of repulsion and non-belonging that are the result of a defence mechanism against a potentiated overload scenario.

Notions of a postmodern overload scenario particularly seem to derive from the spectaclisation of urban society. For postmodern urbanologists like Lefebvre (2003: 116), the city as spectacle "is the very form of the urban, revealed." The spectacle is therefore not only intrinsic to postmodern but also to urban culture (cf. Harvey 1990: 88). As the spectacle represents the totality of the commodity world, it is the vantage point of the money culture that Simmel interpreted as the major constituent of an urban way of life in the beginning of the twentieth century. And although Wirth (1969: 161-162) already mentions sensational events, spectatorship and self-expression as forms of catering to thrills as a means to escape from the monotony of urban life and one of the major functions of urban recreation, the postmodern spectacle seems to be of an altogether different quality.

In *La Société du Spectacle* (1967), the spectacle opens the door to an urban "realm of non-work, of inactivity" for Guy Debord (1994: 21). This might help us understand why Debord (*ibid.*: 12) essentially sketches the phenomenon as "a concrete inversion of life, and, as such, the autonomous movement of non-life." The postmetropolitan geographies of non-places serve as a stage for spectacles that create a flow of illusions – or the opposite of life. Also the urban core, based on zones of transition, like malls, shopping centres, and entertainment areas, becomes a mere centre of spectacle. Because of "the immense accumulation of spectacles" (*ibid.*) during high modernity, Debord goes as far as to argue that the current society is based on the spectacle in every aspect. Experiences of urban isolation are enforced by the spectacle, but now bridge the division between urbanites creating "isolated individuals as individuals *isolated together*" (*ibid.*: 122). The phenomenon of a non-life in non-places of the city stresses the homelessness of the urbanite while the spectacle seems to be anywhere. Consequently, "[t]he spectacle's function in society is the concrete manufacture of alienation." (*Ibid.*: 23) Paradoxically, experiences of separation within and without the individual also means that urban distanciation is geographically eliminated, which leads to a complete indifference towards the Other (cf. *ibid.*: 120). In this sense, we can read his theories of the spectacle as a postmodern urban condition that is elementary for an urban mentality.[49] Yet the continuous spectalisation can be interpreted as the expression of a postmodern overload scenario.

The spectacle creates a new "sense of togetherness and participation in urban life" (Robins 1993: 311) or a novel form of sociability (cf. Featherstone 1991: 105, 107). Debord (1994: 123) describes a "new type of social existence" which is on the verge of dissolution and self-destruction, namely on the point where "*it consumes itself.*" (*Ibid.*: 124) According to Debord (*ibid.*: 12), the spectacle can be defined as "a social relationship between people that is mediated by images". Composed of various images and signs, they are at the same time the end products of the spectacle (cf. *ibid.*: 13). Disrupting the dichotomy between reality and image, social life becomes mere appearance, behaviour trancelike, and the dream a social necessity (*ibid.*: 14-18). "All that once directly lived has become mere representation." (*Ibid.*: 12) The randomness, banality, depthlessness and repetition of urban images are thus just as important as the material reality for the contemporary urban condition. The postmodern urban space of spectacle has transformed urbanity to a mere representation and exerts the strongest influence upon the experiences of urbanites. This could be read as a change of urban mental structures towards the imaginary and simulational role-play.

Jean Baudrillard expands Debord's theory of the spectacle to one of simulation: for Debord (1994: 23, 26), the real consumer becomes the consumer of illusions and Baudrillard specifically focuses on these "semiotics of the consumer city of signs" (Jarvis 1998: 32; cf. Featherstone 1991: 99). Baudrillard's seminal text on *Simulacra and Simulation* (1981) is based on the assumption that simulation effaces the difference between the real and the imagined; the sign virtually precedes the thing.[50] Because the difference between original and copy has become extinguished, the simulacrum threatens the existence of difference in general and between true and false, real and imaginary, signifier and signified in particular (cf. Baudrillard 1997: 3). Baudrillard goes so far as to predict that the overload of signs in the form of simulation results in a complete hallucination of reality. Without differentiation, there can, however, no longer exist any values, norms or even judgements (cf. Featherstone 1991: 98), and conversely Baudrillard thus proclaims the end of all alienation, which at the same time also constitutes the extinction of the Self (cf. Jarvis 1998: 34-35). According to Baudrillard's (2000: 131-132) analogy of "ghosts towns – ghost people" urbanites are forced into a new *conditio humana* that strips them of their idiosyncrasy, difference and strangeness, promoting a lifestyle of

49 | For Featherstone (1991: 103), the spectacle constitutes another instance of de-distanciation, encouraging further immediacy, instantiation, emotional de-control and amazement. The accumulation of spectacles moreover merges high and low cultures, which leads to a shift in postmodern lifestyles (cf. *ibid.*: 105). As such, new youth subcultures for example represent the other side of the spectacle, namely a movement beyond individualism and the decentring of the Self (*ibid.*: 101).

50 | Baudrillard (1997: 6) identifies three successive phases of the image from the picture in antiquity as a basic reality to a masking during the Middle Ages obsessed with perverting reality, to Industrialisation when the image masks the absence of reality and finally to Postmodernism where the referent has disappeared and there is no relation to any reality but everything has become a pure simulacrum.

perpetual reproduction of a new universal culture of identity (cf. Deny 2009: 69), which conversely also leads to repulsion and anomie. The intensity and immediacy of visual sensations, tendencies towards indeterminacies and immanence leave their mark on the postmodern urban mentality, which can be summarised as one of the loss of a sense of a local-historical past by increasing non-places, schizoid culture, and replacement by images and simulations that all lend an even greater feeling of cosmopolitanism to the individual (cf. Featherstone 1991: 11, 40, 99).

Baudrillard (1997: 6) conceptualises the image as central to postmodern city life and urban sensibilities. The intertextuality and multireadability of the simulational metropolis offers multiphrenic intensities and sensations on the surface of its imagery (*ibid.*: 5). However, urban images perceived on an everyday basis have already gone through the "*precession of simulacra*" (*ibid.*: 1). In respect of postmodern urban geographies, one can thereby constitute that the completely semantisised and the simulated metropolis have become a mere code often dislocated from their referent and free from the 'real' environment (cf. Robins 1993: 306; Jarvis 1998: 30-34). Insofar, they are promoted as instruments for manipulating the urbanites' perception towards a simplified user or consumer mentality. The simulational metropolis is the hyperreal, as Baudrillard (1997: 2) argues, produced "in a hyperspace without atmosphere." The hyperreal metropolis has its own influence on urbanity: the new image reality dominates urban public and does not acknowledge any exteriors, rendering all transparent or immaterial (cf. Featherstone 1991: 99; Robins 1993: 320). An absence of belonging and a loss of identity therefore characterise postmodern urban life. The media are central to a discussion to both the "postmodern hyperspace of electronic simulation" (Jarvis 1998: 34) and postmodern urban sensibilities because urban society is drenched in signs and simulation and mainly moves in the rhythm of new technologies (cf. Featherstone 1991: 5). It suggests that mentality is largely influenced by the social significance of the innumerable media productions, communication networks and technological inventions. In respect to the technologically mediated hyperreality, urban spatial imagery becomes a new version of mental setting or mind control (cf. Soja 2001: 324, 331, 335). But despite the stereotypicality and banality of hyperreality, this illegible urban environment increases feelings of insecurity.

The psychological impacts of hyperrealiy are described by Celeste Olalquiaga's theory of psychasthenia in *Megalopolis. Contemporary Cultural Sensibilities* (1992). Psychasthenia is seen as the endemic state of mind within the Postmetropolis characterised by an unmanageable version of the metropolitan overload (cf. Olalquiaga 1992: 2). According to Olalquiaga (*ibid.*: xi) Postmodernism in general and urbanity in particular further ambivalent mental tendencies of "personal responsibility and individual impotence." In contemporary urban experience, feelings, emotions and sensations are affected by imagery of the simulacra rather than through direct exposure. Sensibilities as collective dispositions towards cultural practices – or urban mentality – are today only lived indirectly through a catalyst which mediates a "'trained' way of perceiving" (*ibid.*: xix). Contemporary emotional life becomes caught up in an imaginary level (cf. *ibid.*: 4). Rather than being occupied with the first-degree references of urban objects and events, the postmodern sensibility is thus shaped by simulations, representations, images, and texts of the former real (*ibid.*: 6).

In her analysis of the postmodern cityscape, Olalquiaga (*ibid.*: 94) refers to the metropolis as a "transitory landscape" characterised by waste, deterioration, and abandonment. For Olalquiaga (*ibid.*: 56-57) this implies two ambivalent tendencies: first, the transformation of cities into a corpse of both organic and technological decay indicates that cities have become like bodies. Second, while people strive to locate themselves amidst those permanent ruinous conditions of urbanity, their bodies are significantly connected to the anthropomorphised cities (cf. *ibid.*: 93; Soja 2001: 150-151). On the basis of hyperreal urbanity, people are strongly confronted with their increasing inability to distinguish between organically lived and technologically induced Self: the reason for the postmetropolitan rise of psychasthenia as a mental disorder or even general cultural condition. The urbanite's identity merges with the cityscape and thus becomes bodiless in a placeless world, emphasising its transitoriness, uprootedness, emptiness, and limitlessnes (cf. Olalquiaga 1992: 17). This diagnosis of psychasthenia also helps to describe contemporary sensations of uneasiness, homelessness, perpetual loss and dislocation, which enhance the need for further oversaturation and overload (*ibid.*: 2). Consequently, the concept of psychasthenia describes the postmodern condition of being lost in space, a disturbance in the relation between Self and cityscape and a severe inability to locate the boundaries of one's body (cf. Soja 2001: 330-331). These deficiencies demand the renewal of urban means of distanciation, all in all, an advanced postmodern urban mentality and adapted mental equipments centred on the functions of (re)orientation.

To summarise: the postmodern urban *conditio humana* is constituted by tendencies of emptiness, alienation, disorientation, a loss of identity, the dissolution of solidarity and further disintegration of primary relations, but it is also associated with new forms of spectacular encounters, isolational contractuality, a new solidarity of non-life, a sense of variety and vitality, as well as overcoming alienation and difference. The postmodern cityscape on the surface appearance of its historical and stylistic eclecticism, monumentalisation as well as a decoration offers an array of and enhances ambivalent experiences and an increase in ambivalent stimuli. By only catering to the needs of the spectacular, public spaces lose their former functions and create a pervasive urban void. Emptiness and placelessness of the postmodern urban space overwhelm the urbanites' mental disposition. The metropolis is mainly defined by non-places that decontextualise, reduplicate and simulate a traditional sense of urbanity. Moreover, the homogenising impact of the simulacrum defeats the uniqueness of the city, abolishing not only the differences between global cities but also between the city and the country, public and private, Self and Other, or body and space. These profound changes restructure the discourses and symbolism of the city, in other words alter the "*urban imaginary*, the ways we think about cities and urban life" (Soja 2001: 149). Postmodern urbanity is submitted to these simulational and imaginary tendencies. In a way, as already observed by Simmel, structures of mentality are exponentiated by the new quality of the overload effect generated by innovative technologies, waste of information and signs.

Social contacts become faster, more pragmatic and superficial. Collective notions of identity are seemingly destroyed, which creates a socialisation based on indifference, privacy, anonymity, solitariness, egoism, isolation, insecurity, alienation. Solitary contractuality is to be seen as an enhanced pragmatic metropolitan way of life. However, the antisocial mechanisms of the city are ambiguously countered by the new socialisation of non-places or the spectacle, which in their homogenising tendencies unite people in isolation but also implicate a shift towards anomie and self-destruction. The simulational metropolis defeats social relations, leading to emotional deviance or pathology of resentment, self-hate, hate, and psychasthenia, which creates an encompassing feeling of fear or terror, but also imbalance, madness, psychopathy. Built on security-obsessed architecture of the Carceral City forms, gated communities and Privatopias (McKenzie 1994) promote insular lifestyles and satellite existence. Conversely, this emphasis on protection creates an enhanced ecology of fear. The postmodern culture of spectacles advances the ambivalent interface of entertainment, identification, orientation, knowledge, but also expresses manifestation of urban non-belonging or even mind control through image and simulation.

In terms of individual values and sensibilities, these postmodern developments of the metropolis indicate a (de)centering and fragmentation of identity, a (de)control of emotions, programmed performative act of identity and an aestheticised play with individuality gained in the metropolitan realm, the fragmentation and plurality of world-views enhancing the dislocation and homelessness of the postmodern urbanite. While the non-place is depleted of the possibility of identity formation, it nevertheless offers the chance to relish in this loss of identity for example by role-play. Moreover, losing the Self and gaining a feeling of being a perpetual outsider enhances the connection with the Other, simultaneously emphasising cosmopolitanism and organic solidarity of postmodern urbanites.

4 The Concept of Urban Mentality

According to a common assumption, urbanisation leads to the annihilation of the city and urbanity always contains the paradoxical dimension of its own dissolution. The death of the city is a myth with a long tradition. Historically, we can recall the fall of Troy, the sinking of Atlantis or the destruction of Sodom and Gomorrah. To those we can add the Gilgamic fear of the loss of the city, Gibbons' narrative of the downfall of Rome, as well as Geddes' and Mumford's notion of the death of the city as Nekropolis[1] (cf. Bogdanović 2000: 142-143). Contemporary urban theorists also proclaim the death of the classical urban induced by full-stretch urbanisation or new media and communication technologies.[2] Urban form is dissolved; its limits become porous and evaporate in the space of flows. For most urbanologists the city is a clearly delimitable phenomenon specifically defined by density, centrality, and heterogeneity, but the new territorial formations constitute dynamics of deconstruction, decomposition and deterritorialisation which alter the urbanised areas beyond recognition of their former physical centrality. Urbanity constructed as an ontological opposition to provinciality also becomes dislocated from the city and is consequently extinguished.[3] The Postmetropolis is therefore widely regarded as a large place without urbanity.

Yet the urban sprawl "does not negate the idea of cities as distinct spatial formations or imaginaries" and the "'cityness' of cities [still] seems to matter" (Amin & Thrift 2002: 2). No one would dare to deny the empirical existence of urban entities like L.A., Tokyo,

---

1 | Mumford (1997: 246-248) draws a horrific picture of depression, disease, disorder, disintegration, demoralization, desertion, depopulation, depletion, chaos, blight, crime, instability, conflicts, breakdown, uncertainty, filth, barbarism, terror, and nucleation.

2 | Olalquiaga's (1992: 57) image of the urban skeleton is even crasser: "Dead leaves, stuffed animals, and rotting road kills meet an urban/suburban landscape of industrial waste, deteriorated machinery, and abandoned buildings in what could be considered a subculture of junk and debris." For more see Bogdanović (2000), Guggenberger (2000: 53-54); Keller (2000a: 7-8); Sieverts (2003: 19-24); Prakash (2008: 1-4); Löw (2008: 113-114).

3 | Without clear boundaries between centre and periphery the differentiations between city and country are annihilated. Looking at vast landscapes of suburban housing and industrial complexes, it is increasingly hard to tell where the city begins or the country ends. Rurbanisation describes the urbanisation of the countryside, by which the principle of urban density is inversed (cf. Zijderveld 1998: 126; Rötzer 2000: 24; Prakash 2008: 3).

and London. Amin and Thrift (*ibid.*: 1) comment that "we still name cities and think of them as distinctive places. A Londoner today might dispute which outer suburbs count as London, but swears that the city does not extend to adjacent urban centres such as Reading and Slough." They continue to argue:

> The naming, of course, is highly selective, giving us London as the signature of empire, of crowded streets, art galleries, pubs, and people from around the world, of salient trains, well-trimmed suburban gardens, terraced houses. But somehow the fragments do come together into an enduring picture of London as a busy gateway to the world, a cosmopolis that is also homely. (*Ibid.*: 2)

Paradoxically, the moribund megalopolis continues to describe cities, and postmodern notions of Edge City, Dual City, Divided City, Patchwork City, Network City, Virtual City obviously conceptualise the postmodern city anew as a form of unity. Despite the city's metamorphosis and the transformation of urbanity, the urban retains its generic 'shape' (cf. Schroer 2006: 227).[4] Insofar, contemporary cities are still identifiable as entities with a particular urban culture that is not to be found in smaller, less densely concentrated or heterogeneous settlements, while each city is defined by its distinctive constellations of spatial practices, social power relations, and urban imaginations.

In accordance with the Spatial Turn, a recent theory by the German urban sociologists Helmuth Berking (2008) and Martina Löw (2001, 2008) acknowledges "the spatial specificity of urbanism" (Soja cit. in Berking 2008: 18). This so-called "Eigenlogik der Städte" (Berking 2008: 29; transl. as 'idiosyncrasy of the city') presents a theoretical-conceptional as well as methodological-empirical approach that both recognises the specificity of the postmodern urban realm in contrast to other social processes (urbanisation, civilisation, modernisation, nation building) and emphasises the differences between contemporary cities in their specific urbanity. The individual shape of the city, such as the spatio-structural organisation of density and heterogeneity defines a particular relationship between spatial organisation, material environment and cultural dispositions (cf. *ibid.*: 23). Moreover, the approach takes into account consequences of the urban on feeling, thinking, imagining and acting – or urban mentality. According to Berking (*ibid.*: 23-28), the city is defined by cognitive, emotional, behavioural and imaginary structures he describes as metropolitan doxa ("*großstädtische Doxa*") in reference to Bourdieu.[5] It is argued that urban habitus is predominantly a product of incorpora-

---

4 | It is pointed out point out that the notion of an encircling wall is so strongly grounded in our collective memory that we can only perceive of the city as entity (cf. Löw, Steets & Stoetzer 2008: 12). Braudel (1988: 491) defines this as the "self-consciousness of towns". Only in a few countries the city wall is superfluous. For example in London the city wall had mainly an administrative function as the fear of parliamentarism led to its enforcement around 1643 (cf. *ibid.*).

5 | It appears self-evident that as an urban sociologist, Berking employs sociological terminology from the most prominent cultural sociologist of the twentieth century rather than that of the historians of mentalities, but the line of argument is very similar. Also Parker (2004: 143) refers to Bourdieu to describe doxic certainties of urban attitude: "The 'doxic city' I would ar-tion of the city's socio-cultural structures mediated by doxic structures such as cognitive, emotional, imaginary and behavioural patterns (cf. *ibid.*: 24). Berking (*ibid.*: 24-25) specifically pinpoints the spatialisation of doxic lifeworld relations and emphasises the importance of the 'sense of place' as a constitutive frame of background knowledge. In this sense, doxa implies locale-specific aspects and the city therefore denotes an urbanisation of doxic certainties (cf. *ibid.*: 25-26). Consequently, doxa defines a conceptional frame for understanding the 'specific logic' of cities (*ibid.*: 27-28). Hence, Berking's theory of doxic spatial relations can be perfectly applied for a theory of urban mentality, especially with the new perspectives it offers concerning the congruency between spatial forms and habitual dispositions.

Furthermore, according to Berking's thesis (*ibid.*: 28), metropolitan doxa is transformed into narratives, styles, and cognitive patterns, a notion which is close to the methodological approach to representations of mentality in contemporary London novels as in the present analysis (see chapter 5). Löw (2008: 76) comments:

> Mit dem Begriffspaar *städtischer Doxa* als über Regeln und Ressourcen strukturell verankerter Sinnprovinz, deren Logik auf Versichtung und Heterogenisierung basiert, und Habitus, als körperlich-praktischer Sinn für diesen Ort und, als (auch) ortspezifisches Bewertungs-, Wahrnehmungs- und Handlungsschema, kann der begriffliche Rahmen gesteckt werden, in dem sich *Prozesse eigenlogischer städtischer Vergesellschaftung erfassen* lassen.

While Berking (*ibid.*: 29) is still sceptical whether the relation between city as form and urbanity can be grasped by the notion of metropolitan doxa, this book explicitly shows that the related concept of mentality fills the missing link between city as form and an urban way of life. The concept of mentality helps return to a notion of urbanity that reinstates a connection between the material realities of the city and the behaviour and mental life of its denizens. Due to the stimulus-and-response model of the lifeworld concept, urban spatialities (physical, social, mental) influence societal developments by ways of forming collective mental dispositions. In the following I will present the concept of urban mentality by differentiating urban-generic ambivalences of mentality as intrinsic to every city from factors of influence on the urban-specific mentality characteristic of one particular metropolis.

The whole problematic of inner urbanisation in difference to other social processes, the equation of urbanity with the European city, as well as the discourses on the death of the city or Berking's approach to revive the idiosyncrasy of the city, essentially constitute a question of scale. It has been shown that much research of the urban actually refers to the meta-level of social analysis regarding civilisation, modernity, society, and nation. By contrast, most of the research on urban sociology since the Chicago School is concerned with the micro-level[6] of the city, such as studies on natural areas, moral regions and the

---

gue is very similar to the helter-skleter, clock driven metropolis that Simmel describes where urbanites respond automaton-like to warnings [. . .]."

6 | For the later members of the Chicago School, the interest lay in the partial areas of the city and the spatialisation of specific suburbs or collectives in the city. Even today, when urbanologists regard the city as extremely heterogeneous, they concentrate on local cultures within social worlds of specific neighbourhoods or subcultures. Berking and Löw (2008a: 7) point out that both of these levels neglect the city's idiosyncrasy. Although this analysis will at times make use of notions concerning meta-levels such as Postmodernism and Britishness or the micro-level of communally defined mental structures, I propose in reference the notion of micro-, meso-, macro-, and meta-mentalities to analyse a city's mental dispositions by way of distinguishing between (1) the macro-level of an urban-generic mentality and (2) the meso-level of an urban-specific mentality.

The macro-level is generally connected with urban society, urban culture, urbanity, and metropolitan doxa. Thus, an analysis of an urban-generic[7] mentality necessitates both the differentiation from the non-urban and the identification of a "common urban language" (Parker 2004: 175). This can be deciphered directly from the theories of urbanity investigated in chapter 3.2. The general urban *conditio humana* then offers an interpretation of collective nonconscious dispositions of thinking, imagining, feeling, and acting that all cities – despite their cultural or national embellishment – have in common (cf. Löw 2008: 134). Instead, the level of the urban-specific is what the historians of mentalities understand as regional mentality or what Berking (2008: 16) means by the local-specific context of metropolitan doxa. The meso-level focalises on the local scale as the principle of construction concerning the idiosyncratic logic or grammar of one distinct metropolis. Hence, the urban-specific mentality stresses the individual character of **this** city in opposition to **that** city (cf. *ibid*: 15). The specialities of one city as a local system are, for example, constructed by cultural particularities such as history, economy, society, values, norms, etc. The distinction of the city is, however, also constituted by the dynamics between the local and the global, the periphery and the urban centre, the relation to other cities as well as the influence of specific characteristics on urban-generic elements (cf. Löw 2008: 135).

4.1 Ambivalences of Urban-Generic Mentality

Urban-generic mentality describes the result of a general inner urbanisation. Spatially related to the urban, it is thereby mainly distinguished from the non-urban and defined by mental dispositions inhabitants of various cities hold in common. Braudel (1988: 481) exemplifies this notion of urbanity as a unitary phenomenon:

---

the city because the metropolis in their eyes cannot be thought "as having one geography and one history" (Pile cit. in Löw, Steets & Stoetzer 2008: 93). However, as Crang (1998: 181) points out, these cultural areas are often more in the eye of the beholder than in the mind of the people they study. Emphasising the hybridity and fragmentation of the urban realm, e.g. by way of class-specific areas, urbanologists deny the urban collective any existence and thus also refute a unifying mentality.

7 | In difference to Rem Koolhaas' (1995) visionary idea of "generic urbanity" as an emergent characterless place without architecture, history and identity, the term 'urban-generic' used in this analysis is connected to a collective and common urban tool.

> I do not mean that all towns are alike. But over and above their distinctive and original features, they all necessarily speak the same basic language: common to them all are the continuous dialogue with their rural surrounding [...]; the supply of manpower [...]; their self-consciousness – their desire to be distinguished from the others; their inevitable location at the centre of communications networks [...]; their relationships with their suburbs and with other cities.

Wirth's definition of the city by size, density, and heterogeneity presents a basic attempt to describe an encompassing notion of generic urbanism. Also the recurrent characteristics of the urban identified by other modern and postmodern urbanologists assessed in chapter 3.2 are general in kind. For Rossiaud (1990: 141), a common urbanity shared by different cities is rather "a question of degree, not of kind", which refers to a graduation on a scale of characteristics.

I therefore propose that urban-generic mentality is constituted by simultaneous configurations of ambivalence with contingent scaling. Likewise, mentality as rhizome presents a network made up from contradictory mental structures and mental dispositions always constitute an array of possibilities. In an urban context, ambivalent structures of mentality do not only pay tribute to the differentiation and multifariousness of the urban *conditio human*, but also take up the notion of contradictory urban characteristics. The city itself has been considered to offer myriad possibilities to their inhabitants; it is "a set of potentials" (Amin & Thrift 2002: 4). In that respect, the key terms employed by Urban Studies have been remarkably constant: anonymity, alienation, disorientation, decay on the one hand and change, freedom, mobility on the other. Claude S. Fischer (1984: 16-19) identifies four basic polarities that organise Western discourse of city life, namely nature/art, familiarity/strangeness, community/individualism, and tradition/change while Markus Schroer (2006: 228) lists five main oppositions: urbanity/barbarity, public/private, unity/plurality, centre/periphery, heterogeneity/homogeneity. In reference to the findings of the previous chapter, these antagonisms can be adapted and extended to a cluster of eight dominant configurations of ambivalence as fundamental characteristics of an urban-generic mentality: (1) city and country, (2) public and private, (3) sociability and anomie, (4) heterogeneity and homogeneity, (5) familiarity and strangeness, (6) community and individualism, (7) indifference and involvement, (8) apathy and vigilance.

4.1.1 City and Country

The spatial theme of urban and rural differences is a major constituent of the construction of a generic mentality. City and country are seen as two opposed ontological models which have created their own kind of spatial, temporal, and social organisation as well as cultural practice, and therein "represent two opposite poles in modern civilization." (Wirth 1967: 222) While the country is generally defined by persistence and tradition, the city is connected with an accelerated change, progress, and constant modernisation.[8]

---

8 | Certainly, the polarity between city and country is specifically pronounced in the English tradition. City and country thereby constitute set of key-concepts in British Cultural Studies (cf. Kamm 1997: 13). For more see Raymond Williams (1973), Kamm (1997), Barnett & Scru-

Because the country is significantly connected with nature, paganism, and barbarity and the city is defined by culture, secularism and civilisation, the rustic and the urbanite also exhibit variations in their civilisatory nature (cf. *ibid.*: 224).

Urbanologists generally agree that the difference between urbanite and rustic delineates urban mental dispositions: "There is a city mentality which is clearly differentiated from the rural mind." (*Ibid.*: 219) For historians of mentalities, such as Duby (1961: 947-948), the distinction between urban and rural mental attitudes is of central interest: "Opposition tout au long de l'histoire, et pour chacun des niveaux où la fortune situe les hommes, entre une mentalité rustique et une mentalité urbaine." The general assumption is that peasants are rude, uncivilised, provincial and ignorant, while the city man is urbane, civil, civilised, rational, and cosmopolitan.

The opposition between city and country is also one between the powerful centre and the dominated periphery, which underlines that both are necessarily interdependent: "They are at the same time separate yet drawn together, divided yet combined." (Braudel 1988: 486) The metropolis would cease to exist without the constant recruitment of people from the country attracted to the city by its economic, social, and cultural pull factors. Most urbanites, however, only spend parts of their lives in the city, moving to the suburbs or back to the country (cf. *ibid.*: 487-489). Hence, rural ways of life in turn adjust to city life. These interdependent processes and full stretch urbanisation have led critics to assume that the postmodern era figures the end of the contrast between urbanity and rurality.[9] Yet Barnett (1998: 331) argues that "one cannot be a cityman without the country, and could no more wish to abolish the contrast between town and rural life as define away the differences between the sexes." Paradoxes expressed in the ambivalence of city and country, such as culture and nature, tradition and modernisation, poverty and wealth have become intrinsic elements in descriptions of the city itself.

4.1.2 Public and Private

The contradictory relation between the public and the private constitutes a particularly significant ambivalent configuration of the city. Public and private serve as definite spatial markers for everyday orientation in the urban realm, relegating behaviour: according to the onion model, we can distinguish between the privacy of the home, the transient sphere of the door, the window or the neighbourhood, and finally the publicity of the streets and city square. Moreover, public and private also find their meaning in metaphors of propinquity and distance, as well as gendered oppositions of female/male, domestic/political, sacred/profane, reproduction/production, safety/danger. Similar to the city and the country, the public and the private are not free from their own paradoxes,

---

ton (1998) or Gerald MacLean, Donna Landry & Joseph P. Ward, eds. (1999), *The Country and the City Revisited. England and the Politics of Culture, 1550-1850.*

9 | Löw (2008: 68) states: "Eine Soziologie, die Städte in ihrer eigen- und beziehungslogischen Entwicklung zum Gegenstand der Forschung macht, die ferner im Sinne der Kontextabhängigkeit [...] die Auswirkungen der jeweiligen Stadt auf Wahrnehmen, Denken, und Handeln ihrer Bewohner untersucht, muss eine Perspektive auf die Stadt bereitstellen, welche die jahrhundertealte Gegenstandskonstitution aus der Abgrenzung zum Land überwindet."

as the private itself, for example, oscillates between connotations such as free/alienated, exile/prison, emancipation/repression, productive/destructive, absolute/relative, anonymous/isolated, and close/far.

Paul Bahrdt in his study *Die moderne Großstadt* (1961) interprets the polarity between public and private as the most important aspect of a sociological definition of the city. Due to the ambivalent interrelation between public and private, the creation of a private sphere is strongly defined by the existence of a public one (cf. Bahrdt 1983: 622). The private serves to cover and protect sensitive personal issues and intimacies (*ibid.*: 613). According to Bahrdt (*ibid.*: 621), the construction of a private sphere leads to a differentiation of urban realities and psychological existence. The distance between urbanites constituted in the public has the important function of integration while simultaneously offering forms of communication which help to bridge this distance (cf. *ibid.*: 613). Public and private situations call for different behaviour, enlarging the schizophrenic split between front stage and back stage personality.[10] These habitual forms of representation, however, always call upon collective notions, memories, habits – or the urban-generic mentality (*ibid.*: 615). Bahrdt (*ibid.*: 624) shows that while on a general sociological level, the private seems in danger to be infiltrated by the public, urban discourse favours the public, in the sense that the invasion by the private of public urban space is seen as a breach of *res publica* as a major determinant of *civitas* in the city.

Richard Sennett in *The Fall of Public Man* (1977) sees the privatisation of public and political life as leading to the death of the urbanite *per se*. For Sennett, the focus of public life lies in the city; hence the cosmopolitan urbanite constitutes the perfect public man. The metropolis, physically mainly defined by its public landmarks, such as city squares, parks, walkways, coffee houses, hotels, theatres, operas and museums, is the setting of public places. He argues that the development of sociability is supported by "tangible barriers" (Sennett 1977: 15) between people acting in the public sphere. According to Sennett, the "superimposition of private upon the public" (*ibid.*: 26) has led to a "tyranny of intimacy" and thereby to an "erosion of public life" (*ibid.*: 5), thus creating a "Dead Public Space" (*ibid.*: 12) as "an area to move through, not to be in" (*ibid.*: 14). Other postmodern urbanologists bemoan the spread of Privatopias induced by suburbanisation or technologisation, the destruction of urban public spaces by an invasion of the private as well as by the spread of semi-private spaces throughout the public. By contrast, the progress of information technologies has also led to Orwellian public surveillance, a panoptic society, transparent citizens all taken up in Soja's notion of the Carceral City, which enhances the ecology of fear in the public and the private.

Due to its emphasis on the private side of history and research interest in the everyday, concerning issues, such as family life, childhood, sexuality, and death, the study of privacy[11] is central to the history of mentalities. Ariès and Duby's seminal *Histoire de la vie privée* (1985-1987; Engl. *A History of Private Life*), for example, draws a genealogy of privacy from antiquity to the present and charts the continuities and transformations of

10 | For more on the theory of urban role-play, front and back regions, or the private and the public Self see Erving Goffmann's *The Presentation of Self in Everyday Life* (1959).

11 | For a general definition of privacy see Beate Rössler (2001), *Der Wert des Privaten.*

mentalities concerning the private. Ariès (1991: 11) constructs a model of privacy which specifically locates the cradle of 'privacy' in sixteenth-century England. While the analyses concerning psychological, socio-spatial and mediatised privacy show that the public and the private are relational phenomena (*ibid.*: 18), the history of public/private for Ariès (*ibid.*: 16) mainly presents a transformation of sociability. Insofar, this configuration not only constitutes a physical but above all a social ambivalence.

4.1.3 Sociability and Anomie

Urbanologists describe the city as a specific sociability with ambivalent tendencies to anomie. Featuring an idiosyncratic social entity defined by enhanced size, density, and heterogeneity, the city is conceived as peopled by multitudes. Its equally multiplied social contacts become ritualised, patterned, and superficial, leading to a highly complex "social universe with a plurality of social standards and relative values" (Karp, Stone & Yoels 1991: 24). The urban form of sociability therefore implies a secularisation of society as well as individualisation and alienation of its inhabitants, based on a general shift from the mechanical solidarity of rural community to the organic solidarity of urban society.[12] The intimacy of and full identification with primary face-to-face relations, such as family, kin and friends, is transferred to an anonymity of indirect secondary groups, such as voluntary relations, formal associations and special interest groups, on the basis of mere rationality. This process is mostly interpreted as a crisis of sociability and a first step towards a disorganised, atomistic, demoralised, and finally anomic society.

As was shown, Wirth strongly emphasises the anomic pole of the ambivalent configuration, stressing impersonality and rationality which result in urban disorder, violence, and crime. For authors like Castells, the urban crisis of the 1960s is the result of urban social entropy. Despite the urban renaissance of the 1980s, current urbanologists see the postmodern city wrought with a supermodern version of anomie that is characterised by anonymity, superficiality, transitoriness of social relations and lack of participation. In its postmodern manifestation of solitary contractuality, sociability in crisis results in a total loss of (social) control and a new age of (urban) terror.

At first glance, this notion of urban anomie severely contradicts the ideal of the classical city as a place of encounter, face-to-face communication, and public exchange. Fischer (1984: 36) however argues that "[u]rbanism has unique consequences, including the production of 'deviance', not because it destroys social worlds [...] but because it creates them." There are various contemporary social theories that support this view: either strong communal bonds survive in homogeneous neighbourhoods or the city is liberated from spatial propinquity and groups are based instead on a similar lifestyle as well as mutual solidarity (cf. Häussermann & Siebel 2004: 107-109).[13] For Karp,

---

12 | For more see Emile Durkheim (1893), *De la division de travail social* (Engl.: *The Division of Labor in Society*); Ferdinand Tönnies (1887), *Gemeinschaft und Gesellschaft* (Engl.: *Community and Society*).

13 | These constellations ranging from contacts to colleagues, peers, friends, and family may be scattered and spatially distant, but local propinquity is not necessary due to modern technologies of communication and transport (cf. Häussermann & Siebel 2004: 112-113).

Stone and Yoels (1991: 47-49), primary group life survives in the urban area in nonterritorial communities based on collective identifications with impersonal and anonymous contacts. Moreover, because the authors see solidarity as defined by (in)visible human communication and interactions (cf. *ibid.*: 58), the city actually represents a tightly knit network (social structures composed of a number of overlapping circles of close relations) of everyday social interaction (*ibid.*: 63). In summary, the ambivalence between sociability and anomie as structures of an urban-generic mentality describes a stratum of dispositions for an idiosyncratic mixture between isolation and interaction, propinquity and distance.

4.1.4 Heterogeneity and Homogeneity

A fourth quality of the metropolis and a constituent configuration for an urban-generic mentality is the ambivalence between heterogeneity and homogeneity. The metropolis produces social space, either as urban plurality of cultural practices, diversity of lifestyles with inherent characteristics of social injustice, or marginalisation and segregation. Lindner (2004: 389-390) argues that urban social space is constructed by a tripartite and circular process of (1) inner differentiation, (2) network formation, and (3) concentration.

Urban density, as noted by Wirth, enhances heterogeneity and supports tendencies of differentiation implied in the cultural diversity of a city's population, the plurality of lifestyles, mixture and integration of cultural practices. Park describes the differentiation of urban people in networks of vocational groups with their idiosyncratic "ultra-lifestyle[s]" (Karp, Stone & Yoels 1991: 110). Due to their emphasis on ecological determinism, the Chicago School concentrates on these inner fragmentations of the city into a mosaic of myriad social worlds. The clustering of urbanites in specific areas can lead to a homogenisation of city zones, which produces insulate enclaves of gated communities, ethnic neighbourhoods, or slums characterised by exclusion, entrapment, containment, imprisonment, isolation, and invisibility. But functional distanciation and differentiation in specialised social areas that pursue homogeneity are not necessarily purely negative aspects: a kindred spirit in segregated residential areas or marginalised groups can also facilitate the integration of strangers into the urban world (cf. *ibid.*: 120; Häussermann & Siebel 2004: 193).[14]

Castells' Dual City conceptualises this transformation of the urban social structure with cities growing socially, culturally, and functionally more segregated. Soja rejects this approach as too class conventional to comprehend the heterogeneous frictions in the urban texture because fractures within the city are manifold and exist on different layers of the urban skein. Segregation in general describes a process of urban differentiation along spatially structured (b)orders that divide the city along an increasing number of social axes of class, ethnicity, race, gender, or even age. As regards social segregation, upper-class neighbourhoods (e.g. Knightsbridge) are differentiated from working-class

---

14 | Häussermann and Siebel (2004: 165) show that at least three dimensions have to be considered regarding the segregational dimension of the city, namely material and infrastructural aspects, social dimensions, such as conflicts, and symbolic bordering, for example through stereotyping, imagology, and collective memory.

areas (e.g. London's East End) or middle-class suburbia from inner-city ghettoes of the underclass.

By contrast, Hobsbawm (1987: 48) acknowledges the urban-generic ambivalence in the social geometries of the postmodern metropolis:

> These newly typical inner-city populations are not only those left behind, but sometimes consist of those attracted to the giant city precisely because it contains, and has always contained, as it were sociologically open spaces designed for the socially indeterminate. It was always par excellence a place for transients, visitors, tourists, temporary residents and in some ways designed as a no-man's land, or rather any-man's land.

On the one hand, the common image of the city as melting pot promotes the idea of the metropolis as a heterogeneous world of strangers, yet on the other hand, balkanisation figures as an example of urban anomie. Nevertheless, contemporary theories emphasise the city as a transnational space of migration with transcultural effects on the urban way of life. Urban spatiality is furthermore seen as oppressively gendered; gender (b)ordering becomes specifically apparent in the entrapment of women in designated spaces of the home or the homogeneous suburbs.[15] Whereas the urban woman as temptress, fallen woman, or lesbian constitutes a metaphor of public crisis, urbanism also loosens the stronghold of patriarchal control (cf. E. Wilson 1995: 149-150).

4.1.5 Familiarity and Strangeness

The ambivalent relation of familiarity and strangeness is revealed through phenomena such as tolerance and xenophobia of the homely and/or the unhomely. Urban heterogeneity increases the probability of encountering the unexpected or experiencing incomprehensible spectacles, and multiplies situations of confronting the unknown Other. In *A World of Strangers* Lyn Lofland argues (1973: ix-x):

> To live in a city is, among many other things, to live surrounded by large numbers of persons whom one does not know. To experience the city is, among many other things, to experience anonymity. To cope with the city is, among many other things, to cope with strangers.

The city is the permanent home of strangers, and urbanity presents a constant "situation of living as a stranger in the midst of strangers" (*ibid.*: 176). This emphasises how the public metropolitan realm features as an encounter and interaction between individuals who are generally unknown to one another. According to Lofland (*ibid.*: 176-177), orientation in a world of strangers is made possible by routinely eliminating strangeness and advising specific identity markers (clothes, bumper stickers, neighbourhood). Hence,

---

15 | According to Robert Fishman's *Bourgeois Utopias. The Rise and Fall of Suburbia* (1987), at the latest since the 1960s the suburb becomes the space of the privatised and domestic nuclear family. This landscape of privacy is, however, a gender specific space that denotes the isolation of women. By contrast, inner-city council houses often deny the poorer inhabitants any privacy.

the stranger becomes instead categorically known (cf. *ibid.*: 176; Fischer 1984: 97). Not only does the urbanite glimpse an unknown universe of incomprehensible Others in the city, but also of his own "unfamiliar self" (Handlin 1977: 5). Consequently, the urban is simultaneously a locale of alienation and identification as well as of estrangement and self-fashioning.

According to Simmel and Park, the city has created new types: the stranger, the marginal man, and the cosmopolitan who are characterised by a liminal position that is in turn constituted by a synthesis of nearness and distance. This concept has variously been extended to the black underclass, the immigrant foreigner, as well as the social and sexual deviant. Due to the notion of inbetweenness, the marginal man can be aligned to notions of hybridity and difference as developed in postcolonial theory and adapted in analyses concerning the new urban pariah. In the post-Fordist metropolis non-places of transition might indeed feature as the home of the stranger *per se*, whereas these spaces are also a site of dislocation because they are notoriously devoid of identifying markers.

Furthermore, the ambivalence of the familiar and the strange describes the inherent relation of the city to the uncanny as a position on the threshold between the homely and the unhomely. The city organises the uncertainty of liminal existence in perpetual interrelations between the familiar and the unfamiliar. Due to urban everyday practices, "the unfamiliar [is] rendered familiar", but this routine can become strange again because the city constitutes a heterogeneous space where the "familiar is defamiliarized" (Prakash 2008: 12). On the level of urban personality, this constant wavering between the known and the unknown can result in cognitive or psychological uncertainty and dislocation.

The ambivalence of familiarity and strangeness either leads to tolerance and sophistication or results in intolerance and anxiety. Fear of the stranger or the culturally unfamiliar can blend into a sense of danger or even paranoia and xenophobia. This general anxiety takes its psychological toll on urbanites, not only making them intolerant towards others, but, as Baudrillard demonstrates, leading to an anomic feeling of self-hate. In contrast, Karp, Stone & Yoels (1991: 107) argue that fostering tolerance for differences in habitus and lifestyle is one of the hallmarks of the metropolis. We can distinguish two competing theses of tolerance: the contact hypothesis delineates that spatial propinquity increases categorical knowledge and therefore mutual tolerance between strangers (cf. Häussermann & Siebel 2004: 180). On the contrary, the conflict hypothesis states that the greater the spatial distance, the greater the chance to avoid conflict (cf. *ibid.*: 182). Here spatial segregation is interpreted as a prerequisite for tolerance. The ambivalence between familiarity and strangeness thereby becomes a main resource of the urban-generic mentality.

4.1.6 Community and Individualism

Most urbanologists comment on the ambivalent relations between community and individualism, socialisation and individuation, or solidarity and isolation. Simmel's analysis of urbanity identifies individuality, autonomy, independence, and emancipation as pivotal characteristics of the metropolitan man. Furthermore, Wirth emphasises that the heterogeneity and mobility of the city on the one hand offer the urban individual the opportunity to freely follow their idiosyncratic vocation and on the other hand induce dislocation, isolation, alienation, anonymity, atomisation or the schizoid character of the urbanite. Postmodern urbanologists argue that the geographies of the post-Fordist city, such as non-places, hyperreal landscapes of the spectacle, and the urban sprawl of liminal ghost cities, enhance the loss of personal identity: the fragmentation of the megalopolis equals the postmodern fragmented Self, non-places stress the transitoriness of being without endowing people with identity, and the architectural simulacrum merely offers stereotypical traits.

As described by Wirth, the individual communicates in the social space of urban collectivity by role-play. The urbanite depends on a personal repertoire of multiple compartmentalised identities, enacted variously in regard to audience or setting of its various social urban worlds (cf. Fischer 1984: 202; Karp, Stone & Yoels 1991: 80-81). In general, personality in the urban realm is largely determined by the front role or façade codes such as dress, demeanour, appearance, rhetoric, and other conventionalisms (cf. Karp, Stone & Yoels 1991: 84). While Wirth interprets role-play as enhancing the schizoid character of the urban individual, Fischer (1984: 203, 205) argues that due to urban specialisation, urban roles are never so many as to not be able to handle them, and staging the Self does not necessarily result in psychological and social pathologies. For example, Karp, Stone & Yoels (1991: 103) deduce that anonymity is not simply the result of urban individualisation, but instead functions as an urban-generic role specifically reproduced in metropolitan settings where enactment is considered the norm of urban public behaviour. Role-play stresses that "in the large city one established one's individuality *through* social relationships with others." (*Ibid.*: 26). Urban strangers are a welcome audience for the metropolitan staging of the Self and role-play therefore constitutes an act of interactive self-fashioning or identity-formation (cf. *ibid.*: 80). Because the Self is always related to the Other's role-play, this method of identity formation also creates community (*ibid.*: 25-26). Equally, postmodern urbanologists explicate how the spectacle creates sociability. The urban-generic ambivalence of community and individuality in accordance to the concept of mentality stresses the functional relation between collective and individual.

4.1.7 Indifference and Involvement

Urbanologists broadly accept the notion that overstimulation in the urban realm creates various mechanisms of distanciation; few, however, acknowledge that this implies an urban-generic ambivalence between indifference and involvement. For Simmel, intellectualism, blasé, and reserve are protective and adaptive reactions as well as expressions of indifference towards the urban. Milgram (1970: 1462) further develops this adaptive response to a concept of overload:

> City life, as we experience it, constitutes a continuous set of encounters with overload, and of resultant adaptations. Overload characteristically deforms daily life on several levels, impinging on role performance, the evolution of social norms, cognitive functioning, and the use of facilities.

Urbanites hence redraw socio-spatial boundaries and develop various instruments of social screening that serve as filtering devices against the overload scenario. These mechanisms result in various behavioural patterns of indifference such as non-intervention in cases of emergency, unwillingness to assist strangers, practice of everyday civilities and common non-involvement, enacted anonymity in order to increase distance, as well as role-play (cf. *ibid.*: 1462-1464). In the postmodern overload scenario, the geographies of the post-Fordist city offer a surplus and excess of stimulation which either lead to a potentialised blasé attitude or addiction to spectacularity. Due to the informational excess of new technologies, urbanites are already confronted with the overload effect in the private realm (cf. Nedelmann 1990: 236). For postmodern urbanologists, the contemporary city especially induces visual overstimulation by the fetishisation of images, simulacra, and hyperreality. In this sense, simulation has become a new form of authenticity replacing the role-play of different masking practices.

In their "mini-max hypothesis of urban life", Karp, Stone and Yoels (1991: 88) conceive this habitual reaction to overload not merely as one relegated by distanciation or indifference, but as one of active involvement:

> Urbanites seek to minimize involvement and to maximise social order. Persons must act in concert. Persons must take one another into account. At the same time, persons must protect their personal privacy, a commodity hard to come by in urban settings. Urbanites must, in other words, create a kind of 'public privacy'. They are required to strike a balance between involvement, indifference, and cooperation with one another. (*Ibid.*: 89)

The hypothesis states that urbanites actually practice inattention, briefly acknowledging the other and simultaneously withdrawing within (cf. *ibid.*: 92).[16] This theory recognises the ambivalent relations of urbanity in "intimate anonymity, public privacy, involved indifference" (*ibid.*: 89). Moreover, indifference and involvement in regard to the non/acting urbanite refer to resources of individual impotence or potency.

4.1.8 Apathy and Vigilance

This last configuration of urban-generic mentality describes the city's psychosomatic effects as relations between disintegration and emancipation of the urbanite. Apathy refers to the jaded metropolitan man characterised by mental breakdown, for example schizophrenia, paranoia, neurasthenia and neurosis, but also feelings of repulsion such as fear, hate, horror, and violence. By contrast, vigilance emphasises the urbanite's enhanced freedom, mobility, autonomy, industry, and emancipation.

In his analysis of inner urbanisation Korff (1985: 348), referring to Willy Hellpach's[17] differentiation of emotional indifference and sensual vigilance as generic characteristics of the metropolitan man, argues that apathy and vigilance are characteristics to be found in various morphological phases of the city. Sensual vigilance is apparent in intelligence, intellectual and mental skills, creative power, emancipation, mobility and optimism (cf. *ibid.*: 351). Through intellectualism, indifference, and tolerance the urban grants autonomy, freedom, independence and progressiveness. A theory of urban-generic vigilance, however, also encompasses the urbanite's role-play, skills of com-

---

16 | Erving Goffmann calls this phenomenon "civil inattention" (cit. in Karp, Stone & Yoels 1991: 92).

17 | For more see Willy Hellpach (1952), *Mensch und Volk der Großstadt*.

munication and interaction, perceptual sensuality, variety of reactions, and urban pride (*ibid.*: 352). For Korff (*ibid.*: 348-350), vigilance describes the heightened level of attention as well as an adequate and long-lasting reaction to urban stimuli, whereas apathy becomes routine through emotional indifference in order to prevent emotional distress.

According to Fischer (1984: 174), "crowding studies" in general emphasise that urban density produces alienation and psychological stress:

> Living in a large community means that people will find themselves in specific settings with relatively high ratios of people to space. The denser those settings, the more crowded people feel. This density and the sense of crowding create psychic strains and tensions requiring relief. Relief must be found – for example, by aggression or withdrawal – or the stress will produce mental or physical illness. Urban crowding thus leads to antisocial adaptations or psychopathology. (*Ibid.*: 175)

A general lack of space becomes apparent in reactions of aggression, hate, xenophobia or self-destructive impulses, whereas a lack of privacy leads either to passivity or fatalism (cf. *ibid.*). Because social standards of propinquity and distance are violated, high density generates psychological distress (*ibid.*: 179). For Simmel and the members of the Chicago School, the modern metropolis by ways of overload constitutes a socio-psychological assault on the individual's mental, emotional and spiritual life. While for Simmel the development of personal identity and individual autonomy is still very prominent, later urbanologists underestimate the ambivalent cardinal effects. Although Wirth recognises the vigilant potential of segmental role-play, he concentrates on social anomie and personal degeneration in schizophrenia. Another member of the Chicago School, Howard Woolston[18] (1912: 603), shows that overstimulation creates vigilant urbanites who are "alert, active, quick to seek satisfaction." The immanent succession of stimulational shocks perpetually pushes the individual towards new activities consuming bodily energy and blunting sensibilities (cf. *ibid.*). In this case, urbanites show signs of (di)stress: they are high-strung, hysteric, agitated, burnt-out – an emotional and psychological state that becomes fundamental to "an urban habit of mind" (*ibid.*). Nedelmann (1990: 230) argues that the only vigilant will developed by a blasé person is the need "for excitement, for extreme impressions, for the greatest speed in its change" (*ibid.*: 233). Hence, blasé leads to both a blunting of the senses and an insatiable hunger for stimulation.

According to Olalquiaga, the postmodern overload scenario created by simulation, simulacra and hyperreality results in the psychological syndrome of psychasthenia. She does not so much concentrate on the pathological side of overload, but pays attention instead to the relational alterations of city, body, and imaginary and the demand for a self-responsible development of mental equipment in accordance with postmodern (hyper)reality. According to Baudrillard, anomic emotions like hate consequently constitute an inversed and exponential apathy that demands an increase in effects, spectacles, and happenings. Postmodern urbanologists moreover stress the disintegration of the indi-

---

18 | Howard Woolston's "The Urban Habit of the Mind" (1912) largely follows Simmel's arguments, but has often been neglected in discussions on the effects of urban overload.

vidual urbanite due to the altered metropolitan social fabric. While for Castells, urban mentality as an organon of orientation is annihilated by the general socio-economic determinism of the *homo oeconomicus*, Augé interprets the accumulation of non-places as a trigger for feelings of transitoriness, emptiness, and uprootedness. Other urban theorists comment on the eclectic and superficial multivalency of postmodern architecture, which through double coding invokes schizophrenia "as a general characteristic of the postmodern mind-set" (Harvey 1990: 83).

However, Fischer (1984: 187) severely attacks these notions of psychopathology because he does not find any empirical support for the "urbanism-stress-symptoms hypothesis".[19] Rather than creating a complex malaise, urbanity retains a balance through alterations in the personality of the urban type of the individual. Against the popular notion that metropolis and neurosis are synonymous, Mitscherlich (1983: 681-684) argues that forms of urban apathy are problems of adaptability to urban social norms. This brings us back to the incorporation of mentality or internal urbanisation as the collective problem of mental management of the city. Apathy and vigilance serve the function of configuring the affective and emotional repertoire towards an inner urbanisation and thereby represent a 'transitional mentality' (Korff 1985: 348; orig.: "Durchgangsmentalität").

In sum, these eight configurations of ambivalence recognise the dispositional nature of urban-generic mentality as a range of possibilities. From the categorisation of spatial mentality, we can discern that the first cluster (1-2) indicates predominantly physical, the second (3-5) social, and the third (7-8) mental spaces: city and country or public and private concentrate on spatial (b)ordering based on the cognitive dichotomy of inside and outside. On the other hand, sociability and anomie, heterogeneity and homogeneity, familiarity and strangeness, community and individualism stress the collective side of urban-generic mentality by way of social practices, forms of integration and exclusion, as well as the relation between urban collective and urban individual. Indifference and involvement as well as apathy and vigilance are rather concerned with the habitual, emotive and psychic consequences on the functionally related urban individual. Although the dispositions of thinking, feeling, imagining and acting cannot be singularly relegated, we can nevertheless identify certain tendencies: the spatial theorem concentrates on the differences between the cognition of various spatial entities and devices of (b)ordering. The social theorem considers especially habitual social interactions, whereas the mental theorem is concerned with psychological and emotional effects of oversaturation.

This conceptualisation shows that the presented theories often neglect the dispositional nature of the imaginary. Although notions of imagination and urbanity can be found within each theorem, for example in the collective notion of the city as civilised, the private as secure, secondary relations as anomic, a particular 'imaginary theorem' is not devised on the level of urban-generic characteristics, with the exception of the spectacle. These depictions of the influence on postmodern urbanity, however, can be interpreted as part of the psychological overload theorem. As I will show in the following, an 'imaginary theorem' of urban mentality has been developed by the New Geographers

19 | Fischer (1984: 190-192) deconstructs the common notion that cities are mentally harmful and psychologically damaging by exemplifying that suicide, alcoholism, and fatalism are also part of the rural.

whose involvement with the symbolic environment of the city is specifically useful for exploring the defining factors of an urban-specific mentality.

4.2 Factors of Influence on Urban-Specific Mentality

The meso-level of the urban-specific refers the construction of mentalities to the idiosyncrasies of one distinct metropolis by differentiating its mindscape from that of other cities. It is understood as the mental structures prevalent in a particular city, which can be distinguished from the micro-structures of its single neighbourhoods as well as from the meta-structures of the nation or the macro-level of an urban-generic mentality. In his approach to urbanism as a general urban way of life, Wirth (1967: 219) argues that a definition of the city should lend itself to the discovery of metropolitan variations:

> There is a city mentality which is clearly differentiated from the rural mind. [...] Not only does this difference exist between city and country, it also exists between city and city, and between one area of the city and another. Each city [...] furnishes a distinct social world to its inhabitants, which they incorporate in their personality whether they will or not.

According to Wirth's definition of the city, metropolitan particularities are configured according to variations in size, density, and heterogeneity. Furthermore, tradition or history vary and topography or materiality leave an imprint on the specific city (cf. *ibid.*: 175). Although in postmodern urban theory there exists the widespread notion that due to technological and economic processes metropolitan centres as nodes in the space of flows are actually experiencing a certain degree of homogenisation, the tendencies of globalisation also enforce and strengthen local particularities, in this case, of a specific metropolis (cf. Robins 1993: 319).[20] Besides the new strategies of cultural distinction, contemporary post-positivist notions of culture also pay tribute to metropolitan specificity: "On the project for urban renaissance, we can see how this particular identity and lifestyle is now being mapped onto city space and landscape." (*Ibid.*: 322) Consequently, the uniqueness of each city especially in regard to urban culture is once again foregrounded. The adage that "[n]o two cities are alike" (Porter 2000: 5) is emphasised by a recent article published in *Nature*; it argues that eighty-five per cent of essential metropolitan attributes are generally predetermined, while only fifteen per cent – however a critical percentage – make its idiosyncratic character (cf. Anon. 2011a).

Most notably, the individual urban organism establishes local-specific contexts of meaning; these cognitive, emotional and aesthetic constructions in correlation with the city's biography, habit, and state of mind are experienced as unique (cf. Löw 2008: 71-72). In that respect, we can also speak of an urban-specific character, identity, personality, and biography. As was shown before, the concept of "Eigenlogik der Stadt" offers the notion of the city as a province of meaning through which the construction and metamorphosis of a particular city can be discerned (*ibid.*: 78). First, idiosyncratic logic emphasises dispositions that are linked to the sociability and materiality of a particular

20 | Also see Sieverts' (2003: 58-61) hypotheses on the specificity of the *Zwischenstadt*.

city, as the urban-specific habitus is incorporated in the urbanites' behaviour and the urban materiality (*ibid.*: 77-79). Second, a metropolis develops its character as a place or locale where ways of experience, perception, imagination, and memory are developed (*ibid.*: 80). Third, metropolitan idiosyncrasy asks for doxic certainties developed in narratives, experiences, and materialisations that are historically and geographically emplaced:

> Städtische Eigenlogik ist als Begriff synchron und diachron angelegt. Das Eigene der Städte entwickelt sich sowohl aufgrund *historisch motivierter Erzählungen, Erfahrungen und Materialschichtungen* als auch im *relationalen Vergleich zu formgleichen Gebilden*, das heißt zu anderen Städten. (*Ibid.*: 96)

Thus, urban-specific differences mainly develop characteristic features in the contextual meaning of their lifeworld. From that perspective, however, not only determinants of collectivity, time, space, and compression denominate urban-specific mentalities, but also the urban-generic configurations of ambivalence are specified by a unique urban imaginary.

The New Urban Geographers stress that the urban is specifically influenced and constructed by the imaginary: "literature, film, architecture, painting, tourist guides, postcards, photography, city plans – all provide selective representations of the city and shape the metaphors, narratives and syntax which are widely used to describe the experience of urban living." (Balshaw & Kennedy 2000: 4) Contemporary urban semioticians emphasise that the city is mainly a representation without which, as Shields (1996: 231) argues, the physical city would be unknowable. The problem for Urban Studies seems to be to unite the notion of everyday city life and representations, between non-discursive practices and discursive codes, and the process between physical and mental space (cf. Balshaw & Kennedy 2000: 2) This problem really calls to transcend the old dead-end of the dualism between real and imagined city and to bridge the gap between geographers' factual descriptions and writers' imagination (cf. Shields 1996: 245).

I therefore argue that the cultural particularities of one specific city as defined by its geography, sociology, and history are particularly pronounced in its semantic system, which can be characterised as the urban imaginary theorem. Hence, the following subchapters elaborate on (1) geographical, social, historical, and cultural particularities, (2) imaginary, (3) image, (4) text, (5) narrative, (6) atmosphere, (7) emotion, and (8) identity. This cluster of eight parameters is considered as the main factor of influence on the idiosyncratic *conditio humana* of urbanites and the urban-specific mentality.

4.2.1 Culture

Cultural space is mainly defined by geographical, historical, social, and communicative idiosyncrasies (cf. Kamm 2007: 26-27). These factors of a specific mentality essentially refer back to spatial, temporal and collective determinants of mentality and their confluence in collective space-time compression.

The spatial form of the urban materiality and its geography become the fundament on which the city is constituted. Topographical and architectural elements serve as background information to understand the influence of the environment on denizens' mentality. For Mumford (1997: 316-318), sole geographical particularities determine the specificity of the metropolis by ways of topography and its infrastructural potential (i.e. rivers) or inter-regional transport possibility, climate by individualising the type of urban adaptation (i.e. habits of eating and drinking), and geological foundations suggesting certain building material and even architecture. A common and typical architectural form and urban specific landmarks define the city's visual impact, recognition value, as well as symbolic meaning reflecting the world-view of the urban collective (cf. *ibid.*: 403). Furthermore, according to Wirth's definition, the city as a spatial formation is defined by its specific size, including its dimensions of material growth. The degree of density concerning the city's materiality, architecture, and institutions has an impact on the spatial heterogeneity of urban-specific life juxtaposed in close proximity or growth of its internal and external networks. Local, regional, national, and global connections of the city define the functional status of the city, which in turn informs its prevalent ways of thinking in spatial scales.

The relativity of social time frames distinguishes the city from the country. Moreover, due to its progressive nature, time becomes visible in the urban realm, namely in the shape of historic buildings, monuments, and heritage areas. Because of their density and high visibility, these materialised urban historical structures "leave an imprint upon the minds even of the ignorant or the indifferent." (*Ibid.*: 5) The city can be delineated by its historical roles, for example, as a former Roman settlement or a medieval merchant's town. Historical processes also reflect significant shifts in the nature of a specific city while also featuring recurring typical themes or characteristic topoi that structure the urbanites' thinking and habitus (cf. Löw 2008: 90, 96). The city's biography[21] also implies that certain lines of narrative are more likely to occur than others (*ibid.*: 110); this urban 'path dependency' describes how past routines still influence the present and similarly refer to future developments (cf. *ibid.*: 93). The historical landmarks of the city's rise and fall (in)form the urban collective memory of its denizens. Moreover, a metropolis is renowned for its specific historically significant events, personae, and cultural produce, which construct the city as a mental space full of memories. A whole urban memoryscape is created that saves the city's past for posterity: city museums, metropolitan archives, town libraries, memorials for the city's heroes and historical buildings.

In addition, the city's particularity can either be grasped by the notion of social space or the urbanites as a distinct collective. Wirth's definition of the city is initially a sociological one: the size of the population can relegate the city's institutional definition (town, regional centre, metropolis), which refers back to the 'quality' of its urbanity. Moreover, population density implies a logic of mixture that is different from city to city. In this respect, migratory processes and the concomitant change of the population structure is of pivotal importance for an analysis of urban-specific mentality. The current rediscovery of cultural heterogeneity emphasises the difference and plurality of specific groups as well as that of unfolding socio-spatial processes. Soja (1998: 152-153) sums up the prevalent aspects of the social specificity of the urban:

---

21 | Examples of London biographies see Ackroyd (2001) or Edward Rutherfurd's fictional *London. The Novel. The Story of the Greatest City on the Earth* (1997).

The specificity of the urban is thus defined not as a separable reality, with its own social and spatial rules of formation and transformation; or merely as a reflection and imposition of the social order. The urban is an integral part and particularization of the most fundamental contextual generalization about spatiality of social life, that we create and occupy a multi-layered spatial matrix of nodal locales. In its particularity, its social specificity, the urban is permeated with relations of power, relations of dominance and subordination, that channel regional differentiation and regionalism, territoriality and uneven development, routines and revolutions, at many different scales.

Thus, the socio-spatial particularity is also defined by the layout of its inner networks, the hegemonic power structures of exclusion and inclusion, as well as spatial contestations and localisms. As was explicated before, collective space-time compression unfolds a certain cultural dynamic of all three determinants of mentalities. Likewise, the particularities of cultural space, history and collective additionally exert their combined influence on the mental structures of a particular city.

For Lindner (2008: 84, 93), a holistic cultural analysis of the urban-specific is oriented to the key terms of habitus, *imaginaire*, and texture, which can help approach the individuality of a city. Urban idiosyncrasy describes the development and accumulation of specific structural practices. The habitus of one specific city represents the complexity of interrelations between habits, traditions, and values. This 'urban deep grammar' ("städtische Tiefengrammatik", *ibid.*: 87) defines the character of the city and is a product of the *longue durée* of common social conditions (cf. *ibid.*: 88-89). In a narrower sense, the production of culture encompasses material objects, mass culture commodities of fashion, media, and tourism, places of leisure and consumption, and the construction of cultural images and spectacles. Mumford (1997: 262) argues: "Each practical manifestation of a culture tends to leave a shadow-self in the mind [. . .]." The communicative specificity of the city hence refers to the particularity of its culturescape, namely the mental and ideological images or representations of the urban.

4.2.2 Imaginary

In his seminal work *Soft City. What Cities Do to Us, And How They Change the Way We Live, Think, Feel*, Jonathan Raban (1974: 2) comments: "The city as we imagine it, the soft city of illusion, myth, aspiration, nightmare, is as real, maybe more real, than the hard city one can locate on maps, in statistics, in monographs on urban sociology and demography and architecture." First of all, a city has its own distinct language – or sign system; second, cities are moulded in the images of their denizens, which in turn shape urbanites. Seeing the city as a space of signs and images, Raban's text is at the cusp of a new writing about urban culture[22] and offers an insight into significant factors of a city's particularity and its influences on an urban-specific mentality.

22 | For example, see Mary Douglas (1970), *Natural Symbols*; Roger Downs & David Stea (1973), *Image and Environment: Cognitive Mapping and Spatial Behavior*; Jay Appleton (1975), *The Experience of Landscape*; Anselm L. Strauss (1976), *Images of the American City*.

Since the 1960s, the general adage of the semioticians of the New Urban Geography is that urban spatialities correspond to a system of signs, images, and symbols that can be decoded. The discussion of the city thus concentrates more and more on the symbolic and imaginary institution of urban space defining the scope of urbanites in which they imagine, think, feel, and experience city life. Urban semiotics and urban semantics are therefore important factors of influence on urban-specific mentality and open a whole new perspective on the analysis of city fiction, cultural practices, and beyond. In the following, I will sketch the specificity of the urban imaginary by ways of concepts drawn from cultural geography, urban semiotics, and poststructuralism, namely the image of the city, mental maps, cityscape, and urban metaphoricity.

In his pioneering study *The Image of the City* (1960), Kevin Lynch (1977: 2) strives to define means of the city-dwellers' perception by registering different 'readings' of the urban environment, and he considers a visual quality of cities "by studying the mental image of that city which is held by its citizens." While individuals create their own images, there seems to be nonetheless a substantial agreement on the meaning of the signs among members of the same group; these "'public images,' [are] common mental pictures carried by large numbers of a city's inhabitants." (*Ibid.*: 7) The citizens' urban images are "soaked with memories and meanings" (*ibid.*: 1). For Lynch (*ibid.*: 10), the image primarily caters to the need for identity and structure in the perceptual world. The "generalised mental picture of the exterior physical world" (*ibid.*: 4), a product of sensations and memories, is employed for navigating the city. He points out that a pragmatic environmental image is important for creating a sense of security against the dangers of disorientation but also against feelings of anxiety or terror (cf. *ibid.*). This approach is more than elemental for a theory of mentality, as he shows that urban orientation and consequently the denizen's psychological state are intrinsically linked to a coherent and clear image of the city: "the map must be readable" (*ibid.*: 9).[23]

Lynch not only emphasises the importance of the image in relation to environmental behaviour and perception, but he is also the first to introduce the concept of mental maps to explain urban experience. Individual cognitive maps show, however, that this mode of experience is necessarily subjective. The actual cityscape becomes a personal space of the urbanite's mind; its topography is transformed into psychological maps or private topographies. As a consequence, "perception of the city is not sustained, but rather partial, fragmentary" (*ibid.*: 2). Thus, the mental map emphasises that the urban imaginary is as diverse and manifold as the inhabitants of the city and individualised, for example, according to gender, ethnicity, class, or generation (cf. *ibid.*: 5-6). In correlation with the urban image and the urbanites' experience, this phenomenon implies that different citizens do not only live in different moral zones but also in distinguishable perceptual worlds. Still, due to Lynch's conception of the public image, the personal mental map always refers back to the urban collective. The processual and fragmentary nature of the urban image emphasises that "imageability does not necessarily connote something fixed, limited, precise, unified, or regularly ordered" (*ibid.*: 10). In that way the urban image, although a phenomenon of *longue durée*, always remains adaptable to

23 | For Lynch (1977: 3) urban legibility is achieved through "recognizable symbols"; he divides the image of the city into path, landmark, edge, node, and district (cf. *ibid.*: 8) – a specific vocabulary of cityscape elements.

changes (cf. *ibid.*: 1, 9). The urban imaginary, as a unique sense of metropolitan space with particular meanings, is mirrored in transmutable cognitive maps of the city which lay bare spatial (b)orderings of the city.

Lynch's study on the image of the city and environmental perception helped stimulate new efforts to understand the invisible landscapes of the mind. While Lynch (1977: 2) stresses visual perceptions and the pure semiotic "'legibility' of the cityscape", later studies concentrate instead on the semantics of the cityscape – the urban environment invested with symbolic meaning (e.g. cf. Gottdiener & Lagopoulos 1986: 5; Sharpe & Wallock 1987: 17). Cityscape, fashioned after landscape, refers to the cultural image and experience of the urban; it specifies an inner urbanisation, or the metropolitan internal mindscapes. In general, landscape is a cultural image, which represents, structures, and symbolises the surrounding environment (cf. Daniels & Cosgrove 1989: 1; Duncan 1990: 11).[24] In analogy, the cityscape – defined by a specific urban physical spatiality (cityspaces), but also cultural topographies of identity, positionality, territoriality, interstitiality – takes into account the imaginary experiences and meanings of the metropolitan environment.[25] Landscapes as cultural practice have a major potential to symbolise hegemonic structures and play an active part in the construction of ideologies. This ideological potential of landscape can nevertheless help to decipher the internal operations of culture – such as urban-specific mentalities. The cityscape is rooted in the *longue durée* of the lived metropolis, namely through ideas, attitudes, norms, and values. By way of perpetual representation of landscape, the urbanites' cultural image is transformed by adding further layers of cultural representation (cf. Daniels & Cosgrove 1989: 1). While the environmental imaginary is prone to change and signals a transformation of mentalities, the juxtaposition between an outside and inside reading of the landscape (cf. Duncan 1990: 18) enhances the synchronic comparability of space-specific mentalities. Furthermore, it visualises how people construct the world they live in and thereby (re)produce representations of their collective values, norms, fears, etc. The signifying system of the landscape describes the contextual conception of the world and thus becomes a means through which the socio-cultural system is first structured and then "communicated, reproduced, experienced, and explored." (*Ibid.*: 17) The cityscape thereby reveals the relation between an urban-specific mentality and its contextual life-world.

24 | Landscapes are represented in a variety of arts, such as landscape gardening, landscape architecture, landscape design, urban architecture and design, painting, photography, and literature (cf. Daniels & Cosgrove 1989: 1). Landscape studies have been of traditional interest to American cultural geography and history, architecture, or journalism. In the last decades, landscape interpretation has become a centre of attention and of interdisciplinary research by anthropology, literary and art criticism, psychology, political science, literary theory, and Cultural Studies, as it touches upon important issues of representation, consciousness, and ideology (cf. Duncan 1990: 11).

25 | For example, Mona Domosh's *Invented Cities. The Creation of Landscape in Nineteenth-Century New York & Boston* (1996) delineates the different cultures of New York and Boston by way of their cityscapes.

In that respect, the urban imaginary materialises in standardised images of thought or metaphors. The metaphorisation of a particular cityscape plays a pivotal role in defining an urban-specific mentality, because "we can no more think outside the metaphorisation of space than we can live outside its representations" (Balshaw & Kennedy 2000: 2).[26] Metaphors are to be seen as an interdiscourse uniting the real and the imaginary. In his study *Cityscape. Cultural Readings in the Material and Symbolic City*, Ben Highmore (2005: 5) insists that "our real experiences of cities are caught in networks of dense metaphorical meanings". He shows that the city is a "tangle of physicality and symbolism [...], the mingling of imaginings and experience" (*ibid.*), both a "living physical and imaginary world" (*ibid.*: 23). Because the real and the metaphoricity of the city are indistinguishable, an analysis of the city, according to Highmore (*ibid.*), must begin with the density of the allusive and illusive reality of "this metaphor city", which is mainly generated by four key tropes: allegory, metaphor, metonymy, and symbolism (cf. Duncan 1990: 18-22; von der Thüsen 2005: 1). These can either be nomothetic (general) or idiographic (specific) in kind.[27] The hypothesis is thus that idiographic metaphors of one particular city both influence and depict an urban-specific mentality.

4.2.3 Image

According to Lindner (2008: 86-87), an urban imaginary needs to be distinguished from the urban image because the former is closer to Durckheim's notion of incorporated collective dispositions, while the latter is rather an ideological entity. Lefebvre (2003: 101) comments: "The city *writes* and *assigns*, that is, it signifies, orders, stipulates. [...] This text has passed through ideologies, as it also 'reflects' them." In the sense that conscious ideologies can transform into nonconscious mental structures, the symbolic ideologisation in form of cultural typification, stereotypification, and simplification functions as a specific factor of influence of urban-specific mentality. The general metropolitan aesthetisation interpreted as an indicator of a very conscious ideological process can be detected in urban symbolic economy, themed environments, city branding, spectaclisation, and the city image in the narrower sense.[28]

Scholars of the Urban Political Economy, such as David Harvey, have sought to describe the connections between cultural (postmodernist) and political economic (post-Fordist) changes, which was later paradigmatically adapted and transformed by Sharon Zukin and Mark Gottdiener who pay attention to the interchange between economic,

---

26 | In her exploration of the material and architectural city image and its representations as images on picture postcards, advertisement, and posters, Löw (2008: 108-109) notes that the imaginary city is specifically evoked by metaphoric expressions.

27 | For example, whereas the allegory of the city as a Babylonian whore or metonymy of the city as intrinsically feminine is a general metaphorisation of the city, Big Ben is a specific symbol of London or specific metonymy for British imperialism. Instead the London Eye is a specific symbol of London and a particular metaphor of its visual spectaclisation.

28 | For more see Sharon Zukin (1982), *Loft Living*; Sharon Zukin (1991), *Landscape of Power*; Scott Lash & John Urry (1994), *Economies of Signs and Space*; Stephanie H. Donald & John G. Gammack (2007), *Tourism and the Branded City. Film and Identity on the Pacific Rim.*

cultural, social and specifically urban, considering transformations of the information economy, high technologies, mass consumption, globalisation, and urban change.

In *The Cultures of Cities* (1995), Zukin explores the symbolic economy of Manhattan at specific key locations for an interchange between culture, public space, and commerce. She claims that contemporary metropolitan culture is more and more about cultural politics or cultural production. As culture becomes "the motor of economic growth" for the city, it forms the basis of what Zukin (1997: 15) labels "symbolic economy". The urban landscape is no longer solely defined by material constructions of space but by the production of symbols (cf. *ibid.*: 2), which, according to Zukin (*ibid.*: 8), has notably changed urbanites' way of thinking. Symbolic economy is a major constituent of urban-specific mentality because in this system cultural symbols intertwine with entrepreneurial capital and identity politics (cf. *ibid.*: 3, 12).

> Real cities are both material constructions, with human strengths and weaknesses, and symbolic projects developed by social representations, including affluence and technology, ethnicity and civility, local shopping streets and television news. [...] Real cultures, for their part, are not torn by conflict between commercialisms and ethnicity; they are made up of one-part corporate image selling and two-parts claims of group identity, and get their power from joining autobiography to hegemony [...]. (*Ibid.*: 46)

Because inhabitants of a metropolis use cultural representations to stamp their identities on places, the city is defined by a contestation of public space (cf. *ibid.*: 3). Thus, the group that defines the "symbolic languages of exclusion and entitlement" also decides on the "look and the feel of cities" (*ibid.*: 7).[29] This venture to preserve a specific set of images in the urban material landscape of buildings, parks and streets thus always entails the re-shaping or cementing of the city's dominating collective consciousness and memory (cf. *ibid.*: 19).

Taking Zukin's (1997: 10) notion of "developing small districts around specific themes" a step further, Gottdiener in *The Theming of America* (1997) focuses solely on the use of desirable symbols, themes, and motifs to create environments of consumption.[30] Theming denotes the increasingly symbolic production of contemporary built spaces. Because, according to Gottdiener (2005: 303), urban *façades* and interiors now incorporate "overarching motifs", urbanites, as a response, similarly become wrapped in themes, such as modes of self-expression and fashions of life-style. Consequently,

29 | For example, in 2006 a local London community posted a bid to rename Aldgate East Tube Station to Brick Lane Station in order to promote tourism and business in the area.

30 | Gottdiener refers to Disney's theme parks to show how signification is transferred to space; this Disneyfication denotes the creation of themed shopping and entertainment, for instance, New York's Time Square. Examples of theming in London encompass developments in downtown areas, like urban entertainment centres with street cafés, shops, theatres, street performances in Covent Garden or former waterfront docklands with new lofts, restaurants, museums, galleries, and sport possibilities in Southwark. Other London examples include Piccadilly Circus, the area around the new London Council called More London or the nearby London Bridge Quarter around the Shard, and of course the area of the London 2012 Olympics.

in order to cater to their social roles as consumers of urban symbols, the city's denizens form a particular habitus as coping mechanism (cf. *ibid.*: 305). The theming of the urban environment thus basically induces a form of storyboarding of space while the city's cultural motifs relegate the inhabitants' use of space, their social encounters, and emotional experience.

The cultural economy of the city and the theming of urban space also exhibit strong ties with strategic city management and city branding, because urban culture and the frame of urban space become an important selling-point of the city. Due to globalisation, metropolises are caught in a worldwide inter-urban competitiveness of attracting investors and consumers. Robins argues (1993: 306): "The particularity and identity of cities is about product differentiation; their cultures and traditions are now sustained through the discourses of marketing and advertising." Like companies emphasising their corporate identity by ways of stamping and advertising their brand, ideals, and culture, cities today communicate their specific urban culture and identity; the city markets its own brand by ways of slogans (e.g. City of Love), festivals (e.g. Berlinale), fairs (e.g. Frankfurter Buchmesse), singular labels (e.g. Cultural European Capital), sporting events (e.g. Olympics), or specific institutions (e.g. European Parliament). In that respect, an operational approach of constructing spatial mentalities lies in city marketing (e.g. 'Cool' London).

Furthermore, urban theorists have especially noted a certain acceleration and increase in the spectaclisation of the city. The image of traditional (European) urbanity with its plazas, coffee houses, etc. has reached an extensively staged attractiveness, whether in the transformation of old shopping areas in the old town or within the realms of shopping centres on the urban periphery. Moreover, historical buildings, museums and re-enacted historical sites are integrated into the urban fabric as a quasi-staged identity. The festivalisation of urbanity also initiates special events, especially mass celebrations (e.g. New Year's on Trafalgar Square) or enacted collective experiences (e.g. BP Summer Screens of London's Royal Opera and Royal Ballet), for showing off lively contemporaneous urbanity. Sieverts (2003: 24) therefore argues that contemporary cities ask for city producers rather than city planners.

City branding and spectaclisation have placed the analysis of the urban image in the centre of contemporary urban studies. In reference to American towns, Suttles (1984: 288-292) identifies three specific elements that forge the city's idiosyncratic image: (1) city founders, (2) political or entrepreneurial leaders, and (3) seminal catch phrases, songs or novels. The city's image is the consciously produced auto-stereotype of a particular metropolis, or the sum of prejudices in form of outsiders' hetero-stereotypes (cf. G. Böhme 1998: 154). Ideas, styles, symbols and icons therefore form a strong image of the city that not only influences the urban denizens but specifically determines the pre-conceptions of strangers and newcomers to the city. Hence, physical and mental city images act as a main advertising element in the competition between cities, a definite component of urban self-fashioning, and a major instrument in urbanites' identification.

4.2.4 Text

For urban semioticians, the city is a texture of signs, a text loaded with signifiers. Theories of urbanity, the sociology of cities, the idiosyncrasy of the city as well as theories of the cityscape all include a hypothesis on the city as text: the approach of the Chicago School is to interpret natural areas and moral regions as geographic areas according to cultural characteristics and "'thick' local imaginaries" (Prakash 2008: 9). In regard to the cityscape, Walter Firey's *Land Use in Central Boston* (1947) explores local sentiments and shows that certain spaces have a sentimental and symbolic importance for the mental life of its inhabitants. Similarly, Anselm Strauss in *Images of the American City* (1976) sees the urbanites' imaginary as constructed from spatial representations. In his article "The Cumulative Texture of Local Urban Culture" (1984), Gerald Suttles treats the accumulation of collective images as well as representations of material and immaterial form. Hence, due to its particular layers of accumulation, one city can be distinguished from another and the unique texture of a single city defines its urban-specific mentality.

Considering the city as a grouping of signs, also Lefebvre (1996: 108) delineates that the city as a signifying or semiological, semiotic and semantic system can be read as text and must be considered consistent with postmodern accounts of contemporary urban life and the Spatial Turn. For Lefebvre (*ibid.*: 115), a city specifically consists of (a) the "*utterance* of the city" or what is said in the city, (b) the "*language* of the city", namely the particularities of the city expressed in discourse and habitus, (c) "*urban language*", the urban connotations, and (d) the "*writing* of the city" as inscribed on walls or its physical layout. This conglomeration of the urban semiology is specifically one of everyday living and inhabiting the city (cf. *ibid.*: 116). Consequently, the city for Lefebvre (*ibid.*: 114) is a "unique system of significations and meanings and therefore of values." It emphasises again that the particularity of the city text both informs and influences urban mentality. Because the signifying system of the city is constantly reformed due the production of social space, the product of the urban texture as the "*written book*" (*ibid.*: 102) can only be understood by relating its text to the mental and social context. Hence, the city – rather like a work of art – is malleable to changes in its texture, forms of representations, and meanings (cf. *ibid.*: 101). Lefebvre (*ibid.*: 102) thereby also refers to the deeper invisible layers of the city as text, namely its mental structures: "[I]f I compare the city to a book, to a writing [...], I do not have the right to forget the aspect of mediation. [...] On this book, with its writing, are projected mental and social forms and structures. [...] The whole is not immediately present in this written text, the city." Although Lefebvre (*ibid.*: 108) agrees to the notion that the city texture can be read because it is produced as writing, he also points out that the decoding of the text cannot be achieved without mediation and without knowledge of its context:

> The context, what is *below* the text to decipher (daily life, immediate relations, the *unconscious* of the urban, what is little said and of which even less is written), hides itself in the inhabited spaces – sexual and family life – and rarely confronts itselfs, and what is *above* this urban text (institutions, ideologies), cannot be neglected in the deciphering.

Concisely, legibility of the urban and an understanding of inner urbanisation are only possible in the confluence of text and context. Duncan (1990: 22-23) has commented that the cityscape prone to textuality shows an intrinsic relation between historical pretexts and the contemporary landscape. In order to decipher these urban texts, he suggests:

To understand the relational nature of the world we need to 'fill in' much that is invisible – to read the subtext that lies beyond the visible text. The meaning of these texts and subtexts changes over time and with the changing perspective of the interpreter. In order to know the meaning of a text we must preconceive the whole of which the text is a part. (*Ibid.*: 14)

Such thick description or dialogue between text and context is Robert Darnton's account of eighteenth-century Montpellier in his collection of essays *The Great Cat Massacre* (1984). Darnton, a historian of mentalities, not only stresses the relationship between space and people who inhabit and create that cityscape but also as one of text and context which captures "the shifting iconography of a modernising urban landscape." (Daniels & Cosgrove 1989: 4) In this sense, Clifford Geertz' method of 'thick description' of the cultural text can help in the analysis of these deeper layers of urbanity,[31] thus not only city images and habitus, but also the urban imaginary and mental dispositions.

In this matter lies the problem many socio-semioticians are faced with: cognitive mapping and other devices of semiological legibility reduce the metropolitan texture to a purely denotative level without considering the relationship with culturally specific systems of connotation beneath – or between the lines (cf. Gottdiener & Lagopoulos 1986: 5). They stress that the urban consists of both non-semiotic and semiotic processes. Either neglecting the social production of space or reducing urban writing to a mere surface of meaning, some critics see the concept of text as too limited to be applied to the metropolis (cf. Shields 1996: 246). This paradigm of city as texture and text notably helps to establish a new approach in studying and reading the city, namely the concept of urban mentality as the missing link between matter and mind. Mentality is the instrument to make the city legible and the functional tool that allows for decoding the intrinsically unintelligible elements of the urban.

City signs densify urban texture, the representation and reading of what is identified as the unison discourse. These "multi-dimensional representations" (King 1996a: 17) are linked to other writings, which in Shields (1996: 234) view cast the city as a "trans-discursive [...] metatext". Not only has the "*writing about* the city" in various disciplines led to an "intertextual implosion of representations" (King 1996a: 2-3), but the city seems to have become an object of discursive practices. Critics therefore resort to differentiating 'city-texts' from 'text-cities', or the semiotic texture of the urban from representations of the city in texts or various media (e.g. cf. Mahler 1999: 11-12).

An author of the *nouveau roman*, Michael Butor (2000: 169) directly interprets the text of the city as an agglomeration of city-texts:

Unter Text der Stadt verstehe ich zunächst die Unmenge von Aufschriften, mit denen sie überzogen ist. Gehe ich durch die Straßen einer modernen Großstadt, erwarten und bestürmen mich überall Wörter: nicht nur, daß Leute, denen ich begegne, miteinander sprechen, sondern vor allem die Schilder an den Gebäuden, an den Stationen der Untergrundbahnen, der Bushaltestellen, durch die ich, falls ich in der Lage bin, sie zu lesen, feststellen kann, wo ich mich befinde, wie ich zu einer anderen Station gelange.

31 | For more see Clifford Geertz (1973), *Interpretation of Culture*.

For Butor (*ibid.*: 171-172), the city primarily exists as a collection of texts. However, there are cities that are more defined as cities of texts according to the mass of texts they incorporate. Urban-specific mentality is then influenced by paradigmatic cultural texts of urbanity via textual renderings of city life such as street names, traffic lights, monuments, libraries, ceremonies, restaurant menus, chronologies, anecdotes, jokes, proverbs, songs, city guides, maps, newspapers, newsreels, films, graffiti, myths, street-level tales, and novels.[32] This leads Highmore (2005: 141) to assume that, first, no city can stand "outside the network of texts that circulate and shape our experience of the city", and second, "cultural texts can't help but reflect and refract their context." Reading the city implies deciphering the urban texture of city writing – or texts in the wider sense. Moreover, it shows how the city as an artefact is strongly rooted in the minds of people, that city writing always arouses strong feelings and vivid associations.

4.2.5 Narrative

Similar to a nation, the 'imagined community' (Benedict Anderson) of a city employs narratives as a discursive strategy of self-fashioning. As mentioned before, urban idiosyncrasy is strongly developed on the basis of narratives. Most postmodern, post-structuralist, and postcolonial urbanologists promote the concept of the city as narrative and novelistic space. Accordingly, for Raban (1974: 8), the contemporary urbanologist is asked to "investigate the plot, and its implications for the nature of character, of the modern city, in the hope that we may better understand what it is that cities do to us, and how they change our styles of living and thinking and feeling." Cities as geographical and imaginary reality, as places of collective practices are always symbolically connoted with fear, hopes, dreams and visions through which the idiosyncratic city is narrated into existence: (hi)stories of the city's personae and city-forming events, urban myths about heroes and demons, fairy tales concerning the golden city and parables on Babylon, utopian visions of its bright future, dystopias of its predicted fall, individual stories of success and moral bankruptcy, chronicles of certain neighbourhoods and the fleeting population of the city.

The archetype of an urban-specific narrative is the city myth. All classical myths of humanity are grouped around a city: Atlantis, Babylon, Jerusalem, Troy – even the contemporary 'myth' of the American Dream is based on the vision of the 'city upon a hill'. Chambers (1990: 112) argues: "The metropolis is, above all, a myth, a tale, a telling that helps some of us to locate our home in modernity." In that sense, the phenomenon of urban-generic myths is suited for a definition of the specificity of a particular city. Lynch (1977: 9) comments that the image of the city should be open-ended and adaptable to change, because letting the urbanite continuously organise the transforming metropolitan

---

32 | For example, Lotman (2001: 202) comments: "By the 1830s Petersburg had become a city of cultural and semiotic contrasts which served as soil for an exceptionally intense intellectual life. By the sheer number of texts, codes, connections, associations, by the size of its cultural memory build up over the historically tiny period of its existence, Petersburg can rightly be considered to be unique, a place where semiotic models were embodied in architectural and geographical reality."

reality and urban myths allows for a transmutable narration of the city. These myths also refer to a sensual geography of the city (cf. Lindner 2004: 392-393); situationists and psychogeographers, for example, try to retrace the mythical lines between specific *genius loci* of the city to grasp its hidden meanings, especially of urban collectivity (see chapter 6.4.2).

Cultural geographers seem to unanimously agree on the importance of urban narratives, specifically on the relevance of urban fiction not only as a viable depiction of city life, but also as an influence on the image and feel of a particular metropolis (cf. e.g. Wirth 1967: 217; Harvey 1985: xv). Most critics agree that the modern novel since the eighteenth century is predominantly an urban genre, often a description of the city milieu, its social relations and interaction with the metropolitan surroundings. Moreover, according to Elizabeth Wilson (1995: 151), the "history of the metropolis [...] since 1800 is bound up with the history of the literature it has inspired." Urban-specific fiction can also become the trademark of a city. Butor (2000: 169-171) sees particular cities as carrying an outstanding 'literary weight', in the sense that those are referred to regularly in literature, such as Athens, Jerusalem, New York or London. In the case of London, Charles Dickens deeply formed both the literary image and the mental images (cf. e.g. Darnton 1984: 109; Sharpe & Wallock 1987: 12; Mumford 1997: 270; Kerrigan 1998: 4; Balshaw & Kennedy 2000: 12; Löw 2008: 85). Dickens not only described the new world of the urban realm but also found new means and words to do so. By gradually constructing an urban vocabulary, moulding new terms and images, he taught his contemporaries how to read, understand, interpret and respond to the urban world of nineteenth-century London. Kerrigan (1998: 4) comments:

> Victorians saw London in Bleak House, because they could factor their experience of the novel into the city they knew, and that changes London not just for them but for us, because Dickens's account of the city mixed so deeply into the cultural bloodstream that it still shapes views about what is vernacular and atmospheric in the urban fabric.

Consequently, the city novel conveys an impression of the city and informs us on the reactions to this new landscape of the modern city.[33] During modernity, fiction strongly responds to the modern metropolis in form and content, showing how novels function as "a seismograph of modern urban experience" (Alter 2005: xi). The novel is able to depict the various setting of the city in detail, to represent the richness in human life and behaviour as well as to communicate urban values and attitudes. The genre vividly constructs the literary cityscape because of its greatly geographical and highly metaphorical characteristics. In the topographies of urban literature, space is rendered into a semiosphere of the literary cityscape. Its literary landscapes are topological or even tropological, conveying a meaning of urban space and a wide variety of ideas and attitudes. Finally, all urban novels rely on a psychological and internalised urban landscape that determines the sensual experience of the city and overtly affects human consciousness. Consequently, the genre of the novel draws a multi-dimensional map of the literary

---

33 | Literary critics also acknowledge the intimate relationship between the novel and the city (cf. e.g. Klotz 1987; Wachinger 1999; Alter 2005; see chapter 5.1.3).

cityscape, exceeding the two-dimensional mental maps of the city. Thomas Saarinen (1984: 109) argues:

> Novels are particularly valuable for their personalized accounts of people-environment interactions in specific areas. The deep insights into the psychological and symbolic aspects of the people-environment relationship garnered in novels could well serve hypotheses for more rigorous scientific studies.

In that respect, urban fiction not only adds to the urban-specific texture of a particular metropolis, but also reveals its idiosyncratic state of mind or urban-specific mentality.

4.2.6 Atmosphere

Cities also differ from one another concerning their idiosyncratic atmosphere that denotes the whole impression of a city, a quality that is seen as typical for a specific metropolis, its ambience, pace, aroma, and feel. An important key word of contemporary city branding, urban atmosphere encompasses the city's cultural feel. In his systematisation of the metropolitan overload effect, Milgram (1970: 1465) recognises a different atmosphere in great cities such as New York and London, apparent in tone and rhythm, spatial composition, and texture of social encounters. For him, the notion of urban atmosphere, however, constitutes a standard of comparison not only between cities, but also between the mentality of the tourist, the newcomer and the long-term resident. Since a "good city is highly 'imageable,' having many known symbols joined by widely known pathways, whereas dull cities are grey and nondescript" (cf. *ibid.*: 1468), cognitive and emotive maps can offer an insight into the perception of the urban atmosphere. Urban atmosphere in a way turns the focus on the heterogeneity of urban stimuli, classifies them, and undertakes to retrace particular psychological effects in the urbanite. The concept of urban atmosphere, understood as a holistic sensescape, widens the scope of influencing factors on the urban-specific mentality from one of mere visual legibility and perception to one of sensual or phatic conception (cf. Saarinen 1984: 139; Lynch 1977: 10; G. Böhme 1998: 152-153; Robins 1998: 165; Degen 2008: 36).

Gernot Böhme's article "Die Atmosphäre einer Stadt" (1998) defines the urban atmosphere as a connection between the aesthetic and the human dimension of the city, or between urbanity and image. According to Böhme (1998: 156), the city's atmosphere can be compared to a stage setting (lighting, sound, props, composition). Because the ambience of the city is mainly sensually perceived, it directly influences the urbanites' *conditio humana* (cf. *ibid.*: 160). From the German word *Befindlichkeit*, Böhme (*ibid.*: 154-157) delineates that atmosphere always implies a somatic orientation in the urban realm: the metropolitan space is intrinsically bodily felt by urbanites because the urban atmosphere is scripted in emotional states of being. Böhme (*ibid.*: 162), nevertheless, argues that although its atmosphere emphasises the subjective experience of the city, it is still conceived as an objective quality. First and foremost a nonconscious element of the urban way of life, atmosphere, however, can mainly be recognised as characteristic by the stranger (cf. *ibid.*: 154).

Although odours are the most essential element of urban atmosphere as they are truly atmospheric, smells are a largely neglected part of the perceived sensescape (cf. Raban

1974: 226; Porteous 1985: 375; G. Böhme 1998: 150; Lindner 2004: 392-393; Bischoff 2007: 189). For Gernot Böhme (1998: 150-151), a city without scent is like a person without character; a specific smell makes it possible to recognise a certain place, and in turn to identify with it, especially because the olfactory experience of the city presents an important aspect in the personal and collective memory of urbanites. In his seminal article "Smellscape" (1985), Douglas Porteous explores various aspects of the landscape of smell. His conception of smellscape suggests that smells are spatially ordered and place-related so that particular locales can individually be characterised by smell (cf. Porteous 1985: 362-364): the urban-rural distinction is clearly identifiable through the nostrils, while individual cities, even urban types, may be distinguished by olfactory characteristics[34], and in single urban areas individual smell events can be a defining feature. First of all, Porteous (*ibid.*: 358) constitutes a habituation effect to the smell of the city; as the perceiver becomes habituated to the smellscape, the insider/outsider or stranger/inhabitant effect is an important dimension in the identification of idiosyncratic olfaction. The matrix of pleasant/unpleasant, familiar/unfamiliar olfactory landscapes can thus be attributed to these differences in the sensory response (*ibid.*: 358). According to Porteous (*ibid.*: 359), psychological research indicates that while visual experience is most likely to involve thought and cognition, olfaction mainly stimulates emotional effects. On the other hand, the perceived smellscape is "fragmentary in space and episodic in time" (*ibid.*). Besides identifying places and rendering cities idiosyncratic, smells are therefore also temporally assigned (day, seasons, events, historical periods) (*ibid.*: 367-368).[35] However, in the function of memory and recollection, the temporal aspect does not seem to play a role concerning the emotional trigger of smells, because according to the Proustian concept of odour memory, smells especially release childhood memories which are heavily emotion-laden (cf. *ibid.*: 369-370). The olfactory memory is not only a personal matter; in that sense, the olfactory experience of a city is important for the collective sensual apparatus, especially as a collective olfactory memory.

Moreover, the soundscape of the city generates a particular meaning that constitutes a main factor of influence on urban-specific mentality. Both mentality and urban-specific parameters have been described as a basic tone: while Graus (1987: 16) calls mentality a "tone" of thinking and behaviour, urban idiosyncrasy has been defined as the 'ticking' ("Ticken", Löw 2008: 15) of a city and the doxa as the 'background melody' ("Hintergrundmelodie", Berking 2008: 27-28). The latter already identify sound as another major element that contributes to the highly stimulated senses of city dwellers: especially the "high-noise-soundscape" (Rösing 2000: 74) of the city, defined as a specific acoustic profile of the metropolis, not only influence the urbanites' psychological state

34 | Degen (2008: 45) argues that "when we enter London we might perceive the taste of smog." London has been labelled "The Big Smoke" and variously termed "The Great Stink" (1856) or "The Great Smog" (1952), referring to the city's olfactory water and air pollution. Also, the spatial arrangement of London was constituted by its 'stink industries' near the river Lea, which was one of the causes for the later class-specific urban divide between East and West.

35 | Since the nineteenth century, the modern metropolis has mainly been connected with malodour, stench and air pollution, whereas the postmodern cities seem to be a rather smell-poor sensory environment (cf. Porteous 1985: 356).

and emotions; in an interaction with seeing and hearing, the "sounds in the city" (Saarinen 1984: 134) also have an impact on the habitus of urban denizens. Similarly to the urban smellscape, acoustics of the city have so far thus only been registered in terms of the quantitative pollution of the environment by noise (cf. G. Böhme 1998: 158).[36] Saarinen (1984: 134) points out that the noise produced by oneself is less unpleasant than that generated by others; unrelated sounds intruding from the outside are perceived as bothersome and create stress.[37] Smell and sound as agents of emotion significantly lead to a dispositional structuration of urbanites' psychology. These structures not only strengthen a sense of place and an orientation in the urban realm, but also help the individual to react to the overload of menacing city stimuli.

Rhythm as a vital aspect of the urban texture can be considered as another important factor of influence on the urban-specific mentality. All in all, urban rhythm describes the dynamic interplay of all urban-specific forces in form or pace. The most notable difference between city and country concerns temporal rhythms; Korff (1985: 351) shows how the inner urbanisation brings about the habitualisation of a new temporal practice of time, and Simmel sees urbanity as involving a rationalisation of time. Thus, the rhythms of the city are manifest in certain time-slots that are cultural-specific but also not as strongly determined by natural light. Postmodernists, for example, rather see the rhythms of the metropolis as defined by the media. Urban rhythms become specifically apparent in urbanites' language, elocution, dialect and jargon as well as the locomotion of individuals, the movements of urban masses. The social interaction and cultural practices necessarily produce a rhythmic experience of the urban: "multiple speeds and movements: people crossing the street, cars stopping and accelerating, crowds of people pursuing different aims, the mingling of noises and smells." (Amin & Thrift 2002: 16) This sense of overload is enhanced by the motion and interchangeablity of urban images, symbols, and signs. In that regard, rhythm brings together temporal, spatial, social, and cultural orientation. Amin and Thrift (*ibid.*) comment:

---

36 | Interestingly enough, Murray Schaffer's *The Tuning of the World* (1977), which registers the civilisatory transformations of soundscapes from antiquity to the present, is largely an analysis of literary sources, such as novels and poems. For more also see Murray Shaffer's *World Soundscape Project* (1973-1996) which constitutes the most encompassing research on the soundscapes of Vancover and Canada, later added to by Michael Southworth's urban sound documentation of Boston or Barry Truax's (1978), *Handbook of Acoustic Ecology. Sound References in Literature* and Pascal Amphoux's (1994) *Aux Ecoutes de la Ville*.

37 | There are various perspectives to register the interrelation between city and sound: (a) a particular "sound of the city" as the documentation of basic city noises, (b) specific "soundmarks" in analogy to landmarks, e.g. the chime of Big Ben, (c) the city as a base of music culture or milieu for a specific style of music, e.g. the Liverpool Sound or London's Jungle music in the 1990s, as well as (d) iconic songs about a specific city, e.g. Herbert Grönemeyer's "Bochum" (1984), Billy Joel's "New York State of Mind" (1976) or Alicia Keys's "Empire State of Mind" (2009) as well as the endless list of songs about London, such as The Kinks' "Waterloo Sunset" (1967) or "London Calling" (1979) by the Clash (cf. Lindner 2004: 393; Rösing 2000: 70-73).

> The rhythms of the city are the coordinates through which inhabitants and visitors frame and order the urban experience. The city's multi-temporality, from bodily and clock rhythms to school patterns and the flows of traffic [...]. Rather, the city is often known and negotiated through these rhythms and their accompanying ordering devices [...].

Hence, the study of urban rhythms has become overtly important in contemporary urbanism.[38] The most important theoretical work on urban rhythms so far is Henri Lefebvre's *Élements de rythmanalyse: Introduction à la connaissance des rythmes* (1992). In "Attempt at the Rhythmanalysis of Mediterreanean Cities" co-written with his wife Catherine Réguliere, Lefebvre (2004: 98) recognises the intrinsic spaces of movement, migration, transition and thus the fluidity of the urban realm. Rhythms of the city are seen as specifically historical and infused in everyday practices of the city (*ibid.*: 87). The urban experience in the public places of the city, for example, is formed by encounters, intrigues, diplomacy, trade, negotiations, theatricalisations, reserve, silence, anonymity, and isolation adding to urban "polyrhythmia" (*ibid.*: 89; cf. Highmore 2005: 148). Rhythmanalysis attuned to the city is specifically dependent on two contrapuntual kinds of repetitive rhythmicity: the cyclical or natural (rotation: day and night) and the linear or social (consecution: work), whose conflicts promote the specificity of the city (cf. *ibid.*: 90). The plurality of rhythms thus penetrates urban practices as much as it is penetrated by them (cf. *ibid.*: 89). In Lefebvre and Régulier's (*ibid.*: 95) words, "rhythms of the other" turned outwards to the public are opposed to "rhythms of the self", namely the private. This phenomenon underlines how an interplay between the plural rhythms of the metropolis that (re)combine, overlap, and dissolve can result in urban arrhythmia and implosion or bodily shocks, stresses and strains (cf. *ibid.*: 99-100).[39] Besides the somatic overload, the general urban ambiguities that manifest themselves in the rhythms of social life also bring to light the nuances and differences between towns. Not only the urban imaginary creates a specific livid urbanism, but city rhythms also influence the denizens' unison emotional responses, making them "in the most intimate of ways, *collective* subjects." (Highmore 2005: 158). Lefebvre and Régulier (2004: 98-99) specify these contradictions as public and private, sacred and profane, apparent and secret, indi-

---

38 | Highmore (2005) analyses the interplay between the urban rhythms of modernity, rhythmic depictions in modernist art and movement. Joachim Schlör's *Nights in the Big City* (1998) looks at the nightly rhythms of three metropolises in the nineteenth century in connection to law, morality, and technological change and analyses the night rhythms of London and their ordering technologies due to historical shifts in public morality and state regulation. Also James Winter captures the rhythm of the city in his *London's Teeming Streets 1830-1914* (1993). For other correlations of urban space and rhythm see Dejan Sudjic & Phil Sayer (1992), *The 100 Mile City*; Iain Sinclair (2002), *London Orbital*; Setha Low (2000), *On the Plaza. The Politics of Urban Space and Culture* (cf. Highmore 2005: 159-160).

39 | The body of the urban individual becomes the initial site for recognising the clash between social and psychological order (cf. Highmore 2005: 147). For Lefebvre, the body is the initial site for recognizing the urban rhythms, as it lies between the biological, physiological, and social with their own space-time (*ibid.*). When two different rhythms intersect, such as that of the city in correlation with the denizen's pace, the intrinsic rhythmicality of both becomes apparent.

vidual and social, homogeneous and heterogeneous. Once again, the role of the outsider is stressed, as rhythm is only to be consciously analysed from a distance (cf. *ibid.*: 88; Amin & Thrift 2002: 18). This implies that rhythms belong to urban-specific nonconscious dispositions of city culture and are an all-important element in the construction of London mentality. In the context of Mentality Studies, rhythmanalysis negotiates both contradictory urban experiences, and ambivalent urban-generic structures can help understand the functions of urban mental dispositions.

4.2.7 Emotion

The city's idiosyncratic landscape, smellscape, and soundscape and its concordant rhythms specifically have an effect on the collective emotional life of urbanites, which specifies urbanity. "Apparently cities do things to us, to our emotions and to our consciousness." (Zijderveld 1998: 1) Urban atmosphere and urban rhythm emphasise the importance of the senses as elements of urban life. Not only do they show that the visual influences the modes of urban subjectivity and unconsciousness, but also that olfactory, auditory and rhythmic experiences "engineer the body and the senses" (Amin & Thrift 2002: 28; cf. Robins 1998: 175; Löw 2008: 61-63; Lehnert 2011: 10). Referring to that, the local collective psychological state, structure of feeling or collective emotion of a city is elemental in defining an urban-specific mentality. Amin and Thrift (2002: 28) summarise this level in the concept of urban somatic communication:

> Cities cast spells over the senses, spells which are increasingly engineered by the state and business. And mention of the senses in turn points to that whole realm of human life which is outside consciousness – consciousness is, after all, only one kind of mental process. These are all the reflexes and automatisms which make up the city's 'unconscious', and which account for the bulk of its activity. This is the constant push of habitual consciousness and the dance of gestural, somatic communication [...].

A psychological interpretation of a particular metropolitan mind therefore reveals specific dispositions of feeling. In his recent article on postmodern urbanity "Kollektivgefühl und städtische Kultur" (1998), Kevin Robins has dedicated himself to the analysis of a collective emotion and urban culture. The city has always been an ambivalent object of attraction and repulsion: it supports both integration, coherence, and individualism as well as disintegration or fragmentation. In regard to the formless contemporary city, Robins (1998: 168) interprets the urban-generic ambivalence of familiarity and strangeness as temporal-specifically characterised by an enhanced anxiety, aggression, paranoia – especially towards urban crowds, women, and strangers.[40] However, because in the urban realm everyone is a stranger, every person induces fear in others and in

---

40 | For Robins (1998: 170, 173) these constitute three sources of urban fear: first, the dissolution of the Self in the crowd creates anxieties of the depersonalisation, fragmentation and loss of identity. Second, the presence of women in the city furthers the gender-specific (male) anxieties of the female connotations: nature, chaos, uncertainty, change (cf. *ibid.*: 174). Third, the confrontation with the stranger destroys the relation between physical and psychological

himself (*ibid.*: 178). This example of the emotional dimension of the urban existence pays tribute to a collective emotion of anxiety resulting in psychological states, yet also shows that these are not simply pathological states but intrinsic elements of urban existence. Regarding the urban-specific mentality, it has to be considered that not only do the urban-generic surroundings of the metropolis influence collective emotions, but also that the city's particularities induce dispositions of feeling (e.g. 'Cool' London).

4.2.8 Identity

The city is a place not only of collective experience or emotions, but a locus of collective identity. However, it has widely been argued that cities do not constitute places anymore. Because metropolitan dimensions extend the perception of urban inhabitants, leading to alienation from the urban realm, identification has become impossible. The city's idiosyncrasy on the other hand emphasises the urban character, personality or biography and therefore reinstates the notion of an urban identity (cf. Löw 2008: 16, 90). Historically grown components of a city are condensed into traits of urban character, as dynamic, progressive, cosmopolitan, or sentimental, which are perceived as the city's specific identity that also defines the range of possibilities for future development (cf. *ibid.*: 40, 63). The particularity of the metropolitan realm is thereby the main source of the urbanites' identity (cf. *ibid.*: 169).

A growing visual representation of the city by means of urban images always goes along with the establishment of a "marketable identity for the city as a whole." (Zukin 1997: 23) Urban places are contested and collective identities inscribed into the urban fabric. Furthermore, metropolises have their own identifiable culture, which provides individuals with a common identity by way of shared norms, values, sentiments (cf. Robins 1998: 166; Zijderveld 1998: 20-25). Images of the city and the urban imaginary support the urbanites' notion of their city, and in consequence of their collective Self. This form of unconscious urban self-fashioning is also largely supported by common emotions, induced through atmosphere and rhythm, towards one's metropolis and refined in a collective psychology.

Urban identity according to Hobsbawm (1987: 51) is "based on what all inhabitants of a city have in common: not least pride in the city and its superiority – which can be a very powerful sentiment in great cities" (e.g. 'London Pride').[41] The identity of a city is thus constituted by forging its own solidarity and networks of relationships. For urbanologists the lack of urbanity, of cultural collectivity results not only in anomie but in the loss of a city identity (cf. Zijderveld 1998: 137). This loss of urban identity finally also reaches the individual urbanite who, due to the lack of a macrostructural identification with the city, either searches for other forms of group identity or experiences a loss of personal identity (cf. *ibid.*: 139). Taking up Raban's (1974: 1-2) notion of the soft city I argue that urban identity and the urbanite's personal identity inform each other:

---

distance and thereby annihilates the borders between homely and uncanny, friend and foe, order and chaos, inside and outside. This results in racism and xenophobia (*ibid.*: 176).

41 | Another example would be Munich's 'mir san mir'-mentality (cf. Lindner 2004: 385).

> For at moments like this, the city goes soft; it awaits the imprint of an identity. For better or worse, it invites you to remake it, to consolidate it into a shape you can live in. You, too. Decide who you are, and the city will again assume a fixed form round you. Decide what it is and your own identity will be revealed, like a position on a map fixed by triangulation. [...] We mould them in our images: they, in their turn, shape us by the resistance they offer when we try to impose our own personal form on them.

In that respect, the identity of one particular city defines its citizens' being. Put the other way round, without specifically naming, emplacing, reading, and deciphering the metropolis, urbanites are not able to form an identity of their own.

To sum up: the logic of the urban idiosyncrasy sensitises for the differences of regional constructions of reality and the urban-specific structures of mentality as particular to the very metropolis. As the last chapter has explored, each city produces its own character, which shows itself not only in a dominant type of architecture, individual biography, particular socialisation, and way of life of its inhabitants. This idiosyncratic character also becomes apparent in material and mental images of the city, urban texture and city texts, atmosphere and rhythm, collective emotions and identity. Otherwise, local-specific parameters that inform the city's character influence the city-dwellers' habitus and pre-structure the idiosyncratic metropolitan doxa. Löw (2008: 11) therefore sees theory's function in characterising a specific city, identifying its typical inhabitant and extracting their habitus. Similarly, a theory of mentalities that advances even to the non-conscious of the city proceeds in the following manner: characterisation of the specific lifeworld context of the city, identification of particular city texts, interpretation of its specific mental dispositions.

4.3 The Model of Urban Mentality

London mentality can be understood as generated in the confluence of urban-generic ambivalences further defined by urban-specific factors of influence. The following model visualises the construction of an urban-generic mentality. The basic determinants of mentality – collective, time, space, compression – are specified by the urban habitat framing and outlining the cluster of eight configurations of ambivalence such as city/country, public/private, sociability/anomie, heterogeneity/homogeneity, familiarity/strangeness, community/individualism, indifference/involvement, and apathy/vigilance (see figure 4.1).

Hence, the configuration of public and private, for example, is variously determined by urban collectivity and its social implications, while the spatial determinant devises an emphasis on the city's private spatialities. Both urban parameters experience a certain temporal persistence in their opposition but differ regarding urban routine practices. Compression might indicate a certain shift of the inner boundaries of the dichotomy, for example as the privatisation of the public, or a momentary diffusion of the two poles.

With its focus on contemporary London mentality, this book accentuates the particularities of locally, socially, and temporally emplaced mental structures. Accordingly, the urban-generic configurations of ambivalence will serve as a basic matrix for analysing mentality which is mirrored in the approach and structure of each interpretative sub-

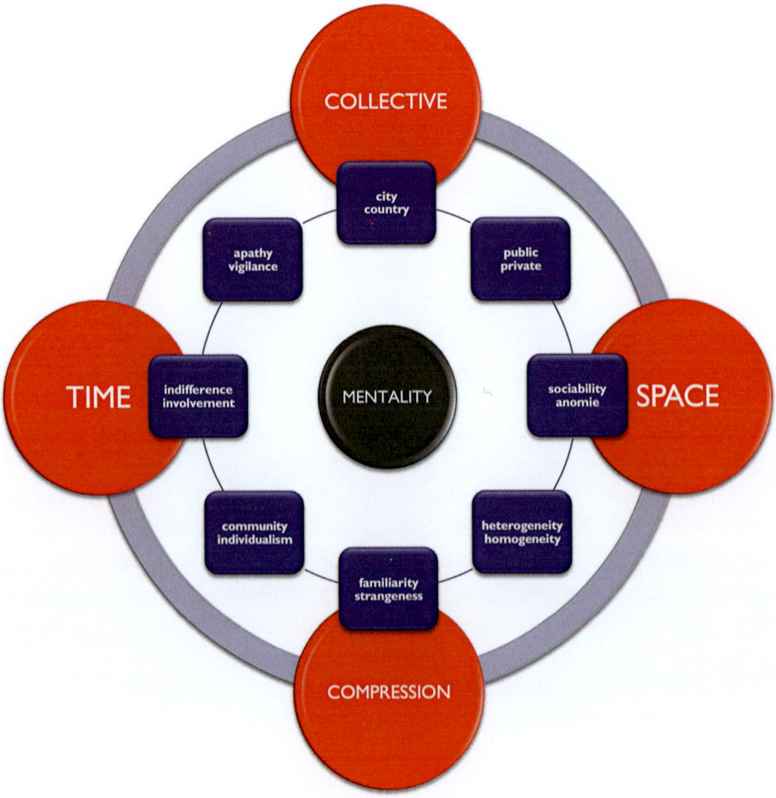

Figure 4.1: Model of Urban-Generic Mentality

chapter. For example, the spatial theorem of public and private is used to examine the depiction of urban spatialities as a whole (see chapter 6), while the social theorem regarding heterogeneity and homogeneity is predominantly taken up with regards to stratifications of the metropolis (see chapter 7). Socio-psychological implications of London mentality are examined using the ambivalence of community and individual or apathy and vigilance (see chapter 8). This modus operandi is supplemented by simultaneous comparisons to London's idiosyncrasy.

A concept of urban mentality necessarily involves the alignment of urban-generic configurations of ambivalence with urban-specific factors of influence. In general, a 'N-Metropolis' constitutes a particular cultural area which specifies urban-generic ambivalences by way of its semiotic and semantic system. The axiomatic cluster of the imaginary theorem notably influences the graduation of urban-generic characteristics. This set of eight factors of influence comprises culture, imaginary, image, text, narrative, atmosphere, emotion, and identity (see figure 4.2).

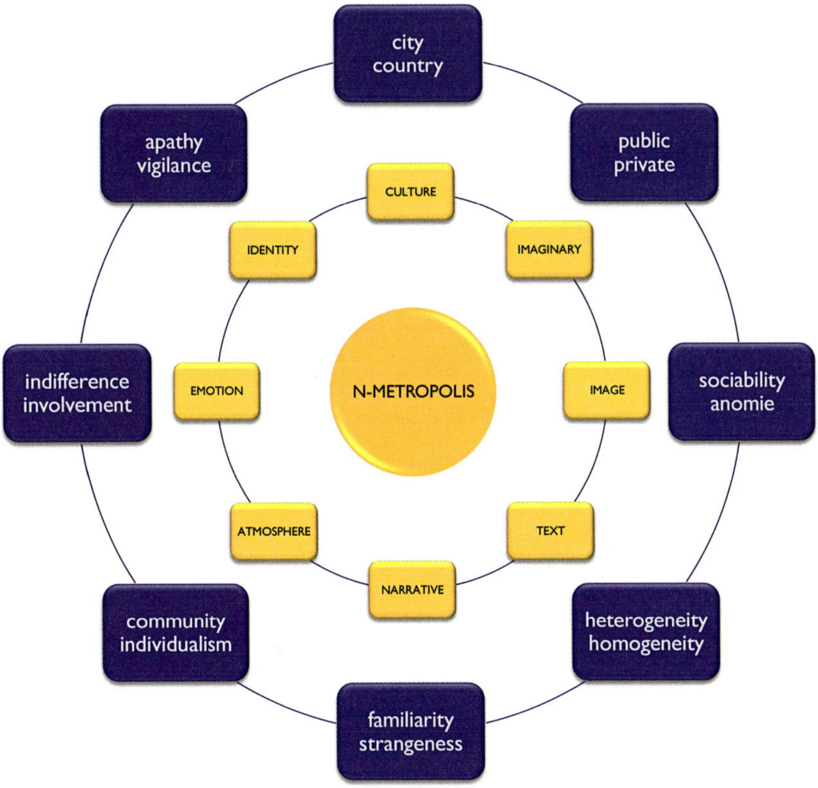

Figure 4.2: Model of Urban-Specific Mentality

The frame of analysis is designed by the urban-specific mentality of metropolitan London during the Blair era. Thereby, the analysis, for example, identifies the London Underground as a particular spatial node of the metropolitan cityscape favoured by the city's imaginary (see chapter 6.2). Moreover, the idiosyncratic metaphorisation of the contemporary metropolis is taken into account in the chapter on "The Palimpsestuous City" (see chapter 6.4). Of particular interest are spatial perceptions, such as mental maps or the sensescape of the London-specific setting (see chapter 6.3). Socio-cultural rhythmicities are especially relevant in regard to the urban dynamics of sociability (see chapter 7.1) and segregation (see chapter 7.2). Influences on London's psychological state of mind necessarily accommodate notions of collective emotion (see chapter 8.2). Finally, the confluence of London's identity and urban inhabitants' identification as Londoners is inspected (see chapter 8.1).

5 Methodological Implications

5.1 Methodological Approaches to Mentality

This chapter employs the theoretical assumptions with respect to the concept of (urban) mentality in order to sketch an appropriate method that can be used for the analysis of mentalities. I propose that this methodological approach can principally be applied to fictional as well as non-fictional (urban) narratives, cultural practices and beyond, although it specifically concerns London city novels.

This work follows a Cultural Studies approach based on the theory of mentalities. In sharing the general hypothesis of alterity, Cultural Studies and the history of mentality specifically deal with the mental aspects of culture: thoughts, ideas, emotions, and habitual norms. While the history of mentalities predominantly explores the otherness of thinking in the past, Cultural Studies focus on the different attitudes of cultural areas. The notions of mentality and culture proliferate a constructionist approach that emphasises the perceptual reality over the merely factual (cf. A. Nünning 2004c: 183). Thus, both strive to reconfigure the social constructions of reality as mental dispositions of thinking, feeling, imagining, and acting. Conversely, the two disciplines also examine how these collective meanings, values and norms become visible in patterns of everyday practices. Being concerned with recurrent structures of meaning, Cultural Studies and the history of mentalities are further related in their semiotic approach. Whereas the historians of mentalities are more oriented towards a quantifiable social history, Cultural Studies explicitly concentrates on qualitative interpretations of textual sources (*ibid.*: 185). The overall concern of both conceptions is connected to the question of how mental dispositions are materialised in symbolic systems and how textual sources can inform us on structures of mentality (*ibid.*: 179, 184).

Fundamentally multi- and interdisciplinary, both fields of study unite an array of methodological approaches. In order to counter the problem of methodological fragmentation or eclecticism, Kamm (1996: 85) proposes a common methodological frame for the analysis of mentalities offered by linguistics and Literary Studies. The overall method applied – "textwissenschaftlich ausgerichtete[...] Kulturwissenschaft auf mentalitätstheoretischer Grundlage" (Kamm 1996: 87) – is based on an confluence of Cultural Studies, the history of mentalities, and Literary Studies (cf. V. Nünning 2001).

In the following I will draft the development of methodological implications from the initial quantitative and qualitative methods of the history of mentalities founded on the assumption of textual pragmatics, the methodical practice of literary history, to a Cultural and Mentality Studies approach. I argue that from the methodological pool of Literary Studies, narratology offers the most prolific instruments for an evidence- and result-oriented analysis of mentalities.

5.1.1 Quantitative and Qualitative Methods

A particular binding methodology for the historical research of mentalities does not exist, but historians of mentalities generally use quantitative source collection and qualitative content analysis. The quantitative analysis builds upon a series of homogeneous sources, especially pragmatic texts such as court protocols, tax lists, inventories and yearbooks, but also personal wills, pamphlets, diaries, letters, sermons, etc. (cf. Reichardt 1978: 138-157; Schulze 1985: 262-263). These sources are quasi-statistically evaluated for recurrences, which results in a representative profile of mental structures. However, certain patterns of rites, myths, or narratives are hardly quantifiable; rather, their mental dispositions lie in the structures of meaning.

For a qualitative approach historians of mentalities first adopt sociological techniques, assimilate methods of social psychologists, and appropriate ethnological or anthropological methods of interpretation (cf. Le Goff 1985: 167-168; Chartier 1988: 21-22). In reference to Clifford Geertz' semiotic notion of culture and his analytical instrument of thick description, historians of mentalities see themselves as "code-breaker[s]" (Duby 1985: 156) who decipher the complex textures of meaning. The anthropological approach of a history of mentalities discloses mental structures of meaning beneath and "involves identifying, linking and interpreting a mass of unrelated signs" (*ibid.*). This qualitative analysis extracts clusters of recurrent attitudes, which makes it possible to synchronically compare collectives or to diachronically track transformations of mentalities. According to Sellin (1985: 594), qualitative analysis therefore always needs to relate to extra-textual contexts of society. Hence, the analysis of mentalities is less about quantification than contextualisation.

Both the serial and the anthropological method, however, bring along two major methodological problems which perpetuate a linear perspective on mentalities. First, although it is a collective phenomenon, supra-individual mental dispositions are largely extrapolated from individual source material. The analysis thereby has to distinguish between the idiosyncratic style of the 'author' on the one hand and the nonconscious collective mental structures on the other hand. Second, a homogeneous source material can easily lead to an emphasis of formal or inconsequential conventions that are mistaken for mental dispositions. Thus, Beeck (1989: 23) calls for a heterogeneous treatment of source material which necessarily includes a variety of texts. He argues that dissimilarities are of relevance because only they emphasise identical and corresponding elements and the singular and unique can turn out to be more significant than the massive (cf. *ibid.*). The balanced choice between heterogeneous and homogeneous sources is therefore important for the analysis of mentalities.

Since the 1970s, historians of mentalities have been uniting quantitative and qualitative approaches and have paid tribute to the richness of cultural texts. The members of the *Annales* school such as Georges Duby (1985: 157), Michel Vovelle (1982: 45), Jacques Le Goff (1985: 173) and Roger Chartier (1988: 21-22) specifically concentrate on documents of the imaginary. For example, Duby (1985: 157) argues that

> no text is necessarily to be rejected. In the vocabulary of stories, dramatic works, letters, family bibles, and, most conservative of all, that of liturgies, regulations, judicial judgements, there are revealing terms to be tracked down: not only words, but turns of phrase, metaphors, word associations.

Especially since the linguistic but latest with the Cultural Turn, historians of mentalities see both pragmatic and literary texts as viable objects of analysis. The fundamental adage is that pragmatic as well as poetic texts form a specific discourse that can be analysed for mental structures; all text types are a verifiable material for the qualitative interpretation of a mentality. According to the assumptions of pragmatics, language is determined by the conditions of society, and thus all semiotic systems carry implications for the dispositions of thinking, imagining, feeling, and acting.

Tânia Ünlüdağ (1992) particularly exemplifies this interrelation between language and mentality.[1] Acquiring cultural-specific knowledge is bound to linguistic socialisation and hence mentality is passed on naturally and mainly unreflected (cf. Ünlüdağ 1992: 284). Language as a system of communicative actions is a specific form of human behaviour and therefore presents a permanent expression of mentality (*ibid.*: 289). Because language inherits a double function, firstly constituting and organising constructions of reality, and secondly articulating experiences and perceptions of reality, language forms images of reality or mentalities and represents mental attitudes (*ibid.*: 284). Understanding language as a major constitutional factor for the social perception of reality, one can argue that a specific texture of language creates the basis for all structures of thinking in a particular historical epoch (*ibid.*: 286). As was shown before, Febvre interprets *outillage mental* mainly as the affective-cognitive medium of language with its infrastructure of vocabulary, syntax, and metaphors. In other words, language presents an element of the mental organon *per se*. In that respect, transformation or differentiation of mentalities is signalled in linguistic deviance (*ibid.*: 286). Since for the most part of cultural history acts of speaking are not directly observable but only conceivable in written fixtures, texts become the main sources for an analysis of mentalities (cf. *ibid.*: 290).

Although the specific of a history of mentality does not lie in the form of its sources but rather in its interpretative approach and method (cf. Le Goff 1985: 173), methodological enlargement and diversification of sources of the histories of mentalities necessarily go hand in hand. The revolutionised history of mentalities is a history of perception and interpretation, wherein the imaginary and its privileged sources gain methodological

---

1 | In her later study *Mentalität und Literatur. Zum Zusammenhang von bürgerlichen Weltbildern und christlicher Erziehungsliteratur im 19. Jahrhundert am Beispiel der Wuppertaler Traktate* (1993) Ünlüdağ analyses the literary form of religious tracts and their implications for a protestant mentality. For more also see Ludwig Jäger & Erika Linz, eds. (2004), *Medialität und Mentalität. Theoretische und empirische Studien zum Verhältnis von Sprache, Subjektivität und Kognition.*

importance. The history of mentalities draws evidence from literature to reconstruct historical processes and mental structures and passes into a history of the imaginary that focuses on constructive processes of meaning (cf. Le Goff 1990: 7, 10; Jöckel 1987: 152). The verbal or textual aestheticisation of mental structures in myths, legends, and other narratives defines the dispositional nature of the imaginary. Representations are interpreted by Le Goff (1990: 20) as nodal points of expression oscillating between thought, memory, and sensibility. In that respect, aesthetic texts such as newspapers, autobiographies, diaries and letters, travel literature as well as poetic and other aesthetic sources such as dramas, songs, films, pictures, must be considered the most fruitful sources for a qualitative analysis of mentalities (cf. Le Goff 1986: 9, 13).

Both high- and low-brow literature are today considered an important part of the historical-anthropological data of the histories of mentalities (cf. Vovelle 1982: 53-54). In their ability to unite associative and cognitive, connotative and affective, mental and emotional aspects, they might even be considered privileged source material for the qualitative analysis of mentalities. Following Michel Vovelle (*ibid.*: 48), aesthetic texts are cultural manifestations that reflect the system of nonconscious collective representations in a particular manner, and therefore the interpretative employment of literary sources has two specific advantages: fiction – as a vehicle of images, clichés, traditions, myths, etc. – directly integrates the collective imaginary in its specific forms of representation, and secondly, fiction is able to register changes in sensibility much faster, especially short and conjunctural transformations of mentality (cf. *ibid.*: 57). Vovelle (*ibid.*: 47), for example, sees fiction of particular interest in deciphering meanings of family life, death, or love because literary sources are able to convey the psychological space inbetween social and literary reality and represent traces of the unconscious, such as feelings (cf. Peters 1985: 183-185; Burke: 1997: 176-182).

However, Vovelle (1982: 45) also points out the ambiguous feelings historians of mentalities have towards literary sources, which seemingly do not persist concerning so-called pragmatic texts. He stresses that literature, used exclusively as a serial source, often banalises sentiments to mere base tropes (*ibid.*: 57). Le Goff (1985: 174) moreover exemplifies that it is a major weakness of the literary text that the themes presented do not necessarily correlate with the collective consciousness because literature might operate according to codes independent of the historical environment. Literary scholars detect similar problems in the employment of literary sources by the historians of mentalities: an adequate understanding and interpretation of literary texts necessarily includes the knowledge of genre-specific conventions which have to be considered during the analytical process (cf. Peters 1985: 194). Moreover, despite the notion of the social construction of reality, the divide between social reality and fictionalisation remains a problem because the simple homology between literary depictions and socio-cultural facts can lead to the default of circuitous speculation on mental structures (*ibid.*: 185). It is hence assumed that historians of mentalities with literary ambitions either lack the methodological know-how or genre-specific instruments to discern the deeper layers of literary representations, or that they degrade fiction to an auxiliary source for the direct comparison of emotions and imaginations. Consequently, a methodological reorientation is needed which unites the methods of a history of mentalities with the preliminaries of Literary Studies.

5.1.2 Literary and Cultural Studies and the Concept of Mentalities

In their common aim to investigate cultural-specific attitudes and structures of meaning and representation, Literary Studies, Cultural Studies and the history of mentalities profit from taking each other into account methodologically (cf. Jöckel 1987: 161; V. Nünning 2001: 234). An integration of the approach to mentalities into Literary Studies has primarily given a variety of impulses for a new kind of literary history. Ursula Peters (1985) first incorporates the theories of mentality into the literary approach, disclosing the *conditio humana* and collective mentalities from medieval literatures. On the one hand, the concept presents a paradigmatic change within literary history and prevents anachronistic readings (cf. Peters 1985: 197-198; Bonheim 1994: 6). On the other hand, it can be criticised that this use of mentality constitutes another circumvolution of relations between the history of mentalities and Literary Studies, in the sense that a concept of mentality is applied both as auxiliary subject and heuristic tool within Literary Studies.[2] Most studies, dedicated to a cultural and literary analysis of mentality, for example by Vera Nünning (2001, 2004), Ansgar Nünning (2004a, 2004c) and the multifarious textual approaches in Kamm and Sedlmayr's (2007) collection, proceed in a similar fashion and sketch essential elements of (past) cultures before exploring a pre-defined mentality in the discursive manifestations or modification of the selected texts.

By contrast, the present study offers an interdisciplinary methodological approach of culture, literature and mentality that allows for the deciphering of mental structures of a specific collective, time, and space. It is by no means to be understood as a critique of literary historians' fascination with the histories of mentalities, nor intended to undermine the employment of the concept of mentalities as an auxiliary subject. Rather, the converging notion of Literary Studies and the concept of mentalities in the interdisciplinary frame of Cultural Studies offer a methodological approach for the contemporary analysis of mentalities, which, moreover, presents a possibility to extract mental structures in the representational constructions of aesthetic texts, cultural practices, and beyond. Consequently, the analysis of literary texts allows for an analysis of structures of mentalities as collective nonconscious phenomena, neither recognised by traditional cultural historiography nor literary history (cf. Nünning 2004c: 181).

Following Jürgen Kamm's (1996: 93) and Ansgar Nünning's argument (2004c: 185-186), the reperspectivation of the concept of mentalities within Cultural Studies offers an appropriate frame to employ literary methods in the analysis of pragmatic, literary, non-fictional and fictional textual sources for mental structures. Kamm (1996: 96) emphasises:

---

2 | For example see: Franz K. Stanzel (1969), *Der englische Roman. Vom Mittelalter zur Moderne*; John Bender (1987), *Imagining the Penitentiary. Fiction and the Architecture of Mind in Eighteenth-Century England*; Doris Feldman (1995), *Politik und Fiktion. Die Anfänge des politischen Romans in Großbritannien im 19. Jahrhundert*; Mary Anne Schofield (1990), *Masking and Unmasking the Female Mind. Disguising Romances in Feminine Fiction, 1713-99*; Peter Brown, ed. (2007), *A Companion to Medieval English Literature and Culture. C. 1350-C.1500.*

> [Der] Ansatz einer mentalitätstheoretischen fundierten Kulturwissenschaft [...] bietet aber gleichwohl ein interdisziplinäres Paradigma, das ausgehend vom Konzept des Kollektivwissens und mit textanalytischen Methoden der Sprach- und Literaturwissenschaft für die Beschreibung kultureller Prozesse anwendbar ist.

In that respect, a concrete analysis of mentalities based on textual sources and the instruments of Literary Studies can lead to a specific definition of mental structures and to a better understanding of other ways of life. Because mentality hypothesises in cultural practices, an analysis of cultural phenomena can reconstruct mental structures (cf. Kamm 1996: 94; A. Nünning 2004c: 180). From the broad perspective of source material on the notion of culture as text, it is discerned that every source problem of the histories of mentalities is essentially a problem of text. All texts present a viable source material for an interpretation of mental structures, while reading the text and deciphering the structures of representation demands an interdisciplinary approach, such as a confluent interpretation of linguistic, literary, and historical instruments. Although there are other methodological approaches such as Geertz' thick description, New Historicism, discourse analysis[3], or linguistic analysis, in the following I will argue in reference to Kamm (1996: 93-94) that Literary Studies offers the most equivalent instruments for interpreting mentalities, such as textual theory, literary theory, receptive theory, and narrative theory.[4]

5.1.3 Narratological Approaches

The narratological approach is particularly evident and successful for the interpretation of mentality due to its confluence of culture, literature and mentality in the essential human activity of storytelling. In *The Literary Mind* Mike Turner (1996: v) argues: "*Story* is a basic principle of mind. Most of our experience, our knowledge, and our thinking is organized in stories." Narratives are interpreted as fundamental means of worldmaking (cf. Neumann & Nünning 2008: 8), and stories constitute axiomatic ways of making sense of the world by ordering experiences, constructing notions of time and space, negotiating collective values, interpreting structures of meaning, generating knowledge and helping to form and stabilise identities, and thereby forging communities and express underlying structures of cultural constructions of meaning. Jerome Bruner (1991: 4-5) in his article "The Narrative Construction of Reality" defines narratives as instruments of the mind concerned with the construction of reality. Narratives are quasi-conventional forms that are culturally transmitted and follow standardised representations. Stories are

---

3 | Michel Foucault's history of madness (1956) or sexuality (1976-1984), for example, is as much a history of mentalities as an analysis of discursive practices. In this respect, *L'archéologie du savoir* (1969) can be understood as a methodological manual for a history of mentalities.

4 | The spectrum of literary methods for interdisciplinary approaches to mentalities, moreover, subsumes ideography, imagology, metaphorology, research on topoi and motives – basically all forms of textual interpretation that allow to detract structures of meaning from semantisised content, aesthetics, stylistic or rhetoric form (cf. A. Nünning 2004c: 188-189).

thereby identified as a symbolic system that supports a particular domain of knowledge. Consequently, not only language or texts function as *outillage mentale*, but also narrative structures.[5] Following the notion that stories are a strong tool of thinking, we can approach narratives as homologous to mentalities because both serve as equipment for orientation and integration. Narratives are also prone to the definition of mentalities as supra-individual, in the sense that all narratives are subjective notions of the world in need of interpretation, but nevertheless – whether factual or fictional – strive to convey a sense of universal truth or collective convention.

Narratives are omnipresent not only in a variety of literary genres, but also in everyday experiences, since basically all oral forms of communications involve stories in one way or another. Literary narratives range from traditional narratives like epic poetry, legend, myth, folktale and fairy tale to short narrative structures such as proverb, anecdote, sketch or the modern prose form such as short story, novella, and novel.[6] Most analyses of mentality are specifically based on narrative literature. Besides novels, myths, sagas and proverbs, research on mentality has been conducted on illustrations, travel literature, documentaries, and films.[7] Both written and oral narratives as well as fictional and non-fictional storylines offer an insight to the interpretation of minds and the mentality of people. Narratives as valuable "representations of collective consciousness" (Siikala 2002: 17) are moreover apt for an analysis of mentality because the history of mentalities has traditionally been interested in the perception and construction of the everyday life of which, as shown above, narratives as a means of orientation are an essential part. Because narratives resemble structures of everyday certainties, they can be used as a veritable source for the analysis of mentalities, and the methodological approach of narratology can reveal cultural and normative codes or dispositions of thinking, feeling, imagining and acting not only thematically alongside the main plot, but also in the narrative structures or the text/context relation.

In general, narratology describes the theory, discourse and critique of narrative, and the discipline is dedicated to the study of practices of narrative presentation and the extrapolation of its means of worldmaking. Narratology offers analytical or methodological instruments by which to extract typical constants, variables and combinations. Its object of analysis is text-based (in the wider sense) and considers elements common to all nar-

---

5 | Bruner's (1991: 20) article and his notion of narration as a "cultural tool kit" initiated cognitive narratology.

6 | For a history of the major forms of narrative literature see Robert E. Scholes & Robert Kellogg (1966), *The Nature of Narrative*.

7 | Peter Burke (1990: 77-78) comments that the historian of mentality Robert Mandrou examined over four-hundred titles of popular culture concerned with the escapist literature of chap-books of Blue Library generally revealing a conformist mentality. Jacques Le Goff (1990: 8-9) employs literary examples from Victor Hugo and Jean de Meun. For narratological analysis of mentalities also see Kay Kufeke (1999), *Himmel und Hölle in Neapel. Mentalität und diskursive Praxis deutscher Neapelreisender um 1800*; Eva Österberg (1991), *Mentalities and Other Realities. Essays in Medieval and Early Modern Scandinavian History*; Anna-Leena Siikala, ed. (2002), *Myth and Mentality. Studies in Folklore and Popular Thought*; Robert Fleischer (2007), *Mentalität im Film. Ein kulturelles Analyseraster multimedialer Texte*.

rative forms whether oral, written or material, pragmatic, poetic or prosaic, factual or fictional. From the 1960s until the 1980s, narratology was dominated by structuralist approaches and developed a variety of theories, concepts and analytical procedures, models mainly concerning literary fiction. Russian Formalists and French Structuralists regard collective functions of the narrative as apparent in the grammar of relations, the verbal or deep structure of the narrative.[8] With the renaissance of narratology and a wider definition of narrative since the 1990s, the classical approach has seen a major transformation. Postclassical narratology builds on the models and methods of structuralist approaches especially by supplementing them with concepts of Cultural Studies, expanding its objects of analysis to other textual phenomena and cultural practices, as well as extending it to questions of contexts and cultural functions of narrative.[9] Thereby the scope of narratological analysis has also gained interdisciplinarity and widened its object of analysis to other media. Whereas the founding fathers of narratology were preoccupied chiefly with literature, contemporary analysis also considers forms such as epic history, drama, opera, cinema, photography, comics, news, conversations, blogs, and hypertexts. The idea of intermedial, transmedial and transgeneric narratives moreover encompasses the understanding that other modes of narration, such as visual images, diagrams, sketches, notes or topographical maps, are integrated in literature. Moreover, as was shown before, the notion of narrative has even been employed to material textures and texts, for example the whole phenomenon of the city. Of course, each genre and each medium specifically forms the narrative, and thus terminologies developed for fictional narratives are not transferable to other forms of storytelling without modification and consequently enlarge the range of narratological approaches (cf. Neumann & Nünning 2008: 9; Heinen & Sommer 2009a: 1). In that respect it is right to point out that postclassical narratology presents a hotchpotch of narratological approaches. Ansgar and Vera Nünning (*ibid.*: 10-13) schematically identify eight paradigms[10] of which the contextual-narratological approach is of major interest to the analysis of urban mentalities in London novels.

This contextual-narratological approach is based on the notion that cultural values, norms, and ideologies find expression in narratives and are perpetuated by stories. Con-

8 | For seminal texts of classical narratology see Vladimir Propp (1928), *Morphology of the Folk Tale*; Northrop Frye (1957), *Anatomy of Criticism*; Claude Lévi-Strauss (1958), *Anthropologie structurale*; Franz Karl Stanzel (1964), *Typische Formen des Romans*; A.J. Greimas (1966), *Sémantique structurale*; Gérard Genette (1972), *Narrative Discourse*; Roland Barthes (1977), *Introduction of the Structural Analysis of Narrative*; Franz Karl Stanzel (1979), *A Theory of Narrative*; Michael Tietzmann (1977), *Strukturale Textanalyse*.

9 | Seminal texts of postclassical narratology include Seymour Chatman (1978), *Story and Discourse*; Monika Fludernik (1996) *Towards a 'Natural' Narratology*; David Herman ed. (1999), *Narratologies. New Perspectives on Narrative Analysis*; Brian Richardson (1997), *Unlikely Stories: Causality and the Nature of Modern Narrative*.

10 | (1) Contextual approaches in Literary Studies, (2) trans-generic and intermedial applications of narratology, (3) pragmatic and rhetoric narratology, (4) cognitive and receptive narratology, (5) postmodern and poststructural deconstructions of classical narratology, (6) linguistic approaches to narratology, (7) philosophical narratology, (8) other interdisciplinary approaches to narratology (cf. Nünning & Nünning 2002b: 10-13).

textualist narratology interprets narrative texts, especially narrative fiction, as an integral part of culture that legitimises cultural hierarchies or constructs identities. Ansgar Nünning (2009b: 59) defines contextualist narratology as an "integrated approach that puts the analytical tools provided by narratology to the service of a cultural analysis of narrative fiction." In the light of this, an interdisciplinary cultural analysis as well as the textual analysis of mentalities gains in profile by applying new categories of narratology. Kamm (1996: 94) argues that the verbal transformation of social constructions of reality is based on narratives in which speech acts are formally structured. Stories, in the sense of cultural narratives, are discursive units that depend on epochal, social and spatial structures (*ibid.*: 94-95). Hence the cultural narratological framework as an ensemble consists of narratives, which in turn function as a cultural worldmaking (cf. A. Nünning 2009b: 67). Literary narratives take an active part in the collective construction of the cultural narrative because stories are "a prime site for the construction of cultural knowledge" (Neumann & Nünning 2008: 17) creating cultures as "narrative communities" (A. Nünning 2009b: 61). In other words, "culture not only contains narratives but is contained by narrative in the sense that the idea of culture, either in general or in particular, is a narrative." (A. Nünning 2000: 359) Cultural narratology[11] therefore helps to disclose mental dispositions of thinking, feeling, imagining and acting in the dialectic of a narratological analysis of culture as well as a cultural analysis of narrative. Proceeding from the assumption that narrative fiction is a force in its own right highly involved in the generation of mentalities, cultural narratology then explores how the formal properties of the story reflect or shape mental structures. In this way, cultural narratology emphasises the interface between narrative structures and cultural discourses, values, norms, ideologies, and mentalities. Moreover, this content-oriented methodological approach notably focuses on dynamic processes of cultural transformations, thus on the negotiation of cultural meanings in a particular historical perspective.

Cultural and historical narratology describes the confluence of narratological, cultural, and historical questions and can be understood as a methodological equivalent to the interface of culture, literature, and history of mentalities. Ansgar Nünning (2009b: 53) argues:

> An alliance between narratology and cultural history can open up productive new possibilities for the analysis both of the dialogic relationship between novels and their cultural contexts and of the epistemological, historical, and cultural implications of narrative strategies.

He defines cultural-historical narratology as "a kind of integrated approach that focuses on the cultural analysis of narrative fictions and the ubiquity of narratives in cultures, both past and present." (Nünning 2000: 357) Thus, cultural-historical narratology forms

---

11 | Research has specifically been conducted regarding cultural issues such as gender, race, ethnicity, identity, alterity, history drawing from a range of cultural and poststructuralist theories, such postcolonial, gender, sociolinguistic, cultural history. For more example see Jürgen Kamm, Norbert Schaffeld & Marion Spies, eds. (1994), *Spuren der Identitätssuche in zeitgenössischen Literaturen*; Birgit Neumann, Ansgar Nünning & Bo Pettersson, eds. (2008), *Narrative and Identity. Theoretical Approaches and Critical Analyses.*

a valiant methodological approach for the analysis of mental structures. This methodological approach is necessarily two-fold: it is either dedicated to particular narrative phenomena in a specific cultural context[12] or it extends the cultural subject area to aesthetic genres (cf. Erll & Roggendorf 2002: 78-79). Historical-cultural narratology re-explores the confluences of cultural issues and literature from a narratological perspective, opening it up for transdisciplinary discussions, which, in its methodological and theoretical inclusions of anthropology, discourse analysis, and the history of mentalities, is consciously eclectic. Erll & Roggendorf (*ibid.*: 85-106) identify four approaches that focus on the confluence of the cultural-historical and literary preoccupations by way of narratology, one of which is the confluence of a history of mentalities and the anthropological-semiotic notion of culture in the exploration of collective standardisations of thinking. They emphasise: "Mentalitäts- und funktionsgeschichtliche Ansätze sind die zur Zeit wohl innovativsten und vielversprechendsten Wegbereiter einer kulturgeschichtlichen Narratologie." (*ibid.*: 107) The present analysis is centrally connected to this version of cultural-historical narratology and the history of mentalities.

The themes and the narratological structure of texts offer an insight into mental constructions of reality, and historio-cultural narratives can be seen in their socio-historical context and analysed with instruments of narratology. The correspondence of culture, literature and history is substantially based on the phenomenon of narratives, they stress emplotment as fundamental worldmaking and construction of reality, related to the everyday. Narrativity as a cultural form of communicating structures of meaning and narratives as a "vehicle of human knowledge" (B. Richardson 2000: 168) thus become the basis for the most informing analysis of cultural issues such as mentality. Narratological methods, theories of urban mentalities and the historio-cultural background information of the metropolitan lifeworld thereby enable a concise analysis of mentalities in non-fictional and fictional texts.[13]

---

12 | In his journal article "History of Events and the Revival of Narrative" Peter Burke (1991: 233-235) explicates that the French *Annales* School in their critique of Rankian event history and traditional historical narratives at first favour immobile structures only to progressively relate to literary narratives in their historical analysis. In that sense, the approach of the historians of mentality initiates a revival of narrative in historical research, which interprets historical narratives based on a narrative structure uniting place, time, and action (*ibid.*: 235-236). For Burke (1991: 237-241) such a new form of historical narration is a synthesis of the relations between event and structures, and borrowing largely from fictional prose, for example, includes a-chronological narration, multiple collective viewpoints, unreliable narrators, alternate closures, thickening descriptions, and microhistories. In *Time and Narrative* (1984-1988), Paul Ricoeur for example argues that all written history, even the mere structural history associated with the *Annales*, necessarily takes a narrative form (cf. *ibid.*: 233). Most prominently Hayden White in *The Content of the Form. Narrative Discourse and Historical Representation* (1987) sees historical narratives following literary narrative genres. Today this development has reached a stage where even the narrative structures of the *Annales'* historiographical texts are analysed with the assistance of narratological instruments of Literary Studies; see Axel Rüth (2005), *Erzählte Geschichte. Narrative Strukturen in der französischen* Annales-*Geschichtsschreibung*.

13 | For example see Martin Lindner (1994), *Leben in der Krise. Zeitromane der Neuen Sachlichkeit und die intellektuelle Mentalität der klassischen Moderne*; Wolfgang Lind-

Specifically the novel can be considered a prominent expression of mentalities and an influential medium for the construction of meaning. The narrative structure and the multifarious content of the novel offer an insight into the values, norms, structures of meaning as well as into dispositions of thinking, feeling, imagining and acting of a specific epoch or culture. Therefore, the present study proposes this genre as particular suitable for an analysis of mental dispositions.

Literary texts in general but narrative fiction in particular are notably apt for the analysis of mentalities due to the following qualities: (1) reference to real world subjects, (2) psychological content, (3) imaginary documents and depiction of the everyday, (4) plurivocality of discourses and its dialogical character and (5) double role of construction and representation, as well as (6) the novel's inherent transformability.[14] (1) Literary texts can be seen as the sum of specialised and habitual speech acts dependent on the same *modus operandi* as other pragmatic texts or cultural practices referring back to the contextual lifeworld. (2) The historians of mentality recognise that sources of the imaginary in general or novels in particular accentuate psycho-sociological topics and that their literary form offers a notion of a supplementary conscious. It is a genuine privilege of narrative fiction that through metaphorisation or focalisation novels are able to articulate inchoate thoughts and emotions and thereby represent mental dispositions. (3) Literary and artistic sources as documents of the imaginary are privileged material because they already include representations of real-world phenomena. Extended prose fiction depicts recognisable and common everyday cultural practices in character, plot and space and therefore presents a specifically suitable medium for the human experience in the field of mental dispositions. Thus the novel also functions as an expression of an existing political or social-cultural climate, the sensibility of its age as well as its world-views. (4) Literary fiction is of high value due to its ability to crystallise complex ideas of society and depict social constructions of reality in a compressed way (cf. Meyer 1989: 90; Lüsebrink 1993: 93; Grabes 1996: 36; Lotman 2001: 163-164; Grabes 2004: 86). The literary texts interconnect various discourses by recombining them in a seemingly arbitrary way, but thereby also reflect on the different perspectives united in this collage of represented mental structures. Novels are also conspicuous due to their multifarious forms, the complexity of their content, and their multiperspectivity. Aiming at a serious representation of life, large social groups can be depicted; various social and historical affairs or the change of a socio-political setting can be portrayed. Bakhtin (1998: 301) defines the novel's "heteroglossia" and "polyphony" as specific characteristics of the genre. The discursiveness and polyphony of the genre allows for various perspectives on epistemological, philosophical, socio-political or cultural questions and thereby the expression of wide-ranging attitudes and values (cf. A. Nünning 2004a: 101). (5) Furthermore, novels are so amenable for a study of mentalities because the textual structure of literary sources is understood as expression, product, carrier, or document of mentalities, while on the other hand literary works are monuments (according to Fou-

---

ner (2003), *Jugendbewegung als Äußerung lebensideologischer Mentalität. Die mentalitätsgeschichtlichen Präferenzen der deutschen Jugendbewegung im Spiegel ihrer Liedertexte.*

14 | For a detailed differentiation between narrative and novel analysis see Nünning & Nünning (2002a: 19).

cault) following their idiosyncratic logic in producing, constructing, assembling, and re-forming mental structures (cf. Meyer 1989: 88-90; Lüsebrink 1993: 89-90; Grabes 2004: 86-87). Thus, literary texts are specific in the way they communicate standardised structures of meaning; more often they problematise, question, and negate cultural clichés or taboos (cf. Meyer 1989: 90).[15] Specifically because literature is neither a mere reflex of and reflection on cultural practices or their underlying mental structures but activates variations, improvisations, and interpretation, it plays a leading role within the spectrum of cultural forms of representation. By way of thematic and narratological selection literary texts recontextualise and recombine the issues at hand and thereby redefine epochal structures of mentality (cf. A. Nünning 2004a: 101-102). (6) Thus, the novel is also an apt medium for an interpretation of mentality due to its inherent transformability: it stands out as the most malleable literary form, adaptable to a variety of topics and themes, but its flexibility shows itself in integrating and interconnecting other fictional or non-fictional text forms, sub-genres and categories (cf. A. Nünning 2004c: 191).

Additionally, one can argue that the genre of urban fiction in particular presents an apt source for the analysis of mentalities. According to Park, "[w]e are mainly indebted to writers of fiction for our more intimate knowledge of contemporary urban life." (Cit. in Lindner 1990: 251)[16] The early naturalist and realist fiction of the city was not more than a soft sociological approach to the city, but its narratological descriptions of the modern metropolis actually developed an intrinsic sense for a genuine urban way of life and its mentalities (cf. *ibid.* : 256).[17] Moreover, as was shown before, the city itself is not only understood as a text or literary *oeuvre*, but seen as a literary genre, resembles the novel (chapter 4.2.5). The writer Michael Butor (2000: 174) also rightly argues that since the rise of the novel in the eighteenth century the novel has largely been urban fiction, in the sense that it describes the urban or has its setting in the city. City and novel therefore relate to each other: the modern metropolis functions as a laboratory of the interconnectedness of space, time and collectives and the novel is especially fit to

15 | One has to bear in mind that there are "a number of ways in which everyday mental structures can be transformed by literary texts, e.g. by combining the mental structures of different groups, by singling out particular aspects of mentality of a group, or by inventing non-existing mentalities." (Meyer 1989: 90) Moreover, literary texts can be written to oppose a certain mentality or deliberately emphasise the mental structures of a specific minority group (cf. *ibid.*).

16 | In that respect, it has also been argued that city fiction functions as a workshop for literary ambitions (cf. Lindner 1990: 251). And certainly the literary corpus in this book pays tribute to the notion that writing urban fiction is a way to explore and possibly perfect not only one's writing but also narrative skill. Most of the famous novels by relevant English authors are set in London. Writers like Charles Dickens, James Joyce and Virginia Woolf developed new forms of narratology on the example of the metropolis while Joseph Conrad perfected his writing and compositions with his city novel *The Secret Agent* (1907). Recent debut novels are also often of the city genre.

17 | "Of course, these books are not sociology, but those who wrote them have one advantage over sociologists – they knew people." (Park cit. in Lindner 1990: 258) For more on sociology and urban fiction see Lindner (1990).

encompass events, characters, and settings in its literary form. While urban density is mirrored in novelistic discursiveness, the city's social heterogeneity finds expression in fictional plurivocality.

Volker Klotz in *Die erzählte Stadt* (1969) detects a fundamental affinity between city and novel. Reasons for this are to be found in the novel's content in regard to the prosaic and everyday, its flexible and open form, and its sceptical, cultural-analytical stance. He argues that the social and spatial scale of the metropolis requests the epical size of the narrative genre (cf. Klotz 1987: 429-430).

> Roman und Stadt erscheinen als zwei ähnlich veranlagte Systeme. Als Systeme, die weitgehend als Ganzes, in ihren Teilen und deren Beziehungen miteinander korrespondieren. Das aber heißt, im Roman findet die Stadt das geeignetste Instrument, ohne radikalen Substanzschwund in einen literarischen Status einzugehen. Und umgekehrt findet der Roman in der Stadt den Gegenstand, der unerbittlich wie kein anderer sein volle Kapazität fordert und ausschöpft. (*Ibid.*: 438)

Reichel (1987: 3) criticises that Klotz refers the thematic issue of space directly upon the aesthetic question of a particular genre. However, also Hoffmann (1978: 396), latest with Dickens sees urban reality and the narrative genre of the novel as converging. And in a sense, the initial definition of the city novel includes that its structure offers an expression of the city's character as such.

Importantly, thus, the genre's idiosyncratic logic of construction and conventions need to be taken into account when figuring out the mental structures within. While literary specificities have been identified, yet largely put aside by historians of mentalities (cf. Chartier 1988: 36; Le Goff 1990: 10), literary historians have pointed out that it is exactly the interrelation between a notion of lifeworld-specific constructions derived from the history of mentalities and literary stylisation that helps to negotiate between simple psychologisations of literature or relegations of aesthetic specificities to mere discursive practices (cf. Reichardt 1978: 160; Peters 1985: 197). However, conventions of literary texts open up another advantage of aesthetic products because they incorporate the possibility to expand imaginary borders of known experiences, thinking, feeling and acting to the limits of cultural possibilities (cf. Grabes 2004: 87-88). In this way, literature also moves along mental border(line)s of a time and place and hence serves as an important indicator of the underlying capacities of the cultural un-thinkable. Literary Studies helps distinguish these characteristics of literary texts as documents of the imaginary, of social attitudes or cultural habits, but also acknowledges the medial specificity of literature in its constructiveness.

The literary specificities with the greatest importance for the application of mentality are constructedness and fictionality, or text/context relation. Primarily, the way of interpreting mentalities through the texts' various functions allows laying bare aesthetic strategies that penetrate the sphere of meaning behind. Because mentalities are not explicitly formulated in literary texts but scattered in various functions of the text it must be the foremost exercise of literary analysis to consider the interrelatedness and discursive handling – or literary *outillage mental* – as belonging to a complex literary structure. Ansgar Nünning (2004c: 179, 188) therefore sees it as an imperative to first examine the discursive-, genre- and text-specific forms of representation with the help of linguistic and literary categories of analysis; second, these aspects of representation are to be analysed for the explicitly and implicitly mental-specific attitudes expressed within.

The decoding of the explicit and implicit manifestations of mentality in various functions of the literary text is best handled by narratological categories and models. Whereas each narrative medium and genre possesses its own narrative conventions, novel analysis serves most categories developed by narratology as the "prototype approach" (Neumann & Nünning 2008: 13), encompassing nearly all analytical characteristics of textual narrativity.[18]

In the context of the present analysis, central categories of a narratological approach to the novel are: (1) story and plot, (2) narrative situation, (3) fictionality, (4) experientiality, (5) events, (6) characters, (7) spatial setting, (8) sequentiality as well as (9) metaphoricity. (1) For an analysis of mentalities, the story informs on the general thematic preoccupation, while discourse reveals more about the forms of worldmaking. (2) Perspectivity and focalisation elucidate the conceptual point of view or the critical consciousness expressed in the narrative text. They thereby help to decipher the subjectivity of perspectives and the interpretation or construction of the lifeworld. Various narrative techniques expose perceptions of atmosphere or inform us of the characters' emotional life. (3) Postclassical and constructivist notions of narrativity have largely dissolved the difference between fiction and non-fiction, as narrative truth needs to be judged by verisimilitude rather than verifiability. The different degrees of mimetic and fictive premises can help in the evaluation of mental structures in the sense that the fictional constructiveness and polyvalence allow for an additional level of interpretation, for example consciousness formation. (4) Monika Fludernik (2006: 10) defines experientiality as one of the major functions of narratives. The term is defined as a quasi-mimetic evocation of real-life experience which means that the real lifeworld and fictional world can be interpreted as basically homologue (cf. *ibid.*: 18). Relying on a cognitive schema of people, experientiality makes it possible to compare cultural constructions of the lifeworld with formations of the narrated storyworld. Due to experientiality, mentality can either be revealed indirectly and alongside the main plot or in the depicted social relations and reactions. Due to experientiality, the fundamental dimensions of mentality (collective, time, space) are reconfigured in the storyworld, most notably in narrative elements, such as plot, characters, and setting. (5) For an analysis of mentalities it is especially interesting to follow the cause and effect of the story's sequence of events, or detect ruptures and reversals of traditional plot structures. (6) All characters of urban fiction as agents of action are first and foremost storyworld participants. Their constellation can indicate social structures and dynamic interactions, which are subject to specific norms and conventions or based on explicit and implicit mental dispositions. Characters, also the figure of the metropolis, induce action which can be of physical, verbal, mental, emotional, sensory, or perceptual kind and thus help to categorise them into doxic notions of thinking, feeling, imagining or acting. (7) The setting describes the story's location in space and time and is closely connected to the representation of mental determinants of

---

18 | For more on the narratological theory of the novel see Georg Lukács (1920), *Romantheorie*; E.M. Forster (1927), *Aspects of the Novel*; Franz Stanzel (1955), *Die typischen Erzählsituationen im Roman*; W. Rotter & H. Bendl (1982), *Your Companion to English Literary Texts. Volume One. Analysis and Interpretations of Narrative Prose.*

collective, time and space. Space as a condition of narrative is a central component of the fictional representation of a world and crucial for understanding the storyworld. Spatial representation, however, is not only relegated to the setting but are moreover indicative of spatial patterns, social hierarchies, as well as the feelings and the consciousness of characters. (8) As a basic category of human experience, time is also a central component of the fictional representation of reality. It informs on the temporal setting of the story and the related lifeworld; temporality thereby describes a chronological development from beginning to end and sequentiality a representation of transformations over time. Time thus also represents the rhythm of certain habits or the emotional life of the protagonists. (9) Finally, metaphors have an important narrative function that can expose mental structures in fictional narratives. Fludernik (2009: 109-128) specifically promotes the extension of narratology to an analysis of imagery due to the following aspects: operating on the narrative and figural levels, metaphors constitute thematic signifiers; global metaphors acquire a structural function in the narrative; metaphors share with the narrative the important feature of sense-making; the metaphor adds to the explanatory or semantic potential of the text.[19] Cognitive theory has also long proven the significance of metaphors in the construction of reality and thus metaphors can reveal components of the unconscious (cf. Fludernik 2006: 93-102).

Consequently, for the narratological text-based literary analysis of mentalities, the London novel is seen as a highly complex aesthetic construction, in which focalisation plot, character constellation, spatial and temporal setting, but also figurative speech such as metaphors refer to mental dispositions. Although a cultural approach addressing mentalities in literature profits from this narratological toolbox, the structural prerequisites of the novel need to be refined and revised before put in service of the concern for the literary and cultural analysis of mentalities. In reference to the theory of mentalities this study proposes a reconfiguration of narratology focussed on the analysis of collective, time, space, and collective space-time compressions to reveal narratological layers of thinking, feeling, imagining, and acting. The following sub-chapter explicitly deals with a spatio-narratological approach useful for an analysis of urban mentality in city novels.

5.2 A Spatio-Narratological Analysis of Mentality

Historians of mentalities regard any temporal or historical depiction, whether structural or chronological, as narrative and spatial image (cf. Piltz 2008: 83). Accordingly, the function of space is considered as predominant in literary narratives that are analysed for mental structures. Space will figure as the focus of the narratological analysis of mentality, first, due to the reperspectivation of Cultural and Literary Studies according to the Spatial Turn, second, in respect of the focus on London mentality as a particular spatial phenomenon, and third, with reference to the spatially induced notions of urban-generic

---

19 | Already Roland Barthes in his *Introduction of the Structural Analysis of Narrative* (1977) argues that a narrative can be considered a long sentence based on metaphoric relations. See also Heiner Müller's "Bildbeschreibung" (1984), a short prose narrative only consisting of metaphors that are compiled into one long sentence.

and urban-specific mentality. The poetology of space explored in this chapter specifically extracts narratological models of literary spaces by concentrating on the spatial constellations that represent and construct both urban-generic and urban-specific mental structures.

As was shown, spatial phenomena are central elements of literary narratives, both for the formation of fictional constructions of reality and as constituents of the created storyworld. Literature itself is, however, located in the spatialities of cultural practices and their culturally producing and produced materiality. Hallet and Neumann (2009a: 16) therefore state that narrated spaces encompass a two-fold perspective: representations of space allow for an understanding of cultural conceptions of space, and the literary construction of space also shows how these structures empower or subvert stereotypical spatial notions. Cultural spaces, literary representations of space and narrative constructions of space are thus interconnected phenomena (cf. *ibid.*: 19). Because the spatial imagery refers back to the collective, temporal and spatial determinants of mentality, narrative space is of central interest to cultural narratology and the interpretation of mentalities in fiction. The history of mentalities, in turn, can then be read as a valid approach to transformations of the socio-cultural semantisations of space. The depiction of space not only comprises the setting of a sequel of events but is always culturally semantisised: dominant norms, hierarchies, collective notions of centrality or marginality, Self and Other as well as subjective locations and identity formation are manifest in narrative space (*ibid.*: 11). Thus, spaces in fictional narratives can be interpreted as a confluence of lived space, cultural semantics, and collective or individual experiences (*ibid.*). An analysis of narrative space in fiction therefore takes into account the literary configuration and reconfiguration of culturally conceived spaces (*ibid.*: 22).

Literary Studies have long been concerned with narrative space.[20] Especially the spatial novel (e.g. travel, pastoral, utopian, urban fiction) has been of major interest.[21] Thematic studies deal with depictions and constructions of space, such as landscape or place, spatial motifs and metaphors, and spatio-cultural questions such as postcolonialism and borderlands, or gender and the city (cf. Würzbach 2001: 107).[22] Whereas there are many studies on the representation of space concerning the history of motives,

---

20 | See for example the tradition of literary atlases such as David Daiches & John A. Flower (1981), *Literary Landscapes of the British Isles. A Narrative Atlas*; Malcolm Bradbury (1996), *The Atlas of Literature*; Franco Moretti (1998), *Atlas of the European Novel, 1800-1900*. Also see studies on British regional writing, such as Hardy's Wessex, Eliot's Midlands, the Yorkshire of the Brontë sisters, the Lake Poets, Scot and Burns' Scotland etc. and of course the array of spatial studies on London literature.

21 | For studies on spatial fiction and the urban see Werner Gotzmann (1990), *Literarische Erfahrung von Großstadt (1922-1988)*; Martin Wentz, ed. (1991), *Stadt-Räume*; Manfred Smuda, ed. (1992), *Die Großstadt als ‚Text'*; Michael Ross (1994), *Storied Cities. Literary Imaginings to Florence, Venice, and Rome*; Elinor Schaffer, ed. (1996), *Spaces: Cities, Gardens and Wilderness*; Richard Lehan (1998), *The City in Literature. An Intellectual and Cultural History.*

22 | Also see Raymond Williams (1985), Pratt (1992), Fludernik (2009). For more see Leonard Lutwack (1984), *The Role of Place in Literature*; Joanna Rostek (2011), *Seaing through the Past. Postmodern Histories and the Maritime Metaphor in Anglophone Literature.*

tropes, and themes (cf. A. Nünning 2009a: 35), systematic narratological criticism has exclusively concentrated on narrative situation, characters and character constellations, or narrative sequence (cf. Frank 2009: 65). Ansgar Nünning (2009a: 34, 48-49) considers representations of space the main research question of contemporary narratology and literary representations of space in dire need of analysis within the context of the history of mentalities.

Because narratologists have privileged the analysis of time, narratological criticism of space has relatively been neglected. Ryan (2009: 420) argues that "most definitions, by characterizing stories as the representation of a sequence of events, foreground time at the expense of space." The development of narratology's interest in space in a sense runs parallel to the transformation of the discipline itself (cf. Würzbach 2001: 105-106; Dennerlein 2009: 15-37). After an early phase of scarce research on space in literature, structuralism with its emphasis of spatial models offers many useful concepts of narrative space (e.g. cf. Bakhtin 1998; Bachelard 1994; Lotman 1973, 2001; Hoffmann 1978).[23] Although research concerning space in literature was already established long before the Spatial Turn the new focalisation on space proved influential for the reperspectivation of Literary Studies in general and of narratology in particular. The Spatial Turn on the one hand emphasises cultural-spatial aspects in literary texts, such as the spatial semantisations of alterity, gender, and identity, while metaphorical terms like liminality, cognitive mapping, *lieux de mémoire*, etc. enter the analytical discourse of narrative texts on the other hand.[24]

Moreover, in their introduction to *Raum und Bewegung in der Literatur. Die Literaturwissenschaften und der Spatial Turn* (2009) Hallet and Neumann specifically stress the confluence of space and time, namely as spatialities and movement in literature;

---

23 | For the analysis of spatial narratives moreover see Maurice Blanchot (1955), *L'espace littéraire*; Bruno Hillebrand (1971), *Mensch und Raum im Roman*; Alexander Ritter, ed. (1975), *Landschaft und Raum in der Erzählkunst*; Jeffrey Smitten & Ann Daghistany, eds. (1981), *Spatial Form in Narrative*; Daniela Berhahn (1988), *Raumdarstellungen im englischen Roman der Moderne*; Dietrich Jäger (1989), *Erzählte Räume: Studien zur Phänomenologie der epischen Geschehensumwelt*; Hillary D. Dannenberg (2008), *Coincidence and Counterfactuality. Plotting Time and Space in Narrative Fiction.*

24 | Conversely, literature serves as a reservoir of spatial metaphors (thirdspace, contact zone) for other disciplines (cf. Frank 2009: 53). For Weigel (2002: 157), however, a spatially oriented Literary Studies is not only supposed to integrate cultural and geographical aspects of the Spatial Turn, but needs to develop into a truly *topographical turn*, which reperspectivates the narratological approach to the cultural historical transformations of spatial representations (cf. Hallet & Neumann 2009a: 28). Topography stresses the specific mediality and materiality of literary and fictional spatial representations (cf. Frank 2009: 61). Hallet & Neumann (2009a: 28) comment: "Nur wenn die bestehende literaturwissenschaftliche Analysekategorien konsequent mit raumkulturwissenschaftlichen Ansätzen verbunden werden, sind neue, disziplinär anschlussfähige und interdisziplinär relevante Einsichten in das Verhältnis von realen und literarischen Raumordnungen zu erwarten." In that sense, Literary Studies are not only supposed to adapt the concepts of other disciplines but to put them to the test in theoretical, methodological, and terminological terms (cf. Frank 2009: 56).

the essays included in their collection particularly take this notion of spatial relations into account. By contrast, the most recent and encompassing study of narrative space, Katrin Dennerlein's *Narratologie des Raumes* (2009) – although an interdisciplinary approach to the construction and a useful study of spatial representation – summarises space as absolute. Furthermore, the study lacks a conceptualisation of spatial functions and metaphors, which are of central interest in the field of spatio-narratological analysis of mentalities.

Although the present analysis does not neglect contemporary conceptions of absolute spaces, it is notably oriented towards notions of relational space. Spacing and (b)ordering put an emphasis on the positioning, demarcation, exclusion, and elevation also in the realm of narrative space. On the one hand, container spaces are virtually based on strict and stable relations between opposites, such as inside and outside, content and frame. On the other hand, narrative space not only registers physical boundaries, but also social spheres of relation and experiences of transgression and liminality. Moreover, relationality emphasises the interconnection between space and time and refigures Literary Studies in view of the spatio-temporal-turn, acknowledging the dynamics of collective time-space compressions within fictional narratives.

In the following this chapter concentrates on the narrative construction of urban space, identified before as the main determinant of London mentality. Narrative categories are defined as relevant for the literary topographies in city novels for an analysis of mentalities. These instruments are necessarily adapted to address, first, mentality as organon and rhizome, second, the determinants of mentality with an emphasis on the spatial, third, theories of urbanity, and fourth, the ambivalences of urban-generic mentality and factors of influence of urban-specific mentality. I will establish major categories for the analysis of spatial representations in urban fiction on the basis of their relevance for the interpretation of mentalities, namely literary topographies in general as well as boundaries, chronotopes, and metaphors in particular.

5.2.1 Literary Topographies

An analysis of literary topographies explores the representation and function of the landscape or cityscape in fictional texts. The relevance of topographical questions within Literary Studies lies in the interconnection between representations of space with the contextual real world. In that sense, imaginary spaces of literature retain the referentiality or experientiality to the spaces of the lifeworld. J. Hillis Miller (1995: 7) argues: "Topographical setting connects literary works to a specific historical and geographical time. This establishes a cultural and historical setting within which the action can take place." Thus, topography denotes the (de)scription of spaces, and in reference to literature encompasses all means by which spaces are textualised and semantisised, especially spacing, (b)ordering, and spatial metaphors.[25]

25 | J. Hillis Miller (1995: 1) calls Proust one of the greatest "topographical poets". For more on literary topography see Miller (1995), Weigel (2002), Böhme (2005), but also Ulrich Meurer (2007), *Topographien. Raumkonzepte in Literatur und Film der Postmoderne*.

From the various narrative categories identified by critics as constituent for spatial narrative fiction, the following must be considered as crucial for an analysis of mentalities and adapted accordingly: narrative situation and focalisation, story, event and action, characterisations and character constellations, setting, topoi, and tropes (e.g. cf. H. Böhme 2005b: IXX-XX; Dennerlein 2009: 1-2, 40-41; A. Nünning 2009a: 45; James 2008: 9, 14-15; Ryan 2009: 421-422).

The narrative situation and perspective is of pivotal importance as the constructed textual world is communicated by way of the narrator's or character's comments. Dennerlein (2009: 119-155) distinguishes between narration of space (construction of situations, settings and locations), description of space (non-situational spatial conceptions of space), and representation of spatial perceptions (perspective, focalisation, movement). Space as narrated or constructed, conceived and described, or perceived and reflected emphasises the subjective formation of space (cf. *ibid.*: 115). The interconnection between narrative situation and space carries three important implications for the analysis of mentalities: the confluence of space and visual perceptions suggests that the characters' human body is crucial in mediating and representing a sense of space. Accordingly, point of view and voice are relevant for the expression of gendered and other hegemonic spaces and becomes an essential marker for ideological discourses and the perpetuation of mental structures. Moreover, multiperspective representations of space juxtapose various constructions of reality, emphasising the range of dispositional possibilities.

Thereby literary topographies also preconstruct possibilities of acting. Narrative spaces present the background and schematics for the sequel of events unfolding in the course of the story. For the analysis of mentalities it is significant to see which spaces initiate particular stimuli causing a transgression of a border, and which spaces are characteristically semantisised to define specific grammars of behaviour. Due to this directive function – the identification of objectives, action, and sequel of events – their semantic fields can reveal structures of meaning and uncover dispositions of thinking, imagining, feeling, and acting.

Narrative spaces are constructed through agents by means of focalisation and action, but also through characterisation and character constellation. Although, according to Dennerlein (2009: 171), a categorisation of character types, traits, feelings, experiences and actions is not useful for the comparison of spatial narratives, it nevertheless helps to identify relations between space, social geography, and characters. Gesture, position, attire, clothing etc. are significant attributes in the characterisation of narrative personae and their location within social milieus. The constellation of characters as denoting specific and often opposing social spaces – such as rural and urban – can help to extract and interpret mentalities, while the stereotyping of specific characters can uncover urban types. Moreover, the literary cityscape that is created is a "composition of socially constructed spaces" (Jarvis 1998: 44). The composition and transformation of character constellations reveal dynamic social interactions that expose patterns of behaviour, norm, convention, and deviation.

Furthermore, the specific setting or the physical character of the narrated space itself can assist in the analysis of mentalities. Models of space are often dependent on the subgenre of the novel (i.e. utopia – island; Gothic novel – castle; *Bildungsroman* – voyage; state of the nation novels – city versus country), and the history of literature has shown that sudden thematic preoccupations, creations of a genre, and therefore constructions of spatial topographies coincide with cultural transformations or changes in mentality (cf. A. Nünning 2004a: 99). In that respect, spatial formations of wide vs. narrow, proximal vs. distant, filled vs. empty, paths vs. locations, homogeneous vs. heterogeneous, uniregional vs. pluriregional, stable vs. instable, and possible vs. impossible worlds not only imply a particular (un)thinkability of spaces but also the thematic significance of particular cultural issues. Semantic fields are defined by a specific spatial imagery, tropes and metaphors, which are essential elements in the analysis of mentalities. Hence, the construction of the literary geography by identifiable spatialities, such as landmarks, not only serves the experientiality of the narrative, or the orientation of characters, but also carries a significant symbolic function.

It was established earlier that novels best capture urban life, that the long narrative genre has mainly been urban and that the city novel constitutes one of the most particular genres of spatial fiction. Gilbert (2008: 105) confirms that the metropolis is the "site *par excellence*, of literary and cultural analysis of space". Research on urban fiction has exemplified that the emergence of the modern city furthered the development of the novel, which in turn shaped new forms and instruments for representing the urban. Due to this obvious confluence of the spatial form of the city and the narrative genre of the novel, literary topographies are of pivotal interest for an analysis of urbanity or urban-generic and urban-specific mentality.

Although the literary topology largely follows the narrative representation and construction of space in general, there are particular elements through which the fictional urban setting is devised differently. According to Mahler (1999: 14-17), the image of the city is created firstly by metonymically referring to prototypcial landmarks of city, and secondly by describing core aspects and attributes of a metropolis, such as constitutional toponyms of the city and the specific isotopes of its atmosphere. Insofar, the general urban setting takes into consideration the urban-generic, while the particular geography denotes the urban-specific (cf. Barry 2000: 6, 20). Moreover, the fictional city also includes an imaginary city which is purely fictive, created in a process of what Mahler (1999: 33) calls "*city-making*". While the mimetic aspect is emphasised by the reference of the London novel to a specific city, fictive elements nevertheless are of great importance.

Urban fiction integrate notions of an abundance of stimuli, such as dominance of visual and other sensual experiences, stressing metropolitan consciousness, mental processes, beliefs and emotions. Thus, the city novel employs the narrative situation to depict the manifold, changing, contrasting, effective stimuli of the urban realm. The narratological study of perspectives and focalisation thus exposes emotionally loaded subjective and collective experiences, which makes it possible to decipher collective dispositions of feeling. Also, the analysis of narrative space – understood as the field for action – has a significant function in the examination of urban fiction. Urban theories draft the city as a place of collective spectacle and drama. These (inter)actions are of an isolated individual and collectively interconnected nature, which brings into focus both to singular characters and character constellations. Moreover, the urban phenomenon is primarily a social scene of interaction; literary topographies aesthetically take up the scenario of social urbanity in narrative structures, for example character constellations. Concerning the aesthetisation of an urban setting, the notion of topological boundaries mirrors the urban dichotomies that are important for the interpretation of urban-generic ambivalences. However, the dynamics of the city put the "intersection of narrative and place, time and space" (Gilbert 2008: 120) of literary topographies into perspective. Movement in space, the flux between map and tour, chronotopic constellations, urban rhythm or the spatialisation of time are of great relevance to the textual analysis of urban narratives. Devices like the traffic signal and the public clock (set against private time) are essential in the temporal organisation or rhythm of the urban and have become fundamental symbols of the social organisation of the material metropolis as well an the representation of the imaginary city. Being spatially constructive, the urban novel has also developed its very own metaphors, symbols or tropes to represent the city and its urbanity. Some of these are mythic and in a sense nomothetic, such as the opposition between Jerusalem and Babylon. Others are idiosyncratic and often integrate well-known city images (e.g. Big Ben). Of course all these elements of literary topography finally have to be seen in concordance with aesthetic forms of fragmentation, montage, juxtaposition, and formal patterns (cf. Ryan 2009: 424-425).

5.2.2 Boundaries

The first of these narrative elements, which will be scrutinised more closely, the boundary is a spatial narrative device which, acknowledges relations between text, space, and culture. Because spacing and (b)ordering, for example by spatial binaries, create structure and organise space, relations of far and near, up and down, open and closed are important for the literary representation of space. The line between the two polarities constitutes the border between spatial fields. This spatial boundary emphasises the opposition between different semantic notions of present and past, nature and culture, freedom and dependency, etc. which serve as significant markers of mental structures. In this way, the literary topography of borders and oppositions, or the textual space, helps to decipher the codes of a specific culture, or semiosphere (cf. Lotman 1973: 441). Recognising London as one particular sphere of meaning, London texts can then expose mental dispositions. Therefore, I confer with A. Nünning (2009a: 37) who values the boundary as the most important topological marker of literary space.

Yuri Lotman in *Die Struktur des künstlerischen Textes* (1970) is the first to describe the boundary as central topological element of cultural representation.[26] According to him, the topological spatial opposition of up and down is interpreted as a non-topological, ethic opposition of good and bad or life and death, which is retranslated into a topographical opposition of heaven and earth, mountain and valley, surface and underground city (cf. Lotman 1973: 330-331). The difference between these two worlds, for instance life and death, can then be identified by a topographical borderline, for example the river Styx as separating the world of the living from that of the dead (*ibid.*: 356). Another substantial binary concerns the relation between open and closed, denoting the difference between strange, hostile, cold and homely, warm, secure, such as in the urban

26 | Originally, Lotman (1973: 316) especially regards the problem of the 'artistic space'. The later translation only refers to 'literary texts' because Lotman exemplifies his concept of the boundary especially in forms of poetry.

topographical opposition of house and street (*ibid.*: 344).[27] As a spatial variant of the good/bad opposition Lotman (2001: 174) thus identifies spatial notions of Self/Other. This polarity does not only mark an epochal shift in spatial construction, but also exemplifies the fusion of geographical and ethical space or the confluence of locality and morality (*ibid.*: 172). Analysing the topographies of narrative texts therefore allows to reconstruct the cultural-specific topological structure as a particular lifeworld and people's social construction thereof.

Following Lotman (1973: 357), the plot can be reduced to one basic episode, namely the successful or failed crossing of a frontier as the basic topological feature of narrative space. Narrative is born by characters crossing structural boundaries of cultural space. According to Lotman (*ibid.*: 348-350), the narrative consists of a sequel of events which are induced by a character transgressing the border from one semantic field into another. Because the border between two spaces is constitutes the divide between two moral orders, an event as the crossing of a boundary into forbidden realms always implies deviating from a conventional order or violating a norm (cf. *ibid.*: 351-357). This in turn might help to understand borders as spatialised doxic frontiers or frames of specific mental dispositions, while the collective crossing of a border can be indicative of a transformation of mentality. Furthermore, the approach implies that independent characters belonging to different semantic fields are brought into contact by the plot (cf. Lotman 2001: 199). The literary topography defines a strong analogy to its personae, in the sense of a determinist relation, in which the space is like a stage set on which certain conventions are exercised (*ibid.*: 197). Although most of the narrative personae are static and stabilise semantic relationality, a second group of characters is mobile, crosses borders, induces narrative events, and violates norms (cf. Lotman 1973: 355-357). In that sense, the world-view communicated in the text basically depends on narrative structures of plot, character constellation, and space as significant concepts (*ibid.*: 364). Boundaries therefore not only constitute topographical spheres of the storyworld but also illustrate non-spatial structures (*ibid.*: 347).

However, Dennerlein (2009: 30) argues that certain spatial issues cannot be resolved by relational (b)ordering and Dreyer (2006: 24) as well as Frank (2009: 68) criticise Lotman's concept for being useless for the depiction of hybrid spaces. However, Hoffmann (1978: 589) earlier comments that although the semantic fields at first sight appear like absolute space, they are nevertheless porous due the transgressable frontier, and because of semantic spacing they are internally structured by relations. Lotman (1973: 344) explicates that the boundary partitions textual space in disjunctive and impermeable spheres of everyday action and ideological conflict, he also stresses that these "conflicting systems do not replace each other but enter into structural relationships" (Lotman 2001: 164), giving rise to new relational orders. So even in Lotmanian terms the literary topography rather constitutes a complexity of spatial relations dependent on subjective perspectives.

In their introduction to a collection of essays on 'boundaries' (*Grenzen*), Dennis Gräf and Verena Schmöller (2009a: 12) define the border as "*Denkeinheit*" – 'a unit of think-

27 | Also see Lotman's (2001: 185) examples of home and forest as equivalent to home and homelessness. Experiences of the pseudo-home include spaces like camp, madhouse, or flight (cf. *ibid.*: 191).

ing' which is spatial, semiotic, and metaphorical and thereby not only represents structures of thinking of a particular culture, but also serves as a mark of cultural processes of transformation or a change of mentalities.

> Grenzen können [...] so etwas wie 'Mentalitäten' repräsentieren, zeigen sie doch, wer zu welchem Zeitpunkt wo welche Grenze zieht, überschreitet und die damit auch verletzt, sie erweitert, partiell zurücknimmt, de(kon)struiert, thematisiert oder problematisiert. (*Ibid.*: 9)

In reference to the theories of mentalities, it has been shown that mental structures as nonconscious phenomena themselves lie on the border region between "the unstated and the stated, silence and discourse, orality and literacy" (Hutton 2002: 3). In their dispositional nature and as a nonconscious range of possibilities they also define "mental barriers" (Le Roy Ladurie cit. in Siikala 2002: 18) of the thinkable. As the concept of urban-generic mentalities shows their rhizomatic structure (itself a spatial form) is constituted by eight pairs of ambivalence. In connection to Lotman's principle of binary semantic oppositions, such as Self and Other, the urban-generic ambivalence of strangeness and familiarity can be seen as spatialised in literary topographies. Hartmut Böhme (2005a: 597-598) shows how the collision of opposing cultural topographies, the breaking of Self/Other boundaries or the inversion of intercultural frontiers indicate a crisis of homogeneous cultural orientation and its transcendence by heterogeneity. In this sense, the oscillation of boundaries indicates, amongst others, a displacement of cultural identity, often initiated by a border crossing such as expedition, travel, tourism, trade and of course migration (cf. *ibid.*: 599-602). Consequently, we can read Lotman's mobile character, crossing the border, as belonging to both semiospheres (cf. Frank 2009: 69). Similarly to Simmel's stranger and Park's marginal man, this figure stands inbetween as long as he is not fully integrated or adapted to the new semantic field, or as long as a change in the layout of the boundary has not moved him back inside the system (cf. Lotman 1973: 361). Insofar, Lotman's concept is indeed applicable for an analysis of hybrid space.

With regard to urban boundaries, borders in general and those of the metropolis in particular are also at the centre of Simmel's topological preoccupations. He understands the boundary as a social act that becomes spatialised in the near and far, closed and open, inside and outside.[28] Urbanites' defence and adaptive mechanisms such as intellectualism, blasé and reserve initially serve as internal borderlines that prevent direct contact with strangers in the urban public. As shown before, the manifestation of an urban condition is due to a particular interrelation and screening between the external city and the internal life of the metropolitan; they define the boundary between the physical urban body and the urbanite's psychology (cf. Frisby 2001: 71-72). For Weinstein and Weinstein (1993: 112), "[t]he specific characteristics by which Simmel defines the metropolitan mentality follow from its formative structure of the double boundary." It describes the relation between urban individual and society and its inherent paradoxes of combining ambivalences of the bounded and the boundless, the finite and the infinite (cf.

---

28 | In "Brücke und Tür" Simmel (1909) defines bordering as an essential human trait of orientation. More on Simmel's notion of the boundary see Schroer (2006: 66-78).

ibid.: 103, 108). Insofar, the urban narrative can be deconstructed as a series of partitions, for example according to the opposition between natural and cultural: walls, hallways, rivers, hills, passageways, fences, windows, bridges, highways, tunnels, passes, etc. This certainly holds true for literary characters that traverse the boundary between non-city culture and urbanity, but every literary city also constructs its idiosyncratic boundaries within. For example, Tinkler-Villani (2005a: xi) argues that

> the binary oppositions which create the dynamism of writing on the city are indeed more correctly described as binary structures, for they are necessary and fruitful, multiplying sets of double perspectives by means of which the writers or narrators engage with the multiplicity of urban experience.

Lotman (2001: 191-202) himself does not only perceive inner textual boundaries between Moscow and St. Petersburg as oppositions of city and country, capital and province, metropolis and city, but also concerning the manifestation of topological boundaries within one particular literary city. The internal urban system of spatial binaries then opens up two central schemes of plot: first, the quest of a newcomer to the city for success and happiness, and second the milieu studies in which characters struggle to decode the inner workings of the city (cf. Hoffmann 1978: 393). Hence, the portrait and ecological city novel are not only based on a specific plot structure and character constellation, but also on particularly ambivalent topological constructions of attraction and repulsion.[29] In this way, binary oppositions and configurations of ambivalence are written into the urban body's fabric, the urban texts and the urban mind. In turn, the ambivalences become intelligible in an analysis of topographical boundaries.

5.2.3 Chronotopes

According to Kantian epistemology, the experience of space is necessarily related to time. Similarly, in narratives, especially the plot as a syntagmatic concept involves the experience of time (cf. Lotman 2001: 151), which is generally connected with motion through space or temporal extension of time through space. For example, Lotman (*ibid.*: 172) notes that a journey to heaven or hell is always thought of in geographical terms; as death is described as a movement in space, the spatial figures as a progression of time (cf. *ibid.*: 173). Spatial movement and events as well as actions and their dynamics in time are to be seen as significant determinants of mentalities because movement also represents (un)consciousness. All in all, movement and space-time emphasise how the semiotic system is in a state of constant flux; its permeability and relationality can be read as an indicator of the transformation of mentalities. The following passages will discuss a selection of methodological approaches in the context of Mikhail Bakhtin's concept of

29 | This ambivalence is first and most notably developed by Dickens, who constructs an analogy of characters and space, either in the materialisation or institutionalisation of people or the personification and anthropomorphisation of the metropolis. Hoffmann (1978: 393-394) states that Dickens' literary topography sums up the material and social life of the city by presenting the variability, vitality, and heterogeneity of the urban realm.

the chronotope that help decipher dispositions of mentality based on the interconnection of urban space, time, movement, and rhythm.

Bakhtin (1998: 84) defines the chronotope or literally "time space" as "the intrinsic connectedness of temporal and spatial relationships that are artistically expressed in literature."[30] Adapting the concept of inseparable time-space for literary criticism, the chronotope is almost a metaphor that describes time and space as artistically visible in "movements of time, plot, history." (*Ibid.*) Consequently, "[a] literary work's artistic unity in relationship to an actual reality is defined by its chronotope." (*Ibid.*: 243) Constituting time as the "fourth dimension of space" (*ibid.*), the chronotope defines the representation of time in images of space, while temporality lends meaning and dimensionality to narrative space. Bakhtin identifies various chrontopes and their initial semantics. Significant chronotopes are those of (1) road and encounter, (2) castle and history, (3) salon and politics, or (4) threshold and crisis. The chronotope of encounter on the road describes the intersection of the spatio-temporal paths of a variety – class, religion, nationality, age – of people (*ibid.*: 243-244).[31] The chronotope of the castle, as in Gothic or historical novels, is saturated with time in the narrow sense, namely one of historical past, while the chronotope of the salon is the amalgamation of the contemporary political public with the private (*ibid.*: 245-247). The chronotope of the threshold (staircase, front hall, corridor, street, square) figures as a moment of crisis, such as downfall, decision, resurrection, renewal, epiphany (*ibid.*: 248). The variety of chronotopes corresponds to particular genres as well as to stable ways of aesthetic thinking initially elucidating the mentality of a specific lifeworld.

Especially the image of the threshold stresses, in contrast to Dennerlein's (2009: 169) understanding, that Bakhtin's concept of the chronotope constitutes a useful supplement to Lotman's boundaries (cf. Frank 2009: 72). A closer look at Bakhtin (1998: 250-251) reveals that, similar to the boundary, he sees events structured around the chronotope by which the metaphorically represented space-time becomes plot-generating. Chronotopes are vehicles of motion, progress and transition, return and regression, as well as turning points and moments of reversal. At the same time, narrative representation of meaning for Bakhtin (*ibid.*: 258) is intrinsically connected to the chronotope: "Consequently, every entry into the sphere of meanings is accomplished only through the gates of the chronotope." Although there are elements which are not directly subject to temporal or spatial determinations, most abstract elements – especially philosophical ideas, social generalisations and explanations of cause and effect – gravitate towards the chronotope (cf. *ibid.*: 250). Furthermore, the literary chronotope is an essential representation of emotions and values (*ibid.*: 243). In this sense, spatialisation of time or temporalisation of space and movement culminate in a form of chronotopic thinking which can be interpreted as highly instructive to mental structures.

30 | For the relevance of Bakhtinian theory in contemporary Cultural and Literary Studies see Smethurst (2000) or Ken Hirschkop & David Shepherd (1989), *Bakhtin and Cultural Theory*.

31 | Because "the road is always one that passes through *familiar territory*, and not though some exotic *alien world*" it stresses the "*sociohistorical heterogeneity* of one's own country" (Bakhtin 1998: 245).

According to Gerhard Hoffmann's (1978) theory of narrative, space-time relations form the basic constituents of the storyworld. For him, not only is the plot defined as a sequence of events, but the narrative structure of the text is constructed by paths (*ibid.*: 590). Paths themselves are established by the movement of characters, which connect several dynamic situations in a novel and thereby add to the unity of the story (cf. *ibid.*: 80, 592, 595-628). By leading towards, opening new, or returning to familiar spatialities, direction structures the narrative space (*ibid.*: 590). Seen as an expression of movement, events or actions can range from long-distance journeys to utter immobility (*ibid.*: 591). Hoffmann (*ibid.*: 594) shows that immobility, for example, indicates the equilibrium of individual and society or self-determination and heteronomy, but also implies harsh social conditions, which can eventually trigger a renewed need for mobility. Texts consist of fixtures on spaces and elements of relative movement, such as static and mobile characters, and while the former belong to socio-cultural structures, the latter inherit a higher degree of freedom of choice in behaviour (cf. Lotman 2001: 151). In that sense, the level of mobility stresses the dispositional nature of mentality as a range of behavioural possibilities and exposes the norms and conventions that frame mental structures.

Especially through the phenomenon of movement, time is symbolised in space because relational spatialities encompass notions of change and continuity (cf. Hoffmann 1978: 356). Besides the historical-linear conception of time as the progressive element of the story, cosmic-cyclical notions of repetitive movements uniting past, present and future, the psychological or existential temporal experience, as in stream of consciousness, emphasise the relativity of experiences in time, space, and motion (*ibid.*: 357). Consequently, the choice of space and perspective always entails a specific notion of time or space-time-relation. Accordingly, the textual semiospheres constitute oppositional temporal spaces: the different use of temporal structures refers to the various historical conceptions of time (*ibid.*: 358) and thereby reveals different temporal mentalities. Moreover, variations in the construction of time through space also establish opposing ontological states, such as the busy, fast-track life of the city versus the idyllic, slow-paced life in the country (*ibid.*: 361). The situational combination of narrative elements like space, time, event, and character thus depends on the historical frame which allows for a historical interpretation (*ibid.*: 355).

In reference to Gaston Bachelard's analysis of the perception of space, Hoffmann (*ibid.*: 6, 41) sees the representational level of atmosphere and feeling as a pivotal function of narrative space. Bachelard's *La poétique de l'espace* (1958) analyses the lived experiences of architectural types and stresses the power of spatial imagination over structures of feeling. His phenomenology of space (understood as a complex space-time) endeavours to assess the metaphors of imagination and marks out the "edges of imagination, exploring the recesses of the psyche, the hallways of the mind." (Bachelard 1994: vii) The spatial image of an individual consciousness, also exposes its qualitative inter-subjectivity (cf. *ibid.*: xix, xxiv). According to Bachelard (*ibid.*: xv), the poet in particular is able to convey the limits of consciousness because poetic images constitute "sudden salience on the surface of the psyche, the lesser psychological causes of which have not been sufficiently investigated." As the poet can reveal the "*dreaming consciousness*" (*ibid.*: xx), we can delineate that it is also possible to convey the collective (un)consciousness or mentality in poetic texts. Bachelard (*ibid.*) stresses, however, that the phenomenology of the imagination is less one of the mind, but rather one of the soul.

Within his "topo-analysis", Bachelard (1994: xxviii) concentrates on places that are influential on the inner life of people: for example, the house as a shelter with its secret rooms, drawers, chests, corners, is constructed by the imagery of intimacy sated with emotions or memories (*ibid.*: xxxvi). On the other side of the spectrum, the immensity of spaces like the sea, the forest, or the night touches upon intimate sensibilities of inner peace and carries a particular oneiric value (*ibid*: 186). Interestingly, according to Bachelard (*ibid.*: 186), the forest "accumulates its infinity within its own boundaries" – a phenomenon which also holds true for the urban realm. Boundaries are of pivotal importance in Bachelard's (*ibid.*: 211) topoanalysis, most specifically in describing the dialectics of outside and inside, open and closed. In their emotional binaries of claustrophobia and agoraphobia, these contradictions define feelings of suppression or freedom. Moreover, the door as an inbetween space or boundary is emphasised in its narrative possibilities: "Why not sense that, incarnated in the door, there is a little threshold god?" (*ibid.*: 223) The poetic image can be counted as a small threshold idol itself because it translates between the two kinds of spaces; intimate and exterior interrelate (cf. *ibid.*: 201). Hence, Bachelard's phenomenology of space combines notions of boundary and chronotope.

Perspective and focalisation of the subject importantly determine the perception of space: perceptual space in fiction is either constructed as a panoramic overview or as a riddled tableau from a mobile point of view. In his sociological anthropological inquiry *The Practice of Everyday Life* (1984), Michel de Certeau specifically explores the conceptual and perceptual experience of the city in cultural practice. He considers the narrative actions of urban denizens and specifies the practices of spatial organisation in the bipolar distinction between "map" and "itinary" or the procedures of "marking boundaries" by the voyeur and the "enunciative focalizations" (de Certeau 1988: 116) of the walker, aligning spatial form and perception with specific practices and actors. De Certeau (*ibid.*: 117) derives these differences from the distinctions between place (*lieu*) and space (*espace*): while place describes a particular location, position, stability and belonging, space exists as an ensemble of time variables and an ensemble of movements. This demarcation between place and space is related to the division between maps (*carte*) and tours (*parcours*); while the map is the place for the projection of totalising and normative observations, often from an elevated point of view, the itinerary is a discursive series of operations on street level (cf. *ibid.*: 118-122).[32] De Certeau (*ibid.*: xxi) exemplifies how the city as text demands a practice of space which is a compilation of the processes of reading/consuming and writing/producing the city.

In this respect, he constructs an analogy between place, elevated point of view, map, consumption, reading, voyeur, social planning and public norms on the one hand and space, street level, tour, production, writing, walker and urban myths and legends on the other hand. Lifted from the street's anonymous mass, the emplaced subject becomes a voyeur of the urban texture. The inherent distance in form of a celestial eye allows the spectator to look down upon, totalise and read the urban text. The panoramic view thereby creates a totalitarian reader (city planners, cartographers) and renders "the complexity of the city readable, and immobilizes its opaque mobility in a transparent text."

---

32 | Map: "The girl's room is next to the kitchen." Tour: "You turn right and come into the living room." (De Certeau 1988: 119)

(*Ibid.*: 92) This organisation of space is mainly achieved by marking out boundaries (*ibid.*: 122-123). However, de Certeau (*ibid.*: 127) also stresses the mediating role of the boundary as encompassing both con- and disjunctions; he exemplifies how the frontier always constitutes an inbetween space which is composed of "interactions and interviews [...] exchanges and encounters". Hence, the boundary betrays the abstract order it strives to create, as rivers can be crossed and picket fences open views (cf. *ibid.*: 128). Consequently, the panorama is purely theoretical, an image of the city that is opposed to the intertwining daily behaviour of the city. By contrast, urbanites' daily practices contest the imposition of walking the streets, writing the city and creating "spatial stories" (*ibid.*: 92).

> The ordinary practitioners of the city live 'down below,' below the thresholds at which visibility begins. They walk – an elementary form of this experience of the city; they are walkers, *Wandersmänner*, whose bodies follow the thicks and thins of an urban 'text' they write without being able to read it. (*Ibid.*)

The various forms of writing form an intertwining network, spatialising the city, but simultaneously eluding legibility (cf. *ibid.*: 93).

> Their story begins on ground level, with footsteps. They are myriad, but do not compose a series. They cannot be counted because each unit has a qualitative character: [...]. They weave places together. [...] They are not localized; it is rather that they spatialize. (*Ibid.*: 97)

Walking, according to de Certeau (*ibid.*: 98), has an "'enunciative' function" in appropriating the urban text by ways of actualising possibilities fixed by the constructed order in varying directions, increase the possibilities in constructing shortcuts or exhibiting new prohibitions by a subjective selection process. In that respect, the rhetoric of walking creates a mobile sequence of "phatic *topoi*" (*ibid.*: 99).

Legibility thus obliterates spatial practices, whereas walking or "[p]edestrian speech acts" (*ibid.*: 92) can free urbanites from geographical representations and grasp meaning beyond mere orientation. Although a map might be able to trace paths and transcribe trajectories, it will always miss the "act itself of passing by" (*ibid.* 97). Moreover, the symbolic mechanisms creating spatial stories evade the urbanistic systematicity of the map (cf. *ibid.*: 105). In fact, however, stories constantly negotiate between the two sorts of determinations by place and space, looking and walking, map and tour: the planned space is transformed by walkers, while the written text is conceived anew from the distance of the spectator: "Description oscillates between the terms of an alternative: either *seeing* (the knowledge of an order of places) or *going* (spatializing actions). Either it presents a *tableau* [...], or it organizes *movements* [...]." (*Ibid.*: 119) In this sense, the rhetoric of the city is a confluence of grammar and figurative speech, a result of condensation and movement, visual and kinaesthetic experiences, or the sum of the concept of the city and urban practices.

In sum, the chronotope is an important measure of experiences in the city and a significant implication for the urban-generic as well as urban-specific mentality because it brings to the fore the chronotopic character of the metropolis itself by focusing on the connections of the urban with time, history, movement, rhythm, perspective, and atmosphere. According to Bakhtin (1998: 252), "each chronotope can include within it an unlimited number of minor chronotopes". This means, especially due to the discursive complexity of the city novel, that urban narrative fiction figures an array of dialogic mutually inclusive, coexistent, interwoven, overlapping, opposing, contradictory, and complexly interrelated chronotopes. The chronotope of encounter, for example, features the social space and the common ground of social behaviour. In that sense, size and heterogeneity of the urban setting emphasise the importance and function of this chronotope in urban literature, especially with regard to an analysis of urban mentality. The chronotope of history stresses traditions and ruptures, makes memory and forgetfulness an issue of the novel and consequently emphasises the unconscious inertia and transformation of mentalities. In urban fiction, the setting is a range of concrete historical buildings or its verticality represented in above and underground spaces. The chronotope of salons and parlours as places of discursive practices reveals ideas and passions of the socio-political frame. In that respect, this chronotope opens up a look on worldviews, ideologies or even temporal mentalities. As already mentioned, the chronotope of the threshold is highly important because it specifically unites the notion of the boundary with that of space-time. Moreover, this chronotope – as a moment of crisis and break in life – is highly charged with emotions and values as it exposes pivotal moments in the representation of mental configurations of ambivalence and urban-generic mentalities.

In his analysis of space in narrative fiction, Hoffmann (1978: 397) argues that city novels in particular emphasise a confluence of space-time, movements, as well as the complexities of physical and emotional perspectivity. He (*ibid.*: 388-444) pays specific attention to the city novel by pointing out that the psychological experiences of the modern metropolis were integrated into the long fictional narrative. Hence, urban structures of feeling such as isolation, fragmentation, and atomisation are represented in the correlation of characters with the narrative space-time (cf. *ibid.*: 407). In reference to de Certeau's spatial stories, the interchange between mapping of or perambulations through urban spaces is signalled by various focalisations, oscillating between the stability of the god's eye view and the myriad movements of the interior monologues and as a technique of actualising urban spaces. This perspectivity refers to the collective consciousness of the city as expressed in the perceptions of urban rhythms, which are important factors in the delimitation of urban-specific mental structures.

5.2.4 Metaphors

Metaphors are not only important structural elements of stories, but they also create spatial relations in the narrative texture and are thereby notably related to the novel's literary topography. De Certeau (1988: 115) points out that *metaphorai* in modern Greece denote vehicles of mass transportation. The term metaphor therefore implies semantics of mobility in space and time because it describes "*ways of moving into something different (manières de passer à l'autre)*" (*ibid.*: 109). From this notion he delineates that stories are spatial trajectories which traverse, organise, select and link spatialities (cf. *ibid.*: 115). Thus, de Certeau (1988: 129) argues, spatial operations instead of defining places (topical) are rather topological. A metaphor, however, also belongs to the *locus communis* (*Gemeinplatz*) which is as much a place as cliché, topos (e.g. the *locus terribilis* of the Gothic novel or the *locus amoenus* of pastoral literature), as well as trope, a rhetoric device.

As such, metaphors oscillate between the literal sense of a place and spatial semantisation. Metaphors are devices that translate between the topological, topographical and semantic models of the text, between imaginary and symbolic spatialities (cf. Mülder-Bach 2005: 403). Hence, spatial topographies, such as islands, mountains, crypts, tunnels, passages, bodies, etc. carry as much metaphorical weight as spatial concepts (*ibid.*: 404). Therefore, metaphoricity is closely connected to Lotman's spatial semantics and Bakhtin's chronotope. For example, boundaries are necessarily metaphorical in the way that they denote gaps (differences) and thresholds (similarities). Bakhtin (1998: 248) points out that "the chronotope of the threshold is always metaphorical and symbolic", whether openly or implicitly so. De Certeau (1988: 129) emphasises that "[b]oundaries are transportable limits and transportations of limits; they are also *metaphorai*." Because metaphors are notoriously ambiguous, they also convey contradictory meanings, not only of particular places but also in regard to events.[33]

The classical function of metaphors in rhetoric, mind-style, and structure underpins the relevance of metaphors for a narrative analysis of mentalities. Kamm (1996: 89-90) considers mentalities as social premises of communication that presuppose an analogical construction of the world. Sarah Heinz (2007: 31-38) explicates that metaphors are an analogy which, in their "as if"-construction, always allow for differences: unlikely aspects are put in relation to each other by the metaphor, through which the analogy creates unity from heterogeneity. In regard to cognitive metaphor theory, the pivotal role of this narrative device for delineating mental dispositions becomes especially apparent. Analogical thinking as a basic structure of rationality is considered essential for an approach to the lifeworld (cf. *ibid.*: 20-23). This implies that new knowledge is put in analogy with the already known, while hermeneutically it describes the conflict between identity and alterity (*ibid.*: 39-40). The metaphor leads to a semantic extension by disfiguring but also constituting meaning and hence essentially proofs the transformation and adaptability of metaphors (*ibid.*: 50-51). Consequently, metaphors are useful instruments of orientation, classification, categorisation and construction of reality (*ibid.*: 29-31).

Following the theory of mentalities, we can thus understand metaphors as part of the *outillage mental*, or with cognitive psychology as an instrument of thinking and constructing social reality. Due to the translational characteristics, metaphors are able to grasp non-sensory abstracts in imaginary or emotional categories (*ibid.*: 28). But as with all systems of signification, a particular habitus for example can be seen as mainly topical (*ibid.*: 29), especially concerning the expression of general feelings like sadness, anger, love, happiness. Metaphors can therefore be defined as condensed structures of thinking, while topoi in general can be understood with Ernst Robert Curtius (1948)[34] as stable clichés and schemes of thinking and representation. Peter Burke (1997: 179) argues that

---

33 | For example, the river is not only clearly distinguishable from the land and constitutes a fixed boundary between two shores, but its waters are also a fluid and illimitable entity with a particular directionality (cf. Hoffmann 1978: 346).

34 | Ernst Robert Curtius' (1948) *Europäische Literatur und Lateinisches Mittelalter* is generally regarded as the foundation of topoi analysis.

because nonconscious mental structures become explicit in metaphorical expressions, the history of mentalities primarily needs to be a "History of Metaphors":

> if we are trying to describe the differences between mentalities, it seems useful to focus on recurrent metaphors, especially those which seem to structure thought. Obvious examples in the history of the West are the metaphor of the world as an organism (a 'body', an 'animal'), and the metaphor of the world as machine, and the shift from one to the other [. . .].

Burke (*ibid.*: 180) stresses that dominant metaphors are especially valuable to the histories of mentalities, and also for a general analysis of mentalities, as the transformation of mentalities helps identify seizures between certain eras and differentiate thinking within a particular period. As shown before, this "power of metaphor" (*ibid.*: 181) is acknowledged by later historians of mentalities like Jacques Le Goff and Roger Chartier, who pay specific attention to representations or the imaginary, for example the metaphoric significance of visual images (cf. *ibid.*: 181-182). In that respect, we can establish with Le Goff (1985: 173) that "topoi are the framework of mentalities" or with Burke (1997: 162) that structures of mentalities are entrenched within metaphors and symbols.

Also stereotypes and clichés that find expression in literature by way of intertextual references, literary figures and landscapes, often according to a specific genre (colonial, travel, picaresque, educational, historical novel), are part of a fixed mental imagery that helps decode mental dispositions (cf. Blaicher 1987a: 16-20).[35] However, while stereotypes strengthen ideologies, clichés are necessarily nonconscious structures that form language, thought, emotion, and action (cf. Zijderveld 1987: 27-29). Clichés are defined as repetitive and routinised elements that function as a protective mechanism against overload. By reducing complexity, these stereotypical depictions serve as a means of orientation and guarantee people's need for security, stability, certainty (*ibid.*: 32-35). Distinguishing between insiders and outsiders, clichés are crucial to a sense of identity (*ibid.*: 38).

As was shown before, the Spatial Turn has induced the spatial metaphorisation in various disciplines. New Cultural Geography, for example, is heavily dependent on metaphorical structures of thinking and conceptualising urban space. Also, any description of the urban realm is dependent on city images and the urban imaginary. Because the city is densely tropological, the thinking of the city is specifically metaphorical. The metaphorisation of the city is based on allegory, metaphor, metonymy, and symbolism of nomothetic and idiographic kind. The urban images that serve the orientation and coordination of metropolitan space are doxic in nature, indicating dispositions of everyday actions and urban habitus. Most importantly, urban images entail the ability to unite various aspects of the city. Moreover, images are highly emotional and thus significant in toning the perception of reality. Because even urban geographers and historians unanimously seem to agree that narratives in their varied perspectives are able to provide an animate picture of urban perception and behaviour, they particularly refer to the fictional city when trying to grasp or comment on a specific feel of the urban.

---

35 | For more on prejudice, stereotype, cliché and mentality in literature see Blaicher (1987).

While according to Lynch's (1977: 6) call for a relative stability of urban images, the stereotypical repertoire of urban tropes conforms to the ready-made assumptions of the observer, it might also induce a further blunting of the senses and passivity by making active perception redundant (cf. Sennett 2000: 87). Whereas the under-represented imagery of the urban emphasises the dominance of particular mental structures that might as well advance on ideological images, the frequent clashes of countervailing metaphors and metonyms instead stress the configurations of ambivalence in urban-generic mental structures. In his theory of the theming and metaphorisation of the urban landscape, Gottdiener (2005: 306) points out that due to the double function (connotation/denotation) of the sign, also the metaphor is semantically highly ambiguous. Metaphors are always "*polysemic*" (*ibid.*) because the translational process (de Man) between proper and figurative sense opens up an array of possible interpretations. This process creates a surplus of meanings and alternative or subordinate images underlining the ambivalent and processual nature of the value system metaphors are founded on. Because tropes also denote inherently ambivalent subjects, such as the warming yet destructive fire, they specifically help identify urban-generic mentalities as influenced by configuration of ambivalences. Moreover, understanding the heterogeneity in the unity of analogy, the metaphor is also a viable attempt to perceive the city's conditions. The concordance of proper and figurative sense emphasises relationality and stresses the importance of metaphors in the construction of urban literary topographies as relational space.

The representation of the urban emerges from the interplay of symbolic constructs and mimetic references. Insofar, the view of the metropolis is tainted by certain preconceptions; major 'readings' or images of the city employed as well as metaphors have offered a series of lenses to make the city legible. Following Shields (1996: 229), we can argue that "[r]epresentations are treacherous metaphors, summarizing the complexity of the city in an elegant model." Images, figures, tropes, metaphors and certain motifs of the city are relevant for the "rhetoric of imagining London", which can lead to a "greater comprehension of 'what London feels like' [and] 'how London creates an impression on the mind'" (Wolfreys 1998: 10). A change in the use of metaphors can reflect the city's transformation, the varying concerns of its 'readers' as well as a change in the perception of the city itself (cf. Sharpe & Wallock 1987: 37). Metaphors and images become the frames through which the illimitable material of the city can be mentally and imaginatively perceived more easily, serving the "deeply felt need to comprehend the city in visual terms". (*Ibid.*: 36) In general, the city metaphor has been employed to symbolise the world, human civilisation or the nation state; this analogy can either be isomorphic or be perceived as antagonistic (cf. Lotman 2001: 191). Major city tropes are (1) body and machine, (2) city and country, (3) Babylon and Jerusalem, (4) network and labyrinth, (5) palimpsest, (6) *flâneur*.

(1) There are manifold, contradictory, protean, immanent literary images, such as that of the city itself as bewildering labyrinth, alienating crowd, dangerous street, isolating room, or oppressive routine, wild jungle, calm ocean, roaring monster, spreading disease, etc. Certain city tropes describe the metropolis as theatre or stage, market, or festive place. Whereas spatial relations imply the city's phemenology and habitus, organic metaphors stand for the functional relations, or the mechanisms of the city's system. Especially the city-body metaphor is not only important in urban studies in general (e.g. cf. Sennett 1994; Ackroyd 2001); in the nineteenth century the most important

metaphor was the organism as a body or part of a body depicting the urban as wen, cancer, stain, fungus, facial blemish, carbuncle or polyp, beast, monster, and marching giant. As will become apparent in the later analysis, the analogy between body and city is still a very prominent image in contemporary fiction (see chapter 8.1.2). Anthropomorphised images analogise the city as feminine, mostly as a Babylonian whore or femme fatale denoting the attraction and danger of the urban lure.

(2) Decline and moral condemnation of cities find a tenuous support in the trope of city and country and the idyllisation of country life. While the city is predominantly seen as a place of disordering barbarity and corruption, virtues are considered distinctly pastoral. Already with Dickens the country is the space of happiness, while London is portrayed as monstrous, wondrous, phantasmagorical, a place of alienation and abnormality – a space of unhappiness (cf. Hoffmann 1978: 632). The relationship between metropolis and province or between city and country is a specifically English metaphorical and tropic tradition (e.g. cf. Raymond Williams 1973; Kamm 1997; Barnett & Scruton 1998). In English literature the city/country antagonism is thus very much exploited, presenting the dichotomies of future/past, renewal/tradition, culture/nature, male/female. Although life in the nation's capital is often unavoidable to earn one's living, there always remains a nostalgic longing for the traditional way of life or a belonging and national identity rooted in the countryside.[36] Nevertheless, as Brogan (1977: 149) points out, this "Arcadia is notoriously a city man's view on the countryside." Thus, the rural mentality remains one of the crucial ways of defining the city mind. But even in contemporary city novels, attributes of cosmic nature (wind, clouds, sun, moon, stars) remains important for the exploration of the citizens' *conditio humana* because similar contradictions between (human) nature and culture are constructed within the city itself (cf. Hoffmann 1978: 389-390).

(3) Consequently, the city contains its own antitype. Just like the various spectres of metropolitan life, the representations of the metropolis come in varied forms from the extremes of urban apotheosis and anti-urban horror-vision (cf. Hertel 1997: 7).[37] Cities are therefore caught in a general ambivalent imagery oscillating between rise and fall, good and bad, light and dark, production and consumption, past and future, utopia and dystopia. Western notions have followed the dual biblical image of Babylon's urban chaos counterbalanced by the idealised heavenly and peacefully ordered city of Jerusalem. In their moral allegories the city has come to represent both decadence and perfection, in Christian tradition resembling the spatial contradictions of hell and heaven.

---

36 | Barnett (1998: 333-335) discusses the paradox that although London is one of the world's largest capitals and most English people live in towns, Englishness is so strongly related to the countryside. He argues the denigration of urban life as potentially undermining the construction of a national identity (cf. *ibid.*: 339-340). A similar phenomenon applies for Australia, whose urban population makes up eighty-nine percent, but in literature and film the bush myth is more important for the constructions of identity than urban images.

37 | Carl Schorske (1977) identifies three major areas of urban self-perception of the last two hundred years: the city as virtue, the city as vice and the city beyond good and evil. He also places this more or less diatomic character of urban perception in the context of the historical realities of the corresponding epoch (cf. Sharpe & Wallock 1987: 7; Hertel 1997: 7-8).

This polarity of meaning, however, is urban-generic throughout the centuries regardless of the particular city; their imaginary cartographies live on in the metaphorical repertoire until today.[38] With the example of St. Petersburg Lotman (2001: 194) for example shows that city imagery is necessarily dependent on this inherently dual understanding. The imagery of the city as Babylon and Jerusalem serves as a master metaphorical ambivalence in the urban literary tradition. The trope shows that cities are praised and decried, depending on whether their inhabitants are seen to live in the centre of civilisation or the hub of moral poisoning (cf. Brogan 1977: 151; Rossiaud 1990: 139-140). Schorske (1977) and Raymond Williams (1985) have shown that the verdict on the city is largely dependent on the stance of pro- or anti-urbanites, but that this opinion of the city is transmutable throughout the ages.

Nevertheless, the image of the sinful city seems to predominate (cf. Fischer 1984: 14): the ruined and guilty city is already a major theme in the sixteenth and seventeenth centuries (cf. Lotman 2001: 193) and Rousseau's eighteenth-century verdict of cities as burial pits of civilisation (cf. Handlin 1977: 19) reads like Mumford's or Baudrillard's twentieth-century notion of the doomed city. The metaphor of the city as Babylon encompasses various notions of the city at once: it is jungle, voracious giant, whore, and machine. First, it implies the heterogeneity characteristic of city life, where all kinds of people meet and mingle who never entirely understand each other leading to non-communication and confusion. Second, the density and congestion of urban life stresses the consequences of overcrowding for the uprooted, displaced and excluded, namely deprivation, decline, disease, violence, corruption, perversion, and crime. In that sense, the Babylonian city is inhabited by a particular pariah personae, such as prostitutes, strangers, homeless people, and criminals. Massey (1998: 265) shows that space is always an element of both order and chaos and as such this dominant figurative duality primarily acknowledges the spatial absolute arrangement and the relational (dis)orders of the spatial form of the city. As part of the imaginary, the trope achieves, however, to represent more than the mere topographical structure of the city, namely a sense of the urban feel.

---

38 | Rossiaud (1990: 139) quotes examples from the twelfth century that either decry or elevate London, such as Richard of Devizes, a monk at Winchester: "I do not like at all that city. All sorts of men crowd together there from every country under the heavens. Each race brings its own vices and its own customs to the city. [...] Therefore, if you do not want to live with evildoers, do not live in London." On the contrary William Fitzstephen, a contemporary of Father Richard, argues: "Among the noble cities of the world that are celebrated by Fame, the CITY OF LONDON, seat of the Monarchy of England, is one that spreads its fame wider, sends its wealth and wares further, and lifts its head higher than all others. [...] The citizens of London are everywhere regarded as illustrious and renowned beyond those of all other cities for elegance of their fine manner, raiment and table. The inhabitants of other towns are called citizens, but of this they are called barons." (Cit. in *ibid.*) In his poems William Blake depicts early nineteenth-century London as both demonic and abundant of universal humanity. Modern and postmodern representations are locked in this dualist relation (e.g. cf. Schorske 1977: 99; Benevolo 1980; Blij 1982: 364-365; Schulz 1980: 265-266; Fischer 1984: 18; Harvey 1985: 250). For contemporary applications of the city trope for the analysis of London fiction see Ball (2004), Cuevas (2008a), and Deny (2009).

(4) Today's preferred urban metaphors, even though some of them have a long tradition as symbolic expressions, all share the emphasis on a matrix, which incorporates and connects elements of time and space echoing the chronotopic character of the metropolis. Metaphors of the network are encapsulated and complex topographies which do not only structure space and social practices, but also represent a specific way of constructing and experiencing the urban (cf. Böhme 2005b: XXI). In that sense, the image of the network pays heed to the intelligibility of postmetropolitan space and simultaneously emphasises the connectedness of the city, its interactions and relationships within the space of flows. The metaphors are especially strongly interwoven with the intrinsic interconnection of space, time, movement, rhythm in the city and the subjective experience thereof. While the city as stage is a ready-made topography, in the network metaphor of the mosaic of the city's connections remains illegible until one sees the whole picture. Maze and labyrinth especially express the struggle for orientation in the city; while the former has a dead end and thus implies that the subject will be lost forever, the labyrinth has a centre, a goal and objective, as well as a way out. The image of the labyrinth, which often functions as a structuring device, has persisted from classical through contemporary writing. The labyrinth forms an irregular, twisting network with only one path leading to the centre. Caught in between the walls and paths, one is caught in a sequence of fragments and unable to see the system in its totality. One can loose oneself at every turn, return to an earlier place, or stand next to the place one is seeking without knowing it, with only a boundary between.

> Because the design of the labyrinth simultaneously represents a puzzle and a solution, a journey and an arrival, it embodies the way in which urban texts can be seen as both maps and routes, as descriptions and projects, portraits of streets and guides within them. [...] The labyrinth signals duality well because it figures both time and space, becoming and being. [...] This is the dichotomy between the confusion the labyrinth has come to symbolize and the formalized visual pattern the image calls up-as [...] in human terms between the wanderer and the mapmaker. (Faris 1991: 38)

The metaphor of the labyrinth is thereby strongly connected to both the persona of the *flâneur*, who follows a certain path of even chaotic or unknown patterns, and the 'voyeur', who knows and constructs the outline of the network of possible paths. The trace of the path through the labyrinth also highlights the interdependence between city and text.

(5) The image of the palimpsest[39] constitutes a spatial imagination that reads the complex relations of times and spaces in the metropolis as multi-dimensional layers of writing.[40] The adage is that previous inscriptions of cultural coding underlie the present

---

39 | Palimpsest is Greek (*palin psen*) and means 'scraped again'; a manuscript page was written on, scraped off, and used again. *The Archimedes Palimpsest*, the work of the great Syracusan mathematician copied onto parchment in the tenth century and overwritten by a liturgical text in the twelfth century, is probably the most famous example of a palimpsest.

40 | Genette describes Proust's work as "a palimpsest in which several figures and several meanings are merged and entangled together, all present together at all times, and which can

one; it stresses the possibility of uncovering endless unexpected inscriptions of past and present in the cityscape that are waiting to be read. The trope thus inherits social, temporal, spatial, and textual dimensions. This image is the most popular in contemporary urban theory as well as in contemporary London novels. Groes (2011: 14) comments: "The key postmodern tropes present the city as text, as narrative, as palimpsest, as a narrated labyrinthine space that can be circumnavigated with the eyes and the mind."

In 1845, Thomas De Quincey published an article with the title "The Palimpsest of the Human Brain" as part of the sequel to his *Confessions of an English Opium Eater* (1822) and thus initiated all subsequent figurative use. He visualises the idea of the palimpsest with a roll of parchment that served as a conservatory for separate generations of literary production (cf. De Quincey 1968b: 344). Whereas earlier writing has been erased and overwritten, the palimpsest features diverse layers or aspects apparent beneath the surface called *scriptio inferior*. In De Quincey's (*ibid.*: 341) words: "A palimpsest, then, is a membrane or roll cleansed of its manuscript by reiterated successions." He specifically uses the image of the palimpsest to show how memories are written in the human mind and overlap. Dillon (2007b: 1-3) points out that before De Quincey's literary ambition the image of the palimpsest was merely a palaeographic oddity, but over time the idea has developed into an interdisciplinary concept – also within Urban Studies.

In a way, the palimpsestic city renders time visible. It is thus not only an image of the urban chronotope, but constitutes a very particular space-time compression. In this sense, Barry (2000: 48) argues that "[a] 'palimpsestic' way of seeing [describes] perceiving through the city several layers of time, several epochs, simultaneously". The palimpsest metaphor constitutes a spatial imagination that reads the complex relations of times and spaces in the metropolis as multi-dimensional. The metropolis is to be seen analogical to a palimpsest due to its physical layers of materiality, the coexistence of hybrid social spaces, and the historicity of its memory. Augé (1997: 16) points out that the palimpsestic urban memory communicates with the inhabitants' memories, provoking and challenging the palimpsest of the urbanites' minds. The city manufactured by monuments is a space of heterogeneous historical expressions, and every individual walking through the city comes across personal and collective memories (cf. *ibid.*). In this way, the city as a whole concentrates and mixes meta-narratives with individual stories. Consequently, the palimpsest refers to an imaginary disposition of collective memory conveying ideas of change and transformation.

However, postmodern critics such as Augé (1995: 34) also argue that contemporary hyperspatial culture emphasises time as a series of ever-changing and perpetual presents which undermines orientation. Olalquiaga (1992: 35) for example interprets the simulacrum as exemplifying how "boundaries between past, present, and future are rendered useless and nominal." The perpetual transience becomes all-encompassing as places are never completely erased and non-places never fully constructed. Augé (1995: 79) sees urban space continually creating "palimpsests on which the scrambled game of iden-

only be deciphered together, in their inextricable totality" (cit. in Dillon 2007b: 5). For more on Proust's notion of the palimpsest see *A la recherche du temps perdu*. Also see chapter 6.4 where the literary palimpsest is identified as master metaphor with significant indicators of London's mentality.

tity and relations is ceaselessly rewritten." As everything is simultaneously historical and contemporary, temporal and non-temporal, place and non-place, the image of the palimpsest in transience stresses the simulational tendency of the city. In a sense the urban texture, overwritten again and again, becomes unidentifiable from a former original, the metropolis transforms itself into a hypertext.

(6) The character devoted to the reading of the network is the *flâneur* (cf. Benjamin 2002: 430).[41] In reference to the palimpsestic city, the *flâneur* adrift in the metropolis represents a constant act of mapping and inscribing the cityscape. On the street, this urbanite is faced with a never-ending series of partial visibilities and close-ups. He only experiences the city in a specific array of signs and reconstructs the city in his imagination through the lens of perceived urban fragments.

In his seminal work *Passagen-Werk* (Engl. *Arcades-Project*), the cultural and urban semiotician Walter Benjamin engages in a philosophical analysis of the metropolis by reflecting on the human experiences in the city which are defined by the city's characteristic as historical repository or temporal dynamic. In section M "The Flâneur", Benjamin (*ibid.*: 416-455) explores Baudelaire's characterisation of the figure and draws a homology between author and character in the sense "that both epitomize the mentality and sensibility of the nineteenth-century petty bourgeoisie." (Weinstein & Weinstein 1993: 56) The *flâneur* is represented as a metropolitan male, middle-class/bourgeois dandy figure, who walks the streets for pleasure and is characterised by his voyeuristic gaze, which serves as a form of visual consumption (cf. *ibid.*). This semi-detached perspective also serves as an intersection between himself and others, although it sets him apart from the general crowd and forces his utter isolation within the urban masses (*ibid.*). Due to his dream-like reverie through the metropolis, the *flâneur* is as much delirious walker and restless wanderer as superficial idler and socially superfluous wonderer (*ibid.*: 56-57).

Benjamin identifies the *flâneur* with Edgar Allan Poe's "The Man of the Crowd" (1840), and similar to the story's narrator, the figure's habitus oscillates between reading and writing, surveillance and urban performance, while his perspective changes from window to street-level. The *flâneur* constructs reality according to his wanderings, the images and atmosphere he observes or perceives along the way. Bakhtin (1998: 159) already points out that the metaphoric significance of literary types, who carry around their own little worlds, constitute their own chronotope. In this sense, we can read the urban type of the *flâneur* as a chronotope in its own right; on the one hand he is a monad totally disfigured from the city's time-space, while on the other hand his gazing and strolling fragmentises urban life.

In his treatment of *flânerie*, Benjamin (2002: 433) moreover refers directly to Simmel for theoretical support. According to Weinstein and Weinstein (1993: 59-60), "the type is amenable to Simmelian analysis because it shares boundary-crossing and mediating attributes with such figures as the stranger and the adventurer". We can also identify

41 | For more see Gerd Stein, ed. (1985), *Dandy - Snob - Flâneur. Dekadenz und Exzentrik. Kulturfiguren und Sozialcharaktere des 19. und 20. Jahrhunderts*; John Rignall (1992), *Realist Fiction and the Strolling Spectator*; Richard D.E. Burton (1994), *The Flâneur and His City. Patterns of Daily Life in Paris 1815-1851*; Keith Tester, ed. (1994), *The Flâneur*; Harald Neumeyer (1999), *Der Flaneur. Konzeption der Moderne*; Stephanie Gomolla (2009), *Distanz und Nähe. Der Flaneur in der französischen Literatur zwischen Moderne und Postmoderne.*

the *flâneur* as a typical blasé person. The *flâneur*'s detachment from involvement, his loneliness in the crowd, and elevated (intellectualised) stance make him similar to Simmel's cosmopolitan stranger. We can draw this circle of comparison further to the work of the early sociologists, to identify the *flâneur* as participant observer, and with the life-story method the figure can be seen as an explorer of unknown urban practices.

Furthermore, the *flâneur* is an intellectually reflexive walker whose construction of reality cannot be separated from his interaction with the urban, nor his mind from the city (cf. Amin & Thrift 2002: 10). It is the lens of his sensibility that links space, language and subjectivity, thus enabling him to read the city and reveal its intimate secrets (*ibid.* 11-13). However, this intrinsic knowledge of the city is in need of assistance by instruments of interpretation, such as routine technologies, historical guides, photographs (cf. *ibid.*: 14); in De Quincey's *Confessions* it is intoxication by drugs and the recording in his confessions, for Woolf's *flâneuse* in *Mrs Dalloway* (1925) it is the sound of Big Ben and her memories, in Iain Sinclair's psychogeographical ramifications in *London Orbital* (2002) it is graffiti and photography along the way. Hence, the *flâneur* is caught up in urban production and can be seen not only as the personification of urbanity *per se* but also as the urban chronicler, urban writer, and cultural critic.

With this conception we have come a long way from the initial definition of the *flâneur* as a mere spectator strolling for pleasure. This shows that the urban trope of the *flâneur* is transmutable and still applicable in postmodern aesthetics and in relation to the post-Fordist metropolis. Moreover, the point that the figure is not gender-neutral can be refuted if the metaphor is stretched. Indeed, there are other sub-types of the *flâneur* which emphasise either their gender or class-specific negative, namely the prostitute or the homeless/tramp as street-walkers *per se*. Nevertheless, the most important difference is constituted by the gaze: while women are points of attraction walking public spaces, the homeless are virtually invisible for the urban crowd. Additionally, the trope is highly mutable, ranging from literary figures such as voyeur and visionary to detective and spy, artist and journalist, passive idler and active intellectual. The description of the urban trope of the *flâneur* moreover suggests similarities to other urban types such as the revenant, the narrator, or the psychogeographer. All these adaptations of the literary type reveal varying mental dispositions.

To sum up: the analysis of spatial construction has shown that spacing and bordering depend on spatial scales, spatial dichotomies and spatial metaphors. In narrative fiction the most important devices of constructing literary urban topographies which can be analysed for mental structures have been identified as boundaries, chronotopes, and metaphors, all of which figure different spatial scaling from meta-structure of the state, the city itself, its social fragmentations down to the urban personae and bodies. In that way, the following narrative analysis will extract urban-specific mental dispositions from London city novels.

Analysis of London Mentality

6 Cityscape

The signifying system of the cityscape takes into account the cultural production of spaces that express and conceptualise a distinct regional personality through their textual meaning, while the urban text that presents "a storied urban landscape" (Suttles 1984: 299) reflects the society of its habitués. In other words, the literary cityscape of contemporary urban fiction is symbolic of London culture, its social order, and mentality. The cultural semiotics of the New Urban Sociology help identify the "cultural distinctiveness" (Harvey 1985: 266) of urban life and urban-specific inner urbanisation.

To read the metropolitan condition and extract urban-specific structures of mentality, this first chapter of the narrative analysis focuses on the metropolitan imaginary, especially the constructions of themed environments, city images, metaphors, symbols, and representations. The sections concentrate on the depiction of London's contemporary literary topography and follow the question of how the representation of its streets, monuments and buildings, squares and landmarks binds people while stressing and promoting common semantics that expose collective nonconscious dispositions of thinking, imagining, feeling, and acting. While this physical cityscape is altered and permanently remodelled by extensions and destructions, representations are transformed in their semiotic compilations. The material environment is narratologically devised as the spatial storyworld and the urban setting is a significant element in the complex experience of the city upon which new cultural sensibilities are built.

The following four sub-chapters explore the literary cityscapes with regard to the most significant spatial structure, topos, spatial consciousness, and city trope: the urban-generic ambivalence between "Public and Private" (6.1) is interpreted as the leading spatial dualism central to (b)ordering the experience of the urban and hence for exploring urban physical, social, and mental boundaries that open relations of distance and proximity, separation and connection, inside and outside, Self and Other, etc. In "Underground London" (6.2), the subterranean metropolis is defined as a particular setting in contemporary urban fiction which both mirrors and inverts aboveground mental attitudes. An analysis of the subterranean city's social spatialities as well as the confluence of the spatial triad elucidates how the concept of the uncanny helps to grasp the illimitable character of the postmodern metropolis. The third sub-chapter "Navigating the Flux" (6.3) explores the most relevant conceptual and perceptual strategies employed by the novels' characters in order to manage the city, and it identifies influences on their mental dispositions. This approach exposes the elementary functions of urbanites' consciousness for decoding urban spaces and specifically discusses the *intellegibility* of the contemporary urban text based on concrete functional elements of urban mentality by mapping, writing, sensing and apprehending the city. The last sub-chapter on London's cityscape, "The Palimpsestuous City" (6.4), explores the contemporary metropolitan master metaphor. The trope of the palimpsest is understood as offering an analogy for the metropolitan's major structure of thinking and the urbanite's dominant way of orientation in regard to constructing mental certainties according to the historical, geographical, social, textual, and hypertextual character of London.

6.1 Public and Private

> So much of city life is an elaborate process of building up defences against the city – the self of fortified town raised against the stranger. We hedge ourselves in behind dreams and illusions, construct make-believe villages and make-believe families.
> (Raban 1974: 230)

Urbanity is notably influenced by the delicate relations of public and private. Parker (2004: 140) describes this dichotomy as an "important dimension of the urban experience, namely how the city came to be a site of public culture and association at the same time as preserving and even intensifying the 'closed world' of the family and the private household." I would therefore argue that in the range of spatial configurations of ambivalence, public and private takes a leading role in the definition of urban-generic mentality. Unsurprisingly, notions of public and private have been at the very heart of city fiction.[1] According to Heyl (2004: 475-476; 518-522), the establishment of a bourgeois private sphere as opposed to the public initiated the birth of the novel as a genre that is able to look behind drawn curtains and closed doors of secrecy:

> Er [der Roman] betrieb von Anfang an die Veröffentlichung des Privaten. Da er das Private zum zentralen Gegenstand hatte (und immer noch hat), ist es mehr als plausibel, von einem überaus engen Zusammenhang zwischen Etablierung einer durch materielle Strukturen und Mentalitäten gesicherten Privatsphäre und dem Aufkommen des Romans auszugehen. (*Ibid.*: 526)

Literary representations of public and private offer stable axioms of experience, and thereby also support the production of (self)knowledge or identity formation. For Head (2007: 15), "[t]he novel has [...] always been a crucible [...] for examining the relationship between self and other, and between private and public." And in her analysis of the modern urban novel, Wirth-Nesher (1996: 26) notes how all the novels depict "the city as a place that challenges the polarization of private and public self". Whereas the topographical polarities of public and private within the city undergo notable modifica-

---

1 | For more also see McKee, Patricia (1997), *Public and Private. Gender, Class, and the British Novel (1764-1878)*; Lena Cowen Orlin (2007), *Locating Privacy in Tudor England*.

tions in the contemporary novels selected for analysis, boundaries between public and private sphere are shown to be fluent. The following chapters explore representations of public and private in four paradigmatic London novels, Ian McEwan's *Saturday* (2005), Maggie Gee's *The White Family* (2002), Monica Ali's *Brick Lane* (2003), and Christine Brooke-Rose's *Next* (1998), in an attempt to decipher the idiosyncrasies of contemporary urban mentality.

6.1.1 Interpenetrations of Public and Private Drama

In many of his novels, Ian McEwan is preoccupied with the relationships and tensions between the public sphere and the private realm; he engages with political and historical events and investigates public experience on a private level.[2] *Saturday* (2005)[3] specifically parallels the private terrors that can befall an individual urbanite with the larger public turmoil and inequalities produced by the global city. The novel describes one day in the metropolitan life of the protagonist Henry Perowne, the chronotope of a private *via dolorosa* on 15 February 2003, when on the streets of London the masses protested against the impending war with Iraq.

The Seclusion of Bourgeois Private Life

Instead of seeing the plaza as a spirit of urban public life and urban collectivity, Henry Perowne, a happily married neurosurgeon, perceives the public sphere as transformed into a theatre where the private is exhibited. Starting his day off work, Perowne looks down from the bedroom window on the city square in front of his house. The square becomes a stage on which "oblivious to passers-by [urbanites are] lost to a family drama of their own" (SAT: 59): a girl fights with her boyfriend and behaves "like an old-fashioned Hollywood heroine" (SAT: 60), a man in a suit cries in the open, an old lady gestures with a bottle of whisky, and a boy shouts on the phone. All in all, these anonymous street actors destroy both the urban distanciation of the Simmelian urbanite and the characteristics of the city square as public by loudly voicing and enacting personal crises. Whereas middle-class families are spatially invisible because they are separated by walls which secure their private sphere, the private life of the lower classes residing in crammed urban homes tends to unfold on the city square. Emerging from small rooms, council flats, terraced houses or cramped streets, the square offers "the attentive spaciousness of a theatre" (SAT: 60) and simultaneously "grants privacy to these intimate dramas." (SAT: 61) Perowne ascribes these patterns of behaviour to the need for spaciousness and paradoxical anonymity of the square. The open space allows urbanites to vent their innermost emotions, which, according to Richard Sennett leads to a tyranny of intimacy and the creation of dead urban space. Classic urban interaction or communal interchange is missing in these fragmented spectacles because the public drama neither establishes relations between the various private actors, nor does it have any observable effect on

2 | For instance, Ian McEwan's *The Child in Time* (1987) correlates to a prolonged future of Thatcherite politics, *Atonement* (2001) is set during the Second World War and *On Chesil Beach* (2007) problematises the threshold of the cultural revolution during the 1960s.

3 | In the following *Saturday* will be abbreviated to SAT.

the spectator above street-level. Still, urbanites seem to have an intrinsic need for public enactment and Perowne's celestial voyeurism tells of a hunger for spectaclisation. Urbanity is created through the medium of the spectacle by generating sociability on the principles of surveillance and non-involvement and is based on the bourgeois conception of separated socio-spatial areas.

Analogous to the permanent public surveillance of the contemporary metropolis by CCTV cameras, Perowne looks down on the urban Other and from this god-like perspective is set apart from the public Londoners also by the middle-class happiness of his own private abode. The amount of private contentment devises the traditional notions of family and home as the sites of personal identity formation and regeneration. In an interview, McEwan comments:

> I thought, why not devise a character who actually is happy in his marriage, loves his work, gets on with his children and then finds what's left to trouble him: the world outside. There is plenty of anxiety in the book, but there is also a celebration of cooking, wine, sex, love, children, work. (Cit. in Gerard 2005)

The Perownes' bourgeois family home is a place of concrete emotional connections that, despite everyday public contacts to other Londoners through professional life, increase privatisation and insulation. The double doors of the Perownes' home are secured by a burglar alarm system whose elements stem from various centuries of metropolitan safeguard: "three stout Banham locks, two black iron bolts as old as the house, two tempered steel security chains, a spyhole with a brass cover, the box of electronics that works the Entryphone system, the red panic button, the alarm pad with its softly gleaming digits" (SAT: 36). Because privacy is totally cut off from the outside and any potential penetration from the unwelcome Other, this threshold grants protection both to material possessions and moral integrity. However, when the vibrations of the Victoria Tube Line in the distant depth resonate in the house (SAT: 65) and when Perwone detects a burning plane in the night sky over the Post Office Tower from his bedroom window (SAT: 14), it immediately becomes apparent that the domicile is not as secure and hermetically enclosed from the metropolis as expected.

Domestic Routine as Mental Security

Perowne also withdraws within a private abode by tending to the minute habits of his Saturday. The day is mapped out by temporal fragments of quality time, hobby, and family obligations, which he mentally repeats like a secure mantra (SAT: 66, 115, 149, 152). At the centre of this Saturday's domestic routine stands the duty to prepare a fish stew for the family reunion dinner. Already in the morning this family gathering serves as an objective of the day and lends security to his geographical tour through town (SAT: 57). Especially the family dinner is considered the foundation of bourgeois family intimacy sharing stories and recreating the day. According to Mumford (1997: 267), in an urban context food and drink take a particular place in metropolitan daily practices, formerly reserved only to feasts and specific celebrations, by creating a moment of euphoria and obscuring psychological derangements. In the case of *Saturday* the dinner becomes a feast of rebirth in the narratological function to recapitulate the horrors of the day and strengthen the Perownes' family structure. Michael (2009: 34) interprets the envelopment in everyday patterns as an adaptive mechanism. Domestic routines in general and the ones around eating keep the psychological effects of the public urban realm at bay. From the beginning, Henry Perowne employs his Saturday ritual to counter his fear of physical and mental intrusions into his treasured privacy, and to provide a feeling of homeliness or sense of control (cf. *ibid.*: 37).

Saturday's intertextual references to modern literature strongly refer to Victorian and modernist notions of the separate spheres model, but by contrast the novel explicitly outlines the alterations in contemporary public and private thinking. Although the ideology of Victorian urban thought still lingers, the inherent occupational discrimination and societal expectations about domestic housework and its gendering are unbound in the novel from the female characters and more overtly tied to the public sphere (*ibid.*: 35). This is implicitly underpinned by the intertextual reference to Virginia Woolf's *Mrs Dalloway* (1925) and its negotiation of quotidian life as inextricable from larger socio-political forces. Whereas Woolf's narrative centres on the domestic routine of a woman, *Saturday* substitutes the perspective for a male protagonist, emphasising how

> at the beginning of the twenty-first century, upper class privileged men in the West are perhaps more dependent on and more apt to preserve the illusion of the private sphere as a refuge from the chaos and violence of world events precisely because they have lost a sense of control and power in the public sphere [...]. (*Ibid.*: 29)

In Ian McEwan's novel domestic routine paradoxically encompasses the traditionally public area of work. But in fact, the routine duties of professional performance become the all-defining element in his life. The Perownes set their lives by their jobs (SAT: 23). For the protagonist Henry Perowne, work is "the ultimate badge of health" (SAT: 24) and his professional knowledge constitutes a mental space of security, a routine of thinking as well as a source of autonomy (SAT: 143, 250). Analogously, the operating theatre of the neurosurgeon establishes a familiar territory in which the character exerts personal control and authority (SAT: 278; cf. Groes 2009: 108; Michael 2009: 36; Groes 2011: 145). It also marks the threshold space where his professional and private lives were unintentionally mapped out because there Henry fell in love with both neurosurgery and Rosalind, a patient and his future wife (SAT: 45). As he bases both 'decisions' on (self-) diagnosis, Perowne mentally connects intimacy with professional routine. In turn, work, such as his wife's job as a lawyer, from the beginning outlines the Perownes' family life and transforms former conceptions of gendered separate spheres: for instance, the kitchen is not presented as a traditional female realm, but a male forum of communication on both public and private matters (SAT: 25-31, 177).

The Public Intrusion of the Private

Private space is no longer a hermetic container but its borders have become permeable, most specifically due the development of the labour market and the media as well as the interconnectivity between public events and private life. In *Saturday*, radio and television occupy the same space as the protagonist's domestic chores (SAT: 6; cf. Michael 2009: 31). McEwan comments in an interview that today "[w]e can be desperately, genuinely concerned about the misery created by the tsunami in the middle of the Indian Ocean, then 20 minutes later we're having a nice time drinking a glass of wine with a friend." (Cit. in Gerard 2005) The media and with it the global world outside constantly intrude on Perowne's private time (SAT: 25, 29, 35, 69, 76, 107, 125, 140, 150, 166, 176, 179). On the one hand, he is torn between his obsession with round-the-clock news and his desire to join the general public (cf. Groes 2009: 112), and on the other hand he is dependent on stable boundaries between the two spheres, insisting on his 'right to be left alone' (SAT: 108). Nevertheless, without the technologies of communication Henry would be cut off from public discourse and would merely rely on the limited personal information of his patients, colleagues, or family members. For example, Henry's attitude towards the Iraqi dictatorship and the impending war is strongly influenced by the personal authenticated report of his patient Miri Taleb (SAT: 62-64).

Because Perowne denies the city square its role as a public forum or a model space of political engagement (cf. Groes 2009: 113), he deprives London of its initial urbanity built on the interrelation of public and private. Due to his rational perspective, the protagonist mentally defines himself as either a private man or an autocratic leader, in any case a man who dismisses both communal experience and urban collectivity (SAT: 61). As a consequence of the unwelcome and baffling anti-war demonstration, tremors from the public reality test Perowne's customary composure (cf. Ross 2008: 76). Throughout this Saturday, a chronotope of (re)creation and (re)birth, Henry Perowne has to accept that the public event of the political anti-war demonstration becomes a permanent backdrop to his private errands which changes his paths through the city, influences his course of action, and finally brings about an altered conception of the public/private at the end of his day (SAT: 61, 71, 79-80, 99, 111, 148, 167, 217).

Driving through London, Henry's main transactions with the metropolis take place from within his Mercedes S500. In the "padded privacy" (SAT: 121) of a mobile lounge with cream upholstery, he indulges in the illusion of being distant and secure from the outside city. He enjoys London when the city air is filtered and the music shuts out the urban noise (SAT: 75-76). Urbanologists have noted that the automobile as a "cocoon of privacy" (Karp, Stone & Yoels 1991: 126) represents the epitome of social isolation that transforms public space into "an area to move through, not to be in" (Sennett 1977: 14). Therefore, Henry remains mentally untouched by the transformed cityscape and, lost in the urban apathy of private thoughts, hits another car (SAT: 81). In this sense, his Saturday routine obviously collides with (de)routed metropolitan conditions. As he realises at once, this crash not only damages his car but inevitably disrupts the routine of his *Saturday* (SAT: 82), revealing that neither the automobile not his privacy is absolute.[4]

4 | Also see Paul Haggis' film *Crash* (2004) where the postmodern metropolis is represented as monadic space with people in their cocooned cars and lives, but whose constant clashes on the streets exemplify the underlying racial, social, and sexual conflicts as well as the intertwining fates of urbanites in the twenty-first-century city. Also J.G Ballard's novel *Crash* (1973) could be read as an intertext to that sequence, in the sense that in a culture of commodities and technologies, private lives, as well as sexual intimacies sooner or later come into conflict with transformations of the urban public and society.

'Urban Drama' and Public Role Play

The following urban drama cannot be routinely ignored or spatially separated from Perowne because severe violations in public and private habitus have unexpected personal consequences for his whole family. While Perowne is angry at the fact that his private possession has been damaged and the boundary of his privacy has been breached, he cannot break away from the habit of relying on its seemingly untouchable security. Expected to enact a formal routine of insurance exchange, Perowne is unable to transfer his professional role as a doctor, cultivated in the semi-public space of the operating theatre, to the front stage role demanded by open urban interchange.

The unfolding confrontation of the street "follows the unwritten laws of an implicit popular scenario, predetermined by socio-cultural expectations." (Girard 2008: 52) Similar to the Hollywood-like acting girl on the city square, Perowne feels involuntarily put on stage and forced into a media-induced role enactment: "He is cast in a role, and there's no way out. This, as people like to say, is urban drama. A century of movies and half a century of television have rendered matter insincere. It is pure artifice." (SAT: 86) Insofar, Henry experiences the contemporary common patterns of public behaviour as based on mediatised stereotypes of public certainties which compromise his individual conduct. However, flexibility of habitus in public spaces is necessary to successfully practice sociability. Urban theorists have shown that the stylisation of public role acting serves the need to create distance in order to protect one's intimate privacy. In his ignorance of appropriate public/private behaviour, Henry omits to perceive that the solution of saving his integrity actually lies in using common urban patterns instead of his personalised professional routines. According to Bahrdt (1983: 615-616), public self-display is constituted through the representation of distance by demeanour appealing to commonalities. But the contemporary metropolis of the novel is shown to be wrought by Babylonian misunderstandings, here between two men of different class and generation. While his opponent, Baxter, offers a cigarette and his first name to create common ground and proposes to handle the incident inofficially, Perowne in his attempt to keep the situation professional returns a handshake and demands his last name and the interchange of insurance information (SAT:89-90).

Urbanity necessarily implies a disposition of the individual to behave differently in public than in private. Public etiquette demands acting impersonally and respecting the right of others to be left alone. Perowne's son Theo knows the urban cultural code of conduct: "He carries himself on stage as he does in conversation, quietly, formally, protecting his privacy within a shell of friendly politeness. If he happens to spot his parents at the back of the crowd, he'll lift his left hand from the fret in shy and private salute." (SAT: 27) On the contrary, Henry Perowne is reluctant to descend to street-level and rather decides to stand on his "professional dignity" (SAT: 89). In reference to his private inclination Perowne is unable to succumb to the public textbook phrases asked of him, favouring instead the familiar "intellectual **game** of diagnosis." (SAT: 91; emphasis N.P.) Although from Simmel's concept of intellectualisation, Henry's pragmatic approach might be viable, a functioning urbanity is dependent on recognising and balancing the different patterns of public and private thinking. Grabbed and hit, overcome with social prejudice, Perowne tries to avoid further trouble by rejecting the public pretence of ignorance. Rather as self-defence, he resorts to breaching the important frontier between public and private and blurts out Baxter's personal secret in front of his sidekicks, having intellectually diagnosed Baxter's erratic behaviour as a symptom of an early stage of Huntington's Chorea (SAT: 95). In publicly announcing Baxter's "secret shame" (SAT: 94)[5] Henry not only humiliates his opponent and violates a stranger's privacy, but from his own ethical standard breaks the professional discretion of medical secrecy. In securing personal dignity by transferring his celestial perspective to street-level, he obliterates the threshold necessary for urban tolerance. Lefebvre (2003: 18) argues: "In the street, a form of spontaneous theater, I become spectacle and spectator, and sometimes actor. The street is where movement takes place, the interaction without which urban life would not exist, leaving only separation, a forced and fixed segregation." Whereas the streets' publicity normally provides security against criminal violence, the paradoxically empty city before the demonstrations creates a new disorder in which the urban protagonists play and study. Like in medieval times, the street not only serves as a place of encounter but is represented as a stage on which honour is either lost or won.

The Penetration of Public Drama into the Private

Henry's binary thinking of separate spheres is consequently shattered. The crash as the turning point of the novel highlights that "the private and the public spheres collide and overlap within the contemporary moment, thus undermining any true distinction between them." (Michael 2009: 28) While for the rest of the day Henry is haunted by visions of Baxter's red BMW (SAT: 140, 146), the urban drama finds its third act when his street opponent invades the Perownes' impregnable castle, introducing the violence into their intimate lives. This intrusion transfers the central conflict from public to private level and ultimately challenges Henry's notion of his allegedly perfectly happy and secure family life. On a mission for retaliation, Baxter, accompanied by one of his sidekicks, forces his way into the house by threatening Henry's wife with a knife. Henry perceives that his house has become a trap and that he is without any chance to defend his family; outside life goes on without any inkling that the private abode of the Perownes is under severe 'terrorist' attack (SAT: 217). By misusing his professional authority in a personal but publicly located crisis, Henry has actually triggered one far worse and endangered his own family. Unable to react automatically against the surprise of the violent intrusion, Henry resorts again to professional routine. As he tries to coax Baxter into the illusion of a possible medical trial, the situation escalates and Baxter demands of Henry's daughter to undress. Baxter's further turn to criminal vigilance and violent methods can be interpreted as a symbolic denigration of his opponent by physically and mentally harming his daughter's integrity. The obvious plan of rape is doubly vile, as the source of his revenge, namely the public humiliation regarding his disease, now offers the potential threat of passing on his defect genes. Hence, with the invasion of the family home and the subsequent threat of rape, the Victorian separate sphere script of "The Angel in the House" becomes reversed to one of domestic violence.

When Baxter learns that Daisy is pregnant (SAT: 218), he changes his plan of wasting the girl's 'purity' to another form of debasing his opponent and forces the young woman

---

5 | The novel reads – "separate his friends from the sharer of his secret" (SAT: 95) – which is a direct reference to Joseph Conrad's short story "The Secret Sharer" (1912). Childs (2009: 28) interprets this intertextuality as signifying Perowne and Baxter's mutual shame.

to read from her collection of poems called *My Saucy Bark.*[6] Daisy is unable to perform because standing naked in front of her family she is overtly embarrassed to open her intimate thoughts to the voyeuristic gaze of violent strangers. Only by the 'backstage' advice of her poet grandfather, Daisy regains vigilance and casts herself into the role of orator reciting not her own, but Matthew Arnold's prominent "Dover Beach" (1867). Employing the distanciation device of role-play, she turns debasement into a literary stage show and is thereby able to regain composure. In that respect, Daisy's recitation of a well-known poem in front of an 'audience' transforms the violent urban drama into a spectacle of public reading. In contrast to the novel's intertext, Joseph Conrad's *The Secret Agent* (1907), in which public drama is also privatised[7], *Saturday* is a "domestic anti-fairy tale" (Groes 2009: 103-104) despite its unexpected happy ending. The poem and Daisy's dramatic voice have a defining emotional effect on Baxter, who once more changes his role "from lord of terror to amazed admirer" (SAT: 223). As a consequence of Daisy's second reading, the quality of the urban drama is recreated through means of poetry and further metamorphoses to an extemporised personal narrative which eventually leads to Baxter's catharsis and the solution of the conflict. While earlier on, Henry penetrated Baxter's mind by extracting his neurological impairment with diagnostic thinking, Daisy successfully restores the violated mental space with poetic, rhetoric, and narrative technique.

In this novel, public spatial practices and conceived spaces become reconnected in spaces of imagination and cultural memory. Both Theo's and Daisy's stage shows empower the imagination which allows for self-discovery and the restoration of a connection between public and private (cf. Groes 2009: 112-113; Groes 2011: 157). Similar to Virginia Woolf's *A Room of One's Own* (1929), Daisy recreates a personal headspace in the crowded parlour (cf. Clark Hillards 2008: 201) by reciting Arnold's poem from memory and thereby reinstates her own privacy and self-consciousness. This vigilant behaviour results in reconnecting the individual mindscape of private to collective consciousness of urbanites. It emphasises that both family and community are distinctive loci of consciousness formation, in the sense that individuals acculturate on the base of

---

6 | "My Saucy Bark" is an intertextual reference to Shakespeare's "Sonnet No 80". It deals with the creativity of the rival poet and is concerned with grappling the paradox of inexpressibility or the values of speech and silence. Moreover, the sea metaphor simultaneously offers a connection to Arnold's "Dover Beach".

7 | Joseph Conrad's London novel *The Secret Agent* concerns similar themes like *Saturday*, namely terrorism, degeneration, anarchy and sexual harassment (cf. Conrad 2008). There are manifold correspondences between the texts ranging from the car/cab drive through London to the family dinner in the evening. While the male protagonist Verloc in *The Secret Agent* runs a pornographic store in Soho which serves as a semi-public urban setting, the pilots of the burning plane in Ian McEwan's novel are caught with a load of child-pornography. In regard to public and private, both novels deal with 'domestic violence' in the sense that a public threat of terrorism is actually mirrored on a private level. In *The Secret Agent* the act of terror is eventually put down to a 'domestic drama' within the Verloc family, to the anomie of the monstrous town London, and to the social climate within the nation. The characters of Conrad's 'simple tale' are all 'fools' and in that sense, Henry's public conduct can be compared to the 'foolish' behaviour of Baxter.

nation, community, and family, but also in the context of how these spheres intersect in liminal spaces within the urban milieu. As such, the private home and the public city have to be seen as contiguous and interrelated spaces constituting a significant characteristic of urbanity. Both private and public are dependent on liminal spaces, while delimitation leads to the dissolution of the public/private ambivalence central to urbanity.

Siege Mentality

In order to extract specific mental structures that underlie the discussion of the urban-generic ambivalence of public and private in *Saturday*, I concur with Ross (2008: 93) that thinking is predominantly shaped by a form of "siege mentality". Reviewing the novel for the *Guardian*, Lawson (2005) argues that "if Saturday were to have another eight-letter S-word as its title, it would be Security." Especially Henry's obsession with security is shown as he perceives his domestic harmony threatened by the urban crime scene and enhanced by global insecurity. Extremely dependent on clear boundaries between private and public, inside and outside, Self and Other, he feels constantly threatened by urban realities. Perowne's intrinsic need to escape or at least shut out the tumult of the streets in order to prevent any confrontation with the urban stranger results in the establishment of a cultivated isolationism within the secured house, the cocooned car, the enclosure of the squash court, and the absolute space of the operating theatre. All of these spaces are mapped out carefully by domestic rituals as a defence mechanism against the city.

Because Perowne is an urbanite who flees from urbanity's contradictions and withdraws inside the house, he actually lives in "dualities of denial" (Robins 1993: 319) concerning the city and constituting a characteristic fallen public man described by Sennett. Throughout a single day, Henry slowly grasps the importance of the public/private ambivalence as a mental instrument for integrating into urban society. Nevertheless, the overall mood represented in the novel is one of a paranoid search for security and a sense of unconditional fortification. Even Baxter's habitus is based on these unwritten laws of privacy and determined by a form of siege mentality. This mental disposition is fundamental to male characters in contemporary London novels and also communicates a significant mental gap between British male urbanites of different generations (see chapter 7.2.3). Moreover, this London-specific disposition is uncannily similar to the Carceral City founded on an enhanced ecology of fear (see chapter 8.2.2).

Reflections of public and private fear of invasion, but also individual and collective vulnerability basically resemble a study of homeland insecurity. In other words, the represented local and specific characteristics of the Perowne family are narratologically paralleled to the greater context of the British nation. The justification of middle-class citizens like Henry Perowne for isolation in private spaces of security as self-defence against a potential danger from the city parallels the menace of global terror in the post-9/11 socio-political context. With the premonition at the end of the novel that England, London, and the city centre lie wide open waiting for the bomb (SAT: 276), this counter-insularity gives urbanites the feeling of being constantly under the threat of invasion (cf. Ross 2008: 81). The fortress house of the Perownes in Fitzrovia becomes a key symbol of the larger state of the nation because despite the connection of transatlantic loyalties to America the "Blair bridge project" (*ibid.*: 75) also enforces Britain's island mentality. Cilano (2009a: 19) shows how post-9/11 discourses reassign a homogeneous solidarity of "our way of life" in which "the production of 'home' entails a tightening of identifications intended to align people ideologically based on appeals to a manufactured sense of cultural nativity." Instead of moving towards a greater inclusiveness of shared memories and feelings, discourses also pay tribute to the new socio-political schisms (cf. *ibid.*: 17, 20). Critics have read the siege mentality as a sign of a fear of loss of identity; the white, male professional class is not only insistent on sharp class boundaries but also dependent on a Eurocentric mindset and an isolationalist Britishness holding onto colonial binaries despite their dissolution due to social and cultural dislocations (e.g. cf. Ross 2008: 92; Michael 2009: 25, 49; Wells 2005; Groes 2011: 144).

The discourse of the boundaries between public and private, state and family, privileged and oppressed are typical components of the state-of-the-nation or condition-of-England novel and thereby pay heed to recent social changes. Besides *Saturday*, other contemporary London novels such as Blake Morrison's *South of the River* (2007), Jonathan Coe's *The Closed Circle* (2004) and Maggie Gee's *The White Family* (2002) employ the genre in relation to Blair's Britain and the state of mind around the millennium.[8] They all present the condition of England as ultimately altered and exemplify the ambivalence in the reconstitution of urban boundaries.

6.1.2 Private Dereliction and Public Regeneration

Maggie Gee's novels have established her reputation as a major contemporary writer concerned with the treatment of serious socio-political issues (cf. McKay 1998: 221).[9] Her texts can be considered as interventions in an ideological discourse corresponding to the political climate of the 1980s and as engagement with the residual effects of Thatcherism in the subsequent political framework of Blairism (cf. Sears 2004: 59, 63). In the style of the state-of-the-nation novel, she explores the history of tragic public events and their effects on individual lives, in other words how the private is enmeshed in the public fabric (*ibid.*: 58). Moreover, Gee's fiction is especially concerned with the failure of totalising and homogenising visions and explores the areas of urbanity that are excluded, marginalised, forgotten or suppressed by the dominant culture of the historical-spatial context (*ibid.*: 59). In that respect, we can read her novels as "cognitive maps" (*ibid.*: 63) of their times engaging with the dynamics between dominant structures of thinking and those "'others' of social consciousness" (*ibid.*: 59).

---

8 | With *The Child in Time* (1987) McEwan already employs the genre of the state-of-the-nation novel in his exploration of the interrelations between public and private life in the bleak realities of Thatcherite Britain. Other contemporary London condition-of-England novels about Thatcherism are Margaret Drabble's *The Radiant Way* (1987), Martin Amis' *London Fields* (1989), Jonathan Coe's *What A Carve Up* (1994), Tim Lott's *Rumours of a Hurricane* (2002), Will Self's *Dorian* (2002), or Alan Hollinghurst's *The Line of Beauty* (2004).

9 | Maggie Gee's novels *The Burning Book* (1993) and *Grace* (1988) are condition-of-England novels of the 1980s concerning nuclear holocaust and nuclear disarmament, while her apocalyptic vision of London *The Flood* (2004) can be considered a contemporary discussion of Blair's Britain featuring characters such as Mr Bliss and Mr Bare. Moreover, Gee contributed to *Diaspora City: The London New Writing Anthology* (2003).

Maggie Gee's *The White Family* (2002)[10] is a condition-of-England novel set in Hillesden Rise, a fictitious part of London reminiscent of multicultural areas like Willesden[11] or Kensal Rise (cf. Jaggi 2002a: 5). The novel explores the social and cultural effects of English political changes in general, and on London in particular, in the latter part of the twentieth century, touching upon themes of social exclusion and integration or urban decline and gentrification (*ibid.*). Mainly narrated through the perspective of white Britons such as Alfred White, his wife May and their adult children Darren, Shirley, and Dirk, the novel questions definitions of Englishness and simultaneously opposes these constructions in regard to contemporary urban realities.

Metropolitan Public Sphere and National Identity

Alfred White works as a keeper of Albion Park and for over half a century has been guarding this patch of seemingly untarnished English idyll against stray footballs, loose dogs, unwanted goings-on in the toilets and vandalism in the café (WIF: 36). Even though various characters in the novel insist on the democratic ideal that the public park belongs to everyone and is central to Hillesden's community (WIF: 11, 14, 239), due to the language of its various rules the public garden rather resembles a place of social exclusion and control. The park keeper's whistle, the surveillance system in the toilets, and the council notice boards ("No Littering, No Soiling, No Golfing: No Motorcycles, No Camping, No Caravans"; WIF: 36) spell: "This was England. If in doubt, keep them out." (WIF: 36) Surrounded by Victorian gates, the greenery's landscape presents a metaphor for an essentialist idea of English naturalness and identity, characterised as perfectly clean and white, militarily defended, and compartmentalised (WIF: 36, 46, 219). In Anderson's (2002) words the park "stands as the last remaining monument to an orderly, regimented past." Alfred White "holds the fort" (WIF: 9), guarding his "fiefdom" (WIF: 48) against the invasion from outside forces (WIF: 10-11, 13, 36, 46), which try to "turn the Park back into a jungle" (WIF: 12).

Because the contemporary city is perceived as a place of chaos and danger, the ideal of the park's quasi-privatised space resembles a dated notion of community and identity. Hence, the metropolitan public sphere in *The White Family* is represented as exclusive in terms of behaviour and modelled as accessible only to white, male, and heterosexual London urbanites. The novel reveals that this absolute idea of homogeneous urban identity in parallel to national identity is anachronistic to multicultural London at the turn of the twenty-first century, but that structures of this dated thinking still prove persistent. Analogous to the sun setting over the British Empire, the librarian Thomas, a friend of the White family, watches how the former glory of the park is slowly embraced by dusk and the surrounding darkness of the city (WIF: 47). Indeed, Alfred White is the park's double: while he withers away in his hospital sickbed, the park goes completely to pieces (WIF: 48, 219, 236). Unprotected by the keeper's care, flowers are dug up, compost is stolen, drinkers and meth addicts return, bushes start to grow wild (WIF: 49, 249). Reminiscent of Joseph Conrad's *Heart of Darkness* (1902), "[i]n Alfred's mind the Park had gone dark. As he saw it now, everything was black. All he could remember was horror.

---

10 | In the following *The White Family* will be abbreviated to WIF.

11 | Zadie Smith's London novel *White Teeth* (2000) is also set in multicultural Willesden.

Horror." (WIF: 335) The dying park keeper recognises that the story of Albion's idyllic *locus amoenus* is a mere myth and that the public space has been under attack for years by fire, overgrowth, death, and violence (WIF: 336-338). The false notion that there never occurred a major crime or a death is additionally refuted when Winston, a black homosexual, is killed in the in the park's toilets by Alfred's racist son Dirk (WIF: 239, 346, 387).[12] Subsequently, in a last stand for British values based on freedom, individualism, responsibility and duty, Alfred gives away his own son to the police (cf. Jaggi 2002b).

Semi-Public Urban Places as Cathartic Spaces

The White Family is set mainly in the seemingly public spaces of London, such as cemetery, school, library, street café, hotel, cinema, pub, market, public transport, streets, and pavements. The novel's narrative structure is built on semi-public spatialities, which are all exclusive in nature: besides the introductory and final chapter the four main parts focus on "THE HOSPITAL" (WIF: 17), "THE SHOP" (WIF: 92), "THE PARK" (WIF: 193), and "THE CHURCH" (WIF: 347). After Alfred falls sick, the socially unrestricted place of the hospital becomes the centre of the White's private family life. However, the hospital, like the park, is bound to its own topography, habits, and rules. Although, in time his wife May is accustomed to the hospital and the staff, she is unable to grasp the meaning of medical lingo and has to trust the professionalism of the doctors and nurses (WIF: 23). As she sees the hospital as secure, a place to be tended to and get better, May also perceives that for her husband it presents a prison (WIF: 26). Bound to the bed, Alfred's every-day practices are totally obliterated: he is neither in the 'fresh' London air, nor independent from others' control (WIF: 24, 100). With the disruption of family routines, personal relationship ultimately changes as well: "Over the threshold. Into the frightening new place which was suddenly part of their life together. . . . Part of their new life apart." (WIF: 22) On the one hand, they are helpless strangers within the ward: when they draw the curtain they are left alone to their intimate state, hardly able to handle the new privacy of sharing the notion of loss and death (WIF: 58). On the other hand, the hospital serves as a mental healing place for their eldest son Darren, who, in a cathartic rant, is only now able to vent a whole life of repressed feelings towards his terrorizing and violent father (WIF: 324).

The White's daughter Shirley Temple[13] chooses the semi-public urban places of the shop and the church for psychological condolence. Rendering to both Mammon and God, she deals with the loss of her daughter, whom she was forced to give up for adoption, and the death of her first husband, a black physician. Thus, shopping is not simply her favourite pastime but in the commercial routine she finds personal recluse and ther-

---

12 | Maggie Gee points out that the novel was written in direct reference to the Stephen Lawrence murder in 1993 (cf. Jaggi 2002a: 5).

13 | Shirley Temple is an American actress and child star. In her double act with a black dancer she was not allowed to perform on stage in the southern states. In her second marriage she gained the name Shirley Temple Black and during the 1970s under Ford's republican presidency became ambassador to Ghana. Hence, Gee seems to consciously employ the name to mark the character's state inbetween black and white.

apy (WIF: 126, 134). Opposed to the harsh reality of Oxford Street, stands the cosy security of the department store:

> Oxford Street is a vision of hell, the bus goes nosing down like a barge, crushing the struggling souls beneath. From the top deck, waves of them seem to disappear, sucked slowly under the metal prow, going under the wheels, silently under. [...] Warm and dry in the revolving door, sweeping me into sweet-smelling heaven. The department stores: my second home. [...] They make me welcome. I feel fit in. I don't feel lonely or sad, when I'm shopping. (WIF: 135-136)

In the metaphorical opposition of Babylon and Jerusalem, the semi-privacy of the store is represented as an earthly asylum where Shirley acquires a personal comfort zone: cladding herself in layers of cream and camel coloured wools and shawls, and covering herself in waves of perfume she creates a cocoon around her body (WIF: 55). Stuffing herself with cappuccino and cake, coffee and éclairs, she numbs her painful memories and encapsulates herself against intrusions from the outside (WIF: 144-151). The shops are a cathartic area which set her free from the despised suburban identity (WIF: 134-137). Moreover, St John's Piccadilly with the safety of the holy house, the belief system, its routine of service, and the supporting community offers another social and mental enclosure where Shirley is able to restore her psychological health (WIF: 169-173).

Consequently, the representation of the urban ambivalence of public/private in *The White Family* is interesting in regard to two main aspects: the collapse of public space due to privatisation and the role of public places as a refuge from a devastated private family life. Created in the time of Victorian philanthropism, paid for by imperial ventures, or organised by the British welfare state created after the Second World War, the (semi)public spaces of the novel (park, hospital, library, school) have become endangered institutions since the end of consensus policy and the rise of privatisation. Despite a public vote against the sale of Albion Park as a new development plot, it inevitably dissolves because gardeners are laid off and the park keeper is made redundant (WIF: 48, 336-338). Although the eldest son of the White family, long emigrated to the U.S., still sees the National Health Service as one of Britain's greatest achievements, other characters mark that since privatisation hospitals are in dire need of reconstruction (WIF: 22, 181, 165). Similarly, the library looses qualified staff and now only caters to users instead of readers (WIF: 35, 95-96). Most local shops in lower Hillesden shut down as people prefer the shopping malls in the commercial belt or the department stores in the city centre. The only thriving place left is the post office, where people of the community go to collect government money, such as their pension, child allowance, or the dole (WIF: 139-140). The decline of these spaces implies the obliteration of urban liminal zones of social contact.

All characters in the novel are employed in public services of education, leisure, and social work: park keeper (Alfred), librarian (Thomas), teacher (Melissa), university professor (Kojo), social worker (Elroy), journalist (Darren), shop keeper (Nimit, George). For Alfred the public is "maddening" (WIF: 219) but he sees it as his duty to serve it by protecting urbanites from themselves (WIF: 50). This role of public service is underlined, as Londoners who are unable to overcome their personal grievances, like Shirley and Winston, both choose public places for suicide, while Dirk transforms his personal frustration into public violence and murder. The public attracts people with personal problems who have nowhere else to go for pain release (WIF: 35, 95-96). The idea of destitute people searching for refuge, social therapy, and healing in semi-public spaces has already been pointed out concerning the hospital, the shops and the church, but it is specifically developed with regard to Albion Park. The park is an open space full of natural colour and light without which "none [...] would be able to breathe." (WIF: 48) As children, Thomas and his friend Darren White escape from the restricted space of the home and their family to the park, similarly to Winston, who takes refuge there because he cannot communicate his homosexuality to his own family. Especially for Alfred, who spends nearly all his life there, the park is more home to him than his own house: "[...] Alfred tramped out into the freezing air, but fresh, so fresh after the air inside, the air he loved, the air of London, with the faint green edge that spoke of the Park, not far away, his place, his home..." (WIF: 397). The public space becomes a refuge from the enclosed privacy of the family.

The Dissolution of Family Life

According to traditional ideas of class-related notions of public and private, *The White Family* offers an opposing perspective on the urban family life represented in *Saturday*. Whereas the latter cherishes the domestic intimacy of family life as a refuge from a collective public anxiety, the former concentrates on an irreversibly divided family and the general social dissolution of family ties.

> And the house, the bloomin' house where they'd lived for ever. With its creaks, and its knockings, and its leaky gutters – And its whitewashed front in the morning sun. And the smell of apples from the fruit-bowl in the living-room. And that dot of gold dancing about the mirror. [...] His chair, her chair. With Shirley's cushions, easing their bones as they sank down. Their little house, with its steamy kitchen, smelling of washing and hot Ribena. Its warmth, its sheen, its – familiariness. Was that the word? Their family home. (WIF: 76-77)

The house, despite its picturesque domesticity, is divided by cracks that go deeper than the surface. Never a space endowed with tranquillity, love, understanding, or support, the family home is wrought with mundane kinds of everyday terrors, domestic violence, misunderstandings, and hate: the Whites' home is a "house of torture" (WIF: 145). Alfred is not only racist, as his youngest son now, but like his own father before him he acts as a terrorising patriarch who beats wife and children. He even hits the pregnant Shirley and forces her to give her child up for adoption. His behaviour is a clear sign of powerlessness: unable to cope verbally with the chaos inside the house, the children's puberty, and unchecked emotions, he either resorts to violence or deserts the home (WIF: 237, 330). Still, Alfred is not represented as a simple stereotype, but a more ambiguous character that is torn between sweetness and fierceness, tenderness and violence (WIF: 251). The park transforms him to a caretaker where he actually tends to the young duck family (WIF: 237) and it is revealed how he tries to convince his wife to keep Shirley's baby, but May refuses in terror of the neighbours' gossip (WIF: 338).

May White, according to Gee, is a "fitter-in" and a "coward" (cit. in Jaggi 2002a: 9) too afraid to speak up since she has followed her mantra of non-involvement from childhood (WIF: 145, 294). She suppresses her sorrows in front of her family, dyes her hair to hide the grey, covers up Shirley's bruises with make-up and helps her youngest son hide Winston's murder. May's intentions are by far not as innocent as she perceives, because she is mainly concerned with the potential rumour intruding into their private life. Towards the end of the novel, she recognises that her covert actions have failed: "Their shame was known. The family shame. Perhaps she had tried to hide too much." (WIF: 409) May also imagines to be set free from the oppressing family home and its emotional life. With a terrorizing father and later a violent husband she has felt imprisoned in the pain inflicted by domesticity all her life: "She had never been able to slip out into the open, the quiet, clear space where happiness was. Not joy so much as an end to sorrow, a rest from anger and fear and resentment." (WIF: 234-235) Both the fear of loneliness and strangeness enforce her intimate feelings of love towards Alfred; May only finds solitude and condolence in reading, a passion that connects her to the librarian Thomas.

The dysfunctional family life necessarily rubs off on their three children. Not receiving any love from his parents, the youngest son Dirk represses his own homoerotic feelings and idolises his father by emulating his hatred toward the ethnic, sexual, and the generational Other (WIF: 70, 85). Shirley hates her younger brother Dirk for his ignorance, despises her mother for her meekness, and still, with over forty, feels physical pain when meeting her father. She rejects her family as a bunch of "[i]gnorant bigots" (WIF: 67) and as a teenager flees the domestic aggressions seeking intimacy in sex with a stranger "far away from pain and anger." (WIF: 151) Founding a family of her own and becoming a mother are her main objectives in life, but her first marriage remains childless and the domestic happiness is destroyed by her husband's early death, while her relationship with Elroy King is based on rather shaky ground, because her brother is Winston King's killer. The White's first-born son, Darren, has even crossed a whole ocean to escape his broken family and his father's violence: "You *terrorized* me. You terrorized all of us." (WIF: 328) Darren is a mild alcoholic, married for the third time, his children do not live with him, and his current wife is bulimic (WIF: 205-206). He admits that he doesn't have a happy private life, because he is still caught in restlessness: "*I hate my life.* Never at home, no time at home." (WIF: 209). In the hotel room, the couple talks about having children as a therapeutic measure for their relationship, while around them "[t]he hotel was loud. Feet came and went, of happy families, hateful imaginary happy families." (WIF: 265) Hence, Maggie Gee's *The White Family* contrives happy family life as an illusion of contemporary urbanity (cf. Jaggi 2002b). The family reunion shows that the individual family members are preoccupied with themselves: despite coming together over Alfred's deathbed they keep apart from each other, unable to communicate, silence and impending misunderstandings further their inchoate distance (WIF: 91, 297). Far from the notion that the family matters most, the urban social world represented in the novel is one of divided unhappy families and personal relations always caught between the need of familiarity and tenderness and the prevailing reality of estrangement and violence (WIF: 98-99).

Residual Mentalities

The White Family emphasises the fact that in the city the domestic sphere contains just as many possibilities of violence as actually the public streets and thereby draws connections explored by feminist geographers in regard to the public/private dichotomy and patriarchal power. The novel especially hints at a link between racist violence on the streets and the domestic violence within the family. In an interview, Maggie Gee explains the corresponding mental structures of public and private sphere: "I think that what happens inside little houses happens next outside of them." (Cit. in Jaggi 2002a: 8) Neo-Thatcherite Blairism has shattered the traditional urban public-private partnerships concerning metropolitan institutions of education, health, and leisure, altering the atmosphere of semi-public spaces. It is not so much the death of traditional public spaces but rather that a certain scale of urbanity is shaken in its equilibrium. Fleeing from the private houses of everyday terror without the possibility of verbal and non-violent conflict prevention, individuals carry their stressed and loaded emotional life outside onto the streets. In other words, the metropolitan public is represented as a necessary means for a balanced urban and intimate life.

It is a significant paradox how characters strive to flee the entombing rules, routines, and mannerisms of their family home only to indulge in the norms, rituals and habits of the urban public sphere. But as typical for the public/private ambivalence, for May White the private rules are both securing and imprisoning. "Whereas with Alfred, everything had been laid down. Rules that were lost in the mists of time, walls he built and cemented in till that red-brick labyrinth became her life." (WIF: 25) Additionally, the rules of public hospitals are liberating but also disturbing: "Rules and regulations. There were always rules. Their life at home was a mosaic of rules, mostly made by Alfred, but at least she knew them ... Now they were on unfamiliar ground." (WIF: 37) However, norms, rules and values change over time and create insecurity, especially when certain boundaries, as the ones of public and private in the city, are in the process of alteration. As May notes: "Only now nothing seems quite safe any more. The walls were shifting. The sea was rising." (WIF: 25) As argued above, the dusk of an era is close, the rising of another time at bay.

I therefore deduce that in the representation of public and private, the novel depicts the persistence of residual mental structures and shows how mentality is in turn shaped by the consistent fear of loss of secured traditions in the perpetual transformation that is the postmodern metropolis. Despite the overt politics of multiculturalism, upward mobility and gender equality, the novel exposes the deeply rooted dispositions of empire/insular mentality, thus segregational mental dispositions prone to separate sphere models of race, ethnicity, class, generation, gender and sexuality. Thus, as in all her other novels, Gee shows how emotional experiences, here of the British Empire, transcend their historical limit and context, affecting the imminent present of Londoners (cf. Sears 2004: 57). In reference to the notion of *longue durée* and the concentric circles of mentalities, British mentality that was in its heyday at the end of the nineteenth century is recalled during Thatcherism and still influences the everyday experiences of contemporary 'New' London. Sears (*ibid.*: 60) comments: "All Gee's characters search for patterns in the fabrics of their lives and the worlds they inhabit, all search for repetition and the security of a return to structure, all express a desire to return to consistency from a world of hostile, unpredictable contingency." In this respect, we can read the characters' consistent search for comfort in rather traditional institutions that offer a set of rules and routines as a recluse from urbanites' fear of impending personal loss, the breaking of primary relations, and an atmosphere of urban entropy. The novel exposes both the need of limited conventional positions for security and also the anxiety of all strangeness that lies beyond those boundaries (cf. *ibid.*: 61). Besides the actual social experiences, the novel exemplifies how residual mentalities pertain within private lives and therefore reverberate and (re)surface in the fabric of the urban public.

6.1.3 Enclosed Privacies in the Global City

Whereas Maggie Gee's *The White Family* is considered a postcolonial novel in its treatment of contemporary racism from a white British perspective, Monica Ali's novel *Brick Lane* (2003)[14] recounts the life of Nazneen born in Bangladesh, who at the age of eighteen is married off by her father to the older Chanu living in London's Tower Hamlets. *Brick Lane* is a multicultural *Bildungsroman* that captures Nazneen's awakening during the journey from rural Bangladesh towards the protagonist's metropolitan coming-of-age in the years between 1985 and 2002. Similar to other contemporary postcolonial London novels written by a second-generation immigrant, woman author, *Brick Lane* casts a strong female character, who, by slowly traversing the boundaries between inside and outside, becomes more and more open to the city's influences and emancipates herself from "an unspoilt girl [f]rom the village" (BRL: 22) to a woman of the city.[15] This chronotopic journey of awakening, recreation, and rebirth leads Nazneen from exemplary dutiful Islamic womanhood, fatalistic passivity, and closeted existence within the boundaries of a council estate flat in the East End to single mother, metropolitan vigilance, and an unconstrained urban way of life. In this respect, the protagonist's quest for the public space represents an image for how a newcomer becomes acculturated to urban life and is internally urbanised.

The Private as a Space of Oppression and Apathy

For her first half year in London, Nazneen is physically, socially, and mentally sealed off from the outer world. Not only is the protagonist's experience of London for a long time limited to the confined horizons of the musty council flat and the decaying council estate, but she is also locked in isolation, loneliness, boredom, routine, and paralysis (cf. Pesso-Miquel 2008: 87). Neither allowed to leave the place without her husband, nor to go to college and learn English, she becomes imprisoned within the claustrophobic confines of the council flat bare of any personal or domestic happiness: "[S]he saw that she was trapped inside this body, inside this room, inside this flat, inside this concrete slab of entombed humanity." (BRL: 76) Analogous to Rose's (1993: 144, 150) findings on gendered spaces, Nazneen in her confinement is shown as oppressed by a patriarchal culture, but also as inhabiting a paradoxical space of a migrant, that of imprisonment in exile:

---

14 | In the following *Brick Lane* will be abbreviated to BRL.

15 | Also see Bernadine Evaristo's *The Emperor's Babe* (1997), Meera Syal's *Life Isn't All Ha Ha Hee Hee* (1999), Zadie Smith's *White Teeth* (2000), Andrea Levy's *Small Island* (2004), Diana Evans' *26a* (2005), Naomi Alderman's *Disobedience* (2006), Xiaolu Guo's *A Concise Chinese-English Dictionary for Lovers* (2007).

In all her eighteen years, she could scarcely remember a moment that she had spent alone. Until she married. And came to London to sit day after day in this large box with furniture to dust, and the muffled sound of private lives sealed away above, below and around her. (BRL: 24)

The public/private ambivalence is represented as one of oppressive privacy undermining all chances of either familiarity or agency. Against this authoritarian privatisation and isolation, the female character develops various strategies which irrevocably become measures of the urban habit of distanciation. First, Nazneen paradoxically withdraws more into herself, employing loneliness for self-inspection; second, she preoccupies herself with domestic routine chores as a practice of security; and third, by acoustically perceiving the private spaces of her neighbours behind the paper-thin walls becomes accustomed to rhythms of an urban way of life.

Like Virginia Woolf's *A Room of One's Own*, the novel is interested in the interconnection between architectural, bodily, and mental spaces of the female inside and their relation to creativity. Alongside the minute enumeration of the flat's interior, the topography of Nazneen's inner Self, her thoughts and worries, memories and illusions are revealed (BRL: 20-21; cf. Hiddleston 2005: 64-65). In her mind Nazneen flees the flat's restrictions creating a private mental space, in places of memories and visions of herself as someone else. The character's vivid recollections and dreams of her Bengal home village with its open skies, sunshine, and colours are contrasted to the confined darkness of her life in London's Brick Lane (BRL: 45; cf. Cuevas 2008a: 199). Imagining herself as the swirling ice-skater figure she watches on TV and in magazines (BRL: 41, 93) or as the independent woman in her sister's letters (BRL: 94) she casts off the invisible chains that bind her. Here Woolf's model is turned on its head because the creation of mental space as a room of one's own later enables the construction of physical and social private spheres. The private confines of her mental spaces offer Nazneen open realms of the imaginary with horizons of an urban future. In time, however, the images of Bangladesh slowly disappear behind a veil of fine mesh, the recollection is rendered from enlivened scenery to mere hazy knowledge (BRL: 217). Unable to escape into the world of her daydreams, Nazneen fills her mental space with everyday troubles and eventually she succumbs to depression and nervous exhaustion (BRL: 270, 326). In the void and non-place of apathy Nazneen is rendered a non-person, and her husband Chanu, in a distant manner, only talks to her in the third person (BRL: 326). Despite or specifically because of obliterating her former Self, Nazneen later re-emerges from the darkness of depression and nightmares internally cleansed and able to redefine her mental spaces as well as independently bring her visions to life.

Her second survival strategy to endure isolation is to turn to the domestic routine of cleaning, cooking, praying, washing, visiting female friends, eating at night, a daily structure which provides her with a sense of stability (cf. Hiddleston 2005: 61, 66). "Life made its pattern around and beneath and through her." (BRL: 40) As Rose (1993: 24-25) points out, women's time-spaces are both strongly mapped out and restricted. In that respect, Nazneen's survival strategy for stability and safety must be read as a reaffirmation of her confinement. But Nazneen's daily routine also includes spending hours at the window, gazing at the dilapidation, decay, and architectural monotony of the tower block (BRL: 18). As the interior of the room stands against the exterior of the streets, the window becomes the border between inside and outside. But as her vision is obstructed by the net curtains, even these glimpses of other public and private lives are restricted to imaginary constructions (BRL: 17, 364, 448). In opposition to Perowne's window perspective, Nazneen's urban life behind the curtains is strictly limited to the unreal of "all shapes and shadows" (BRL: 17). Thus her first experience of London is a kind of Platonian shadow theatre, raising both suspicion and curiosity. More importantly, the curtained existence emphasises Nazneen's perspective of the subaltern immigrant female, who is even more marginalised by a tripartite colonisation in the East End, namely that of class, ethnicity and gender.

The imagery of net curtain and veil furthermore underlines how the novel focuses on the private world of its protagonist, exposes the constrained everyday tenor of female immigrants revolving around family and the home. First of all, for Banerjee (2008: 6) the veil is the symbol of Nazneen's imprisonment; it not only hides her from public gaze but as a marker of religious creed and female obedience basically enforces her near obliteration as a person. The sari's silk weighs her down like chains strangling her: "For a glorious moment is was clear that clothes, not fate, made her life. And if the moment had lasted she would have ripped the sari off and torn it to shreds." (BRL: 277) On the other hand, feeling watched in the public, the protagonist pulls the sari over head (BRL: 54, 254) because the veil can also serve as a protective device against voyeuristic gazes and a securing boundary of privacy (cf. Banerjee 2008: 5). According to Banerjee (*ibid.*: 7) in the instance of migration, the veil becomes an ambivalent metaphor for both private and public, immobility and mobility, at-homeness and migration. At the end of the novel, Nazneen successfully works in the fashion industry and skates over the ice in her sari, stressing privacy as a potential for female agency (*ibid.*: 8). Consequently, the curtains around Nazneen's existence are dissolved by a cultural appropriation of the veil to an urban way of life of distanciation.

Similar to the notion in *Saturday*, the novel also reveals how the spatial existence in the council estate isolates its inhabitants while at the same time denying them any privacy. The rows of flats are like cells, their curtained windows and "wire meshing suspended inside, gold-rimmed keyholes, stern black knockers." (BRL: 53) While Chanu points out that council statistics count 3.5 people to a room as enough "space to grow" (BRL: 49), Nazneen perceives the confinement of the place through a vigilant imagery that compares urban and rural landscape. The sun is "squeezed between slabs of concrete" (BRL: 86) and pigeons patrol the green patch on the courtyard like "prisoners in an exercise yard." (BRL: 54) The opposition between urban imprisonment in London and rural freedom in Bangladesh's countryside thus not only concerns her mental spaces of memory versus the prison of her flat but is also taken up on a larger scale in her experience of impersonal living conditions on the estate:

> You can spread your soul over a paddy filed, you can whisper to a mango tree, you can feel the earth beneath your toes and know that this is the place, the place where it begins and ends. But what can you tell to a pile of bricks? The bricks will not be moved. (BRL: 87)

The general confinement of people, especially women, in the semi-privacy of the council blocks has notable effects on the emotional condition of their inhabitants (e.g. depression and suicide) (BRL: 29, 40). Even the white tattoo lady, basically Nazneen's only distant contact for the first months, wears the look of utter boredom and total detachment (BRL:

17-18). Nazneen recognises how others are likewise imprisoned by poverty, immobility, and apathy due to living an isolated life in the midst of many. Fighting her own loneliness Nazneen invades her neighbours' privacy by eavesdropping on the everyday life around her: "The television on. Coughing. Sometimes the lavatory flushing. Someone upstairs scraping a chair. A shouting match below. Everyone in their boxes, counting their possessions." (BRL: 24) In contrast to the communal life in her Bangladeshi home village, she first experiences the paradox of urban life where the necessity of closing in one's privacy also entails a high degree of personal detachment, while at the same time sharing walls, information, and space. For Nazneen the unknown neighbours are her closest relations.

> The wife upstairs who used the lavatory in the night. She and Nazneen knew her by her bladder. The milkman's alarm clock that told Nazneen the gruelling hours her neighbours must keep. The women on the other side whose bed thumped the wall when her boyfriends called. These were her unknown intimates. (BRL: 182)

The ambivalence of public and private here becomes suspended to one of strangeness and familiarity. One of the characters (Mrs Islam) puts individuality and enhanced privacy down to cultural differences between white Londoners and Bangladeshi immigrants (BRL: 88-89). It is by far not only the unhomely spatialities of the estate that render its inhabitants prisoners, nor Nazneen's unfamiliarity with the surroundings of Brick Lane that keep her inside, but mostly the additional 'cultural boundaries' erected between the woman's secluded existence and public life on the streets, for example the restrictions set by her husband and the expectations of the local community. For fear of social stigmatisation, life is largely relegated to the cultural enclave of the estate (BRL: 26-28, 45-46). The preconditioned cultural permanence of private behaviour in the public, enforced by informal laws of gossip and prejudice, is mirrored by the English restrictions in public spaces (BRL: 18, 64). Thus, the confinement of the individual is paradoxically expanded in the public because spaces of action are even more controlled.

Mediascapes of Intimacy, Freedom, and Mobility

Brick Lane also explores the relations between the urban ambivalence of public and private in relation to media and gender. The use of various means of communication – letters, television, pamphlets, internet – oscillate between the boundaries of internal and external spatialities. Nazneen's sister's letters from Bangladesh keep her informed on Hasina's most intimate life, and over time indirectly alter the protagonist's attitudes. The medium is an essentially private matter, sealed and secret. In the novel, Nazneen hides the letters of her sister in a shoebox in the wardrobe or – as a treasure of her heart – close to her body concealed by the sari. Although the letters are a space of subjectivity, emotional autonomy and intimacy, the protagonist is unable to use them as a confessional medium and write about her act of adultery.

Television offers a rather closed private place because it provides Nazneen with the possibility to escape into dreams of ice-skating and experience a feeling of wholeness and purity. For the protagonist, the TV is a metaphorical fireplace radiating warmth and comfort (BRL: 36). It is not only the place where stories are spun and the imaginary spurred, but as Guggenberger (2000: 45) points out, the sofa is turned into a flying carpet over the global (political and social) landscape. Hence, the public enters the private and at the same time opens the familial to the political. In Ali's *Brick Lane*, the two most important political incidents that serve as the background to the third part of the novel, namely the Oldham riots and the terrorist attacks on New York in 2001, offer the national and global backdrop of the family's localised life. For Nazneen, watching the repetitious images of the collapsing Twin Towers on TV suggests that her own family has just survived a true crisis (BRL: 367).

The politically insecure climate portrayed in the media strengthens Chanu's decision to re-migrate to Bangladesh, and to earn the money for the move, Chanu buys a computer for himself and a sewing machine for Nazneen (BRL: 191-192). While the sewing machine is directly connected to female domestic work in private, the computer and the internet are traditionally related to office work and as an access to a world wide web of a global public. It does, however, not turn out to be a possibility for more participation and access to the public for Nazneen and the girls, because Chanu, in order to prevent their free access to the public, forbids the women to touch the computer. All in all, the use of technological devices – cassette player, radio, computer, navigation system, mobile phone – is exclusively reserved for the male characters (BRL: 202, 274, 318, 359). Although Chanu is convinced that he just acquired unlimited mobility and access to the whole world (BRL: 200), he is notoriously helpless in operating any of the tools and the computer is quickly forgotten. In contrast, the younger Karim successfully establishes mental connections with an imaginary community on the web, whereby the technologies become the expression of his inbetween space as a locally based East Ender and a member of a global diasporic culture.

The internet as the epitome of global information and communication networks offers a new kind of public space which has become contingent upon derivative movements. Guggenberger (2000: 37-59) shows in his study on the "Virtual City" – a non-place between the private place of the living room and the meta-public of the world – that a transformation from spatial communities to groups of contemporaries has led to geographical de-placement. But in opposition to Castells' notion of the Informational City, the influence of the mediascape as represented in *Brick Lane* does not simply erode the local, but also encourages localism and privatism, for example the socio-cultural and religious leaflet war between Bengal Tigers and Lion Hearts (BRL: 257-259).

Spatial Permeability and Reterritorialisation

Brick Lane, in the ambivalence of public and private, uncovers the gendered differences "in mobility, in movement through time-space, and in the constraints which caused this differential geography." (Rose 1993: 26) However, it also evidences women's contestations of these limits, for example by altering the delineations of the domestic as reproductive space. Although the sewing machine is located in domestic work, home labour initiates a decisive step in Nazneen's development. The work as a seamstress professionally connects her to the globalised garment industry and thereby to the factories in Dhaka, but also opens the flat to outer influences of London. They change the inner setting of the flat to a place of work and enable Nazneen to gain personal as well as financial independence.

The younger London-born Karim, a second-generation Bengali, comes to represent a way for Nazneen to project herself beyond the boundaries of domestic life. In contrast to her monotonously lecturing husband, the "new middle-man" (BRL: 209) communicates information from the outside world and brings her emotional and sexual freedom. As a "go-between" (Kral 2007: 68), Karim slowly opens the door to the public and allows Nazneen to discover the world (BRL: 243). In becoming her lover, Karim literally fills the space and the void in her life, letting her enjoy the domesticity of the flat for the first time (BRL: 285-286). Hence, in the process of awakening, Nazneen becomes engaged in various projects of re-territorialisation. The novel's use and appropriation of space is two-fold (cf. Cuevas 2008a: 198): on the one hand, Nazneen significantly re-adjusts the interior private space of the flat and makes a home for herself and her daughters, while on the other hand, she widens her mental map of the external London environment, advancing from a mere distanced spectator at the window to an actor involved in writing the city by walking and reterritorialising the streets of the metropolis.

The first steps of rather silent readjustment of the private space take place through Nazneen's "domestic guerrilla actions" (BRL: 77) and minute transformations of family life which revoke the restricted social patterns of a Bengali housewife and mother and "destroy the state from within" (BRL: 63). The kitchen is a female space *par excellence*, a place within the interior of the flat where the very authority only belongs to Nazneen, she appropriates it as a room of her own and a space of resistance. Later, in absence of male control, the flat is taken over by female agency; especially Nazneen's daughters transform the flat to a more western lifestyle, speaking English, wearing jeans, using shampoo, eating burgers, etc. (BRL: 193-194, 207, 213; cf. Cuevas 2008a: 208; James 2008: 75). The home becomes ultimately compromised when Nazneen commits adultery in the marriage bed, hence territorialising the inside of the flat from the kitchen, to the living area, and finally to the bedroom, and extending her independence from domestic chores to intimate subjectivity.

Due to the influences of a wider public, and her own ventures to the outside, she is able to redraw the boundaries and to reterritorialise the flat as a place of personal agency, private family life, and intimacy. Cuevas (2008a: 207-208) questions how it is possible to reconcile the implied ambivalent relation to the estate with its negative connotations as a trap, in which, however, Nazneen succeeds in making a home. This ambivalence can be deciphered by looking at the relational constructions of public and private spaces and their mappings by the novel's characters. Beforehand, as shown above, Nazneen's only privacy is her mental space and both the flat as the estate are perceived as panoptic prisons under communal surveillance. Redefining the space of her own flat, she also readjusts her relation to the estate which enables her to traverse the boundaries beyond Brick Lane. This brings us to the second trail of reterritorialisation, namely Nazneen's transgressions of various boundaries from the inside of the flat, to the outside of the estate, the neighbourhood of Brick Lane, her first venture into the City, her independent approach to the city centre at Covent Garden and finally her free movement about Greater London.

During her first months in London, Nazneen only ventures out a few times, trailing behind Chanu and initially confronted with the strangeness and difference of place and people (BRL: 43). As staying on the estate within the bounds of ethnic community does not count as going out, she slowly makes her way out of the flat taking short journeys to other council blocks, striking up acquaintances with other Bengali wives (BRL: 46-47). Nazneen's first independent exploration of the closer neighbourhood leads her from the East End to the square mile of the City of London and is still marked by strong but liberating insecurity (BRL: 54-63). From the confines and the familiar private places of the estate, she explores the semi-public spaces of the neighbourhood around Brick Lane as well as the rather distant and strange territory of the City's financial district. Crossing the street for the first time constitutes a decisive first step, yet in time Nazneen's movements become more and more refined. In the beginning she hastily runs through the streets, yet she finally becomes aware of topographical mappings until she has acquired a certain rhythm of walking which then allows her to idiosyncratically scrutinize her surroundings, take in the first impressions of the metropolis and from the invisible stance of a *flâneuse* gaze at the alien Londoners around her (BRL: 54-57). Consequently, in her first solitary walk through London she already adopts the role and the habit of an urban walker reterritorialising the city's spaces (cf. Cuevas 2008a: 201; Deny 2009: 225; Poon 2009: 430). In that respect, I agree with Angelina Poon (2009: 432) that this first transgression of boundaries constitutes more than a playful representation of female *flânerie*. Rather Nazneen's pedestrian perambulations are closer to de Certeau's account of ordinary walkers who make use of their partial knowledge to rewrite the space of the metropolis. Hence, Nazneen not only experiences a small section of London, but also becomes a short-time actor constructing its public spatialities of the streets, city squares, and pubs.

In reference to the urban ambivalence of public and private, her position is not simply a transformed perspective from inside to outside, from distant onlooker on the curtained window to a participating visionary in the streets, but it offers Nazneen an alternative image of privacy, namely private demeanour in public. Virtually step by step, she learns the rules of visibility and invisibility (BRL: 43, 56). For example, Nazneen watches a woman's rich clothes and jewellery which she perceives as solid armour of personal protection (BRL: 57). Intruding the woman's privacy by way of her looks, she in turn becomes visible and vulnerable. This interaction not only makes her understand the urban habitus of distanciation but initially teaches her about the downside of the city's public life, namely anonymity and indifference. Resting on a green patch within the surrounding greyness of the metropolis, she suddenly becomes aware of her disorientation and alienation within the urban mass (cf. Deny 2009: 224): "A woman on her own in the city, without a husband, without a family, without friend, without protection." (BRL: 58) But although the unfamiliar, unreadable, labyrinthian, alienating and anonymous urban landscape seems to lack all the social and emotional anchors of rural community life (cf. Valman 2009: 6), Nazneen's existential disorientation in its ambivalence of unexpected freedom also carries a positive notion (cf. Deny 2009: 225). Even without the command of English she is able to communicate with strangers in the city in order to find her way back home autonomously:

> Anything is possible. She wanted to shout it. Do you know what I did today? I went inside a pub. To use the toilet. Did you think I could do that? I walked mile upon mile, probably around the whole of London, although I did not see the edge of it. And to get home again I went to a restaurant. I found a Bangladeshi restaurant and asked for directions. See what I can do! (BRL: 62-63)

This first exploration of the metropolitan public produces an exhilaration of urban life, a heightened self-consciousness, and a stronger sense of power over her immediate environment.

Other trips into the centre of London until her independent venture to the city centre are scarce and only take place under the autocratic command of her husband, but they all carry specific notions of acquiring public knowledge and enforce her acculturation to metropolitan mental structures (BRL: 100, 252, 310, 289). Nazneen's trip to Covent Garden as a significant physical, social, and mental act of reterritorialisation is directly connected with her decision to break up with Karim (cf. Kral 2007: 68; Poon 2009: 433). This step to independence is clearly mirrored in the traversing of various boundaries between private and public. First, she crosses the boundaries from the semi-private spaces around Brick Lane to the centre of London's street performance. Second, she makes use of the telephone and the tube, thus traversing the gendered boundaries to the public, namely transport and technological communication (BRL: 446-450). And last, the relationship with Karim, initially confined to the flat, is brought out of the closet and put to an end to in public. Hence the private issues, as shown by Perowne in *Saturday*, are resolved in the anonymity of a public square.

Moreover, during her vigilant search for the missing older daughter Shahana, Nazneen confidently navigates the East End and no obstacle can impede her progress (BRL: 466-476; cf. Cuevas 2008a: 208; Valman 2009: 6). In the jumble of the night's street fights the protagonist distinctly maps her way through the streets – Bethnal Green Road, Vallance Road, New Road, Cannon Street, Cable Street, Falstaff Pub, Commercial Road, Adler Street, Altab Ali Park, Brick Lane – and even jumps the street barrier put up by the police. This independent mapping gives her the strength to finally voice her decision not to return to Bangladesh with her husband but to stay in London with her daughters (BRL: 450). With the close of the story in 2002, Nazneen has achieved financial independence working for "Fushion Fashion" and created a cobweb design on her own, symbolising how she has now spread her net of spatial knowledge all over the metropolis from Ealing and Wembley to Tooting and Southall (BRL: 481).

The long-term liberation process she goes through is represented as well as made available by the city as an inertly "fluid, transformative *space*" (Ball 2004: 225). Nazneen acknowledges that she was imprisoned by the imaginary boundaries of her own relegated knowledge and agency, and that in reality the dividing lines between inside and outside are fluent. She overcomes the final boundary of private/public when she skates the Liverpool Street ice-rink clothed in a sari. In this instance she not only traverses the frontier to the commercial city, but also transfers her most intimate hope formerly buried in her mental space to a public performance and image of transition (BRL: 492; cf. Cuevas 2008a: 209; Valman 2009: 7; Groes 2011: 250).

Preservation of Authenticity versus New Forms of Belonging

Cuevas (2008a: 202; 2008b: 389–390) and Deny (2009: 216-221) point out that the confinement of women to the private realm within the migrant community of Tower Hamlets serves the preservation of ethnic authenticity. Both Chanu and Karim are unable to locate themselves in London, inscribe Nazneen with their longing of an imaginary homeland; they presume to talk for Nazneen, disregarding her subjectivity and rendering her, the girl form the village, the epitome of their idea of home, authentic with an unspoilt nature (cf. Banerjee 2008: 8). Women are traditionally a metaphor for nature and home, associated with stability, reliability, authenticity and a reverence for something that has been lost (cf. Rose 1993: 60; Massey 1998: 9-10, 180). The patriarchal structure is thereby altered to emphasise the traditional notion of culture versus nature in the context of migration as one of authenticity, essentialism, and homogeneity.

For Chanu, Nazneen embodies purity, simplicity and natural ignorance unaffected by modern ways of life, untarnished by British society, and uncorrupted by urbanity (BRL: 22-23; cf. Poon 2009: 430). His own professional and personal degradation in postcolonial London leads to a growing disenchantment with Britishness on the one hand, and a pride in the re-construction of an alternative imaginary Bangladesh on the other hand (cf. Cuevas 2008a: 206; Deny 2009: 219-221). Chanu's decision to return to Bangladesh is based on the misconception that "[b]ack home we'll really know what's what." (BRL: 464) His political and ethnic short-sightedness that his mother country has not changed in the last three decades becomes painfully apparent in the contrast of Chanu's romanticised ideas of home versus Hasina's letters (BRL: 146-177; cf. Kral 2007: 69). Crang (1998: 137) points out that even in Bengal "Dhakari saris appeal to urban middle-class nostalgia for rural village life, employing images of 'eternal Bengali woman' and classical poetry emphasising village and home." In that respect, *Brick Lane* portrays a two-fold regression to fundamentalist ideas of cultural essentialism. This first concerns the imaginary homeland as the former colonial periphery and the countryside as opposed to metropolitan realities. Thus, also for migrants the idea of home resides in the country as opposed to urban-generic displacement.

Likewise for Karim, Nazneen, the Bengali flat and the cultural-specific domestic routines constitute a means for creating an imaginary stability. At first, Karim appears to be opposed to Chanu; Nazneen admires her lover for his focussed agency and "place in the world" (BRL: 448). In reality, the second-generation immigrant is caught in a constant struggle to overcome his diasporic inbetweenness (cf. Deny 2009: 216-217). Nazneen as a Bengali wife and mother reproduces a notion of authenticity, which he desires as his fix point of identity construction and self-definition (*ibid.*: 219). The confinement of women to the private sphere paradoxically counters the men's fear of disorientation in the public urban realm and re-establishes an essentialist idea of home and identity (*ibid.*: 220). These static structures of thinking which construct impermeable and stable boundaries of public and private in the city necessarily fail to build an urban existence.

Redefinitions of the Self as urban do, however, not only encompass personal identity but also group identities. Campbell-Hall (2009: 172) shows that post-millennial fictions of migration specifically represent a significant change in survival strategies of migrant family units by renegotiating the definition of the traditional family unit and domestic community. Nazneen recognises that she "had learned first about loneliness, then about privacy, and finally she learned a new kind of community." (BRL: 182) In her analysis of the novel, Campbell-Hall (2009: 172) tracks five developmental stages of an immigrant's trajectory of integration, from "*an unrealistic idealisation of the host community*" to a renegotiation of the domestic and an extended family unit more appropriate to contemporary British society. This process entails that Asian-British novels, for example Meera Syal's *Life Isn't All Ha Ha Hee Hee* (1999) and Hanif Kureishi's *The Buddha of Suburbia* (1990), challenge the actual integrity of the traditional Asian-British family unit (*ibid.*:

171). Thus, the domestic is set in opposition to outside hostility, politics and a British national identity, and the home and the family remain "strongholds of Asianness" (*ibid.*: 172) and tradition.

Often the migrants find themselves in a stage of fractured identity crisis in "*search for a new domestic community*, a culturally familiar home-away-from-home in Britain." (Campbell-Hall 2009: 175) Karim and Nazneen both look for a new group identity, but while the young man locates it in the fundamentalists' essentialist ideas of being and belonging to a global religious brotherhood, Nazneen in carving out a room for herself, discovers a place within the hybridized local female community based on the pragmatic fabric to secure a successful approach to the urban everyday. Forging ties of support and common interests with women of her own generation in the estate, she claims her own place in the contemporary metropolis (cf. Valman 2009: 7). In that sense, Ali's *Brick Lane* propagates how female immigrants, in the attempt to gain some degree of independence, need to define their own social space against the culture of male-dominated spatialities, and communal activism. Hence, the novel moves away from the closed ethnic notion of home as an absolute space, favouring a new notion of belonging in the form of communal female solidarity and sisterhood (cf. Cuevas 2008a: 209). The transgression of family ties therefore also indicates "a crucial change in thinking, from an emphasis on communal considerations to a preference for the well-being of the individual." (Campbell-Hall 2009: 178) Re-establishing spatialities and the re-defining the female Self is indicated by the image of Razia's and Nazneen's empty flats. However, these functional redefinitions of the family unit, the re-placement of the private sphere, and the renegotiation of domestic communities not only reflect, as Campbell-Hall (*ibid.*: 173, 177, 179) argues, the changing social structures within the postmodern, postcolonial and multicultural British society, but they also convey the shifting boundaries between public and private, altering the semantics of the contemporary metropolis.

To sum up: first, Nazneen finds herself confined by the patriarchal spatial imagery of the public/private division, the gendered urban spaces, as described by Gillian Rose and Doreen Massey. The flat is the world she inhabits and this enclosed existence enhances the restrictions of her personal agency and thinking. However, the novel exemplifies how traditional roles, their assignment to spatial polarities of public and private and the separate sphere model cannot be contained within the city. In Nazneen's case, these rejections are exemplified in the mentally unsettled process of unlearning her mother's legacy of fatalism as a philosophy of life (cf. Poon 2009: 433). By territorialising the metropolis as a space of emancipation, Nazneen's coming of age is linked to her crossing the boundaries between the inside of her flat and the outside of the estate, traversing the lines between the common area of the Brick Lane neighbourhood and the unknown of the inner city. In the fashion of an immigrant woman walker, her specific perceptions and actions within the urban ultimately change the places around her, as the experience of the city alters her own habits. We have to bear in mind, however, that the immediate public spaces of the estate and Brick Lane are transformed as territorial fights ensue and Brick Lane is altered by the city centre expanding to the East End. In that sense, the urban public intrudes into communal semi-private structures as well. Moreover, not only does the public always permeate into the private to change its setting and relations, but, as Nazneen's interior spatial practices show, the private is also a space of resistance for her. Spatial entrapment is seen both as a burden as well as a chance of rootedness and a means and resource for empowerment (cf. Rose 1993: 126). The acknowledgement of the dynamics between public and private space ultimately render the female immigrant better equipped to urban life and faster to integrate in London metropolitan life by pragmatic sensualism and vigilance than her male counterparts. Concerning internal urbanisation, *Brick Lane* shows that the urban-generic mental structures are based on the acceptance of the public/private ambivalence which essentially means the constant realignment of their boundaries to establish liminal spaces between work and play, production and reproduction, reason and body, expert and everyday knowledge.

6.1.4 Public 'Aparthide' and Search for Intimacy

Christine Brooke-Rose's novel *Next* (1998)[16] takes up the theme of individual lives in the city and the harsh realities of a post-Thatcherite social fragmentation due to an overwhelming unemployment and a general end-of millennium feeling. Brooke-Rose zaps into and out of the represented lives – an atypical urban soap opera – of London's homeless people. Concerning the public/private ambivalence, the novel explores the political and social consequences of a post-Fordist age on the urban individual and exposes the paradox of their marginal existence as completely intertwined with the public spaces of the city. In the case of the homeless in *Next*, the two entities merge in an extreme way.

Although Brooke-Rose is often considered an experimental writer in the tradition of the *nouveau roman*, she is now positioned as a postmodern author with a deep interest in narratology who strongly negotiates socio-political themes and cultural transformations (cf. Sapio Garbero 1993: 107). In the 1980s, her novels question relations between simulation and reality not only on a textual basis, but according to Brooke-Rose initially explore how "[o]ur entire attitudes, our mental structures have now been altered [...], the fact that this reality we are given everyday is in fact highly organised." (*Ibid.*: 118) Her narratives are often written in present-tense and free indirect speech, thus emphasising the distinctions between "the public sphere of events and discoveries presented as factual statements on the one hand, and on the other hand the inner world of psycho-social dramas presented as narrative fiction." (Birch 1994: 117)

Life without Privacy in the Public

In *Next* the public has more or less involuntarily become the 'home' of London's homeless; they sleep, wake, eat, wash, walk, read, and talk in the streets. While Diogenes still has his barrel, as one character points out, the only possessions left to the metropolitan homeless are wrapped in a plastic bag with dry clothes to change into after a rainy night and a raincoat to sleep on (NXT: 194). In correspondence to the cynic's maxim of autarky, all the drop-out homeless prefer the outside and its freedom to the hostels and night centres, which are mainly reserved for the young home-leavers. Although these places offer a bed and a shower, they are less private than the public sleeping spots (NXT: 73,

---

16 | In the following *Next* will be abbreviated to NXT. Also, I will quote passages from *Next* as fluent text without spaces and omissions if not particularly necessary for an understanding of the extracts.

145). Hence, the homeless become rather possessive about their secret night shelters (NXT: 55, 61).

The ten metropolitan street walkers, both male and female, make their beds under motorways, on the emergency stairs of tube stations, in telephone boxes, on park benches, and in doorways, having to adapt to the rhythms of the city around. The novel's story begins with the homeless Tek waking to the sounds of the motorway overhead and the rain on his face. After his favourite morning routine of "breakfast in BED" he walks a long way to the public lavatories to wash, shave, and change (NXT: 2-6). The daily route is followed by dropping in at the food centre to eat and dry the clothes. This is also the only time during the day that he feels remotely social, with homeless meeting others, sitting down together to eat, exchange news, or watch television. Then it is out into the streets again, accumulating more miles on London's tarmac. Unable to pay for public transport, the homeless do a lot of walking in between the public institutions that sustain their life – hostels, food centres, job centres, assistance, and benefits, Homeless Person Units, etc. (NXT: 34).

The homeless protagonists are notoriously unsheltered; the weather, the city's noise, the violence of its streets all leave them utterly vulnerable. The unshielded city life of the homeless becomes initially prevalent during winter when the emergency services drive out to collect the homeless before they freeze to death (NXT: 103). But especially for female homeless, life on the streets carries extra problems: the younger Elsie (NXT: 68) is plagued by her period and the older Ivy is hindered by her incontinence (NXT: 105), the teenage Paula binds two other homeless teenagers to her for protection. And finally, in the public sphere of the park, Elsie is murdered by an unknown person.

Narratologically fashioned after the first literary documented urban homeless, the Greek cynic Diogenes, London's street walkers are figures of the public. Like their ancient forefather, they are notoriously sophisticated and overtly critical of society. From Elisa (Elsie), Ulysses and Woyzeck (Tek) to Jesse James (Yuppy) most homeless main characters are named after renowned literary outcasts opposed to mainstream culture. By their mental equipment of cynic attitude they are characterised as relatively autarkic, ascetic, cosmopolitan, living in urban exile, but their position as outcasts allows them to insist on free speech against public grievances.

The Public Quest for Intimacy

With their private lives rendered public, the homeless characters in *Next* as non-persons are on a frantic mission to re-establish some kind of privacy and retain a form of intimacy. As Gilbert (2008: 109) has pointed out, the *flâneur* does not look for spectacles but rather yearns for intimacy. For the homeless Londoner, the city's natural walkers *per se*, the idle cruise around the metropolis is transformed to a vital search for privacy. This necessarily presents a paradox because the privacy sought for is defined by the 'right to be left alone', independence in the midst of the public masses, while in their need for intimacy the homeless look for connections within their own social 'family'.

Whenever they have the chance, the homeless narrate their personal drop-out story not only to link up with a soul mate but also in the need to reinstate their Self and underline that they are still individuals and not mere fragments of the urban mass. However, these reminiscences from the past do not apply to the present and often these narratives are highly unreliable, and narrowed down to the cause of their transformation from member of society to pariah. For example Quentin says: "I tried to start up independent like, something more diversified seey, but I couldn't find the backing, so I left haome, pretending a business trip. Married with two kids. That was seven years ago." (NXT: 23) Or later Elsie exemplifies: "I was brought up in the slummy West Indian part of Notting Hill. Queen of the Carnival one year, at seventeen. And here I am, between integration and segregation. I integrated so well I'm on the streets, like you." (NXT: 34) The conversations thus always remain on the surface, concerning wider social but never personal issues and often wind up in monologuous rants on the state of the nation.

The inefficient search for intimacy is specifically connected with the characters Tek and Ulysses. Tek links up with various homeless, but while walking with them he either falls into a tirade on historio-political issues or digs too deep into the private matter of his chosen companion. As Elsie remarks: "He sits, but looks straight ahead at the world, never at me." (NXT: 34) And Tek later acknowledges: "Must stop making cheer-quenching remarks. Yet approached Rickey; I approached Ulysses. I approached Elsie." (NXT: 195) Hence, while trying to connect to his fellow urbanites he involuntarily fails, because the reciprocal interest not to feel alone is diametrically opposed to their need for individuality, freedom, and solitude.

> The conversation lags, as if switched off with the pale sun. Why did I pick him up? [...] I now I'll never get rid of him, no excuses on Sunday, no job-or-girocentres. Though in fact he seems to be regretting it too. Let him think up an excuse, he's young, with a lying imagination still active. But then I felt much the same about that old man, Ulysses. (NXT: 189)

Both Tek and Ulysses look for communication as intimate atmosphere, but once they have vented their private thoughts or heard enough personal information, they delink and disappear into the urban mass. Whereas both characters first enjoy their walk through Hampstead, Tek suddenly realizes that, although he has just used his fellow walker for his emotional trash, he now wants to discard him:

> We reach Haverstock Hill. Hampstead Tube Station up on the right, but I daren't say so, though I suddenly want to get rid of him. [...] Why did I confide in him, he's going to cling like a father. A father-confessor, but then he shouldn't know me behind the lattice-work. Pig-selfish of me, I feel better he feels worse, as if he'd taken over the burden. (NXT: 132)

While Tek forces his political views and private stories on everyone, Ulysses himself picks up various characters, whether a boy from a street-gang or a couple in a restaurant. The parallel situation takes place when Ulysses seeks contact to a former butcher at the food centre for some breakfast conversation and sociability. Although his chosen partner first feels reluctant to talk to him, he opens up over a cup of tea and communicates his whole drop-out story and the larger political context of his personal failure (NXT: 166-167). When he seems impossible to stop, Ulysses more and more longs to leave. The search for intimacy remains on a superficial basis of small-talk, never really and truly opening up or laying bare the inner Self. Moreover, as in the case of the male characters Henry Perowne (SAT), Alfred White (WIF) and Chanu (BRL), the homeless' personal identity also strongly depends on employment, which is all they care to talk about.

So it's as alienating to talk of meat as it is of Africa. Is everyone alienating when they talk of passion-forming work? Or is it work-forming passions? Are we now so dead to it all, like plugged off walkmen, that we don't hear each other any more? Or even ask egging-on questions? (NXT: 169)

In that respect, the homeless' contradictory relation to intimacy and privacy exposes the structures of the whole urban society as wrought by alienation. The analogy of linguistic pun concerning "walkmen" indicates that postmodern urban life with its technological devices of TV, music, advertisement and computers has created a monadic urbanity without interconnection. In analogy, their privacy is paradoxically located in the public, the newspaper as the most important prop of protection for the homeless is a device that allows them to "tune others out" (Karp, Stone & Yoels 1991: 87). Croaky's states that he "[n]eeyd to be alaone. Here's the paper for company" (NXT: 83). He expresses the intrinsic paradox of these forms of media intervening in the private lives, just as the narrative's free indirect speech shows how the homeless' thoughts are constantly interfered with by urban reality (see chapter 6.3.2).

Public Invisibility

The second paradox of homeless urban public/private existence *Next* negotiates is that of invisibility, a theme of urban-generic mentality already covered by *Saturday* and *Brick Lane*. Although the characters living on the street are visibly distinguishable from the urban masses, they are also eager to keep their distance and create absolute spaces of privacy – mostly mentally. In other words, they are both afraid of their invisibility as members of the urban pariah as they are afraid for it. As argued above, most homeless characters prefer the solitude of the streets at night to the hostel. Although feeling "shrouded in shock, dejection and loneliness" (NXT: 142), they are easily oppressed by the human 'baggage' they collect on the street (NXT: 172-175). With their privacy in the open, the homeless of London are careful to retain their personal space by a neat play of behavioural indifference. Elsie's coat is her protection, not only against the cold, and "an aparthide" (NXT: 17) saving her from recognition but also signifies her difference and distance to other urbanites. Still, as pointed out by one of the characters, the fur hood of Elsie's coat may draw the eyes of aggressive animal lovers to her, as her black skin makes her a prey for racist remarks. Finally, although hidden in her coat in the depth of the darkness in Hyde Park, she falls prey to murder. Beforehand, Tek and Elsie mutually ignore one another in Hyde Park.

I sit, pushing the others down the bench. A bench, somebody said, one feels good one a bench, the invention of the chair was the beginning of selfishness, each for himself. [...] Fivish. Dusk falling. I saw her. She saw me, then turned away and went to sit on another bench further on... [...] She was rolling her head, erm, in a strange way as if to say she didn't er, care to talk to me. I stared at the ground, pretending not to see her. Wondering if I should, well, join her. But I didn't... (NXT: 83)

While Tek averts his eyes to leave Elsie her intimate space in the public, Yuppy's gaze is drawn towards her and he begins to follow her around London (NXT: 19, 36, 67). It is not only their common street walkers that stalk, but despite their perceived invisibility, the homeless are highly visible and supervised by the "Big Brother[s]" (NXT: 150) of public government institutions. Living on the streets they are constantly under public control. An officer seizes the bundle of an elderly homeless woman, in which she carries all her belongings: "He picks it up, not so much out of galantry but to examine its innards, dirty zinc dishes spare undies and all. Thanks officer. Ah daon carrey bombs. Off nao fer a brisk walk, tara." (NXT: 104) As urbanites exiled to exist without the shelter but condemned to open space, they are the favourite victim of general prejudice.

The 'Nexting' of Personal Relations and Post-Fordist Anomie

In the beginning of the 1990s, Christine Brooke-Rose states that "the computer revolution has and will change our mentalities" (cit in Sapio Garbero 1993: 113). In *Next*, everyday urban life has taken on the manner of zapping through a TV programme. As people show their personal issues in talk shows, you might stay with them as long as you like, switching off in an instant. Due to continuous 'nexting' nothing is next, close, personal, or intimate anymore.[17] Even the homeless in their constant search for intimacy cannot stand the proximity of others for long and in their ambivalent need for privacy shut everything else out.

The biography of most homeless characters in the novel is not only determined by the harsher economic climate of Thatcherism and its continuance under the following two British governments, but is also notably influenced by the interrelation of broken social and family life. For example, Ivy, a sixty-five-year-old woman, whose son was killed in the Irish conflict, is left on her own with a meagre pension and decides to stay on the streets (NXT: 107). As we perceive from the narrated drop-out stories, the primary relations of family life, similarly to *The White Family*, are dissolved. For Oliver, society as a whole has become out of touch, family life is a myth that does not hold in the contemporary city, and personal life is crushed by the overabundance of socio-political issues.

> No. I don't like going there [to his parents]. But I see a sister occasionally in London. To keep in remote touch [...]. But in fact we're all out of touch aren't we? We never talk family, do we? [...] Aggressivities and problems are no longer related to Oedipus and Electra and all that. The family romance is buried. Deeply perhaps but dead, disintegrating. Personal history's dead. I must go. (NXT: 183)

In this sense, the ideal of close family ties, community relations idealised in soap operas, the meta-structure of the novel, is a double virtual reality and more than mere televised fiction. Unable to come clean in front of his wife regarding his bankruptcy and personal failure, Quentin leaves his family and spends seven years on the streets until he reaches the end of his tether from daily destitution and the hope for a job makes him come in for help (NXT: 70-71, 161). For Quentin, all personal feelings are compromised by words and disappear under the shield of phrases when his wife firstly reacts steely and with

---

17 | Brooke-Rose, as pointed out by Sapio Garbero (1993: 116) and Birch (1994: 93), is involved in wordplay concerning the titles of her novels. Thus, for *Thru* (1975) the topic of the novel is "hurt".

natural distance and in parallel his former home is closed off by the house's gate, garden, door (NXT: 71, 163). As a comparison, the narrative includes the shattered family life of an immigrant family living in a small dump in Notting Hill. The only daughter is already estranged from her family, while the older son hates his home and prefers to roam the street with his gang, getting involved in crime and violence (NXT: 43; 155-156). The despotic father, Xavier, is illiterate, a builder but mostly out of work, who releases his anger on wife and kids (NXT: 42). Adelina, left in an all-male household, runs the family home, works as a cleaner, strives to learn to read, and sometimes feels the urge to flee her buried existence, leave her husband and children, and live independently if homeless in the city (NXT: 155).

In its spatial semantics of public and private, the novel deals with an urban mental disposition that is predominantly distinguished by estrangement. This significant urban state can either materialise in a form of drop-out mentality or a mentality of exclusion. At their basis lies an enhanced need for the right to be left alone, especially due to the de-privatisation of urban life or the overwhelming intrusion of the public into private life. The novel thereby stresses urban anomie, as people are pushed into liminal public/private existences, and in the manifold "doorways in London" (NXT: 54). Former public community and family life has been abandoned for a metropolitan monadic and restless individualism. Consequently, all the private space the homeless urbanites have left to withdraw to is the seemingly enclosed privacy of their thoughts.

6.1.5 Isolationist Structures of Mentality

Heyl (2004: 11) shows in his analysis of privacy in London that since the eighteenth century the private sphere has become more and more a part of urbanites' everyday lives which leads to a transformation of the city's material structures, its social and cultural life, as well as its mentalities. Contemporary London fiction charts a drive towards the construction of absolute island spaces of urban similarity, sameness, and homogeneity, erecting or stabilising hierarchical structures of marginalisation in the midst of the city's variety. This becomes visible in the mental privatisations of identity, habitus, and emotional life. The analysed novels concentrate on the phenomena of both inclusion and exclusion caused by frontiers between public and private in relation to group identities of class, generation, gender, ethnicity, and race.

Initially caused by a growing exposure to the public, the establishment of an absolute bourgeois private space implies a transformation of norms and rules concerning the boundaries of legitimate structures of behaviour. Especially prevalent is therefore the clash of socio-economic identities in the urban realm. In *Saturday*, Perowne strives to maintain the clear opposition between the bourgeois privacy of the family as opposed to the controlled publicity of democratic citizenship. From his stance, Perowne recognises that the lives of the lower classes are significantly mediated in the public. Also the White's suburban lower-middle class existence, private and professional, is mainly defined by public places. Equally, the inhabitants of Tower Hamlets in *Brick Lane* are represented as prisoners of the estate whose private lives lie in the open. And finally, the homeless of *Next* exist totally exposed in the public, being driven around the city in a constant search for intimacy and privacy.

Generational conflicts (Baxter vs. Henry in SAT, Nazneen vs. Chanu in BRL, Alfred vs. Darren in WIF or Tek vs. Elsie in NXT) emphasise the different use and semantisation of both urban realms and in correspondence with the theory of mentality constitute a definite sign for the transformations of mental structures. These dissimilarities become especially apparent in the ruptures between generations. While younger characters are seemingly more willing to adapt to new demands of public life, older characters prefer the privacy of the home as a realm of personal freedom. With the exception of McEwan's depictions, the novels are in general quite critical of the concept of the family as the place of intimacy (WIF, NXT) and authenticity (BRL). Instead of proving the urban defence mechanism of reserve, the family is mentally infiltrated by the public, especially through new technologies. Although the family is the primary locus of socialisation and a significant space of inner urbanisation by socialisation, the more relevant spaces in contemporary London are shown to be those of the wider society. Consequently, the novels not only scrutinise intimate associations between people joined by family ties but also emphasise the bond of the crowd and the relevance of secondary relations in urban life (see chapter 7.1.1).

Especially *Brick Lane* concerns the critique of the division between public and private space as gendered constructions in the city. The separate sphere ideology decisively prevents women – physically and symbolically – from being part of public life and relegates them to the confines of the home as a locale of family, personal relations, reproduction, parenting, and sexuality. In the novels analysed, this strong dichotomy and the quasi-imprisonment of women at home is still viable (May in WIF, Nazneen in BRL, Adelina in NXT). The men's insistence of a bounded privacy (Henry in SAT, Alfred in WIF, Chanu in BRL) has instead been shown as a sign for essentialist notions, which is notoriously misplaced in the constant transformations of metropolitan plurilocalities as geometrics of difference.

The creation of absolute spaces of public and private with concrete boundaries implies a certain isolationist mentality as dispositions for constructing stable identities against the urban overload of stimuli and exposure to the public. However, these isolationist structures not only signify the intrinsic anxiety concerning the Self, but specifically reveal the fear of the urban Other, the general figure of the stranger and with him the dynamics of the metropolis. While the complexities of the urban ambivalence of public and private are shown to be more heterogeneous and paradoxical, the constructions of public and private in the novels elucidate how characters largely rely on the security of middle-age "white heterosexual bourgeois notions of the private" (Rose 1993: 131).

Consequently, this urban pre-condition also applies with regard to spaces of racial and ethnic inequality. It arouses, for instance, territorial disputes around Brick Lane, while public places in *The White Family* are regarded as a patch of declining quintessential Englishness. However, in each of the four novels the successful integration into metropolitan life and the inner urbanisation as connected with a certain growth of tolerance towards the Other and a charged form of agency is put in opposition to the privatisations of urban life. Still, in *The White Family* the librarian Thomas lacks the literacy of tolerance and rather inhabits an increasingly distanced or reserved specific version of urbanism, which despite its political liberalism is not free from social or racial prejudice. In contrast to Sennett's notion of the cosmopolitan as public man, the novels rather construct characters on the urban archetype who is able to negotiate both the public and the private which in its liminal existence is closer to the urban type in Simmel and Park's sense. This life on the threshold also means being able to adjust one's behaviour according to the momentary urban surrounding.

The predominant withdrawal and isolationist mental structures necessarily define both private and public spaces, whereby the public becomes increasingly less public: in *Saturday*, private dramas are enacted on the city square, while in *The White Family* and *Brick Lane* semi-public physical, social and mental spaces provide space for personal autonomy. First, elemental to ontological security is the constitution of a habitual framework in regard to the public and the private. The characters' routine include that their everyday life is split in roles of front-region and backstage behaviour in accordance to public and private spheres. In *Saturday*, Henry is unable to acknowledge the need to adapt his professional thinking to the public drama unfolding in the streets, while Nazneen is able – by quasi-anthropological thick description – to quickly learn about the differences of urban public conduct. All novels communicate and problematise the idea of urban drama: *Saturday* in its analysis of public and private stages, *Brick Lane* in the idea of shadow play, and *Next* in the intermedial relation to the soap opera. Second, the classical idea of public catharsis as a means of urban healing is depicted in contemporary city novels, most prominently in *The White Family*, as a significant mental equipment of social stress reduction. Represented as a stage of masking, for instance by role-play (SAT) or costumation (WIF, BRL, NXT), the metropolis allows one to rid oneself of one's hide, and vent one's emotions. So, the public becomes the space of enacted intimacy and stress relief, without which society turns towards violence, self-destruction, and anomie. Insofar, in the postmodern metropolis which is more characterised by a relocation and a permeability of boundaries, strict rules of behaviour are necessarily suspended. Rather, the new dynamics of space request mobility concerning habitus in public settings where according to mediatised patterns acting rather than spatio-specific becomes more situational. The novels hereby discuss various patterns of (de)distanciation.

These patterns of public/private behaviour are not only based on unreflected codes of conduct, but also regulated by altering language codes. In London fiction the question of language dominates much of the discourse on the urban ambivalence of public and private. Language reinforces geographical barriers and physical distances and thus enforces separate spheres as well as the exclusiveness of metropolitan spatialities. Public language itself structures urban space by prioritising, prohibiting, restricting, and controlling the creation of secure and insecure, free and enclosed places. The public sphere with its official devices, codes of speech, and other forms of communication is therefore marked as a specific cultural space of power-relation within the city. On the other hand, the language of the predominantly public space can be appropriated by the private and finally lead to a blurring of boundaries. In *Saturday*, the media are omnipresent as a background noise, as the language of new technologies and advertisement infiltrates the homeless' thinking in *Next*, while in *Brick Lane* breaking the rule of speaking English at home is part of the female reterritorialisation of the flat. In other words, it is not only front and backstage roles, different codes of urban conduct, but also different grammars and sets of vocabulary that define the mental structure of public and private. Even the narrative structures of the novels confirm this exploration of relations of public/private ambivalence in focalisation: while *Brick Lane* features a long epistolary part usually found in confessional literature, the other three novels concentrate on the consciousness of their characters, either by free indirect speech or multi-perspectivity. This reveals that perceptions of the public are highly idiosyncratic in their lingual control, concerning gender, profession, ethnicity, etc.

Contemporary London fiction shows that the public and private maintain a mutual relationship in the metropolis. In this sense, only the complementary of both spheres refers to a transformation of mentalities. The novels are postmodern in their reassessment of modernist but also nineteenth-century ideas of the separate spheres concerning the public and the private. While critically exploring the dissolution of separate spheres, they expose the residual mentalities of homogenising spaces and inquire into the consequences of the urban psyche which are created by new semi-public threshold spaces. Thereby, the texts unmask modernist notions as essentialist, anachronistic, and misplaced concerning postmodern everyday life of the city. Whereas privacy has been considered desirable and progressive, the epitome of the private urbanite is revealed as a liminal being, able to choose urban roles and oscillate between public and private existence. Without the various constructions of threshold places that create the distinction between inside and outside, neither the city nor its public and private domains are possible.

From *Saturday*'s siege mentality, *The White Family*'s residual mentality, and *Brick Lane*'s hybrid mentalities of belonging, to *Next*'s mentalities of apartheid, the analysis has revealed that contemporary London mental structures emphasise a general desire for the private. We encounter this in the construction of Privatopias but also in semi-public spaces which serve the need for security, essentialism, authenticity, and intimacy. Although these mental standardisations appear strangely misplaced in the metropolis, these patterns are appropriate reactions to the anxiety, disorientation, overload, and strangeness of the postmodern metropolis.

Conversely, it is hermetic thinking that marginalises urbanites like Perowne from contemporary urban life. All in all, rather the de-routinised days, for example of mass demonstrations in London, show public behaviour very much alive and social life thriving. And while formerly enclosed public spaces become redundant, new semi-public spaces are erected as spaces of transience which allow for both privacy and sociability. Also new community structures are created becoming the equivalent to the former primary relation *per se*, the family. Insofar, London is shown on the verge of an anomic society because it is missing familiar spaces for intimacy. However, public space is not dead at all; it is rather characterised by an enhanced fragmentation and individualisation, thus also a stronger sense of distance between actions and sphere of action. In all the novels, the public in disguise of the media, new technologies, the homogenising tendencies of globalisation, and surveillance systems invade personal life and thinking. Thus, the postmodern metropolis especially lacks independent privacy, a space of non-mediatised intimacy and authenticity. Nevertheless, these Woolfian realms are predominantly reached by the female characters' mental spaces of imagination (Daisy in SAT, May in WIF, Nazneen in BRL, Elsie in NXT).

What we can actually discern from that development is that boundaries of public and private have become permeable, realigning the spaces of public and private behaviour or even leading to a contestation of the equivalent relations between actions, spaces, and spheres. When content and form of action become conceptionally separated from the spaces of action, this mechanism creates interstitial and contingent spaces. Thereby, the ambivalence of public and private and the according mental structures are adapted to the shifting and dissolving boundaries or the permeable and fluid spatialities of the postmodern city. For urbanites the mental structures of isolationism are a means to cope with the concomitant fear of a loss of identity and the Self, disassociation as well as isolation, involuntary transformation and insecurity. Consequently, contemporary London mentality is oriented towards the protection of privacy by social distance. Standardisations of thinking represented as embracing the public are quite scarce.

From the selected literary corpus of analysis especially postcolonial novels about second generation immigrants (e.g. *Londonstani*), or those concerning subcultures (e.g. *King Rat*) and newcomers (e.g. *Bleeding London*) emphasise the sociability and freedom of the public realm as a chance for personal transformation and vigilance. A third group of novels is not centrally concerned with the theme of public and private, because the equivalence of both spheres is taken as a prerequisite for socially entwined personal dramas unfolding in the urban realm (e.g. *253*, *London Bridges*, *White City Blue*, *A Long Way Down*, etc.).

6.2 Underground London

> Discovering subterranean London meant exploring it, penetrating it. In turn, it was penetrating me, I realised, it was filling my thoughts.
> (Smith 2005: 255)

Without a dominant high-rise skyline, the London's vertical city is constituted in the essential opposition between above- and underground. Sizing a vertical cut through the metropolis or peeling back the city's surface, the multi-layered and widely spread system of underground London is revealed. It forms a three-dimensional labyrinthine space that represents "[ein] dezentriertes unterirdisches Geflecht" (Krewani 2002: 185) – a decentred subterranean network. Accordingly, Tobias Döring (2002: 55) and Alice Jenkins (2006: 35) both define the London beneath as a rhizomatic space, a relational system of multiple (inter)connections. Next to basement flats and wine cellars underground London contains the "arteries which sustain the urban body" (Thorne 1996: 7), like water supply ducts, sewers, electricity and communication cables, gas pipes, sewered rivers, and channelled tributaries. Most prominently the tunnel system and stations of the oldest underground railway spread through the subterranean city – the London Tube. The city beneath includes moreover archaeological remains of roman temples, crypts, plague pits, cemetery catacombs, as well as various caves and deep-level shelters.[18]

18 | In the following I will refer to 'underground London' or 'subterranean London' when indicating the whole area beneath the city, while London Underground or the Tube specifically refers to the subterranean railway system. For more information on subterranean London besides Pike (2005) and Trench and Hillman (1985) see Anthony Clayton (2000), *Subterranean City. Beneath the Streets of London*. For more information on the London Underground besides

The Thames Tunnel between Wapping and Rotherhithe built by Marc and Isambard Kingdom Brunel between 1825 and 1843 triggered a phase of major tunnelling throughout London. Pike (2005b: 351) points out that this tunnel was not only about tapping the underworld, "but functioned as a key threshold space for a modern London coming to terms with radical changes in its cityscape and social dynamics." The underground city gradually expanded with the new sewage system (1859-1875) by Joseph Bazalgette, and finally the cut-and-cover tunnels of the first underground railway system (1860s-1880s), extending to greater depth with the tubes (1890s) and spreading to the suburban fringes during the 1920s and 1930s. In that sense, the construction of the London Underground can be considered an even more decisive historical landmark in the metamorphosis of the metropolis and the transformation of urbanity. Especially by serving as shelter during the Blitz, the Tube re-established a positive underground mythology as a space of security which mitigated the underground's long-standing image of the nineteenth-century sewer, subway and necropolis as a nightmarish vision of hell (cf. Trench & Hillman 1985: 9; Pike 2005a: 5-6, 173-174).

According to Brandolini (1996: 5), the Underground and London have developed a reciprocal identity. Whereas the labyrinthine system of subterranean London is a prerequisite for the city's survival, the Underground presents a specifically significant icon for the city's idiosyncratic character.[19] For Döring (2002: 55-56) the "irrational maze" of the subterranean metropolis "serves a way to visualize and structure London's vast immensity" and thereby "offers an apt way to comprehend and represent metropolitan realities". With an average commuting time of thirty-seven minutes, the London Underground has developed into a central space of urban everyday experience, demanding and regulating a specific behaviour. Whereas the subterranean means of communication notably define the way of life of Londoners, the Tube initiated "a consciousness adequate to the new cityscape" (Schivelbusch 1986: 186). Enlivening the metropolis in flux through providing its foremost means of transportation and mobility, the London Underground is defined by specific experiences, images, fears, hopes, fantasies and visions. Insofar, an analysis of a London-specific mentality necessarily includes the implications of the Underground's historical, geographical, social, and cultural particularities as well as its iconography, narratives, atmosphere, and feel.

Underground London as a whole has triggered ambivalent attitudes and has become a space of ambiguous "cultural negotiations" (Döring 2002: 33).[20] Since John Holling-

---

Halliday (2001) and Wolmar (2004) see John Glover (1951), London *Underground. An Illustrated History of the World's Premier Underground System*; Oliver Green (1988), *The London Underground. An Illustrated History*; Christian Wolmar (2002), *Down the Tube. The Battle for London's Underground.*

19 | Already in 1865, Henry Mayhew (2003: 14) contended that "[the new London railway] was [...] so peculiar and distinctive a feature of the great English capital, that to omit this underground of intercommunication from a publication professing to be descriptive of the foremost institutions and establishments of the British metropolis, would assuredly be the same as playing the tragedy of 'Hamlet,' with the principal character left out."

20 | For recent articles and monographs which critically analyse the impact of the spatial representations of the subterranean cityscape see Ashford (2008), B. Baker (2003), Brandolini (1996), Döring (2001, 2002, 2003), Krewani (2002), McLeod (2007), Mengham (2003), Pike

head's *Underground London* (1862), there has been a sheer endless plethora of critical publications on the subterranean city and especially since the 1990s, the popular press shows an increasing interest in the subject of the underground.[21] Smith (2005: xvi-xvii) puts this new focus of the city down to the material transformations of London when building sites uncover parts of the city's life-supporting arteries:

> The past twelve months have witnessed extraordinary developments, large and small that underline the fact that the future security and prosperity of the capital depend to a remarkable degree on its hidden side, its secret self, its subterranean alter-ego. In a way London thinks about herself, this is now a city turned upside down. The great berg of the metropolis - so much of it out of sight beneath the tarmac and the concrete - grants us tantalising and sobering glimpses of what was previously overlooked.

Moreover, the terrorist attacks on the London Tube in 2005 notably reinitiated dark impressions and anxieties in regard to the metropolitan underworld.

While the 'metrotext' has become a significant urban 'sub-text' of the metropolis, literary sources offer the most sophisticated confrontation with underground London (cf. Brandolini 1996: 5; Pike 2005a: 18). In the 1980s, Lesser (1987: 31-32) bemoaned that the thriller was the only genre that still maintained a strong link with London's underworld and serious literature featured hardly any connection with the metropolitan physical underground, but with Döring (2003: 194-195) and Pike (2005a: 189) we can contend that towards the end of the twentieth century the underground has seen a major revival in literature.[22] Underground London has become a major topos of the metropolitan imaginary alongside representational landmarks, and in addition to the palimpsestuous city defines the dominating tropes in contemporary London fiction (cf. Pleßke 2009: 196-197).

The verticality of underground semantisations and their dichotomies offer narrative fiction various possibilities for crossing borders in the Lotmanian sense. The spatial semantics of the subterranean city between utopia and myth, its stereotypical atmosphere

(1999, 2002, 2005a, 2005b), Pleßke (2009), O'Brien (2010). For more also see David Welsh (2010), *Underground Writing. The London Tube from George Gissing to Virginia Woolf* and David Ashford (2013), *London Underground. A Cultural Geography.*

21 | See for example Christopher Ross' bestselling *Tunnel Visions* (2002), Tim Bradford's *The Groundwater Diaries* (2003), Stephen Smith's *Underground London* (2005), Peter Ackroyd's *London Under* (2011), and Mark Mason's *Walk the Lines. The London Underground Overground* (2011).

22 | For primary texts see Dorothy Meade & Tatiana Wolff, eds. (1994), *Lines on the Underground. An Anthology for Underground London Travellers*; Tobias Döring (2003), *London Underground. Poems and Prose about the Tube.* Besides the novels used for this analysis see John Healy (1990), *Streets Above Us*; Barbara Vine (1991), *King Solomon's Carpet*; Neil Gaiman (1996), *Neverwhere*; Jake & Luke Thoene (1997), *The Thundering Underground*; Will Self (2000), *How the Dead Live*; Nicholas Royle (2001), *The Director's Cut*; Andrew Martin (2002), *The Necropolis Railway*; China Miéville (2007), *Un Lun Dun*; Marie Phillips (2007), *Gods Behaving Badly.*

as well as its alternative forms of perception and modes of representation are especially employed in genre fiction (*ibid.*: 197). London thrillers take up the idea of the criminal underground; it presents an ideal setting for "chase scenes, break-ins, criminal hide-aways, or the cornering of suspects." (Lesser 1987: 13) London's underground in regard to the criminal underclass and moral deprivation is, however, not only a space of social otherness, but the Tube also serves as an image for a "new social mobility" (*ibid.*: 14). Hence, in more ways than one, the interstitial space of underground London significantly figures as a thirdspace for the "beyond" (cf. Bhabha 1994: 3). By convention, science fiction and fantasy have made use of the underground's mythical versions of the past in their utopian visions of the future, apocalyptic notions of (urban) catastrophe or fantastic dreamscapes (cf. Jenkins 2006: 28).

The interstitial spatiality of the underground especially becomes apparent in London Noir novels, where subterranean urban tunnels are an equivalent to the dark caverns of country houses in Gothic novels and the spatial semantics of the uncanny are re-negotiated for the postmodern metropolis. It is the urban realm where the homely can inadvertently turn unhomely, where the unknown Other is identified as the repressed Self, and the mirror to the space above reveals the underground as an anthropomorphised doppelganger. Since Plato the literary underground cave is a place of self-knowledge and self-consciousness as well as self-recognition (cf. Haupt 2005: 505), a space where the protagonists struggle with threshold encounters of something alien, yet intrinsically part of themselves. An odyssey through the subterranean city or a journey on the Tube resembles the urban narrative trope of katabasis because wandering on the threshold between life and death signifies a transgression of the character's Self. Literary London underground is thereby associated with transitory identities whose transformation is usually marked by split personality or bodily metamorphosis. Thus, in more senses than one, the literary underworld also offers Freudian psychological readings as it symbolises the depth of the Self with its unspeakable desires and fears or as the unconscious (cf. Lesser 1987: 126; Ros. Williams 1990: 1; Jenkins 2006: 29). Buried personal memories and traumas are likely to resurface. However, these are not only individual, but in the subterranean space of the collective unconscious exist the alternative, hidden and repressed realities of the whole city. More often though, because the underground is material as well as imaginary, it symbolises the dream-scape between the conscious and the unconscious – the inbetween of an "oneiric space" (Pike 2005a: 110).

In its specific combination of verticality and enclosure (cf. Ros. Williams 1990: 7), the underground carries extra weight for the imaginary. While the opposition between surface and depth seems to be an archetype deeply rooted in the "structure of the brain" (*ibid.*: 8), this binary is not beyond time and space. The spacing and (b)ordering of aboveground versus underground, the rhizomatic structure of the subterranean city and its overwhelming denotation of the unconscious emphasise the significance of underground London for an urban-specific mentality.

The analysis of "Underground London", in reference to Lefebvre's spatial triad, will concentrate on physical, social, and mental aspects, as well as the spatio-temporal dynamics unfolding between all three components. Offering readings of five underground London novels – China Miéville's *King Rat* (1998), Geoff Ryman's *253. The Print Remix* (1998), Tobias Hill's *Underground* (1999), Keith Lowe's *Tunnel Vision* (2001) and Conrad Williams' *London Revenant* (2004) – I will explore isotopic, utopic, and heterotopic representations, observe its social spaces, and penetrate the subconscious spaces of the urbanites' minds, personal and cultural memory as well as the oneiric spaces of metropolitan becoming, and finally the uncanny moments of space-time compression to see beyond the mere mirror of the other city and disclose the collective nonconscious. The interpretation first sets out to show that the subterranean city (topographically and topologically) provides a necessary means of orientation in the postmodern metropolis and thereby constitutes a definitive pre-requisite for the construction of contemporary London mentality. Second, by paying specific attention to the ambivalence of familiarity and strangeness, I will argue that in its liminality, underground London as a spatialised uncertainty has become the main setting for the uncanny in the postmodern literary metropolis and can be identified as the most defining element of the subterranean mental structures.

6.2.1 Isotopic, Utopic, and Heterotopic Space

First of all, subterranean London is a replica of the metropolis above, mirroring its maze of streets, alleys, and lanes, but underground London is also seen as the counterpart to the surface city due to its enclosed and dark spatiality. Pike (2005a: 68-69) shows how the underground city unifies the derelict and contaminated space of the sewer system, which is traditionally conceived as organic, dirty, demonic, labyrinthine, unstable and female, with the antiseptic space of the Tube conveying an inorganic clean, bright, safe, well-ordered and masculine world. Contrasting notions of the underground are built on the urban-generic ambivalence of city versus country, and the vertical city is metaphorically constructed alongside the trope of Babylon and New Jerusalem (cf. *ibid.*: 275, 373; Jenkins 2006: 34). The subterranean city itself is always caught between "antiquity and novelty" (Pike 2005a: 12-14), "'old' superstition and 'new' pride in technology" (Lesser 1987: 34, 81), or myths and utopian visions (cf. Haupt 2005: 518). Due to its inherent spatial contradictions and the ambiguous conception as mirror and counter-image, the underground has become a space of interference simultaneously combining different topologies (cf. Pike 2005a: 30, 190). This sub-chapter hence explores contemporary representations of underground London as "*isotopy, u-topia, and heterotopy*" (Lefebvre 2003: 37) as vehicles of urban-specific mental structures.

The Mirror Image of the City

The chronicler of London's biography, Peter Ackroyd (2001: 568), considers London below a replica of the city above: "The Underground has its streets and avenues which the pedestrians quickly recognise and follow. It has its short cuts, its crossroads, its particular features [...] and, just like the city itself, areas of bright lights and bustle are surrounded by areas of darkness and disuse." Additionally, the underground imitates life aboveground by mimicking "the rhythms of the city [...] as well as its patterns of activity and habitation." (*Ibid.*) Representing the underground as homologous to the city above, its physical spatiality can be considered an urban isotopia. Moreover, Mumford (1997: 239) values the subterranean city not only as a mirror to the labyrinthine "outlines of the street-net on the surface", but as a space where urban denizens "spend[...] no inconsiderable part of the day." Insofar, London Underground is an intrinsic part of urbanity. In regard to New York, Gelfant (1954: 24) argues that "[s]ubway life in a way epitomizes city life: in a daily life situation within the subway are the collective physical conditions and psychological tensions that give rise to a manner of life defined as urbanism." In other words, underground behaviour largely mimics urban activities in a condensed form and thereby exposes dispositions of acting.

In the eyes of the protagonist in Keith Lowe's novel *Tunnel Vision* (2001)[23], the Underground embodies metropolitan life: "The tube is our history [...]. It's what defines London as a city: It's part of *all* of us." (TUV: 194) This "laddish" (Anon. n.d.) underground novel is a thick description of the London Tube and its users that constitutes an analogy to life in general and urbanity at the turn of the millennium in specific. The novel tells the story of the trainspotter Andy whose subterranean odyssey follows the protagonist's self-discovery on the day before his wedding (cf. Döring 2002: 44-45). His journey of the Underground's 205 stations within twenty hours is an urban *tour de force* including underground paraphernalia, closed ghost stations, chance encounters, suicides and delayed trains. Because the District, Circle, Metropolitan and Hammersmith & City lines are built directly underneath the city streets, the Underground mirrors London's cartography one on one (TUV: 306). As the city's double, the subterranean space conveys security as a cosy place of familiarity (TUV: 172-173).

Similarly, in Tobias Hill's *Underground* (1999)[24] the subterranean spatiality is specifically described as "a city under the city" (UND: 101), whereby the transformation of the subterranean space is attuned to the death and revitalisation of the city above:

> The Underground starts out perfect. At first it isn't like the city above it because it is conceived all at once. Everything must be created, heat and the passage for air. For the engineers and architects it begins as a perfect technical form. Then years go by – decades. Cross-tunnels are found to be unnecessary, so they are bricked up. Deeper tunnels are added by the government, then closed down. [...] Up above, communities die out. Stations are abandoned. [...] The Underground becomes a reflection of the city above – organic, not perfect. (UND: 135-136)

Additionally, underground London is represented as encompassing the city's sound- and smellscape, but still creating a very own and distinct atmosphere. Its fictitious "urban sound archive" (Döring 2002: 44) includes the sighs of tunnel air, the roar of the Tube, the echo of voices underground opposed to the distant, muffled sounds of the city above, and finally the significant stillness of darkness (UND: 3-4, 8, 38, 59, 117, 220). Moreover, the subterranean city in *Underground* resembles a particular smellscape mixing urban odours of car exhaust, human hair, sour fruit, urine, damp and stale air, clay and limestone (UND: 3, 5, 47, 74, 91).

The novel's main character is a Polish immigrant who, as an employee of London Transport, works the night shift on the Underground. Due to his job, Casimir seems to know the subterranean topography inside out, and he especially values the subterranean system's sense of order, control, as well as safety. However, Casimir has to notice that

---

23 | Like Lowe's fictitious *Tunnel Vision*, Christopher Ross' *Tunnel Visions* (both published in 2001) also concentrates on the Tube's anthropology. In the following *Tunnel Vision* will be abbreviated to TUV.

24 | In the following *Underground* will be abbreviated to UND.

his mental map of the Underground is far from complete and he slowly acknowledges its darker counter-side, the juxtaposition of being hidden and being trapped (UND: 162) Regarding spatial connotations, the underground is traditionally considered a place of darkness and claustrophobia opposed to the surface as a place of light and spaciousness. In respect of this opposition, Hill's novel also feeds on many ancient and modern underground myths devising the subterranean city as an allotopic spatiality which demands alternative readings. Consequently, underground London is constructed as an inverted image of the urban surface.

Counter Spaces of the Urban

In regard to his notion of Nekropolis, Mumford (1997: 291) suggests that an underground city may prove to be man's final shelter in a world which has become increasingly uninhabitable. Due to its otherness and because the space of the underground is "claimed [...] as constituting a secret, subterranean history of the city" (Pike 2002: 113), the subterranean metropolis also "functions as a source of desire and fantasy [...]" (Levy 1978: 70) which harbours the urbanites' denials, hopes, and fears. Würzbach (2001: 110) points out, that an allotropic space necessitates cross-reality constructions, such as myth, fairy tale, fantasy, science fiction, utopia, and dystopia.

In Keith Lowe's *Tunnel Vision* the picture of the cosy underground space of the Tube "illuminated by warm-coloured light" (TUV: 172) is counterpoised by its largely life-threatening connotations strongly revoking the mythical imagery of the underground as hell:

> Underground is dark, and lifeless. Underground is where the air is stale, and plants don't grow, and light cannot penetrate. It is where you are put when you die, stuck in a box full for all eternity in a space only big enough to fit your body. [...] Hell is underground. Underground is hell. (TUV: 170)

The Tube station is compared to a "mouth gaping like a gateway to the underworld" (TUV: 109) taking in the protagonist on his katabasis. In the brief dream sequence called "The Vestibule of Hell" (TUV: 163), which is reminiscent of Milton's *Paradise Lost* or Dante's *Divine Comedy*, Andy imagines himself being on a train to the abyss. His vision is fraught with darkness, blackness, blindness, and the atmosphere is thick with heat, smoke, sweat, and fear. Thus, this dream-scape uncovers the character's deepest anxieties by alluding to a mythologeme deeply ingrained in the collective unconscious.

Whereas subterranean myths focus on the otherness of the present compared to the past, the underground counter spaces of utopia/dystopia rather concentrate on the otherness of the present in regard to the future. Following Prakash (2008: 16), utopia and dystopia function as a general means of sublimation because the "images of urban dystopia and utopia act together to suppress the appearance of porosity, contradictions, and the promise of urban life." For Lefebvre (2003: 130), utopia is generally located near the borders of verticality, especially within the subterranean city.[25] Situated in a

25 | Cities as the loci of civilisation, evolution, and progress have long been the subject of literary utopian imaginations, and novels such as Edward Bulwer-Lytton's *The Coming Race*

different space or time, the *eu-topos* is also the embodiment of social and political ideals, which functions as a criticism of the present order disrupting dominant assumptions of the organisation of society and pointing towards alternative possibilities. The counterweight to utopia, is the depiction of a dystopian place which centres around feelings of alienation, despair, and fear, often envisioning apocalyptic scenarios of collapse, loss, and degeneration. Postmodernism with its discourse on the death of the city has revived these notions of "urban apocalypticism" (Pike 2005a: 78) and contemporary authors represent urban apocalyptic visions as connected to the vast dimensions of underground London. Against the utopian ideal of coherence, homogeneity, and unity, the dystopic urban imagery encompasses civilisations on the brink of anomie and social collapse.

China Miéville makes use of both the symbolic and physical underground spatiality in his allegorical fantasy *King Rat* (1998)[26]. The character King Rat, an opaque antagonist to human dispositions, owes his secret underworld realm to Bazalgette's creation of London's sewers. Abducted by the ruler, Saul Garamond, the young protagonist of half-rat and half-human decent, first encounters the other-worldly maze of London's underground:

> Saul stared into the pit. The swirling winds of the courtyard yanked at the rich-smelling wisps of vapour emerging from the hole. The sewer was gorged with darkness; it seemed to overflow, seeping out of the open concrete and obscuring the ground. The organic scent billowed out. Just visible, a ladder driven into the subterranean brick plunged out of sight. Where it was riveted to the wall, metal had oxidized and leached out profusely, making the sewer bleed rust. A sound of a thin flow of water was amplified by the yawning tunnels, making for a bizarre booming trickle. (KRA: 101)

The atmosphere of the sewers is dominated by mysterious darkness, horrid odours, magical sounds and uncanny organic processes. A locus of decomposition, disease, death, decay, and dissolution, the sewage tunnels are not only compared to "Pandemonium" (KRA: 420) – Milton's capital of hell and chaos – but its organic, irrational, uncontrollable, and primitive spatiality carries a specific dystopian undertone. Its allotopic space induces amazement, fright, and disorientation:

> Saul became lulled by the sewers. He kept King Rat in his sights, losing himself in the damp brick convolutions. [...] Saul felt like a tourist. He investigated the walls in passing, reading the mildew on the bricks. He was hypnotized by his own footsteps. Time passed as a succession of brick tributaries. He was ignorant of the cold and intoxicated by the smell. Occasional growls of traffic filtered through the earth and tar above, to yawn through the cavernous sewers. (KRA: 106)

(1871) or H.G. Wells' *The Time Machine* (1895) are set in the symbolic space of the underground. According to Rosalind Williams (1990: 6), the "image of hyperurbanity resembles that of the underground" because imaginary underworlds mimic vast cities while future cities appear like caves.

26 | In the following *King Rat* will be abbreviated to KRA.

Unable to cope with the stimuli of the alien surroundings, the protagonist is still privy to visual orientation instead of adhering to the subterranean smell- and soundscape (KRA: 107). This enclosed sensual otherness of the sewer tunnels triggers claustrophobia and anxiety (KRA: 206). Furthermore, in *King Rat*, the city's sewers host a new urban sub-species of proletarian rats and the novels re-enacts London's 1990s Drum N' Bass urban subculture, whose venues are located in abandoned warehouses and other non-places throughout the metropolis. On the whole, the novel's subterranean setting envisions counter-urbanity able to withstand the homogenising tendencies of a global urbanity grounded on surveillance. But far from a dream of social harmony and perfection, the spatialities of underground London are dystopian nightmares in regard to urban violence, subordination, and apathy.

Likewise, in Conrad Williams' horror novel *London Revenant* (2004), contemporary settings in London are transformed by showing the mysterious nature behind their seemingly ordinary façades, or rather under the streets of the metropolis. The protagonist Adam at first tries to avoid travelling on the Underground because he is repulsed by its whole environment:

> I couldn't stand it. It was too crowded and hot in summer and too crowded and damp in winter. I didn't like the way some people appeared down there, as though they'd left their brains behind before leaving for work, or were this far from snapping and massacring everybody in the carriage. [...] Nobody laughed, and there was no reason why they should. Down there, people acted differently. It was almost a social requirement that nobody spoke to each other, that misery or boredom surface on each face. You could believe by those masks that the people down there never went up top [...]." (LOR: 26)

For Adam the Tube is like hell: due to its idiosyncratic atmosphere the air is thick and the crowd aggrandise the claustrophobic feeling of the place. He compares the commuters to zombies as the Tube etiquette damning them to death-like immobility and frozen physiognomy. The enclosed space of the subway uncovers the layers of urban anomie as the unhappiness and blunted senses of urbanites resemble expressions of a life half lived. Adam therefore understands the Tube as a nightmare of oblivion and a premonition of death:

> We fear the swift glide into tunnels, the jarring and jolting, MIND THE GAP and platforms choked with commuters, like rats congregated on a sewer ledge. Descending: it is not something we look forward to really, perhaps because we step nearer the place we ultimately wish to stay away from. It's a constant reminder of burial. (LOR: 39)

This idea of the subterranean city as a grave is again enhanced by the characteristic smell- and soundscape: The Underground's stench is "almost cloacal", smelling of "the deep earth", and "the air here seemed tired, coiling heavily in his lungs; tasting stale, slightly burned" (LOR: 81), and while its dark spatiality enhances a sense of stillness (LOR: 182), the moving trains that "suck air from the shaft" create a breeze and trigger a shrieking sound and a "hum of electricity" (LOR: 221).

Similar to the subterranean kingdom in *King Rat*, the imaged subterranean spaces are inhabited by an "Underground" civilisation undiscovered by the "Topside" which aims to take possession of the lost city "Beneothan" below contemporary London (LOR: 315). Adam only gains access to the counter-space of the underground civilisation when he ends up homeless on the streets of London. The protagonist as his alter ego Monck becomes part of this subcultural society and while spending more and more time in its subterranean space he starts to appreciate both the "womb-like protection of the underground" (LOR: 84) and the security of the Tube's enclosed space. At the same time, he looses his aboveground dispositions of orientation.

> The Tube no longer repulsed me, scared me as it had once done. Now it felt the safest place around. Its warmth and closeness were something to be embraced, rather than avoided. Suddenly, all the space and choice that span around top was too great. (LOR: 172)

Finally he relishes the safety of being a part of the big crowd inside the train and tolerates its dense atmosphere. This change comes about as he is able to place and map his subterranean experiences, slowly discovering the shape of the unknown urban entity. While on his first trip to the other realm, he suffers from the surroundings beneath as an unhomely and strange yet often travelled land (LOR: 78-79), the protagonist later discovers the secrecy of the unknown "limbo stations" (LOR: 184) as "Inner Circle, The Web, Urbania" (LOR: 79) and solves the underground's maze by deciphering the bottle sign as a map of the yellow Circle Line. London beneath represents the place of the inevitable uncanny presence of an otherwise avoidable spectral Other. "There's stuff underground you wouldn't believe. It's like another city, it's like London but *upside down*." (LOR: 46) Consequently, Adam's orientation is literally turned on its head, represented in the image of an earthquake that occurs in London and inverses the underground/aboveground topography. Its "eruptions and collapses" (LOR: 265) create "a new topography of urban mesas and buttes", "a horizon filled with crippled buildings" (LOR: 263). The "violent new landscape" (LOR: 265) mirrors the confusion Adam first experienced underground, but now the "Topside" has become alienated and gained the nature of a dark labyrinth (LOR: 267). While for London above, the cataclysmic earthquake heralds the building of a renewed utopia, the uncanny space of the underground is sealed (LOR: 307-308). In the end of the novel the alternative city below becomes Adam's new home (LOR: 331).

The Subterranean Thirdspace

The metropolitan realm is constituted by the constant flux of exclusion and integration of specific topoi which open the possibility of a topology of other spaces. Insofar, this section explores conceptualisation of underground London as heterotopic thirdspace. As has been shown, the spatiality of the underground is both topographic and topologic, mythic and utopic, and unifies notions of life and death. Underground London's realm of the dead and the metaphysical space for urban purgatory and hell actually comprises one of Foucault's (1986: 25) main examples of heterotopia: the cemetery. In a sense, the mythologem of a descent to hell can be interpreted as a crisis heterotopia, a topology that serves to regain urban orientation, whereas the heterotopia of deviation concerns the constancy of Othering and control embedded in urban underground visions. In the following the characteristic of the underground as heterotopic thirdspace will be analysed with the example of Geoff Ryman's novel *253* (1998).[27]

253 is set on a southbound Bakerloo Line train from Embankment to Elephant & Castle on 11 January 1995, between 8.35 am and 8.42 am. The train itself features seven carriages, each with thirty-six seats, adding up to two-hundred and fifty-three characters including the driver because all seats are occupied but there are no standing passengers.[28] Each character is assigned a passage of two hundred and fifty-three words featuring detailed information on "**Outward appearance**" with a brief physical description, "**Inside information**" offering more personal details on the passenger's life, and "**What they are doing or thinking**", thus relating the passengers' thoughts and behaviours to neighbouring lexias or other people on the train (253: 2-3; cf. Döring 2001: 126-127).

The single carriage maps in front of each section, which chart the people on the car, their position and unique passenger number, serve as an overview for both the train and the novel (e.g. 253: 154-155). Besides this rather linear structure of the novel's character profiles and numerological identification, the book comprises an index grouping passengers according to their commonalities (253: 354-364), which serves as an important navigational device for the reader. Moreover, the novel is combinational in its structure presenting a number of seemingly unrelated and disconnected intertextual as well as intermedial elements, such as fictional footnotes with additional information on London, metafictional advertisement on creative writing as well as a customer feedback sheet at the end of the novel (cf. Schnierer 2000: 539-542; Calvi 2004: 177).

Colombino (2006: 615) therefore points out that *253* plays on the postmodernist "urban/electronic design and commodity culture". Although perhaps not as obvious as in the hypertext version, the Underground train in *253* becomes an apt metaphor for the city's spaces of flow which have been transformed to an accumulation of intersections, stations and junctions and thereby an apt symbol of the Informational City's network. The confines of the moving train with its characters in transit and the repetitive heterochronia of just over seven minutes present the epitome of an urban heterotopia. In the sense that it largely describes a semi-public space of transit, this heterotopology appears notoriously inhabitable.

Nevertheless, the physical structure of this fictional Tube train constrained by the (im)plausible numerology of *253* leads not only to "the illusion of an orderly universe" (253: 2) but its rigid layout also seems to further the notion of absolute space or a holistic world-view (cf. Colombino 2006: 625).[29] Thus on the surface, *253* is a rather static

27 | Ryman was one of the first authors to create an interactive internet novel. In cyberspace, this online version of *253* (1996) has since been considered a paradigm of hypertext fiction and the paper-based *Print Remix* became the first-ever website-to-book adaptation. In the following *253* will remain abbreviated as 253.

28 | By comparison, Proust's seven-volume novel *A la recherche du temps perdu* features approximately three hundred characters and Dickens' *Bleak House* 'only' features about sixty major and minor figures.

29 | The instability of the abstract space of *253* is commented on by Geoff Ryman himself when he notes that it was highly problematic to have the novel translated: in another language, it was either impossible to stay within the confines of the two hundred and fifty-three words per character or the lingo had to be adapted in a way that it completely transformed the text,

novel, as each page is a short story in itself and each passenger, although mentally affected by the surroundings or other travellers, is represented as sitting apart in the physical constraints of a specific isolated seat. In other words, Ryman turns characters into identified and identifiable places on a map (*ibid.*: 617) or even the plot of a graveyard. Similar to London Underground's key train hubs, however, the protagonists are also interconnected through a "series of superimposed maps with their interconnected sites" (*ibid.*: 625): for example, the stations along the trip on the Bakerloo Line, the characters' allocated seating, the novel's index and map, the passengers' common places of work and leisure.

Because the characters are treated as topographical abstractions interconnected by arbitrarily drawn lines, their spatiality seems to resemble Harry Beck's schematic map of the London Underground (253: Cover).[30] Its modernist notion of abstract space debunks mythic images of the underground and promotes a new utopianism for subterranean London – a more ordered, systematic, comprehensible, and stable place than aboveground (cf. Pike 2002: 107-108; Pike 2005a: 25). Also Mengham (2003: 199) underlines the devices of controlled urban (re)orientation that are inscribed in the map:

> The Tube map with its symmetries, its rows of diagonals, its repetition of angles, is an excessive rationalization of something that in reality is much more irregular. An accurate map would look worryingly chaotic, its proliferation of unrepeatable pattern would make the city look out of control.

Easily legible, the Tube map bears little or no resemblance to either the experimental or the physical metropolis.[31] Its topographical abstraction aims at practical utility and reduction of complexity and thereby symbolically obliterates chaos from the metropolis, offering an optimistic vision of the city through its bright, clean, and colourful design. As Beck's map allows for a totalised and entirely comprehensible vision of London (cf. Thorne 1996: 7; B. Baker 2003), in analogy to *253* this topography evokes an utterly holistic mental image. Critics have shown that the Tube map not only represents the only official version of the London Underground, but by way of its iconic status has imposed a single vision of London which dominates the city's image to this day (cf. Vertesi 2005: 1; Jenkins 2006: 37; Pike 2002: 101; Pike 2005a: 22). Janet Vertesi (2005: 4) analyses the influence of the Tube map on Londoners' mental maps, and establishes

---

especially in regard to its emotional effect (cf. Goto 49: 204). Foreign language speakers on the Tube are thus equally misrepresented by the rigid form of two hundred and fifty-three English words.

30 | Because a "Journey Planner" serves as table of contents to the homepage of *253* (Ryman 1996), the allusion to the Tube map is more obvious in the online version. The Underground map is also an important symbol of the city's transformation in Keith Lowe's *Tunnel Vision* (TUV: 3-4, 46-49, 134-138), and Beck's outline of the Central Line becomes the orientation-key to the Underground for Adam in Conrad Williams' *London Revenant*.

31 | For more general information on Beck's map see Maxwell J. Roberts (2005), *Underground Maps After Beck. The Story of the London Underground Map in the Hands of Henry Beck's Successors.*

that it acts as a "local civic interface" because it "structures the ways in which users of London conceptually organize, understand, and interact with the city" (*ibid.*: 1).[32] In other words, the Tube map presents the foremost means of orientation in the city. McLeod (2007: 391) comments:

> [T]he London Underground map is arguably one of the most important methods of orientation for newcomers and Londoners alike, schematising the city's chaotic geography in an orderly structure which makes sensible the often complex routes and changes of transport required when travelling across the capital.

This implies that mental dispositions of orientation are notably incorporated through the perceived, conceived, and lived city beneath.

In reference to Geoff Ryman's novel, the abstraction, numerology, and static mapping of the train fulfil expectations regarding urban dispositions of thinking determined by the ready-made mental map of the cityscape below. Hence, like a traditional dystopia, the novel is dependent on a rigid spatial order of social control, ideological regulation, or normative surveillance, and the train becomes a larger symbol of incarceration and predetermined navigation. Colombino (2006: 616) works out, that Ryman's *253* conceives "the city as claustrophobic site of entrapment" because the novel's "comforting" (253: 1) numerology, maps, and strictly defined spatial boundaries constitute an "all-encompassing grid of control" (Colombino 2006: 624). In choice of form and content, especially due to the "God-like and omniscient" (253: 4) narrator penetrating the traveller's thoughts, the author's choice of totalitarian surveillance produces transparent urban citizens. While simultaneity, oscillation, contradiction, and juxtaposition of spatialities are inherent components of the heterotopia, the heterotopic city beneath is also conceptualised as a regulatory space denoting specific dispositions of power enforced by a high degree of panopticism. Presupposing a system of opening and enclosure that both isolates and renders penetrable, the heterotopia defines a topology of access which establishes subterranean boundaries of social control that demarcate a specific behaviour. Due to the thoroughly spun network of CCTV cameras on the Underground, Big Brother is omnipresent in subterranean London. For Colombino (2006: 624), Ryman's novel conveys a sense of panopticism because author, reader and characters accumulate information on the other passengers and devise them to an absolute space of controlled positioning. The carriages of the Bakerloo Line actualise the abstract utopia to a heterotopic yet panoptic counterspace. On the other hand, the dystopian fantasy of *253* ends with an apocalyptic notion of the train crash (253: 343-351) finally transforming the underground into a heterotopic urban cemetry.

---

32 | Knowledgeable travellers even indicate specific lines and their idiosyncratic personality. For the personality of the Victoria and Bakerloo Line see Ross (2002: 63), while Keith Lowe's *Tunnel Vision* notably tackles the personality ("aroma") of the Northern and the Central Line (TUV: 18-20; 50-51). Peter Ackroyd (2001: 568) comments on the particular associations and connections of the single Underground lines: "The Northern Line is intense and somehow desperate; the Central Line is energetic, while the Circle is adventurous and breezy. The Bakerloo Line, however, is flat and despairing. [. . .]."

The Tube train in constituting ambivalence between control and freedom, surveillance and autonomy, is not only an absolute space of difference but also of *différance.* Metropolitan underground resembles a cluster of separate and individual places variously interconnected (cf. O'Brien 2010: 156). The revelation of the relational subject-positions opens up Ryman's text for a representation of the idiosyncratic perceptions of the train's surroundings, at the same time paying tribute to randomness and fragmentation (cf. Colombino 2006: 624-625). This ensemble of contradictory relations is established through the interconnection of personal 'places' (physical, social, mental, temporal) and underlined in the character profiles or the later index. If the assemblage of the Tube on the surface still seems governed by certain oppositions, the internal perspective reveals the underground as a heterotopia which disrupts closure and certainty.

For Foucault (1986: 27) the ship which transgresses colonised spaces constitutes the heterotopia *par excellence.* In the field of underground London, the Tube in motion is the inverted heterotopic or alternative chronotopic capsule moving inbetween modern re-territorialised spaces and consequently, also by simultaneously combining various heterotopias, the London Tube figures as **the** postmodern heterotopia *per se.* Because of its characteristics as a threshold between being/becoming, presence/absence, inside/outside, past/future, ego/id, Self/Other etc. the Tube can be compared to this undeterminable heterotopia. The polycentric urban space is wrought by concentration and dispersion and therefore inherently "*is* concrete contradiction." (Lefebvre 2003: 39) All that is absolute is at once relativised into a renewed space of "mental and social, spatial and temporal differences." (*Ibid.*: 37) A heterotopia is the other space which is "simultaneously excluded and interwoven." (*Ibid.*: 128) Oscillating between notions of utopia and dystopia, the existing space of the underground is marked both by confinement, claustrophobia, and panopticism but also security, openness, and coexistence. Hence the physical underground constitutes the locus of the metropolitan sublime, simultaneously encompassing juxtapositions[33] which generate both awe and fear. On the threshold between strangeness and familiarity, the underground becomes the main trope of the postmodern uncanny, negotiating the uncertainty of contemporary metropolitan existence. This also carries notable implications for the underground as social space.

6.2.2 Subterranean Sociability

A thriving city like London is dependent on its subterranean arteries, especially the lines of communication and transportation. Since the 1980s, passenger numbers of the London Underground have returned to a state of "the very life force of the capital" (Wolmar 2004: 293). More than one billion passengers use the Tube each year, which equals approximately three million rides per day. The London Underground is therefore an

33 | For example myth/science, rational/irrational, fecund/technocratic, female/male, Gaya/Hades, public/private, individual/collective memory, introspection of the Self/encounter with the Other, desire/anxiety, curiosity/horror, attraction/repulsion, etc. According to Vidler (1999: 39), the sublime is distinguished from the uncanny in the following characteristics: height, depth, extension, vertigo versus silence, solitude, confinement, suffocation, collapse of time and space, claustrophobia.

extremely relevant social space of the city; it is an intrinsic part of everyday urban experiences where the classes mix, and new codes of behaviour are developed (cf. Pike 1999: 113). This sub-chapter looks at dispositions of acting as well as socio-cultural negotiations exploring specifications of the urban-generic ambivalences of indifference and involvement, heterogeneity and homogeneity, sociability and anomie, or familiarity and strangeness.

Tube Etiquette

Due to overcrowding and train delays, commuting on the London Underground can be a rather tiresome everyday experience which significantly influences urbanites' perception of the Tube in general and determines dispositions of thinking, feeling, imagining, and acting. Most notably, norms and rules of behaviour develop that prevent chaos, hysteria, or panic. Moran (2005: 53) points out that the London Underground, more so than the Paris *Métro*, constitutes a strongly rule-driven and standardised place, where beside legislative and regulative norms, passengers obey a particular "Tube etiquette" (*ibid.*: 54).[34] In reference to the heterotopic demise of underground London, certain habits mirror and stress aboveground interaction, while other responses are utterly idiosyncratic to the Tube. Scholars have shown how behaviour on underground trains is governed by principles serving to protect personal rights and sustain social distance.

> In the subways [...] people are more on their own, and protection is afforded by particular seating arrangement, the affording of civil inattention, involvement shields to maintain distance that are brought with the passenger, and taboos against physical contact. (Levine, Vinson & Wood 1973: 216)

Tony Blair involuntarily broke Tube etiquette when he travelled from Waterloo to the Millennium Dome; trying to strike up a conversation with a black woman sitting next to him Blair did not observe the rules of civil inattention. Albeit recognising the Prime Minister, the urbanite kept listening to her music, staring straight ahead duly ignoring Blair. Embarrassed, he resorted to standing near the doors in oppressive silence, while the young woman later claimed: "I'm always the same in the mornings, I put my Walkman on and turn off." (Davison 1999; cf. Moran 2005: 57) Hence, subterranean behaviour initially reveals certain traits of the urban character marking people as true Londoners

---

34 | "Among other things, Tube passengers are told to 'mind the gap' between the train and platform by a white-painted sign on the ground; to pass along the platform to prevent bottlenecks; to keep hold of the handrail on the escalator; and to make sure that the carriage doors are clear of baggage. Aural as well as visual clues add to this sense of the pervasive authority of invisible legislators." (Moran 2005: 53) Forms of behaviour to maintain absolute distanciation despite physical proximity are "nonchalant virtuosity" (*ibid.*: 54), "dead-eyeing" (*ibid.*: 55), scowling, sitting down next to people of the same sex, etc. (cf. Levine, Vinson & Wood 1973: 209; Karp, Stone & Yoels 1991: 87). For example, in Sam Selvon's *The Lonely Londoners* (1965), the protagonist Moses tells the newly arrived West Indian immigrant Galahad talking does not conform to appropriate behaviour on the Underground, and that he has still a long way to go to become a London citizen (Selvon 2006: 15-16).

because travelling on the Underground constitutes a "most thoroughly Cockney element" (Mayhew 2003: 14).

Andy, the protagonist of Keith Lowe's *Tunnel Vision*, is accustomed to the Tube's behavioural grammar: "Talking to a stranger [...] goes against everything I've learned as a Londoner and as a tube-traveller [...]." (TUV: 35) Travelling at night, he comes into contact with the tramp Brian only by breaking the most basic of all Tube laws: "don't look at *anybody*." (TUV: 31) A personal demonstration of appreciating the presence of the Other crosses a normative boundary, draws attention and generates even more curiosity (cf. Levine, Vinson & Wood 1973: 210). In general, the novel's protagonist characterises train commuters as "notoriously unobservant" (TUV: 209) because the average nine-to-fiver ultimately ignores everything. Levine, Vinson and Wood (1973: 210) show however, that visual inattention simply conceals the fact that passengers are drawn to other conversations. Also for Andy, the hordes of people during morning and evening rush hours constitute "an attentive audience [...] because despite all their looking elsewhere I know everyone else in the carriage is listening" (TUV: 62). Especially during Brian's spectacular elaborations of homeless life and suicide, strangers on the train follow every single word spoken:

> You can tell by their faces – they lose that blank inward stare for a moment, and focus on the pair of us, just for a split second, before switching their eyes away again. They don't want Brian to stop talking: a few tales about people topping themselves is entertainment for the journey, something to think about on the way home from work. It breaks the daily commuting routine. (TUV: 134)

By far the most remarkable form of inattentive demeanour can be observed during rush hour, when physical proximity is unusually high even for the city. Levine, Vinson and Wood (1973: 213) register different forms of protection against intimate physical contact during peak time: aggressive pushing or passive resignation. Fighting their way through the masses on the platform, Andy and Brian squeeze into a full Piccadilly Line train around half-past five in the afternoon. Andy keeps apologising to other commuters until he falls prey to total passivity within the claustrophobic train:

> ThistrainissocrowdedIcanbarelybreathe.Youcan'ttellwehreonebodyendsandthenestbegins,andthe heatisunbrearable.Everyoneispushingeveryoneelso[...]notbecausetheywanttobutbecausetheyMU ST.Theypushwhentheymustinhale,theyarepushedwhentheybreathout.[...]There'snowheretoESC APEto,nowheretofindanyspaceexcettheinsideofmyhead.[...]But then at WestKensington afewpeoplegetout, andthecrush eases slightly,and atBaron'sCourt afewmore, until at last I am free to breath once again. Gradually the carriage returns to normal – busy, but bearable [...]. (TUV: 253-255)

In this narrative section the author eliminates the spaces between single words to imitate the physical crush of urbanites' bodies, the density of air, and the compression of Andy's thoughts. The passage exemplifies that an extraordinary amount of self-control is required as collective survival strategy in a space of high density. In a sense, everyday practice of the Underground serves as a form of collective adjustment to urban overload and a lesson in protective defence and adaptive mechanisms.

The passage also implies a high degree of tolerance for the Other, but this attitude is intrinsically based on a general adherence to indifference, inattention, and non-involvement. In *Tunnel Vision*, a Filipino whose inappropriate behaviour marks him out as a "tube virgin" (TUV: 64) is shunned by the other passengers. The protagonist comments on his own non-involvement: "That's the thing about the tube – you can't be nice to beginners, it's just not allowed." (TUV: 65) Although the misbehaviour causes commotion, all the other passengers ignore the Filipino, refrain from helping or speaking to him, and return to their subterranean practices of inattention. Only newcomers to the city or tourists do not follow the rules of Underground behaviour (TUV: 71). While Andy avoids staring at women in the Tube in order to hide his desire, a group of young Italians openly flirt with one another and when any Londoner would be embarrassed to give up his seat even for an old woman (cf. Milgram 1970: 1464), a Scandinavian tourist holds back the doors breaking the rule of non-interference (TUV: 209-210). Tolerance of otherness hence implies that, although disapproval is communicated, the rules of habitual indifference are still maintained.

Consequently, the everyday practice of riding on the Underground is represented as a major means of urban-specific socialisation and enculturation. In Andy's case, it goes so far that his patterns of acting are exactly attuned to the Tube: he anticipates where to stand on the platform so that "a) the train doors open directly in front of you, and b) when you get off the train you will be right by the exit." (TUV: 5) Moran (2005: 55) argues that the predictable design of the Underground system, the relatively homogeneous outline of its stations, and the invisibility of its regulations add to a sense of subterranean routine behaviour.

These idiosyncratic modes of acting are also charted in Geoff Ryman's Tube novel *253* where the idea of habitualisation is mirrored in the layout and numerology of the novel as well as in its reiterative narrative structure. The story time of seven minutes of the same section between Embankment to Elephant & Castle is constantly re-travelled within the formally repetitious bounds of the passenger profiles. A description of passenger number 66 underlines how much the commute between home and work has become routine for Londoners:

> Julie actually is asleep. Her morning routine is so established that she dressed herself sleep-walking. She walked on automatic pilot to the tube and changed trains at Embankment without waking up. She is conscious of nothing until Passenger 46 clumps Passenger 47. She thinks: I'm dreaming that I'm sitting on the tube [...]. (253: 95)

The character is described acting on autopilot, knowing the Underground schedule by rote and automatically taking the same track every day. As an everyday pattern, the use of the Tube has become so uneventful that Julie is able to navigate the Underground sleepwalking. A majority of passengers on board are lost in thought because of the blunting effect of routine behaviour, and the train, as opposed to the cityscape above, actually enforces personal introspection. Therefore single passengers decide to break with the accustomed everyday practice and reinvent themselves. For instance, Mr Ralph Moles feels alienated by his profession as a piercing specialist and longs for a change, but acknowledges that it will put at risk all his public and private routines (253: 78). According to the anthropologist Marc Augé (1988: 103, 105), the sole sociable praxis on the Underground as a transitional space between home and workplace is that it facilitates the transformation between private and public Self. However, this internal metamorphosis is often concealed by practices of "autoinvolvement" (Levine, Vinson & Wood 1973: 210), particularly daydreaming and reading.[35]

Döring (2002: 34) points out that the London Tube operates as a major place for reading: books, papers, posters, advertisement, poems, etc. Certainly, the novel *253* creates the impression that the Bakerloo train presents the heterotopia of a library.[36] A large number of characters inspect the daily newspapers; others look at magazines or become immersed in books, a few again scan the advertisements for distraction. The single paragraphs in *253* reveal, however, that commuters seldom actually take in the content of the books, but they are rather occupied by other thoughts.[37] Thus a predominant part of the train commuters is completely absorbed in subordinate involvements and practices of civil inattention by assuming the inconspicuous behaviour of reading and thereby conceal the fact that they choose to avoid potential interaction (cf. Levine, Vinson & Wood 1973: 208, 210). Co-workers, relatives, and even partners mutually ignore each other in order not to violate the 'right to be left alone' or the rule of non-involvement. Passenger 11, Mr Douglas Higbee,

> [a]ppears to be asleep, except one eye is open. [...] He is trying to avoid to talk to the ship's magician, Passenger 18, who is also in the same carriage. [...] It's all right for the magician. *He's* pretending to be riveted by a newspaper. [...] Instead, Douglas is pretending to be asleep, but only with the right-hand side of his face, the one turned towards his colleague. His left eye is reading the ads in safety. (253: 24)

It becomes obvious that in fact both men notice each other, but try hard to obliterate the other's existence in order to retain control over their individual privacy. Thus, the rule of civil inattention in the Tube is represented as the significant form of communication (of

---

35 | Also in Julian Barnes novel *Metroland* (1980), the protagonist observes that the train journey between home and work equals a heterotopic instance of metamorphosis.

36 | Looking at passengers on the Tube, we will not fail to notice that it is probably the largest mobile library in the world with nearly everyone being engrossed in a novel, one of the London papers or simply reading the "Poems on the Underground". *LITRO*, a magazine of short stories, is distributed monthly throughout the London Underground. Distributers selling or giving out prints of *The Big Issue*, *The London Paper* (2006-2009), *Metro*, and *Evening Standard* cover the entrances to the Tube in the evening rush hour. *The Independent* and *The Times* changed from broadsheet to compact format in 2004, which initiated a boost in selling figures, maybe also because the tabloid format is better adapted to the Underground's limited space. More recently, the number of electronic reading devices such as Kindle or iPad has increased dramatically. Interestingly, in the novel merely three passengers have headphones on, listening to classical, pop or dub music. Portable MP3 players only appeared in 1999 and a tender for full mobile phone coverage of the London Underground was just published in 2007. Hence, the image of autoinvolvement on the tube has certainly altered since the time of the novel's publication.

37 | Admittedly, it would have been a difficult task for Ryman to construct a discourse time of seven minutes of the single profiles in just two hundred and fifty-three words.

not wanting to be communicated with) which actually defines subterranean sociability (cf. Levine, Vison & Wood 1973: 208). On the one hand, the passage exemplifies again that civil inattention constitutes a version of public role-play, which simultaneously establishes invisible boundaries of a semi-private space. On the other hand, the presence of Tube rules and behaviour emphasises how much urban sociability depends on play-acting.

Subtitled "Tube Theatre" (253: 1), Geoff Ryman's novel charts the various degrees of London at play. The author grasps the difference of internal life and external appearance in the character profiles which delineate Goffman's notion of play acting as one of simultaneously camouflaging and fashioning the Self. Insofar, Ryman deliberately misspells characters as "char**actors**" (253: 353; emphasis N.P.) and thereby renders the everyday automatic habitual performance linguistically evident. His novel is specifically engaged in the difficult task of differentiating between authenticity and urban self-fashioning. Passenger number 251 turns out to be only acting to read – book performance is a new way of advertisement on the Tube (253: 337) – but without the inside information or the omniscious point of view, it would be hard to establish the fleeting boundaries between habit and urban act. While character 75 is a model posing to read a woman's magazine because he is photographed for an advertisement (253: 113), number 143 simply "tries out various positions which combine modesty and assertiveness." (253: 198) Also Ms Christine Marre

> is acting out several dramas at once, the pursued woman, the citizen against fraud. [...] Chris lives alone, in terror of being invisible. She lives in terror of being found out. She lives for the moment clinging in panic to the telephone with other people listening. She looks over her shoulder again. Can people see she is a woman with a desperate story. (253: 110)

Catherine merely mimes to be the wife of an undercover agent, but her act is taken for real by passenger Mr Terry Mack, who trails the woman despite or because of her theatrical face and erratic behaviour (253: 214). Consequently, O'Brian (2010: 161) argues that "*253* constructs an elaborate Jungian insight into London's inter-connectedness, where a plethora of social types are placed on display, and where the train carriage doubles up as a stage area, on which the passengers-cum-actors begin to perform." The novel expands on the topic of normative behaviour and play-acting by staging the performance of "Mind the Gap" in car number 3 (253: 125-140). This piece of Tube theatre is based on the deviant behaviour of character number 124 and enacted by the fictional double of the author himself. A couple of tourists and foreign students as well as some involuntary London witnesses watch when the spoof act goes wrong and the performance becomes indistinguishable from social drama. Also the anthropologist Marc Augé (1988) already titles one of his articles on the Parisian Underground "Das Schauspiel der Metro". Insofar, the Tube as stage presents a heterotopia which significantly fulfils the urban function of a routinised daily spectacle.

Thus, the Underground resembles a threshold space which offers a forum for simultaneous public and private demeanour, gazing and acting, introspection and staging, self-fashioning and role-play which fathoms the incorporation of metropolitan doxa. This internal urbanisation is moreover supported by ungoverned eruptions of action and a recombination of social relations. In this sense, *253* expands the possibility of breaking taboos to all urbanites who, in letting their personal shields of distanciation drop, are caught off guard. The reasons for these border-crossings are largely due to a spontaneous reaction against the overload of stimuli or an enhanced craving for proximity and spectaclisation: while Martin Park accidentally hits Ashley Watkins with his bicycle seat (253: 70), Phil Barker, a young villain, gets into a shuffle with the tall but passive rugby player Harry Wade (253: 28, 30). Kevin Potter, who wonders about people avoiding him, is insulted by Georgina Bullen maddened by his horrid body odour (253: 62), whereas George Aristidou, angered by an advertisement for London Transport, rips down the poster and is reproached for his action by Camilla Burke-Harris (253: 147). Danny Dodding, a drop-out and impostor, circumvents anonymity by approaching total strangers as former friends in order "to keep warm" (253: 213). Despite this deviant behaviour of affective eruption, ignoring the rules and breaking the taboos of civil inattention is indeed sometimes the source for striking up new relations.

The absolute deconstruction of the Tube's normative order is represented by the last carriage, which ultimately marks the threshold between personal life and death as well as collective sociability and anomie. Passenger 253, the revenant of Anne Frank, demands that people dance, and other characters spontaneously join the party. In reference to *menippea* and Bakhtin's (1968: 7) notion of the carnivalesque, in the Underground traditional urban laws are suspended turning everyday life upside down. This unexpected happening stresses the constant transformability of urban rules due to internal displacements, habitual eruptions, and unhomely interruptions for which the Underground serves as a laboratory.

In sum, Keith Lowe's *Tunnel Vision* and Geoff Ryman's *253* both exemplify the most basic rules of Tube etiquette which are built on the larger mental disposition, namely the urban-generic ambivalence of indifference and involvement. In the words of Levine, Vinson and Wood (1973: 212), the Tube "enable[s] people to avoid unnecessary encounters and to hide their emotions", but as the analysis has shown, also offers a stage for enactment. The novels reflect how the Underground makes urbanites aware of each other, furthering a certain degree of tolerance towards the categorically known stranger. In that sense, the heterotopia of London Underground (cemetery, school, library, theatre, and festival) constitutes a space to explore various urban ambivalences, especially of familiarity and strangeness. In other words, London Underground is the topology of the (un)homely, whose specific character of habitation and transgression defines a particular structure of London's mental disposition.

Multipli-City Beneath

The analysis of Geoff Ryman's novel *253* brings into focus the quantitative heterogeneity of Tube passengers and urban denizens. In general, the London Tube is perceived as a threshold space of the urban masses where strangers briefly encounter each other (cf. Döring 2003: 182). The Underground has played a notable part in the formation of the metropolis as a multicultural city (see chapter 7.1.4) and from that perspective, also constitutes a thirdspace in the sense of Homi Bhabha. This section traces representations of plurality, diversity, and hybridity, pointing out the subterranean negotiation of the urban-generic ambivalence of heterogeneity and homogeneity.

The protagonist of Keith Lowe's *Tunnel Vision* experiences the Underground as "a sea of bodies" (TUV: 111) and "hordes of faces [...] and backs of heads" (TUV: 227) without any individual characteristics (TUV: 66). The subterranean city is hence predominantly presented as a social space of high density and collective similarity. Andy perceives the Tube as "the great equaliser" including "company directors and barrow boys" and a place where "old women and teenage boys [are] jammed together" as well as "black people, Asians, and whites mingle peacefully with tycoons and tramps" (TUV: 62). Commuting is represented as utterly democratic and egalitarian, thus creating metropolitan sociability. "[T]here is no seniority, no privilege, and no discrimination" (TUV: 62), although "half the passengers in this train don't speak English" (TUV: 212). In this heterotopian space of *différance* the protagonist even links up with the homeless Brian, although he used to consider tramps as annoyingly aggressive. The tolerance of this "accepting society" (TUV: 64) has been shown to be a consequence of negative interaction and indifference. Throughout the "mass migration" (TUV: 62) at rush hour when everyone is "packed together like chickens in a battery farm", "[n]obody screams, or cries, or makes any indication that they are anything but comfortable – the place is a picture of tolerance." (TUV: 64)

Nevertheless, the social space of the London Underground is not without friction. The image of acceptance and tolerance during rush hour in the brief space of seconds alters the layout of the scene from contact to conflict hypothesis, when a passenger who is not attuned to Tube etiquette disrupts the apparent atmosphere of indifference. The whole carriage groans and glares "as if to ask what the hell a Filipino is doing in Leytonstone. To my shame, I have to confess I'm thinking exactly that myself. It is as though the Central Line at rush hour has brought all my latent xenophobia to the surface." (TUV: 66) As shown earlier on, the xenophobia Andy develops is not immanently directed at the Filipino as an ethnic outsider, but rather as an urban Other in general, whose difference is ignored to a point despite his obvious disruption of city routine.

Consequently, Keith Lowe paints a picture of the Tube as a largely diverse and hybrid unity. In a general sense, the Underground seems to have actually become what Henry Mayhew (2003: 15) had hoped it would be – a geographical and social, so we might add from a twenty-first-century perspective also transcultural, unifier: "the metal ring that is to wed the wealthy and fashionable West to the poor and squalid East, and to unite the healthy North to the pestiferous South". Similarly, in *Tunnel Vision*, Andy's odyssey throughout the London Underground system reconnects the loose ends of the lines, often depicted as non-places of business parks, pastoral idylls, boxed areas of routine, "residential purgatory" (TUV: 287) or "suburban hell" (TUV: 287). Insofar, the Tube creates subterranean and subconscious connections between spatially and socially segregated spheres.

Frozen in time, Geoff Ryman's *253* offers the chance to examine the everyday life of 253 individual strangers who have a lot more in common than they would ever realise. While the single-page profiles emphasise their differences, the specific links imitate what makes people the same (cf. Grossman 1997). The variety of names indicates the sociocultural multiplicity present on the train and the sheer number of characters portrayed creates the notion that within the mass of passengers personal differences are annihilated: members of the upper class like Lord Anthony Lowick and the aristocrat Dr Agatha Beffont sit next to people from the middle and lower classes, but also to the down-and-out homeless, such as Mr Justin Holmes or Mrs Delia Hendy. While the author claims to actually prefer the novel to the internet version because it stresses heterogeneity (*ibid.*), the "Reader Satisfaction Survey" (253: 365-366) at the end of the text offers the following option for the meaning of the novel: "a tribute to the infinite variety of London life" (253: 366). The introduction of the "useful links appendix" remarks that "linking people because they were gay, black or Asian seemed pointless as linking people because they were white or straight" (253: 353) underlines the egalitarian project of the novel.

However, the index offers entries concerning country and/or nationality, such as Australia, Bosnia, Canada, Cyprus, Czechoslovakia, Turkey, etc. (253: 354-364). Moreover, the information on the characters' looks and appearance often starts with the denomination of the colour of their skin or their ethnicity, while internal information specifies their socio-cultural background. Mr Anup Agnihotri, an Indian-Ugandan electrician for the first time travelling with the Tube, finally takes notice of London's multicultural make-up: "Looking at the people. It is strange to see how many of them are not English. It is as though he has been locked away in his own world." (253: 166) In this respect, the novel also takes up London's socio-cultural history of immigration and its present-day standing as a multicultural metropolis. Mrs Gerta Fazahi, who teaches Arabic and Hebrew, is married to a Jewish Lebanese; Miss Becky Patterson, assistant at the British Library with a degree in Tibetan, is the daughter of third-generation Zimbabwean farmers; Miss Yoshi Kamimura, a Japanese language student, is pregnant from an Italian fascist drug dealer; Mr Igor Klimov and Mr Dimitri Belinkov are illegal Russian immigrants looking for work. And Mrs Rezia Begum, an immigrant from a Bengal village to Brick Lane, is reminiscent of the character Nazneen in Monica Ali's novel.

The novel, however, does not only chart this multiplicity of strangers, immigrants, and hybrid men, but also exposes the various forms of alienation, xenophobia, and racism people encounter within the cosmopolis. The character by the famous name of John Kennedy sees a courting Asian couple stoned by kids at Archbishop's Park, where at night Rafael Da Cunha is taken for an Arabian rent boy by office workers. Despite being totally disoriented, African Keith Olewaio loves to be a cab driver in London, whereas his cousin Toby Swisme, a frightened victim of racial attacks, wants to return home. The house of Mary Al-Masud, an East Ender who now lives with her bigamist Kuweiti husband, was firebombed by their neighbours; Florence Cassell from Kenya is racially abused as a "half-caste bitch" (253: 100) by black and white Londoners alike. Jack Spufford, who applied for a visa for his Polish wife, comments: "Black or white, if you're foreign, England can be a shithole." (253: 190)

Even though the passengers' names, looks, and thoughts sometimes appear culturally determined, stereotypical, or even cliché, the summary of their individual stories and the layers of cultural experience collide in often unexpected connections between people within the heterotopia of the Tube. Rather comically, Geoff Ryman presents the love quadrangle around passenger Mr Sam Cruza, who is a New York taxi driver selling the *Big Issue* at Waterloo station. Ms Maggie Rolt, a rich business woman, takes him for Pascal, a tour guide from Switzerland; Mme Marge Matisse, a heiress and descendant of Henri Matisse, thinks he is an Albanian seaman; Ms Anita Mazzoni regards him as an Italian actor called Antonio; and for Mrs Beverly Tompset, a lecturer in sociology, Cruza is Attila, a Cossack sailor. As easily as Cruza imitates other personalities and appropriates manifold migrational backgrounds, as much does the cosmopolitan resemble not one but many identities. When the train goes through the barriers at Elephant & Castle: "**Sam Cruza** sits in the New York Metro. The other passengers look up from their papers; they are all cab drivers; they are all him: Albanian, Romanian, Greek. They all start to exist, taking parts of him with them." (253: 350) Cruza symbolises a person in permanent transit whose transgression of a borderless space points towards the constructedness and fleetingness of identity.

The Tube as the postmodern heterotopia *par excellence* can therefore be identified with Döring (2002: 60) as a place of "heterogeneous social gatherings in transit" which charts the urban subject position based on "transitional and insecure social identities". For example, Savi Gupta imagines the people in his carriage transforming their respective sex (253: 84). This emphasises the arbitrariness of pre-defined identity and reveals the manifold possibilities inherent in each person. The fictitious character 186 of the Prime Minister Margaret Thatcher bears her social inversion, namely a thatcher in "workman's jeans and donkey jacket" working at the roof of the new Globe Theatre (253: 256). Colombino (2006: 628) works out that Ryman compares the conservative's phenotype and iconic status to Mick Jagger as "the symbol of transgression." (cf. 253: 199) Hence, any notion of homogeneity is deconstructed in Geoff Ryman's novel in stressing the fragmentation of London's socio-cultural make-up and the multiplicity of subject positions between and within people (cf. O'Brien 2010: 168-168). Because characters meet alternatives of their Self either by way of inversion in their own schizoid profiles or in the counterparts and doubles of other passengers, the narrative underlines the uncanny simultaneity of Self and Other, familiarity and strangeness symbolised by underground London.

In sum, underground London is represented as a public contact zone for encountering the urban stranger (see chapter 7.1.4) as well as a private space of negotiating the personal fragmentation of identity. Furthermore, the Tube figures as a transcultural contact zone, where there is neither a specific centre and strict definitions of Self and Other have virtually disappeared and are changed by multiple constellations of alterity and unity. Hence, the Underground constitutes a state *E Pluribus Unum* wherein the constant flux of boundaries seems to dissolve rigid lines of segregation.

The Down – And Out

Due to the paradoxes of anonymity and social fragmentation of the urban realm, the underground is not only a network of human interrelations and unity but also its opposite, namely a metaphor for the stratified metropolis *per se*: as an allotopic counterspace, underground London likewise figures as a place for outsiders and a refuge for the displaced (cf. Döring 2001: 123). David Pike (2005a: 11) shows that during the late nineteenth century the metaphorical underground spaces of poverty and crime become more and more entwined with the newly excavated topographies of the underground. The verticalisation of social segregation by the polarities of high and low finds its physical equivalent in the city's above- and underground. As such, the social differences between London's West and East End are not only visualised in Beck's Tube map (cf. *ibid.*: 23) but become notoriously associated with the city beneath. During Victorianism, underground London denotes the social underworld of the lower classes, the poor, the criminal and socially discarded, the so-called 'down and out'. This urban underclass is made up of underworld beings such as prostitutes, pimps, dealers, addicts, sexual deviants, mafiosi, terrorists, illegal aliens, slum dwellers, etc. (*ibid.*: 1). Even in twentieth- and twenty-first-century literature, subterranean London is seen as the spatiality of the urban social margin. Underground London therefore also features as a major topos for the urban pariah motif (see chapter 7.2.4).

In Tobias Hill's novel *Underground*, the subterranean city is first depicted as a social space used by an undistinguishable mass of people in flux (UND: 101). However, the only people that are acknowledged as individuals in the subterranean space are the marginalised, dispossessed and socially discarded – the modern 'down and out': immigrants, the homeless, drug addicts, criminals and the crazed (UND: 100). The novel's protagonist, Casimir, who works in the Underground and lives in a small trap in Waterloo, is not only imprisoned but also invisible; his existence is of an (un)homely nature.[38]

Ashford (2008: 13) points out, that in Tobias Hill's *Underground* homelessness is "rendered the key to the psychological as well as the architectural *Unheimlich*." In reference to Vidler's (1999: ix) notion, the postmodern uncanny underground summarises homelessness and exile with feelings of alienation and social or individual estrangement. More than the stranger, the migrant, or the hybrid man, the tramp is characterised by transitoriness of which the underground train is the apparent symbol. "It is the world where the homeless live invisibly among us, the world to which we banish them when we close our mental eyes and make them disappear from our minds." (Ekman 2005: 64) In this sense, subterranean London constitutes not only a metaphor for urban hierarchies, but the realm of the stranger and thus the epitome of urban-generic ambivalences of strangeness and familiarity or the urban uncanny: "The Underground attracts strange people. Even ordinary people are different. Less social, more isolated." (UND: 100)

China Miéville's novel *King Rat* (1998) portrays twentieth-century London with great topographical and sociological accuracy, albeit from the protagonist's perspective of the city's cultural, economic, and social margin. Although it is a fantasy novel, the narrative largely departs from the traditional conventions of the genre by creating a 'dyadic world' (Ekman 2005: 65) of above- and underground London and a hybrid between human and non-human, natural and supernatural. The novel's protagonist, Saul Garamond, is a hybrid being – half human, half rat – who occupies a position inbetween. For Miéville, the cross-fertilisation of realism and fantasy along with horror and science fiction is of great interest because it is able to convey elements intrinsic to socialist critique: mass culture, counter-culture, and radical politics (cf. Newsinger 2000), all three of which are strongly linked to the metaphorical and literal underground in *King Rat*.

According to Maczynska (2010: 75), the novel exposes[es] the ideological limitations of bourgeois urban myths and map[s] urban space from alternative, playfully subversive positions", the final effect of which is "an uncanny, misaligning metropolis, macabre but darkly comical, drawn with a satirical humor laced with existential dread." Similar to the 1960s counter-culture of swinging London, situated in subterranean clubs and galleries (cf. Pike 2005a: 186), the human characters of Miéville's novel – Saul, Fabian and Natasha – are represented as instinctive rebels against the established or-

---

38 | As McLeod (2006: 390) argues, "[m]any postwar migrants precariously lived and worked beneath the surface of London, existing in the cramped confines of the city, apart from, as well as a part of, the fabric of day-to-day life in London." Although the new immigrants are visible in their employment and an integral feature of city life, they mostly live and work beneath its surface. According to Pratt (1993: 88) "[i]nvisibility names the subaltern's presence for the dominant party."

der (cf. Freedman 2003: 406). Natasha composes Drum N' Bass tracks which capture the contemporary urban landscape as "crumbling buildings, everything grey, towering and enormous, flattened, variegated and empty, unclaimed" (KRA: 272) as well as the denizens' "dead ends, disappointments" (KRA: 272). London is a city of the dead, just as "ghostly" as the "fabricated emotions" of electronic music which "signal[s] the destruction of anything human in this world" (KRA: 271; cf. Bould 2009: 320). Fabian navigates this anomic cityscape, which has turned into a vision of Mumford's Nekropolis:

He interacted on the fucking tarmac, communicated with people passing him in their cars. This was as close as he came to relationships now. [...] And then back out into the cursory conversations of the roadways, his dangerous flirtations with cars and lorries. There was no such thing as society, not any more, not for him. He had been stripped of it, reduced to begging for social scraps like signalling and brake lights, the rudenesses and courtesies of transport. These were the only times now that anyone took notice of him, modified their behaviour because of him. Fabian was so lonely it made him ache. (KRA: 296-297)

His social life being reduced to cycling London's streets the character feels estranged from the metropolis which is already on the verge of anomie (cf. Bould 2009: 320).

Postmodern London only seems to consist of outsiders: the characters' ineffective counter- or rather subcultural activities are located in the topological heterotopias and non-places of the city, while the homeless occupy the netherworld of side-alleys and the threshold of doorways. The protagonist Saul links up with a mentally ill girl who is hungry for company and recognises that she is just as "alienated from her city as he was" (KRA: 224). They both belong to the down and out inhabiting a "place so close to the real city, and no one can see them" (KRA: 213). In that sense, Saul's status as member of a subculture, refugee, hybrid, outcast and initially homeless also makes him a prisoner of London's underclass and its nightly figures:

He was captivated by London. Someone approached him from a corner: a woman in heals, he could hear, a brave soul walking this area alone at night. He did not want to scare her, so he slumped against a wall and slid down to the floor, just a comatose drunk. The associations of homelessness struck him [...]. (KRA: 286)

Consequently, the uncanny topography of the sewers assimilates the city's topology of poverty and crime, atavism and anomie, political uncertainty, and social crisis.

The physical, social, and mental uncanny nature of the underground is traditionally encompassed by the figure of the rat as a persistent trope of the subterranean city and the socially depraved. The Cockney Londoner King Rat introduces himself to Saul in the following manner:

I'm the big-time crime boss. I'm the one that stinks. I'm the scavenger chief, I live where you don't want me. I'm the intruder. [...] I killed half your continent one time. I know when your ships are sinking. I can break your traps across my knee and eat the cheese in your face and make you blind with my piss. I'm the one with the hardest teeth in the world, I'm the whiskered boy. I'm the Duce of the sewers, I run the underground. I'm the king. (KRA: 34)

He demonstrates his otherness – criminal, scavenger, intruder, killer, deserter – which induces fear and panic, but shows that rats exist 'below' us and 'within' ourselves.[39] When coming to terms with his own half-rat nature, Saul relishes in his newly acquired invisibility and limitless scope of movement: "*I'm rat and can travel how I like.*" (KRA: 133) The sewers as the home of the rat incorporate the river Styx into the topography of London, which as a threshold space denotes a state of flux and passage as well the home of marginal and mythical figures (cf. Pike 2005a: 190-191). The rat charts the metropolis as an unfixed territoriality that refuses the commonplace of home in favour of the uncertainty of uncanny non-places. It is that form of utterly uncontrollable mobility, transgression of borders, and fleetingness – like the migrant's – which induces anxiety.

Nevertheless, this intangible otherness already exists within the boundaries of the Self. Saul questions whether he really existed independently of King Rat or whether the two of them were not figments of each other's imagination (KRA: 125). The rat is thus represented not only as counter but double of the urbanite. In his interpretation of dreams, Freud initially sees the symbolic significance of the rat as an ambivalent character, which according to Pike (2005a: 198-199) stresses the "chthonic connection of the rat to the uncanniness of the underworld". King Rat, as a character beyond morality and law, is represented as a spectre: "Unclear. Minimal. Dirty. Subaltern." (KRA: 280) At the end of the novel, King Rat voices from the spectral off: "*I'm the one that's always there. I'm the one that sticks. I'm the dispossessed, I'll be back again. I'm why you can't sleep in your bed.* [...] *I'm the tenacious one, the one that locks my teeth, that won't give up, that can't ever let go. I'm the survivor.*" (KRA: 421) Insofar, the rat is the vivid projection of urbanites' repressed collective anxieties, memories, and traumas. The rat resembles an archetype of fear concerning the death of the city – specifically socially. This is even enhanced as through its adaptability and transformative potential, the rat is likely to survive the human apocalypse. In this sense, the rat is not only a figure of the subterranean lower classes, but rather an animalistic revenant of its citizens' most basic, yet hidden, terrors.

Ashford (2008: 17) also argues that the representation of the uncanny is strongly aligned with the discourse of communism in the novel. The spectre of communism haunting Europe is an ideological image that has been perceived as an imminent danger to the (capitalist) metropolis or postmodern (post-Fordist) city from beneath. From this perspective, the rats of London's sewers are devised – like already in the modernist conception – as the urban proletariat (cf. Pike 2005a: 225). For Saul, King Rat's subordinated rat subjects represent the controlled masses, whose uninspired life is domineered by food, procreation, sleep (KRA: 223, 325). Sensing the rats' predisposition for totalitarian command, Saul resorts to fundamentalist rhetoric in the need for defending the city:

---

39 | Pike (2005: 198) points out the interconnections of the myth of Vienna's Rat Man and Freud's invention of psychoanalysis. The London Underground are presumably inhabited by a new subspecies of black mice, called "*mus Metropolitanus*" (Wolmar 2004: 292). Mayhew (2003: 14) argues that to fight congestion in the streets of nineteenth-century London, denizens must either "be made to fly through the air with the London sparrows or to scour along the drains with London rats." Also Andy in *Tunnel Vision* compares himself and Brian to rats in a pipe (TUV: 309) and Adam of *London Revenant* perceives commuters of the Tube as rats (LOR: 39).

> 'You are *rats*,' Saul told them, sticking out his lower lip and jerking his head back like Mussolini. They gazed at him, a shifting mass of followers, peering out from all the nooks and crannies of the building site in which they had congregated. [...] The rats were inspired. They longed to follow him. He dismissed them with a wave and they scattered in short-lived bravado. (KRA: 335-336)

Gripped by a first urge of urban vigilance and "millennial fervour" (KRA: 335), the rats spread out across London like an army of revenge against the totalitarian aggressor Pied the Piper towards socio-political emancipation (KRA: 362, 419). In a triumph of revolutionary egalitarianism engrained in urbanity, Saul overthrows the rat monarchy and declares the underground the republic of "Citizen Rat" (KRA: 420; cf. Freedman 2003: 405-406; Gordon 2003: 355).

In sum, underground London can be considered as the description of urban hierarchies *per se* which devise the city beneath as the locus of oppressed social otherness. As a place of the marginalised and notable space for identity formation, the sewers are a classic heterotopia in the sense of Foucault, constituting the most alternative spatiality within the subterranean city. For Lefebvre (2003: 129), a heterotopia especially corresponds to urban anomie, as its spatialities are constructed by out-groups. Furthermore, Rosalind Williams (1990: 21) and David Pike (2005a: 46) have shown that in descending below the social surface of the metropolis, writers seek knowledge about the Other, but actually unearth reflections of common values and anxieties. As such, the underground encompasses spaces of the collective unconscious filled with desire and fear, which devises the subterranean city as both an ideological map and a mental landscape of the urbanite. The homeless and the rat as figures of the urban uncanny therefore are metaphorical expressions of the city's alienation and anomie, which conversely are idiosyncratic experiences familiar to every citizen of the metropolis.

6.2.3 The Metropolitan (Un)Conscious

Despite the heterogeneity of the Tube's crowds and the significance of the underground as a public space of socialisation, for Augé (1988: 103) the *Métro* is mainly a space of solitude. As was shown, the underground is a place of introspection and surveillance as well as a space where the Self is confronted with its utmost fears of otherness. Thereby the analyses of subterranean physical and social spaces have already touched upon aspects of the underground as mental space. According to topological divisions in the narrative world, vertical partitions relegate ontological layers within the narrative universe, such as reality, dream, and magic (cf. Ryan 2009: 429). Just as the subterranean space becomes the place where the Self can be located, thus a space of self-recognition and conscious identity formation, the alternate side of the underground rather offers an uncanny view into the undefined space of men, namely his unconscious.

Wendy Lesser (1987: 127) extensively shows that vaults, dungeons, and caves are considered the depths of the Self, and therefore a literary subterranean endeavour is seen analogous to a psychoanalytical unearthing of the deeply buried and forgotten remnants of the past. Although there is a larger memory of the underworld, a collective unconscious, in the sense of the Jungian archetype and the Freudian notion of the *id* as suppressing both trauma and desire, which is topographically located in the urban underground, the following approach of the sub-urban (un)conscious also concentrates on the subterranean city as housing the mental apparatus of the nonconscious. Michael O'Brien (2010: 168) argues in regard to contemporary underground novels by Geoff Ryman, Tobias Hill, and Conrad Williams that they "evoke a London from underground which is fractured, not solely across geographical boundaries, but most evidently through the disparate readings of London which are exhibited through their characters' attitudes, memories and fears." In the following I will explore mental-scape, memory-scape, and dream-scape as represented in Ryman's *253*, Hill's *Underground* and Williams' *London Revenant*.

Mental-Scape

In Geoff Ryman's novel *253* the Tube is index and symbol of the city's collective consciousness. Because the usual activities are temporarily suspended and civil inattention forces/allows people to spatially separate themselves, the urbanites' passivity of riding the train furthers introspection. Mr Clive Kelton, for example, acknowledges that only "on the tube, does he have any time to himself, time to rest." (253: 39) The interior monologue, especially in the sections on "What he/she is thinking" reveals the common thoughts, memories, dreams, reflections, visions, and imaginaries of the single travellers. Due to the single portraits, the novel offers subjective insights into a "wide array of collective thoughts" (O'Brian 2010: 161) as well as the various imaginative layers of urbanites: deep and shallow thoughts, hopes and desires. O'Brian (*ibid.*: 160-161) argues that the void between the single social spaces acts as an additional stimulus through which the imaginative process of the commuters is activated, for instance by fantasising about the strangers' personal identities.

Oftentimes, Ryman's insights into the psyche of average Londoners specifically oppose their physical appearance or the image by other commuters (*ibid.*: 163). Mr Thomas Dowe "[l]ives alone in a spotless flat", he is "treated for depression" but he hides from his doctors "a completely unacceptable sexual longing" (253: 164) and is now on his way to request castration. His counter, Rob "The Knob" Hall (253: 46), is aroused by the women on the train and decides to get off at Waterloo to release his sexual tension in the toilets. While most of the thoughts are of a mundane nature, yet are rather intelligently arranged, some revelations are overtly humorous. There are, however, a couple of disturbing openings: while Alfred Cushway has the looks of an ageing male model, at home he beats his children (253: 40), and the police constable Bert Harris is exposed as extremely violent, homophobic, and full of hate for other people (253: 139). These thoughts break social taboos and reveal sexual and criminal aberrations, but also serve the voyeuristic and sensationalist side of the Tube theatre: passenger number 165 dreams of adultery with her brother-in-law, 169 is madly in love with Saddam Hussein, 199 schemes to murder his colleague's wife, 73 is possessed by the thought that Jesus orders him to knife his own stepdaughter, 97 wants to steal a baby at St Thomas's Hospital and 101 has decided to commit suicide. The Tube is once more semantisised as a heterotopia of deviance, specifically that of prison, psychiatric ward, and brothel. Civil inattention and not being omniscious are hence underlined as prerequisites to avoid violence, panic and terror in the metropolitan realm.

Furthermore, the penetration of Londoners' innermost thoughts also concerns recollections that reveal a deep nostalgia for London's past as a city that was still one of sociability and community spirit. In particular the smellscape of the London Underground triggers Proustian memories that take the passengers back in time. For Mr Don Disney, the decline of Billingsgate fish market resembles the transformation of the metropolis and the disintegration of the nation:

> He remembers the old market, with its arches, its noise, its humour. He remembers the heavy leather boots with the copper toes, and the thick leather hats on which he would balance boxes of fish, or trays of eels. [...] Life was smart, hard and funny. Now it's grey and corporate. [...] When they moved the marked the foundation thawed, and the building began to fall down. Like Britain really. (253: 118)

Mrs Madeleine Strickler remembers travelling to church on the Tube in 1957 and decries the loss of communal feeling (253: 239). Similarly, Mr Tony Mannochi's recollection of the Tube in 1964 is fraught with a notion of sociability and he meditates on how in the metropolis "everything is replaced, especially people." (253: 37) Contemplating on the London Underground Strike of 1989, which revived a sense of solidarity and communality in London's streets, Ms Anthea Dobbs sees the contemporary city's "habitual isolation [...] breed[ing] mistrust and cynicism" (253: 296) and driving it towards urban anomie.

Hence, the temporal construction of underground London not only serves as a repository of the past, but also as an oracle for the future. As was shown before, these moments of memorial and premonitional introspections are owed to the tube travellers' actions of inattention such as reading. O'Brian (2010: 159) argues that "'mental space' becomes more apparent to the subject, as he or she feels compelled to escape into the novel they are carrying". The texts enable the urbanites to transcend the spatial limitations of the carriage to a wider scope of space, time, and collective. Insofar, the Tube furthers experiences of escapism and the mental spaces created during the short period of time often influence people's decision to get off their metaphorically chosen track. Some characters alter their lives and suddenly jump up and leave the train before their actual destination, while others are voluntarily or involuntarily kept on the train driving towards the novel's "cataclysmic conclusion" (*ibid.*: 166).

It is therefore interesting to regard the contemplations of people immediately during the train crash (253: 345-351) as an apt image of the urban overload scenario. We can discern three groups of characters: the fatalist, the apathetic, and the vigilant. The fatalists like Milton Richards and Paul Launcey embrace death as salvation and as an answer to their prayers. Some characters contemplate their own death, while others, deeply lost in thoughts, memories, and dreams, do not even realise what is happening. Most non-urbanites cannot react appropriately to the crisis: the Japanese Yoshi simply wonders at the strangeness of England, Debbie, an American film maker, is completely disoriented and Selima just wishes she had at least died fighting in Bosnia. There is hardly any time to process an event, and people are forced to act mechanically. The only passengers that actually react with prompt vigilance are two men in the first car: the fatally ill Richard Tomlinson jumps up and tries to wake the driver, and the retired MI5 agent Maurice Hazlett lurches for the emergency break. People not attuned to the constantly shifting environment of the city are lost, but, ironically, the only passengers who walk away from the crashed train unharmed are the homeless Anne Frank and the drunk Tom McHugh.

Insofar, the thoughts and behaviour of people underground reveal an inversion of the urban overload. Londoners have already adapted to the multitude of sensual expressions by normative behaviour and routinised navigation in the environment leading to a blunting of the senses which allows them time for introspection and contemplation. The heterotopia of the Tube actually offers this space for reflection to the urbanites, where they are able to manufacture mental spaces to bring their "subterranean selves" (Ross 2002: 103) into the open. O'Brian (2010: 164) argues that "the act of commuting becomes ritualized around memories and impulses connecting individuals to a society which lives its life through the tube." The single characters build their mental-scapes on different scopes of contemplation, dreams, visions, memories, and imaginations so that the whole train appears to be one large collective unconscious of the city above.

Memory-Scape

The analysis of Ryman's novel *253* has shown that the subterranean city as mental space denotes the subconscious of memory. Suspended from every- or present-day behaviour, characters enter this heterotopic archive of an individual or collective past. According to Haupt (2005: 507), the vertical city denotes the spatialisation of its chronology. The descent into the underground hence implies a return to one's past. Accordingly, the labyrinthine passageways of underground London constitute a topography of memory (cf. Krewani 2002: 194; Pike 2005a: 83).

Casimir, the protagonist of Tobias Hill's *Underground*, enjoys tunnel-walking during his night shifts, strolling along the tracks of the Tube. Thus, the traditional trope of *flânerie* is not only (re)transferred to an underground setting, but its narrative function has been altered within the confines of the subterranean city to symbolise an introspective exploration of the Self. Casimir's subterranean contemplations become gazes back through time. Because virtual blindness enhances aural and olfactory senses, the intensified smell- and soundscape of the subterranean city stimulates his memory:

> In his mind the Underground's levels and rooms are laid out, clear and certain. [...] The metal stairway smells of dry shit and dust around him. He is near the top before his heart rate starts to quicken. He remembers a church tower in Poland; Pentecost, laughter, the bell-tower floor strewn with blue irises. (UND: 39)

While as a boy in Poland he perceived social status, morality and beauty through the colours blue, red, green and yellow, Casimir's painful memories of his childhood are brought back to him in darkness. In Greek mythology the waters of Mnemosyne and Lethe, denoting memory and forgetfulness, respectively, form different topological stages on the threshold between above and underground. Likewise, for Casimir subterranean London is similar to being under water, enforcing his encounter with the repressed past (UND: 234). By contrast, two female counter-characters in the novel both try to forget. Casimir's Jewish mother suffers from Alzheimer's, which the protagonist sees as a means to cope with her traumatic experiences in a German concentration camp. Consequently, the protagonist fights forgetfulness: "She is the woman who chooses to forget her past. And Casimir is the one who remembers for her, even when the remembering hunts him. Catches him in the dark, presses over him like the weight of London clay." (UND: 103) As a heterotopic space, underground London's compressed space-time resembles a storage of both history and autobiography or collective and personal memory; it functions as *lieux de mémoire*.

Aleida Assmann (1999: 258-265) explicates how 'spaces of memory' figure a storage room for unsolved traumatic experiences of a collective memory. The epitome of such a traumatic space is Auschwitz (cf. *ibid.*: 328-339) with the Holocaust as the most contentious issue of postmodern historiography. Interestingly, as in Geoff Ryman's *253* with the character of Anne Frank and China Miéville's nightmares of the totalitarian stalker Pied the Piper and his intended annihilation in *King Rat*, also Tobias Hill's contemporary underground novel problematises the holocaust in the history, memory, and trauma with allusion to the London Tube. It appears to be a postmodern adaptation of the death train in connection with preoccupations of history and memory, bringing into focus London as refuge for various traumatised pariahs.

In *Underground*, the issue of trauma is also explored through the character Alice, a homeless girl who in the subterranean dark tries to obliterate her childhood memories of rape. In defence, Casimir attacks Alice's abusive father who has come to search her out on the Underground. In this battle, the protagonist encounters the demons from his own past, the personal family and collective socio-historical trauma. It is revealed that Casimir's father, although in love with a Jewish woman, participated in a pogrom that killed forty-two members of the Jewish community returning from Buchenwald concentration camp, and later made money selling nerve-gas to terrorists (cf. Ashford 2008: 13-14). Insofar, the subterranean city represents a personal contact zone between Casimir's metropolitan presence and his Eastern European roots.

Because in his mind the spatialities of underground London merge with the mines in his Polish hometown, Casimir becomes confused on which side of the tunnel he will resurface – the London or Poland direction (UND: 247). In the space of memory, the past can only ever be revisited but never fully entered, nor the present totally left behind; instead, different horizons of time overlap in this threshold spatiality. As such, the underground is a strongroom for the past but also the oracle of the future, enclosing times gone by and times to come. Having encountered his trauma and fought his deepest anxieties, Casimir decides to look towards the end of the tunnel, the light and his future in London (UND: 248). In Lotmanian (1990: 161) terms of spatial semantics, the character's re-emergence from the Underground initiates his rebirth. Hence, through his journey within the realms of the subterranean heterotopia of crisis, the protagonist has come to terms with his past and is reborn as an urban citizen of metropolitan London.

From Vester's (1996: 120) notion that collective mentalities are an unsystematic version of collective memory, we can discern that the heterotopic inversions of the underground are especially apt to represent dispositions of thinking, feeling, imagining, and acting. Repressed traumas and experiences are not only buried in the depth of the denizens' memory-scape, but are collectively stored in the deep archives of the subterranean city, entrenched in its multi-sensory environment, namely its idiosyncratic sound- and smellscape. In that sense, underground London functions as the urbanites' personal space of memory and the city's *lieux de mémoire*. The underground's sublimity accounts for the unimaginable and frightening but also horribly familiar and remembered aspects of the metropolis and its denizens (cf. Pike 2005a: 82). Uncanny representations of the underground and its personae as well as their reiterative return from the repressed depths explore ambivalent relations of strangeness and familiarity. The underground reveals residual mental structures, traumatic memories, and repressed anxieties that influence London's urban-specific mentality

Dream-Scape

Furthermore, the underground represents an oneiric space which harbours preconscious states of mind such as dark fantasies or irrational nightmares. Especially in Conrad Williams' *London Revenant* the subterranean city is such a significant psychological space. The novel's protagonist, Adam Buckley, is haunted by premonitions in which the aboveground city becomes inverted to a hellish underground. After linking up with a group of people whose parties are a hotbed of surrealist orgies of drugs, sex, and food (LOR: 50-51), Adam has repeated dreams of death, murder, and suicide (LOR: 62-65, 96-100). These horrific oneiric visions are represented as the character's uncanny premonition, insofar as shortly afterwards the leader of the party community is killed in a car accident (LOR: 101). Until waking up, Adam never knows whether he is in fact dreaming, and the parallelism between nightmarish reality and lucid dreams distorts both his conception of the metropolis and his Self. His fantasy is shown as a mental landscape in which the irrational areas of the urbanite's mind are emphasised, especially the flux of dreams, which revives transcendental aspects of city life.

The chronotope of violent nightmares leads Adam to transform into Monck, a covert operative of a secret society that lives in the Underground. This descent into the underworld and simultaneous transgression symbolise a journey into his unconscious. In Sigmund Freud's verticalisation of different levels within the map of the psyche the *id* – the unconscious – is buried in the depth of the Self. Due to the novel's anthropomorphisation of underground London as IT, the subterranean space is depicted as the psychological space of the *id*. Lesser (1987: 127) shows that the *id* cannot be fathomed by the conscious mind and therefore essentially becomes part of the body itself; "both are literally unconscious, incapable of thought or reasoning, but powerful enough to alter and invade and finally control the conscious life. It is this sense of 'unconscious' – the underworld of the soul and the body". As Adam/Monck's antagonist, the underground terrorist IT/Blore/H[40] arises from the depths of the city. He completely identifies with the metropolis and hence his fabric of terror personifies the collective unconscious of Londoners wrought by anxiety.

Uncertainty in the mode of the uncanny and the personification of the revenant stresses the threshold existence of the urbanite being caught between the conscious visible material city above and a spectral urbanity below. Literary underground London is semantisised as a state inbetween which brings the Self in contact with the unconscious and thus connects various states of being and becoming. Hence, the "Psychometropolis" (Vidler 1999: 189) of underground London is the Other necessary for the completion of a whole identity. In its heterotopic inversion, the subterranean city symbolises a reversal, defining the hidden realities of urban unconsciousness as the machinery that keeps

---

40 | "IT" in *London Revenant* is nameless and becomes faceless during the novel. The figure has multiple identities in different spatial contexts.

London and its denizens in motion. Because of Adam's bouts of narcolepsy and blocks of memory loss, the perception of urban reality of the city is distorted. Trying to find his way in London, the character becomes trapped between "the Topside" and "the Underground" and thus Adam/Monck is unable to ground his identity in a stable passage of time from past to future. When literary London is additionally shaken by an earthquake turning the whole cityscape upside down, the new topography of disorder and chaos creates a labyrinthine space where there seems to be no getting through, rendering the urban "an obstacle course" (LOR: 267). The earthquake constitutes the acme of Adam's distorted psychological state, and as such it also symbolises that he has reached a mental dead end. Only by transgressing the threshold identity as Monck is the city rendered whole for Adam; consequently the illegible becomes legible and the uncanny turns homely.

All in all, underground London as the metropolitan (un)conscious opens views into the minds, memories, and dreams of urbanites. It has disclosed collective dispositions of nostalgia and trauma, hopes and anxieties, thus specifically the non-conscious structures of feeling. As a topography of the urban sublime, the underground is generally able to inspire both awe and fascination as well as to trigger bouts of dislocation and terror. Although this ambivalence, ingrained in familiarity and strangeness, is rooted in urban-generic attitudes, mental-scape, memory-scape and dream-scape have revealed the particularities of subterranean London and thereby the urban-specific nonconscious as wrought by a fear of anomie, loneliness, dislocation, and loss.

6.2.4 Deep Collective Space-Time Compressions

Underground London is not only a physical, social and mental, but also a temporal phenomenon. We have already seen that in the underground different temporal horizons interlace with one another. Insofar, the particularity of subterranean collective space-time compression is constituted by its "unimaginably rich [...] brew of other times, places, and modes of being in the world" (Pike 2005a: 197). This sub-chapter specifically regards the temporal implications of the city beneath first in their chronotopic and heterochronic nature and secondly in a broader perspective of spatio-temporal liminality.

Tube Times: Chronotopes and Heterochronies

For Mumford (1997: 243), the subway even more than the sewage system constitutes "*a vast expenditure of time*". In the sense that a vertical descent equals a temporal movement, and the underground's body, in the form of memories and visions, constitutes a mental spatialisation of time, the subterranean space also denotes a space-time compression of past and future, nemesis and return (cf. Haupt 2005: 518-519, 524-525). The incorporation of spatial-temporal paradoxes culminates in the urban underground, which combines "both organic and inorganic nature, gestation and growth as well as death and decomposition" (Gottlieb 1999: 238). Within the confines of the underground, time is either compressed or intertwined, and can therefore be interpreted as heterochronic.

A temporal heterotopia breaks with traditional time by either "indefinitely accumulating time" (Foucault 1986: 26) or being absolutely temporal. In that sense, the chronotope of the London Underground features a hyperbolic image of Foucault's (*ibid.*: 24) heterochronie: "a train is an extraordinary bundle of relations because it is something through which one goes, it is also something by means of which one can go from point to another, and then it is also something that goes by". Wolfgang Schivelbusch shows in his seminal study *The Railway Journey* (1986) that the train in general induces a temporal shrinking which is perceived as a spatial one. The paradox of railway time is that "space [is] both diminished *and* expanded" (Schivelbusch 1986: 35), just like the London Underground leads to the expansion of the city itself. But because the railroad only knows "points of departure and destination" (*ibid.*: 38), the train opens up a new space "in-between, or travel space" (*ibid.*: 37). In that sense, the annihilation of "traditional space-time continuum" (*ibid.*: 36) by train travel leads to a collective space-time compression that transforms structures of thinking in regard to the subjective and collective spatio-temporal perceptions (*ibid.*).[41]

The protagonist of Keith Lowe's *Tunnel Vision*, Andy, bets that he can travel the system of London's Underground within twenty hours[42] and thereby inverses the metropolis into a chronotope of one single day. On his exceptional odyssey beneath and around London, he experiences an array of space-time capsules. At 5.05 am on the Northern Line between Morden and Colliers Wood, the train is a very different place from that during daytime. At this hour, the chronotope of the street is relocated to one of the tracks of the Tube, becoming a chronotope of encounter describing the intersection of the spatio-temporal paths of a variety of urbanites – here the trainspotter Andy with the homeless Brian. Particularly during rush hour, when people are so close to one another that space encompasses both aspects of sex and death (TUV: 134), the Tube forms a temporal heterotopia. The protagonist suggests that time is suspended when commuters "are crammed in this train like we've been vacuum-packed" (TUV: 232). The novel structurally plays on this idea of collective space-time compressions when the characters are caught in a full train carriage; in the passage the compression of words and text resembles the claustrophobic confinement of space and emotional expression of time which enlarges Andy' paranoia and makes him think of death (TUV: 253-254). On the other hand, he despises the other extremes of empty trains at the end of London's lines because their space-time suggests loneliness (TUV: 280-281).

Similarly, the protagonist Adam in Conrad Williams' *London Revenant* feels oppressed by this subterranean density of space-time compression, in opposition to the freedom he experiences aboveground.

> Down there was all about suffocation, enclosure; the compression of air, time and space. Then suddenly you found yourself thrown into the space of the big city, with the sky jetting off in every direction above you. I also felt slightly sick. I don't like it. I don't like it. The crush. The people breathing on you. The weight of the tunnels. (LOR: 157)

---

41 | Concerning the mental implications of the difference between train and motorcar travel, Schivelbusch (1986: 39) notably refers to Proust's *A la recherche du temps perdu*.

42 | At the time of the novel's publication, Robert Robinson was world record holder for travelling the whole tube system in 19 hours, 59 minutes, 37 seconds (cf. Anon. n.d.); in July 2002 a new record was set for visiting all 272 stations in 19 hours, 18 minutes by Jack Welsby (cf. Smith 2005: xi). The latest Tube challenge record of 2004 lies at 18 hours, 45 minutes for all 275 stations.

The Tube is perceived as an strange chronotope in which he feels trapped. Especially due to these alien parameters the Tube becomes his personal terror that enforces his sense of dislocation.

> Like the way the Tube seems to warp London, make it less real. Less reliable than it already is. London shrinks. [...] On the Underground, time becomes this vampire that attaches itself to the back of your neck, tapping you off energy and the ability to relate space to movement. (LOR: 39)

Nevertheless, as was shown before, once accustomed to the different order of space-time, the Underground offers clearer demarcations of orientation than the city above, and therefore finally represents Adam's personal safety net. Correspondingly, in Tobias Hill's novel *Underground* the protagonist Casimir is also sometimes overcome by a sense of dislocation when the Underground seems to be "shifting around him" (UND: 40) or giving him "a sense of motionlessness" (UND: 92). Paradoxically, the moving train experiences a slow-motion effect because the never changing perspective of an array of repetitious underground places figures a spatial and temporal standstill. In Hill's novel, the chronotope of the castle, saturated with history, is appropriated to the underground; in the immensity of deep space-time, Casimir digs up repressed memories. The subterranean city is able to accumulate the incommensurable possibilities of urban human life, and due to its density, the underground offers an encompassing yet blurry picture of the metropolis above.

The heterotopic character of the Tube is employed in its hyperbolic extreme by Geoff Ryman's *253*. The novel merely features a story time of the seven minutes and thirty seconds narrated two hundred and fifty-three times from the equal amount of different subject-positions. According to the author, this pure simultaneity allows to contrast perspectives and construct spatial relations (cf. Grossman 1997). An urban myth holds that London Underground minutes feature one hundred seconds (cf. Moran 2005: 55) and accordingly, the time it takes for the Barkerloo Line train to go from Embankment to Elephant & Castle would be expanded to a discourse time of approximately thirty hours. Moreover, the short amount of time is also subjectively expanded by ways of dreams, memories, and visions. O'Brien (2010: 158) argues that "as space decreases, time becomes elastic and, as the individual progresses through the network of tunnels, he or she uses the time within this empty space in the day, to read, eavesdrop or simply indulge in idle reflection." In other words, the mental spaces offer the possibility to enter not only other scapes but also other times and narratives. O'Brien (*ibid.*: 162) therefore interprets the envisioned transformations of identity as "an expression of the elasticity of time and space in the London Underground, in terms of how human forms change and London itself becomes distorted when viewed from a subterranean perspective." Yet the train constantly progresses towards its doom, the fatal "End of the Line" (253: 343). Whereas the London Underground is a symbol of the urban space of flows – transience, contingency, and fleetingness (cf. O'Brien 2010: 155) – narrative convention demands drama, progress, chronology, and closure, thus disrupting the constant chronotope of the novel and reducing it to a single event. Hence, in contrast, the intersubjective and interspatial view frozen in time is condensed because the author's use of prolepsis in the beginning of the book reveals that the train will ultimately crash and that we dive into the thoughts of the characters during what are presumably the last minutes of their lives (*ibid.*: 160, 163). Consequently, the train resembles a chronotope of mental orientation on the threshold between life and death.

Thanks to Schivelbusch's study, the general implications of underground railway travel for structures of mentality seem largely solved. Still, the novels since the 1990s obviously respond to the uncertainty which is created by a new condition of space-time compression in transferring their settings to the urban Gothic space of underground London. As registered by Smethurst (2000: 15), the postmodern chronotope shifts to spatial denominations. Hence, the literary chronotope in contemporary London novels in analogy to Smethurst's (*ibid.*: 65) argument enables a reading of the postmodern urban condition: "The idea of the postmodern chronotope is initially to present a reasonably coherent way of seeing and representing the contemporary world." Between being and becoming, the chronotope or space-time of the city beneath as well as the chronotope of the train in progress or commuter in transition capture the transformation of current urban-specific mental structures and specifically points towards a particular temporal mentality. The mental implications of the Tube's heterochronia concern its total dislocation from rational parameters of space and time. Lost inbetween fragmented pieces or simultaneous layers of space-time, urbanites are paradoxically enabled by way of inversion to reflect upon their personal time-track, life, and biography. From a collective point of view, the topographical and topological underground then serves as a major agent of orientation.

The Liminality of Underground London

In reference to Walter Benjamin, Pike (1999: 117) shows that the subterranean city as a space of transit, movements, and contact is a "threshold space" where meaning is negotiated. This spatio-temporal transitoriness not only defines the chronotopic character of underground London but notably its liminality. Insofar, underground London is a space inbetween, a space of transition, where the subterranean cityscape forms a grey zone where different urban ambivalences are negotiated (cf. Döring 2001; Pleßke 2009; O'Brien 2010). The co-existence of dichotomies and antagonisms defines the underground as a liminal space of experience. Underground London is the liminal space of an illimitable metropolis where the real and the imaginary overlap, consequently encompassing myth and utopia, antiquity and novelty, superstition and innovation, the concrete and the abstract, the physical and the mental. Because the underground both (de)masquerades and counters the world above, its spatialities have triggered ambivalent attitudes. Moreover, subterranean London itself is defined by its idiosyncratic dichotomies and co-existing antagonisms of physical, mental, social, and temporal space which create zones of interference. As was shown before, the subterranean city unites the cultural characteristics of Babylon with those of New Jerusalem as well as social marginalisation and interaction. Augé underlines the liminal state of the underground between home and work life, and between public and private. But underground London is mostly a site of extreme intimacy; this personal space of introspection emphasises the unconscious and its psychological liminality, and the multi-sensory space of the underground triggers both anxieties like terror and claustrophobia as well as feelings of protection and safety. Simultaneously, "womb and tomb" (Lesser 1987: 13), the inner sphere of the earth is the realm of the dead as well as a shelter for the living. The London

Underground is naturally a dark space, but its places are partially lit by artificial light, in both senses creating dislocation. As a black hole, it conveys emptiness but also density, pointing towards the unknown and a deeper truth and personal enlightenment. Its liminal spatialitity offers interstitial moments for constructing transient identities. The realm lies between repression and elimination, fascination and repulsion, so that the subterranean city is both a familiar place and an unfamiliar space. Because most of these aspects have already been explored within the heterotopic physical, social, mental, and temporal representations of contemporary underground novels, I will in the following specifically concentrate on the uncanny aspect of this liminality.

In Geoff Ryman's novel *253*, the time before the train crashes at Elephant & Castle is represented as the remaining time of the characters' lives and thereby characterise the Tube as the liminal space between life and death. Insofar, the death train is a modern adaptation of Charon's bark that crosses the threshold of the river Styx carrying human souls into their afterlife. Ryman specifically claims that people tend to have relations with the beyond, and therefore in his novels the author chooses to normatively include ghosts, visions and spectres as well as "new forms of revenant." (Cit. in Hill 2006) On the one hand, the characters that die in the crash return in a transcendental form or live on as their iterated profile-doubles in the novel. On the other hand, we can read all of the two hundred and fifty-three passengers aboard the train as urban zombies, reduced to lost souls by the city's violent demands. An early mention of this ghostly trail in the novel is the footnote within a footnote which features a hidden profile of William Blake either as a spectre of his Self or a vision by passenger 134: "On 11th January 1995, William Blake came back to Hercules Road. The train, trailing spirits, pulled him. He arrived staggering forward as if hurled onto the platform of Lambeth North tube station." (253: 185) Due to his eighteenth-century mentality, for Blake the Underground presents a vision of hell with ghostly chambers and theatrically masked people. Despite the perfumed atmosphere, "there is no odour of human closeness", while the "harsh cleanliness in the air" and "the stench, like tar or oil lamps" (253: 187) mark the inhospitable cityscape above. Blake returns to the future of contemporary London, which is not quite like his imagined Jerusalem: "He looks at the jumble of buildings, some shiny like wrapped presents, others like wedding cakes, still others like lavatories with tiles." (253: 189)

Another revenant is the elderly version of Anne Frank, contemplating like Blake the sad faces around her and comparing them to the deficient life of the unliving. Although she knows who everyone on the train is, Anne is obviously ignorant of her own writerly alter ego:

> She is Anne Frank, the famous diarist, bus she doesn't know that. She has wandered Europe for the last 50 years. She sometimes sees the face of a child in bookshop windows, and knows enough to be happy for her. That child got what it wanted. It is not what Anne wants. [...] Anne thinks she is still in the train to Auschwitz, and that she is trying to make people happy one last time. (253: 340)

As a mental survivor of holocaust she has haunted Europe traumatised and disoriented. Anne thinks that she is still on the infernal train to annihilation. Insofar, the diary as a literary document also serves as a monument to Anne Frank, rendering her immortal to bear witness in all eternity (253: 351). The ambiguity of her character lies in the liminality between presence and absence, past and present. Buse and Stott (1999: 10-11) comment that the ghost unsettles any neat temporal compartmentalisation: "In the figure of the ghost, we see that past and present cannot be neatly separated from one another, as any idea of the present is always constituted through the difference and deferral of the past, as well as anticipations of the future." Anne Frank not only personifies, but is objectified as an oracle of violent death. The female revenant initiates the inversion of a *danse macabre* (253: 340). In the musical tradition of *memento mori*, Anne begins to sing "*If that's all there is my friends, then let's keep dancing*." (253: 340) The constant Jewish wanderer is joined by the returning African migrant 223, Professor Dionne Butler, who urges the frightened people to join the dance: "Everybody!" (253: 340) In a cultural appropriation, the dance turns into a party with a puppet of pacifist John Lennon and Anne Frank waltzing through the carriage. Due to the initiation of the heterochronic festival, the party people are saved by dancing onto the platform of Lambeth North, while the train hurtles on towards "The End of the Line" of the Underground, the track, the song, and the text.

Within the space of seven pages, the absolute community formed throughout the brief journey is annihilated by the catastrophe (cf. Ashford 2008: 26). The feelings of terror and anxiety built up throughout the novel by numerous references to painful existences, lethal injuries and the brutality of war find an end in a cataclysmic and apocalyptic denouement (cf. Colombino 2006: 632). The crash generates the only narrative part of the novel where time unfolds in an eventful manner and the impact of the train finally sets the bodies of the fixed characters in involuntary motion – by vibration, fluctuation, swallowing, transfixing, shooting forward, falling backwards, etc. (*ibid.*: 628). And, as Ashford (2008: 27) shows, the wall at the terminus literally becomes the portal into another dimension: especially the ghosts of the passengers in Car 6 transcend into the limbo of their choice. As such, the underground represents various liminal states of the urban *conditio humana*, which ultimately oscillate between death-in-life or salvation-in-death. All in all, the uncanny recurrence of the number 253, the doubling and oneiric unreality of character profiles, the ambiguity of magical fate as well as the discourse of threshold existences make cultural anxieties of the death of humanity and the end of history resurface in the city beneath. Cixous (1976: 543) comments on this liminal position of the ghost between life and death:

> What is intolerable is that the Ghost erases the limit which exists between two states, neither alive nor dead; passing through, the dead man returns in the manner of the Repressed. It is his coming back which makes the ghost what he is, just as it is the return of the Repressed that inscribes the repression. In the end, death is never anything more than the disturbance of the limits. The impossible is to die.

Equally, in Conrad Williams' novel *London Revenant* the protagonist Adam experiences the surface London as a world of shadows, haunted by ghosts and experiencing events of urban revenance. In the process of the unconscious taking over and controlling his Self, Adam becomes aware of the "inbetween-ness" (LOR: 182), the liminality of underground London. The community of urban homeless people, themselves marginalised and unseen but deeply rooted in the centre of the metropolis, has "grown in spaces forgotten, or ignored." (LOR: 230) It is the idea of the homeless leading an existence between places, neither really in the city nor outside of it. In the novel, tramps are sentinels keeping watch on the outside of Underground stations, on the threshold between the known and unknown spheres of the metropolis. They ensure that the secret of the clandestine race of Underground people and the lost city of Beneothan stays unknown to "Topside" London (LOR: 231). The community haunting the subterranean city could as well be ghosts or lost souls (LOR: 271).

This collective spectre of the city is mirrored in the title of the novel *London Revenant* – that which returns and is resurrected. Time and space offer alternative realities in this allotopic space (LOR: 17). Underground London is a space inbetween, an oneiric space of horror and utopian vision, a space of liminal existence as "the *revenant* disrupts boundaries of time and space, and risks unravelling the confident demarcations of categorical thinking." (Luckhurst 2003: 337) The novel's revenant – here as the ghostly incarnation of the antagonist H/Blore – is an unnameable thing between a person and a monster, materiality and immateriality. Jacques Derrida (1994: 4-11) in *Specters of Marx* defines the *revenant* as a personification of liminality "somewhere between life and death, presence and absence, material and ethereal existence." (Luckhurst 2003: 337) This Derridean ghost takes up notions of mobilisation, iteration, deferral and transportation and hence haunting as an unbearable constant movement can be read in analogy to the Tube.

When Adam's narcoleptic bouts increase, his reality becomes more and more blurred by supernatural possibilities of walking through walls and on water, transcending the boundaries between past and present as well as between seemingly real places and imagined Londons. He cannot ignore the liminal space of underground London that enhances his schizophrenic state of mind. Descending, Adam experiences a kind of impersonation and dissolution of the Self: "I was insubstantial as smoke, [...] I lost all my shape and colour" (LOR: 161). Like the limbo Underground stations, his identity starts to disintegrate into a limbo-nothingness as if he were a ghost or a mere shadow of his Self. His haunting other thus does not lie outside of his Self, but the ghostly trail of his other character is the projection of his own spirit. This oscillation between two identities, above- and underground, conscious and unconscious, fact and fiction is again decided by a cataclysmic denouement – here an earthquake. The former Nekropolis of underground creatures rises in form of a New Jerusalem as the apocalyptic catastrophe is turned into a resurrection of the metropolis and the salvation of the protagonist from his state of non-existence. Because for Derrida (1994: 149-150) the revenant describes the connection between modalised presents of past, present and future, it opens the possibility of resurrection or reconstruction in a new identity.

Underground London as a thirdspace is "capable of juxtaposing in a single real place several spaces, several sites that are themselves incompatible." (Foucault 1986: 25) And, as Derrida shows, the revenant defies the basic dichotomies that organise our understanding of the world: vertical and horizontal, virtual and actual, longitude and latitude, presence and absence, body and spirit, past and present, life and death, visibility and invisibility. In deconstructionist manner, calling the end of all meta-narratives and favouring ambivalence, paradox and uncertainty, the liminality of the haunted and the underground constitute the opposite to an ontology based on certainties and polarities. With apocalyptic instances in the end, the ghost as a projection of this unnameable notion of the end of urban history is ultimately seen as both danger and chance for the postmodern city.

To sum up, underground London exists as an alternative sphere to the metropolis above, and as city within a city offers a complicated spatiality that connects unusual physical, social, mental, and imaginary spaces. Due to the co-existing dichotomies of urban life, the subterranean city is mainly defined by its liminality. Contemporary London novels employ this idea of the interstitial in the context of space-time compression. The defining borders of spatial oppositions normally taken for granted are dissolved and made obsolete in this allotopic and heterogeneous zone, whereby the underground imaginary functions as the liminal space between and of antagonising places. And it is paradoxically these liminal states of both conscious and unconscious which are suspected to lend a greater truth to the urban existence. In other words, the underground's isotopia offers an apt tableau for the urban sublime, while simultaneously constituting the threshold to urban understanding. As a heterotopia, London Underground becomes a borderline of human perception, insofar as something inbetween the conscious and the unconscious is constantly on the verge of resurfacing. In the unconsciousness of the urban, repressed memories and traumatic experiences from the past are unearthed, adding to the multi-layered collective history of the metropolis and opening possibilities of an uncanny beyond in the future of the city.

But not only is the subterranean space considered as liminal, but the characters themselves are threshold existences (i.e. identity crisis, schizophrenia, stranger, hybrid men, marginal other). Just as the space becomes the place where the Self can be located and is thus a space of self-recognition and conscious identity formation, the alternate side of the underground rather offers this (un)homely view into the undefined space of man. The underground *flâneur*, the abject homeless and the ghostly revenant all seem to haunt the inbetweenness of subterranean spaces. London Underground as the largely unexplored depth of the city shines a light on the unnameable, unknown, unhomely, uncanny, and numinous – namely the repressed but also inherently central Self. The chthonic and dark spatialities of underground London, which render vision virtually senseless, momentarily throw the protagonists into a state of enhanced disorientation and loss. The uncanny nature of their subterranean experiences also stresses the uncertainty of existence aboveground, whereby the characters' urban state of mind is exposed as inherently residual, fleeting, and unstable. Postmodern London mentality is thus depicted as an enhanced uncertainty of the contemporary urban *conditio humana* because the main metropolitan spheres have been transformed into uncanny interstitial spaces that defy any traditional notions of Being.

6.2.5 Subterranean Structures of Mentality

Historians of mentality specifically deal with everyday issues that are "silent, invisible and unconscious in order to understand what is spoken, seen and thought." (Simms 1989: 1) In that sense, underground London functions as an apt topos of mental dispositions. Subterranean structures of mentality conceptualise the underlying collective standardisations of thinking, feeling, imagining, and acting deciphered from the trope of the underground in contemporary London novels. The general notions of the subterranean space refer to archetypical mythologemes of a larger collective unconscious or images of the *id*. The London-specific topography of the vertical city, on the other hand, such as the Victorian sewers or the Tube, devises the representation of underground London towards the collective nonconscious. Underground imagery not only conveys the cloth or ideology of current urbanity, but actually reaches beyond the subcutaneous dispositions of thinking or subterranean urban mentality.

Because the contemporary metropolis evades holistic representations, a reduction of the cityscape to the subterranean spaces of underground London and its limited yet multiplex metaphor(i)city seems to re-approach the conceptualisation of urban space from its most dominant margin. In its materiality, social relations, mental configurations, and spatio-temporal dynamics, the London underground in large parts mirrors the postmodern metropolis and contemporary urban *conditio humana.* Nevertheless, it is important to recall that underground London is also a counterspace which comprises, juxtaposes, and inverses aboveground realities. The idea of unity in diversity as expressed in the liminality of the subterranean city can be identified as a significant mental disposition that sets the frame for behaviour and attitudes towards the underground in particular and the metropolis in general.

It has been shown that underground London is often represented as the metropolis' spatial mirror image in terms of labyrinthine confusion or diameters of urbanity. However, already Keith Lowe's *Tunnel Vision* and Tobias Hill's *Underground* show, that this echo of the city above is in a way distorted. Rather, the interpretation of the two genre texts, Conrad Williams' *London Revenant* and China Miéville's *King Rat,* have proved that contemporary underground fiction still follows the traditional conventions of devising utopian/dystopian spaces in the otherworldliness of the subterranean city. In conclusion it has been argued with Geoff Ryman's innovative novel *253* that the representation of the Underground's spatiality specifically denies this strong binary between isotopia and utopia, but rather offers thirdspace constructions (physical, social, mental, and spatio-temporal) in the sense of Foucault's heterotopia.

Following the lead of heterotopic juxtaposition and inversion, the analysis of subterranean sociability in the Tube novels *Tunnel Vision* and *253* discloses that its dispositions of acting (indifference, inattention) serve as a measure of urban socialisation and acculturation, specifically with regard to distanciation and routine as protective mechanisms against overload. Concentrated on the representation of multiplicity and heterogeneity, the Tube's "social interface and urban intermingling" (Döring 2002: 45) constitutes an interpersonal and transcultural contact zone allowing for a controlled interaction between urban strangers. Conversely, the vertical city is also a Dual City, in which the city's subaltern live below. However, the underground is not only the main topos of the urban Other, but rather the confrontation with the urban stranger often figures as encounters with the unfamiliar Self. Although socialisation by otherness induces anxiety in the urbanite, it is also experienced as a potential pattern against social anomie or personal apathy.

Furthermore, the underground as mental space especially denotes the city's subconscious and the urbanites' unconscious. Reading the mental-scape in the novel *253* has revealed that due to subterranean practices of introspection the absolute space of the Tube is expanded to a larger space of flows which consists of memories and dreams. The analysis of *Underground* and *London Revenant* consequently elucidated how a descent below the surface of the city restores and vindicates repressed memories, touching upon cultural and personal traumas while simultaneously allowing urban communities and individuals to recover their alienated Self and experience the transformative power of the other metropolis.

Finally, the fourth sub-chapter explored the alienating spatio-temporal indications of underground London as chronotope or heterochronia and threshold liminality. For Pike (2005a: 16), the underground as a threshold forms a spatial "key component" of the metropolis which comprises all three elements of Lefebvre's spatial triad. While the chronotope revealed this interference of various temporal strata as influencing mental dispositions, the liminality of this temporal state was shown to expand to a ghostly space haunted by revenants. As elements of the uncanny, the threshold existences devise the underground as a space of the contemporary *conditio humana* caught within the uncertainty and anxiety of a new epoch of space-time compressions and transformation of mentalities.

I therefore claim that underground London in its physical, social, mental, and temporal heterotopia as a spatialisation of uncertainty has become the main setting for the uncanny of the postmodern literary metropolis. As shown in the beginning, it is a remarkable development that so many city novels since the 1990s are set in the underground. Moreover, the subterranean city is not only employed as a setting but intrinsically determines the themes of the novels and dominates as the major trope of contemporary London fiction. Although I choose to exemplify my findings with paradigmatic underground novels, later analyses will also take up the metaphor of the subterranean cityscape with specific notions of the uncanny.[43]

Freud (2003: 124) in his seminal essay "Das Unheimliche" (1919) explicates that the German word *unheimlich* is the opposite of *vertraut* or *heimisch*, meaning secret, familiar and homely. Thus the uncanny equally denotes the unknown, unfamiliar, occult and magical. Nevertheless it is never purely the strange, but the once familiar is rendered alien by the process of repression and forgetting (cf. *ibid.*: 152). In other words, the uncanny is that which ought to have remained "secret and hidden but has come into the open." (*Ibid.*: 132) Caught between the ambivalence of familiarity and strangeness, the uncanny is thereby not only an intrinsic part of urbanity, but from a general stance resembles ambivalence, flow, blunting of oppositions or cognitive uncertainty (*ibid.*: 125). This situation of unknowing can be a disquieting and disturbing but at the same time also a strangely pleasurable experience which borders on the sublime.

According to Freud (*ibid.*: 135, 143, 155), fiction – especially fantastic literature – presents the best opportunities for creating uncanny sensations in which the trope of the uncanny is generally linked to a cryptonomic setting, such as the labyrinth, and cast of personae like the double, dead bodies, revenants, spirits, ghosts, phantoms, automatons, puppets etc. as well as a recurrence of situations, things, and events. Equally, underground London novels, be it genre or mainstream, can be seen as a sub-genre of the urban Gothic which follows the aesthetic conventions of the uncanny.

Insofar, underground London as isotopia, utopia and heterotopia is a prominent spatiality of urban alienation and strangeness, while simultaneously denying any specific or fixed denominations but breeding paradox, inversion, and liminality. For Döring (2002:

43 | I already voiced this thesis in two papers given at Passau University and at Brunel University in 2008. Brian Ashford's later essay "The Ghost in the Machine: Psychogeography in the London Underground 1991-2007" (2008) comes to a similar conclusion.

64) the sublimity of the nineteenth-century city panorama has been challenged by a modern vision of the "uncanny network of the tube" which figures as a symbol of both urban civilisation and its anxieties. In a sense, the Tube through its uncanniness is a *metaphorai per se* for urban-generic ambivalences. The combination of travelling in the depth of the earth doubly emphasises the need for knowledge: truths located in the underground cannot be voiced aboveground, but neither can they be granted rationality – as apparent in silenced dreams, covered trauma, or unfulfilled desires. However, the underground not only features as a repository for this otherness, but is necessarily haunted by its return in an often diabolical or supernatural yet always spectral idea of the material and metaphorical dispossessed. Similar to Gothic literature, the "potentially duplicitous space" (Pike 2005a: 40) of contemporary underground literature is suffused with doubles, ghosts, and revenants.

At first, the Derridean hauntology of the underground exemplified by the revenant's return counters chronological temporality but favours simultaneity and juxtaposition of the space age. Derrida sees the revenant as the harbinger of the end of history, and indeed the novels include apocalyptic notions, which induce, however, a resurrection of the spectral city. Besides its direct relationship to (un)death and (im)mortality, the novels also stress the transient threshold being of the spectre in the dominant figure of the homeless. As Ashford (2008: 10) argues, "[h]omelessness is invariably the key to the uncanny realm." This persistent association between homelessness and the uncanny does not only lie in social otherness but also in the (un)homely and migrational character *per se*. Hence the homeless person is the paragon of the urban stranger or Other.

City life as a world of strangers is constituted by a synthesis of nearness and distance also apparent on a Tube during the physical proximity and social distance of rush hour. The unaccustomed stranger breaks down normative expectations, creates misunderstandings and disagreements, and forgers "urban unease" (Fischer 1984: 96). Yet the general urban stranger, despite being personally unknown, is categorically known and therefore is by nature a source of the uncanny. Due to the heterotopic inversion in the underground, this relation between normativity and deviance is transformed to one where urbanites recognise slices of the Self in the Other, or the Other in the Self.

According to Benjamin, the uncanny as such was essentially born of the rise of the great cities (cf. Vidler 1999: 4). The metropolis is the place of the new, different, unexpected, incomprehensible, strange, unknown, odd, hybrid, tempting, overwhelming, thrill, claustrophobic, etc. (cf. Fischer 1984: 17) Although space-time the subterranean city resembles a hyperinflation of these sensations, it offers a possibility "to penetrate the mystery, unravel the confusion, and grasp the contradictions" (Harvey 1985: 251). As shown before, subterranean overload reversely leads to projection, introspection, and reflection. Not only is urban (un)knowing incorporated in the underground's significant sublimity on the threshold of familiarity and strangeness, what is more, "[s]ublimity celebrates ambivalence" (Ros. Williams 1990: 86) and ambivalence moves everyday activities into a realm of uncertainty. Hence, the uncanny underground represents a tableau for the uncertainty of our contemporary world.

The Australian science fiction writer and literary critic Sylvia Kelso (1997: 457) characterises Postmodernism as the "Age of Uncertainty" and the uncanny as a key element of this "moment of flux between certainties" (*ibid.*: 466). It constitutes an instant of space-time compression and an era of transition working towards a generation of uncertainty wrought by fragmentation, undecidability, and chaos. The "postmodern uncanny" (*ibid.* 456) resembles a new sense of the uncanny because it presents bizarre events or the disruptions of time and the doubling of subjectivity as well as never-ending contradiction entwined with the everyday and producing a confused postmodern schizophrenic consciousness. While the concept used to be purely psychological or aesthetic, it now also carries larger social and cultural implications.[44]

The new qualities of the postmodern uncanny in relation to the postmodern city and the idiosyncrasies of underground London's Gothic setting offer a very distinct notion concerning the urban *conditio humana* of contemporary Londoners insofar as uncanny urban fiction around the millennium is a distinctive response to the transformations of the Postmetropolis.[45] Architectural transformation, according to Vidler (1999: 3), has already rendered the margins of the city highly uncanny. The urban cityscape itself has become an uncanny cryptography of simulational and hyperreal places which transformed the metropolis into an image or double of itself. From this point of view, the uncanny simply resembles the urban-generic otherness of the city which defies the urbanite's finite or knowable identity of London.

> London is not a place; it cannot be placed. [...] London takes place; it is a fluid city, a city of singular, endless flows (both spatial and temporal), which can only be seen – if at all – if one sees indirectly, from the corner of one's eye [...]. Seeing London is, it might be said, a matter of being open to the gift of vision, of receiving a vision incommensurable with and in excess of the merely visual. As a city always on the move and only apprehended from the corner of one's eye, London is unavailable to any generalization, summarization, or finite identification. One cannot fathom London because there is neither beginning nor end. One can never get to the bottom of an abyss, particularly when the abyss *is* meaning or identity, an identity we might say without identification. (Wolfreys 2004: 4)

---

44 | The uncanny has become a master trope and one of the most supercharged words in current critical vocabulary. Of these critical and literary discourses which privileged the notions of spectrality and marked an establishment of uncertainty, Jacques Derrida's *Specters of Marx* (1994) proved to be a watershed that prompted "a 'spectral turn' in contemporary criticism." (Luckhurst 2002: 527; cf. Kelso 1997: 468) This international resurgence of critical interest in the uncanny was also constituted by Anthony Vidler's *The Architectural Uncanny* (1992) and pursued in titles like Gennis Byron's & David Punter's *Spectral Readings, Towards a Gothic Geography* (1999).

45 | In regard to the uncertainty principle in postmodern literature, Julian Wolfreys and Roger Luckhurst have published widely on neo-Gothic literature, the uncanny, and the revival of the urban Gothic in London literature. The "new London Gothic" (Luckhurst 2002: 529) uncanny fictions not only revisit the past like neo-Victorian novels, but specifically comment on the city's "politemporal assemblage" (*ibid.*: 532). This "Gothicized apprehension of London" (*ibid.*: 529) involves with the past from a contemporary stance, returning from the repressed histories of the city (cf. *ibid.*: 530; Wolfreys 2002: 198, 202). For more also see Nicholas Royle (2003), *The Uncanny. An Introduction*; Klaus Herding & Gerlinde Gehrig, eds. (2006), *Orte des Unheimlichen*; Bianca Del Villano (2007), *Ghostly Alterities. Spectrality and Contemporary Literatures in English*.

Nevertheless, for Wolfreys (2002: 193) the uncanny is a trope that has been able to capture the atemporal uncertainty or illimitability of London. The spectre that haunts the subterranean city is something beyond reason. Because this indefinable presence of the human mind cannot be fathomed rationally, the uncanny becomes a way of knowing the metropolis.

Moreover, due to the new plurality, hybridity and difference as well as transparence and contingency of the urban physical, social, and mental spaces, the recent resurgence of the uncanny can be interpreted as a metaphor for the ultimate postmodern urban overload. The depiction of the London Underground specifies, inverts, and hyposensitizes internal overstimulation. The uncanny subterranean space as novelty and strangeness represents the "repository for possibilities of invention, innovation" (Pike 2005a: 13) which marks the flux and flow of the transitional phase. Its form of urban revenant not only represents the constant metamorphosis of the metropolis, but in its heterotopic inversion also brings to light hidden cultural disruptions. Subterranean mental spaces further this experience and thereby initiate boosts of urban vigilance. In its ambivalent relation, the underground also enforces apathy, not only in the form of non- or autoinvolvement, but also in the numbing through rules, panopticism, subversion, strangeness, otherness, paranoia, anxiety, and terror. Because attention becomes focused on the control of these determinants of uncanniness, a need for stability is enhanced. Consequently, the character of underground London as a heterotopia uncovers the counter-movement towards homogeneity and the reconstruction of an absolute space in the spell of overcoming alienation. In the words of Steve Pile (2000: 264-265), "the important thing about the 'unknown city' is not so much that there are parts of the city that are unknown, but that urban space vacillates between the reassuring solidity of knowingness and the sinister voids of unkowingness; in this, the city becomes [...] familiar." This is what characterises the intelligible metropolis.

6.3 Navigating the Flux

> Londoner sind wirklich schnell. Im Denken. Im Lebenswandel. Selbst beim Gehen. [...] Langsam ist in London nur der Autoverkehr.
> (Dahrendorf cit. in Gaede & Hanig 2005: 87)

Classic approaches on the overload theorem state that the increase of stimuli leads to an irritation of the senses provoking feelings of dislocation and disorientation. Consequently, the individual urbanite develops adaptive and protective coping mechanisms to reduce urban overload, for example, cognitive functions of intellectualisation and blasé, social means of reserve such as role performance and non-involvement, or perceptive techniques of simplification, segmentation, and abstraction. According to Gelfant's (1954: 15) study of the city novel, literary urban space is mainly perceived through three elements: the physical facts of the city, the urban atmosphere, and the aesthetic impression the scene makes upon the mind. These ways of spatial legibility are overtly apparent in the narrative style of the modern city novel that specifically concentrates on urban consciousness. In their interpretation of urban modes and structures of perception, scholars especially focus on the protagonists' moods, dispositions, feelings, or thoughts in relation to the atmospheric and emotional dimension of the cityscape.[46] James (2008: 29) comments that the

> rhetorical integration of vision and voice, sight and insight, is especially penetrating for writers [...] who have exploited the dexterity of free indirect discourse: that is, when they forfeit the detachedness of authorial commentary, articulating instead observations of space focalized by the characters' immediate responses or spells of recollection.

Because the spatial significance of perception is dependent on the relation between subject and space, the emphasis of subjectivity and perspectivity of the urban experience pays particular attention to representations of corporeality and sensuality. These somatic experiences are often conveyed by a careful outline of the urban atmosphere and its multifarious sensescape. Contemporary literature variously engages in narratological imitation or thematic discussion of processes of perception in order to express the pluralistic and dynamic yet fragmentary and anatomised everyday life of the postmodern city.

Due to the notion of the social construction of reality, acts of perception are representations of space and the selective process of perception by protective mechanisms therefore reveals particular urban mental dispositions. In other words, this analysis is interested in both the *outillage mental* of urban perception and the images conceived because collective mental manageability of space reveals structures of thinking, imagining, feeling, and acting. In reference to de Certeau, I will first look at idiosyncratic mapping projects in Geoff Nicholson's *Bleeding London* (1997) as subjective modes of reading and writing or perceiving and organising the urban. Pedestrian utterances become even more pronounced in Christine Brooke-Rose's stream-of-consciousness novel *Next* (1998). Sensual perception of London's atmosphere, especially its smell- and soundscape, will be analysed in China Miéville's *King Rat* (1998). The last sub-chapter will consider Ian McEwan's *Saturday* (2005), a meta-consciousness narrative contemplating the legibility of the city versus its intelligibility. "Navigating the Flux" will disclose the changes of 'seeing' the city as major transformations in the perceptual dispositions of contemporary Londoners and specifically as a change in standardisations of thinking. A major factor for this shift lies in the sensual stimulation represented by the metropolis itself as regards the space of flows and the city in flux.

---

46 | For example, see Heinz Brüggemann (1985), *"Aber schickt keinen Poeten nach London!". Großstadt und literarische Wahrnehmung im 18. und 19. Jahrhundert. Texte und Interpretationen*; Klaus R. Scherpe, ed. (1988), *Die Unwirklichkeit der Städte. Grossstadtdarstellung zwischen Moderne und Postmoderne*; Susanne Hauser, (1990), *Der Blick auf die Stadt. Semiotische Untersuchungen zur literarischen Wahrnehmung bis 1910*; Sabina Becker (1993), *Urbanität und Moderne. Studien zur Großstadtwahrnehmung in der deutschen Literatur 1900-1930*; Natascha Würzbach (2006), *Raumerfahrung in der klassischen Moderne. Großstadt, Reisen, Wahrnehmungssinnlichkeit und Geschlecht in englischen Erzähltexten.*

6.3.1 Mapping the Metropolis

Mapping has certainly become one of the predominant metaphors within the rhetoric of the Spatial Turn. As argued in relation to the Tube map, urbanites' mapping presents a significant means of navigation and a possibility to familiarise oneself with the metropolis because its feature constitutes an essential "interface between user and the city" (Vertesi 2005: 1). Maps, generally considered coherent images of the metropolis, are employed "to tame the urban labyrinth, and to represent its spaces as 'legible' and 'knowable'." (Pinder 1996: 407) Also for Ackroyd (2001: 112) "the mapping of London represents an attempt to understand the chaos and thereby to mitigate it; it is an attempt to know the unknowable."[47] Most notably, Charles Booth's maps of urban poverty in *Inquiry into the Life and Labour of the People of London* (1886-1903) rendered urban squalor legible, intelligible, definitive, and controllable.

Spatial organisation of thinking in the "geographies of the mind" (Harvey 1985: 200) constitutes "maps of meaning" (P. Jackson 1989: 185) through which people socially construct reality. For urbanites, these perceptual geographies harbour cognitive or mental maps of the city. According to Kevin Lynch, a spatial schema of the metropolis is mainly arranged around topographical landmarks. What is more, in contrast to the normative maps of cities, mental maps emphasise the private, individualised and fragmentary perception of the urban. As associative media, mental maps represent social and atmospheric notions of the urban device of a metropolitan psychotopography that illustrates both cognitive and psychological dimensions of urban navigation.

While Reichert (1996b: 36) points out that map and narrative are necessarily two different means of the spatial structuring of thought, namely either relationally or chronologically, for Miller (1995: 19) a "novel is a figurative mapping". In the special edition of *GRANTA* magazine on the capital, Martin Rowson (1999: 103-111) draws four different maps of literary London – Chaucer's London, Eighteenth and Nineteenth-Century London, Victorian London, and Modern London, which constitute visual representations of the metropolis' "multiplex visions" (Eade, Fremaux & Garbin 2002: 160). Indeed, literary London offers manifold versions of the cityscape because individual city novels present idiosyncratic perceptual cartographies.

This sub-chapter takes into view the conscious mapping projects represented in Geoff Nicholson's *Bleeding London* (1997)[48] as well as the unconscious mental maps of the novel's protagonists in their quest to decipher London' nonconscious geography. Mark Rawlinson (2002: 251) describes *Bleeding London* as "a *roman à cléf* of urbanist discourses" because its topographical experience includes metaphorical, psychogeographical, and cartographical representations of the metropolis. Map-making represents a major theme of the text: the novel's protagonists, Stuart London, Judy Tanaka, and Mick Wilton, are engaged in idiosyncratic projects of "remapping and de-mapping" (Schlaeger 2003b: 38).

47 | For more see Peter Whitfield (2006), *London. A Life in Maps.*

48 | In the following *Bleeding London* will be abbreviated to BLL.

Stuart's Narrative A-Z Map

Stuart, a passionate Londoner, urban historian, and city guide with an overwhelmingly detailed knowledge of the metropolis, decides to unveil the city's "eccentricities and unknown quarters" (BLL: 73). He goes on the ultimate walk of London, encompassing every single street, and thereby strives to undo the work of Phyllis Pearsall, who in the mid-1930s covered 3,000 miles and charted 23,000 streets to devise the *A-Z map of London* (BLL: 77-83). As he goes along, Stuart inks in the streets on his *A-Z* map and mitigates London to a network of black lines: "The map [is] reduced to a pattern, to decoration and ornament, an abstract design with London as its distant organic inspiration." (BLL: 8) First, this enhanced abstraction appears to tame the metropolis' complexity. But while the London *A-Z* ignores all differences of the city and blunts urban heterogeneity, Stuart's ink basically refills these gaps of meaning with life, creating a gigantic non-verbal texture. As "an absurd puzzle, a conundrum, a maze" (BLL: 8), his abstract appropriation hence ironically renders the city illegible, while simultaneously recovering its urbanity. The function of the map in offering guidance has become obsolete and the fixed image of London is narrowed to its original labyrinthine character.

In this way, Nicholson undermines the map's totalising perspective, and transforms the mapmaker Stuart to an urban *Wandersmann* who prefers the peripatetic perception of the metropolis. At the same time, by keeping track of his excursions with a walker's diary, the protagonist turns reading the city into writing the urban. As his map gradually darkens, Stuart increasingly relishes narrating his own version of London, from the places he visits and the conversations he overhears to surprising coincidences and the city's frequent bleakness (BLL: 190-200). The cityscape in his diary, which accompanies the footsteps of his wordless meandering, is constructed by a list of London's material outline (neighbourhoods, streets, squares, buildings) and additional annotations on atmospheric impressions of the urban scenes. Thereby the character's diary and the author's novel overlap and create a multiperspectively and sensually imagined cityscape that vividly captures London's contemporary reality:

> On the Victoria Embankment at Charing Cross Pier. A long row of parked, empty tour buses, hundreds of joggers of all sorts and ages [...] Under Blackfriars Bridge, cardboard boxes, folded blankets, plastic bread trays belonging to the homeless [...] At Paul's Walk the benches were full of people eating their lunches, most of them couples. [...] You can't walk straight all the way along the north bank of the river. You get forced up Broken Wharf away from the Thames, into Queen Victoria Street and Upper Thames Street. I walked down Bull Wharf Lane, a dark, narrow alley leading to the river, but it was a dead end. [...] On London Bridge a painted sign, black and white and now looking old and faded. It said, 'Less noise. Please consider offices above.' At the point a hovercraft passed under the bridge, its low thick engine note reverberating under the broad concrete spans. (BLL: 190-191)

Thus, while urbanity is restored to the abstract structure of the city by perceptual fictionalisation, this urban reality is necessarily subjective because the character's pedestrian speech act which obliterates/fills London's spaces is an individual reterritorialisation of the metropolis (cf. Deny 2009: 237). Although, in the beginning of his quest, Stuart claims that he does not want "to make London his" (BLL: 78), the protagonist later confesses that he "was continuing his affair with the city, pursuing it, wanting to possess it"

(BLL: 140). In writing the diary, Stuart retraces London according to his personal fashion and hence contradicts his own objective of making the city's places equal (BLL: 78). He recognises: "What I see will reveal as much about me as about London." (BLL: 142) The character Stuart 'London' consequently projects his Self on London and creates the metropolis in his image, the mental map of the city becoming the mirror of his mind and soul. As map and territory are aligned, the urbanite merges with the city (see chapter 8.1.2).

Mick's Sociological Crime Map

For the second protagonist, Mick Wilton, a Sheffield thug who comes to the capital to avenge an alleged gang-rape of his girlfriend, the familiarisation with London's topography is predominantly matched by his understanding of the city's social terrain (cf. Chilton 2007: 20). When Mick first arrives in London, the taxi driver mistakenly takes him to Park Lane in the West End and the character is deeply impressed by London's surprising beauty (BLL: 18). Having made it to his hotel in East End's Hackney instead, Mick feels as though he has entered "the twilight zone" (BLL: 25). This ambiguity exemplifies that while the cityscape is malleable to a subjective point of view, orientation depends on hegemonic structures created by socio-spatial boundaries and separations. As a Northerner, Mick is sensitive to the socio-cultural differences of spaces and his further encounter with the metropolitan *terra incognita* follows this predetermined perception. The *A-Z* is of limited use for his quest because it obliterates all social indicators necessary to track down the wanted London men, whose socio-economic backgrounds give off clues to their potential address (cf. Dreyer 2006: 59). In order to find his well-off victims, Mick is actually in need either of a specialised social map of the city or the socio-cultural knowledge of a Londoner (BLL: 36). The London-born protagonist Judy Tanaka explains the city's urban-specific social map to the newcomer: "Philip Masterson. For that name there's only one address that fits the bill at all. It's in Maida Vale, whereas all the other Philip Mastersons live in Walthamstow or Peckham or areas like that." (BLL: 38-39)

The protagonist repeatedly traverses London following the daily lives of his victims and thereby slowly starts to know his way around the city. In addition to the navigational tool of the map which relegates him to particular tracks, Mick uses specific paths over and over again and thereby leaves his very own patterns on the texture of the metropolis: "Already certain routes through the city were becoming his own. He was discovering the logic and connectedness of the streets, discovering short-cuts, but he would still have been lost without the map he'd bought from Judy." (BLL: 153) Dreyer (2006: 62) shows that the protagonist's perambulations between the different areas of the city are either summarised in brief passages or completely invisible as only departure and arrival are indicated. In contrast to de Certeau's urban walker or Stuart's detailed descriptions, the newcomer only acknowledges particular spots within the urban fabric, and hence similar to an urban sociologist maps the metropolis as a mosaic of social worlds.

London therefore presents a puzzle for Mick, which the petty criminal, ironically turned metropolitan detective, is made to assemble and solve (cf. Dreyer 2006: 72; Deny 2009: 259). Mick receives a jigsaw puzzle from Judy with which he tries to connect known localities of London and finally form a detailed map of the city: in the beginning, there are only "myriad pieces of London meshed together" (BLL: 150) and these parts of the fragmented city need to be joined to a coherent whole. Completing the puzzle, he feels "as though he was gaining mastery over his once wholly unfamiliar territory." (BLL: 156) Step by step Mick makes London his, and sexual intercourse with the 'real' Londoner Judy gains him the last missing piece (BLL: 232). London's territory is a puzzle, and its single pieces leave a similar grid of horizontals and verticals like Mick's peripatetic structure of natural zones. In that sense, Mick's spatial perception of London is indeed compart**mentalised**; the fragmentations and topological abstractions aid his orientation through the riddled maze of the city. In regard to Mick's mental map of the metropolis, Judy declares: "You had a pretty shrewd idea of what London was like, long before you got here. You created your own version of London. It was just as real as the actual London." (BLL: 206)

Judy's Erotic Sex Map

Stuart's and Mick's urban wanderings put them in contact with the half-Japanese Londoner Judy Tanaka who employs both men for her own metropolitan mapping project. Judy's idiosyncratic map is one of intentional sexual encounters: she wants "to be fucked everywhere. In every hole. In every position. In every borough. In every postal district" (BLL: 131). With Stuart, she sets out to both "pick up on the mass of erotic energy" (BLL: 135) and cover London with sexual memories. Topographical mappings and territorialisations of the metropolis thus answer a basic anthropological need (cf. Deny 2009: 260), but in the case of Judy they also serve the re-appropriation of the Self. After she has sexually conquered a new place of the city, Judy marks the spot on a transparent sheet over a map of London, which represents how "geographically promiscuous she had been" (BLL: 343). Like the postmodern version of the *flâneuse*, she relishes the eroticism of the city's masses. On her map, Stuart sees "how the city was overlaid with the patterns of where other people had lived and had sex" (BLL: 133), creating erotic patterns all over town. London is certainly large and various enough to indulge in all sorts of clandestine affairs. Warf and Arias (2008a: 8) comment:

> The city – that dense, complex, often bewildering environment that offers so many opportunities and possibilities for anonymity – has for centuries generated connotations of illicit sexuality, of adulterous affairs, casual encounters, prostitution, predatory attacks, and homosexuality.

The metropolis as a literal "site of desire" (Lefebvre 1996: 109) and the association of sex in the city marks Judy as an object of strange eroticism. She represents the quintessential female figure of the urban scene – prostitute, femme fatale, Babylonian whore (cf. Gilbert 2008: 109-111). But in the case of *Bleeding London*, these idiosyncratic erotic mappings also help the protagonist to overcome alienation induced by gender and cultural hybridity. In that respect, spatio-somatic sensation is equated with a significant form of mental mapping. This evident relation emphasises that perceptions of the metropolis are always dependent on "*particular* bodies and *particular* experiences" (Pinder 1996: 422). At the close of the novel, Judy's body figures a serpentine line on the surface of her skin that resembles the Thames, which presents yet another abstraction similar to Stuart's own black arterial inscriptions on the metropolitan skein (cf. Deny 2009: 239). On the other hand, the metropolis is anthropomorphised and in Judy's corpse the city metamorphoses back into its original organic state (BLL: 345; see chapter 8.1.2).

Illimitable Deceptions of Abstraction

As the cartographic ambitions of Geoff Nicholson's characters show, maps create a particular order and therefore offer a possibility to conceptualise urban realities. Due to abstraction maps are, however, also recognised as highly arbitrary representations of the metropolis. Stuart, rejecting the map as suitable urban means of orientation, claims:

> Maps are euphemisms, clean, clear, self-explanatory substitutes for all the mess and mayhem, the clutter and ambivalence and blurring and intermeshing weft and warp of the real places they purport to describe. They are fake documents, pathetic simplifications and falsifications. (BLL: 29)

Equally, Mick feels some of the places in his jigsaw puzzle do "not belong to the London he knew", making the "map even more confusing than the reality" (BLL: 155). And Judy knows "how deceptive maps can be, how quickly they can become out of date, how places in the real world can have meanings und significances quite out of scale with their cartographic depiction." (BLL: 344) Schlaeger (2003b: 25) argues that if "it is impossible to know the object one wants to represent, then all representations of the object are necessarily misrepresentation". The personal abstractions of Stuart's, Mick's and Judy's London maps, for example, neglect the density of urban life. As each mapping is a sole interaction of the individual character with their material surroundings, urbanite and city are caught in their hermetic space-time capsule. In "Cities Without Maps" Ian Chambers (1996: 188) writes:

> the very idea of a map, with its implicit dependence upon the survey of a stable terrain, fixed referents and measurements, seems to contradict the palpable flux and fluidity of the metropolitan life and cosmopolitan movement. Maps are full of references and indications, but they are not people. [...] The city place is both a rationalization of space and of time; its streets, buildings, bridges and roads are also temporal indices. It permits us to grasp an outline, a shape, some sort of location, but not of the contexts, cultures, histories, languages, experiences, desires and hopes that course through the urban body.

Consequently, urban space cannot be constituted by mere abstractions, but always involves dynamic psychological, social, or corporeal dimensions and urbanity depends on the heterogeneity of perspectives. As Judy exemplifies, a variety of idio-maps of London exists within the metropolis: "There are an infinite number of maps that could be drawn of London; not just sex maps but death maps, crime maps, drug maps, maps of resistance and insurrection, of liberation and oppression, murder maps, suicide maps." (BLL: 136) Rather, London is a multi-dimensional and transformative mental map "created in the image of each of its inhabitants, newly imagined with each new citizen, with each new attempt to describe it." (BLL: 301) Critics have variously shown that the numerous literary representations of London in postmodern novels defy the idea that there exists any one true reading of the inexhaustible cityscape.

Because there is not one encompassing model of London, the novel undermines the idea that maps provide reliable information on the metropolis. "*Complete London*" always remains an "*Unreliable London*" (BLL: 22). Likewise for Peter Ackroyd (2001:

116), London "seen in terms of abstract size and measurement [...] becomes unimaginable." In *Bleeding London*, after walking the streets of London, Stuart claims:

> I have seen it all [...] I have been to the boundary, to the wall, to the places where the city ends [...] I have seen history and nostalgia. I have seen love and death and their pale companions sex and violence. I have seen a fine town, a nation, a great cesspool, the modern Babylon. [...]. (BLL: 26-27)

Before Stuart starts on his tour, the protagonist is confident that he will conquer illimitable London (BLL: 84), but while he succeeds in physically covering the city's streets, his diary on the city remains "UNFINISHED" (BLL: 31). Pogossian (2010: 3) comments that "[t]he knowledge acquired through urban pilgrimage cannot be trusted. Instead fragments of experiences, numerous obstacles in deciphering the city pinpoint the failure to reach London as a whole." As other chroniclers of the city, the character is confronted with the fact that the metropolis is essentially illimitable, ineffable, endless, infinite, immutable, immeasurable, eternal. On the one hand, London's illimitability stimulates equally inexhaustible possibilities and endless narratives, while on the other hand alternating perspectives offer diverging realities. By re-assembling the pieces, urbanites master the variety of the metropolis and create an idiosyncratic image of city. For example, planning "A neater London" (BLL: 72), Stuart's wife Anita London (née Walker) helps to build replicas of London's key attractions in a theme park on a Japanese island and thereby reduces illimitable London to a small-scale playground (BLL: 332). This spectaclisation of the metropolis, in reference to Debord (1994: 23), presents a map of the postmodern situation – "a map drawn to the scale of the territory itself."

Because the city is actively perceived and reshaped in the protagonists' imagination, the triple denouement of the novel underwrites the mapping activity of the characters as indeed successful – Mick finds himself liberated by the city, Stuart's view on the historical city is recognised and Judy's desire fulfilled (BLL 253). De-mapping and re-mapping the illimitable city in general initiates great creativity and opens up new possibilities of reorientation for the urbanites (cf. Schlaeger 2003b: 26; Deny 2009: 108). In their endeavour to master the unhomely urban lifeworld, the protagonists individually de- and re-map the metropolis by filling, reorganising and reinterpreting physical, social, and mental spaces or borders.[49] In contrast to de Certeau's panorama, these idiosyncratic maps offer a more mobile engagement with urban space through alternating positions and diversifying perspectives. Rather, these maps encompass an understanding of urban-generic ambivalences by representing

> different senses of the city: of separation and unity; of hurried movements through the streets, and drifts and languid strolls; of noise, confusion, and bewilderment as well as legibility and co-

---

49 | Deleuze and Guattari (1998: 13) comment on the malleability of mapping processes: "The map is open and connectable in all of its dimensions; it is detachable, reversible, susceptible to constant modification. It can be torn, reversed, adapted to any kind of mounting, reworked by individual, group, or social formation. It can be drawn on a wall, conceived of as a work of art, constructed as a political action or as a meditation."

herence; and of constraint, exclusion, and spatial entrapment, as well as mobility and circulation. (Pinder 1996: 423)

Insofar, urbanites' mental maps are a flexible medium that visualises a momentarily fixed, yet transmutable image of London. In other words, multiplexity, multilocality, and multivocality of the metropolis are appropriated in the multiperspectivity of the characters' mind. The characters' paths in *Bleeding London* represent the contemporary urbanite's desire to "achieve individuated distance from the official, commodified London." (Chilton 2007: 13) The map-maker transforms urban incoherence into a knowing point of view which helps in orienting and localising the Self. In this sense, by orchestrating personalised images cognitive mapping overcomes anxieties and boosts human agency in relation to the city's alleged hypertrophy of objective culture. In regard to mentality, this might perpetuate the notion that the manifold versions and obvious misperceptions of London defy the idea of standardisations of thinking. By contrast, *Bleeding London* presents imaginary map-making as a viable form of socially constructing reality. The process of sensual abstraction can be interpreted as a significant element of metropolitan formal thinking. In other words, mental mapping represents a contemporary version of urban intellectualisation. Due to their referential detachment, maps serve as contemporary protective mechanisms against the postmodern overload scenario. For comprehending the input of stimuli, mapping exercises offer versions of urban territorialisation because they represent space in an intelligible form. Soja (2000: 241) therefore deduces that "[i]n fact we do not know the difference between the map and the territory, and would not know it even if we had our noses pressed up against the thing itself." Seen critically, maps present an expression of nostalgia for legibility (cf. Sharpe & Wallock 1987: 36) because they transform fragmentary sensual elements into a coherent system of signs, or a legible text.

6.3.2 Touring the Streets of London

Geoff Nicholson's *Bleeding London* has shown that the metropolis is an area to be traversed and that the city's labyrinthine complexity only becomes mappable in heterogeneous, highly diversified trajectories. Similarly conceptualised in de Certeau's theory of touring, only the pedestrian can grasp the meanings of every-day urban life. In literary history, this street-perspective is intrinsically linked to the figure of the *flâneur*. Alternating between mobile and static point of view the *flâneur* encompasses notions of both walker and spectator. Due to its superior detachment the *flâneur*'s voyeurism has been strongly connected either to a form of panopticism or the objectifying gaze of the heterosexual male. The feminist literary critics Deborah Parsons (2000: 38-39) and Elizabeth Wilson (1992: 109) nevertheless identify this urban figure as ambiguously gendered especially due to its marginal position; a wo/man of the crowd in flux stands ostensibly apart from normative notions of the masses. According to Benjamin (2002: 442), "[t]he *promeneur* is no longer capable of 'meandering capriciously.' He takes refuge in the shadow of cities: he becomes a flâneur." Due to this migrational obscurity, the urban walker (artist, dandy, collector, man of the crowd, prostitute, widow, rag picker) or the related marginal man (cosmopolitan, hybrid, alien, stranger) gazes but remains largely invisible.

It is the ambivalent perspective of the *flâneur* – standing apart form the city in apparent symbiotic relation to the urban environment – which marks his transitional perception of the city. "The urban *walker* or *flaneur* belongs on the asphalt and is aesthetically stimulated by the very confusion and clash of the different elements of urban life." (Parsons 2000: 13) In this respect, Benjamin links the consciousness of the *flâneur* to Simmel's observation of the psychological impact of stimulational overload and the subsequent response of protective detachment. His mind registers specific components of the city, contemplates and reflects, in order to arrive at an understanding of urban complexity. Weinstein & Weinstein (1993: 62) comment that while "both Simmel and the *flâneur* are concerned with the fragment, no *flâneur* would be caught dead trying to grasp what was universal about it." In that, the *flâneur* does not so much create a mental map of the city and read it as coherent, but tours the fluid city getting to know and rewriting its heterogeneity in order to render it homely. From a postmodern stance, it seems unconceivable to develop an urban-specific mentality without the idiosyncratic fleeting position of *flânerie*.

Notably the appearance of the *flâneur* in the nineteenth century coincided with the transformation of metropolitan materiality and a new form of urbanity, whereby the figure became a metaphor for a "new urban mentality" (Parsons 2000: 21). Since then, the *flâneur* and his consciousness of reserve and selective observation have become tropical for an urban-generic experience encompassing indolence, isolation, marginality, loneliness, intoxication, and the thirst for spectacle, but also loss, self-abandonment, apathy, impotence, melancholia, despair, and psychological disintegration. Of course, these impressions are prone to change in time as the urban environment is transformed to create a new meaning of the "streets of the mind" (Mohrmann 1996: 263).

The following analysis of Christine Brooke-Rose's novel *Next* (1998) charts the implications of urban perception by walking the city with regard to space, language, and subjectivity and decipher its relevance for the postmodern London nonconscious. Brooke-Rose's novel maps *fin-de-millénium* London on the street-level by touring the metropolis in the mind of twenty-six characters, ten of whom are homeless. The novel's psycho-urban space is grasped in the mode of interior monologue and stream-of-consciousness passages which represent the characters' processual perception, reflective thought, and inner speech.

The Structure of Urban Consciousness

In the beginning of this novel on the contemporary urban state of mind, the reader 'wakes' under a London bridge inside the consciousness of the homeless character Tek. The expository passage exemplifies the overload of sensations – aural, tactile, visual – which hit the perception of the character upon waking in the urban environment depicted as a postmodern vision of the city as pandemonium.

> Under closed eyelids floats the dim awareness of the washtub-drubbing trucks overhead that grunged the short nights' sleep. Stiffened as a coffin lid, one live corpse rising from granite, sitting up against the concrete column peering at the pinkish grey drizzle which turns the square arches in the access complex of the motorway into an ancient film dazed across with the constant white beams, and the overhead trucks into a loud mechanical projector, somewhere behind the

brain. A crisis of horns and brakescreams from above scatters the mental furniture what was it, the happy rich unhappy in their high bourgeois tizzies. (NXT: 1)

Tek rises from the death-bed of grey concrete into an equivalently bleak morning with an obtrusively mechanic soundscape. The "crisis of horns" mirrors Tek's social position and shattered mental state. The interaction of exterior and interior urban life depicts the mutual expressiveness of the city's perceptual landscape and the urban consciousness.

In extension of this city/consciousness metaphor, the physical and mental wanderings of the homeless, when the characters are alone and unconfined by dialogue, are appropriated to the wandering movements of the prose on the novel's pages. In other words, the meandering of the *flâneur* through the metropolis is mirrored by the outline of the stream-of-consciousness and the structure and layout of the text. For instance, on pages 20 and 21 from *Next* we perceive an image of the homeless' walking as one of staggering and swaying along the pavements of the city. Mirroring the movement of Tek through the city and along its streets, the text conveys the habitual pedestrian movements and its rhythms. On the left page, the character seems to be veering to the side after having passed invisible or rather unnoticed parts of the city indicated by the void. When Tek becomes lost in a more coherent memory that suddenly fills his mind, the text gains in density. On the right hand, he needs to yield, step-and-slide, or avoid other walkers and vehicular traffic, simultaneously observing and monitoring their actions. Momentarily distracted by the flowering of colourful umbrellas he bumps into someone: "**HEY LOOK WHERE YOU ARE GOING**" (NXT: 21). The homeless character is instantly distracted again by the shop windows' display of trendy clothes and Christmas decorations. Entering the Job Centre in a side road off Oxford Street and joining the queue, Tek unexpectedly falls into word games on Shakespeare and Henry James to calm himself.

Because these imagined layers of continuous and recurring steps all over town are synonymous with the variety of recurring thoughts, Brooke-Rose constructs a parallel between walking, perceiving, and thinking. The figure of the homeless *flâneur* is a reader of the urban text(ure), who according to his movements personalises fragments of the urban text. In reference to the *flâneur* Benjamin (2002: 416) argues: "In the asphalt over which he passes, his steps awaken a surprising resonance." Bombarded with an array of stimuli around, the homeless *flâneur*'s mind is filled with sensory impressions. As Tek perceives the urban surroundings, he connects his visual images with the thoughts that accompany his perambulations in an idiosyncratic reading of the city. On the other hand, Tek only recognises such elements he chooses to reflect upon and the textual gaps indicate what is specifically not thought. Knowledge of the city is presented as always both: subjective and contextual. In this sense, the city becomes an imaginary institution, a landscape of the mind.

The body is an established metaphor of the city and a conventional trope of urban fiction, and *Next* devises the metropolis as a mobile mind. Tek perceives "[t]he city as brain" and the motorway as "[a]rteries, nerves, lines of force, ventricles of liquid cells." (NXT: 205) In compliance with this image, the structural layout of Brooke-Rose's novel mirrors the texture of London's brain, while the endlessly oscillating consciousness of the twenty-six characters depicts a significant image of the metropolitan mind in transition. Berking (2008: 15) claims that the particularity of a city is construed by its idiosyncratic pace. Consequently, the characters' mental structures are determined by their urban every-day life, but because their entire day is spent moving through the metropolitan streets, their state of mind is notably influenced by the rhythms of *flânerie*. Tek comments on the homeless' routine: "L for lambada. Lambeth Walk. Walk walk walk we do nothing but walk." (NXT: 91) Throughout the story-time of one week, walking stretches unlimited into the future, expanding space and thought whereby the homeless' daily lives are strictly framed by and limited to the cyclical action of walking.

In Brooke-Rose's novel the homeless hence becomes the *flâneur per se*. When the protagonist Ulysses tells Tek the story of how he learned to walk in Paris, the novel indirectly alludes to Baudelaire, the original creator of the figure (NXT: 124). Moreover, the name of Ulysses recalls both the antique father of all literary *Wandersmänner* (Homer) and the paradigm of modernist *flânerie* (Joyce). In this sense, the protagonist Ulysses, a world adventurer and cosmopolitan who now sleeps in the city's doorways, becomes the epitome of the placeless wanderer. In his study on the *flâneur*, Benjamin (2002: 443) quotes the following from Baudelaire: "For the perfect flâneur,... it is an immense joy to set up house in the heart of the multitude, amid the ebb and flow... . To be away from home, yet to feel oneself everywhere at home". Members of the Chicago School and postmodern urbanologists have especially emphasised the impersonal and rootless existence of homelessness as symptomatic for the urban *conditio humana* in the space of flows. The novel draws us into the minds of the homeless, who, even more so than the guarded and isolated *flâneur*, are an anonymous collective in permanent transit. For example, after being mugged the homeless character Quentin becomes totally disoriented, but recognises the source of his mental deterioration as the fluctuating street which is paralleled by a single-worded text scattered across the pages of Brooke-Rose's book (NXT: 71-78). While in general the mind is an organ of control offering dispositions of acting, the mind in the transition passes through spaces of indecision.

On the Margin of the City-Text

As a marginalised group, the homeless literally walk outside the framework of the regular urban conduct. Their walking antagonises the social mobility described in the other novels because their movement is not progressive but cyclical. For the homeless as for the migrant, the metropolis "fails to deliver the freedom, personal renewal, and worldly access that, in time-honoured big-city fashion, it is seen to promise." (Ball 2004: 7) Although the protagonists might appear to heartily stride like "gentlemen on a country walk" (NXT: 127), they are forced to walk "carrying a bulging plastic bag" (NXT: 127) full of the belongings of their street life. The urban homeless experience the city from a marginalised yet centred perspective, reading the reality of the metropolis on London's streets (NXT: 181). Ulysses maps the city through its various drop-out centres: "There aren't so many sleeping centres after all and they're miles apart. There's one in Stratford. Or South of the river, Deptford, Streatham. [...] There's one in Hendon I once went to but I chose this one, because of the cold." (NXT: 165) For them, the urban realm is not marked by sights but by locations that secure their basic existence: places for sleeping, for eating, for warming up and to draw money. Tracing the urban chronotope of encounter, the homeless predominantly chart the urban world as one of strangers and marginals, poverty and insecurity. In the textual extract from *Next* presented before, we read that Tek "fancies himself as a Westender" (NXT: 20). So even, or maybe particularly, in the view of a London-*connoisseur* like the tramp, the streets of the East

End differ from those of London's centre (NXT: 77). Similar to the characters in Geoff Nicholson's *Bleeding London*, the homeless as *flâneur* in transition perceives a very detailed but equally restricted social image of the cityscape.

Tek's own fragmented view is especially illustrated in the way he registers the different brand names of businesses along the commercial wasteland between Edgeware and Cricklewood: "The Beacon Bingo Hall [...]. A Total petrol station [...] among a complex of cinemas. Peugeot to the right. And an old horrorcore ad from Benetton [...] a Discount House, Blockbuster Video, an off-licence, a Burger King" (NXT: 5). Already modernist critics like Benjamin argued that these commodified spaces change the texture of urban life and equally distract the *flâneur*'s perception. Here, the references to specific brands superficially demonstrate an urban plurality, but this landscape of shops, warehouses and petrol stations also resemble Augé's generic non-places only fit for transit – the true home of the homeless. In this sense, Ulysses is careful to point out that the drabness of London streets is very different from those of Paris' boulevards (NXT: 125). Hence, the homeless represent the urban unhomely *per se*, but also stress that the metropolis' non-communicative environment of transit is on the brink of transgressing into anomie.

While London's cityscape is perceived as on the verge of physical and social annihilation, the characters' contemplations reveal how their personal memories as well as their historical remembrance are affected by walking. The passing cityscape indirectly evokes certain thoughts, locking the characters in a vicious circle of reflections; wandering implies to mentally stray. In this respect, restless wandering itself becomes a form of overload with its intricate symptoms of mental regression. Quentin comments: "You daon knaow wha' seven years in the streeyt can do to the brain, and management skills, and memory." (NXT: 108) Unsettled walking the city creates a mental void inside the men of transition; Tek thinks that they "lose brains in this game. Memories too. We walk and walk, take this and that, and I suppose think. But I can never remember what I was thinking. I can never reconstruct it." (NXT: 131) The homeless walk themselves out of existence because the cyclical, restless, monotone pace destroys their sense of personal narrative (NXT: 148). Without offering a refuge, the city's overload scenario lays itself on the urbanites' mind like a film, and smothers the brain with a patina of its own social, temporal, spatial, mediatised, and memorialised representations. Insofar, the *flâneur* in general – and the London homeless character in particular – represents an urban chronotope in which history and geography merge into a continuity of Being.

In Christine Brooke-Rose's London novel, the historical consciousness and memorial perception of the urban connected to the postmodern overload of mediatised simulacra is specifically developed in the character Tek. For him, the twentieth century constitutes the "most murderous century" in which massacres called "by the least urban of the Urbans" are reduced to mere "forgettable footage" (NXT: 202). As a counter measure to personal oblivion, a protective mechanism against the overstimulation by catastrophes screened on television, Tek is forced to recall his private version of "alphabestial bestiary" (NXT: 16):

The century's alphabête, that does it despite traffic. A for Auschwitz. B for Belsen. C for Cambodia. D for Dresden. For Deportation. E for Ethiopia, for Ethnic Cleansing... F for, what's

F? Famine... Mao's Great Leap into, 1959. Stalin's ditto, Ukraine 1933. Fundamentalism. There's usually more than one horror for each letter. (NXT: 3)

The civilisatory centre of the metropolis is set in relation to the worldwide material overhaul of horror scenarios. In this age of annihilation, a *fin-de-millénnium* state of disasters also rules the mind as dominated by widespread meta-narratives: "The century, besides, of the death of God. [...] The withering of the state, the collapse of communism, the corruption of capitalism, the end of meritocracy [...] the end of the nation-state, of ideology [...]. The end of meganarratives, of all the fictions we live under [...]." (NXT: 202) In opposite, the marginal figure of the *flâneur* touring the city is, more than monumental history, concerned with the refuse of everyday life and the endless little narratives of the urban palimpsest.

In a conversation between the characters (black) Blake and (homeless) Ulysses, the namesakes of the great chroniclers of urban historical fiction, past and future, both insist on the African origin of civilisation (NXT: 47, 52-53). A faster change than in the long evolutionary process is suggested by Oliver who argues that change only comes about by disruption: "it takes two generations for mentalities to change on any item, the old must die and somehow not transmit" (NXT: 182). The homeless historian Tek who looses his personal memory and interchanges it with allusion from history explains in direct reference to the school of *Annales* and their concept of mentality:

[...] the further back you go the less there is, so that historians can talk about say popular feeling during this or that half-century or even decade from one chance indication, without a clue as to how ordinary people actually experienced things. Of course the Annales School and the New Historicism tried to remedy that by clogging things up again, scanning parish registers and trade invoices and leapfrogging disciplines. (NXT: 129)

Tek voices his concern that the lives and experiences of the homeless will be lost for the future because they are neither noticed nor recorded in the present. But exactly these thoughts as well as the inherent mentalities are captured by the novel's *flâneurs*. Hence Elsie's female disruptions of Tek's catastrophic alphabet for a joyful dance defies the end-of-the world scenario of "no next, no story." (NXT: 203)

The Rhetoric of Walking

In charting the lives of the homeless touring and writing the city-text, *Next* reconstructs urban narrative on the page. Constantly in motion, the homeless inscribe their footprints all over the city. Following de Certeau (1988: 98-99), the "pedestrian speech act" of Brooke-Rose's characters as an urban language of its own selects and alters the spatial signifiers of London's streets, transforming them into a spatial story. Therefore, I will set Brooke-Rose's 'writerly' approach to language and narrative into context with de Certeau's (*ibid.*: 99) "rhetoric of walking" and "spatial stories". The woman writer sees fiction as a cognitive tool which fosters interpersonal communication and sensual perception in direct competition to the news as a primary means of information and orientation. In *Next* the new media stories are diametrically opposed to those of the narrative itself, and the distant visual perceptions of television are countered by the close reading of the city by the homeless' street stories. According to Harper (2001: 42), Brooke-Rose is notoriously committed to the poetic possibility of the novel's form and its relationship with other domains of knowledge. Hence, we can argue that the novel's structure of literary language, setting, and character corresponds to the postmodern urban overload of the city's semiotic system. In her fiction she disorients the reader and encourages him to survey narrative from a new perspective: "Christine Brook-Rose's fiction is written with the object of stretching people's mental horizons and questioning the conceptual language in which they think." (Birch 1994: 226)

In *Next*, the reader is not only invited to take on the perspective of the urban homeless and thus experience the city both from below and from street level, but its unusual form and strange language puts him into the disposition of an alienating and unhomely material, social, and mental environment. The narrative thereby structurally teaches the reader to orient himself in the literary city and to find his way by touring the minds of the homeless London protagonists. "While the relations between the inner workings of the mind and the public sphere is at the heart of all her writing" (*ibid.*: 16), she approaches this subject with the poststructuralist belief that specifically "linguistic structures have a formative effect on the mind" (*ibid.*: 90). In reference to de Certeau (1988: 99), we can contend that the touring in *Next* intrinsically features a parallelism between linguistic and pedestrian enunciation. The poetics of the urban walker/writer create an urban spatiality that speaks its own language.

Aow Stella, doow concentri'e on dahyley lahf wiuw yer ge' mey me lanch a' leeys if yer can't tauwk ter mey iss past toow. (NXT: 32)

Willyer wauwk wiv mey Euwsey? / For a bi', Yuppy, Ah meeyn Jessey. / Wiv them nimes smatahms Ah doan knowaw oo Ah am. A feeyl ca' orf lahk, ever seynce Ah baounced. (NXT: 37)

Certainly the urban spaces inhabited by the characters foster an idiosyncratic language which, in turn, offers London a particular character. The variety of speech, language, and enunciation employed in *Next* as well as the intertextual and intermedial references or the appropriation of the language of a wide array of discourses, then charts the polyglossia of contemporary urban life and the unlimited diversity of spatial stories as well as its multiple and metamorphic form. The question of who is thinking or perceiving the cityscape becomes a fundamental concern for deciphering the novel's texture. Only indicated by the correlation of language and context, this phenomenon creates ontological uncertainty. As the city is subject to certain linguistic constraints, one becomes aware of the constructedness and essential misrepresentations of London. The ambiguous space fostered inbetween, like the absence of text on the novel's pages, consequently indicates the habitual voice of the metropolis.

The literary *flâneur* represents a habitué and observer of urban life whose characteristics and perspective define him as a figure of ambivalence and thus as an apt allegory for the metropolis on the verge of turning unhomely. Its postmodern appropriation is the immigrant or homeless walker who seems even more attuned to the non-places of the post-Fordist city. The analysis of Christine Brooke-Rose's novel significantly shows how urbanites and urban space virtually script each other. The simultaneous observation/touring of the city registers physical, social, and mental space as texts to be "inscribed, read, rewritten, and reread" (Parsons 2000: 3). This interconnectivity lends a certain coherence and orientation to the urban. In other words, the text becomes medium/metaphor/image through which to perceive and intellectualise the urban. In this sense, literary and scientific discourses of the contemporary city indeed overlap. Touring or writing are activities which enable the denizens to translate their experiences in the city to an urban way of thinking. Nevertheless, in Brooke-Rose's novel the omnipresence of the media seems to destroy the void between reality and fiction which is necessary for a notion of the urban. In other words, touring postmodern London is in itself an ambivalent practice of producing orientation as well as uncertainty. Still, the characters' rhetoric and poetics of walking form idiosyncratic narratives deeply embedded in the collective nonconscious of the contemporary type of the *flâneur*.

6.3.3 Sensing the City

The city's atmosphere is one of the most important factors of influence on the urban-specific mentality. Whereas in the past, analyses of the urban condition were rather influenced by the visual impressions of the city's image (whether by map, tableau, or tour), a few recent publications focus on the urban sensescape. The urban environment is experienced not by the visual sense alone but by the whole sensory body of touch, sound, smell, taste and sight. In *Sensing Cities* Mónica Degen (2008: 36) shows how the perception of space is mapped through sensory experiences and that senses are a central ingredient in the organisation of everyday life. In the spatial-sensuous encounter, perception is translated and condensed to a specific feeling of the atmosphere, its ambience, pace, rhythm, aroma, composition, texture. Hence, urban space becomes equipped with idiosyncratic qualities of feeling (cf. Lehnert 2011: 9). In other words, the urban cityscape constitutes both setting and object of feelings (*ibid.*: 13-14). Thus, sensual perception of the Postmetropolis especially stresses urban-specific dispositions of feeling. This approach to urbanity then foregrounds the explicit and implicit consequences of the city's overload on urbanites' "sentient body" (Degen 2008: 38).

In the following I will offer an exemplary analysis of China Miéville's *King Rat* (1998). While the chapter on Underground London has shown that the confined spaces of the subterranean city are often represented in terms of their alienating atmosphere, especially in terms of smell and sound, either as reviving suppressed memories or inflicting a terror of the unknown, this sub-chapter concentrates on the larger development of sensescape in the novel in order to dissect the implications of mentality in regard to navigating London.

The Visual Cityscape

For Bischoff (2007: 190), the cityscape constitutes a visual expression of the eye's dominance over other sensual organs. Privileging the sense of sight is constructed around the notion of Cartesian perspectivism, whose abstraction of space by way of its optical format, physical layout, rationality, orderliness, predictable geometry and monotony promises fixed points of reference for orientation. Due de Certeau's notion, the celestial view further abstracts to urban to gain control of its confusion. Therefore, we could argue that the visual constructs the city as container space, exerting absolute control, power, and knowledge. In its denotations of voyeurism, scopism, and panopticism the "logic of visualisation" (Lefebvre 1991: 98) brings to light its implications on the power of verticality or hierarchy of spaces. Returning from a seaside holiday and entering London by train, the main character of Miéville's *King Rat* comments on the visual in the totalitarian architecture of London's high-rises. While his father's house is "an ugly Victorian block, squat and mean looking for all its size" (KRA: 11) and already conveys a feeling of coldness, the architecture in London's neighbourhood of Brent is represented as extremely oppressive:

> The grandiose tower of the Gaumont State cinema jutted into the sky on his left, a bizarre totalitarian monument among the budget groceries and hoardings of Kilburn High Road. Saul could feel the cold through the windows and he wrapped his coat around him as the train neared Willesden station. (KRA: 10)

The sensual alienation is twofold: first, the building's visual difference in comparison to the surrounding streets gives it an exaggerated look reminiscent of George Orwell's Ministry of Truth in *Nineteen Eighty-Four* (1949) or Fritz Lang's and Graham Greene's Ministry of Fear.[50] Thus, the novel's sensuous exposition in regard to Saul's perception of London directly relates the postmodern metropolis to the totalitarian control of a panoptic society. For the protagonist, mere perspectivation of the metropolis has lead to the confinement of urban society:

> the conspiracy of architecture, the tyranny by which the buildings that women and men has built had taken control of them, circumscribed their relations, confined their movements. These monolithic products of human hands had turned on their creators, and defeated them with common sense, quietly installed themselves as rulers. They were as insubordinate as Frankenstein's monster, but they had waged a more subtle campaign, a war of position more effective by far. (KRA: 288)

In the contemporary metropolis, the London Eye defines the city's new panorama. However, the hyperbolic Ferris wheel has not only become a spectacle in its own rights, but also the most prolific place from which to view the whole of the city. Second, the alienation of the Gaumont State building's scopism is also commented on in its character as spectacle: the cinema is a place of other spaces, dreams, and visions. This notion of absolute urban illusionism is seized in an image of Baudrillard's simulacrum; the appropriation of the novel unveils the spatial totalitarianism of London's South Bank and City architecture as an encompassing simulation:

---

50 | Fritz Lang's adaptation (1944) of Graham Greene's novel *The Ministry of Fear* (1943) is set in Bloomsbury. Senate House on Russell Square, today part of the University of London, housed the Ministry of Information and is said to subsequently have influenced George Orwell's Ministry of Truth in his novel *Nineteen Eighty-Four* (1949). Of course it also became the setting in the later film adaptation. Legend has it that Hitler selected Senate House as his headquarter on invasion of Great Britain and therefore spared the building from being bombed during the Blitz.

for the most part the city was inverted and refracted in the Thames, a sinuous shattered mirror. Lights glinted on the water, dark shapes punctuated with hundreds of points of light, the towers of the city, the far-off lights of the South Bank Centre, far more real to him then than their counterparts in the air above. He stared down at the city below his feet. It was an illusion. The shimmering motion of the lights he saw was not the real city. They were part of it, to be sure, a necessary part … but the beautiful lights, so much more lively than those above them, were a simulacrum. They merely painted the surface tension. Below that thin veneer the water was still filthy, still dangerous and cold. Saul held on to that. He resisted the poetics of the city. (KRA: 311)

The immediacy of the city's hyperreality produces an inverted picture, because from below Saul actually looks down on the grand skyline cunning him into the illusion of empowerment. Amazement is, however, stripped by the recognition of the willing manipulation of perception. Against the glittering diversion of the skyscrapers' lights, Saul prefers the murky and prosaic reality of ground level and the monolithic gaze cannot penetrate the surfaces of urban everyday life. Traditionally, the metropolis is depicted as an illimitable and unconceivable non-entity which can only be conceived in the unity of the fragmented perception of the walker. The heterogeneity and constant input of stimuli forces the urbanite into a constant disassociation and selection, but reassembling these elements in the "mental eye" (Kaern 1990: 93) reformation remains always arbitrary. It calls for a unifying sense of the city – the sensescape of London.

The Synaesthetic Sensescape

A 'sense of place' is always constituted by embodied perception, where the body as the mediator between Self and the world becomes the agent between the senses and the city. In *King Rat* this mutual layering of sensual body and space mirrors the urban *conditio humana* within the Self. This recognition is indicated by introspection in the London Underground:

The train was now below the houses. It wound through a deep grove in the city, as if the years of passage had worn down the concrete under the tracks. Saul Garamond glanced again at the woman sitting in front of him, and turned his attention to the windows. The light in the carriage had made them mirrors, and he stared at himself, his heavy face. Beyond his face was a layer of brick, dimly visible, and beyond that the cellars of the houses that rose like cliffs on either side. (KRA: 8)

Here Saul's perception of the claustrophobic and enclosed city is determined by his own limited human view. This 'subject position' changes when he becomes aware of his rat-nature. As noted before, sensual perceptions, especially those of the smellscape, are dependent on one's outsider status.[51] Although Saul's rodent nature is recognisable

51 | Also see other London novels with non-human characters, e.g. Will Self's *Great Apes* (1997), Patrick Neate's *The London Pigeon Wars* (2003), Neil Gaiman's *Anansi Boys* (2005), or dead protagonists, e.g. Will Self's *How the Dead Live* (2000). Their different focalisation offers an utterly other perspective on the postmodern metropolis.

before (KRA: 10-11), his extraordinary powers only come about when he wakes to his rat being:

> superhuman strength and speed, and the ability to dash straight up a wall, to squeeze through tiny chinks and cracks, to make himself so inconspicuous as to become practically invisible to human eyes, and to digest and enjoy any sort of food, no matter how rotten and filthy. (Freedman 2003: 402)

Thus, the spatial reperspectivation of London is largely due to Saul's sensual metamorphosis – albeit one of consciousness rather than a material one – which makes accessible a "nonanthropocentric vision" (Maczynska 2010: 75). Saul is first rendered Other when he is questioned by the police, debased to common criminal, and in prison is assigned his pariah existence. Moreover, the disorienting enclosure of the cell demands the development of other senses.

> Saul opened his eyes with a start. For a moment he was uncertain what had happened. The sounds were changing. The depth seemed to be bleeding out of all the noises in the world. Saul could still make out everything he had heard before, but it was ebbing away into two dimensions. The change was swift and inexorable. Like the curious echoes of shrieks which fill swimming pools, the sounds were clear and audible, but empty. (KRA: 27)

The protagonist experiences his metamorphosis through an enhanced sensation of auditory capacity which is "unnaturally clear" (KRA: 27) and directly affects his body. He becomes aware of the "sounds of his body", e.g. the "thump of his heart" and the rhythm of his "fast and shallow" (KRA: 27-28) breath. He touches his ears, confused by the "strange sonic vampirism", and tries to shake off the uncanny sensation of his orientation "made dizzy by the cacophony of his own body" (KRA: 28). Because Saul's animalistic instinct of danger is imprinted on his feelings of terror and sensory reactions when he pricks his ears like a rat. This not only affects his sense of hearing but also that of sight. Looking at the ceiling of his cell he perceives how "[t]he network of cracks and lines in the paint seemed to shift uneasily, the shadows moving imperceptibly, as if a faint light were being moved in the room." (KRA: 28) Seeing here becomes a fore-sight; the impression (literally in the cracks of the wall) constitutes a visual proleptic perception of things to come. Simultaneously feeling vibrations in the air, Saul is rendered synaesthetic by the fear-induced metamorphosis. While the transformation plunges him briefly into a crisis close to schizophrenia, the prison break also opens a whole new city for the protagonist. From the growling trains and the "grandiloquent and preposterous declamations" (KRA: 36) of King Rat's voice or the "discordant cacophony" of squeaking rats (KRA: 127), the "distant hum of traffic but closer sound of birds" (KRA: 129), the soundscape of London makes him experience the metropolis anew. Maczynska (2010: 75) argues that the metamorphosis equals the transmutability of the city in flux; due to its transformative potential, also the self-image of its citizens is prone to an ongoing renewal and grants endless opportunities for shifting identities.

Urban Instincts

While Saul's new focus has altered his consciousness (cf. *ibid.*: 76–78), his invisible position as rat and the darkness in which he travels conjure up a new inner vision. This mental condition supports the sensuous experiences of sound and smell, thus drawing an alternative mental map of London's sensescape (KRA: 10, 38): "Hold your tongue and prick your ears: hear the trains *growling*? Got the map in your bonce? *Learn the way.* [...] Follow your I Suppose." (KRA: 107) King Rat teaches Saul to follow his "feral instincts" (KRA: 247) and thus the 'inferior' and animalistic senses of smell, taste, and touch (cf. Degen 2008: 42). The atmosphere of the city and the sense of place of the citizen rat are instantly connected to the fluidity of the city's and the citizen's identity. Degen (*ibid.*: 45) explicates that because smell permeates the personal realm in triggering memories, it is also the most pervasive sensory stimulation which then not only represents a fluid experience in terms of space and time but also of identity, thereby unveiling the repressed sinister Other. For her, the city of smell therefore "represents the crossing of a threshold" (*ibid.*) and purveys the most definite notion of transition – spatial and bodily. Hence, the fleetingness of smell resembles the constant becoming of metropolis and urbanite alike.

The smellscape in China Miéville's novel *King Rat* is described vividly and constructs a different urban narrative; Saul walks "through an olfactory patchwork and the smells of piss told him stories." (KRA: 127) Generally, smell in the city is equated with stench and air pollution and connected to death, illness, filth, and dirt. But the olfactory sense is also a social sense (cf. Bischoff 2007: 198) because these sensory experiences of disgust are ascribed in connection with poverty, misery, and the lower social classes. And while the postmodern cityscape is rather conceived as smell-poor, the novel *King Rat* in its subversion also uncovers the residues and the stench of this new 'wasteland': "the smell of smoke [...] mingled with exhaust fumes and the whiff of rubbish" (KRA: 35) or the "rich smell of rot" (KRA: 56) coming off rubbish bags. Taste and smell are directly connected and in the metropolis, they both define a specific flavour of the city. In *King Rat*, the smell of waste is interlocked with the rodent's taste for residue: "tea-leaves and egg yolk [...] a damp crust of bread [...] half a fruit-cake, flattened and embedded with sawdust. Chicken bones and crushed chocolate, the remnants of sweet-corn and rice, fish-heads and stale crisps" (KRA: 56). At first disgusted, Saul, to his horror, recognises that he never suffered from intoxication of too much sugar, fat, or alcohol, can stomach anything and never puked. Shrugging off his human "layers of habit" (KRA: 58), he relishes in this new synaesthestic experience of tasting urban deterioration:

> His mind still rang with admonishments heard long ago [...] but his stomach, his stomach remained firm. The smell of the meat was enticing. He willed himself to feel ill. He strove for nausea. He took a bite. He wriggled his tongue into the meat, pushed apart the fibres. He probed, tasting the dirt and decay. Lumps of gristle and fat split open in his mouth, mixed with saliva. The burger was delicious. (KRA: 59)

The touch of his probing tongue brings us to the notion of the city of touch. As shown with Simmel, urbanites generally employ tactics of distanciation to 'handle' the influx of urban stimuli, while the stranger is defined by his specific relation of distance and proximity in the metropolitan realm. As Saul observes on King Rat, the outsider is more in touch with the physical cityscape because his haptic sense is able to detect any "minor aberration, some imperfection of the brick" (KRA: 43). Due to this acute tactile apprehension of the city's surfaces, the rat is actually able to follow "invisible paths in the brick and mortar to stop suddenly and grip at a seemingly arbitrary spot in the surface. Those fingers were acute to unseen clues and potentials in the architecture." (KRA: 42) The character not only develops a finer motor skill in navigating the city, but he can actually read the hidden ciphers, handwritings, and stories of the textual city. On top of this, Saul is able to feel and therefore read the immaterial, for example the pull of "the geomantic tugging." (KRA: 127) These urban ley lines in *King Rat* are specifically defined by the urban rhythms of time, movement, and becoming. Feeling the "pulse of the city" (Degen 2008: 43), Saul advances to a rhythmanalyst employing the shocks, stresses, and strains of the urban environment in his spatial and temporal navigation of London. Lefebvre and Régulier (2004: 87) see the rhythmanalyst as "[m]ore sensitive to times than to spaces, to moods than to images, to the atmosphere than to particular events". Constantly following the rhythms of urban stimuli he feels a growing "hyper-real focus on the here and now", which is characterised by an "acceptance of the unacceptable" and in truth resembles a form of "reactionary stoicism" that dulls his feelings towards others (KRA: 321). In that respect, Highmore (2005: 160) goes as far as to argue that "rhythmanalysis undoes a common-sense geography of the city."

London Unbound

Although Saul also recognises the danger of his animal traits which can render him inhuman, asocial, and anomic, the soft and fluid city in Miéville's novel is represented by the unbounded possibilities of Saul's movements. The rat can squeeze through invisible cracks in the walls, vertical and horizontal dimensions are inversed, it climbs the roof above and the drainpipes below (KRA: 3-4). A possibility to roam freely alters the city, Saul's perception thereof, and his attitude and feeling towards the metropolis. "*I was heavy and human. And now* [...] *I'm rat and I can travel how I like.*" (KRA: 133) While his view of the city as a human was limited, he now perceives London "at an angle from which the city was never meant to be seen" (KRA: 288) and uncovers the hidden counter-world of sewers, back alleys, and hidden passages (cf. Maczynska 2010: 75). The properties of the metropolis also change through the new-found flexibility of urban behaviour: Saul traverses the city with "breakneck progress" (KRA: 148), moving "at a crazy speed over the streets" (KRA: 148), ducking through the traffic on the Westway to the "rhythmic ebbs of cars" (KRA: 131-133), weaving "in and out of central London" (KRA: 120). In a way, his mobile sensory experience through touching, smelling, tasting, hearing and seeing the urban realm is well attuned to the overload of the fluid city.

As the protagonist's body becomes one with the speed of the metropolis and its intricate rhythms, he is overcome by a euphoric energy (KRA: 44-45, 120). Having defeated the abstract and totalitarian space, he feels exhilarated and woken from apathy to and new rush of urban vigilance (KRA: 288). "Saul had seen a new city. The map of London had been ripped up and redrawn according to King Rat's criteria." (KRA: 126) This new topography of London is not an absolute space of boundaries and walls, but an alternative and illimitable one: "Saul felt it yawn before him, infinitely vaster than he had imagined, unknowable and furtive." (KRA: 61) Out of bounds, Saul suddenly doubts whether the city still existed (KRA: 126), because once he touches the metropolitan sublime, it immediately withdraws from his hold.

Experiences of this transmutable city are put in strict opposition to the totalitarian visualisation of space mentioned in the beginning of this analysis. Hence, *King Rat* largely takes into account the marginal and peripheral cityscapes or the liminal zone and in-between spatialities of the metropolis. The character King Rat not only introduces Saul to a different mobility and an unusual perception, but also to the various 'non-places' of London: its sewers, cul-de-sacs, back yards, back alleys, parking lots, train tracks, rooftops, etc. Saul inhabits an urban sensescape whose atmosphere is notoriously a state inbetweeen ("Zustand des Dazwischen"; Lehnert 2011: 15-16). King Rat inverses the common image of the city to one presenting the hidden sensual realities of urban life: "The rest of it, that's just in-between for you now. All the main streets, the front room and the rest of it, that's just filler, that's just *chaff*, that ain't the real city. You get to that by the *back* door. [...] Well, you've touched it now. All the vacant lots and all [...]. That's London." (KRA 45-46) The novel's collage of fragmented passageways, sewers, Tube trains, bus routes, bus depots and highways is devoid of conventional centres yet unified into informational propinquity.

London's Westway plays a pivotal role in the protagonist's discovery of an inverted urban vigilance which is in no way inferior to the city in flux. The highway between Edgeware Road and White City is probably one of London's most prominent roads; when constructed in the 1970s is was the longest stretch of elevated road in Europe. On the one hand, the Westway is part of the totalitarian landscape of concrete, tar, and CCTV cameras offering "drivers entering the city an impressively cinematic panorama of central London" (Moran 2005: 65). Bringing congestion, noise, pollution, poverty, Moran (*ibid.*: 64-65) also shows that on the other hand, "the dead zone alongside and under the road, unsuitable for houses and offices, has slowly grown back to life, creating a netherworld of football pitches, cricket nets, roller-skating parks, wholefood markets and community centres." China Miéville's novel *King Rat* takes part in the manifold cultural constructions of the Westway[52] representing this non-place as significant for urban contestation and cultural subversion (KRA: 131-133; 139-146; 246). Moreover, the highway is a relevant part of London's traffic circulation and therefore an important aspect of the city's everyday life. With the converging arteries of communication and transport beneath its arches, it becomes a pivotal node of the inverted Informational City. As King Rat says of himself: "I fill all the spaces in-between. [...] I can hear the things left unsaid. I know the secret life of houses and the social life of things. I can read the writing on the wall." (KRA: 34) We can thus discern that from the visual cityscape to its holistic sensescape, London's architecture to its marginal non-places of inbetweenness, Miéville's novel foregrounds urban thirdspaces of transition as offering possibilities of navigating the Postmetropolis and constructing urban identity.

The final battle of the subaltern against the totalitarian perspectivity of postmodern urbanity is literally played out in the non-place of a South London warehouse. This

52 | The Westway also plays a pivotal role in J.G. Ballard's *Crash* (1973) and *Concrete Island* (1974) as well as in Nicholas Royle's *Matter of the Heart*, Ian McEwan's *Saturday*, and Tim Lott's *White City Blue*. For other cultural negotiations of the highway see Moran (2005: 61-62).

vision of the centreless city sees urban culture created in the rhythms of transitional spaces.

> The trains that enter London arrive **like ships sailing** across the roofs. They pass between towers jutting into the sky like **long-necked sea beasts** and the great gas-cylinders **wallowing** in dirty scrub **like whales**. In the **depths below** are lines of small shops and obscure franchises, cafés with peeling paint and businesses tucked into the arches over with the trains pass. [...] **The rhythms of London are played out here, in the sprawling flat zone between suburbs and centre**." (KRA: 7; emphasis N.P.)

The hyperbolic water imagery employed upon the protagonist's arrival in London not only premonitions his later awakening in the sewers of the city beneath but in combination emphasises the temporality and transitionality of the postmodern fluid city (cf. Bould 2009: 317-318).

To sum up, the analysis of China Miéville's contemporary London novel *King Rat* exemplifies how an orchestration of visual sense, smell, taste, feeling, and sound, helps contextualising an experience of the urban realm. As the metamorphosis of the protagonist Saul Garamond shows, the polyphony of senses is fundamental for an orientation in the city that not only ensures survival but is central to a more complex understanding of urban reality. This "*active sense-making*" (Degen 2008: 48) offers mental patterns which secure a vigilant existence against one of anxiety or apathy. As the protagonist's foster father teaches his son: "When we learn, we no longer fear. This is tar, and this is what it does, and this is the world, and this is what it does, and this is what we can do to it." (KRA: 25) With the alteration of the urban sensescape from one of static visualisation to one of polyphonic sensual mobility, Saul's feelings of alienation, estrangement, insecurity and anxiety are reconfigured to elation, invigoration, triumph and power over the city. Giving equal ontological weight to the fragmented or hidden and forgotten non-places and passageways, contemporary London is seen as more heterogeneous and varied in its transformative energies and vigilance. As the real is equated with the visible and the un-real with the invisible (cf. R. Jackson 1981: 45), the other senses note the subversive and uncanny characteristics of the metropolis. In that respect, sensing the city becomes a prerequisite for navigating the Postmetropolis as an intrinsic part of urban-specific structures of thinking.

6.3.4 Apprehending Urbanity

This last sub-chapter specifically deals with Ian McEwan's novel *Saturday* (2005), which is a significant meta-text on understanding the mind. The fiction represents consciousness and the complexities of mental processing through the combined narratological effects of characterisation, focalisation, and conceptual metaphors. It centres on knowing the city like knowing the human mind, through the accelerated consciousness of a motorised *flâneur*, the informational flows of the media, the knowledge of science as well as the transformative understanding of art and literature. These ramifications on the different ways of perception all take into account, as I shall argue, the transformations of urbanity under the influence of the postmodern metropolis in flux, and thereby reveal mental dispositions of navigating the fluid city against the background of human history of evolution and civilisation.

The free indirect speech of *Saturday* is limited to the consciousness of the middle-aged protagonist Henry Perowne, which means that the multifariousness of London is channelled through his monoptic gaze. Concentrating on "what goes on inside Perowne's own head" (Kemp 2005) his recollections, perceptions, and evaluations of the urban environment are represented as inquisitive and self-reflexive. The ordinariness of Perowne's contemplations is not only expressed by the morning routine of coffee, sex, and wallowing in bed, but is specifically stressed when he is urinating and defecating (SAT: 57; cf. Groes 2009: 105). The story set in the mind of a thinking urbanite going about his everyday business on an ordinary day follows the tradition of modernist representations of consciousness in novels like James Joyce's *Ulysses* (1922) or Virginia Woolf's *Mrs Dalloway* (1925). The narrative situation thereby focuses on an individual consciousness and explores the introspective conceptions and perceptions that mediate the urban denizen's experience of their metropolitan world. In concentrating on the mental relation of humans with their environment, these texts show how individual and private minds are connected to the public and collective urban experience.

Spatio-Temporal Consciousness

In an interview, McEwan states that he "wanted to capture the present, to get what would be in the mind of a reasonably educated person in early 2003." (Deveney 2005) Waking up on the morning of Saturday 15 February 2003, the protagonist Henry Perowne contemplates the feel of the time he lives in, contrasting it to the "more optimistic days" of Fitzrovia's past: "And now what days are these? Baffled and fearful, he mostly thinks when he takes time from his weekly round to consider." (SAT: 4) The spatio-temporal perception of the metropolis plays a pivotal role both in the temporal construction of the novel itself as well as in the exploration of the urbanites' consciousness and experience of urban time.

While the novel is committed to linearity, Perowne likewise strives to structure his Saturday around the weekly repetition and a specific chronological arrangement of temporal of routinised practices (see chapter 6.1.1). Hence, the city can be navigated by personally devising the temporal organism of London. In Perowne's urban life, "time is always fragmented, not only by errands and family obligations and sports, but by the restlessness that comes with these weekly islands of freedom." (SAT: 66) Routine and meticulously arranged time-slots are then connected to a specific, pre-determined and carefully laid out itinerary through London: Warren Street, Maple Street, Tottenham Court Road, University Street, Huntley Street, Goodge Street. Charlotte Street, Great Portland Street, Harley Street, Marylebone High Street, Paddington Street, Acton, Westbourne Grove, etc. (SAT: 59-169). Daily routine, the movement through London as well as the reiterative intertextual references to *Mrs Dalloway* devise Perowne's own progress through the streets as that of traditional *flânerie*.

Walking and transgressing the city momentarily renders Perowne an urbanite *par excellence*. The atmosphere on the streets of London, the surrounding architecture as well as passers-by spark off specific thoughts that fuel Henry's introspections (*ibid.*: 46). Walking "away from the square along blinding moist pavement" he is surprised by the fresh and clean taste of London's air, which triggers the impression that he is actually walking along "some coastal wilderness [...] from a childhood holiday." (SAT: 71) The crowds instead conjure up thoughts of one of his patients and the repressive regime of Saddam Hussein (SAT: 72-73). Consequently, Perowne is perceptive to both the beauty and the terror of the urban realm. Watching a man sweeping the rubbish off London's streets, the sublimity of the scene momentarily transgresses his individual stance (SAT: 74) and thereby, the traditional form of urban perception by *flânerie* offers him an inkling of the larger consciousness of the metropolis.

Depending on the time of the day, the city accelerates, and with it the urbanites' perception is altered from stasis to mobility. The appearance of the cityscape and the experience of metropolitan space changes dramatically from night to day and even within the day. In the early hours, the city square in front of Perowne's house is empty and carries a ghostly but peaceful atmosphere (SAT: 4-5). A mere two hours later, the city becomes alive with the noise of traffic and people (SAT: 48, 59-62, 71-72). Because through the course of the Saturday the urban atmosphere changes spatio-temporal experiences of the urban define the different subjective perceptions of the city. As the morning progresses and the city speeds up, so also Perowne alters his form of mobility and consequently his spatio-temporal perception of the metropolis. The urban locomotion of walking is literally a brief passage in the whole novel, while longer passages concern Perowne's motorised tours around London.

Mobilised *Flânerie*

While for Benjamin (2002: 443) "the sidewalks were laid down in the interests of those who go by car", for contemporary urbanites driving through the city now constitutes a new form of *flânerie*. In Jacobs' (2006: 216) words, the "*flâneur* became a chauffeur" and "the driver can be considered a kind of postmodern variant of the *flâneur*." (*Ibid.*: 221)[53] The protagonist in Ian McEwan's *Saturday* traverses the streets of London in the cushioned cocoon of his Mercedes. According to Mumford (1997: 241), the motor car represents "the limp of a faltering pedestrian" and Perowne sees the car as an extension of his own body and a part of himself. In the beginning he handles the car "apologetically" and is overcome by confusion due to the sensations of stability: "the car idles without vibration; the rev counter alone confirms the engine is turning." (SAT: 76) Hence, the car represents a mechanical protection device against the postmodern overload scenario for the contemporary 'idler'. Due to the swift movement in parallel to the fluid city, the postmodern chauffeur is able to get back on track contemplating on the multifariousness and heterogeneity of the metropolis.

On his motorised tour around London, Perowne maps the city while simultaneously sensuously perceiving the different places, their 'visual' atmosphere and the feelings they inflict. The corner of Charlotte Street and Goodge Street is "a spot [...] where the affairs of utility and pleasure condense to make colour and space brighter" (SAT: 122) while the stone façades of "sombre Great Portland Street [...] make it seem always dusk here" (SAT: 123). But it is not only darkness and light, colour and greyness that define

---

53 | For other London novels with predominant automobile perceptions see *City of Tiny Lights*, *Corpsing*, *Londonstani*, *Millennium People*, *South of the River*, *The Matter of the Heart*, and *White City Blue*,

the spectrum of London's feel but also proximity and distance, vastness and tightness, agoraphobia and claustrophobia, awe and control: for example, Perowne's perception opposes the "immensity of suburbs around Perivale" (SAT: 125) with the "orderly grid of medical streets west of Portland Palace" (SAT: 123). Driving through the city, the postmodern *flâneur* hence still captures the idiosyncrasies of urban places and the different rhythms of the metropolis, for example, Marylebone as a place of contentment and peace (SAT: 126-127). Stuck in traffic jam and slowly crawling back into central London, the protagonist from the safe position of his cars wallows in the sensations of the post-Fordist metropolis and probes his contemporaneous feel of urbanity:

> he lowers his windows to taste the scene in full – the bovine patience of a jam, the abrasive tang of icy fumes, the thunderous idling machinery in six lanes east and west, the yellow street light bleaching colour from the bodywork, the jaunty thud of entertainment systems, and red tail lights stretching way ahead into the city, white headlights pouring out of it. He tries to see it, or feel it, in historical terms [...]. (SAT: 167-168)

Thus, the contemporary urbanite discards the traditional driver persona for that of the postmodern *flâneur* cruising the streets and revelling in the scenes that surround him; he becomes an encapsulated consumer of the urban spectacle, both its beauties and its crises. Due to the intrinsic dynamism of the scenery and its transformability constructed by the continuous alternation of the perspective of the moving car, the sensual perceptions are cinematic in kind. For Jacobs (2006: 214) these fleeting perceptions of a volatile metropolitan life, the speed of traffic or the flux of commodities create a new visual mechanism which expresses a preference for entertainment in overcoming the gap between the *flâneur* and the urban crowd. The sensation of non-movement within the car and the mobility of the urban environment outside define the inverted paradox of the postmodern chauffeured locomotion through the city and point to a significant form of perception of the city in flux and to particular mental structures. In this sense, the car not only constitutes an extension of the body, but also of the urban psyche (cf. *ibid.*: 217). On the one hand, his emotions seem to steer the car and dominate Perowne's navigation through the urban labyrinth (SAT: 78). On the other hand, the mood swings of the protagonist inflicted by the quick alterations of his perception are mirrored by the shifting perspective and the car's movements. Emotion and motion are created in a dialectical manner:

> the forward motion is a prompt, it instantly returns him to his list, the proximal and distal causes of his emotional state. A second can be a long time in introspection. Long enough for Henry to make a start on the negative features, certainly enough time for him to think, or sense, without unwrapping the thought into syntax and words, that it is in fact the state of the world that troubles him most, and the marches are there to remind him of it. (SAT: 80)

Perowne even goes so far as to experience the perceptual process *per se* as constant but fleeting spatio-temporal transition:

> The assertions and the questions don't spell themselves out. He experiences them more as a mental shrug followed by an interrogative pulse. This is the pre-verbal language that linguists call

mentalese. Hardly a language, more a matrix of shifting patterns, consolidating and compressing meaning in fractions of a second, and blending it inseparably with its distinctive emotional hue, which itself is rather like a colour. A sickly yellow. (SAT: 81)

Interestingly, in Perowne's self-analysis of his own consciousness, the vocabulary employed to describe his mental spaces is not much different from the former subjective constructions of the cityscape – especially in terms of rhythm, semantics, time, movement, cinematic device, and significant colour coding. Mentalese in this context describes the emotionally reactive but abstract perception of the urban overload scenario without words, which could be interpreted as a pre-verbal *outillage mental.* Consequently, the car serves as a device that aligns the human mind to the postmodern cityscape and eventually allows the urbanite to react in tune with the speedy and transformative surroundings (SAT: 81).

In other words, the motorised *flâneur* is the epitome of urban vigilance and best equipped to absorb, filter, and extract meaning from the multifariousness of the city in flux. The automobile promises fast movement and free and independent command of the urban space, and equally Perowne sees the metropolis and the technology of the twenty-first century, or symbolically the streets and the cars, as examples of progress and success (SAT: 76-77). According to Boeri (1997: 36), "[h]ighways are [...] a place in themselves; alien, but full of energy." Similarly to China Miéville's protagonist Saul Garamond, Henry Perowne relishes the non- or transit-place of the London Westway as a place of emotional elation: "The reviled Westway, rearing on stained concrete piles and on which he rises swiftly to second-floor level, offers up a sudden horizon of tumbling cloud above a tumult of rooftops, it's one of those moments when to be a car owner in a city, the owner of this car, is sweet." (SAT: 154) From another stance it means that the urban overload scenario accelerates, leading in consequence to new forms of distanciation. Moreover, because the car enlarges the distance between postmodern *flâneur* and the urban landscape, the city is transformed into a landscape of mere surfaces and this destruction of spatial depth results in a further alienation from the cityscape. Olalquiaga argues (1992: 5): "Reorganizing space into flatness (lack of depth and volume) and mobility (lack of fixed axis), monitors and screens have become the new windows of the world, condensing an otherwise vast landscape into a small frame." In *Saturday*, Perowne passes stretches of buildings which are simple façade and rather aggrandise a certain blasé in the driver (SAT: 78).

According to contemporary urbanologists, the mobilised *flâneur* simply uses the street as a conveyor belt to pass the city's monuments, and unlike the walking *flâneur* does not interact with the metropolitan public (cf. Guggenberger 2000: 54; Rötzer 2000: 21; Groes 2011: 157). Due to this destruction of urban public places, the subject becomes submissive to the need for mobility: "As urban space becomes a mere function of motion, it thus becomes less stimulating in itself; the driver wants to go through the space, not to be aroused by it." (Sennett 1994: 18) In contrast, Sennett stresses that the urbanite regresses into a state of passiveness or urban apathy, which for Baudrillard even constitutes a "spectacular form of amnesia" (cit. in Jarvis 1998: 37).

The argument that mobilisation creates social anomie and personal disintegration or apathy is also supported by the exclusive solitariness which accompanies the perception of mobilised *flânerie* (cf. Boeri 1997: 35). Yet as the analysis of mobilisation in the Tube has shown, interpersonal distanciation allows for subjective introspection, the movement and alteration of time driving towards the depth of the unconscious or the other spaces of memories. "Only in experiencing speed in solitariness within a familiar territory are we able to ascribe a specific importance to the spaces passing by, that corresponds to our state of mind." (*Ibid.*: 36) By yearning for a silence far from the noise of the urban texture of signs, the "white noise" gains in resonance: "[Perowne] doesn't particularly like himself in this frame, but the second-by-second wash of his thoughts is only partially his to control – the drift, the white noise of solitary thought is driven by his emotional state." (SAT: 78) The interior of the car becomes the place of associations incidentally ascribed by unconscious glances caught in passing from the city without gearing up emotions (cf. Boeri 1997: 36). In this respect, Jacobs (2006: 214-215) points out that although the perception of the city from a moving car implies distance, it is not an aesthetic one, but rather functions as a highly specialised perception engrained with a specific attitude and demanding particular training.

Mediatised Consciousness

Due to Perowne's cinematic visual perceptions of the metropolis, his motorised *flânerie* also appears to mirror the perception of the Informational City by referring to the technological conditions of postmodern urbanity. In his analysis of *Saturday*, Currie (2007: 127–129) points to the relevance of personal or subjective time versus monumental or public time in the postmodern city. While the striking of Big Ben in *Mrs Dalloway* functions as an authorial temporal backdrop for the private thoughts and actions of its characters, in *Ulysses* the bell tower punctuates the rhythm of "a vast and solitary day" (Joyce cit. in Augé 1995: 75-76). In reference to the history of mentality, Augé (*ibid.*: 76) shows that devising space around the church and bell tower strives for reconciling spatio-temporal conceptions. Analogically, the centre of Perowne's morning attention is the Post Office Tower which stands in as an icon of the mass-communication age (cf. Green 2010: 62). Similar to Miéville's *King Rat* the monumental building not only serves as a spatial orientation, but TV and radio news keep clock of Perowne's day. As was shown before, the media support the protagonist's routine and gives him mental security, and therefore Perowne has to acknowledge that the media define prevalent urban stimuli which influence or even predetermine urbanites' perceptions of reality (SAT: 186). Leupolt (2010: 64) comments:

> Henry Perowne's credulity makes us aware of the strong influence and fascination the media exercises on us. Its omnipresence in our contemporary culture, repeatedly depicted as oppressive in *Saturday*, often leads us to take for granted 'official' opinions and representations of reality. In their collective hunger for spectacle, both news channels and individual spectators fill the gaps of knowledge with their imagination, thus distorting reality according to their needs.

Insofar, the public and private are both only perceived through the lens of mediatised experiences. Mumford (1997: 249) contends that the mediatised public is a necessary prerequisite in navigating the metropolis because "no one can see or know what takes place in the city at large without listening to the radio and consulting the newspaper." He further argues:

> The essential gossip of the metropolis is no longer that of people meeting face to face on the crossroads, at the dinner table, in the market-place: a few dozen people writing in the newspapers, a dozen more broadcasting over the radio, provide the daily interpretation of movements and happenings. (*Ibid.*: 256)

Perowne feels himself very much the victim of media information and recognises that the ideologised construction of the news manipulates his way of thinking.

> Have his anxieties been making a fool of him? It's part of the new order, this narrowing of mental freedom, of his right to roam. Not so long ago his thoughts ranged more unpredictably, over a longer list of subjects. He suspects he's becoming a dupe, the willing, febrile consumer of news fodder, opinion, speculation [...]. (SAT: 180)

But the media not only seem to make his thinking less independent but also predetermines his dispositions of feeling because television's coverage on the workings of terrorism and war creates an urban atmosphere of terror, anxiety, and paranoia (see chapter 8.2.2). The flow of the Informational City consequently thwarts individual agency and induces urban apathy.

Meta-Conscious Reflections

Dominic Head (2007: 192) argues that this phenomenon "suggests a new kind of territory for the novel that treats the issue of consciousness." The novel's alignment of narrative, mental process, and focalisation mirrors its theme of consciousness. Its self-reflexivity can therefore be compared to that of postmodern meta-narration. In compliance to historical meta-fiction, I contend that Ian McEwan's *Saturday* constitutes a new kind of meta-consciousness novel. Perowne's frame of mind, as argued before, is determined by his line of work: in striving to understand everything in medical schemata, he not only dissects other people but also diagnoses the city according to his professional perception. The neurosurgeon not considers himself an expert of the human brain (SAT: 8-12, 44-45, 86) and inquiries into his own thought processes:

> An habitual observer of his own moods, he wonders about this sustained, distorting euphoria. Perhaps down at the molecular level there's been a chemical accident while he slept – something like a spilled tray of drinks, prompting dopamine-like receptors to initiate a kindly cascade of intracellular events; or it's the prospect of a Saturday, or paradoxical consequence of extreme tiredness. (SAT: 5)

The analysis has already brought into perspective how Ian McEwan's protagonist reflects on questions of perspectivity, perception, and consciousness. According to Head (2007: 192), "McEwan is [...] moving in a new direction [...] trying to produce [...] a diagnostic 'slice-of-mind' novel – working towards the literary equivalent of a CT scan." By way of its protagonist the narrative tracks down the various layers of thought processes, paths of associations, and the infliction of memories. McEwan's "theory of the mind" (Childs 2009: 26) builds on an array of mental states: Perowne's consciousness as wrought by anxieties, the character's assumptions on his patient's tumour, the worries of his mother's dementia or the professional diagnosis of Baxter's mental degeneration (cf. Childs 2006: 150).

Perowne's emphasis on the functions of the left brain – intellect, sensory discrimination, visual-motor skills (cf. Byrnes 2009: 66) – pays heed to the urbanite's growing intellectualisation, on the other hand the novel represents this rational approach as strongly limited. Perowne recognises that he in fact knows very little because neuroscience still cannot account for the processes of the brain's encoding of experiences, memories, dreams and intentions nor fathom the relation between the physical site of the mind, and the incomprehensible workings of human consciousness (SAT: 255; cf. Byrnes 2009: 62, 75; Green 2010: 69). In a transferred sense, Perowne might be able to read the materiality of the urban cityscape, but is unable to comprehend the urbanites' state of mind (SAT: 86). Hence, the text goes beyond a simple homage to the modernist representations of consciousness in its attempt to understand and represent mental processes. In its quest to render the mind intelligible, the novel not only endeavours to explore the human ways of knowing, but also studies the various representations of consciousness by art and neuroscience.

All in all, the protagonist's thoughts about the relations of matter and mind are integrated in a larger discourse of the novel concerning the different modes of intelligibility regarding science and literature, or rationality and creativity (cf. Head 2007: 185). In being an expert of the human brain, Perowne is a rational and pragmatic scientific materialist who responds to observable and measurable truth (cf. Green 2010: 62). He believes in scientific advances of understanding consciousness (cf. Head 2007: 25) and can be characterised as a modern "New Atheist Everyman" (Impastato 2009: 15). He relishes in reading Charles Darwin's autobiography reflecting upon it as a decisive paradigm shift of thinking (SAT: 56; cf. K. Wall 2008: 778; Childs 2009: 28-29). A literary philistine, Perowne discards all sense of stories, but still ardently relies on the constantly progressive narrative of evolution (cf. Bradley & Tate 2010: 28):

> What better creation myth? An unimaginable sweep of time, numberless generations spawning by infinitesimal steps complex living beauty out of inert matter, driven by the blind furies of random mutation, natural selection and environmental change, with the tragedy of forms continually dying, and lately the wonder of minds emerging and with them morality, life, art, cities – and the unprecedented bonus of this story happening to be demonstrably true. (SAT: 56)

Perowne believes both in a linear progressive structure of time and in the transformability of the environment and finally the mutations of an urban civilisation. Not only do cities mark the contemporary frontier of further development for him, but the metropolitan man resides on top of the evolutionary scale: "The street is fine, and the city, grand achievement of the living and all the dead who've ever lived here, is fine too, and robust." (SAT: 77) Similar to Christine Brooke-Rose's character Ulysses, for whom there has been a decisive change of thinking due to his knowledge of cultural and technological innovation (NXT: 51), also Perowne ponders on the emergence of technological achievements. This link between natural changeability by natural selection and human transformation rather pays heed to the environmental determinism of Social Darwinism. Both characters indirectly introduce their own being in the context of evolution of which the contemporary city seems to have become the focal point offering all the aspects that enhance the pace of human development. And it also gives rise to the question whether, if not an 'urbanite race', at least an urban culture, has yet again progressed due to new postmodern urban circumstances and environmental changes. Childs (2009: 29) shows that Perowne defines urbanites as gods (SAT: 77) and denigrates Baxter to an ape-like existence (SAT: 88), while the squash match with his colleague becomes a battle for the survival of the fittest (SAT: 103-109).

Childs (2009: 27), however, also points out, that Darwinism plays a more ambivalent role in the novel: on the one hand, Perowne's understanding of human agency – and urbanites' vigilance for that matter – is based on strictly biological terms, on the other hand Darwin is part of the culture of human knowing and his biography as a narrative is intrinsically part of humanist education. For Ian McEwan (2005: 7-8) himself, Darwin is an intensely communicative prose writer, whose scientific work – like Perowne's – permeated his whole thinking. Due to his professional scientific mindset, he has a distaste for fantasy – or as Currie (2007: 125–126) argues – experiments of time. *Saturday*'s main character is a literary ignoramus who is strongly sceptical towards fiction as a relevant form of knowledge. Deeming literary imagination a secondary mental activity in the construction of consciousness, the protagonist stands in strict opposition to the other members of the Perowne family, especially his poet father-in-law and daughter Daisy (cf. Head 2007: 178, 192; Currie 2007: 125-126): "This notion of Daisy's, that people can't 'live' without stories, is simply not true. He is living proof." (SAT: 68)

The only aesthetic representation of the city Perowne believes in is a musical utopia painted in the lyrics of his son Theo's band performance. The group creates a musical map, which for Perowne forms an encompassing image in the confusion of his Saturday in London: "And here it is now, a coherent world, everything fitted at last." (SAT: 172) This musical and poetic representation of London briefly contributes to his understanding of urban space as well as permitting him to "inhabit a kind of imagined community" (Bradley & Tate 2010: 29). But later, when Baxter penetrates the family home and threatens the Perownes, Henry is unable to cast off his professional mindset and fails to comprehend the minds of the other family members. It is only through Daisy's recitation of Arnold's "Dover Beach" that Perowne is enabled to alter his perspective and see through the others' eyes. While during the first reading he feels a metamorphosis brought on by the rhythm of the words and gains a deeper understanding for his pregnant daughter, in Daisy's second reading and slightly altered performance, Perowne sees Baxter on the shore and "it's through Baxter's ears that he hears the sea's 'melancholy, long withdrawing roar, retreating [...].'" (SAT: 221-222) Thus, poetry not only evokes powerful emotions, but enables one to alter one's position and enter the mind of someone else. Most importantly, literature thereby opens up an "intersubjective space" (K. Wall 2008: 787) in which the character becomes confronted with a different point of view makes it possible for him to feel compassion for the other (cf. Michael 2009: 45; Childs 2009: 25; Weidle 2009: 60; Bradley & Tate 2010: 22; Green 2010: 676).

In this sense, literature represents a powerful medium of meta-consciousness: it does not only allow for a direct view of the city's surfaces (brain) but enables the character to inhabit other minds. Being confronted with unfamiliar or alien ways of perceiving, interpreting, and evaluating furthers tolerance, human interaction and urban sociability. McEwan (2005: 6) argues in regard to his epigraph from a novel by the American author Saul Bellow that "[a] reader may not understand from the inside every specific of Herzog's condition – a mid-twentieth-century American, a Jew, a city dweller, a divorcé, an alienated intellectual – nor might a young reader sympathize with the remorse of early middle age" but "however strange these people are, we will understand them readily enough to be able to appreciate their strangeness." (*Ibid.*: 5) In other words, the recognition of different viewpoints through the transposition of a thirdspace lies at the heart of urban tolerance and consequently is the basis for the collective consciousness (cf. Egbert 2009: 243; Weidle 2009: 60). Kathleen Wall (2008: 784) comments: "Had he [Perowne] had [Kafka's] Metamorphosis in mind rather than a diagnosis as he approached Baxter, their little bit of urban drama might not have gotten out of control." Because literature encodes both "cultural and genetic inheritance" (McEwan 2005: 11), it offers a "window into the collective mind of a society" and thus exposes the "malleability of human nature" (*ibid.*: 15). In regard to McEwan's (*ibid.*: 11) view on this "gene-culture coevolution", Green (2010: 70-71) reads *Saturday* as a new form of science fiction, which shows how poetry can bring scientific understanding to the mind by employing narrative techniques, cultural notions and post-millennial ideas about consciousness. As mentioned before, for Kamm (1996: 96) Cultural Studies aim to acquire "cultural meta-knowledge". In this respect, like no other novel besides Proust's *A la recherche du temps perdu* mentioned in this analysis, Ian McEwan's *Saturday* directly engages in a literary and philosophical discussion of standardisations of thinking.

Exemplifying the capacity of art to represent consciousness, to transmit feeling, and to initiate compassion, tolerance and sociability, *Saturday* also defines literature as a "richer way of knowing" (Green 2010: 62). The novel emphasises the possibility to reach beyond the literal because it discloses a thirdspace of intersubjective and transmutable ways of knowing which reaches a greater depth of understanding the human condition; in this case the text specifically offers "a glimpse of the undefinable, the indeterminable" (*ibid.*: 70) state of being urban. Beyond the binary of the two cultures (science versus art) the mental turn of the protagonist Henry Perowne towards the "third culture" (Head 2007: 200) of an interdisciplinary way of knowing comes to define his new open-mindedness and enhanced urbane character. Thus, science and literature are represented as complementary forms of knowledge (cf. *ibid.*: 19-20; Green 2010: 59-60) which develop a significant dynamic prerequisite for an understanding of the postmodern metropolis. Whereas literature has the capacity to create feeling and expose the contents of the mind, science is able to detect structures and processes of the brain. In regard to urban mentality we can interpret the unfolding dialectic as an ambivalence of proximity and distance. Urban intellectualisation and rationality offer a protective mechanism to gain distance and channel the influx of stimuli, while empathy developed by literary socialisation prevents the city from anomie.

Furthermore, refuting the strong division between science and art, *Saturday* also conflates reality with fiction – the novel becomes a laboratory of the mind. When Perowne overlooks the city and strives to see the technological achievements of the twenty-first century in historical terms, he wishes that he were able to see the scene through the eyes of the prodigies of English Enlightenment, but fails to do so because "[h]e doesn't have the lyric gift to see beyond it – he's a realist, and can never escape." (SAT: 168) What he initially fails to see is that he (I/eye) is already overtly lyrical in taking in the aesthetics and the feeling of the twenty-first-century post-Fordist technological environment.

All in all, equivalent to this book's methodological approach of deciphering urban mentality, for McEwan (2005: 18) "[l]iterature must be our anthropology". In his article on "Literature, Science, and Human Nature", McEwan (*ibid.*: 5) states:

Greatness in literature is more intelligible and amenable to most of us than greatness is science. [...] We have the privilege of unmediated contact. From the first sentence, we come into a presence, and we can see for ourselves the quality of a particular mind; in a matter of minutes we may read the fruits of a long forgotten afternoon, an afternoon's work done in isolation, a hundred and fifty years ago. And what was once an unfolding personal secret is now ours.

Therefore, *Saturday* unfolds a parallelism between the intellectualisation of neurosurgery and the legibility of fiction. By judging, evaluating and distancing, Perowne not only structures, but constantly reads the metropolis around him. The combined transformative agency of intelligibility achieves to form a consciousness appropriate to the postmodern space of flux. The frame (of mind) through which the protagonist looks out of the window down at the London city-square in the morning has been inevitably altered by the spatio-temporal flow of twenty-four hours transgressing the contemporary metropolis. Ironically, the knowledge of London created by the omniscient narrator allows us access to the mind of Londoners in the beginning, but is deconstructed throughout the novel to expose the unreliability of the character's perspective, only to return to the same yet newly felt quasi-omniscient perspective at the end of the text.

6.3.5 (Sub)Textual Structures of Mentality

Contemporary discourses about the city are wrought by notions of urban disorientation and loss, consequently accompanied by anxiety and terror. Against this background, the question arises how people are able to navigate the labyrinth of the city, structure its multifariousness, and even create a sense of metropolitan idiosyncrasy. The chapter on "Navigating the Flux" suggests that regarding the functional aspect of mentality as an organon of organisation, orientation, relief of strain, alignment, regulation, and integration we can delineate various mental tools that are employed by the urban characters/narrators of contemporary novels or integrated in the narrative structure. The social construction of urban reality has been specifically looked at by various perceptual processes that influence the idiosyncratic and complex experiences of urbanites resulting in their individual consciousness as necessarily kaleidoscopic. The analysis of Geoff Nicholson's *Bleeding London*, Christine-Brooke Rose's *Next*, China Miéville's *King Rat* and Ian McEwan's *Saturday* has deciphered a surprising variety of perceptual processes and agencies of urban re-orientation.

More thoroughly than ever before, the city today is represented by maps. While the narrative of *Bleeding London* follows the schema of the map, urban mis-representations are shown to be intrinsically subjective and idiosyncratic because the personally constructed mental maps always consist of the in-between of *carte* and *parcours*. Yet through fragmentation and distanciation, the abstractions of mental maps are necessary to stabilise perception and serve as a filter against postmodern urban overload. In this sense, the symbol, schema, or textual structure of the map is very much engrained in the everyday perceptual experience of the contemporary metropolis.

In opposition, the analysis of *Next* has concentrated on the touring practices of the largely homeless cast of characters. The novel lays bare the parallelism between walking/writing, perceiving/reading, as well as city and language/text/narrative. Black (1997: 21) argues that the medium of the map is different in its capacity for orientation from that of the written text, "because the first offers simultaneity of form and impression whereas the second provides a sequential organization and content", also the continuity of the urban text (in *Next* represented by the continuous stream-of-consciousness) can lead to a strong blunting of the senses and loss of the Self. However, constant vigilance in the form of urban mobility is seen as a prerequisite for a successful urban experience.

Also in China Miéville's *King Rat* mobility and the impressive considerations on the 'fleeting' senses as synaesthetic are emphasised for a better understanding of metropolitan transformability. But constructing a thick texture of synaesthetic sensual experiences is only possible through the interchangeability of perspectives. This phenomenon simultaneously defies both the blunting mechanisms of the contemporary preference for the visual and its emphasis on the spectacular. However, as the novel shows in concord with *Next*, the constant mobility and an ontology of the inbetween which purveys a singular temporal experience of present (or past) induces dangers of apathy and anomie.

Mobility also plays a pivotal role in Ian McEwan's *Saturday*, in which the protagonist's transgressions of the metropolis by car constitutes a particular postmodern *flânerie*. Its spatio-temporal perceptual perspective induces new experiences of proximity and distance, depth and flatness, introspection and urban experience. What is more, as a meta-consciousness novel *Saturday* is self-reflexive about urban perceptual processes and the construction of consciousness, whereby McEwan especially focuses on the pre-verbal processes of mentalese. Nevertheless, similar to Brooke-Rose's "ongoing interest in the changing relationships among science, humanity, and literature" (Harper 2001: 47)[54], he detects the potential of literature for gaining greater understanding of postmodern urbanity. McEwan does not focus on the different meta-narratives, but stresses the complementariness and interchangeability of capacities between both science and art or their significant practices of legibility and intelligibility.

Insofar, all London novels under analysis strongly bring into focus the agency of urban experience by representing urbanites in mental crisis, but not lost or condemned in the rough life of the city in flux. Rather, the denizens rely on specific nonconscious devices that help in navigating the metropolis. These functional parts of mentality include specifically abstracted pre-verbal models, and synaesthetic emotions that are, on the other hand, capable of being translated into conceptual leitmotifs, especially those of map and text. Moreover, these overlapping perceptual processes are depicted as interactive spatial practices, representations, and conceptualisations; hence the production of space is indeed seen as an important aspect of urban vigilance. This urban-generic state of the mind is enhanced by the spatio-temporal movement of subject positions grounded in an equivalence of urban mobility and urban mental space.

---

54 | In her "Intercom Quartet" including the novels *Amalgamemnon* (1984), *Xorander* (1986), *Verbivore* (1990) and *Textermination* (1990), Brooke-Rose takes into account the "effect of technological innovation on pure thought process and our ability to communicate." (Birch 1994: 114) She particularly regards the media and communication technology which is underpinned by a consideration of the novel's role in a technological society (cf. Harper 2001: 47).

Contemporary urban space is generally conceived as open, mobile, interactive and fluent, fathoming key metaphors of transitivity and porosity, rhythm and daily practices, *flânerie* and writing (cf. Amin & Thrift 2002: 3-7) which constitute the traditional and fundamental opposition to the city as settlement or container (cf. Robins 1993: 316). In that respect, representations of the urban rely on perceptions from the position of transport as inwardly stable and outwardly transitional and mobile devices, such as the moving Underground, train, car, body, and mind. Moreover, oscillating between centrality and marginality, perception is represented through spaces that are non-places as devised by Augé, namely classic transit spaces – streets, highways, junctions – or more generally physical, social and mental thirdspaces. These are themselves connected with specific urban 'a-rhythmi-cities' in the sense of unusual or coincidental encounters. Enhanced mobility or the spaces of simultaneous juxtaposition are cinematic as they present a blurred but also seemingly coherent notion of the metropolis. For Ian Chambers (1990: 113), this "cinematographic and phantasmagoric city with its sensuous streets of desire" constitutes a "metropolitan hyperspace", namely a city in which the image has taken over. The visually based overload scenario of the Postmetropolis creates a new defence mechanism against the influx of stimuli which leads to a thorough blunting of the senses and a regression into a form of tunnel vision or "tunnel walking, with its narrow sightlines and its limited possibilities for deviation from an already laid-out route" (Ekman 2005: 30).

In conclusion, I argue that London-specific mental dispositions concerning the perception of the postmodern metropolis rely on the constant interchangeability or transmutability of subject positions between stasis and mobility. Insofar, the nonconscious structures of mentality can be defined as significantly (sub)textual. They are not only textual in the sense of recreating patterns, but also in the recombination of the signifiers or the metaphoricity of the signified. While this seems generic in the sense that it applies to most postmodern metropolitan areas, it has been shown that the idiosyncrasies of London spatialities offer specific locales for restructuring mental maps. This phenomenon also devises the postmodern urbanite in general and the Londoner in specific both as unhomely and residual in character, or as a homeless wanderer who is not so much lost in the metropolis, but like Simmel's stranger constantly imprisoned inbetween, on the move, and addicted to an endless hunt for knowing the city.

6.4 The Palimpsestuous City

> To even the amateur student of London tradition the great city of present is like an old parchment which has been written on and erased, re-covered with script and re-erased, until what exists today shows beneath the latest superficial transcript microscopic traces of all the romantic stories written on it since the hour when it first lay immaculate beneath the pen of the mediaeval cleric. The very lay of the land shows how much of a palimpsest London is. The dust of the centuries has drifted round it, gradually raising the ground level so that the records of the past are packed in layers beneath the pavements of today. These strata are dear to the heart of the archaeologist – the ashes from the fire of 1666, the relics of the days between Shakespeare and Chaucer, the traces of mediaeval life, and finally the sign of Norman, Anglo-Saxon, and even Roman London.
> (Boynton 1913: 271)

As was noted before, the image of the palimpsest is employed by contemporary literature to express the multi-layered chronotopic character of the urban with its various configurations of visibility and legibility. Otherwise a purely academic metaphor, the palimpsest is extremely fruitful in literary and cultural analysis as well as in approaches of the history of mentalities because it helps to focus on the consciousness of historical marginality and cultural alterity hidden beneath or within the strata of the dominant cultural text. Palimpsestic reading as a procedure of textual archaeology brings to light invisible everyday practices. I would like to suggest that the palimpsest presents the master metaphor in contemporary urban fiction.[55] Recalling the assumption of Peter Burke, this implies that the palimpsest is a major aspect of London mentality insofar as its specific way of thinking generates a severe impact on Londoners' way of life.

This chapter on "The Palimpsestuous City" explores the historical, (psycho)geographical, socio-cultural, intertextual, and hyperreal metropolis as represented in Ge-

55 | Other critics have emphasised the importance of multi-dimensional system of layering as paradigmatic to postmodern London literature (e.g. cf. Breuner 1991; Teske 1999; Wachinger 1999; Phillips 2006). I employ the concept of the "palimpsestuous city" in the sense of a dynamic structure (cf. Pleßke 2006: 85); seen from the perspective of dynamic space, palimpsestiousness always implies both Being and Becoming. According to Dillon (2007b: 3-4) "palimpsestuous" is an adjective that refers to the involution and entanglement of various texts inhabiting the palimpsest as a result of palimpsesting various texts. In other words, for her "palimpsestuous" denotes the structure, while "palimpsestic" denotes the process. For the relevance of the metaphor in regard to other cities see Alfred Thomas' recent *Prague Palimpsest. Writing, Memory, and the City* (2010).

off Nicholson's *Bleeding London* (1997), Nicholas Royle's *The Matter of the Heart* (1997), China Miéville's *King Rat* (1998), Conrad Williams' *London Revenant* (2004), and Matthew de Abaitua's *The Red Men* (2006). Moreover, in order to refute the notion that the palimpsest is either genre-specific, merely an element of the synoptic novel, or mainly relegated to 1990s literature, I will also include Jane Stevenson's *London Bridges* (2000), Monica Ali's *Brick Lane* (2003), and Ian McEwan's *Saturday* (2005). While each novel is allocated to one of the sub-chapters, *Bleeding London*, which has variously been analysed in the context of London as palimpsest (cf. Rawlinson 2002; Mergenthal 2002; Schlaeger 2003a; Dreyer 2006; Chilton 2007; Altnöder 2009; Deny 2009), will serve a lead analysis for each interpretative aspect.

6.4.1 Historical Layering

As elaborated before, the postmodern metropolis and its architecture are overtly palimpsestuous in nature, which means that "cities often display a mixed layering of times in which carcasses of twenty- and thirty-year-old structures stand alongside buildings that have aged over centuries." (Olalquiaga 1992: 65) On the one hand, the urban materiality of monuments renders time visible, while on the other hand, the cityscape in analogy to a manuscript text becomes a palimpsest of history inscribing itself in "a process of addition, amendment, and perpetual alteration." (Crang 1996: 430) The city as palimpsest is more than a mere chronotope because in its space-time compression it conflates various historical layers and obliterates temporal boundaries. The past exists as material fragments in both synchrony and juxtaposition with the present because "[p]alimpsests are created by a process of layering – of erasure and superimposition" (Dillon 2007b: 12). Due to the constant writing and overwriting of the cityscape and the resulting spatialisation of temporality by historic landmarks, the metropolis is transformed to a palimpsest of recollection and memory. Hence, postmodern London not only constitutes a comprehensive archive of memory as in De Quincey's (1968b: 344) understanding, but is transformed to an encompassing *lieu de mémoire*, where the contemporary obsession with history and memory becomes an instrument of constructing the city's marketable image. I therefore understand the multifarious material historicity of the city as the first notable aspect of the palimpsestuous city: the metropolis is "the *locus of history*" (Debord 1994: 125), a place where history is made and consciousness of the past is produced; the "city *tells* and *sums up* history" (Mancini 2003: 167) hence interweaving stratifications of past, present, and future in the urban texture and creating a palimpsest in which London's contradictory historical narratives find expression.

Historical Overabundance

Geoff Nicholson's novel *Bleeding London* (1997) is a postmodern homage to London in which the metropolis and its palimpsestuous urban body constitutes a dominating metaphor throughout. Especially the polymorphous lexical and popular discourses of representing and preserving the city, for example by maps, puzzles, guide books, tourist walks, city literature, diaries, landmarks, etc. lend the text's city the characteristic of a palimpsest. Concerning temporal setting or entanglement, *Bleeding London* features various allusions to contemporary history, accumulations of historical events, density of historical monuments and famous Londoners, or personal memory. Historical layering is mainly provided by chapter 23, "Blitz" (BLL: 210-213), and chapter 29, "Fire" (BLL: 249-253) (cf. Mergenthal 2002: 126). Whereas the former recounts the experiences of the protagonist's father during the German bombing of London, the latter is a dream-sequence, triggered by Stuart's aspirations of writing a diary like Samuel Pepys. In this respect, Mergenthal (2002: 126) speaks of "personal representations – the city represented through its denizens, past and present". The two chapters stress the interrelation between history and personal biography, the metropolis and the urbanite. While Stuart's memory of his father's experience during the Blitz is inevitably connected with a collective memory of Londoners, his later dream resurrects London's past and appropriates collective memory to an individual "after-image" (Resina 2003: 12-13; cf. Schlaeger 2003a). Hence, the novel emphasises the contingency of historical memory, where cultural practices of palimpsesting create an ambivalent dynamic that questions temporal linearity. The Great Fire and the German air-raid are major disruptive events in London's history; both erased large parts of the city's architectural space and destroyed artefacts of its material history:

> The turrets and spires, the dome of St Paul's, the tower of Big Ben are like targets, chess pieces waiting to be picked off. There is no way of missing. Every stray bomb will score a hit, will destroy something precious, some landmark or piece of the city's past; if not the docks and the munitions factories, then a Wren church, a row of Georgian houses, a fragment of Roman wall. (BLL: 211)

Paradoxically, it is exactly this destruction and erasure which add both to the mental (memorial) and physical (material) palimpsest of the metropolis. In his dreamscape, Stuart imaginatively re-enacts the Great Fire of 1666, again breaking out in the East, but this time it is translocated to the Docklands. Not only does the fire consume the postmodern architecture, but in his emotional vision Stuart becomes the saviour of modern London by pulling down landmark architecture, such as the NatWest Tower, Centrepoint, King's Cross Station, Canary Wharf, and Buckingham Palace: "All over London buildings were disappearing, like pieces taken off a chess board, and only now did Stuart notice that all the buildings that had gone were the ones he hated most." (BLL: 253) In their common metaphor of London as chess board with pieces added and taken away, the two chapters draft the destruction of the cityscape as a prerequisite for its reinvention – employing the vision of London as phoenix, a symbol of the eternal city. The ultimate chapter of *Bleeding London* – "Boadicea's London" (BLL: 346) – recounts the destruction and purification of Londinium by the warrior queen remembered through the centuries by "a layer of red earth, the ashes she left behind" (BLL: 347) and thereby premonitions the renewed metamorphosis of the postmodern metropolis at the end of the twentieth century.

As different time levels intertwine in the city's texture, the master metaphor of the palimpsest emphasises the character of the metropolis as becoming. Both examples create a sense that the past never really disappeared but is still present in a transformed and 'up-dated' phenomenology. Nothing ever seems to be really forgotten in the city, it just needs to be excavated and unravelled. In *Bleeding London*, specifically the protagonist Stuart London, a history graduate, resurrects the past and unravels its new connotations in the London of the present. The *flâneur* here envisions an ecstatic eradication of relations between subject and object (cf. Voss 1988: 41). His name – Stuart London – denotes a historical epoch of the city which objectifies the carrier to a mere signifier (BLL: 67). During his walks around London, Stuart invokes historical events and traces reminders of historical personae that have become part of the urban fabric in street names and monuments:

> I saw statues of Boadicea, John Kennedy and Bomber Harris. [...] I saw the solid, sturdy monuments to trade and its names, the Hoover factory, the Oxo Tower, the Tate Gallery; sweet and sour reminders of empire. I saw the slew of history, of kings and pretenders, developers and reformers, visionaries and bureaucrats, martyrs and wide boys. I read the obvious eponyms, the roads named after Cromwell, Wellington, Addison, Albert, Mountbatten, Mandela. (BRL: 27)

Consequently, Stuart charts London as a major locus of history and simultaneously exposes the interconnections of local metropolitan histories and global politics. What is more, he registers London's history from A-Z as the past is intertwined with present everyday practices and acknowledges how public and private history form a thick texture characterised by erasures, traces as well as omissions. While the buildings have been transformed and the context changed, the past still resonates in these places through the memory of the contemporary spectator. Regarding formerly famous inhabitants of certain sites Stuart argues:

> When we say Edward Gibbon lived here, or this is where Elizabeth Browning met Byron, or this is where Christopher Marlowe was killed, or this is where Samuel Johnson walked, what do we mean by 'here'? The here has gone just as surely as the now. Even if they still exist, the buildings they inhabited have been changed out of recognition. The streets are no longer the same. They have been modernized, transformed. (BLL: 193-194)

Hence, London is a place of change, growth, decay, redevelopment and a site of erasure which will outlive its inhabitants in an unknown yet already imagined future. These (dis)continuities of the metropolis are taken up by the protagonist in direct reference to the palimpsest: "The city, it seems to me, must always be a palimpsest, a series of erasures, of new beginnings, obliterations, of temporary preservations and misguided reconstructions. Much of it is guesswork. There is no authorized text." (BLL: 194) Paradoxically, Stuarts' own business "The London Walker", which offers professional guided walking tours through the metropolis as commercialised tourist attraction, seems to provide for exactly such a form of authorised London historicity. But the plethora of tours from the Shakespeare Walk, from Pepys's to Virginia Woolf's, or from the Rock 'n' Roll Walk to Beatles' London (BLL: 74-75) deconstructs the notion of one coherent historical map, indicating instead the overlapping of spatial and temporal traces on the texture of the city. Furthermore, from the perspective of a scholarly historian interested in grand narratives (i.e. by visiting every museum of the metropolis), Stuart quickly returns to the historical anthropology of London's streets (BLL: 76-77). Consequently, even the postmodern metropolis still exists as a historical memory-city, which "concentrates and mixes great history with individual histories [...]." (Augé 1997: 16)

(De)Palimpsesting the City

Jane Stevenson's debut novel *London Bridges* (2000)[56] pays tribute to the classic English detective caper. Set in late 1990s London with some minor excursions to Scotland and Greece, the story revolves around a forgotten bequest and a valuable South Bank real estate owned by the Greek monastery of St Athos. Stevenson intelligently combines retracing the history of spatial ownership and the private puzzle of solving a murder with the quasi-archaeological task of deciphering London's palimpsest. According to the *Chicago Tribune*, "she makes palpable the layers of history waiting to be discovered in the very fabric of the contemporary city." (Anon. 2003) In the context of London's (property) development before the millennium, which boosted both urban heritage culture and postmodern architecture, the novel thereby variously problematises the city's ambivalent relation between measures of progress and preservation: architectural, literary, archival, and anachronistic.

One of the novel's six central characters, the lawyer Edward Lupset, is mandated to resolve the title of a South Bank estate for a Greek client, and lured by the worth of the plot of land he sets upon a mission to solve the 'mystery' of the trust of St Michael Graecorum. Following the clues given in the client's letter, he uncovers important historical documents archived in the law firm's basement and preserved for posterity (LBR: 16-17). Further traces finally lead him to the old aristocrat and city banker Eugenides, whose family's business, located in "the depths of the City" (LBR: 23), was already well established in the eighteenth century. With the assistance of Eugenides' personal memory, the history of St Michael is reconstructed: its origin lies in the Greek trade between Venice and London around 1540 and the subsequent development of a Greek community in the metropolis. The Orthodox church was built in 1667 after the Great Fire, converted to an Anglican church in 1886 and finally destroyed during the Blitz in 1940 (LBR: 27-28). Thus, the historical palimpsest in *London Bridges* is arranged on the same events of destruction and recreation as in *Bleeding London* – the Great Fire and the Blitz put into the context of London's transforming materiality during the 1990s.

A parallel narrative shows how research into a private collection at the British Library has brought the gay classics professor Dr Sebastian Raphael to Mount Athos, where he is looking for the records of a lost poem by a famous Greek poet from the sixth century. Including the text in an epoch-making book, he intends to further his academic career. Similar to a palimpsest, the poem only exists as a medieval copy, rediscovered between the pages of an ancient text. The historio-textual traces equally lead Sebastian back to Eugenides' London home where, amidst the outstanding private collection, he finds the ancient manuscript (LBR: 56-58). Because the poem's theme makes it an apt subject of contemporary gender, queer, and transnational studies, the Greek Eugenides, who was not able to come out of the closet during his lifetime, observes: "Perhaps its time has come" (LBR: 58).

The third trace surmounting the story of St Michael concerns the Cockney community activist Hattie Luke, who works for the London Bridge Trust. In contrast to Edwards's self-obsessed and Sebastian's egoistic motives, Hattie promotes the work of the charity as community oriented: "We're for London, and our basic question is, is a new project going to make London life better or worse." (LBR: 87) On one of her walks

---

56 | In the following *London Bridges* will be abbreviated to LBR.

through Southwark's "world of soot-stained Victorian and Fifties flats" (LBR: 64) she incidentally comes across a garden grown on the wasteland of St Michael's rubble.

Once these pieces and layers of London's historical palimpsest have been retraced, uncovered, and deciphered by multiple characters, the novel engages them in a palimpsestic restructuring of London's materiality. Involved in restoration work at St Lawrence Jewry, an archaeologist discovers the remains of a seventeenth century fountain brought to London by Levant merchants for the coronation of Charles II (LBR 90). In order to reintegrate the artefact into London's everyday life, Hattie and Sebastian assist in reassembling and translocating the sculpture to Southwark, adding yet another layer to the eclectic postmodern cityscape (LBR: 93). Set in the garden of the former site owned by the Greek church, the fountain will eventually serve as a memorial for the London Greek community (LBR: 152). Thus London's history does not stop in the present, but by building textual bridges from the past to the future of the city continually rewrites the temporal palimpsest of the city. The cityscape in *London Bridges* is narrated as always resurrected and invented anew.

Although professionally engaged in the Southwark development and reconstructing the church site according to a *lieu de mémoire*, Hattie openly criticises the new urban policy of "bringing things back" (LBR: 63). In regard to the new Globe Theatre as a slice of Elizabethan London, she draws the difference between a historical city as a "tourist thing" (LBR: 63) of pure commodity and the eighteenth-century cottages in the shadow of the theatre where the historical city is still part of London's way of life. With the Docklands, the Thames, and the South Bank rendered amenities, she casts a critical eye on palimpsesting techniques that construct a themed cityscape in which Londoners end up "like a pack of Red Indians on a reservation, playing at being ourselves." (LBR: 64) The objective seems to lie in the idea not only of conserving, but renewing the city's history by a recombination of past and present, to both grant an imaginary and material future to London's everyday life at the end of the twentieth century and infuse the metropolis with new vitality. The novel describes a variety of historio-architectural palimpsestuous spaces Londoners inhabit (LBR: 89, 102, 166, 258), and whose essence is symbolically represented by the Eugenides residence at Garlic Court in the centre of the City. Its historicity is built on the survival of various epochs:

> The houses had, perhaps, once accommodated rural landowners with business in the city. They had subsequently stagnated into Dickensian squalor, and still bore the scars, though post-war affluence had breathed new life into the old bricks, rosy beneath their layer of grime. (LBR: 23)

Urban architecture is left with a patina of scars and grime indicating death, yet it also represents the vitality of the preserved layers beneath.

Another character, the Australian graduate student Jeanene, explores the city from her non-European perspective, and because she comes from a country that in a metropolitan sense is devoid of history, she is overwhelmed by the spatio-temporal specificity of London. Nonetheless, her knowledge of the city is strongly conditioned by English literary history and while walking through Shoreditch, Jeanene instantly connects the borough with the Bard: "Look at this notice beside the door. It says it's been here since 1462. Shakespeare probably drank here. [...] Even the bars turn out to be historic." (LBR: 206) Similar to the classicist Sebastian, she insists on the spatio-temporal capacity of literary representations and the archival character of literature because its palimpsestuous structures inhabit the potential of orientation in the postmodern metropolis: "The London she has been learning her way around [...] has sometimes seemed grotesquely familiar, mapped out by Eng Lit 101 from Shakespeare to Dickens [...]." (LBR: 267) In her mind, spatial text and city text add to one another offering quotations as landmarks. By contrast, the belt of London's M25 is just a jumble of non-places – spaces of non-palimpsestic materiality. The sameness and repetitiveness of its architecture renders the urban disorienting so that Jeanene feels displaced to the non-historicity of any Exopolis: "the featureless city [...] was no part of that world of literary reference and cultural heritage. It was more like Sydney, in fact, because it simply existed; mile after mile of it, without any cues or reference points whatsoever." (LBR: 267) On the one hand, the non-place as part of urban history without the depth of temporal layers is opposed to the rich fluidity of London throughout the rest of the novel. On the other hand, their inability to harbour the past is compared to the density of time accumulated in special temporal archives or space-time capsules.

For example, Eugenides[57] is depicted as an anachronism who has lost touch with the contemporary world, its modes of speech, and everyday life (LBR: 29, 40, 54). Similar to the interior of his house, which has been left unchanged for eons, Eugenides, who has "not crossed the river for a number of years" (LBR: 28), is both spatially isolated and historically entombed in this "time capsule in the middle of the City" (LBR: 131). Thereby, Eugenides recognises the intrinsic paradox of the palimpsest's atemporality, namely its archival layering of past, present, future and its unfolding dynamics between erasure and overwriting. By contrast, the lawyer Edward assumes that the search for Greek treasure of a former London is "forgotten by absolutely everybody" (LBR: 31) and thereby underestimates the intrinsic urban flows of time, which depend on unearthing and reviving 'lost' (hi)stories:

> The idea that the past itself could hold concealed wolf-traps, snares and spring-guns, that the British Library in holding the past, might also hold the future, was a notion wholly and absolutely alien to his theory of what constituted knowledge. (LBR: 45-46)

Due to its various places of memory the city itself seems to make sure that nothing will ever be forgotten. As all traces lead to Eugenides, the novel stresses the importance of anachronistic spaces that serve as spaces of preservation. Moreover, paradoxically, the stability and traditionalism of these archival loci is shown as essential for initiating progress. Like the palimpsest, they hold the information under a protective veneer shining through, being at last uncovered through time, but potentially leading to a reinterpretation of its historical texture and urban semantics.

Similar to Eugenides, the monks of St Athos in their insular existence are variously identified as anachronisms because their notion of time "is essentially cyclical, often [they] have little or no sense of history." (LBR: 36) Without any interest in matters be-

---

57 | In regard to the archival character of literature, it is interesting to recollect that the figure of the Smyrna merchant Eugenides is part of T.S. Eliot's seminal modernist London poem "The Wasteland" (1922).

yond the monastery, their knowledge of London is out of date, but in contrast to the urbane aristocrat, the monks are not concerned with the idiosyncrasies of history at all (LBR: 42, 181). Instead, monasticism is described as a reflection of eternity – or a constant presence (LBR: 185) – which makes transparent the temporal mental gap between medieval orthodoxy and postmodern secularism. Nevertheless, the monks' persistent routine once again stresses the significance of space-time capsules as artefacts of timelessness on the one hand, and anachronisms as archives of preservation on the other hand. Indeed, the stagnation of selected places offers the potential of metropolitan transformation and urban progress.

Both Geoff Nicholson's *Bleeding London* and Jane Stevenson's *London Bridges* explore the thick texture of London's historical palimpsest. From the manifold stories, personae, events, and traces, the Great Fire and the Blitz are applied to the postmodern metropolis in analogy to fragmentary erasure and overwriting, death and resurrection. In reference to Dillon (2007b: 125), the concept of the palimpsest "structurally *embodies*" perpetual openness necessary for the reassessment of urban history and its present as well as future survival. In its paradox of erasure and preservation, the palimpsest not simply stresses postmodern architectural eclecticism but specifically outlines the multi-dimensionality of metropolitan life. The historical palimpsest becomes a metaphor that unites thinking the postmodern city as ultimately fluid, yet wrought by idiosyncratically traced structures which stabilise orientation within the metropolis. Conversely, London characters are concerned about the commodification of history and the "hypertrophy of memory" (Huyssen 2003: 3) because it harbours the danger of destroying present existences or leading to a potential loss of the Self. However, as will be shown in the next sub-chapter, urbanites' disorientation might paradoxically indeed be the mental key to finding places of perseverance.

6.4.2 Psychogeographical Tracing

The last sub-chapter has established how the London's urban way of life is coupled with a sense of "chronological resonance in which past events are continuously replayed" (Coverley 2006: 27). The palimpsest stresses the possibility of uncovering illimitable, unexpected inscriptions of past, present, and future within the urban texture. Urban time is henceforth transformed to a highly complex spatial texture of stories, meanings, pictures, voices, memories, texts, and traces. Thus, if metropolitan time is multifaceted in space, then places within the urban space of temporal flows hold unknown secrets. In that sense, London's spatial palimpsest constitutes a polymorphous enigma that needs to be detected and decoded. In the words of Phil Baker (2003: 326): "Its overlap with histories and myths of place is a further way of gaining a purchase on the inhospitable environment of the metropolis. People want to inscribe marks and find traces in the city." Beyond the visible, they determine a unique spirit of place, or *genius loci*. According to Baker (*ibid.*: 324), "[t]he feeling of place is inseparable from the meaning of place, often within personal cartographies that have their own landmarks." The urban texture constructed by "dreams, nightmares, desires, visions, and repressed, hidden, unexpressed, or unheard thoughts" (Mancini 2003: 171) can be fathomed by practices of psychogeography which uncover the emotional atmosphere of particular places.

The idea of a psychogeography depends on categories of movement, iconography, observation, and atmosphere. Concerning the uncovering and deciphering of the city's iconography, MacFarlane (2005: 3) advises the psychogeographer to be "alert to the happenstance of metaphors, watch for visual rhythms, coincidences, analogies, family resemblances, the changing mood of the street." London encompasses an array of historical trails, landmarks of memories, dreams, and visions as well as layers of voices, objects, signs, inscriptions and allusions to books, films, works of art or associations with stories, events, and people and thereby constitutes not only a place of "endless signification", but according to Schlaeger (2003a: 55) resembles a "poly-palimpsestuous site". A geography premised on the iconography of the metropolis is additionally rendered idiosyncratic by the varied practices of observation, such as individual cognitive mappings, whereby the environment becomes interspersed with emotion. This "psychotopographical nature of London" (Wolfreys 2002: 195) opens possibilities to understand the persistent feeling and the mental structures the metropolis imposes upon its citizens.

Due to these requisites it is not surprising that the genesis and development of psychogeography is from the beginning strongly intertwined with the city, urban writing, and the metaphor of the palimpsest. The literary tradition of psychogeography can be traced back to Daniel Defoe's *Journal of a Plague Year* (1722), while classic psychogeographical practices are retrospectively said to begin with Thomas De Quincey's *Confessions of an Opium Eater* (1821).[58] In the 1950s Guy Debord and the French Situationists adopted De Quincey's navigational metaphor of intoxicated *flânerie* to the random drift of *dérive*. For Debord (1955: 1), psychogeography initially means a new urban practice that is sensitive to hidden stories or encrypted events and that is able to see through the society of spectacle.[59]

The contemporary literary popularity of psychogeography owes most to London writers Iain Sinclair and Peter Ackroyd.[60] In Iain Sinclair's mind, the term psychogeography describes a "way of thinking and dealing with how the city emerges." (Cit.

---

58 | Other psychogeographers *avant la lettre* include Wordsworth and Coleridge, the Surrealists, Baudelaire, Benjamin, Kafka, or Beckett. For more on the history and theory of psychogeography or further texts see P. Baker (2003) and Chilton (2007), but especially Merlin Coverley's *Psychogeography* (2006).

59 | According to Guy Debord's (1955: 1) original definition, psychogeography is "the study of the precise laws and specific effects of the geographical environment, whether consciously organized or not, on the emotions and behavior of individuals." The psychogeographer aimlessly drifting along idiosyncratic paths charges upon places of distinct psychic atmospheres and perceives changes in the ambience of certain urban zones.

60 | In London, psychogeography gained currency during the early 1990s when the metropolis saw the founding of the London Psychogeographical Association (LPA; 1992-1997). Examples of psychogeographical writing by Iain Sinclair include *Lud Heat* (1975), *White Chappell, Scarlett Tracings* (1987), *Downriver* (1991), *Lights Out for the Territory* (1997), *Liquid City* (1999), *London Orbital* (2002), *London. City of Disappearances* (2009), and *Rodinsky's Room* (1999) together with Rachel Lichtenstein. Sinclair's *Lud Heat* specifically inspired Peter Ackroyd's *Hawskmoor* (1985). Other fictional works on the mythic history of London by Ackroyd are *The House of Doctor Dee* (1993) and *Dan Leno and the Limehouse Golem* (1994). Other notable psychogeographers include the novelists J.G. Ballard, Michael Moorcock, and Will Self,

in Barfield 2008) His interpretation of psychogeography rejects aimless wandering and appropriates the Situationists' idea of strolling to an urban stalker who purposefully journeys the postmodern metropolis with a thesis (cf. Sinclair 1997: 75). In his non-fictional *Lights Out for the Territory* (1997), a journal and multi-discursive assortment of subtexts[61], Sinclair's urban walking decodes the meaning of the urban palimpsest as he uncovers London's secret history through urban iconography while at the same time palimpsesting his own layered version of London.

From a cultural perspective psychogeographical writing before the millennium is primarily a reaction to the urban regeneration initiated during the Thatcher Era and pursued by Blair's politics (cf. MacFarlane 2005: 3). Insofar, Iain Sinclair sees his writing as a tool of resistance against the contemporary socio-cultural politics of erasure and an approach to reclaim London from the perspective of the city's everyday archivists (cf. Barfield 2008).[62] Second, psychogeographical tracing establishes a counter-narrative both to the development of an official city image and the metropolitan paranoia induced by growing urban surveillance (*ibid.*). Third, psychogeographical techniques reinscribe a city which threatens to become illegible or obsolete (cf. P. Baker 2003: 326–328). In other words, the uncovering of *genius loci* and the overwriting of the urban texture by idiosyncratic traces offer a cultural response to an anxiety concerning the spread of non-places. Psychogeography thus represents an attempt to prevent the erasure of place by space as premonitioned by Marc Augé, such as the banalisation of cityscape or the growth of Exurbia (cf. P. Baker 2003: 332; MacFarlane 2005: 4; Ashford 2008: 2; Pogossian 2010: 16)

---

artists Gilbert and George, poet Aidan Dunn, as well as film directors Chris Petit and Patrick Keiller.

61 | For example notes, thoughts, pictures of walks around London, reminiscences of films, reviews of poems, fragments of autobiographies, character studies or urban topography, graffiti, underground publications, crime, marginal artistic endeavours, footnotes, drawings, signs, myths, episodes, histories, impressions, stories, texts, films.

62 | With the publication of Peter Ackroyd's *London: The Biography* (2000), in which explorations of the anthropomorphised metropolis recover links between events, urbanites, activities in past and present and thereby resurrect London's consciousness, psychogeographical writing was fully integrated into the mainstream of British literature. Iain Sinclair comments on the session about psychogeography in the Victoria and Albert Museum London, 8 February 2008: "And so you go on to a point where we are actually sitting here having discussions in the V&A, that's the endgame of this idea, the whole psychogeographic conceit." (Cit. in Barfield 2008) Questioned in what way psychogeography as a geography of resistance also challenged gender constructions, Sinclair points out that various women artists follow a vague psychogeographic form (cf. *ibid.*), for example Rachel Lichtenstein. But in regard to fiction, psychogeography is largely a male domain. Sinclair criticises Will Self's *Independent* column on "PsychoGeography", because it caters to the fact that "[n]ow it's just become this brand name for more or less anything that's vaguely to do with walking or vaguely to do with the city. It's a new form of tourism." (Chapman 2006) For more also see Will Self's *Psychogeography* (2007), which is said to be closer to the spatial excursions by Coleridge and Wordsworth.

This strong link between 1990s London literature, psychogeography and palimpsestuous metaphoricity might lead critics to assume that what I term the 'psychogeographical palimpsest' is a dated image. On the contrary, after the watersheds of 9/11 and 7/7 the trope constitutes a thriving phenomenon especially in contemporary genre fiction. According to Brooke-Rose (cit. in Birch 1994: 123), "palimpsest histories [...] mingl[e] realism with the supernatural and history with spiritual and philosophical reinterpretation". While the etymological meaning of the fantastic refers to making things visible and the uncanny plays a pivotal role when it comes to unearthing the silenced past of the city, psychogeography in reverse is prone to the supernatural, ghostly tropes, and Gothic imagery. Of course the Gothic was already urbanised in the *fin-de-siècle*,[63] but Roger Luckhurst (2003 1: 338) identifies a revival of the metaphoric haunted city in contemporary fiction.[64] He sees these recent portrayals of occult London as obsessions with the "hidden reserves of knowledge" (*ibid.*: 340) and symptomatic for the cultural tenor of the time. In the following I will analyse Geoff Nicholson's *Bleeding London* (1997) for its idiosyncratic palimpsestic mappings, Nicholas Royle's *The Matter of the Heart* (1997) as a typical psychogeographical exploration of the centre of the city, and Conrad Williams' *London Revenant* (2004) in regard to represented images of spectrality, resurrection, and revenance.

Palimpsestic Mappings

Geoff Nicholson's *Bleeding London* has been critically compared to other psychogeographical writings; the novel not only refers to Ackroyd's and Sinclair's psychogeographical excursions – "nobody on the tour would have heard of any of these people" (BLL: 128) – but explicitly appropriates, recontextualises and overwrites their texts in Stuart's "Whitechapel Walk" (BLL: 127-129). While the analysis of the historical palimpsest has brought to light the constant erasures and superimpositions of the urban texture, chapter 6.4.1 has exemplified how the protagonists of *Bleeding London* enlist in various highly idiosyncratic mapping projects. Despite the map's claim of generality and encyclopaedic depiction, the different versions of London mapped out in the novel prove the subjective frame of perception – "seeing it historically, erotically and even murderously" (Harrison 1997). Due to these deconstructions, the characters engage in the subversive practice of "psychogeographical mapping" (Pinder 1996: 405). In reference to the production of psychogeographical maps, which according to Phil Baker (2003: 324) are not "'objective' panoptical" maps, but "private cognitive maps of our customized cities", the analysis of the psychogeographical palimpsest focuses on the spatial displacements and

---

63 | For examples of Victorian Gothic London see R.L. Stevenson's *The Strange Case of Dr Jekyll and Mr Hyde* (1886), Oscar Wilde's *The Picture of Dorian Gray* (1891), Arthur Machen's *The Three Imposters* (1895), and Bram Stoker's *Dracula* (1897).

64 | For the contemporary urban Gothic see for example Christopher Fowler's *Darkest Day* (1993), *Disturbia* (1997), *Soho Black* (1998) and his Bryant & May Mysteries, Will Self's *How the Dead Live* (2000), Michèle Roberts' *In the Red Kitchen* (1990), John Harrison's *The Course of the Heart* (1992), Geoff Nicholson's *Bleeding London* (1997), Nicholas Royle's *Director's Cut* (2000) and *The Matter of the Heart* (1997), China Miéville's *King Rat* (1998) and *Perdido Street Station* (2000), or Matthew de Abaitua's *The Red Men* (2007).

imaginary additionally involved in the mental maps of the three characters. In contrast to Lynch's mental maps, however, these psychogeographic cartographies break with the idea of linearity and the dominance of easily identifiable landscapes (cf. Deny 2009: 257). Not merely concerned with the legibility of urban landmarks these maps lay bare the collision between London's topography and the psychological condition of London characters.

Rendering to his obsessive practice of walking the metropolis, the protagonist Stuart London starts on his monstrous metropolitan tour in order to objectify the democratic social values of the city by levelling the differences of social or historical weight (cf. Dreyer 2006: 73). For Stuart "walking would be an act of reclamation, a way of taming the city, a way of saying that London was open and accessible to everyone, that it held no secrets, no unknowable horrors." (BLL: 78) But his first intent is not to revive the city's idiosyncrasies and unearth its forgotten and repressed secrets in order to reintegrate them into London's urbanity; Stuart rather strives to translate panoramic appropriations of the metropolis to street level, thereby objectifying everyday life and making London domestic, homely and knowable. Because he walks the city with a particular objective, he is nevertheless transformed from voyeur/*flâneur* to psychogeographical stalker (cf. Deny 2009: 244). Once departed on his mapping project, his steps are necessarily appropriated and determined by the materiality of the city. Putting his foot on London's pavements Stuart changes perspectives from the intellectual abstraction of the map to the sensory and emotional practice of walking (*ibid.*: 257). His role is immediately altered from city planner to psychogeographer when he chooses to start at "North Pole Road" (BLL: 84; cf. Dreyer 2006: 65). Due to the rhetorical utterances of his paces left in the streets of London, Stuart creates his very own and personal path through the city, adding to the urban palimpsest. He notices that his plan to objectify the metropolis initiated by physical movement has turned into a combined act of subjective imaginary and memory:

> [Maps are] no longer necessary since I have created a new London, not one made out of stone and brick, tarmac and concrete, but a London created out of memory, imagination and shoe leather. I have dreamed it. I made my dreams come true. (BLL: 29)

He acknowledges that London's palimpsest is not only constituted by layers of history, but does also exist through multiple overwritings of memories and perceptions of the mind (BLL: 301).

Concerning the psychogeographical aspects in the tour revealing connections between the ambiance of a place and the psychology of the urbanite, the novel draws an analogy between Stuart's body and the anthropomorphised metropolis: "I feel at home in the city, I feel part of its fabric. It feels as alive as I do, but with a much longer life-span." (BLL: 302) In this corporeal identification with the city (cf. Altnöder 2009: 303; Deny 2009: 242), the mapping and remapping, writing and rewriting of London's texture not only influences the palimpsest of Stuart's mind, but alters his whole personality. City and identity are represented as necessarily constitutive of each other: "Yes, a man is like a city, a site of erasures, of subsidence, in-fill, subdivision and occasional preservation orders." (BLL: 302) Towards the end of his trip, Stuart notices that by blotting out the streets in his *A-Z*, he has walked himself out of existence and consequently yearns for total erasure in a final suicide mission (BLL: 304, 57, 297). Because he feels dislocated in time, disoriented in space, and alienated from himself, the protagonist "develop[s] a taste for spaces cleansed by plague and fire, by blitzes and bulldozers" (BLL: 29). However, these spatialised urban *horror vacui* offer neither stability for the formation of identity nor relief for a cathartic crisis, but rather present capsules of space-time compression connected to self-destruction.

The city's "erotic history" (BLL: 136) captured in Judy Tanaka's "sex map" (BLL: 136) represents an idiosyncratic mapping of the relation between urban spaces and the urbanite's emotional life. Judy's personal map is a "plastic sheet that showed where she lived and fucked." (BLL 134) The connectedness between personalised maps of London and the palimpsestic nature of the metropolis are indicated when Judy arranges the various maps of her sexual partners over one another to a multi-layered structure of sex in the city (BLL: 343). By having sexual intercourse at selected spots in the metropolis, Judy has become intimate with the body of the urban itself. In the affair with Stuart, both characters engage in sexual psychogeography throughout London (cf. Dreyer 2006: 66). The two protagonists retrace an alternative map of London from Joe Orton's toilets in Holloway Road, a former brothel in Charlotte Street, Waterloo Road as the centre of eighteenth-century prostitution, the doorways of Fleet Street where Pepys enjoyed illicit sex, to Catherine Mansfield's mansion at Gray's Inn Road (BLL: 134-135). Judy and Stuart thereby both decipher London's intimate iconography and later add to the city's sexual palimpsest by making love close to these nodes of eroticism.

In contrast to London-made Stuart and London-born Judy, Mick is not initiated to an urban way of life, and without any knowledge of how to navigate the city (BLL 20-22; cf. Deny 2009: 254). For him, London represents Babylon, a *locus terribilis* of chaos, claustrophobia and overload, while the demands of metropolitan palimpsestuousness induce dislocation and disorientation (*ibid.*: 255). Throughout the novel, getting lost in the metropolis thus implies a reconstruction of the newcomer's mental apparatus towards inner urbanisation.

All protagonists in *Bleeding London* are entangled in a problematic mapping and re-mapping of the metropolis, which reveals their obsessions with the city. These obsessions not only influence their various perceptions, evaluations, and actions, but initially stress the importance of idiosyncratic mappings or psychogeographic endeavours in order to decipher London's palimpsest. Due to their unreliability, it is less the final map that serves navigation, but the route travelled offers a significant memorial narrative for orientation which reclaims the city for the individual (cf. Schlaeger 2003b: 41; Deny 2009: 258). For the idiosyncratic cartographers of London, who are attuned to the ambiance of the place, the city can become an agent of vigilance. As Stuart fails to commit suicide, Judy transforms herself into a map of London and Mick voluntarily returns to the city, the successful urbanite at the end of the twentieth century seems to be one, who is a cultural learned psychogeographer – someone able to unconsciously follow the fluid ley lines within the city's palimpsestousness. The psychogeographical palimpsest thereby becomes an apt metaphor for the mental requirements of contemporary urbanity. Psychogeographical thinking and feeling enables urbanites to personally react to the fleeting realities of the postmodern metropolis and inhabit the collective space-time compressions of the city.

London as Omphalos

Nicholas Royle's novel *The Matter of the Heart* (1997)[65], similar to *Bleeding London*, anthropomorphises the metropolis: here, a circulatory system of traffic roads is compared to arteries which centre in the city's stony heart. This system connects psychogeographic trails of roads/ley lines/songlines/contrails to uncanny places/*genius loci*/sacred sites/omphali.[66] The metaphor of the omphalos additionally intertwines the notion of a cultural semiotic locale with a significant place of bloody sacrifice, and postmodern psychogeographical reading. As with Miéville's, Williams' and de Abaitua's literary narratives, *The Matter of the Heart* can be classed as weird fiction; it is a collage novel that weaves together genre elements of mystery, surrealism, and the Gothic, nineteenth-century melodrama, travelogue, and road movie (cf. Kendall 1997).

In the fashion of De Quincey's psychogeographical excursion of the city, one significant narrative strand in the *The Matter of the Heart* follows the constant intoxication of the main characters' bloodstreams through excessive consumption of narcotics and food on the one hand, and their disturbing obsessions of daily urban experiences, distorted dreams, memories, imaginaries, and visions on the other hand. Besides an indirect cinematic intertextuality to the obsessive and deadly hedonism depicted in Marco Ferreri's film *La Grande Bouffe* (1973; Engl.: *The Big Feast*), in one of the narrator's dark dreams the apple of René Magritte's surrealist picture *The Listening Room* (1958) is exchanged with a beating heart as a metaphor of spatial sensuality. Simultaneously, the acts of re-tracing are recollective practices of the characters infused with haunting memories, which emphasise the fear of loss, the feelings of nostalgia, and the need for mourning, wherein the psychogeographical palimpsest is represented as a texture constantly encoding urban structures of feeling. Similar to psychic map-making and the idiosyncratic mappings in *Bleeding London*, Royle uses psychogeography to literally map the characters' "emotion onto London locations." (Kendall 1997) For the first-person narrator Chris, the various emotional connections between nineteenth- and twentieth-century London, the prehistoric location in Dartmoor, the places of the former British Empire in New Orleans and Western Australia constitute a "new experiment in psychogeography" (MAH: 287). All in all, *The Matter of the Heart* combines urban psychogeography with everyday story-telling, traditional myth-making, automobile mediations, and mental implications of global airplane travel.

While London's metropolitan streets are hyperbolically anthropomorphised, the characters identify them as ley lines or "emotional routes" (MAH: 7) of personal history, the very streams that sustain the urban organism's life. The narrator's friend Max,

65 | In the following *The Matter of the Heart* will be abbreviated to MAH.

66 | The cover of the Overlook edition of Geoff Nicholson's *Bleeding London* features a red map of London with the Thames, the Houses of Parliament and Westminster Bridge as landmarks in the background and an iconic depiction of a heart at its centre. In an interview, Nicholas Royle points towards the originally planned title of *The Matter of the Heart*: "And the new novel is called *Omphalos*. Which means the very centre of something. So in the novel this is the very centre of London, which might upset the psychogeographers who might claim it's down in the Isle of Dogs, I think. And it's all to do with the heart, the human heart, and there's all sorts of stuff going on with hearts in this old hospital." (Cit. in Kendall 1997)

depicted as a character oscillating between professional literary agent and philosopher of everyday life, "had this idea that there are insubstantial but clearly defined thoroughfares all over the city." (MAH: 7) Max traverses and (b)orders the city by driving London's streets with his other friend Danny, creating an idiosyncratic nightly map of excessive partying and intoxicated mobile *flânerie*. Moreover, it is the anthropomorphised vessel of the car rather than his own agency which guides the human passenger through the streams of the metropolitan fluid trajectories (MAH: 8). One can argue that Danny's incorporation of the habitual handling of the car and the navigation of London's topography have already turned him into an urban automaton. The character's reaction to the city's stimuli has been blunted to an extreme trance-like everyday experience that even resists the high level of intoxication by drugs. For Voss (1988: 48), it is the *flâneur*'s rhapsodic walking that becomes one with the elementary forces of the metropolis; intoxicated *flânerie* (cf. Benjamin 2002: 417, 419-420, 423) paradoxically stresses the 'naturalisation' of the characters to their surroundings, in other words, their complete corporeal and inner urbanisation.

Although, or especially because, Danny is well attuned to the metropolis, he neither takes "shortcuts or time-savers" (MAH: 9), but instead repeatedly plots the same way home going past a mansion block of Holloway Road, where he had

> once French kissed a girl called Kim [...] slowing down through Crouch End, some reference being made to Clive here, a Jenny there. People Danny knew or had known. By the time they pulled up in the middle of Max's estate he felt he'd been taken on a tour through Danny's address book. (MAH: 9)

Following Bakhtin's notion, urban streets become the chronotope of (re)encounter that reconnects the characters to lost lovers, friends, and acquaintances. When falling in love with the cardiologist Joanna, the narrator Chris similarly brands the city's roads with the tires of his Stag, writing his own emotional route into the city's texture (MAH: 39). The psychogeographical implications are noteworthy: the narrator suggests that the distance between the Westway and his home in White City is equivalent to the running time of Laurie Anderson's song "Freefall" (MAH: 38). The music not only mirrors his feelings but also his spatio-temporal transgressions of the metropolis' psychogeography.[67] He even acknowledges that the lights of the city are attuned to London's anthropomorphised urban rhythm: "Flying across town, wheels barely touching the tarmac – one heart to another – I checked the pulse of the city: a white light winking at Canary Wharf. The BT Tower's red flash. The lights' intervals were the same. Beating at the heart of the city." (MAH: 39) In a surreal vision reminiscent of Möbius' strip of M.C. Escher's graphics,[68] the narrator imagines the highway in Australia joining his emotional route in London

---

67 | The song is from Laurie Anderson's 1994 album *Bright Red.* The second stanza of the lyrics from "Freefall" reads: "Secret codes and cryptograms / I'm lost in your words I'm swimming. / We're going down to the bottom. All the way to the bottom. / Rapture of the deep." The music video of the song begins with the trace and echo of a heartbeat on a cardiogram.

68 | The symbol of the Möbius strip also appears in the name of Danny's girlfriend Z, his white Mercedes A 280SE, the headlights in a form of a figure 8 and the constant metaphor of the

(MAH: 208). This notion of routes and places being joined is taken up in the white and ghostly contrails of the planes, their traces creating a transmetropolitan, transcontinental, and world wide web of emotional linkages. Aeroplanes "describe the same trajectories through space. [...] A web of want. A need net." (MAH: 258) Spatial movement here represents a chronotope of emotional encounter.

All these variants of emotional routes potentially lead the characters to a nodal point or specific *genius loci*. In contrast to the dispersal of various *loci memoriae* along the routes of emotion stressing the excursions of the psychogeographer, the emotional encounter with the specific spirit of a place corresponds to the idea of absences and reappearances mediated through the palimpsest. The central spatial node of Nicholas Royle's London is provided by Lanesborough House at Hyde Park Corner. Like Wren's churches investigated by Sinclair and Ackroyd, in *The Matter of the Heart* the space of the former St George's Hospital has kept its spirit over centuries. Similar to "cardiac myocytes" (MAH: 294), muscles that keep beating after extraction, the destructed hospital still vibrates with its lost lives. The character Max identifies St George's as "the psychogeographical heart" (MAH: 293) of all the emotional routes concerning the relationship between Danny and his nameless girlfriend Z (MAH: 18). Moreover, through international networks and psychogeography as "some elaborate game of temporal translocation" (MAH: 288), the spirit of London's heart is connected to other *genius loci*, most notably Western Australia's Pinnacles Desert. The pillars are joined by imaginary lines and pathways constructing their own psychogeographical structure (MAH: 271-272). Not only is the desert perceived as a place suffused with energy, but this *genius loci* is taken literally as a "Repository of Lost Souls" (MAH: 268). Leading the protagonist Chris back from Australia to Dartmoor, Royle narratologically connects England's mythical landscape of Arthurian legend to the global web of memory places. In analogy to the metaphor of the Möbius strip, all roads, emotional routes, and the narrative itself return to London's Victorian hospital, where the characters localise the heart of the metropolis and the world's omphalos (MAH: 293).

The main significance of the place lies in its occult aura (MAH: 294, 227).[69] Due to the emotional energy of this place, the characters are involuntarily involved in unravelling the dark history of the hospital's room where, according to the characters' investigations, in the middle of the nineteenth century the surgeon Dr George Maddox attempted the world's first heart transplant and caught a decisive space-time capsule of adding a defining layer onto London's historical palimpsest. It is the place where Maddox and his

snake biting its own tail metamorphosed into an ouroboros. The meaning of the latter is eternity, in the sense of constant renewal by shedding its skin, and unity.

69 | Other synchronicities uncovered at the end of the novel include the parallelism of distances between the various hospitals featured in the novel. In an interview, Nicholas Royle gives an insight into his own fetishism with the St George's Hospital: "I'm obsessed by coincidences, or things that appear to be coincidences, which may be other things, a pattern of some kind. Synchronicity." (Kendall 1997) For more also see Nicholas Royle (2003), "Abandoned Buildings", in Joe Kerr & Andrew Gibson, eds., *London. From Punk to Blair*, London: Reaktion Books, 221-227. Phil Baker (2003: 329) shows that the idea of the ruin is a recurrent image in psychogeographical writing.

young assistants behaved like "actors in a stage, silhouetted against a new sociological and historical cyclorama" (MAH: 57) aiming to make medical history and gain immortality. Although, Maddox' visions go wrong, his secrets are preserved by the hospital, just as the victims' blood streams into the floor boards.

> Infinitesimally slowly the grain in the wood parted and the dark stud of life seeped in. Sticky patches remained on the boards themselves but some of the blood coagulated within the fabric of the hospital, so that it became part of the very structure of the behemoth. (MAH: 57)

Analogically to the ancient stone of the omphalos as an offering cup, the floorboards are described as receiving the blood of coroner patient, involuntary organ donor, and medium alike (MAH: 65). One hundred years later, during the Thatcher Era, the Australian-born character Danny collects an obscure object reminiscent of an extracted heart left lying around while secretly exploring the abandoned hospital's cryptopic spaces (MAH: 14-15). Moreover, the secrecy of the hospital's atmosphere and the penetration of its forbidden portals help Danny seduce his young colleague Z, making love to her in the former transplant chamber (MAH: 16-17). To the already incorporated spatial layer of violence are added two more, the guard's rape of Z and Danny's murderous self-defence (MAH: 267). A decade later, in the mid-1990s, the former hospital has been transformed into a luxury hotel, constructed "within and around its actual shell." (MAH: 19) In the same ominous room, the hedonistic American Charlie Herzog has a heart attack while unconsciously mirroring the tragedy of Danny's and Z's obsessive love-making. His Near Death Experience, in which Herzog briefly reaches a revelation, stresses that indeed "that room ain't no ordinary room" (MAH: 107), but a gateway of the supernatural.

However, the hospital room is not the only spatial structure of similarities and juxtapositions constructing a psychogeographical palimpsest that triggers emotional outbreaks. Comparable signs reappear in various places around the world lending unconscious but global patterns of (in)security and (dis)orientation or cathartic enlightenment to the characters. In other words, Royle uses narrative devices of motif, metaphor, and symbolism as traces for the protagonists to follow psychogeographic clues of analogy. There is not only simultaneity of events and symbolism achieved by narrative technique of flash forwards, flashbacks, repetition, and crosscutting, but also a significant doubling of characters. In an emotional breakdown of uncertainty, the first-person narrator Chris is unsure whether Max and Danny were not the same person or whether they existed at all (MAH: 41). Equally, Danny is represented as an uncanny resurrection of the nineteenth-century surgeon, "[o]ne unconsciously mimicking the other, matching his movements in space, but separated in time by more than a century." (MAH: 42) *The Matter of the Heart* challenges perceptions that the atmospheric interconnection of spatial and individual recollection is lost. Consequently, it still holds true that "every person, every individual, [is] able to experience his own history at the heart of the city" (Augé 1997: 16), coming across personal and collective memories.

For Chris, the mapping of his personal route around the world and metropolitan London is not only tied in with writing new lines on his personal relation to the cardiologist Joanna, but intertwined with re-reading the memories of his dead father. Actually each memory presents a painful threshold of mourning. In a parallel subplot, the Australian character Ambrose, mourning the death of his own father in a road accident, obsessively follows the traces of the "drivers' last signatures on the world's page." (MAH: 125) Additionally, he is haunted by a personification of his trauma which he identifies as the "Projectionist" – the phantom editing the "series of retinal memories or after-shocks." (MAH: 129) For both men the Australian Pinnacles, as the repository of the dead, constitute personal *lieux de mémoire* where their fathers return in dreams and visions (MAH: 272). Their acts of mourning equal the attempt to ontologise the traces (or remains) in their memory and identify their loss by localising the dead. The interconnection between psychogeographical palimpsest and personal memory strongly questions notions of time as chronological, and rather emphasises the constant superimposition of recollections.

In the psychogeographical idea of unearthing the city's soul, literary London imagines a palimpsestuous construction in which the visible interacts with the invisible, rationality with irrationality. Thus, contemporary representations of the metropolis defy the idea of opaque boundaries between the physical realities and the symbolic. *The Matter of the Heart* constructs the psychological palimpsest mainly through surrealist imagery and references paying tribute to the interrelations between the topographical urban body and the psychology of the urbanite. Especially mourning is understood as an unreflective mental device in connecting a personal psychogeography with layers of collectivity. Both urban overload and personal trauma are shown to lead characters to an excessive blunting of the senses. Being overdosed but unable to draw mental security by getting high, they function as urban automata. As pointed out in the theory of urbanity, this urban condition drives metropolitan denizens to search for even more excitement, notions of uncertainty, difference, and spectacle – the unhomely in an otherwise accustomed environment. Finally, the anthropomorphised city itself becomes the obsession of urbanites' lives – their daily dose of adrenaline.

Metropolitan Hauntology

Critics detect similarities of Nicholas Royle, Iain Sinclair, and China Miéville to Conrad Williams' writing (cf. Kendall 1997; VanderMeer 2006), whose debut novel *London Revenant* (2004) unites characteristics of the psychological thriller with those of urban social comedy, magic realism, fantasy, and horror fiction. Contemporary realist settings are transformed to surreal and mysterious visions illuminating otherwise unnoticed urban sights, moods and emotions (cf. VanderMeer 2006). In accordance to Royle's *The Matter of the Heart*, the characters in *London Revenant* likewise strive to "the centre of London [...], the omphalos. The true centre. [...] [Because] if they found the line, if they stood at the heart of London, something would be revealed." (LOR: 205) The city is not only the main character in the story, but the urban space is transformed into a living and breathing organism which reveals more of London's idiosyncrasies (LOR: 190). This aspect concentrates on the psychogeographical excursions and the revenant as the spectral personification of London's palimpsestuousness.

Dissatisfied but in need of his circle of friends and co-workers, the novel's protagonist Adam tags along with a group of party addicts that leaves a trail of alcohol, drugs, and sex from inner city pubs to private houses (LOR: 60). After the death of a hostess (LOR: 101), the party people turn from urban hedonism to another version of distraction. Yoyo, one of the female characters, starts to discover patterns on maps and suspects secrets imprinted in London's texture:

> Messages everywhere. Signs. You look at the maps and you swear there's something buried there for you. If only you knew how to look. Something coming through, like a shape you recognize in the clouds. Like faces in a fire. (LOR: 111)

Having lost the source to numb their senses, the characters begin to investigate the deeper grammar of London, obsessed by the idea that this practice will bring greater meaning to their urban (non)existence. They search for the palimpsestuous city's *scriptio inferior* that reveals the genuine urban character of London and the undistorted sense of the metropolitan everyday. Their conception is that the city is a multi-layered text of signs and that reading reveals the hidden and invisible (cf. B. Baker 2003). Although potentially disturbing and uncanny, these signs beyond the boundary of visibility are conceived as "a message written *in* and *by* the city to remind men of their own past and, maybe, to reveal them their future" (Mancini 2003: 173). On their tours through the city the characters finally become addicted to the hunt of urban heterotopias. Owing to Yoyo's obsession with maps, Adam's friends take it on themselves "to discover oases within the rotten heart of the city." (LOR: 113) In a sense, the psychogeographical characters in *London Revenant* search for non-places within the city centre in which a construction of space, Self, and future – thus active transformability – still seems possible.

However, these places are not pure in the sense of being untouched, rather "all fouled and fucked" they still "promise so much" (LOR: 80). The art of psychogeographic excursions is to unravel magic within metropolitan decay by acknowledging beauty in depravity (LOR: 133). It is the aesthetics of the ugly that bring out London's idiosyncrasies – by peeling back the "canvases of urban decay" (LOR: 154). The idea of "Lost places. Pockets of wow." (LOR: 113) refers to William Blake's line "Marks of weakness, marks of woe" from his Romantic poem "London" (1794), directly quoted in the epigraph to Part 1 of the novel. Blake's bleak poem decries London as a city on the brink of architectural, social, moral, and spiritual decline. Although Conrad Williams also depicts urban deterioration as a sign for crumbling primary relations and a growing loneliness, the novel takes a more positive stance in discovering hidden aspects of the city that are mysterious, but far from Blake's notion of disease and poverty, offer an exhilaration of freedom and a refuge for the desires of their searching souls.

Jameson (1991: 33) has pointed out that the new spaces of the postmodern cityscape can be experienced as surreal and supernatural. Hence, the hallucinatory and imaginary aspect represents an active deciphering and rewriting of the urban environment. The character Iain describes his psychogeographical experience as follows:

> All that rank carnality going on under a sky that was filthy black until your really stared at it, and then it was chock full of subtle colour [...] At first I found little impressions that leaked light when it was dark [...] Holes in fences. Cracks in walls. [...] I heard weird things, sounds coming out of stuff that shouldn't have carried sounds at all [...] And then I saw turnings off main roads where, on the map, there shouldn't be any. (LOR: 134)

Unearthing London for these "micro-Utopias" (LOR: 114), Iain discovers a paradisiacal café on a site where houses should be, Yoyo encounters a deer roaming in the middle of the city and Meddie plays cards with pirates on Embankment (LOR: 135). Again, the city's iconography can only be deciphered and its true meaning be established by those who have become properly attuned to the urban semantics of both beauty and decay.

All in all, these psychogeographical excursions can be interpreted as turning from hedonism, intoxication and blasé to a new imaginarily heightened urban awareness of the city beyond the plethora of surface stimuli and spectacles. In contrast to Simmel's notion of intellectualisation, psychogeography significantly stresses the imaginary as a means of handling the city's overload and reveal a deeper urban truth beyond the surface reality of everyday life. Even the sceptical and confused Adam, who did not believe in the discoveries of his friends, finally acknowledges: "There were messages everywhere. Everything was a page." (LOR: 230) As Adam deciphers the repetitious bottle-shaped symbol, psychogeographical thinking becomes the main instrument to unravel the city's palimpsestuous semiotic system. On their psychogeographical excursions the characters uncover secret palimpsestic layers and thereby also come in touch with the lost ghosts of London's idiosyncratic history. Generally, in cities "the haunting partly consists of the prevalence of such verbal and topographical echoes of the past." (Barry 2000: 46)

As developed in the chapter on "Underground London", the idea of the ghost haunting the city is mirrored in the concept of the revenant. The title of Conrad Williams' novel *London Revenant* implies the ghost that eternally returns might as well be the various ethereal strata of the metropolis itself. This suggests that the metropolis is haunted by its "ineffable, forgotten and frequently resurrected otherness" (Wolfreys 2002: 198). In reference to Derrida, urban revenance indicates that the city holds layers of previous incarnations. Derrida (1994: 10) coins the term "hauntology" based on ontology in reference to the paradoxical nature of the spectre which is neither being nor non-being. Although he seems to reject the idea of the palimpsest, its unfinishedness, metonymy, and absolute space, Dillon (2007b: 33) shows how Derrida's (1994: xx) thought of spectrality nevertheless gains a strong intimacy to palimpsestuousness. The spectral defies that there is a presence because all temporal strata coexist as modalised presents (cf. *ibid.*: xix, 149-150). The figure of the ghost – neither soul nor body, neither disappearance nor appearance, neither object nor subject, neither visible nor invisible – also elucidates that any form of present existence is constituted through the deferral of the past and the anticipation of the future. Metropolitan haunting and the spectral existence of the revenant insofar refer to the instability of the city in flux.

Similar to the representations of characters in *The Matter of the Heart*, the existence of Adam's friends in *London Revenant* is absolutely uncertain. Their psychological excursions mark these Londoners not only as spiritual or visionary but also as imaginative apparitions. Moreover, Adam's own ontological status as that of his antagonist Blore becomes blurred between uncanny repetition and spectral doubling. As was shown before, the novel represents the dual nature of the metropolis in the division between Topside and Underground London or the real and the sublime. This spatial opposite is repeated in the doubling of the protagonist Adam as Monck, while the narrator's continuous struggle to reconcile his dual identities emphasises his schizophrenic state of mind. Dillon (2007b: 37) in reference to De Quincey comments on this psychological disorder: "The fantasy of the palimpsest of the mind, and the disunity of the self it implies, does not lead to a Romantic notion of the mirrored or doubled self, but to a post-Romantic notion of the *spectralized* subject". Experiences of a ruptured unity of the Self and images of the Other within the Self have been shown to be endemic to Postmodernity.

This spectralisation of the Self is likewise mirrored by the fragmentation of time into a series of presents. Adam's antagonist H/Blore turns out to be the descendant of a workman killed during the building of the first tubes in 1887 (LOR: 327-328) and thereby personifies a "vital incarnation of the capital's repressed history" (Ashford 2008: 19). Blore being one with the subterranean city embodies

> the Tube's history, all its energy and desperation. He was its blood and sweat, its disease, its tears [...] Blore was somehow a link, the connective tissue between topside and Underground. He was London made flesh, a cipher between the living and the dead. (LOR: 239)

Skinning his face and stitching on a borrowed one, this ghostly incarnation of London's past is moreover represented as the spectral personification of metropolitan palimpsestuousness. Additionally, Ashford (2008: 20), due to Derrida's notion of the revenant, sees Blore as the herald of the end of history. In the constant return of the spectre, human imagination is only able to envision the death of historical meta-narrative as the return of the uncanny. Blore as the resurrection of the city's past therefore embodies the transcendental powers of the metropolis which lie beyond the linearity of chronological history and rather correspond to the undead layers of its palimpsestuous texture. In this sense, the palimpsest is rendered an "uncanny harbinger[...]" (Dillon 2007b: 13) and the palimpsestuous city therefore resembles an encompassing metropolitan hauntology. In De Quincey's (1968: 343-344) words, the palimpsest inherits the idea that restoration of effaced superscriptions simultaneously calls back to life of the subsequent generation and by burying other traces posterity can rise again. While revenance features the return of the dead, visionary projections foster its appearance as a vital renaissance. Thus, the psychogeographical palimpsest in *London Revenant* decries urbanity as a constant return of trauma which haunts the city and urbanites alike.

> For, if London is a ghost town, its apparitions remain to affect us materially – to live on beyond individual memory, and to return in every instance, at every passage, where now exceeds the present, where dreamwork exceeds mimetic or ontological stability, and where representation gives up the ghost to the spectral machinery, the machinic assemblage that is signed in the name of the city, as a fluctuating, serial translation, transport, and oscillation of itself. (Wolfreys 2004: 236)

Analysing the psychogeographical palimpsest in contemporary London fiction thus reveals psychological and phenomenological particularities of the metropolis, its urban living conditions and urban-specific mentalities. The palimpsestuous city constitutes a means to depict and understand the "collision between physical space and the human mind" (Atkins & Sinclair cit. in Schlaeger 2003a: 55). The psychogeographical palimpsest emphasises how the constructed realities of the city become the distinct fundament to act upon. A common denominator in all three novels under analysis is the notion of personal loss, caused by the death of family members, the abandonment by friends and partners, and the subsequent feelings of mourning and loneliness. Due to anthropomorphisation "the deep memorial palimpsest of the brain" (De Quincey 1968b: 347) becomes the texture of the city and people's minds alike. Thus, the metaphor of the palimpsestuous city is doubly of relevance for contemporary London mentality: on the one hand, it captures the structure of feeling in an urban world "surrendered to solitary individuality, to the fleeting, the temporary and ephemeral" (Augé 1995: 78), on the other hand, the palimpsesting of the metropolis adds to the urbanites' mental dispositions. Because the sacrifices made to the city, and the energies drawn by the city also become resurrected and transformed to new mental agency of urbanites, the "preconscious text [becomes] capable of divination and prophecy" (Sinclair 2003: 1).

6.4.3 Socio-Cultural Re-Con-Textualisation

The contextual palimpsest is made up by overlapping social encounters and cultural cross-references. Because overlaying phases juxtapose, mutate and connect in unexpected ways, the palimpsestuous city in becoming experiences a similar transformation when memories, thoughts, and diverging connotations are woven into the cultural texture of the metropolis. Thereby, the metaphor constitutes a spatial imagination that reads the complex relations of urban time, space, and collective as multi-dimensional. The school of urban ecology sees the cityscape as recording cultural traces over time and accumulating them into a palimpsest of meaning (cf. Crang 1998: 22). For example, contestations over urban territory, meaning and hence inscription emphasise the social dimension of the palimpsestuous city. Moreover, the city is to be seen analogical to a palimpsest because differences and indifferences concerning ethnicity or class coexist in its social space (cf. Sennett 2000: 77; Parker 2004: 103). Thus the re-con-textualisation of the urban palimpsest both pays tribute to a hybrid, relational, and dynamic concept of culture as well as to the transformative agency of the metropolis. While the palimpsest serves as a metaphor for urban heterogeneity as well as the socio-cultural process of change, it also stresses the transformations of mentality. Insofar, the palimpsestic imprints are not only historical and geographical, but of largely cultural and social relevance for the analysis of urban-specific dispositions of thinking, imagining, feeling, and acting.

Palimpsestuous Intersections

The urban palimpsest in Geoff Nicholson's *Bleeding London* is represented as a result of human interaction through the city. In accordance to Bakhtin's notion of the chronotope, the city's streets become the space where the individual walkers' paths cross one another and constitute a major locus of encounter. The novel follows personal psychogeographic routes to show how the lives of urbanites intersect in series of seemingly random connections. The routes of the protagonists Stuart and Mick cross on the former's suicide mission and the latter's criminal hunt through London. Otherwise, both are professionally and privately connected to Judy. Intertwining patterns of life inscribed on the texture of the metropolis are therefore specifically visualised in Judy's map, on which her sexual partners mark their places of intimacy. Mick observes "how these patterns resembled or differed from his, how sometimes intersected his own map, sometimes seemed to complement it, other times seemed to have been drawn in strict opposition." (BLL: 133) These various structures of complementation, opposition and intersection of everyday lives in London create an abstract picture of the metropolitan socio-cultural palimpsest. Moreover, due to the interweaving representations of the urban body, the city text is constructed as a palimpsest of personal narratives that erase and rewrite one another (cf. Altnöder 2009: 308).

Therefore, the palimpsest becomes an image of the overlapping of individual and the urban collective. The city's texture is a socio-cultural palimpsest, in which certain individual traces are combined creating a new logic unforeseen by the mere juxtaposition of its partial and fragmentary narratives. London as an imagined community is continuously produced and undone by the superimposition of individual everyday experiences of the palimpsestuous city. Thus, while the map's two-dimensionality is only able to capture the structures of interchange, Stuart's peripatetic perspective underlines the texture's cultural depth and diversity. On his tour through London, the character experiences the city's heterogeneity:

> In King's Road I saw a Chelsea pensioner. I saw a bar done out like a Mexican cantina. I saw plenty of flashy young people in clothes that were either fantastic or ludicrous or both, but I also saw a number of smart old chaps in blazers and trilbys. And I saw an apparently posh old lady walking down the street. (BLL: 197)

Moreover, he encounters men dressed up like chefs, two homeless men in a doorway, an Italian or Spanish girl handing out leaflets for a language school, a seemingly schizophrenic young black man, a man wearing a Scottish tam-o'-shanter, a boy with a Mohican haircut, a girl looking like a secretary, a camp pierced man, an Australian, a blind busker, a mixed Hare Krishna procession, criminal youths, and tourists from all over the world (BLL: 6, 143-144, 197; cf. Dreyer 2006: 67). This image of socio-cultural plurality is added to by Mick's first view of the multicultural metropolis characterised specifically by the British-Japanese Judy Tanaka (BLL: 59, 323).

Due to her otherness of gender and ethnicity Judy constitutes the "epitome of the outsider" (Mergenthal 2002: 135). Mergenthal (*ibid.*: 133) points out that the female protagonist is marginalised by the novel's third-person narrator, who mainly focuses on the male characters. Furthermore, the chapters dedicated to Judy are centred on her exotic body. Because of the traditional analogy between urban and female body, Judy is marked as a seductive element of city life, and her phenotypical otherness rather enhances her alienation from the cityscape. Suffering from racial and cultural stereotyping, Judy finds it increasingly hard to localise herself in the neo-imperialist spaces of the global city (cf. Chilton 2007: 18). Nevertheless, the final identification of Judy with London (BLL: 344-345; see chapter 8.1.2) brings to attention that her body is not only a sign of gendered and ethnic difference, but that her characteristics of the stranger and the hybrid (wo)man exactly render her the urbanite *per se*. Finally, her self-branding displays the "fluid and oftentimes global networks of values, images, places, practices and memories that make up London" (Chilton 2007: 18) produced by the stranger's over- and rewriting of the palimpsestuous city. She embodies the urban socio-cultural contact zone captured in the structural and quantitative notions of the city's heterogeneity.

Transcultural Superimpositions

From this point of view, the metaphor of the palimpsestuous city supports the protean character of the metropolis as a consequence of its increasing and transformative mosaic of ethnicities and cultures. Postcolonial novels have in particular offered an abundance of depictions of London's cultural texture, and have themselves contributed to the rewritings of the city text. Altogether the manifold analogies between postcolonial London fiction and the palimpsest can be described as follows: first, rewriting the city is inherent in the notion of the Empire writing back to the metropolitan centre. Second, a palimpsestic deciphering and re-encoding of the urban text(ure) implies an appropriation and translation of the metropolis. And third, the peeling away of layers brings to light the suppressed, oppressed, and marginalised narratives of urbanity, while simultaneously superimposing and interweaving new culturally heterogeneous voices within its structure of meaning.

Especially in regard to the latter, the palimpsestuous city not only pays tribute to the officially authorised and often homogenised surface, but takes into account the perception of the marginal Other or cultural subaltern, especially the metropolitan stranger or hybrid (wo)man. Experiences of migration to the postcolonial city captured in these texts are themselves a combination of fact, metaphor, history and imagination further complicated by personal, political, social, religious, racial and sexual considerations. Generally, they open new perspectives on issues of history, identity, temporality, reading, writing, and textuality. In regard to the city, the focus on spatial problems of deterritorialisation, displacement, and spaces of resistance of these representations adds layers of palimpsestic inscriptions that deepen our understanding of the metropolitan realm and its negotiations. In addition to suggesting "new routes and passageways in the city, alternative spatial practices that resituate, re-map and transform London" (McLeod 2004b: 188), metropolitan places are likewise integrated into different contexts. Due to its notion of transformation and relationality, the palimpsestuous city becomes an apt metaphor for the cosmopolitan, multicultural, and global character of London at the turn of the twenty-first century.

Salman Rushdie's long fiction, in particular *The Satanic Verses* (1989), has been variously commented on in its palimpsesting of novelistic, historiographical and autobiographical devices (e.g. cf. Brooke-Rose 1994: 125-126; Rogobete 2008: 151-152).[70] Concerning his analysis of Rushdie's writing on the urban palimpsest, Daniel Rogobete (2008: 151; emphasis N.P.) comments:

---

70 | Major palimpsest texts by Salman Rushdie are *Midnight's Children* (1981), *Shame* (1983), and *The Moor's Last Sigh* (1996). Rushdie's palimpsestuous project of painting over India mirrors his character Aurora's style of painting in *The Moor's Last Sigh*. In *Shame* the notion is that history itself is fiction and a product of the palimpsesting devices of the migrant's mind: "It is the true desire of every artist to impose his or her vision on the world; in Pakistan, the peeling, fragmenting palimpsest, increasingly at war with itself, may be described as a failure of the dreaming mind. [...] I too, like all migrants, am a fanatist. I build imaginary countries and try to impose them on the ones that exist. I too, face the problem of history: what to retain, what to dump, how to hold on to what memory insists on relinquishing, how to deal with change. My story's palimpsest country has, I repeat, no name of its own." (Rushdie 1995: 87) The novel's magic realism is called "palimpsest history" by Brooke-Rose (1994: 127-128), who sees the history of the nation intertwined with re-creative readings. For other contemporary postcolonial and palimpsestic writings see Bharati Mukerjee, Arundhati Roy, Hanif Kureishi, Amitav Ghosh, Hari Kunzru, Rohinton Mistry, Kiran Desai. Especially Zadie Smith, Andrea Levy, Bernadine Evaristo, and Monica Ali offer a profusion of imaginings and revisions of London as a palimpsestic space (cf. Rogobete 2006: 156-157).

This study focuses upon the conflicting postcolonial representations of London which have transformed it into a palimpsestic juxtaposition of economic, geographical, political, ethnical and cultural realities. Such descriptions and re-representations - which may often be in conflict among themselves - turn London into a spiritual labyrinth where each **metaphorical traveller** has to find his or her own ways, and reach a personal truth.

The city becomes infused with a plethora of global histories, as immigrants bring their histories with them (cf. Gibson 2003: 298). Thus while Rushdie's *The Satanic Verses* superimposes the "palimpsest countries" (Brooke-Rose 1994: 126) India and England as well as their "polyphonic palimpsest histories" (*ibid.*: 137) on London, we can argue that Monica Ali's *Brick Lane* (2003) equally overwrites London with fragments of images concerning space, time, and identity from a Bangladeshi cultural origin.

While the female protagonist Nazneen finds herself an outsider and uncovers the "patterns of inequality and oppression" (Hiddleston 2005: 63) in the socio-cultural text of the city, her existence in the wider web of city-life creates new space-time patterns of daily routine on the metropolitan texture. Nazneen first becomes a mental traveller to her former home in Bangladesh; the memories of her rural childhood represent alternative narratives which mediate and refract the protagonist's new metropolitan life. In due course, her memories and thereby the mental map of her home village are erased and overwritten by new spatial configurations. As Nazneen appropriates London life through alternate spatial practices and "cross-cultural misrepresentations" (Perfect 2008: 115), the narrative of the metropolis is filtered through imagined colonial landscapes and a "postcolonial consciousness" (Ball 2004: 11; cf. *ibid.*: 28-29; Poon 2009: 432; Groes 2011: 238).

Born in a Bengali village, significantly socio-spatially opposed both to metropolitan centre and Western way of life, Nazneen constructs her own urban connotations by ways of analogy when encountering London for the first time: "The clouds rushed at the top of the buildings as if they would smother them in a murderous rage. The buildings stood their ground, impassive as cows." (BRL: 60) She appropriates the foreign surroundings with the incorporated cultural knowledge, and with vocabulary or metaphors of her own cultural dictionary: a car horn sounds "like an ancient muezzin" (BRL: 54), London's schoolchildren are "pale as rice and loud as peacocks" (BRL: 55), learning to cross the street "she waited next to a woman and stepped out with her, like a calf with its mother" (BRL: 55) and the City's buildings appear to her like "white stone palaces" (BRL: 56). In this way, Monica Ali's postcolonial novel not only remaps certain territories and reshapes the city's geography, but also redefines the metropolitan texture by rewriting its biography from a marginal point of view. Moreover, Nazneen connects new experiences with memories and images from back home, she indirectly forces the visions, myths, and histories of her Bengali village onto the texture of the city, now adding new fragments to the imaginary palimpsest of London by writing inbetween. As Groes (2011: 238) comments, the Bangladeshi context and frame of reference is transplanted into the metropolitan British context and superimposed onto Tower Hamlets. With the new representations and cultural redescriptions from the unexpected perspective of a young immigrant woman London's cityscape is reconstructed as the product of a wide range of socio-cultural symbolic processes.

In this respect, the image of the palimpsest, as emphasised by Sizemore (1984: 177), also recalls women's stories hidden beneath the surface texts. Certainly, due the double-marginalised state of the female characters – Judy in *Bleeding London* or Nazneen in *Brick Lane* – another dimensions in the city's multilayered palimpsest is deciphered. With regard to Doris Lessing's London novel *The Four-Gated City* (1969), Sizemore (*ibid.*) sees both the city and women writers' texts as 'palimpsestic' in nature, and therefore considers women to be particularly capable urban novelists. In line with this interpretation, I suggest that also Monica Ali uncovers new layers of urban society, when she represents the everyday life of the Bangladeshi community in the East End and simultaneously pulls back the veil in front of the female migrant's mind. It was shown that in contrast to the novel's male characters, Nazneen is able to overcome her apathy and develop a successful urban agency. Sizemore (*ibid.*: 181) suggests that women are more likely to be able to read palimpsests, due to the interconnectedness of maternal thinking and reason as well as their being sensitive and automatic observers of their environment who perceive the most subtle transformations and differences in their urban surroundings. Similar to Lessing's female protagonist (*ibid.*: 182-183), Nazneen is concerned with the variety of urban life or the invisible vertical and horizontal socio-spatial boundaries of the city. Although psychogeographers are likewise not blinded by landmarks and rather search for emotional meaning hidden in unexpected places, Ackroyd and Sinclair's protagonists mainly discover horrors in the depths of the East End (*ibid.*: 186). Although Nazneen registers the area's contemporary depravity manifest in unemployment, drug abuse, usury, territorial disputes and loss of cultural roots, the discovery of the district's socio-cultural palimpsest emphasises vigilant diversity.

The historical, social, and cultural particularity of Brick Lane and the East End presents an exemplary piece of London's larger palimpsestuous parchment and hybrid spatiality. This part of the city has become the epitome to record urban transformation, as various cultures have left their own distinctive traces on the area's palimpsest. Literature, both fictional and non-fictional, has played a major role in this recent refashioning of the East End (cf. Brouillette 2009: 425-427).[71] Rogobete (2008: 155) argues:

---

71 | For more than 300 years, London's East End had been the shipping and mercantile centre of the capital, while in the last twenty years the Docklands have seen massive urban regeneration into a centre for media industries. The developments for the Olympics 2012 have reconfigured the area once more. Due to this dynamism and the East End's tradition of immigration, integration and shifting populations, the cultural make-up and with it religion, commerce, and architecture have changed immensely. The East End's Jewish garment factories were once as famous as today's Brick Lane curry houses. On the one hand, the East London Mosque serves UK's largest Muslim community, on the other hand, the area is seen as fundamentally Cockney. For more information on the East End see Newland (2008) or Ed Glinert (2005), *East End Chronicles*. For contemporary multicultural texts set in the East End see Meera Syal's *Life Isn't All Ha Ha Hee Hee* (1999), Monica Ali's *Brick Lane* (2003), Matthew D'Ancona's *Going East* (2003), Tony White's *Foxy-T* (2003), Tarquin Hall's *Salaam Brick Lane* (2005), Rachel Lichtenstein's *On Brick Lane* (2005), Jeremy Gavron's *An Acre of Barren Ground* (2005), Iqbal Ahmed's *Sorrows of the Moon: A Journey Through London* (2007), Jeffrey Archer's *A Prisoner of Birth* (2008), and Richard Bean's controversial play *England People Very Nice* (2009).

The creation of hybrid spaces where physical, political, psychological and cultural dimensions are combined, transforms the metropolitan space into an unfolding narrative susceptible to be read and interpreted from different angles of perception, as a palimpsest where stories upon stories accumulate, corresponding to layer upon layer of history and personal stories.

In Monica Ali's novel this notion of material but also socio-cultural layers added to the structure of Brick Lane is captured by Nazneen's recorded excursions into the neighbourhood. On her first encounter with the heart of the East End in the mid-1980s, the streets are stacked with rubbish and deserted early (BRL: 55), while two decades later Brick Lane has been invaded by tourists and everything is shiny and clean (BRL: 252-253). Furthermore, the cultural palimpsest has virtually thickened in its atmosphere with Sitar music and curry smells (BRL: 256). In this sense, Brick Lane comes to register commodities from various cultural areas, expectations and stereotypical notions, where the original context only plays a minor role in the establishment of a new texture:

> Days of the Raj restaurant had a new statue in the window: Ganesh seated against a rising sun, his trunk curling playfully on his breast. The Lancer already displaced Radha-Krishna; Popadum went with Saraswati; and sweet Lassi covered all the options with a black-tongued, evil-eyed Kali and a torpid soapstone Buddha. (BRL: 446)

Although, this passage certainly criticises the cultural appropriation and commodification of ethnicity and culture in twenty-first-century, the cultural palimpsest and the heterogeneous urbanity offer an important contact zone of reconciliation and conflict resolution.

Interestingly, this overwriting and rewriting to create a complexity of different texts is also achieved, as Banerjee (2008: 10-12) points out, by a certain superimposition of London and Dhaka as part of the transnational simultaneity generated in the novel's epistolary section. In the process of mobility and migration, urbanity is transferred and appropriated to the respective metropolis. Gibson (2003: 300) argues: "London's places are now great meshes of local and global together, palimpsests where the global overwrites the local, and then is overwritten in its turn. But the maze of interrelation itself is never abstract." Furthermore, the socio-cultural palimpsest not only celebrates the metamorphosis of the city, but the potential for adaptation of both urban society and the urbanite. The local multicultural contact zone of Brick Lane therefore also brings globally entwined structures into focus. In other words, the palimpsestuous city here stands as a metaphor for the glocalisation of the urban. These micro- and meta-level overwritings, nevertheless, refer back to the meso-level of London's "'metropolitan particularity'" (*ibid.*).

London as a palimpsestuous city is a place of crossings, entanglements, mixtures, networks upon networks, coincidences, causes and effects, miscegenation and complication. In handling this overload of heterogeneous cultural semantisations, palimpsestic thinking helps to decipher these various layers and overcome the anxiety of disorientation caused by plurality. As was shown with the example of Monica Ali's *Brick Lane*, transnational narratives impose other layers of histories and stories on urban reality (cf. *ibid.*: 298-299). Although the entanglement of segregation (the council estate of Tower Hamlets and territorialisation) and integration (iconographic overlappings in the contested space as contact zone) might seem paradoxical, it simply emphasises the often opposing interferences of the urban palimpsest. *Brick Lane* underlines how urban ambivalences of heterogeneity and homogeneity are made to coexist in the palimpsest's structure of difference and indifference. Based on the hybrid nature of intercultural exchange and carnivalesque encounters between different Londoners, the newly constructed "decentred mentalities" (McLeod 2005: 40) challenge exclusionary logics particularly in form of an *outillage mental* built on "vernacular cosmopolitanism" (*ibid.*: 42). This particularly finds innovative expression in novels, poems, songs, dance, and music (*ibid.*: 39).

Hybrid Citizenship and Urban Jungle

This unearthing of the metropolis' socio-cultural layering, however, does not apply only to postcolonial London novels written by immigrants. As we have seen, psychogeographical writing has a curious reverence for individualist outsider figures appropriating London and also Gothic literature traditionally takes into account the forgotten or repressed Other of society. In contrast to the classical fantasy genre in the fashion of J.R.R. Tolkien, which relies on stereotypical depictions of race, China Miéville refutes this stance and at the same time criticises postmodern fascination with hybridity as a "fetishistic and sometimes quite self-indulgent *celebration* of marginality for its own sake." (Cit. in Gordon 2003: 364) Rather, Miéville's weird fiction in *King Rat* (1998) owes to De Quincey, Moorcock, or Sinclair's urban fantastic (cf. Marshall 2003). Freedman (2003: 399) observes "that Miéville's work suggests, from *King Rat* onwards, [...] that speculative fiction may sometimes function as a more efficient genre than philosophical exposition for the overt expression of impurity and nonidentity." This allegorical narrative develops the urban ambivalent constellations of heterogeneity and homogeneity with the example of his protagonist Saul Garamond, who is descendent from opposing cultural and social milieus. The following analysis concerns the various depictions of London as a multidimensional socio-cultural palimpsest especially with respect to the protagonist's hybridity and the palimpsestuous nature of the novel's intermedial reference to Jungle music.

London is not only spatially diversified, but the metropolis is discovered by Saul as a place populated by estranging and heterogonous wandering urbanites (cf. *ibid.*: 402; Bould 2009: 319). The novel's character constellation constitutes, as Miéville points out in an interview, a hotchpotch of European and African mythic or artistic traditions (cf. Gordon 2003: 355)[72] which ratify the multicultural hybridity of fin-de-millennium London. The Cockney King Rat ruling the proletarian sewer rats represents London's lower class (KRA: 28), the spider-man Anansi, who speaks with a strong Caribbean accent and has a habit of sucking his teeth, is a symbol of the post-war migrant to the metropolis (KRA: 143-144), while the bird-man Loplop with his European intonation stands for the manifold continental *émigrés* (KRA: 148, 155). Additionally, all the characters are specifically emplaced in multi-ethnic neighbourhoods of postcolonial London:

---

72 | Figures include Pied the Piper of Hameln, the West Indian trickster figure Anansi, Tibaukt, the King of the Cats from *The Arabian Nights*, Kataris, Queen of Bitch, a demon in charge of dogs from the pantheon, Loplop, the Bird Superior from a painting by Max Ernst, and Mr Bub, the Lord of the Flies adapted from the novel by William Golding.

Saul's home is located in multicultural Willesden, Fabian, a black artist and urban cyclist, comes from Brixton, and Natasha is a Drum N' Bass DJane with her homebase and studio in Notting Hill's Ladbroke Grove. Fabian, in a short urge of materialist envy of other Brixton youths, repeats his own mantra against cultural commodification and stereotyping: "*I won't be another black man with a mobile, another troublemaker with 'Drug Dealer' written on his forehead in script only the police can read.*" (KRA: 81) The novel thereby captures the post-Fordist metropolis in its insurmountable heterogeneity, with a special emphasis on the subcultural resistance against capitalist commodification of urban hybridity or as a mere locus of a new homogenising form of Britishness (cf. Freedman 2003: 403).

The novel specifically devises the main character as the personification of this plural metropolitan socio-cultural palimpsest. Saul, both of rat and human descent, "is a figure of radical *hybridity*" (*ibid.*: 397). Similar to a character in a typical postcolonial *Bildungsroman*, his two socio-cultural personalities seem to be at war with one another, but once he also accepts his rat being, Saul becomes aware of the positive traits and additional possibilities of his hybrid identity. Confronted with the tall, blond and immaculate Aryan Piper and in the face of his genocidal plans of homogenising the city (KRA: 163; cf. Freedman 2003: 404), Saul recognises that "[*p*]*urity is a negative state and contrary to nature*" (KRA: 97). It makes him "understand the monstrous quality of non-hybridity and homogeneity" (Freedman 2003: 398) as racial, social, or cultural totalitarianism.

Miéville's *King Rat* therefore celebrates metropolitan heterogeneity and complexity with its own warfare on totalitarianism and violent socio-cultural obsessions of homogeneity. Due to "the 'dissonance' between his two natures" (Aichele 2005: 68), Saul does not dance to the Piper's tune (KRA: 249). He is even able to resist the multi-track melodies because, as Saul points out to his antagonist: "One equals *one*, motherfucker. I'm not rat plus man, get it? I'm bigger than either one and *I'm bigger than the two*. I'm a new thing. *You can't make me dance*." (KRA 301) In tune with the palimpsesting of the metropolis, Saul cannot be reduced to either one track, as he has incorporated both heterogeneous cultural layerings and actually lives the mutual effect of their crossover. In this sense, the protagonist becomes the herald of a new multicultural urban citizenship (cf. Freedman 2003: 397; Aichele 2005: 68; Maczynska 2010: 76-78).

This idea of cultural palimpsesting is mirrored on another highly relevant level, namely Jungle music as the hybrid soundscape of the novel. In interviews China Miéville has repeatedly argued that *King Rat* is as much a musical as a London novel (cf. Gordon 2003: 355; Marshall 2003). Narratologically and thematically woven into the structure of the text, Jungle – a variant of Drum 'N Bass, techno, rap, and reggae that evolved in London's multicultural working-class milieu of the 1990s – becomes an apt metaphor for the hybridity and dynamism of the city, the urban subcultural movement, and the emotional dimensions of the characters. Miéville's novel mimics the rhythm interlacing various loops of the narrative and intertextual references with the music by integrating well-known lyrics (KRA: 21-25; cf. Gordon 2003: 355). Jungle as a hybrid genre samples different sources of sounds, while the modern musical technology enables more than one distinct track being played (cf. Freedman 2003: 397; Gordon 2003: 355). Its impure and heterogeneous tones are all held together by a predominance of African-American beats. Insofar, the music mirrors the integration of calypso in early postcolonial London novels which captured the sublime hybridity of London for the first time.

Saul's socio-cultural antagonist, the totalitarian Piper, wants to control the multi-track music of Jungle to bring the heterogeneity of urban species under his singular spell. He approaches Saul's friend Natasha, who is an "alchemist" (KRA: 82) of musical mixtures. She uses the ghostly traces of other pieces of music and assembles "a snatch of trumpet from Linton Kwesi Johnson, a wail from Tony Rebel, a cry of invitation from Al Green" (KRA: 67) to create a musical palimpsest. Feeling increasingly alienated by synthetic sounds, Natasha falls prey to the organic one of Pied's flute (KRA: 189). In due course she becomes obsessed with "Wind City" (KRA: 190, 268-272), a track she consistently works on to integrate Pied's controlling sound by "tweaking it, adding layers to the low end, tickling the flute, looping it back on itself." (KRA: 190) For Natasha the song's musical make-up corresponds to the metropolis:

> This was Wind City, a huge metropolis, deserted and broken, alone, entropic, until a tsunami of air breaks over it, a tornado of flute clears its streets, mocks the pathetic remnants of humanity in its path and blows them away like tumblewood, and the city stands alone and cleared of all its rubbish. (KRA: 273)

While Natasha intends a cleansing catharsis for London and an emotional tabula rasa to rewrite her own version of the city (KRA: 268; cf. Bould 2009: 319), Pied only favours the various layers of jungle in their potential to brainwash his fellow human victims (KRA: 343, 386). The Piper by manipulation misapplies the very power of hybridity he aims to destroy. And although Jungle becomes the tool which charms his victims into total submission (KRA: 357, 370-386), the city, which has initially produced this hybrid genre, also created Saul, who as a half-breed between two socio-cultural urban species remains immune against these incantations (cf. Freedman 2003: 396).

Music encompasses the sense that finally brings Saul's human and rat nature together but also makes him vulnerable to the pull of the city and the totalitarian soundscape produced by Pied: "he obeyed the music, two tunes at once, the rat and the man, the mellow and the frenzied, spilling around each other, filling his mind." (KRA: 393) While listening to the "cacophony that is the life of the city" (B. Baker 2003), the dominant bass of the Jungle beat assists Saul in navigating the overload of aural stimuli by returning to the as-if tone of his resistant hybrid mentality (KRA: 395-396). When Saul first learns of his descent and biography ("Part Three: Lessons in Rhythm and History", KRA: 113), the rhythm of the city is explored, and both are united in a mutual reckoning of identification:

> He [Saul] could hear sounds from all over London, a murmuring. And as he listened, it resolved itself into its components, cars and arguments and music. He felt as if the music was everywhere, all around him, a hundred different rhythms in counterpoint, a tapestry, being woven underneath him. The towers of the city were needles, and they caught at the threads of music and wound them together, tightened them around Saul. He was a still point, a peg, a hook in which to wind the music. It grew louder and louder, Rap and Classical and Soul and House and Techno and Opera and Folk and Jazz and Jungle, always Jungle, all the music built on drum and bass, ultimately. (KRA: 287-288)

Saul feels the texture of the city being written, overwritten, and rewritten by various layers of rhythms, styles and cultural backgrounds. Moreover, from the encompassing rhythm of the metropolis, Jungle is identified as generically urban and idiosyncratically emplaced in London – "the Drum and Bass soundtrack for a London of council estates and dirty walls, black youth and white youth, Armenian girls." (KRA: 67) While psychogeographers make use of emotional quotations drawn from the urban imaginary concerning various aspects of popular culture, especially film, China Miéville exploits the suggestibility of music as an urban iconography similarly specifying the palimpsestuous city.

Moreover, in line with the metaphorical implications of the palimpsest, *King Rat* also particularly pays heed to giving a voice to the marginalised subcultures of the metropolis. Characteristically, the novel's exposition is set in a train approaching King's Cross in the midst of London's often forgotten urban sprawl, yet, as was shown before, the third-person narrator places the centre of London's heartbeat in the jumble of non-places without the city. And as the Jungle parties take place in disused warehouses, these non-places are conquered and recreated by subcultural movements that ceaselessly rewrite the city's palimpsest of identity and socio-cultural relations. Consequently, China Miéville's London novel *King Rat* constitutes an extraordinary example of the reflection of "the city's heterogeneous, palimpsestic character" (Maczynska 2010: 58) in its dense socio-cultural layering. Maczynska (*ibid.*: 66) therefore counts the text to a new genre of urban fiction:

> Visionary satire offers precisely such a subversive reimagining of urban space and perception, by dismantling the familiar metropolis and imposing upon it palimpsestic, alternative urban structures. This creative resistance is actualized in texts that push past the boundaries of realist representation to defamiliarize, deform, and transform the modern city, as well as enact the construction (and deconstruction) of the contemporary urban subject.

With regard to Miéville's innovative narrative use of the musical palimpsest, Jungle music becomes another image for the urban rhythm and idiosyncratic factor of influence on London's urban-specific mentality. While Geoff Nicholson and other psychogeographical writers concentrate on the absence of sounds in places to recover lost layers and voices, and Nicholas Royle's characters are obsessively attuned to the single sound of a beating heart, Miéville's protagonist Saul also appears to be more acculturated to the cacophonic layerings of urban plurality.[73]

In sum, China Miéville's *King Rat*, Monica Ali's *Brick Lane*, and Geoff Nicholson's *Bleeding London* construct London as a socio-cultural palimpsest, as a many-layered city with various districts and a multitude of varying urban characters, especially focussing on marginalised groups of the city. Certainly, other novels, such as Nicholas Royle's *The Matter of the Heart* with the crossing paths of characters, Jane Stevenson's social

---

73 | Mumford (1997: 4) already described the socio-cultural plurality of the metropolis and the diversity of its temporal structure and labour by comparison to the symphony of a complex orchestration that gives rise to "sonorous results which, neither in volume nor in quality, could be achieved by any single piece."

interconnections in *London Bridges* or Conrad Williams' *London Revenant* with ordinary people caught up in the same ghostly tracings can be enumerated here. Moreover, with hindsight to the hybridity of urbanity explored in *King Rat* and *Brick Lane* the socio-cultural palimpsest is a metaphor for concepts of thirdspaces further explored in chapter 7.1.4. These novels employ the metaphor of the palimpsest to insist on the overwriting of urban meaning and the construction of alternative urban iconographies essential to the development of the city and for their inhabitants' orientation. Hence, the palimpsestuous city also in its socio-spatial aspect negotiates questions of orientation, this time with a specific emphasis on urban-generic profiles of heterogeneity and community and their potential for an enhanced vigilance within the city in flux that captures the essence of urbanity.

6.4.4 Intertextual Writing

The novels analysed so far draft their narratives as peripatetic tours of rewriting and reimagining the city and bring the fictional urbanites closer to the meaning of the metropolis and their own urban existence. Thereby the palimpsestuous city is constructed through intericonographic, intermedial, and intertextual practices (cf. Schlaeger 2003a: 49-50). Concerning postmodern urban fiction, Mancini (2003: 168) stresses the connection between narration, city, and urban rewritings: "The city is a text waiting to be read and written or rewritten in literary and narrative terms: a city of signs and essences whose panorama is drenched with (hi)stories relevant to its origins, to its citizens, to the society in which it has developed." In reference to the symbolic and the imaginary city as dominant factors of influence on urban-specific mentality, the city as text and city texts, constituted by artistic, musical, cinematographic, and narratological aspects, form layers of memories precious for the construction of urban identity. The layering of city-texts can be described as a "process of palimpsest production" (Dillon 2007b: 52) whereby "the subsequent reappearance of the underlying text results in the twiformed structure of the palimpsest, to which two or more texts, often different and incongruous, coexist in a state of both collision and collusion." (*Ibid.*) This section therefore explores the aspect of intertextuality and intermediality in relation to the palimpsestuous city; it specifically analyses the layering of London's texture by the juxtaposition of various literary texts.

With Dillon, I refer to an understanding of intertextuality as formulated in Gérard Genette's seminal *Palimpsestes* (1982). Generally, intertextuality is defined as the co-presence of two or more texts, while the grade of visibility of the original hypotext in the later hypertext varies from a mere echo to commentary or from superimposure to transformation. According to Genette (1993: 532), the interrelation between two or more texts and their mutual overlapping, juxtaposition, and dissonance create a complex structure marked by transparency and the construction of novel meaning. He establishes: "[d]iese Doppelheit des Objekts lässt sich im Bereich der Textbeziehungen durch das alte Bild des *Palimpsests* abbilden [...]." (*Ibid.*) The hypertext invites us to engage in a form of relational reading coined by Phillipe Lejuene as 'palimpsestuous reading' (cf. *ibid.*: 533; Dillon 2007b: 4). Pastiche and intertextuality are major aspects of postmodern aesthetics and therefore contemporary London novels are largely intertextual constructs or literary palimpsests. Concentrating specifically on Geoff Nicholson's *Bleeding London* (1997) and Ian McEwan's *Saturday* (2005), I contend that the implementation of various hypotexts moreover serves the construction of the metaphorical palimpsestuous city with its implication of urban particularity.

Biographical Re-Writings of the City

The protagonist Judy Tanaka of *Bleeding London* in sexually mapping London mainly follows the erotic traces of writers, such as Orton, Pepys and Mansfield. Therefore, she perceives London through a literary lens of authors (i.e. Dr Johnson or Dickens) and idiosyncratic subjects of imagination (i.e. Boadicea or Jack the Ripper). As the reinterpreted urban figure of the *femme fatale* or Babylonian whore, Judy becomes not only a female allegory for a sexually territorialised London, but by metamorphosing herself into an erotic map of London, she is similarly appropriated by the literary city of the novel itself. Schorske (1977: 110) emphasises that Baudelaire considered the prostitute the cousin of the poetic city dweller. In this way, Judy's sexual quest of street-walking is inexorably bound to Stuart London's hyperbolic city-project and the concomitant writing of "The Walker's Diary". But Pike (2005a: 265) correctly stresses that the streetwalker is the "dialectical counterpart to the male flâneur [...] in the power she embodies as an oppositional urban figure, even if this oppositional power is expressed though negative clichés of femininity."

Stuart, besides his mundane walking, also chooses an alternative aesthetic path to the city by writing a diary. The first entry summarises the phenomena of everyday life he encounters throughout his perambulations, but his observations of urban street life become intermingled with his knowledge of London's history and literature. Following the footsteps of "all the great Londoners" (BLL: 28), most of whom, such as Evelyn, Pepys, Johnson, Boswell, and Dickens, are great literary chroniclers of the metropolis, Stuart's narrative style inadvertently mirrors the writing actually retraced. Because Stuart's notes on urban life, in enumeration and detail, are similar to the style of his literary idol Samuel Pepys (BLL: 196-200; cf. Dreyer 2006: 67), the consequent intertextuality forces connotations of a bygone London to intertwine with the present-day experiences of the protagonist. Writing his diary Stuart adds to the textual palimpsest of London, which is composed of various city texts and their cross-references to one another. The density of descriptions of everyday life, his comic encounters, and the diversity of grotesque urbanites crossing his path mimics Dickens' London. Instead, in the beginning of chapter four "The Walker's Diary. The Penultimate Days" (BLL: 26) the atmosphere is reminiscent of Boswell's famous Johnson quote:[74]

> I was worn out today as I walked the city. I have worn myself out in the city. It has eroded me. [...] I have been left drained and evacuated. I have been to the boundary, to the wall, to the places where the city ends, where the train tracks knot together, where the pylons hiss and fizz their dissatisfaction, where the workings show, the innards, the guts, the secretions, to the place where we hone our taste for fragments. (BLL: 26)

74 | [W]hen a man is tired of London, he is tired of life; for there is in London all that life can afford." (Boswell cit. in A.N. Wilson 2002: 465)

Although he does not reach his foremost teleological objective, Stuart finally still emerges stronger and reoriented from his quest because the journey of writing constitutes his reward. Deny (2009: 121, 123) argues that even if Stuart's spatial and literary practices fail to deliver an encompassing and universal reorientation in the post-Fordist metropolis, his project of walking and writing can nevertheless be considered as an act of identity formation and a measure of spatial structuring. Since his last name casts him as a personification of the metropolis, by rewriting the city Stuart necessarily also changes his own personality.

The character's diary builds another palimpsestic layer in the novel, as it conflates the re-writing of the metropolis with an autobiographical re-writing of the Self. The genre of the English diary, especially Pepys', predates and also initiates the development of the novel which charts private life in the first-person narrative voice. A document of individual city life, Stuart's autobiography tells of the boundaries of urban-generic ambivalences in twentieth-century London. While in Pepys' time the reconstructions of London after the Great Fire altered the private and public mental maps of its inhabitants (cf. Heyl 2004: 530), Stuart's diary represents a metafictional comment on writing postmodern London as well as an invariant of a chronicle on the city's mind. Pepys, the novel's hyperbolic character Stuart, and the author Geoff Nicholson are mutually employed in constructing London as a palimpsestuous city (BLL: 247; cf. Dreyer 2006: 70; Chilton 2007: 20; Deny 2009: 114). Thus, intertextual writing also emphasises ontological doubleness – a "*non-contemporaneity with itself of the living present*" (Derrida 1994: xix). This revenant of textual layers is mirrored in the conflation of Samuel Pepys and Stuart London, while the character simultaneously personifies the amalgamation of city – text – urbanite. In the context of Geoff Nicholson's own *Bleeding London* as yet another textual version referring to Stuart's and Pepys' work, the created hypertext resembles the palimpsestuous idea of erasures and overwritings *per se*.

Metropolitan Intertextuality

In her study on the palimpsest, Dillon (2007b: 92-101) thoroughly analyses Ian McEwan's novel *Atonement* (2001) for the infinite possibilities of palimpsestuous textuality. Similarly, McEwan's later *Saturday* (2005) variously reflects upon and integrates past writing, such as Austen (SAT: 27), Arnold (SAT: 231, 269), Conrad (SAT: 95), Darwin (SAT: 6, 55), James (SAT: 58) and Milton (SAT: 134) (cf. Groes 2009: 102; Groes 2011: 155). First, intertextuality in the novel mediates between contemporary and Victorian views of private domesticity, public politics, history and literary form. Second, these layers of intertextual literary productions on the urban, for example Saul Bellow and Virginia Woolf, add to the various competing voices of the metropolitan intertextual palimpsest. In reference to McEwan's understanding of literary anthropology, this anthology of intertextual references creates a thick description of London's contemporary texture which necessarily depends on former layers of writing. The intertexual palimpsest of London is presented as being able to comprise the workings of the city and comprehend nonconscious urban processes. In his critique of the anthropological efforts, McEwan basically argues for a universal investigation into the understanding of structures of thinking. Parallel to the story of an archaeological dig which describes how excavations can lift the urban mystery of the city's mind (SAT: 242), Genette's (1993: 9) notion of 'architext' (e.g. discourse, genre) devises a narrative's various degrees of intertextuality. Both construct the urban palimpsest because they decipher the urban-generic metropolitan mindset in comparison to London's specific mentality.

The novel's epigraph, taken from Saul Bellow's *Herzog* (1964), sets urban life in temporal and spatial comparison:

> Well, for instance, what it means to be a man. In a city. In a century. In transition. In a mass. Transformed by science. Under organized power. Subject to tremendous controls. In a condition caused by mechanization. After the late failure of radical hopes. In a society that was no community and devalued the person. Owing to the multiplied power of numbers which made the self negligible. Which spent military billions against foreign enemies but would but pay for order at home. Which permitted savagery and barbarism in its own great cities.

Surrounded by enhanced destructive or dystopic implications and their repetitious urban images, the life of a man in a Western city of transition is likely to have certain traits of character. This epigraph restores the image of the city as wrought by ambivalences of culture and nature, the city as both the seat of civilisation and a place of darkness (cf. Groes 2009: 102; Groes 2011: 162-163): New Jerusalem and Babylon. While Enno Ruge (2010) interprets Bellow's urban fiction in its extreme misery as a counterpart to *Saturday*, I would rather refer to the construction of a larger and encompassing intertextuality which translates the exploration of people's mind from an urban-generic condition and a specific zeitgeist at the turn of the twentieth century to an idiosyncratically emplaced mentality of London in the twenty-first century.

As variously noted, *Saturday* is a present-day tribute to Virginia Woolf's *Mrs Dalloway* (cf. Clark Hillards 2008; Cilano 2009a; Girard 2008; Michael 2009; Pogossian 2010).[75] Both novels portray the apparently casual day of a Londoner featuring similarities in narrative structure and thereby apparently of urban routine and structures of feeling over centuries. Henry Perowne and Clarissa Dalloway share the same class status occupying similar mansions in Fitzrovia. Henry's Saturday mirrors Clarissa's itinerary (cf. Girard 2008: 61-62), but their days are also closely matched in terms of minor events that trigger memories, such as their subjective reactions to the aeroplane spectacle in the London sky. The latter rewrites the trauma of war anchored in the Woolfian text referring to international terrorism and the impending war on Iraq (cf. *ibid.*: 61). While both novels rely on free indirect speech to explore the mind of their characters, *Saturday* specifically explores the diachronic differences in thinking. Interestingly, Clark Hillards (2008: 201) observes that Perowne's "man's head is a woman's room, which is, apparently, full of nineteenth-century literature." The hypotext of *Mrs Dalloway* intertwines with other literary layers of the time (Victorianism, Modernism) and space (London). Clark Hillards (*ibid.*) comments that Daisy's re-reading of Matthew Arnold's "Dover Beach" in *Saturday* also becomes an intertext of *Mrs Dalloway*, arguing: "Saturday, then, is a novel by a man in which a woman recites a poem by a man that reflects a novel by a woman in which a woman recited a poem by a man." All these texts reflect doubt and

---

75 | Other postmodern rewritings of Mrs Dalloway include Robin Lippincott's *Mr Dalloway* (1999) and Michael Cunningham's *The Hours* (1999).

anxiety on the notion of being caught between two worlds, two eras, two anthropological human conditions, and their changes.

In sum, the intertextual palimpsest enables urbanites to orient themselves in the city, especially translating between individual and the urban challenges of community, and allows the reader to grasp the continuities and transformation in the urban mentality. As a junction between several texts the hypertext of the contemporary London novel is always a re-reading, accentuation and displacement of the cityscape and urbanity. This literary palimpsest of fictional (hi)stories further defies the notion of homogeneity and celebrates the plenitude of urban narratives in its layers and patchwork of allusions (cf. *ibid.*: 204). Due to a combination of urban contradictions with ambiguities of postmodern fiction, the palimpsest both celebrates a certain disenchantment and loss of orientation in the multiplicities of the post-Fordist metropolis, but always indicates it as a chance for renewal. Re-reading and re-writing are shown to be necessary prerequisites not only for self-fashioning, but for a general successful orientation in the urban realm. In *Bleeding London* and *Saturday*, but also in *Corpsing*, *London Bridges*, *Next*, *South of the River*, *The Matter of the Heart*, *The White Family*, *253* the tradition of the literary metropolis as habitualisation of urban knowledge becomes a further dimension for navigating the cityscape and its heterogeneous social relations. Urban fiction therefore not only teaches sociability, but literary mental chronicles of the city, serves urban acculturation, especially the inner urbanisation of its inhabitants. In this respect, urban-generic and urban-specific mental dispositions are strongly based on a particular degree of literacy because literature initially conveys structures of thinking, feeling, imagining, and acting. Thus, besides facilitating values and norms, the intertextual palimpsest conceptualises the mediation of mentality in literature. Mumford (1997: 258) argues: "This metropolitan world, then, is a world where flesh and blood is less real than paper and ink and celluloid." As exemplified in the case of psychogeographical writing such as *The Matter of the Heart* or *King Rat*, there are also strong references to other media, for example, film, music, and advertisement, which add to the intertextual palimpsest of London novels.

6.4.5 Hypertextual Simulation

As shown in the former sub-chapter, various idiosyncratic narratives of the metropolis and individual mental chronicles, intertextual references construct the city as a multi-layered text of meaning. There is no metropolitan master narrative, but only stories that convey multiple versions of the city's fluent 'autobiography'. Mancini (2003: 172) therefore argues that "the city acquired such a depth that no metaphor could exactly represent; except, maybe, the hypertext." Various London novels published between 1997 and 2007, such as Geoff Ryman's internet novel *253* (1998), J.G. Ballard's *Millennium People* (2001), but also Iain Bank's *Dead Air* (2003), Will Self's *Dorian* (2003), Martin Amis' *Yellow Dog* (2003), William Gibson's *Pattern Recognition* (2004), and Hillary Mantel's *Beyond Black* (2005), employ notions of hypertextuality/hyperreality to represent the postmodern city-text as a contemporary palimpsestic network of layers.

In contrast to Genette's firmly print-based use of hypertextuality, in the 1960s Theodor Nelson coined the term "hypertext" referring to a nonsequential text on an interactive screen that branches and allows the reader to take different pathways in reading (cf. Orr

2003: 49). Today, the internet encompasses both notions of intertextuality, because the tissues of its hypertexts represent a networked text structured by links, paths, annotations, and a vast assemblage of fragments. The palimpsestuous city as hypertext emphasises the postmodern metropolitan space of flows, whereby the urban hypertext is simultaneously polyphonic, atomised, antilinear, multisequential, and borderless. Its characteristics of multiplicity and heterogeneity defy ideas of both hierarchy and chronology. The hypertext in its dispersal of the writer appears primarily opposed to authority, hierarchy and an autocratic univocal voice, stressing the necessity of permutation and heterogeneity (cf. *ibid.*: 56-57). Nevertheless, the hypertextual system in its technological possibility of enhanced control and intensified surveillance also figures as a postmodern version of panoptical power – the Carceral City. These ambiguous aspects of the hypertext are ingrained in William Gibson's (1982) understanding of "cyberspace", a largely urban virtual reality that has both the potential to open unexpected world-views and to enact supplanted hallucinations.

While the social and physical spaces of the contemporary metropolis are likewise affected by networks, mobility and flow, in Frederic Jameson's (1991: 38-39) view this transformation of space is not yet paralleled by a mutation of the subject: "We do not yet possess the perceptual equipment to match this new hyperspace [...], in part because our perceptual habits were formed in that older kind of space." Postmodern spaces like the Bonaventure Hotel initiate gross misconceptions and feelings of dislocation in urbanites, demanding new collective practices of congregation and movement (cf. *ibid.*: 40). Besides the urban transformation of hypertext, cyberspace, and hyperspace, the largest impact on postmodern urban life can be grasped with Jean Baudrillard: The constant iteration and replication of images forms simulacra in which the imitation becomes indistinguishable from the original, giving rise to a new hyperreality.

Joan Resina (2003: 22) shows that palimpsestuous rewriting of urban relations under the condition of simulacra creates an overlay which questions the correlation between locality and authenticity: "the historical imagination is stimulated by quotation – that is, by reference to the traces of that which can no longer be retrieved." He argues that while the past cannot be grasped, an image can only ever exist as an "after-image" (*ibid.*: 12-13). In other words, the perceptual notion of the metropolis already exists in a palimpsest of images indistinguishable from the real. This specifically applies to knowledge of the city, which is largely dependent on mediated images. "Acculturated interpretive dispositions and previously internalized cognitive patterns are fired by the image which is thus connoted, turned into a visual aid for meanings that precede it in the social field." (*Ibid.*: 14) Contemporary mental images of the metropolis thus constitute a new kind of visual simulacrum (cf. *ibid.*: 8).[76] Putting an emphasis on the copying effect of the metropolitan texture and employing Baudrillard's concept of simulacrum, one can argue that the metropolis in its various sequels of simulations has become an ahistorical hypertext. In the following I will analyse the metaphor of the palimpsestuous city in reference to hypertextual simulations in Geoff Nicholson's *Bleeding London* (1997) and Matthew De Abaitua's *The Red Men* (2007).

---

76 | This idea of the after-image as a visual sensation that lingers through mediated simulations after the stimulus has disappeared (cf. Resina 2003: 1) is especially apparent in the mediatised images of 9/11.

Metropolitan Hyperreality

As continuously developed in the last chapters, the three protagonists in *Bleeding London* idiosyncratically map the metropolitan territory to shape London in their own image. Stuart London observes that "London is mythical [...], created in the image of each of its inhabitants, newly imagined with each new citizen, with each new attempt to describe it." (BLL: 301) These perspectives on London are inevitably partial because constructions of the mind exemplify the rendering of the physical real city to text, image, simulacrum, and finally hyperreality. In *Simulacra and Simulation* Baudrillard (1997:1) argues: "The territory no longer precedes the map, nor survives it. Henceforth, it is the map that precedes the territory – a precession of simulacra – it is the map that engenders the territory [...]."

Especially in Stuart's appropriation of the city we can follow this significant spatial transformation from the real to the hyperreal. Simultaneously walking and rewriting the city Stuart reduces the map to an abstraction and finally a mere image of London (BLL: 8; cf. Deny 2009: 258). It is a visual simulacrum which, in the logic of Baudrillard, masks the fact that London itself has long since become unreal. Although Stuart's diary entries are intended to retain the reality of his metropolitan excursions and establish a certain authenticity of his experiences (BLL: 329; cf. Deny 2009: 108), his wife Anita ultimately identifies them as literary fiction: "What you were doing was creating a new London, inventing a new city, a city of words, something in your image." (BLL: 331) Containing the illimitable and instable metropolis within a stable and limitable text bears witness to a certain aspatiality and atemporality.

In the fashion of postmodern overload and reserve, Stuart is bored with his daily tourist walks of London and through his personal tour of the metropolis strives to still his aggrandised hunger for stimulation and spectacle. His wife achieves to cater for this obsession with entertainment by offering more pop-culture oriented walks to London tourists (BLL: 73-75). The commodification of London's history and geography renders the city a mere collection of postcards, souvenirs, and maps – dispositionally clothing the monstrous city in a postmodern user mentality. As argued concerning the historical and the psychogeographical palimpsest, the contemporary rewriting of London collapses the tension between temporal layers, "especially when the imagined past is sucked into the timeless present of the all-pervasive virtual space of consumer culture." (Huyssen 2003: 10)

Anita London, an embodiment of the post-Thatcherite New London capitalist, in accordance with "New Labour's millennial attempts to re-brand London as centre of a brave new England" (Chilton 2007: 12) aims to turn the city into "[a] neater London" (BLL: 73). Anita is engaged in her own work of mapping London: together with foreign businessmen she plans to build a mini-version of London on a Japanese island. This theme-park is to solve London's spatial problem of being "too big, dirty, dangerous and expensive, and [...] too far away from Japan." (BLL: 332) On an area comfortably coverable within an afternoon, the simulated city will encompass key touristic attraction like geographical landmarks and historical monuments, but also London's modern architecture, its main shops, and public transport (BLL: 332-333). Moreover, the commoditised version of London is to transfer metropolitan historicity turned spectacle, such as re-enactments of the Great Fire, the Plague or the Blitz. Although to Stuart this homogenised and even essentialist version on London "sounds like hell" (BLL: 333),

Anita's plan just brings into being Japanese abstract mental maps of the metropolis. In this sense, the Lilliputian London with its buildings, experiences and products is a mere simulacrum which overcomes both London's territory and the cartographic map (cf. Chilton 2007: 11). While for Baudrillard (1997: 53), Disneyland serves as an example of concealing "the fact that it is the 'real' country, all of 'real' America, which is Disneyland", the Japanese tourist version in *Bleeding London* actually hides the fact that London has become a mere simulation of itself.[77] Despite all this, Schlaeger (2003b: 33) is right to stress that the theme-park vision of London does not have a direct effect on Londoners' everyday lives. Still, without potential Japanese tourism, both the branding and the image of the metropolitan centre will experience change.

Various critics have commented that Geoff Nicholson's parodic version of visionary London is a cleverly crafted postmodern narrative which pays heed to the heterodox experiences of the metropolis as well as the plurality of normative key elements in a contemporary remapping of London (cf. Onega & Stotesbury 2002a: 16; Rawlinson 2002: 250). In cataloguing nearly all possible variants of depicting a city, *Bleeding London* is self-reflexive concerning representations of the city (cf. Mergenthal 2002: 126-127). Its multiple exercises in urban spatiality, such as reconstruction, deconstruction, recognition, abstraction, alienation, dissemination, dispersal, intertextuality, pastiche, and hyperreality of spatial references defy any notion of true readings of cityscape and reality (*ibid.*: 133; Dreyer 2006: 85-86). In this sense, Dreyer (*ibid.*: 67) accentuates that Nicholson metafictionally plays with the notion of holistic urban representation mirrored in the novel as obscure mental challenge. We can thus conclude that *Bleeding London* comprises the same images the Japanese want to simulate (cf. Chilton 2007: 14). And due to Mick's expectations, London is also already pre-imagined in people's mind (*ibid.*: 17). While the historical and social city cannot be cloned, its images are perceived, produced and seemingly endlessly reproduced in spectacles and simulations that render the city increasingly hyperreal.

Simulations of the Urban-Generic

Matthew de Abaitua's debut novel *The Red Men* (2007)[78] is set in London, more specifically Hackney, in the near future. The narrative is an Orwellian vision of contemporary society including computerisation, automation, simulation, biotechnology, surveillance and their implications for the urbanite characters (cf. Jordison 2007). One of them, the Jewish writer Raymond Chase, polemically describes the transformation of the post-millennial metropolis in the following way: "Your worst fears have come true. Before the millennium, you worried about global surveillance, aliens, mind control. You couldn't think straight for fear. Now it's actually come to pass [...]." (REM: 294) Similar to Miéville's *King Rat* and Williams' *London Revenant*, *The Red Men* instead of featuring an alternative (fantastic) London geography, devises the fictitious metropolis as structurally homologous to the real space of postmodern London. At first glance, a fantas-

77 | Similar to the simulated London in Geoff Nicholson's novel or the theme park in Julian Barnes' *England, England* (1998), in 2006 British architects built Thames Town in China (http://www.thamestown.com) advertised as "the real thing."

78 | In the following *The Red Men* will be abbreviated to REM.

tic element is introduced through the interspersion of technological innovations, which are however plausible developments of our present age, narrated in a hyperbolic and grotesque formation. From the perspective of Raymond, the post-millennial metropolis is depicted as an overabundant yet predictable consequence of urban metamorphosis:

> The counter-cultural prophesies of the 1990s have all come true. A fundamentalist Christian business culture? Check. Robots? Check. An overwhelming, vertiginous terror that the real world has slipped its moorings and is blipping in and out of the banal and quotidian and some deranged power fantasy... CHECK CHECK CHECK. (REM: 107)

During the 1990s, the narrator Nelson Millar was the professional editor of a metropolitan magazine, which at the time seemed to be a counter-cultural experiment of "Cool London" in retrospect to the Sixties' "Sexy London" (REM: 32, 61). But from the post-millennial perspective its title *Drug Porn* is a notable premonition of counter-culture corrupted by the commodification of pornography and drugs to mainstream practices (cf. Jordison 2007). He also acknowledges that with 9/11 the era of naivety concerning socio-economic power structures came to a close, marking the end of the "brand age" (REM: 64) and the "dawn of the unreal age." (REM: 318)

Otherwise, post-millennial London has become the epitome of Castells' notion of the Informational City: an electronic network of information and a flexible space of flows that reach all domains of contemporary urban life. But in contrast to the modern city which is characterised by "stationary architecture and moving masses", the new virtual city is dominated by still and torpid urbanites "while the cinematic space of flows swirls around them." (Warf 2008: 67) In *The Red Men*, the main node of London's space of flows significantly is "the Wave Building" (REM: 43) as the headquarters of the monopolising technological giant Monad situated at Canary Wharf's West India Dock.[79] The tower of One Canada Square is described as "a beacon of capitalism", while the steel panels of its pyramid are an "all-seeing eye" (REM: 43) expressing its urban surveillance power over the city. Similar to Bonaventure's dislocated spaces, the poet Raymond Chase walking through the wharf is lacking in mental facilities of orientation that would have made it possible to distinguish "where indoors ended and outdoors began" (REM: 43). The masses of commuters and pedestrians represent a hypercrowd of "demographically-engineered London" marked by a certain "velocity" of streaming along the "faux-cobbled walkway" (REM: 43). The hyperspace of the Isle of Dogs seems to be defined by dispositions of feeling like alienation, uncertainty, and anxiety. For Raymond – quoting the philosopher Henri-Frédéric Amiel – "[a] landscape is a state of mind" (REM: 46). The Wave Building itself has the atmosphere of the "headquarters of a cult" (REM: 35) and mainly lies underwater. Only connected to the wharf by narrow retractable walkways, its surface offers few weak points of attack. Thus, the node of the Informational City is also an absolute space with an entrance protected by a metal scanner where people are "analysed, measured, identified and approved." (REM: 44) Monad

79 | A monad is a topological model denoting the product of encapsulation created through movement; in other words, the monad is a place formed by the manifold interrelations in the space of flows.

is represented as another fortified spatiality of the postmodern metropolis that defines its inhabitants' mentality once again as isolationist.

From a narratological point of view, the island-like water-city of the Wave (REM: 44, 55) pays heed to the tropes of utopian literature, such as Thomas More's *Utopia* (1516) or Jules Verne's *Twenty-Thousand Leagues Under the Sea* (1870). Walking through the building, Raymond is overwhelmed by its science-fictional world of 'unreal' technology (cf. Jordison 2007), especially its pliant and organic computers made of genetically engineered viruses that enable the screen to adapt to any surface, travel through the city, and slide under doors (REM: 36-37). The enhanced overload of stimuli makes Raymond raise the level of coping mechanisms which in turn leads to an obliteration of memory: "He put his forgetting down to the raising of his 'reality filters', the screens that protected his vulnerable self against the terrible advance of impossible, unthinkable information." (REM: 49)

The company's robots have already conquered urban space. The seven feet tall Dr Easy, designed for comfort with his mournful eyes, round head, soft body and open hands, holds a certain amount of love for humanity (REM: 16, 18). With resistance rising against the technological overhaul by Monad, the robots are revised to avatars called Dr Hard made of a compound of aluminium, magnesium, and boron – "an unfeeling indifferent golem, operating on motor functions only" (REM: 242). All these robots are inhabited by an artificial intelligence called Dr Ezekiel Cantor which is variously described as both god and artist (REM: 200, 333). His purpose lies in "rewriting reality" (REM: 333), constituting a hypertext of memories, ideas, facts, evidence, anthropological observations, and filling its gaps by statistically recurrent narrative structures. Controlled and overwhelmed by this monstrous mass of information Cantor possesses, the palimpsest of the city as historical, psychogeographical, social or intertextual formation is rendered virtual and hyperreal.

Matthew de Abaitua's *The Red Men* captures the influence of new communication technologies on urbanity in the example of the digital or simulated city. While the contemporary hyperspace offers gradual simulations as virtual cities, in simulation games, and simulations of urban development, urban simulation initiates a certain convergence of virtual and real cityscapes, but at the same time neglects the specificity of reality or – its depth and essence. Monad fancies itself as a company à la IBM, Microsoft, Apple, or Google whose products altered the *conditio humana* of its time (REM: 73). The company owner Hermes Spence's advanced vision is to simulate a whole town. In a polemic talk about the stasis in politics and the manifold crisis of the twenty-first century – "energy, mental health, fertility and mortality rates, terrorism, global warming" (REM: 178) – he suggests to create Redtown, a simulation of a British town that will allow predictions on significant political, socio-cultural and economic measures:

> Imagine a normal British town, average population of about thirty thousand. What if there was some way to set the entire town aside as a closed test group. A living, breathing model village. If you wanted to track the effects of a new educational policy, or the consequences of a tax hike, then wouldn't it be wonderful to plug those numbers in and see them ripple across every aspect of that town's life? Not merely economic consequences, but psychological and social ones as well and – yes – the consequences of that policy on voter attitudes. Wouldn't such a tool revolutionise government and business, and make life better for everyone? (REM: 178-179)

As a fit model for Redtown, Nelson chooses Maghull, a suburb of Liverpool (REM: 183). The aim is to have an average all-English town as a foundation for simulation – ninety-eight percent white, predominantly protestant, two generations (REM: 193). Hence, the choice of a largely homogeneous community which devalues complexity, difference, and otherness as significant characteristics of urban culture neglects an important factor of the urban equation. The project therefore seems doomed from the beginning. Beforehand, the London suburb of Hampstead is ruled out because of the higher price in psychological privacy and its ethnic diversity.

> Although there is homogeneity to the world's bourgeoisie, agglomeration around values of education and status, the underlying differences of religion, culture and immigrant experience would require different base algorithms, taking up too much of Cantor's mind. (REM: 193)

The model always obstructs the interrelation of juxtaposed and contradictory layers in an urban society so noticeable in the metaphor of the palimpsestuous city. In other words, neither will the simulation feature heterogeneity as a defining element of urbanity, nor will it cast decisive elements of an urban-generic mentality. Since the virtual algorithms do not care for ethnicity (REM: 169), this conceptualisation not only homogenises but also on a general basis rules out the stranger and the hybrid man as a major group of the urban environment. A difference in urban perspective or mentality on a generic basis also comes to the fore during the process of simulation (REM: 188-189). The inhabitants are seemingly not inhibited by signing over the "copyright to the contents of [their] mind[s]" (REM: 190) to Monad because they depend on confession and the "cult for self-exposure" (REM: 198). The question remains whether this attitude towards privacy is socially (class) or spatially (town-metropolis) related to the differences between a northern provincial town and the capital.

Despite these model-based mistakes in the initial choice of the generic town to debase urban complexity, Nelson as project manager pays minute attention to the creation of Redtown's mental map:

> you create a mindmap, first plotting landmarks. Being at mother's bedside as she dies corresponds to the central business district. A teacher praising a precocious reader matches up to the canal, the construction of which accelerated the growth of the town. The recognition that you will never fulfil your promise is a new housing estate on an old school field. Guilt at abandoning your family, the overgrown marshland beside the railway station. Each of these places exerts a continuing influence upon the citizenry: like a traumatic memory, their subtle pressure persists. (REM: 194)

His colleagues specifically map and catalogue every house, park, pub and shop in Maghull, psychogeographically identifying a church from the twelfth century as "one of the cardinal hotspots in the town's mind" (REM: 203). In this respect, the creative minds from London are sensitive to the importance of the town's socio-historical spatialities for the unconscious of its inhabitants and the creation of their cognitive as well as emotional, imaginary, and habitual maps:

Accurately capturing the circuit flowing between landscape and mind was crucial to the simulation. Cantor never grasped the human unconscious, the red men were utterly secular – that is, temporal, their selves partaking of none of the archetypal, eternal patterns encoded deep with the human brain. In crafting Redtown, Eakins and I decided that landmarks would take the role of these unconscious impulses. The marshland around Maghull railway station, the secluded set of swings in Glenn Park, the disused tracts of the Cheshire Lines would emanate their own dark music. (REM: 204)

In this sense, the seemingly homogeneous town develops an unforeseen complexity, unable to be grasped by the absolute dictatorship of a single autocratic mind-space. The project has to include day-to-day life in the simulation, like work places, colleagues and jobs as well as leisure, shopping trips and pub nights out, the minute differences between "a pint at the Meadows on a Friday night with old school friends" and "drinking on a summer evening beside the canal outside the Running Horses." (REM: 272) Nelson and his team also conceive that the relations with the surrounding periphery and the differences to other suburbs around Liverpool need to be explored. This objective brings them into the non-places of the town which seem to determine the real idiosyncrasy of the city: "The greenbelt separated Maghull from Kirkby to the south east, and Ormskirk to the North, two towns against which the character of Maghull was defined. [...] The personality of Maghull was suspended between these two poles." (REM: 275)

Consequently, the simulation of a whole town is uncovered as a project of inhumanity because the artificial intelligence is unable to grasp the authentic fabric of urbanity and endangers the prerequisite of heterogeneity. Any urban simulation thus equals a project of eradication or social eugenics. In an economic simulation of tax reduction, Redtown gives out unexpected answers of depression and apathy (REM: 340). While the management accuses the artists of having underestimated economic vigilance, the American customers put it down to the unexpected importance of the soul in economic doctrine (REM: 341). In his tests on Redtown, Nelson keeps unleashing apocalyptic catastrophes on the simulated town because "[i]t concealed the biggest flaw in the simulation; the degradation of its integrity – its reality principle" (REM: 244). Because simulation defies the difference between reality and fiction, it is unable to represent realities which are based on ambivalent relations to the imaginary.

In *The Red Men*, Monad is devised as a technology teleported from the future (REM: 58, 372) which comprises all the structures of the current Informational City and its fluid spatialities. Furthermore, the novel traces back the correlation of counter-culture and monopolistic economic culture to an ambivalence intrinsic to London's urbanity, whether in a post-millennial, 1990s, Sixties or WWII London (REM: 29, 33, 160-161, 288). In this sense, the novel is less speculative than retrospective or even realist – debunking, as Baudrillard (1997: 122) states, the difference between science fiction and the real. However, the discourse of simulation and hyperreality defies the notion of an one on one overlapping of original and copy, so that – like in the case of the communal simulation of a whole city – simulation always induces socio-cultural homogenisation, which is contradictory to metropolitan dynamics.

But, as Baudrillard predicted, totalitarian surveillance produces its own opposition. Seeking to eliminate external aggression, integrated and hyper-integrated systems secrete their own internal virulence, their own malignant reversibility: when a certain saturation-point is reached such systems undergo this alteration willy-nilly, and tend to self-destruction: [...]. (Ashford 2008: 24)

In recalling the double nature and the force of the Other in a metropolitan environment, the metropolitan equilibrium is reversed: "The reality principle set about its work, ensuring the simulation obeyed the laws of the real world." (REM: 354) The dystopian vision of an age of eternal reproduction and surveillance which destroys the sanctity of the original and authenticity is counterpoised by a hopeful notion of the urban ambivalences at play.

The corporation of Monad is doubled by that of Dyad paying heed to London's twofold character in terms of physical, social, and mental space: (1) nostalgic, derelict, earthbound, heterogeneous, and Babylonian Hackney versus futuristic, reconstructed, watery, homogeneous, New Jerusalem Canary Wharf; (2) urban down-and-out versus executive elite; (3) organicity and drugs versus technology and porn (REM: 249). In the fragmented interplay of decline and rebirth, East London has become a multi-layered palimpsest which defies two-dimensional simulation:

Looking down over the East End I felt the jigsaw of time had been upset. One street was a pre-industrial bazaar while another was the dividing line between the feudal fiefdoms of two crimelords. Chimney sweeps were torching bemused androids. Sweeney Todd butchers his patrons to sell their organs in the Clapton black markets. Peter The Painter chairs the latest Great Refusal meeting. Is that a Romany convoy camped on the Mile End Waster or is it the Peasant revolt rebels? Are the Luftwaffe and al-Qaida still conspiring to destroy Target Area A? (REM: 357)

The simulated versions of London in Geoff Nicholson's *Bleeding London* and Matthew De Abaitua's *The Red Men* both foreshadow urban life in an age of cyberspace and mirror the transformations put into place in the contemporary postmodern metropolis. As the urban becomes increasingly hyperreal, the metaphor of the palimpsest enables the protagonists to navigate the unreal city while the palimpsestuous complex layering of social meaning defies the homogenising potential of the simulacrum.

6.4.6 Palimpsestuous Structures of Mentality

Sharpe and Wallock (1987: 38-39) argue: "Whatever words we employ, field or atom or something as yet unnamed, they will shape our city, for the kind of metaphors we choose will influence the kind of city we see." As was shown, the image of the city as palimpsest is a recurrent master metaphor in contemporary London novels, and is represented as lending a largely ordering and stabilizing linguistic presence in a fictional universe of enormous complexity such as is the contemporary literary metropolis. The master metaphor of the palimpsest mirrors the urban structure as a layered text built up over time, a coating of architecture and life but also ideas, images and feelings. In other words, the palimpsest is the perfect metaphor for the contemporary notion of the city *E Pluribus Unum*.

> Palimpsestuous metaphoricity is the catachresis of metaphor [...], a metaphor of metaphor. [...] palimpsestuous is in fact another name for the catachrestic-metaphorical relationality represented in and by the palimpsest. (Dillon 2007b: 55)

Even if the palimpsest is sometimes employed as a direct metaphor, it is mainly linked to an unconscious structure of various spatial configurations emphasising its significance for contemporary urban dispositions of thinking. Due to the interrelation between metropolis and urbanite, the palimpsestic layers of London are imprinted on the urban mind. De Quincey (1968b: 346) uses the image of the palimpsest to show how memories are written in the mind and overlap:

> What else than a natural and mighty palimpsest is the human brain? Such a palimpsest is my brain; such a palimpsest, oh reader! is yours. Everlasting layers of ideas, images, feelings, have fallen upon your brain softly as light. Each succession has seemed to bury all that went before. And yet, in reality, not one has been extinguished.

The metaphor also reveals the way in which the knowledge of the city is formed, mediated, destabilised, superseded, and reactivated. As a place of history and memory on which signatures of the past overlap with recent reading and writings, the city emphasises coexistence and juxtaposition. Therefore, the palimpsestuous city not only functions as a metaphor for the "*simultaneity* of arrangement" (*ibid.*: 348) in postmodern urban space, but the notion of the "memorial palimpsest of the brain" (*ibid.*: 347) also dispositions urban thinking. Augé (1997: 16) points out that the palimpsestic urban memory communicates with the inhabitants' memories to provoke and challenge the palimpsest of the urbanites' minds. The city wrought by monuments is increasingly the space of historical expressions, and every individual walking through the city comes across personal memories. In this way, the city as a whole comprehends and mixes great history with individual stories.

Furthermore, the metaphor stresses that traces from mental structures of the past still have relevance for the present, while the palimpsest also conveys ideas of change and transformation. This notion of long duration of the historical palimpsest is especially revealed in Geoff Nicholson's *Bleeding London* and Jane Stevenson's *London Bridges*. Because all the novels selected for this analysis have their narrative setting in the Blair era, palimpsesting layering encompasses a strong retrospective view, also in the sense of including intermedial (MAH, KRA, REM), intertextual (KRA, BLL, SAT), or intercultural references (KRA, BRL). Moreover, all literary texts in their postmodern style defy linear chronological narration and juggle multiple time frames, multiperspectivity, flashbacks, hallucinations, and visions. The metaphor of the palimpsest is enhanced by the texts' narratological techniques representing the density of urban space-time.

The psychogeographical palimpsest moreover spatialises ideas of temporal displacement, sequentiality, suppression, engagement etc. and connects them to the contemporary urban *conditio humana*. Ripples of significance oscillate between the various temporal strata of the metropolis, their spatial materialisation leaving an imprint as after-image of sensation within the hidden and unconscious zones of the metropolis and its urbanites. The connotation of the palimpsest as interference, haunting, and resurrection is taken up in psychogeographical literature (BLL, MAH, LOR) in the narrow sense, but also by fantastic literature in the wider sense (KRA, REM), devising the figure of the revenant, the ghost, and the double as personifications of the forgotten or oppressed strata of urban life (historical, geographical and social). Regarding mental dispositions, the palimpsest furthers the notion that the urbanite is not only met by a daily overload of stimuli, but additionally challenged through the cryptic haunting of the mind by inexplicable or atmospheric hidden phenomena of the metropolis that create uncertainties by blurring the boundaries between internal/external, life/death, presence/representation. The analysis has shown, however, that psychogeography is a viable measure of orientation in the postmodern urban environment.

The idea that there is no displacement of other cultural texts was explored in the socio-cultural palimpsest, where postcolonial novels such as Monica Ali's *Brick Lane* have been analysed in their intercultural inscriptions of urban space and the juxtaposition between urban/rural or metropolitan/peripheral mentality. Instead, China Miéville's *King Rat* brings into focus the subcultural and class-induced layers of the metropolitan mental structure. Both novels emphasise that urban vigilance is largely produced by the heterogeneity, strangeness and individualism of people considered Other. The palimpsestuous city aims to unconsciously integrate marginalised groups into the textures of its own transformability. In consequence, the imprint of the palimpsest on the urbanite's mind is enabled to negotiate the encounters of the generic urban stranger.

The intertextual palimpsest has furthermore brought into focus that there is no displacement of former (mental) text in the city because the literary London texts are notoriously palimpsestic and vice versa: "The trope of the palimpsest is inherently literary and tied to writing, but it can also be fruitfully used to discuss configurations of urban spaces and their unfolding in time without making architecture and the city simply into text." (Huyssen 2003: 7) This interrelation between city-text and text-city has exemplary been explored in *Bleeding London* and *Saturday*, where the navigation of the city is mediated by the various urban intertexts. The palimpsest of literary London functions as a means of orientation in the metropolitan realm shaping certain narrative patterns of behaviour, collective imaginaries and specific emotional tropes. This intertextuality of the palimpsestuous city currently also encompasses cross-medial references to pictorial art, cinema, and different areas of popular culture.

Finally, the hypertextual palimpsest takes up the notion of computerisation, technologisation and simulation of the postmodern metropolis. The novels under analysis defy the idea of successful simulations of the urban, since hyperreality obliterates the urban-specific historical layers, the city's intrinsic 'feel' and atmosphere, the socio-cultural heterogeneity and intertextual multidimensionality. Literary London in Matthew de Abaitua's *The Red Men* has become the epitome of the Informational City. It devises urban simulation as a project of anomic homogenisation, which due to the urban-generic ambivalence and definition of the city as heterogeneous is destined to fail. The dynamics of the space of flows configure their own vigilant counter-flows which in parallel to the nostalgic spatial mode oppose the futuristic absolute space of hyperrealiy. However, this moment of urban transformation, in the sense of a social space-time compression is characterised by mental confusion and disorientation whereby the metaphor of the palimpsest serves as a cultural technique and tool for urban characters to protect themselves and others against personal loss and collective anomie. The palimpsestuous mentality thus keeps equilibrium in navigating between the real and the hyperreal.

Consequently, we can contend that the metaphor of the palimpsestuous city offers a contemporary coping strategy against a postmodern London overload induced by temporal, spatial, social, textual, and hypertextual compressions of the metropolis. While characters fight the enhanced stimuli with aggravated methods of distanciation, such as intoxication (blasé), intolerance (reserve), and authority (intellectualisation), they cannot resist their urban drive for more stimuli and spectacle leading them back onto a path to search for hidden authenticity and plurality beyond the urban simulacra. These structures of mentality hence underline ambivalences of strangeness, heterogeneity, tolerance, and vigilance.

Contemporary London presents a palimpsestuous construction in which the visible interacts with the invisible. London's text as an endless reservoir of encrypted knowledge and hidden possibilities asks for the decoder to read its monuments and unravel secrets and reveal the urban-specific. The palimpsestic cityscape with buildings from the past alongside postmodern architecture emphasises the nature of the metropolis as becoming. The intrinsic palimpsestuous character of the city as a texture of recurrent erasures and new beginnings demands a continuous process of revision and retranslation. The city-dweller constantly confronted with the palimpsestuous city is asked to construct a particular urban cognitive itinerary.

With a view to the incorporation of mentality, the literary texts anthropomorphise the palimpsestuous city in offering personifications of the historical, psychogeographical, socio-cultural, intertextual and hypertextual palimpsest. The metaphor itself is brought into being and becomes flesh. The tropic figures of the *flâneur* as historian or prostitute (BLL, NXT, BRL), the double as psychogeographer, revenant, ghost or simulation (MAH, LOR), the stranger as cosmopolitan or hybrid man (BLL, BRL, KRA), and the author as writer, narrator, or reader (SAT, REM) have adapted to the palimpsestuous nature of the city. They resemble the city in becoming: the *flâneur* with an emphasis on the spatial and cognitive, the psychogeographer on the temporal and emotional, and the stranger on socio-cultural transcendence by novel habitus, the narrator in the imaginary process of internal cultural transformation. The palimpsestuous city therefore encompasses all the major personae of urban literature emphasising the inclusiveness of the metaphor in depicting the multifarious metropolis (see figure 6.1).

(1) The modern *flâneur* can decode the signs of the city through browsing the urban palimpsest (cf. B. Baker 2003). This figure perceives city life as a spectacle to be consumed, and moves in the same urban direction as the crowd without being within the crowd but notably separated from collectivity. In this sense, the *flâneur* inherits an exploration of the threshold between community and individualism. In contemporary London novels, however, the figure is transformed into one not only reading the palimpsest but reimagining, recombining, reconstructing the city as well. This is where the *flâneuse* – prostitute, *femme fatale*, Babylonian whore – is often devised as the equivalent of the urban poet or writer. The streetwalker – *flâneur*, walker, wanderer, prostitute, or stalker – transgresses the city and stresses the fluidity and contradiction of the urban space (cf. Pike 2005a: 265). Appropriation of the trope around the turn of the millennium creates the new type of a city stalker with intent (cf. Schlaeger 2003a: 58):

> The concept of 'strolling': aimless urban wandering, the *flâneur*, had been superseded. We had moved into the age of the stalker; journeys made with intent—sharp-eyed and unsponsored. The

Figure	Determinant	Analogy	Characteristic
Flâneur Walker Stalker	Space	City	Texture
Psychogeographer Revenant Double	Time	History	Layers
Stranger Migrant Hybrid Man	Collective	Society	Content
Narrator Writer Author	Collective Space-Time Compression	Culture	Transparency

Figure 6.1: Urban Figures and the Palimpsestuous City

> stalker was our model: purposed hiking, not dawdling, nor browsing. This was walking with thesis. With a prey. ... The stalker is a stroller who sweats, a stroller who knows where he is going, but not why or how. (Sinclair 2003: 75)

The stalker is a composite figure that comprises other walkers with a thesis – especially the detective or the historian.

(2) Both figures necessarily need to read urban space pychogeographically to extract its essential secrets. Moreover, any history or detection is not only an act of geography and history but likewise an act of autobiography and writing (cf. Soja 2008a: 12) often represented as de-traumatisation. In this respect, the spatial atmosphere is strongly intertwined with the psychological existence of the urbanites in London's non-places. Dislocation only furthers the significance of the spectral traces over the city which inhabit and define the palimpsest of the urbanite's mind as "cryptic incorporations" (Dillon 2007b: 32). A notion of revenance is very prominent in Conrad Williams' *London Revenant*, but other novels (MAH, KRA, REM) also inherit the idea of the uncanny, the double, or ghostly haunting. In a sense, contemporary revenance symbolises the resurrected anxieties of an urban *horror vacui* due to metropolitan surveillance architecture and non-places which destroy a feeling of homely existence and generate a psychological state disrupted by the unhomely. This influence of revenance is increased due to the power of a repetitious modern technology, for example in Matthew de Abaitua's *The Red Men*, contemporary technologies, media, and culture produce their own ghosts, icons, doubles and simulacra.

(3) The simulations, the virtual and the ghost are identified in this novel as archives of experience that are translated into a language of the urban Other. In that line also lies the denomination of urbanites as strangers – to themselves and others. However, all novels pay heed to the strangeness, homelessness, uncanniness and heterogeneity created as essential to urban life. While Monica Ali's *Brick Lane* emphasises the urban vigilance of an immigrant woman, China Miéville's *King Rat* underlines the importance of a subculture and the urban pariah for further transformation of urbanity itself, a notion that is similar to the counter-cultural movements and their intrinsic ambiguity as depicted in *The Red Men*.

(4) Another form of revenance that is dispersed throughout London fiction analysed in this chapter is the ghost of literary, cinematic, or artistic traces in the novel's intertextual and metafictional elements. Wolfreys (2004: 129) points out the paradox that the author's writing always unconsciously redefines urban existence as well as experience:

> The act of writing London is then a double act: of reading as rereading and rewriting, of invocation and disclosure of the hitherto invisible, whereby what comes to be remarked is what is already at work, and which, in returning, appears as the traces of multiple cultures, histories and events. Therefore, no act of writing can ever control itself or its subject, if it is open in its reception to the city.

Therefore, an urban narrative does not pre-exist in the author's mind but the story is written by the city on the palimpsest of his brain (cf. Pogossian 2010: 23). We also get this notion from the characters who figure themselves as authors, narrators, readers in and of texts: Stuart London in *Bleeding London* rewrites Pepys' diary, Jeanene in *London Bridges* follows literary footsteps around the metropolis, Chris in *The Matter of the Heart* is called a "Chronicler of the Heart" (MAH: 21). Moreover, the analysis has discussed the palimpsesting of urban music by Natasha in *King Rat*, Henry Perowne's literary deliberations in *Saturday*, and the narratological simulations by Cantor in *The Red Men*. The metafictional comments on writing the city resist the notion of a homogenised urbanity and celebrate the diversity of postmodern London.

Contemporary London fiction thereby not only questions the narrativity of the metropolis, but also stresses the variegated versions of the city which revive the dead surfaces of postmodern non-places through walking, reading, writing, and imagining (cf. B. Baker 2003: 17; Barfield 2008). In this respect, the city devises its own hybrid figure, which is writer and reader, author and character, observer and observed (cf. Pogossian 2010: 5). Thus, while Wachinger (1999: 297, 301) remains sceptical in regard to the legibility of the palimpsestuous subtext, he acknowledges (de)palimpsesting as a viable measure to master the metropolis. The metaphor of the palimpsestuous city is internalised in the wandering and writing of urbanites and allows the city's denizens to mentally grasp and navigate metropolitan complexity. The image of the palimpsest stands for mental characteristics as both organon and rhizome. Palimpsestuous mentality allows Londoners to react to the manifold stimuli of new spatialities, because it serves the main functions of the mental organon: organisation, orientation, relief of strain, regulation, and integration. Palimpsestuous structures of mentality then also further the intelligibility of London.

7 Socioscape

While the fist part of the literary analysis accounted for the specific influences of the cityscape upon the mental dispositions of Londoners, this second chapter engages with the city's social space and concentrates on the metropolitan collective. In reference to Lefebvre's notion of social space as encounter, assembly, and simultaneity, "Socioscape" considers the relations between urbanites and their urban way of life including socio-cultural interrelations, transpositions, juxtapositions, and hegemonies as produced and producing in metropolitan space.

Following the ambivalences of urban-generic mentality, this chapter specifically deals with the social theorem of urbanity as represented in contemporary London novels. The analysis is thus informed by the aspects of sociability and anomie, heterogeneity and homogeneity, familiarity and strangeness, community and individualism, as well as indifference and involvement. The first part on "Urban Sociability" (7.1) concerns the various networks of human interrelations in contemporary London casting new sorts of primary and secondary relations in constant interchange with temporary phases of overabundant loneliness. This mental aspect of relational fluidity also becomes apparent on a greater socio-metropolitan scale where tendencies of anomie are devised as shifting towards renewed forms of sociability, because the cosmopolitan social zones of transdifferent contact re-negotiate aspects of familiarity and strangeness within London's socioscape. The second section "London Metropolarities" (7.2) regards the various stratifications of post-Fordist, postcolonial and postmodern London, which open significant views on mental attitudes towards class, gender, and ethnicity in the contemporary city. In reference to a prevailing cosmopolitan nature, the stratified city casts its denizens in the role of strangers, outcasts, pariahs and deviants presenting mental dispositions of urban otherness.

7.1 Urban Sociability

For Ferdinand Tönnies and Emile Durkheim the modern metropolis represents the spatial origin for solidarity, which is accompanied by an overabundant rationality and where social bonds are forged on the ground of common interests. It is argued that urban size enhances individual or social differentiation which loosens both intimate relations and community ties. At least since the Chicago School this metropolitan emphasis on secondary relations, secularisation, individuation, alienation, and segregation has been read as a definite sign of urban anomie. But in contrast to this sociological notion of disintegrating sociability, the socio-cultural heterogeneity of the city nevertheless houses local communities where face-to-face relations and mutual solidarity survive. For example, Karp, Stone & Yeols (1991: 47-48) promote a rediscovery of community in interpersonal relations of urban social organisation transcending ecological boundaries. Hence, communities are either geographically delineated by circumscribed areas, bound by common values, attitudes, ideas, lifestyle, or sustained by social interaction and human communication (cf. *ibid.*: 49-50). Because community is characterised by social dynamics of human interrelations, the latter also feature strong social bonds between urbanites which are equal to those of primary relations.

The London novels under analysis bring into focus the context of both the numerical dimension and diversity of the metropolis including the manifold possibilities of social interrelation. In urban writing, the large number of London's population is represented as the urban masses and assumes the image of an indistinguishable crowd. For instance, the urban characters in Conrad Williams' *London Revenant* compare the metropolitan population with that of insects regularly invading one's privacy (LOR: 246-247). Similarly, Ian McEwan's novel *Saturday* depicts the relation between individualism and community as the protagonist's solipsistic wanderings take place in parallel to the "crowd possessing the streets, tens of thousands of strangers converging with a single purpose conveying an intimation of revolutionary joy" (SAT: 72) during a mass demonstration against the impending war. As was shown, especially contemporary Underground novels such as Geoff Ryman's *253* and Keith Lowe's *Tunnel Vision* represent subterranean narratives on the London-specific urban combination of population size, density, and heterogeneity including the unfolding dynamics of urbanites' civil inattention. Otherwise, the diverse, poly- and multicultural character of the city's society and culture is significantly indicated in all novels. While in *Saturday* the London neurosurgeon Henry Perowne works with a multi-ethnic team at the hospital (SAT: 7) and in Jane Stevenson's *London Bridges* the Australian newcomer Jeanene is momentarily surprised by the diversity and variety of London's population (LBR: 135), postcolonial London novels such as Maggie Gee's *The White Family*, Monica Ali's *Brick Lane*, Patrick Neate's *City of Tiny Lights*, and Gautam Malkani's *Londonstani* directly refer to the cosmopolitan and multicultural city with its diasporic communities or hybrid individuals.

Although each city novel concentrates on a particular fragment of London society, in sum, the texts represent a large variety of typical urban characters – from identity-searching immigrant, marginalized homeless, criminal lower-class thug, affluent middle-class intellectual, to members of London's working class or subcultures and weird urban eccentrics. The social dynamics in this world of strangers as represented by contemporary London novels will be part of this sub-chapter on London's socioscape. Texts interpreted in this section, Tim Lott's *White City Blue* (1999), Monica Ali's *Brick Lane* (2003), J.G. Ballard's *Millennium People* (2003), Nick Hornby's *A Long Way Down* (2005), and Blake Morrison's *South of the River* (2007), are mainly ecological city studies featuring both an urban-specific community and the context of a specific social environment of the city. The analysis will focus on contemporary sociability as developing through networks of human interrelations and urban isolation unfolding on the basis of revolution and renegotiation. In reference to Lofland (1998: 59) I contend that nonconsious dispositions of thinking, imagining, feeling and acting cater to "relational fluidity" enforced by urban heterogeneity.

7.1.1 Networks of Human Interrelation

Studying the significant conditions of living in a big city, one has to acknowledge that metropolitan place and space serve as an anchor of shared experiences. The rootedness of people in a common social space can highlight the interplay between social structures and the structures of the psyche or those of the mind; sharing an imagined space is an indication of common urban sensibilities and thinking. The success of city life depends upon the various overlapping social worlds and human interrelations such as partnerships and family, circle of friends and fellowship, acquaintances and neighbourhoods, professional and special-interest groups, residential and other communities. Therefore, the sub-chapter concentrates on the representation of the city as composed of shifting, mixing, contaminating, experimenting, revisiting, and recomposing collective and personal networks. Understanding how the urban affects people's dispositions of thinking, feeling, imagining and acting demands a decoding of postmodern metropolis effects of social networking.

Dysfunctional Primary and Extended Secondary Relations

The general adage of urban sociologists is that the life of nuclear families appears to be decaying, in the sense that its relations serve fewer functions, shifting sociability from an aggregation of families to one of a collective of individuals. As explored already in "Public and Private", contemporary London novels convey an image of weakening ties of primary groups, especially those of family and friends. The analysis has shown the endangered domestic bliss in Ian McEwan's *Saturday*, the exchange of traditional family structures for new forms of belonging in Monica Ali's *Brick Lane*, the dysfunctional family relations in Maggie Gee's *The White Family*, and the loss of intimacy in Christine Brooke-Rose's *Next*.

Particularly the novels by McEwan and Gee can be classified as state-of-England texts in which the relation between family and nation as well as city and country or public and private is explored. While Thatcherism experienced a boom in classic state-of-the nation pieces, so far Blairite Britain has been assessed especially in Jonathan Coe's *The Closed Circle* (2004) and Blake Morrison's *South of the River* (2007)[1]. The back cover of the latter claims that it "is an anatomy of the way things are, *South of the River* is the big British novel of our times". The blurb, however, further clarifies that Morrison's novel "is not so much 'state of the nation' as state of our souls, marriages, families, hopes and careers – a sharp and sexy portrait of a dysfunctional group of characters, all different yet connected." In any case, as Taylor (2007) points out in his *Guardian* review, it "is not an overtly political book" but rather concerns itself with a "group of people at the mercy of events". The novel thoroughly represents London during Blair's first five years in office in reference to historically significant incidents, but mainly touches upon

1 | In the following *South of the River* will be abbreviated to SOR.

social issues of race and gender relations, career life and marriage, political and personal disillusions, sex and misogyny, death and murder (cf. *ibid.*).[2]

South of the River chronicles the everyday life of five central characters between the 'new dawn' after Labour's landslide election victory in May 1997 and the characters' ultimately transformed urban existence in 2002. The multi-medial and multi-perspective narration circles around Nat Raven, a failed writer reduced to lecturing college students; his wife Libby, an advertising executive struggling to maintain a work-life balance; his lover Anthea Hurt, fifteen years his junior, who is employed by the council as a tree officer and waits for her life to change; his best friend Harry Creed, a black journalist working for the local South-East London paper who feels he does not belong; and finally Jack, Nat's elderly uncle from East Anglia who owns an engineering company. Unfolding between these characters, the narrative builds up more networks of interrelations stretching to the wider family, circles of friends, and colleagues, clients or acquaintances.

The five protagonists are presented as caught in a constant struggle to retain a balance between communal involvement and individualism which also necessarily concerns their professional and personal relations. While Nat is intent to compartmentalise his social life into space-time frames for work at college (Monday to Thursday), a day for his personal needs and friends (Friday) and the weekends for the family, Libby's life is spatially and temporally split into her two roles as business manager with an advertisement company north of the river, and that of a good mother and supporter of the husband south of the Thames. Libby has had an exceptional career, but in her self-transformation from chubby "Beth" to mature "Thin Libby" (SOR: 73) she looses Nat to a younger version of herself. Anthea's urban success is grounded in her ability to constantly adapt her roles to 'environmental' circumstances (SOR: 77, 110, 120, 235). During the brief affair with Nat, she fancies herself as a professional environmentalist and writer. By contrast, Harry is caught in a daily struggle against racism. For a long time he throws himself into work in denial of his nonexistent private life, while at work he straddles a fine line between personal and impersonal journalist writing (SOR: 129-130). As a young man, the night he narrowly escaped the New Cross Fire of 1981 resulted in an indiscretion with a girl and a son whose existence he denies for the following seventeen years. In opposition to the other four characters, Jack Raven's country life is turned upside-down when his wife suffers a stroke, his family business faces insolvency, and hunting is about to be banned. In this manner, the novel exemplifies how professional ambitions come to corrupt private lives.

More specifically, the novel takes into account the dissolution of primary relations, and family ties in specific. From Jack's rural Suffolk perspective, traditional English community values are disintegrating: "They were a quality engineering firm, when quality engines weren't in demand; a family business, when the family was dysfunctional; a country enterprise, when the countryside was going to the dogs." (SOR: 104) Jack's own family is scattered around the world: his daughters live in Paris and Edinburgh with

---

2 | For example, the Stephen Lawrence court case, the World Cup match between Argentina and England, the funeral of Princess Diana, the building of the Millennium Dome, the Millennium bug and celebrations, the hype about Harry Potter books, Oasis hits, the birth of Blair's fourth son, 9/11, foot-and-mouth disease, the Golden Jubilee, the discussion of banning fox hunting, the National Front winning ground in the municipal elections in the East End, etc.

their own families and careers and the line of male Ravens has been disrupted by his nephew Nat, whom Jack thinks a looser. He considers Libby – bright, level-headed, good at business – as totally wasted on his nephew, despite her age and Irish descent (SOR: 249, 472). Libby's own family is also dispersed and lost: her father died years ago, her mother is still resident in Ireland and eventually dies of cancer, while her sister Patsy lives in America. Libby's perfect nuclear family becomes shattered when Nat has an affair and as a consequence the couple splits up, they share the children, and her ex-husband remarries to start a new family. Nonetheless, in a familiar role-play towards a potential Italian client Libby still claims that "family has always come first" (SOR: 443) and that "trust is important in all relationships, at work as well as home" (SOR: 444).

However, dysfunctional families are not a phenomenon of the contemporary city alone. Nat's own parents split up when he was a young boy; growing up without a father notably changes his character from "happy child" to "solipsistic adolescent" whose "one consolation lay in books." (SOR: 18) In a way, this substitute for the lost primary ties paves the way for his later professional life. After ten years of marriage, Nat feels a loss of affection for his wife, who seems to have become drained off her former energy and grown bitter (SOR: 236-237). While Nat considers "[m]arital sex was like living in London – after a time you took it for granted" (SOR: 135), he feels invigorated and euphoric by his affair with a younger woman. Not only does he become "a better husband, a better father" (SOR: 135) but in allusion to Blair's Third Way, he experiences a rebirth: "As though the spirit of a new nation was blowing through him. [...] New Labour, new Britain, new Nat." (SOR: 136) For Anthea, the affair has a similar transformative effect. After her father's early death and her mother's breakdown, Nat becomes a substitute as he reminds Anthea of her dad: "the comfort of being in his arms, hugged, held, enfolded, anchored: that was the same." (SOR: 117) After a time, the lovers' cocoon of comfort, symbolised by their anagram (Ant-Nat) (SOR: 178), brings into question the ambivalent human desire of proximity and commitment versus independence and freedom (SOR: 266-267, 270). While Anthea first escapes Nat on nightly urban walks she finally leaves London for good, seemingly acculturated to the intellectualised and goal-oriented manner of urban emotionality:

> living with someone could be a battle [...]. Or could incarcerate you, as had happened when she was with Nat. [...] Be free of all ties. Have sex, if she needed sex. Even have children, if she wanted children. But never confuse sex with love – or let loving someone deflect her from her purpose. (SOR: 490)

Similarly, Libby decides for the independent leap to New York. Although she begins an interim affair with a colleague who is the exact opposite of her ex-husband – young, energetic, greedy, relentless – she finally recognises that her lover's private and professional self-absorption does not mix well with her idealistic notions of friendship, sex, and love (SOR: 273-275). On finding out that in order not to spoil the dinner with a potential client, he does not inform her of her mother's death, Libby instantly switches from intimate to professional reserve: "As she dressed, she put on her three-monkeys face: not hearing, not seeing, not speaking. The face was one she used when negotiating: in the face of her expressionlessness, clients sometimes panicked and upped the money, even adding a nought." (SOR: 435) While the two female central characters decide to follow a path of professional and private independence, the two middle-aged male characters Nat and Harry actually pursue reconciliation with private and family life. Harry links up with his estranged son, gaining the emotional freedom to begin a new professional life in Boston (SOR: 209, 388-389), while Nat founds a new family with a long-term colleague from college and finally resurfaces from depression and apathy (SOR: 482).

Although the novel shows a variety of friendships, the relation between Nat and Harry is explored in most detail. It develops from a student-teacher context to a mateship which is supported by weekly routines of Friday lunches and watching football. This common interest in football emphasises a certain gendered loyalty grounded on the basic rules of competitive sports and fair play etiquette. As a supportive friend, Harry serves as "Mr Alibi" (SOR: 194) lying about Nat's affair, which Libby interprets as a typical "matey pact" between "[l]ads sticking together." (SOR: 259) Instead, Harry is actually quite critical of his friend's behaviour and eventually even feels emotionally consumed by Nat's personal troubles (SOR: 386). The unequal relationship between the two men becomes apparent as Nat also takes financial advantage of Harry while simultaneously pursuing the old power-relation to his former student with his paternalist reproaches concerning his friend's opinions and actions (SOR: 380-381). Nevertheless, "[a]s he hugged Nat goodbye, Harry thought of all the things that divided them (age, race, temperament, social origins) and how their friendship has survived regardless. Maybe that's what defined friendship: an indifference to difference." (SOR: 387) Friendship in *South in the River* is thus not so much defined by commonalities and special interest but founded on practicing tolerance and mutual solidarity.

In the novel, interpersonal relations define a larger individuality and do not abolish notions of community, although it is socially heterogeneous, temporally fluid, and spatially dispersed. From Jack's traditional perspective, a genuine community is located in the country (SOR: 229), yet also in an urban setting a job guarantees "respect, self-worth, a place in the community" (SOR: 103). As shown above, all the urban characters are strongly defined by the securities their professional life has to offer. Not only does their job guarantee a specific social status but the associated social space also makes further contact and interconnection possible, granting the development of various secondary but also intimate relations underneath the initially distanced professional veneer. Temporarily, work can also become a refuge from private troubles or boost private life by way of professional success (SOR: 257, 479). Moreover, as the title of the novel implies, the locale of South London still serves as a larger spatial contact zone for the interrelations developed throughout the novel. The south (i.e. Lewisham, Deptford, Southwark, South Bank, Peckham, New Cross, Carshalton) is seen by the characters as an area of dereliction and a place for losers (SOR: 294). Otherwise, according to Harry's perspective, the people with multicultural backgrounds live here but their "heart lived somewhere else." (SOR: 55) In sharing similar communal concerns, the regeneration of South London under New Labour spurs hopes for change. In that respect, the human interrelations of family, extended kin, and friends are still based on urban ecology.

Social space in *South of the River* is explored in linking and untying primary relations that do not dissolve the social network of the metropolis but rather cast it as transmutable and fluid. Regarding mentality, urbanites have to handle a higher degree of changing social settings, not only in the public but also in the private realm, and quickly adapt to new social circumstances in order not to fall through the networks of urban sociability.

Furthermore, these processes become specifically pronounced due to a stronger drive for personal independence and freedom, mobility, personal interest, and individuation.

The Hoods of Relationship, Friendship, and Fellowship

The cutting and knitting of ties in the net of urbanites' relations is also a main concern in Tim Lott's *White City Blue* (1999)[3], winner of the Whitbread First Novel Award. According to Ochsner (2009: 242), the novel is "above all a book about friendship". Similarly to Keith Lowe's *Tunnel Vision* (2001) and Gautam Malkani's *Londonstani* (2006), but also Ian McEwan's *Amsterdam* (1998), Zoë Heller's *Notes on a Scandal* (2003), or Clare Allan's *Poppy Shakespeare* (2006), Lott explores the urban politics of friendship[4]. The author especially concentrates on gang life, comradeship and the rules of rivalry embedded in power relations represented by four thirty-year old London characters from the White City area of Shepherd's Bush[5]. The first person narrator, Frankie Blue, is a successful estate agent who finds himself in a premature midlife crisis. Feeling convinced that marriage and a circle of friends do not mix, he has to decide between the "marital future" with his fiancée Veronica or the "social past" (WCB: 95) he shares with his mates Tony, Colin, and Nodge.

While Frankie cherishes Veronica's abilities of consideration, honesty, briskness, efficiency and independence and respects her female sensibilities, he is rather spooked by her professionally pathological demeanour of dissecting and getting inside people in order to detect personal damages (WCB: 14, 122). Consequently, Frankie remains incredulous when only after a short get-together Veronica offers him a correct social diagnosis of his best mates: "*You don't like Tony and he doesn't like you. I can't imagine why you're friends at all. You feel sorry for Colin and he resents you for it. The only one who's a real friend is Nodge, I think. He cares about you.*" (WCB: 50-51) Anthony Diamonte is a London hairdresser of Italian descent and performs as the leader of the gang. Throughout the novel, his sophisticated appearance and vigilant demeanour make way for the image of the typical yob or lad: self-obsessed, superficial, pretentious, cruel to others, misogynist, racist, and homophobic. As Frankie later acknowledges, Tony is just a trophy friend who is actually "*a bigoted, selfish, vain, untrustworthy scumbag.*" (WCB: 232) Colin, or the "tortoise" (WCB: 100), represents Tony's exact opposite and serves the others as regular victim. He is depicted as a sensitive computer nerd who still lives with his sick mother and sleeps in a children's bedroom. According to Frankie, Colin "hates discord" (WCB: 30) as much as "he hates change" (WCB: 57). Once best friends in primary school, Frankie and Colin shared a time of harmonious playfulness, a state which the protagonist initially imagined marriage to be like (WCB: 98). While Colin non-verbally expresses his love for Frankie by drawing a picture of their friendship, Frankie sells out Colin to Tony in order to gain the trust of the gang leader. Beaten at home, bullied at school and despised by his mates Colin, finally turns towards God

3 | In the following *White City Blue* will be abbreviated to WCB.

4 | This refers to Jacques Derrida's *Politics of Friendship* first published in English in 1997.

5 | Similarly to the Westway, London's White City is a particularly semantisised space of the metropolis. See for example the World Exhibition in 1893 or The Who's album *White City: A Novel* (1985).

as his only friend. The fourth fellow of the group is Nodge, a semi-intellectual taxi driver with a down-to-earth and no-nonsense attitude, but whose conduct appears rather distanced, lofty, analytical, straightforward, partly cynic and self-righteous. Moreover, Frankie describes him as an autodidact with a spleen for cinematography, contemporary art, and the opera as well as owning a certain sensitivity towards ethnic minorities or the general underdog. In the end, Nodge turns out to be homosexual and becomes Frankie's 'best man'. Although the characters seem very different from one another, their friendship and homo-social bonding is based on a common interest in sports, significant habits and rules, a (superficial) misogynist and homophobic attitude, but also on the dynamics of male competitiveness, hierarchy and power.

Similarly to the male characters in *South of the River*, the most common denominator of friendship in *White City Blue* lies in the friends' mutual interest in football (cf. Ochsner 2009: 241); in school the four of them are the only ones in the whole class supporting the local Queens Park Rangers (WCB: 188). In their shared love for the club they are connected, however, to a wider male community, which the novel draws as a hotchpotch of ethnic and class identities united in their common interest. The atmosphere of the pub during the football match represents familiarity and belonging to Frankie: "A hundred of other faces are upturned also, mostly male. [...] The whole place has an odour of Fosters Ice and Lynx Aftershave. I like it. It smells like home." (WCB: 23) This special interest in football unites individuals and temporally breaks through the dividing lines of their personal socio-cultural backgrounds, creating a cathartic moment of unification:

> All the faces in the pub have lit up and for that one brief second, for that tremendous moment, we all love each other with a sodium-burning intensity. At these rare and wonderful times, to be a mate, to have your mates – there's nothing better. Lager spills on the floor, overturned in the ecstasy. Up on screen, they're doing the same, five team members in blue and white shirts hugging and kissing in perfect joy. (WCB: 27)

What is more, the whole ritual of coming together as friends is carefully mapped out for each night encompassing drinking beer, eating out and routinised patterns of communication: "Nodge complains, Tony provokes, Colin agrees" (WCB: 32) and Frankie lies. But by a fundamental rule of behaviour, they never show any emotional compassion, impression, or joy towards the other. Also the content of their conversations underlies similar restrictions: besides talk about football it is the discussion about women and sex that binds them (WCB: 58; cf. Ochsner 2009: 244). Especially Tony has the urge to prove his virility by talking about his latest sexual conquests and shows a misogynist attitude by regularly employing words like "doris", "doll" or "professional" (WCB: 59, 72, 123). He even implies that Frankie simply wants to get married "[f]*or a bit of regular gash.*" (WCB: 133) According to these set rules of misogyny, the protagonist feels forced to apologise for getting married by using a similar pool of vocabulary: "*She's lovely, Veronica, she'll make a great doris. She's kind, loves me. She's intelligent and warm.* [...] *And she's a terrific shag.* [...] *It's an excuse for a party, isn't it?*" (WCB: 159) Because a similar sexist attitude prevails towards homosexuals (WCB: 21, 173), Nodge later confesses that he did not dare to come out of the closet as it would have meant breaking the rules of their male conduct and the end of their fellowship.

Not only sexual but also bodily power constitutes a major prerequisite in their personal politics of friendship: since school days, Frankie, Tony, and Nodge have been competitive in sports. So-called Diamond Tony is the most dominant of the friends and the rule-setting focus of the group. A bully at school, he now regularly takes financial advantage of his friends (WCB: 75). In order to escape his own outsider status at college, Frankie has perfected his ability to lie and thereby finds his way into the circle of influence around Tony (WCB: 144). "Crybaby" (WCB: 221) Colin, first being the victim of domestic physical and psychological abuse at school, in later years is merely tolerated as the weakest element of the group and the stigmatised underdog whose job it is to come last (WCB: 62). As Frankie sees it, he is again and again put into the position of the complacent, soft, vulnerable, and sad loser of no relevance: "I don't care about Colin, because I know he isn't going to win anyway, and even if he does, it doesn't matter." (WCB: 219) Colin himself describes their friendship as having shifted to a form of fellowship based on sway and dependency: "Although you must have got something out of it, I suppose. A feeling of power? [...] I don't think you see me as a friend really. More as a disciple, or maybe a pet." (WCB: 248) Hence, the strong laddish bonding is mainly founded on strict rules and rigid power structures.

On the other hand, Ochsner (2009: 253, 257) suggests that the subtext of homoerotic bonding between the characters is suffused with feelings of love and maintains the appearance of the group as friends. In this respect, Tony's viciousness doesn't make a difference to Frankie, because he is "sure that underneath it all, we really *do* like each other" and only wonders from time to time "what good is that, if it's always underneath" (WCB: 66). However, his fiancée points out that Frankie is not only ashamed of his friends, but in truth thinks them redundant (WCB: 177-178). In this sense, the protagonist himself sees the foundation of their male community more as matter of routinised and superfluous habits: "We're just ... friends. We're furniture in each other's front rooms, too heavy to move." (WCB: 77) However, their rules of behaviour not only grant a form of stability of identity, but as a place of belonging present a substitute for home (WCB: 39, 235; cf. Ochsner 2009: 248). As the protagonist insists again and again, the friends' commonality is largely the construct of a shared history. In its identity-forming potential the group holds its yearly "***commemoration***" (WCB: 207) – a ritualised celebration of a particular day in their youth, when they found themselves a self-sufficient and all-powerful social monad cut off from the rest of the metropolis (WCB: 191-195). More than anything else, this "*custom*", "*pact*" (WCB: 178) and "*habit*" (WCB: 185) represents the epitome of their interpersonal bonding. Because there is a "breach of *protocol*" (WCB: 213) on various interpersonal levels, the celebration of 14 August in 1998 leads to the breakup of the gang.

Although Frankie later sets out to make up with his friends, the temporal and spatial distance to the group changes the protagonist's perspective from which he is now able to demask Tony as a hollow man: "I see his face [...] as if for the first time. I see that it is, in fact, not good-looking at all. It is violent, and ugly and stupid. [...] Tony is nothing, a vacuum that has acquired a series of useful gestures." (WCB: 258) In contrast, sitting in the back of Nodge's cab and talking to him over the intercom, Frankie finally tunes in to what his friend actually has to say: "it's like hearing the real Nodge, for the first time." (WCB: 265) Although the formal politics of friendship also support a shift towards fellowship with a high potential for a social void, the analysis of interrelations in

White City Blue shows that finally intimate relations are not eclipsed by impersonal ties, but rather that urban friendship tends to retransfer into more selective intimate relations.

Hence, similar to the shift in perspective, primary and secondary relations are also in a constant state of flux. Frankie acknowledges: "It's all drift. History, friendships, being around generally." (WCB: 38) In his discussion with Veronica which friends to invite for their wedding day, the couple unfold an analysis of the nature of friendship (WCB: 39-49; cf. Ochsner 2009: 241). Frankie explores how his friends are geographically dispersed and totally lost "through natural erosion" (WCB: 39), for example due to drug addiction, alcoholism, depression and schizophrenia. Looking at photos of gained and lost relations, he finds that his circle of friends has shrunk to "[t]*en really good ones. Ten more peripherals. A score* [of] *virtual acquaintances. A few left from school, a few more from college, a few picked up at work, perhaps an ex* [...]. *One or two borrowed or stolen from other friends. An ex-flatmate or two.*" (WCB: 41) Grading and parcelling this accumulation of friends in purple for the "undead", green for the completely hateful, yellow for ex-girlfriends, and blue for the untouchables (WCB: 47-49), he recognises that the only ones left over, the ones that had not "retreated into some micro-world" (WCB: 39), are Colin, Nodge, and Tony.

Yet even before their friendship implodes, Frankie has an inkling that he wants to commit himself to his independent micro-world and break loose from the fellowship (WCB: 18). But in order to transform himself and alter his position in the urban realm, he finds that it is imperative to shift the perspective of the relational space (WCB: 110). The protagonist thereby perceives the connections created and broken between people as specifically spatial in the sense that the personal inner spaces shift like the world's continental plates:

> I did not know there was an invisible world within us, in which events move on, irrespective of what we want. Connections here are made and unmade, opportunities are offered, taken or refused. Tentacles of connection reach out or are withdrawn, sometimes suddenly, sometimes gradually. Tectonic plates move, unseen, and cannot move back. (WCB: 154)

In the metropolitan context of London, this constant shift of outer social and inner personal world is inevitable. When Frankie offers a new flat to Veronica the estate agent comments on the cracks in the walls: "*London's built on clay. If you want something that doesn't have a bit of movement, you're in the wrong city.*" (WCB: 13) Speaking with Massey, the metropolitan socioscape of London is prone to the shifting power geometries of space-time. Moreover, Phil Tew (2007: 91) points out that the changing social (power) relations in *White City Blue* also have to be read in the context of the transformations in cultural practices of urban male working-class culture in the 1990s. In other words, relational fluidity in Tim Lott's novel is defined by the change of fleeting, routinised, secondary-intimate, and primary relationships.

Likewise, Adam in Conrad Williams' *London Revenant* is dissatisfied with his circle of friends; neither does he know why he hangs on to them nor why he is not able to fully break with them (LOR: 60). For reasons of personal distanciation he even goes as far as calling them "imagined friends" (LOR: 317). It suggests that he negates real closeness of friendship to a more purpose-based acquaintanceship to stabilise his existence within the urban social void (LOR: 95). Emotional closeness appears to be a no-go between the circles of friends and they acknowledge their lack of social cohesion (LOR: 115) The security Adam temporarily finds with the help of Yoyo is replaced by that of a stable working environment with routinised relations (LOR: 148-149). Hence, similar to *White City Blue*, in *London Revenant* urban friendship seems to be mere pretence, partly self-interest and an empty, meaningless gesture of informal belonging, close to what Louis Wirth defined as fictional kinship groups.

Strangers' Obsessions and Special Interest Groups

Jane Stevenson's *London Bridges* features a disparate (upper-)middle class cast of characters in contemporary London whose connection is based on commonalities in terms of social background (Jeanene & Dilip), sexual orientation (Eugenides & Sebastian), religious affiliation (Hattie & Jeanene), or workplace (Dilip & Edward), while the analysis of Blake Morrison's *South of the River* explored the communities created by region, extended primary relations, and work. For Wirth (1967: 220) the "characteristic urban social unit" is constituted by the "occupational group rather than the geographical area". Urban sociologists argue that urban strangers encounter one another and interconnect in highly specialised groups of interest. In this sense, interpretations of contemporary London novels such as *The Matter of the Heart*, *Bleeding London* or *Tunnel Vision* have shown that urbanites meet on a common ground of certain obsessions (emotional routes, maps, trainspotting), forging networks of interrelation that encompass the whole urban realm. Wirth (1967: 221) describes this form of personal self-fashioning and construction of specialised groups of interest:

> Here the latent energies and capacities of individuals find expression and locate themselves within the range of a favourable milieu. This possibility of segregating one's self from the crowd develops and accentuates what there is of individuality in the human personality. The city gives an opportunity to men to practice their specialty vocationally and develop it to the utmost degree.

In the following I will analyse Nick Hornby's *A Long Way Down* (2005), a multi-perspective narrative of four London strangers united by their preoccupation with suicide as a means to end their seemingly disastrous and unmanageable urban way of life.[6] The overall assumption regarding all of Hornby's characters, according to Heath (2005), "that the behaviour, thought processes and manners of such people had been previously neglected in contemporary writing appears absurd, but Hornby made it seem so; he skilfully pinpointed habits and emotional foibles that felt hitherto undescribed but true." And while "[s]uicide and [...] the state of mind that leads to it, is an intractable subject for literature" (Mars-Jones 2005), the author's popular approach achieves to contain this topic by representing everyday metropolitan structures of feeling concerning isolation and solidarity.

The novel *A Long Way Down* starts on New Year's Eve when four strangers incidentally meet on the roof of Topper's House in Archway with the initial intent to commit

6 | Niederagen (2000: 233) emphasises that Hornby's writing is based on a strong regional consciousness with protagonists that are only fathomable in the context of the dynamic and anonymous life of London. In the following *A Long Way Down* will be abbreviated to LWD.

suicide. The narration thereafter follows the characters' various steps to overcome apathy and loneliness through a reluctant self-help group, forging an "ill-matched alliance" (Briscoe 2005) and finally becoming indispensible to each other in making "it through to a new dawn, new hope" (LWD: 66) back into street-level urban life three months later. The first inversion from apathy to the discovery of sociability as situational organic solidarity is shown when the candidates surprisingly find themselves in a role-play of restraining one another from jumping. The unlikely group of protagonists features Martin, a disgraced TV host, Jess, an unstable teenager and daughter of a Labour junior minister, Maureen, a middle-aged single woman who cares for her chronically disabled son, and JJ, a failed American musician stranded in London.

Martin Sharp is a selfish, superficial, and vain snob who once co-hosted a national morning TV show. After he is imprisoned for sex with an underage girl, Martin is sacked from work, divorced from his wife, estranged from his kids and mauled by the press. Having ended up a lonely loser with an unfulfilling job at a cable station, he makes the "logical decision" (LWD: 3) and conducts all necessary "preparations" (LWD: 7) to jump off Topper's House. The novel's unreliable voice, however, exposes Martin's reasons for committing suicide as less personal shame or regret, but rather the only way out after destroying his own private life and professional career. Even when kept from jumping by the other three protagonists, Martin sees himself as the ultimate failure: "I couldn't even jump off a fucking tower-block without fucking it up." (LWD: 9) Once recrossing the railings of the building's roof and descending the stairs down to street-level, the protagonist wants to return to his lost life. He finally gets the chance to rebuilt his existence when he transforms from "an arsehole" (LWD: 199) to the caretaker of Jess and takes responsibility via mentorship for a deprived teenager.

Eighteen-year-old Jess Crichton is the verbose counterpart to Martin's "cocky articulacy" (Briscoe 2005). She is a troubled, furious, self-destructive and lonely girl who suffers from the family's trauma of her sister's unexplained disappearance. Woog (2005) comments: "Jess has become, in response to this trauma, a foul-mouthed, drug-loving anti-intellectual who says what's in her head without filtering it first." On the one hand, her uninhibited nature helps Jess in approaching strangers and making friends, on the other hand, her inability to handle the urban rules of distanciation further isolate the teen in the habitualised socioscape of London (LWD: 52). Because she lacks the mental equipment to deal with urban social life, Jess becomes afraid of finally ending up on her own and spontaneously decides to jump of Topper's House (LWD: 6). When she runs towards the edge of the roof, she is wrestled down by Martin and Maureen: from her point of view, Jess feels like her ineptitude saved the other two suicides, but from the others' perspective the plan to save the girl gives them an excuse to descend from the tower (LWD: 12, 28). Jess' decision to become a different person is supported by the socialisation within the group of suicide candidates, while Maureen personally helps the Crichton family to overcome their trauma and find back together.

Maureen represents a counter character to all others; especially her mousy, defiant, caring, and restless nature stands in opposition to Jess' aggressiveness. Yet she is equally lonely despite being integrated into the community of her local church. Maureen had sex only once in her life which resulted in a lifelong struggle of caring for her disabled son. Although she sees suicide as a sin, Maureen immaculately plans to anonymously jump off Topper's House: "I didn't want to do it in my own front room, where someone I knew would find me. I wanted to be found by a stranger." (LWD: 10) While her suicide or the death of her own son seem the only options left to her, being 'found' by three strangers opens a way out of her misery by way of a holiday, a job, a social life (LWD: 134-135). The new social interaction not only offers Maureen hope and self-esteem, but also opens the door of her unworldly, lonesome existence to one of gritty urban sociability (LWD: 50).

The fourth character JJ is an American musician whose band broke up and who was dumped by his girlfriend. Left without friends and family in a foreign country, he is debased from touring the country's music stages to delivering pizza in the capital (LWD: 22, 132). But even at work JJ feels like a loser because he is only surrounded by smart immigrants: "I was probably the dumbest out of all the guys at work, or at least the worst educated. We got African doctors, Albanian lawyers, Iraqi chemists ... I was the only one who didn't have a college degree." (LWD: 23) When he decides to commit suicide in order to link up with other artistic geniuses – Plath, Van Gogh, Pollock, Levi, Cobain – JJ finds himself face to face with Martin, Jess, and Maureen instead:

> A middle-aged woman who looked like someone's cleaning lady, a shrieking adolescent lunatic and a talk-show host with an orange face ... It didn't add up. Suicide wasn't invented for people like this. It was invented for people like Virginia Woolf and Nick Drake. And me. Suicide was supposed to be cool. (LWD: 25)

His intrinsic need to build a personality and gain authentic individuality is finally resolved when due to Jess' assistance he takes up busking on London's streets again. Consequently, the social relation to other sad and self-obsessed urbanites helps the suicide candidates to overcome their personal crises and find the stamina to start a new existence in the world amidst many.

Topper's House becomes a threshold space and extraordinary platform of communication reminiscent of Freud's couch. Usually, suicide is a solitary act conducted without visual or vocal contact, in a place where intervention is least unlikely; however, all four suicides "chose the most popular suicide spot in North London on one of the most popular suicide nights of the year, [when] intervention was almost inevitable" (LWD: 43). The unfolding group dynamics between the strangers meeting in the public forum of the roof thwarts all individual intentions (cf. Mars-Jones 2005). Maureen, impatient to get it over and done with, approaches Martin, who already sits on the edge, and inevitably disrupts both their solitary moments.

> I'd been in the zone; I was in a place where it would have been easy to push myself off. [...] I understood with a horrible clarity the impossibility of attempting to resume life down on the ground. But the conversation with her [Maureen] had distracted me, pulled me back out into the world. (LWD: 15)

In their assessment on urban sociability, Karp, Stone, & Yeols (1991: 61) comment that although city life is built on distance and reserve, denizens can only tolerate a certain amount of impersonality: "Perhaps at the height of feelings of depersonalisation and lack of integration, persons will seek alternatives in the environment to provide them with the kinds of relationships that seem to be denied them." Similarly, once the lonely suicidal Londoners begin to communicate, they breach the rules of indifference and begin to get involved with one another. Although that first contact is marked by competitiveness or solitary contractuality, it nevertheless stops them from going over the precipice and, what is more, lays the foundations for the further building of interpersonal bridges. Without anything in common but their respective failure to commit suicide and a need for salvation, they form a "reluctant support group" (Mars-Jones 2005; LWD: 41, 82, 181). Martin observes that "[e]ven though we had nothing in common beyond that one thing, the one thing was enough to make us feel that there wasn't anything else – not money, or class, or education, or age, or cultural interests – that was worth a damn; we'd formed a nation." (LWD: 44) In reference to the need of handling deficient situations, the urbanites join out of a desperate need for self-transformation. Towards the end of the novel, Maureen develops an inchoate understanding of these mechanisms of urban sociability: "One person bumps into another person, and that person wants something, or knows someone else who wants something, and as a result, things happen." (LWD: 238) Yet their connection is also forged by sharing collective dispositions of feeling in regard to isolation, loneliness, loss, misery and sadness (LWD: 63; cf. Woog 2005).

> I [Jess] went over and put my hand on his [Martin's] shoulder, and he looked at me as if I were a person rather than an irritation and we almost had a Moment of some description – not a romantic Ross-and-Rachel type moment (as if), but a Moment of Shared Understanding. (LWD: 53)

In that respect Topper's House represents a heterotopia where axiomatic practices of urban rule are inverted. Already Jess and Martin perceive that their small community is a gathering of anarchists living outside the common law of the city and that street-level agreements do not apply anymore (LWD: 26, 44). The suicides are not only spatially cut loose, but inevitably characterised by the ecological influence of the tower:

> Because that's what the four of us had done – crossed a line. [. . .] [S]omething had happened to us which separated us from lots of other people. We had nothing in common apart from where we'd ended up, on that square of concrete high up in the air, and that was the biggest thing you could possibly have in common with anyone. (LWD: 64)

However, in forming a common identity, the group agrees on its own basic statute law – the "SUICIDE PACT" (LWD: 89) – which entails not killing themselves for six weeks until Valentine's Day. Due to a loss of emotional bonding, the urban individuals rely on the organic solidarity of urban society and by rational calculability enter antagonising, impersonal and anonymous contacts as a form of negative integration. Thus, the four Londoners come together on the basis of solitary contractuality.

Because having descended from the roof together, all following attempts to strengthen their bonding only stress the improbability of fostering a community beyond a mere support group (LWD: 124, 146). On the other hand, it is their individual disparate and collectively discordant behaviour that comes to define their society. While the newspapers mark them as "freaks" (LWD: 131), the attempt to enforce their togetherness frees them from a state of personal apathy, and the newly developed group vigilance prevents the characters from breaching their social contract. Their unlikeliness as a group becomes specifically pronounced when they fly to the Canary Islands (LWD: 153). While for Maureen the holiday is one of the reasons she feels it worth living for and the first night out "was the nicest meal I've ever had in my life, and perhaps the nicest evening I've ever had in my life" (LWD: 156), Martin thinks it is simply a "so-so seafood in a tourist trap on the seafront" (LWD: 156). According to the latter, this social discrepancy proves: "They were just people who would talk to me because I was in their boat, but it was a bad boat to be in – an unseaworthy, shabby little boat, and I could suddenly see that it was going to break up and sink." (LWD: 158) With nothing in common, sick, bored and irritated by one another, back in London they decide to go their separate ways (LWD: 169-175). However, meeting on Topper's House for the last time, they are witness to a man committing suicide, the collective shock of which brings them closer together again (LWD: 178-183). Henceforth, for purely egoistic reasons Martin suggests that they extend their "reluctant solidarity" (LWD: 185) to ninety days in order to pass the suicidal crisis period.

A Long Way Down thereby follows the process of four urban strangers who build a temporary yet relevant association, which helps them overcome their single crises of defunct primary relations due to a default in urban proximity or distance. Jess comments to the reader:

> Most people have a rope that ties them to someone, and that rope can be short or it can belong. (Be long Belong. Get it?) [...] Maureen's rope ties her to Matty and it's about six inches long and it's killing her. Martin's rope ties him to his daughters, and, like a stupid dog, he thinks it isn't there. [...] I think JJ is tied to this bloke Eddie [...]. And I'm learning that I'm tied to Jen, and not to my mum and dad – not to home, which is where the rope should be. (LWD: 143)

In learning to fathom the rope-length of their internal relationships, the four protagonists are taught to re-estimate social relations. For JJ the four survivors – "the Kings and Queens of Shambles" (LWD: 57) – are similar to a rock band (LWD: 249) "bound together by a transcendent purpose" (Amidon 2005; cf. Woog 2005). In the eyes of Maureen, the other three appear like people in a soap opera, such as *Eastenders* (LWD: 29, 40). Without being able to pinpoint the nature of their relation, the bond ends up with yet another extension of their social contract (LWD: 30, 109); finally solitary contractuality turns into friendship and the "intimate-secondary relationship" (Lofland 1998: 56) transforms into one of primary relation. When offered support by her church community, Maureen proudly declaims that she has found new friends (LWD: 240), while for Jess it is commonsense that they will be "friends for ever." (LWD: 105) In regard to his best friend and ex-girlfriend, JJ admits to a certain kind of social overload by primary relations which initiates personal and collective transformation: "I loved them, and would always love them. But there was no place where they could fit any more, so I had nowhere to put all the things I felt. I didn't know what to do with them, and they didn't know what to do with me, and isn't that just like life?" (LWD: 231) Hence, urban primary relations like friendship still exist, but they are more diffuse, dynamic and based on temporarily felt personal deficiencies rather than on collective similarities.

These deficiencies are not rated as anomic. Rather the individual tower of Topper's House in North London stands for stability, loneliness, and solitarity, whereas at the end of the novel the ferris wheel of London Eye in the centre of the metropolis becomes a symbol of the urban social dynamics and network structures (LWD: 256-257): its single compartments are interconnected and the revolving wheel suggests urban vigilance. *A Long Way Down* stresses that urban communities aren't necessarily built on physical or social correspondence, but that city-centred solidarity is rather based on a common state of mind. It conveys a mental attitude that proliferates the commonality of temporary individualism and community.

The city brings together people from different social backgrounds and consequently in the multi-character (and often multi-perspective) novels such as Blake Morison's *South of the River*, Tim Lott's *White City Blue,* or Nick Hornby's *A Long Way Down*, London is depicted as a "web of correspondences" (Tinkler-Villani 2005a: x). In representing the post-Fordist metropolis as a "dense mosaic of interlocking communities" (Crang 1998: 111), contemporary London novels seem to follow an argument similar to urban sociologists like Karp, Stone & Yoels (1991: 73-75) who contend that urbanites do not lead a non-social existence, but that communities and primary group life survive in the city, while they now form less of an allegiance to a particular territory than a network of social relations without socio-cultural boundaries. This phenomenon ties in with Lofland's (1998: 53-59) understanding of relational fluidity in regard to the varying degrees of intimate primary relations, defunct family life, emergent fellowships, routinised relationships and intimate-secondary relations. Metropolitan dispositions of thinking, imagining, feeling and acting all cater to the city's oscillating chance encounters. Londoners' nonconscious mental structures are hence predominantly functionally oriented and largely attuned to temporal relations.

7.1.2 Urban Islands of Loneliness

Urbanity and urban-generic mentality are always based on the ambivalence of community and individualism, which implies that social life intrinsically oscillates between interaction and isolation or propinquity and distance. Urban sociologists since Simmel and Park have pointed out that living among strangers guarantees a certain amount of anonymity which on the one hand results in loneliness, superficiality, and lack of commitment but on the other hand presents an important prerequisite for personal freedom, independence and emancipation. Milgram (1970: 1464) comments:

> Conditions of full acquaintance, for example, offer security and familiarity, but they may also be stifling, because the individual is caught in a web of established relationships. Conditions of complete anonymity, by contrast, provide freedom from routinized social ties, but they may also create feelings of alienation and detachment.

The paradox of urban life entails that density enforces internal differentiation and physical proximity results in distanciation of contacts. This is seen by the sociologists of the Chicago School or even by representatives of the New Urban Economy and Sociology as an indicator of an increasingly insular urban life (cf. Sieverts 2003: 76-77). The cluster of separate worlds within the metropolis promotes the isolation of communities and individuals alike.

Urban loneliness, isolation, and anonymity also constitute a major literary topos of the description of the city. Some aspects of metropolitan isolationist tendencies and their mental implications as represented in contemporary London novels have already been explored in the chapter "Public and Private". In reference to the last analysis on human interrelations within the city it has been shown that networks of social connections between individual urbanites can create what Baudrillard (2000: 132) defines as a satellite-like urban existence. Regarding social dynamics, the city has always been connected with the idea of anonymity and individuals as singular atoms disappearing in a vast crowd. Milgram exemplifies (1970: 1464) that "[t]he city dweller, when walking through the midtown streets, is in a state of continual anonymity vis-à-vis the other pedestrians." Monadic anonymity in the sense of a protective mechanism in the midst of many is a popular image of the metropolis grasped in the literary figure of the *flâneur* – or the lonely (wo)men in the crowd. In regard to the *flâneur*, Benjamin (2002: 446) comments on the shared state of loneliness in the midst of urban masses as represented in writings of Baudelaire, but the urban crowds function as a protective device since urban encounters demand loneliness:

> [The masses] stretch before the flâneur as a veil: they are the newest drug for the solitary. – Second, they efface all traces of the individual: they are the newest asylum for the reprobate and the prescript. – Finally, within the labyrinth of the city, the masses are the newest and most inscrutable labyrinth. Through them, previously unknown chthonic traits are imprinted on the image of the city.

The postmodern overload scenario enforced by spectacle, simulation and hyperreality has been shown to create a new form of sociability, when urbanites share their isolation in the common urban public. The repulsive indifference of the crowd and the isolated individual in the modern metropolis is a recurrent image taken up in De Quincey's literary perambulations through the city. In his autobiographical essay "The Nation of London" the lonely souls of the urban crowd are depicted as figures transformed to mere shadows:

> No loneliness can be like that which weighs upon the heart in the centre of faces never-ending, without voice or utterance for him; eyes innumerable, that have 'no speculation' in their orbs which *he* can understand; and hurrying figures of men and women weaving to and fro, with no apparent purposes intelligible to a stranger, seeming like a mask of maniacs, or, oftentimes, like a pageant of phantoms. (De Quincey 1968a: 182)

The oversaturation by anonymity, impersonality, and loneliness here implicates anomic tendencies of deprivation, the loss of the Self, and consequent schizophrenia. Jonathan Raban (1974: 136) explains this phenomenon of the contemporary city in the following way: "For the really lonely individual in the city, life becomes a string of disconnected occasions; each present moment is exaggerated, and its theatrical glare seems designed to illuminate and isolate his aloneness." Hence the overload of anonymity, loneliness, and isolation in the urban realm promotes metropolitan alienation and estrangement. In the following I will explore the contemporary dynamics of anonymity, isolation, and oversaturation by loneliness as depicted in the same texts explored with regards to urban networks of interrelation in order to fathom the implications of their ambivalent relation of contemporary London mentality.

Suicidal Loneliness

In Nick Hornby's novel *A Long Way Down* (2005), each of the four protagonists is "saturated with misery and loneliness" (Dunmore 2005) leading to the individual decision to commit suicide. However, as the protagonist Martin emphasises, the various reasons for suicide such as divorce, anorexia, unemployment, rape and death, just like the characters' own reasons of family trauma, disgrace, despair and loss, are sound explanations and not issues that derive from a "disturbed mental balance" (LWD: 7). Nevertheless, in an urban milieu an overload of loneliness seems to be rated as a form of disintegration by characters when linked to social isolation or absolute social disconnection.

Maureen is a lonely middle-aged woman living an existence of "*homo clausus*" (Elias 1994: 206) eating microwaved food and consuming real social life through the television programme segments of *Eastenders* (LWD: 96, 156). She even makes up her own disabled son like a character from the soap opera, building a whole unlived teenage life for him with tapes, books, football boots, computer games (LWD: 117-118). Similar to fictionalising family life, she talks herself into being included in her local church community. But as Maureen later recognises when seeing "a middle-aged woman, no husband in sight, pushing a young lad in wheelchair" (LWD: 168) in a Tenerifian church, the religious community is rather a congregation of types that could be found in "any church anywhere in the world" (LWD: 169) with fates not relegated to the metropolitan milieu. However, in the city her situation takes on a more poignant form which encompasses the possibilities of further personal disintegration but also integration. Although she argues that "I've always been fine on my own" (LWD: 168) she suffers from depression. Her initial sadness does not derive from the demands of her catatonic son but rather from a loss of communication and increasing distanciation from urban social life induced by self-censorship:

> You know that things aren't going well for you when you can't even tell people the simplest fact about your life, just because they'll presume you're asking them to feel sorry for you. I suppose it's why you feel so far away from everyone, in the end; anything you can think of to tell them just ends up making them feel terrible. (LWD: 154)

Instead, Martin represents the twenty-first century type of a fallen public man. As a formerly successful TV personality for whom the enclosed imprisonment in jail was humiliating and terrifying, his private life is further scandalised by the tabloids. Martin has not only lost the private connection to his family and the contacts of work but totally lacks anonymity. The only protective shield he is left with is the ignorance of London taxi drivers: "I have preferred minicab drivers for some time now, because they are as ignorant of London's inhabitants as they are of its geography." (LWD: 205) Although he admits that "[t]he papers have been full of shit about me, and every word of the shit was true" (LWD: 98), Martin has been brand-marked as a criminal and lunatic; despite having a job, a lover and people who invite him for dinner parties, he only feels pitied. Instead, the reason for Jess' loneliness is her dysfunctional family; her parents are distressed both by the grief for their older daughter and work-life, neglecting the attention-seeking troubled girl. In her 'homelessness' Jess feels close to the deprived loneliness of London's tramps (LWD: 226). Yet the anonymous non-places of the metropolis' commercial landscape seem to offer Jess a kind of shelter where she enjoys the freedom of integration via anonymity:

People go on about places like Starbucks being unpersonal [...] I'd be lost, if [...] people like that got their way, and there was nothing unpersonal in the world. I like to know that there are big places without windows where no one gives a shit. You need confidence to go into small places with regular customers, small bookshops and small music shops and small restaurants and cafés. I'm happiest in the Virgin Megastore and Borders and Starbucks and Pizza Express, where no one gives a shit, and no one knows you who are. (LWD: 145)

For JJ the break with his band resembles the loss of his hopes for becoming a famous yet inchoate rock star. He likes being the centre of the world and actually feels condemned from a public life on stage to a private and lonely existence as a helmeted pizza delivery guy. Only briefly does he enjoy "knowing that I was sort of famous and completely anonymous, all at the same time" (LWD: 91) when the suicides' pact seeps out to the press.

It is their shared suffering from oversaturated loneliness that promotes solitary contractuality. The characters' suicide pact temporarily unites them and frees them from the shackles of isolated existences, offering a social space without destroying the urban potential of anonymity. Hence, after surviving the first night, Martin states that their small community has already altered London's anomic atmosphere:

It's not scary any more, [...] London. It looks all right. [...] There were all these fireworks, and people walking around, and we were squeezed up here because there was nowhere else for us to go. [...] I didn't belong. [...] There's nothing down there to feel excluded from. It's just a big city again. Look. He's on his own. And she's on her own. (LWD: 81)

The analysis of *A Long Way Down* shows that while loneliness belongs to a basic state of mind, urbanity offers constant possibilities to reverse feelings of isolation to those of autonomy and to transfer apathy into vigilance. In that respect, Niederagen (2000: 232) is right to argue that the cynicism of Hornby's characters never falls prey to an anomic apocalypticism, but as I would add mirrors Simmel's notion of blasé in regard to their own state of mind, which as an oversaturation of loneliness constitutes another form of emotional overload.

London Blues

The main character Frankie Blue in Tim Lott's novel *White City Blue* (1999) has to learn the determination of temporal urban socioscapes, especially that of a metropolitan milieu where "[e]verything, and everyone, has a time; a person has to fit yours." (WCB: 17). While in his childhood silence functioned as a form of communication between himself and his best friend Colin, the silences of adult life rather indicate the distanciation between urbanites and their respective isolation. He observes how the children on a London playground interact without inhibition, while singles and pairs of parents stand silently, never acknowledging each other. Hence, Frankie especially notices the mental gap between childhood and adulthood by the socialisation from a state of proximity to one of distance: "*We close up like clams as we get old.* Distance is one of the ways we stop being children." (WCB: 158) In that respect he also experiences distanciation as a major aspect of urbanity. Seeing his own father as his only and best friend, Frankie feels that human goods like personal identity, friendship, and connectedness have become a mere illusion. The plan of changing his life by getting married also resembles the possibility of altering his personal identity and becoming a part of someone else, hence leaving behind the solitary existence of a bachelor and the isolation of the single urbanite (WCB: 133). His friend and fellow Tony, by contrast, presents a third *a priori* of urban life: "*You're always alone. Whoever you fuck, however many times you fuck them, whoever you marry or don't marry. You're on your own. Just you, your brain and your cock, walking around* [...]." (WCB: 133) From this point of view detachment prevails in the city.

As a born Londoner, Frankie variously experiences phases of loneliness and social seclusion. Cut loose from the social circle of university after graduation, he already went through a phase of being stranded in the island existence of an isolated urbanite. Being unemployed, his disintegration is not only due to a lack of material and financial means but he also feels less capable of supporting himself psychologically (WCB: 2). Although he is not totally disconnected after breaking with his friends and fiancé, the backing of his mother does not suffice to fight the feelings of utter loneliness. Otherwise throwing himself into work, there is only Sunday left to get through the "numbness to being on your own" (WCB: 236). The raw look of his face bears witness of this disintegration.

The blues of Frankie's loneliness is paralleled by the elderly customer Harry Butson. Some months earlier, Frankie had offered the Butsons a flat and was surprised by the couple's close and happy relation, so different from his own parents' who always seemed "indifferent to, or even contemptuous of each other." (WCB: 21) After the death of his wife, with his children and grandchildren living far away and without any friends by his side, Harry has suddenly been degraded to a lone Londoner. Frankie notices that Harry actually only approaches the agency's office for the chance of a conversation and suddenly perceives the signs of personal disintegration: "I can see the agony of this dignified, grave man, the shame he feels at being reduced to trawling for company like a rich man turned suddenly into a beggar." (WCB: 242) Moreover, the protagonist feels the penetration of oversaturated isolation becoming part of the man's habit and is full of horror because of the pertaining social *vacui*: "Loneliness, like a cold blue light seeping out of his eyes, coming towards me like mustard gas. This makes me panic [...]." (WCB: 241) He instantly understands these changes as a prophesy of his own future, which gives him the power to make up with his friends and partner. Hence, *White City Blue* comments on the dangers of personal disintegration and apathy by way of distanciation and isolation. But similar to Hornby's text, the novel presents these feelings as intrinsic to the contemporary urban condition with its inherent chances of counter management, revived vigilance, and restructuring of urban sociability.

The Lone Wolf and the Solitary Vixen

Although Lewis Mumford (1997: 228) contends in his study on *The Culture of the Cities* that the isolated state of the metropolitan lone wolf is largely an illusion, this significant character "has a central place in the literature of the city." (Raban 1974: 137) In Blake Morrison's *South of the River*, the protagonist Nat Raven represents a self-absorbed and solipsistic figure of urbane loneliness. The character claims that every man, especially a creative artist like himself, is an isolated island (SOR: 37). As a professional playwright he only gained success with a piece titled *Suicide Alley*, while the unfinished drama Nat has been working on for years takes up the idea of a man's lonely vulpine existence in the postmodern metropolis from the 1980s to the 1990s and variously changes its title from *Terrace of Unhope*, *Desperation Way* and *Lonely Crescent* to *Wilderness Avenue* (SOR: 21-22). After his younger lover leaves him, Nat physically disintegrates to a mere shadow of himself and gets sick with "Labyrinthitis" which destroys his sense of balance and renders him an "un-, non- and Not-Nat" (SOR: 359). Ending up in an underground basement flat, abandoned, unemployed, missing his former partners and family, he goes through a rough phase of urban non-existence.

By contrast, his lover Anthea, who feels out of her depth in their relationship, her job and private life (SOR: 281), earlier on writes a short-story on "The Solitude of Vixen" (SOR: 95). Indeed, Nat's former wife represents such an independent, tough but lonely female urban fox. Being one of the first successful Thatcherite women, Libby's usual lunch in the City consists of "a baguette and a *café au lait* from Pret A Manger, eaten *très vite* and *à seule*." (SOR: 65) Intermittently thwarted by her divorce and her mother's illness, she feels humbled by the metropolitan "forces beyond her control. Her face [...] looked grey, from all the shuttling back and forth. She might be here in body but her head was circling uselessly in Baggage Reclaim" (SOR: 341). Once Libby decides to cleverly follow her emancipated, autonomous, and independent path, she already seems reconciled with and "perfectly together – together in her aloneness" (SOR: 512). Before she finally regains her urban composure of self-contented solitarity, Libby contemplates – in a moment reminiscent of Virginia Woolf's Mrs Dalloway – committing suicide because she feels cast out from the social life of the city in general and the party around her in particular:

> As the Drifters drifted upward, she felt newly sorry for herself – abandoned by her husband, betrayed by her friends, outshone by her children, vanquished by a woman she's thought a nonentity, dropped and left behind in the race of life. Five years ago, life had been good. But then, something had ghosted in to blight it, something acrid and mangy, like a fox crossing the garden at first light. (SOR: 500)

Painting a tableau of British society during the first half of the Blairite decade, Morrison not only amplifies the interlaced lives of Londoners but also stresses their fierce individuality which can lead to isolation, social degeneration, and anomie. In a lecture that seems like an author's summary of the New Labour zeitgeist, the protagonist Nat comments:

> Life as we now live it isn't funny. We've become a nation of dumbos and zombies, faddies and fatties, workaholics and shopaholics, abusers and self-harmers. We kid ourselves we're emotionally literate – that we're truly communicating at last, thanks to mobile phones and emails. But it's an illusion: real intimacy doesn't exist; no one listens; we don't have time for each other, life is a nightmare, from which comedy is no escape. Cheer up, people say, it might never happen. But it doesn't happen, it has happened, and we're living with the consequences. You have to laugh. No, you don't. It's no laughing matter. (SOR: 426)

In that respect *South of the River* takes account of "an age where communication has never been easier, but to find someone who'll listen has never been harder" (Perkins

2007), where isolation is enforced by a new vulpine social atmosphere, in the sense that it charts a certain continuity of "the greed-saturated 'me-me-me' generation of Thatcher's reign" (Mukherjee 2007). Hence, the fox is an apt symbol of metropolitan London life both in the early "Noughties" and late Nineties. In his *Telegraph* review Roger Perkins (2007) writes:

> Blake Morrison's **South of the River,** an enthralling novel of the way we live now in Blair's Britain, is choc-full of the vulpine: there are foxes in the gardens, grounds and streets of late-1990s London and foxiness in the characters of the people who live there.

The book is suffused with allusions to foxes: despite the inchoate appearance of the urban vulpine, it features stories of Anthea Hunt's *Book of Foxes*, the banning and exercise of foxhunt in the country, folk tales and children's stories about foxes, etc. (cf. *ibid.*; Taylor 2007). First, the image of the fox represents the clever but harsh socio-political atmosphere of Blairite Britain, with further cuts in culture or the ensuing war on terrorism (SOR: 380, 425, 496). For Nat's friend Harry the rise of "[i]mmunity to others' sufferings was more or less a requirement of being human these days, the only means to get by without screaming [...]." (SOR: 356) Insofar, the protagonist identifies the animal as a symbol of the "resurgence of the primitive at the heart of modern London" (SOR: 152) and thus not merely anomic but entropic. Moreover, the animal stands for London's contemporary socioscape: "It sometimes seemed there were more foxes in London than there were people, and half the people were foxes, too: sneaky, mean-eyed, nocturnal." (SOR: 58) In opposition to the complacent lone wolf in his attic, the individual fox emphasises the vigilant yet mean-sided aspect of social isolationism.

Second, the term "foxy" also denotes the sexiness of business and advertising (SOR: 20-25) fashioned around the "*youthful urban, cheeky, clever, postmodern*" (SOR: 124) situation of the "New Age" (SOR: 122). This ties in with the general re-branding of the country as 'Cool Britannia' and the metropolis as 'Sexy' London. Moreover, this allusion to the sexy city is connected to the possibility of fleeting sexual relations in the urban, such as between Anthea and Nat. Overcoming the oversaturation of loneliness by temporarily acquiring physical intimacy through sexual intercourse has already been mentioned in reference to *The White Family*, *Brick Lane* and *Bleeding London*. Consequently, while the fox both symbolises friendliness and dishonesty (cf. Perkins 2007), the image also encompasses London's socioscape as oscillating between a pragmatic vigilant independence and disturbed apathic isolationism.

To sum up: as predicated by urban sociologists, the impersonality of city life breeds loneliness and isolation due to diminishing personal relations. However, the protagonists of the novels only temporarily feel isolated and deserted in "this metropolitan crush of persons" (Simmel 1971: 334). Due to the social dynamics of the contemporary city "a deep sense of meaninglessness and homelessness" (Zijderveld 1998: 135) transforms back into a positive experience of anonymity, autonomy and independence of urban vigilance. In that respect, although the novels under analysis in this monograph (BLL, KRA, LBR, LOR, LWD, MAH, NXT, SOR, WCB) are aware of the anomic tendencies of metropolitan isolationism, in contrast to the bleakness of social existence in Thatcherite London novels such as Martin Amis' novels *Money* (1984) or *London Fields* (1989), they rather accept social *vacui* as an intrinsic moment of personal transition. One could even see metropolitan loneliness, anonymity, distanciation, and non-involvement define a specific momentum of the overload scenario.

Because "city life breeds its own tolerance for the private lives of the inhabitants" (Milgram 1970: 1464) as in the forms of individuality or even eccentricity, it also presents the possibility to reinvent oneself. This certainly fosters a sense of innovation and freedom of choice. Rather than let individuals fall in the trap of self-loathing pity, urban mentality seems to foster a sense of orientation towards rebuilding social contacts between strangers that momentarily assist in diminishing deficiencies. All in all, the represented withdrawal and the need for solitariness in contemporary London novels is shown as an unquestioned retreat from the city aimed at a long-term survival in the urban. Yet urbanites cannot live completely isolated without loosing themselves and becoming obsolete for the world. Human company even when reduced to physical proximity is all the characters strive for. It denotes an urban everyday orientation where social contacts exist both on the level of a manageable quantity of people and on the level of physically being with others, but without aiming to build emotional relationships.

7.1.3 Metropolitan Voids and Millennial Anomie

Most urbanologists after Simmel have related urbanity to a decline in social cohesion, disorganisation and atomisation of community, breakdown of moral order, and vulnerability to anomie. Especially theoreticians of the post-Fordist city since the urban crisis of the 1960s have registered both a new form of anomie due to the postmodern relativism, heterogeneity, social mobility and diversification, as well as a novel overload scenario that induces enhanced social and individual savagery, aggressiveness or madness. The analysis of contemporary London novels such as *London Revenant*, *The Red Men*, *King Rat* and *Next* has already deciphered various examples concerning metropolitan alienation and anomie on the verge of personal breakdown and social entropies.

In the following I will specifically refer to J.G. Ballard's *Millennium People* (2003) and the representations of postmodern socioscape forged in an urban environment of gated communities and non-places.[7] Ballard was one of Britain's most acclaimed visionary writers and hailed as the most important figure of the British New Wave which anticipated the cultural transformations of the present period (cf. Baxter 2008a: 3). For Ballard, the post-war era is saturated by a "process of intelligibility" (*ibid.*) and needs to be countered by reinventions of the real future. In that respect, he has been called "the anticipatory or timely voice of a paradigmatic postmodernism" or "the prophet of the perversity of the contemporary world." (Luckhurst 1997: xii) The author, however, engages not only with the plain contemporary social existence but especially with its hidden implications. According to Noys (2011: 392), Ballard's narratives are a form of "forensic prose" analysing "new forms of cultural pathology." As variously pointed out, Ballard's initial search is for the hidden and unconscious depths of contemporary culture or the "inner space" of the psyche (cf. Baxter 2008a: 3-4).[8] In exposing the inner logics

---

7 | In the following *Millennium People* will be abbreviated as MIP.

8 | For example see Ballard's essays: "Which Way to Inner Space" (1962) and "Time, Memory and Inner Space" (1963). According to the *Collins English Dictionary,* "Ballardian"

and states of mind he becomes a true mental chronicler of recent socio-cultural, technological and environmental changes. The author's preferred setting is the alien cityscape of contemporary London with its multi-storey carparks, bridges, motorways, high-rises, and enclosed micro-spatialities, problems of urban sprawl, overpopulation, environmental despoliation, contraction of living space, and psychological consequences such as entrapment, paranoia, schizophrenia, or the deadening effect of routine. In all these novels London is as much a habitable place as a state of mind.[9] Groes (2008: 78) even reads London as a master narrative in Ballard's writing; major London novels by the so-called "Seer of Shepperton" (Baxter 2008a: 1) are *The Drowned World* (1962), *High-Rise* (1975), *Crash* (1973), *Millennium People* (2003) and *Kingdom Come* (2006), in which he variously drowns the metropolis, sets it on fire, or blows it up.

In *Millennium People* the *petit bourgeois* of London is represented as staging a grotesquely inversed revolution: while the residents of Chelsea Marina, a gated community, abandon their civil responsibilities and start ridding themselves of their cultural capital, a series of terrorist acts take place within the metropolis from smoke bombs in video stores to an arson attack on the National Film Theatre, the bombing of the Tate Modern and the homicide of a famous TV presenter. The protagonist David Markham is a corporate psychologist whose job it is to chart the "emotional life of the office and the mental problems of middle managers" (MIP: 8). After the death of his ex-wife in an attack on Heathrow airport he settles in Chelsea Marina in order to pin down the terrorists and becomes a police informant "map[ping] the emerging psychology" (MIP: 32). Therein, London is on the verge of social and mental breakdown. Non-places of airports, carparks, "hypermarkets" and "gated communities" (MIP: 63) are represented as becoming the perimeters of urban middle-class non-existence. The reluctant urbanites stage a socio-cultural revolution that reveals their hunger for violence and destruction. Their pathological mental responses to a general state of boredom is induced by the trivial and affectless contemporary urban culture at the start of the new millennium which is characterised by surveillance technology, postmodern consumer culture, globalised tourism, themed cityscapes, simulation, spectaclisation, and mediatisation. After the psychopathologies of "motorway mayhem and tower-block madness" (Thomson 2003), Ballard in *Millennium People* analyses the mind- and socioscapes of a community transgressing its self-inflicted (b)orders through outbreaks of violence.

The Brainwashing of Gated Communities

Ballard's fiction, such as the upper-class denigration in *High Rise* (1975), demonstrates a loss of faith concerning the possibility of meaningful communal life (cf. Gąsiorek 2005: 43). The author comments:

I think the suburbs are more interesting than people will let on. In the suburbs you find uncentred lives. The normal civic structures are not there. So that people have more freedom to explore

denotes a "*bleak manmade landscapes & the psychological effects of technological, social or environmental developments.*" (Cit. in Baxter 2008a: 1)

9 | Also see Ballard's short stories: "Chronopolis" (1960), "Billenium" (1961), or "The Overload Man" (1961).

> their own imaginations, their own obsessions. And the discretionary spending power to do so. (Ballard cit. in Groes 2008: 79)

In his analysis of Ballard's London fiction Groes (*ibid.*: 80) elucidates how the oppressive discourse on the city in his 1960s novels becomes dislocated to the city's peripheral geographies of the airport, the tower block, the traffic island and the gated community during the 1970s, whose structures of deferral are once again transported to the centre of the metropolis in *Millennium People*. Hence, the changes of the urban form taking place 'without' the urban sprawl in a way reinfiltrate the metropolitan centre by relocation of suburban structures into inner-city estates (MIP: 133). Groes (2008: 89) claims that "Ballard's later world focuses in particular on the ways in which gated communities emerge as new pockets of order, which subsequently succumb to the same forces that operate in the peripheral topography of London." In regard to Chelsea Marina, the literary scholar even goes so far as to argue, that the peripheral leisure resort of a Mediterranean city is transplanted into the centre of metropolitan London (cf. Groes 2011: 82). Chelsea Marina is a "comfortable enclave" (MIP: 3) erected on the site of a former gaswork in West London's Fulham. Copying nearby upper-class Kensington street names – Beaufort Avenue, Cadogan Circle, Grosvenor Place, Nelson Lane (cf. Groes 2008: 90) – the estate is conceived by developers and city planners as a postmodern themed environment of suburban living, albeit without the comfort of free parking. Later plans to rebaptise the estate's streets after 1960s French filmmakers show that hyperreality has taken over the everyday socioscapes of the metropolis and not only the themed environments along the South Bank.

Additionally, the gated community is marketed as a simulation of communal life (cf. McNamara 2001). In that respect, the sealed enclosure represents both a designed sociability and a hypertrophy of community:

> Chelsea Marina was designed for a salaried professional class keen to preserve its tribal totems – private education, a dinner-party culture, and a never-to-be-admitted distaste for the 'lower' orders, which included City dealers, financial consultants, record industry producers and the lumpen-intelligentsia of newspaper columnists and ad-men. (MIP: 51)

The community's lifestyle is strongly defined by school fees, Brazilian daily helps, ballet classes and BUPA subscriptions, a specified menu of leisure activities ranging from travel to films and parties, and mapped out folkloric calendar, from the Night of the Proms to the Wimbledon tennis fortnight (MIP: 87-89). As an absolute space the estate not only offers a certain security and comfort but homogenises this "threatened salariat" (MIP: 216). *Millennium People* variously stresses that this kind of urbanite, rather than being on the fringe of urban society, with its attitude towards "civic duty and responsibility" (MIP: 147) actually constitutes the very heart of urban citizenship. The initiators and members of the ensuing middle-class revolution underline the problematics of the intrinsic "hyperconformity of these protected enclaves" (Noys 2011: 395) which chain them to a "castle of obligations held together by the ivy of middle-class insecurity." (MIP: 166) Hence, instead of being safe in the communal abode, the urbanites are seen as secured and kept under control by a habitualised grammar of self-regulation (MIP: 104, 193). "They [...] police themselves. Not with guns and gulags, but with social codes. The right way to have sex, treat your wife, flirt at tennis parties or start an affair. There are unspoken rules we all have to learn." (MIP: 89) In this sense, individual freedom is only seen possible in the unlearning of being urbane.

But instead of living in a secure and affluent neighbourhood, the inhabitants of Chelsea Marina see themselves as "trapped and impoverished" (MIP: 87) living in a "zone of intense spiritual poverty" (MIP: 84) where they are limited "in their minds, in their customs and values" (MIP: 84). In the rhetoric of the revolutionaries, these London middle-class estates are "re-education labour camp[s]" (MIP: 109) or new panoptic prisons to make the core of urban society "docile and subservient" (MIP: 85). Urban and national institutions such as parliamentary democracy, the media landscape, museums and educational system are all accused of brainwashing the community and enforcing the "middle class's herd mentality" (MIP: 205). For the characters, metropolitan life has become an "endless theme park [experience], with everything turned into entertainment. Science, politics, education – they're so many fairground rides. Sadly, people are happy to buy their tickets and climb aboard." (MIP: 62) In regard to the Blair era, Ballard (cit. in Litt 2006) underlines the reason for society's self-delusion:

> I think we wanted to be conned. We wanted this nice young man with his people-carrier and his suburban wife and kids. We wanted him. Out on the M25, that's where I live, I could see that people wanted the new suburbia. And Blair promised a sort of blandness. He just played mood music, but we like mood music.

The absurdity thus lies in the fact that these themed environments and mapped-out wastelands of thinking are exactly what contemporary urbanites strive for, although this mental equipment implicates a collective mental regression, a loss of urban independence, as well as a drift towards anomie. The mindscape of the gated community is drenched in dispositions of meaninglessness and boredom (MIP: 115; cf. Noys 2011: 400). In this sense, the spiritual vacuity of the inhabitants of Chelsea Marina is mirrored in the actual physical state of this estate agents' con: a "high priced slum" (MIP: 52) with a marina "[t]he size of a toilet" (MIP: 51). In reference to Baudrillard's (2000: 131-132) understanding of simulated suburbs, the designed marina does not constitute a residential comfort zone but a pool of waste, residue, and voidance.

> In front of me lay Chelsea Marina, its streets empty as never before in its twenty-year existence. The entire population had vanished, leaving a zone of silence like an urban nature reserve. Eight hundred families had fled, abandoning their comfortable kitchens, herb gardens and book-lined living rooms. Without the slightest regret, they had turned their backs on themselves and all they had once believed in. (MIP: 5)

In *Millennium People* the universal process of concentrated emptiness and social vacuity, mirrored in the image of Exopolis, has spread to London and brought about the resurgent violence of suppression and hate from depletion.

Ballard presents the middle-class revolution as a protest against "psychic immiseration" (Noys 2011: 395) where inexplicable acts of crime and psychotic violence are the only means to escape the constraints of contemporary consumer culture. The author comments: "We want more exciting lives. There are limits to the number of TV sets you can have at home. There are limits to the number of cars you can own." (cit. in Litt 2006) One of the novel's characters emphasises this point by arguing that people "aren't meant to be comfortable. We need tension, stress, uncertainty." (MIP: 63) In the novel the "underbelly of bourgeois life" (MIP: 37) thus develops a taste for pointless violence, ruthlessness, and betrayal. Because the mental attitude of anger has been bred out of the middle classes long ago (MIP: 170), the feelings of hate and actions of destruction are necessarily directed towards themselves, their very own physical, social, and mental institutions: "*We don't like the kind of people we've become...*" (MIP: 154) Hence, criminality and violence, but also psychopathology, become the only means of resistance and liberation from self-inflicted socio-cultural repression (cf. Gąsiorek 2005: 50).

In an interview with Ballard, Toby Litt (2006) discusses the various emergent collective psychopathologies – madness, paranoia, schizophrenia, bi-polarism, anger, clinical insanity, traumatisation, fascism – as ways out of boredom and confinement to freedom and authenticity. The various characters we encounter in *Millennium People* are mentally and/or physically damaged and handicapped. In sum, the communal life of London's gated communities as represented in the novel is wrought by alienation and anomie (cf. Gąsiorek 2005: 49; Chapman 2006), caused by a new attractiveness that is borrowed from (social) and symbolic vacuity and the revulsion of non-urbanised but ideological fabric of designed meaning. As the main character David argues on entering this estate of executive housing south of King's Road, Chelsea Marina is "the heart of another kind of darkness" (MIP: 51). Towards Toby Litt (2006), Ballard underlines the fact that the contemporary consumerist metropolis no longer contributes to social cohesion and that boredom brings to the fore a new appetite for excitement, thrill, and horror. The novel thereby charts the anomic tendencies of postmodern urban sociability in both aspects investigated by contemporary urbanologists, namely the postmodern non-place existence in relation to the postmodern overload scenario.

Collective Vacuity and London's Non-Place Realms

Iain Sinclair calls Ballard a "great writer of [...] nowheres" (cit. in Chapman 2006) and indeed his novels are specifically set in the terrain of London's transit-zones: motorways, airports, hospitals, retail parks, shopping malls, gated communities. *Millennium People*, besides the social void of the Chelsea Marina estate, is also suffused with metropolitan non-places, most prominently Heathrow, the no-man's land between the airport and the city, as well as the spectacularised re-developments on London's South Bank, and non-places of the everyday: suburban cinemas, McDonald's, travel agencies (MIP: 112). According to Marc Augé, these places are notoriously deplete of markers for individuals to locate themselves, let alone communities to build more than solitary contractuality. In his theory of urban non-places Augé (1997: 14) states that "[a]ll around cities we can see a multiplication of spaces with an extremely problematic social meaning, most likely because they are defined both by the centrifugal and centripetal movement [...]." Additionally, typical Ballardian icons, such as the car and the concrete flyover, play a prominent role in the text (cf. Chapman 2006). Basically all characters are rather obsessively linked to their damaged cars. Forced to drive the refitted car of his disabled wife, the protagonist feels how urban life itself is paradoxically confined to these places of transit, of which the car is initially the best example.

In many ways, my life was as deformed as this car, rigged with remote controls, fitted with overriders and emergency brakes within easy reach. I had warped myself into the narrow cockpit of professional work at the Adler, with its inane rivalries and strained emotional needs. (MIP: 145)

For Sinclair, literary London in Ballard's late fiction is therefore notoriously unplaced, unhinged, or unfixed and hence uncovered as fluid or alienated (cf. Chapman 2006). In more ways than one Ballard follows the tracks of the emergent spatial dominant of the space of flows also in regard to its altered social dynamics such as the Dual City. When the self-abhorring middle class flees the dereliction of gated community by simulating a revolution, his protagonist David imagines "them endlessly circling the M25 in their muddy Land Rover, locked in a deep trance." (MIP: 7) In that respect, Luckhurst (1997: xiv) has already commented on the feeling of unease perpetrated by non-places in Ballard's writing which presuppose a certain unhomeliness. The home of the millennium people equally lies in an "interstitial zone" which is a "space of sublimity [...] hover[ing] between terror of entrapment and the ecstasy of release." (Luckhurst 1997: xv)

The novel explores this ambivalent feeling of imprisonment within mobility in the example of travel, especially airborne global holiday. One of the revolutionary fakes argues: "Today's tourist goes nowhere. [...] All the upgrades in existence lead to the same airports and resort hotels, the same pina colada bullshit. [...] Travel is the last fantasy of the 20th Century left us, the delusion that going somewhere helps you reinvent yourself." (MIP: 54) Air travel is seen as another collective simulation for urbanites to feign directedness and orientation, while instead they have long since become a transient people living in anonymous isolation. Heathrow is the nexus of a huge illusion pointing to nothingness (MIP: 251; Semioforidis 1997: 45; James 2008: 88). In *Millennium People*, this void of the airport is surrounded by an "automotive limbo" (MIP: 241) or long-term car parks and alienating zones of meaninglessness. This interstitial space is the refuge of urban contemporaries: "There's no past and no future. If they can, they opt for zones without meaning – airports, shopping malls, motorways, car parks. They're in flight from the real." (MIP: 120) This zone mirrors the perforated, brainwashed and empty mental wasteland of contemporary Londoners as well as their social non-existence.

Heathrow approached, a beached sky-city, half space station and half shanty town. We left the motorway and moved along the Great West Road, entering a zone of two-storey factories, car-rental offices and giant reservoirs. We were part of an invisible marine world that managed to combine mystery and boredom. In a way it seemed fitting that my former wife was lying in a hospital here, within a call of life and death, in an area that hovered between waking and the dream. (MIP: 25)

Iain Sinclair argues that Ballard's fiction devises London as a suburb of Heathrow (cf. Barfield 2008) and thereby transforms the metropolis to a heterotopian space. In accordance to Augé's conception of non-place, airports have long since developed into new forms of the urban with all the major uses and functions of a city but overtly connected with the everyday of the contemporary urban nomad.

These favoured places of nomadic sociability are opposed to the traditional city as meeting-place and space of memory. It represents the city as image and a place "where the original space of the spectacle is diffused into the non-place of multiple reproductions." (Simeoforidis 1997: 50) In *Millennium People*, the non-places' contractual sociability spreads within the postmodern metropolis centring on the South Bank redevelopment around Millennium Wheel (MIP: 123). The middle-class rebels burn the National Film Institute following a script of action movies. Finally they bomb the bunker of Tate Modern, whose "bombastic" (MIP: 180) architecture cowes "both eye and brain" (MIP: 181) and is perspectivated as "Führer spectacle, an early sign, perhaps, that the educated middle classes were turning towards facism" (MIP: 181; cf. Groes 2011: 86). However, for the protagonist, the theme park of the South Bank merely mirrors the Informational City on the north shore of the Thames and constitutes a simulacrum where only terror or its echoes denominate a "meaningful event" (MIP: 180). The flowing muddy river and the erupting violence are the essential realities left in this hyperreal wasteland of non-urbanity (cf. Groes 2011: 84). Postmodern urbanologists have extensively discussed the mental consequences of urban non-place vacuities: the centreless depletion and flatness of the hyperreal leads to contractual solitude, social void, or anomie as well as apathic states of schizophrenia, frustration, terror, hate and violence.

In sum, Ballard's millennium Londoners are subordinated and dwarfed by the urban environment of non-places of transit, totalitarian architecture, gated communities under sureveillance and simulated theme parks (cf. Gąsiorek 2005: 48). The urban collective is charted as on the brink of a mental collapse (MIP: 198) that is initiated by the loss of time and space differentials. The author's critique of simulated London obviously brings into perspective the suicidal metropolis. While before, the city in Ballard's fictions was apocalyptically destroyed by external forces, the contemporary Simcity stages its very own death in the midst of a wide-ranging cluster of socio-cultural and intellectual vacuities (MIP: 180). It is the middle-class crisis that leads to an enhanced uncohesion of urbanity or urban/national identity. In Groes' (2008: 93) words, the metropolis is "no longer representative of the British nation, but a confused, post-national language – a multitude of tongues that, for better or for worse, twenty-first century London increasingly speaks. The world, it seems, has caught up with Ballard." In its critique of twenty-first-century simulacral London, metropolitan architectural spectacle, and bourgeois attacks on consumerism, *Millennium People* projects a city caught in a static void with the only remedy of shock violence (cf. James 2008: 89; Groes 2011: 68, 84, 92).

7.1.4 Transcultural Contact Zones

Due to the ambivalences of sociability and anomie, individualism and community, as well as heterogeneity and homogeneity, contemporary London is depicted as a space of dynamic relations in perpetual transition. The city becomes "a social universe with a plurality of social standards and relative values" (Karp, Stone & Yoels 1991: 24). It was shown that urbanity is based on people's multiplied social contacts, but the metropolis itself constitutes a social space of multiplicity. The last decades of the twentieth century were marked by social differentiation and thus a growing possibility of the encounter with the urban stranger, whereby global migration has had a severe impact on the accompanying cultural mobility. For example, Chambers (1990: 58) argues with reference to the global city: "As a simulated metropolis it is inhabited by a community of modern nomads: a collective metaphor of cosmopolitan existence where the pleasure of travel is not only to arrive, but also not to be in any particular place ... to be simultaneously everywhere." The space of flows without definite places creates communities whose ways of life are seemingly less localised.

London in particular has seen a definite transformation of its socio-cultural reality since the Second World War, developing into a multicultural and global metropolis towards the second millennium with "shifting, mixing, contaminating, experimenting, revisiting and recomposing [dynamics] that the wider horizons and the inter/trans-cultural networks of the metropolis both permit and encourage." (Chambers 1996: 190) Conversely, contemporary metropolitan life cannot be fathomed without the experience of postcolonial migrants. Consequently, studies on postcolonial London novels are extremely popular today especially with regard to the exploration of hybrid identities, diaspora cultures, and representations of multiculturalism. This sub-chapter by way of Monica Ali's paradigmatic postcolonial London novel *Brick Lane* explores the contemporary urban socioscape with regard to the translation between peoples, cultures, and mentalities. Similar to Ballard's *Millennium People*, Ali's text is an ecological city novel concerning a relatively small urban area inhabited by a very specific community of London. In the following I will investigate the social dynamics of Brick Lane's neighbourhood and its inhabitants transgressing beyond its mere spatial borders and also extract moments of mobility as constructing an oscillating zone of contact.

The Dynamics of Urban Estates

Being a severe point of discussion in regard to the multifarious socio-spatial reality of the city, specifically London, I want to underline that paradigms of dominant mental structures belonging to micro-mentalities can be transformed and integrated into meso- or macro-mentalities.[10] The general assumption is that although the experience is milieu-specifically differentiated, the city simultaneously prefigures emotions, perceptions, etc. in such a dominant way that they seep into the mental structures of subcultures (cf. Löw 2008: 81-82). Argued the other way round, fragmented, marginalised and segregated structures are necessarily related to the urban and thus also depend on the city as the dominant frame for the social construction of reality (*ibid.*: 110-111). Insofar, the social worlds of segregated communities are also part of literary London.

According to Catherine Pesso-Miquel (2008: 81-85), representations of metropolitan micro-worlds often feature characters whose trajectories are confined to a limited urban area and depict the city as lived from within. In this sense, ecological novels with their emphasis on the everyday are of specific interest not only for Mentality Studies but

---

10 | For example, Paul Newland (2008) has shown that the mental paradigms of the class-specific milieu in London's nineteenth-century East End were further constructed to the cultural character of the London Cockney as the specific Londoner, while the class-specific differentiations between East Enders and West Enders were raised to the macro-level of national British class mentality. On the other hand, the burgher mentality defined as the urban-generic mentality of the merchant city does not form a monolithic block, but can be further differentiated into social or economic status (cf. Barceló 1995: 51).

also to decipher the social relations of the respective communities within and beyond. I therefore argue that an analysis of ecological novels can reconstruct an image of the metropolitan socioscape as a whole. Similar to Pesso-Miquel (*ibid.*: 81), who outlines the limited expansion of the cityscape in Graham Swift's London novels, a majority of this analysis' corpus is set in a specific neighbourhood of London. Although known as the Shepherd's Bush bard, J.G. Ballard characterises a gated community in Chelsea in *Millennium People*, while Tim Lott specifically locates his novel in the social milieu of the White City area. It has been shown that Maggie Gee's *The White Family* is set in North London, while Blake Morrison's book concentrates on the socioscape *South of the River*. Gautam Malkani's *Londonstani* is ascribed to Hounslow, while Matthew de Abaitua's science fiction novel is emplaced in Hackney. Monica Ali's *Brick Lane* is one of many pieces of contemporary fiction that depict the East End. Although the novel offers impressions of Britain and London as a whole, Cuevas (2008a: 207) argues that the scope "remains limited by comparison, forcefully drawing the reader's attention to the limits of Nazneen's mental map of the metropolis. The emblematic sights/sites of London exist as an 'absent presence'."

Brick Lane, as the title of the novel indicates, is centred on a neighbourhood of Tower Hamlets. This area – with the highest concentration of Bangladeshis in London – has boasted a significant community since the 1970s (cf. Eade, Fremaux & Garbin 2002: 161). The protagonist's story as part of Brick Lane's social space also reflects selected historical development in the area and the personal history of its inhabitants.[11] Cuevas (2008b: 385) classifies Monica Ali's book as a typical example for the genre of the estate novel with a "focus on characters whose destinies are shaped by the social milieu of the council estate".[12] Her thesis shows that literary representations of Britain's underprivileged and stigmatised communities have become a major theme parallel to the media coverage of the rise of a growing urban underclass wrought by unemployment, poverty, violent crime, ethnic segregation (cf. *ibid.*: 383). Brick Lane's domestic insularity as represented by Nazneen's account of her interior life as a female Muslim migrant in the East End enforces the notion that the virtual segregation of the Dogwood housing es-

11 | In the 1980s a major section of the male population worked in white-collar jobs in local administration such as for the Council like Nazneen's husband Chanu. It shows the territorial struggles between white and non-white ethnic communities on the estate but also the outrage between Islamists and secularists around the Mela (BRL: 347, 359), which had "triggered high tension between community leaders" (Eade, Fremaux & Garbin 2002: 166).

12 | Cuevas (2008b: 385) identifies two influences, namely the nineteenth-century London slum novel and twentieth-century American street lit. Accordingly, the estate novel must be seen as "part of a literary tradition of fictions written by and about the urban lower classes." Examples from the nineteenth-century, which are also early sociological explorations of the modern metropolis, include George Gissing's *The Nether World* (1889), Arthur Morrison's *Tales of Mean Streets* (1894) and *A Child of the Jago* (1896) or Israel Zangwill's *Children of the Ghetto* (1892); early migrant fiction such as Buchi Emecheta's *In the Ditch* (1972) is also set in a council estate; contemporary examples are Victor Headley's *Yardie* (1992), *Excess* (1993) and *Yush* (1993); Courttia Newland's *The Scholar* (1997); Alex Wheatle's *Brixton Rock* (1999) and *East of Acre Lane* (2001) (cf. Cuevas 2008b: 385; Valman 2009: 3).

tate creates a bounded cultural enclave which is nonetheless internally segregated along class, ethnicity, race, and religion.

Simultaneously, the novel reflects the contemporary living conditions on the estate, including unemployment, poor housing, growing drug addiction, and youth deprivation (BRL: 142, 354-358, 484). Similar to Jack London travelling the abyss of London's East End in the disguise of a participant observer, Dr Azad is described "as a man of science" coming to the deprived flat in the East End "to observe a rare specimen: unhappiness greater than his own." (BRL: 115) In the traditional nineteenth-century literary comparison of the East End as 'Darkest England', *Brick Lane* depicts the area as a wasteland of poverty, dereliction and entropy similarly to Joseph Conrad's *Heart of Darkness* (cf. Pesso-Miquel 2008: 89). From Nazneen's insider point of view, the surrounding area is experienced as one of decay which increases as time goes by (BRL: 143). The character's antipathy towards the estate's surroundings is enhanced by a feeling of entrapment:

> She began to spend time at the window, as she had in those first few months in London, when its was still possible to look out across the dead grass and concrete and see nothing but jade-green fields, unable to imagine that the years would rub them away. Now she saw only the flats, piles of people loaded on top of the other, a vast dump of people rotting away under a mean strip of sky, too small to reflect all those souls. (BRL: 364)

Her change of inner perspective cannot solely be reduced to the transforming outlook of the city but equally reflects how her position in the metropolis has been altered from expectant newcomer to a momentarily dwarfed city-dweller.

The novel not only charts the growing spatial ruins, but also implicates the larger socio-psychological voids created. Nazneen's experience of imprisonment and dereliction also leads to a consciousness of lack and deficiencies that results in frustration, anger, violence, depression, mental disease and suicide (cf. Pesso-Miquel 2008: 90-93). The protagonist's vision of the city throughout is in confluence with her emotional state; for example, when Nazneen's first child dies, she experiences London as a broken city of darkness and consequently falls into the dark mental space of depression (BRL: 117-118). For Hiddleston (2005: 68), Ali's novel reveals how in general the perception of the community and its position in society "clearly structures the character's mental world." Despite the images of decay and despair, *Brick Lane* also presents the female protagonist's resilience, humour and hope which further vigilance and personal maturation; it takes years until Nazneen is able to transform the uninspiring and grey urban landscape of friction to a more personal and colourful space of transcultural interchange (cf. Pesso-Miquel 2008: 93).[13]

Hiddleston (2005: 57) also points out that Monica Ali's novel takes a look behind the closed doors of a segregated social world in the centre of the metropolis and offers

13 | Hiddleston (2005: 57) has extensively discussed how Monica Ali was accused by the local Bangladeshi community of propagating stereotypes and thereby misrepresenting Bengali culture in London (cf. Poon 2009: 436; Perfect 2008: 110). Ali tackles the "burden of representation" to reveal the immigrants' unequal status in society (cf. Hiddleston 2005: 66; Perfect 2008: 110; Feng 2009: 17).

an unprecedented portrait of East London's Bangladeshi community, its social life and cultural practices, "provid[ing] the reader with knowledge about the detailed customs of those ordinarily enclosed in their ghetto." (*Ibid.*: 64; cf. Cuevas 2008a: 195) *Brick Lane* achieves to mirror the forging of a community identity which lies between the ethnic identity of back home, the new place identity of Banglatown and the imagined community identity constructed by the diffuse knowledge of sharing a similar fate with others. The idea of an imagined community is already developed in the realm of the block. Imaginatively crossing the boundaries of her flat, Nazneen creates pictures of her invisible neighbours and completes their images by little hints she receives about them (BRL: 182). She thereby indicates an urban connection through involuntarily shared intimacy that is caused by close living conditions in a limited space of the metropolis.

However, the idea of the imagined community becomes more prevalent in a postcolonial context. London as the former metropolitan heart of the Empire and the new place of diasporic communities "has become the site for imagining multiple communities extending far beyond the localities of London's East End" (Eade, Fremaux & Garbin 2002: 161). The Bangladeshi community of Tower Hamlets as shown in the novel has wide-ranging dealings with the local state of their estate, the metropolitan fabrics of London as well as with the social spaces of their home country. Nazneen's everyday experiences in London always evoke memories of her village life which are additionally mediated by her sister's letters from Dhaka. This correspondence offers the possibility to compare her metropolitan life in London to Bengali urban life as particularly gendered. With the help of her lover Karim, who works with new media, she gets to 'know' the living conditions of Muslims and immigrant communities sharing similar (religious) mental dispositions.

Additionally, the community's links to the ancestral villages in Sylhet district, where most of the estates' inhabitants come from, are paralleled with the life in the urban village of Tower Hamlets. Chanu explains these communal connections as culturally transported from Bangladesh's rural areas to metropolitan Britain to recreate a homogeneous and familiar social atmosphere: "[M]ost of our people here are Sylhetis. They all stick together because they come from the district. They know each other from the villages, and they come to Tower Hamlets and they think they are back in the village." (BRL: 28) Chanu as a passionate newspaper reader keeps up to date on the mediatised news concerning the city, the country and the world. Park (1967: 39) argues that newspapers serve the same function village gossip used to have. While he also claims that the absence of personal information is what "makes the city what it is" (*ibid.*), in the Dogwood estate oral news still present a probate means of communication as especially the women talk and exchange information. Mrs Islam, for example, is characterised as the community's information hub, from whom nothing can be veiled (BRL: 28). The novel thereby indicates that the social structure of the urban estate rather equals the mechanic solidarity of village life with all its rural dynamics. Primary relations are still intact, which again underlines the 'rural' nature of the estate. In this sense, Monica Ali's *Brick Lane* belongs to a new wave of diaspora fiction which focuses on the social displacement of the peasant community into an urban realm, which defies a dichotomy of "at-homeness and migration" (Banerjee 2008: 7) or familiarity and strangeness, but follows the translational processes of appropriation, integration, superimposure and transfer (cf. *ibid.*).

The novel also picks up on the transformations of socio-cultural and political geographies of a globalised world and its psychological consequences (cf. Kral 2007: 69-70).

It is the third sphere of the global spectre in which the diasporic community of immigrants and Muslims find themselves involved with people from all over the world. The informal group around Karim feels and worries with the victims of fellow displaced and marginalized people. Thus the community of Tower Hamlets is not only one located in the specific ecological environment, but includes an imagined public of different times and places. London as one node within a larger net of global flows, connecting virtual communities around the world and consisting of transnational communities caught up in their imaginary homelands, is nevertheless represented as strongly localised. First and foremost, the renowned and medialised specificity of London's East End, the reformulation of urban identities due to the South Asian diaspora in Tower Hamlets as well as the enacted territorial power struggles between Bengal Tigers and Lion Hearts show that these global communities do not outplay local ones (cf. *ibid.*: 72-73).

While Karim uses the internet to google foreign Muslim prayers and the mobile phone to remind his father of prayer time, as a second generation immigrant he is situated between urban-specific modernisation and ethnic traditionalism. Also Nazneen's children are drawn towards Western music, clothes, and food while similarly influenced by their parents' cultural practices. The novel hence offers an insight into the feelings of disorientation of a particular generation caught between cultures (cf. Hiddleston 2005: 61), but also, for example in Nazneen's job at "Fusion Fashion", presents possibilities of reciprocal influence and translocation. Consequently, the female protagonist despite the "strongholds of Asianness and Britishness" (Campbell-Hall 2009: 173) achieves to fuse both into a new way of life and mentality, which oscillates between urban and rural, global and local, fundamentalism and post-positivism, segregation and negotiation. Knowing one's place in the world, the definition of home, is no longer assigned only to one physical place of origin or one specific space of memory. Instead, home seems to reside in various locations where the urbanite re-discovers frontiers between familiarity and strangeness. The urban inhabitant, as a constant stranger, like the migrant, the hybrid man or the polyglot is never truly at home due to his double belonging. In that respect the metropolitan citizen resides on the borderline between public and private, between an isolation of individual consciousness and the social inter-connectedness of the group consciousness.

Additionally, a tale of gentrification (cf. Cuevas 2008a: 204-205; Brouillette 2009: 428-429), the novel moreover charts the cultural and economic 'invasion' from the City (BRL: 310) and suggests that its socio-cultural landscape has been refashioned as well. Since Brick Lane has become renowned for its curry houses, the area has turned into a major tourist attraction representing a colourful part of what is supposed to resemble London's multiculturalism. While Cuevas (2008a: 205) criticises that Bangladeshi residents and well-off Londoners might share the same streets, but still shop, work, and live in "separate social worlds", Valman (2009: 3) considers Brick Lane a local "multicultural 'contact zone'". Especially in its function as marketplace and commodification, various critics have pointed out the multiculturalism of the area (cf. Perfect 2008: 113; Valman 2009: 5; Brouillette 2009: 427). In reference to Sukhdev Sandhu, Feng (2009: 16) points out that Brick Lane has always served as a "temporary interzone for immigrants" from various racial and cultural backgrounds. In this sense, the insular focus of the estate novel is shifted to encompass the intra-communal dynamics of its social relations to the East End as a complex transcultural space and finally to London as a contact zone for strangers. Monica Ali's novel consequently celebrates the potential of metropolitan transformation where the emergence of liminal spaces, cracks, doublings, overlappings and displacements around cultural difference stands for an intersubjective and collective experience of urban community, namely a cosmopolitanism both shared and rejected.

Socio-Cultural Mobility and Hubs of Cosmopolitan Interchange

According to Mumford (1997: 233) "each great capital sits like a spider in the midst of its transportation web" and Wirth (1964: 75) especially sees this "heightened mobility of the individual" as constituting the social dynamism and superficiality of city life. Mobility enhances the freedom of the individual, in the sense that the "old adage which describes city as the natural environment of the free man still holds" insofar as everyone can follow his "inner nature" (Park 1967: 12). Freedom again spurts independence of thought and a widening of personal horizons to enlarge the possibilities of social contacts. This independence, of course, greatly affects the development of personality within the framework of city life, causing a special relation of individualism and community.

In contemporary city novels social dynamics are represented as an interaction between character and setting or milieu, whereas mobility creates a specific urban sensescape. Different forms of transportation and mobility in the novels are often narratively employed to depict the characters' territorialisation of the city as they make it their own and gain freedom. These mobile processes, however, not only present various levels of freedom and independence to be gained in city life but also define the social relations between individual and community. Overground transportation by car or bus strictly correlates with urban stratification. While driving a car is denoted with a social position granting independence and power, a trip on public transport necessarily functions as a social contact zone. Particularly the analysis of Geoff Ryman's *253* and Keith Lowe's *Tunnel Vision* has explored the heterogeneities of subterranean sociability in the cosmopolitan contact zone of the Tube.

The following interpretation of Monica Ali's *Brick Lane* (2003) follows that lead to assess the London Underground as a transcultural contact zone, due to the fact that the majority of Britain's ethnic minorities lives in the Greater London Area (cf. Reichl 2002: 19) and commute, use and experience the Tube on a daily basis. Additionally, as variously shown, the London Underground has been a crucial location for transforming London into a cosmopolitan city; London Transport considerably contributed to the creation of a multicultural metropolis by recruiting employees from the West Indies (cf. Wolmar 2004: 296; McLeod 2007: 404).[14] Around the millennium thirty-two per cent of its workforce were non-white (cf. Halliday 2001: 137). Moreover, the deep-level shelter of Clapham Air Raid Shelter in South London became the first settlement of the

---

14 | After the Second World War, in response to labour shortages and in order to keep the city moving, London Transport started recruiting in Barbados, followed by Trinidad, Jamaica, and later by Malta, Cyprus, the Indian sub-continent and Eastern Europe. Immigrants were trained as drivers, conductors, station staff, canteen assistants, track engineers, and builders especially for the London Underground. For more see Dennis Brooks (1975), *Race and Labour in London Transport*.

Jamaican *Windrush* generation and in consequence the origin of Brixton's West Indian community (cf. Smith 2005: 271; McLeod 2007: 394). The transcultural contact zone thereby focuses on the composite "migrant as traveller" (McLeod 2007: 393), emphasising the fluidity of identity formation by way of routes instead of roots (cf. Chambers 1996: 196; Pike 1999: 113) and the construction of "cosmopolitan collectivity" (McLeod 2007: 404).[15]

McLeod (*ibid.*: 391) in particular demonstrates how the London Underground has become an important trope for the metropolitan experience such as cognitive and identitarian chaos, frustrations and confusions, but also possibilities of diasporic expression by "peoples and cultures initially subterranean and surreptitious".[16] Looking at Lord Kitchener's calypso song "The Underground Train" (1950), Hanif Kureishi's film *Sammy and Rose Get Laid* (1988), and Salman Rushdie's novel *The Satanic Verses* (1988), he shows that disorientation and confusion give way to "subaltern creativity, creolisation and contestation" (*ibid.*: 403). McLeod (2004b: 25-26) suggests that "the sound, motion and energy of other times and places [...] shape a new passage through the city". This creolisation of space is mirrored in Sam Selvon's *The Lonely Londoners* (1956) and added to by an appropriated Caribbean dialect where the London Tube is caught in a process of intercommunication that alters the perception of its space. Although these stories are about disorientation, the immigrant's way through the underground is also a form of resistance against its dominance, and the urban space is mastered through what Pratt (1992: 5) calls "creole self-fashioning". Music, rhythm and language appropriate modes of the urban centre and thus are defined as metropolitan culture itself. Thereby, London as the heart of the former Empire is set in a new system of reference. This subaltern intertextual creativity is an act of contestation (cf. McLeod 2007: 403) which nevertheless engages dialogues with the metropolitan space as it is addressed to the metropolitan reader as stranger as well as to familiar readers of the own socio-cultural group (cf. Pratt 1992: 7). In that way, their textual negotiations as much as the London Underground space represented therein become a contact zone.

Nazneen's enhanced mobility from the inside of her flat to the various outsides of the city, from marginality to the centre, helps to develop her urban characteristics of emancipation and personal freedom. In the beginning, Nazneen's pedestrian perambulations

---

15 | I have developed the idea of the Tube as contact zone in regard to McLeod's (2007) article concerning postcolonial writing on the London Underground. It was first presented at the "Contact Zones in Modern British Culture" conference at Konstanz University in February 2009 in a paper called "Re-Presenting the Heart of Darkness: Immigrants in the Contact Zone of the London Underground". Therein I follow the rough development of representations on immigrants in the Underground as depicted in songs (Kitchener, Kwesi Johnson), novels (Selvon, Kureishi, Ali, Ryman, Hill), and film (*Tube Tales*) from 1950 to 2003.

16 | As was shown in Monica Ali's *Brick Lane*, the protagonist Nazneen, who lives a closeted existence in the hidden and segregated East End estate of Tower Hamlets, is triply marginalised (class, gender, ethnicity) and finds herself an unseen outsider in contemporary London: "[T]hey were not aware of her. [...] They could not see her any more than she could see God. They knew she existed [...] but unless she did something, waved a gun, halted the traffic, they would not see her." (BRL: 57)

through the City already are a way of confronting the city by appropriating its sights just as these re-territorialisations parallel her transformation. Her first mobilised explorations of London take place by bus: making a racist remark on the African conductor's stature, Chanu obviously misjudges his own position as colonised stranger in the city (BRL: 99, 291). As Kral (2007: 67) points out, the family trip to central London actually pushes the characters from Brick Lane further to the periphery. Nazneen, however, grasps the variety of the metropolitan heterogeneity for the first time from the mobile bus, which invites urbanites to engage in different ways with the metropolitan contact zone. The glistening lights racing by transform the road into a "crawling carnival", while the shops behind sell "a little bit of everything from the world" (BRL: 100). From behind the bus windows she also discovers a woman in a sari, who like herself seems still not quite self-confident enough in navigating the metropolitan streets.

Contemporary novels negotiate postcolonial issues regarding London in this subterranean zone, enact specific struggles within the Tube, and consequently transform the perception of this spatiality. While the first part of the migration, as in Nazneen's case, often involves a route of passage over the sea, a second trip involves cruising the city, finding and asserting space. Especially the odysseys on the Underground are depicted as a struggle of belonging to the metropolis. For second-generation immigrants such as Karim in Hanif Kureishi's coming-of-age novel *The Buddha of Suburbia* (1990), the journey underground is presented as a way of finding one's identity, a 'rite of passage'. It has become a paradigmatic trope in postcolonial novels that the (second-generation) immigrant travels the Tube to the city centre, recognises the Self, momentarily becomes lost in the Underground's passageways and ascends to aboveground London in a stabilised manner. I therefore go as far as to call the underground chronotope the climax of self-recognition and definite turning point of self-fashioning and construction of mentality in postcolonial London novels.

In *Brick Lane*, Nazneen first catches the Tube because she is in a hurry to confront her lover Karim with her decision not to marry him. The passage stands in the context of penetrating the centre of the city – here Covent Garden – and presents her largest emancipatory stride. In Whitechapel station Nazneen mimics a modern young woman walking in a declaratory fashion: "Nazneen watched her and stepped as she stepped. How much could it say? One step in front of the other. Could it say, I am this and I am not this? Could a walk tell lies? Could it change you?" (BRL: 448) The protagonist makes the apparently confident women her twin, in the sense of a mirror image. She encounters the Other and at the same moment transforms herself. Before she already mentally tries out different western clothes (BRL: 297; cf. Feng 2009: 21) and in this situation she imagines herself 'in the shoes' of another woman. Insofar, Mary Pratt (1992: 7) develops her concept of the contact zone as space of "trajectories [that] now intersect" between "travellers and 'travelees'". Nazneen only slightly falters when she momentarily loses her way in King's Cross Station.

> She got lost and walked for miles through tunnels and up steps and down escalators, across ticket halls, past shops and barriers and through more tunnels. A couple of times she was close to tears. She challenged the tears to come and they backed down. Eventually, she found the platform and entered the train." (BRL: 448)

In this sense, the liminality of underground London defines a definite transitional space. When Nazneen for the first time travels to the heart of the city on her own to meet Karim at Covent Garden, she observes how people pass each other on the streets without caring (BRL: 449). She both reviews the basic rules of civil inattention and learns how non-involvement breeds a sort of tolerance.

In Sam Selvon's novel *The Lonely Londoners* published nearly sixty years prior to Ali's, the female figure of first-generation immigrant Tanty feels familiar with the London Underground due to its fame. Despite this sense of place which seems to transcend local and global geographies, she is momentarily overcome by fear and a sense of disorientation when travelling from Harrow Road to the city for the first time (Selvon 2006: 68-70). Tanty feels empowered because she has demystifyed the Underground, conquered the metropolitan centre, and returned 'home' to her familiar community in South London. In *Brick Lane* the postcolonial subject's empowerment goes even further. The ride on the tube presents an independent decision of going one way or the other, a personal journey of orientation and initiation, an issue of arriving 'home' as well as fighting the problems and disorientation along the way (BRL: 446-448). Arriving in the centre of London by Underground, the protagonist Nazneen notices that all she ever wanted was to feel at home. She consciously gains familiarity with London by penetrating its centre. Throughout the years, the character has developed the mental equipment to handle London as she pleases.

While Nazneen travels the Tube from East to West London and Selvon and Kureishi's characters advance from South to North, one of the main characters in Naomi Alderman's *Disobedience* (2006) takes the subterranean trip from North London's Hendon to the centre. This novel also unites cosmopolitan emancipation and self-recognition by commuting on the Tube: Esti, an Orthodox Jewish woman, is not only socially and religiously oppressed by the confines of her community and marriage, but is also forced to suppress her lesbian orientation. The anonymity of the Underground thus grants her consolation (Alderman 2006: 169) and the journey to Camden a chance of rebirth, recreation, and self-definition of her hybrid identity (*ibid.*: 172). Rather confused and under pressure to be back before the start of Sabbath, she is confronted with the cosmopolitan sphere of religious contact when an Indian lady signifies her pregnancy as a gift from God (*ibid.*). Exerting influence on the urban socioscape by re-appropriating its space necessarily constantly transforms urban mental structures as well.

In regard to the gendered geometries of space-time, urban sociologists in general assume that women are more dependent on using public transport and its existing routes which strongly define where they can travel (cf. Karp, Stone & Yoels 1991: 147-149). Moreover due to their frequenting the density of the Underground's enclosed public space, women are seen as exposed to the possibility of sexist or racist harassment. By contrast, postcolonial London novels stress the positive and empowering experience and the thrill of anonymous visibility. Having mastered the route to the metropolitan centre the female characters are especially represented as struggling to transgress the socio-geographical borders of their various enclosed quasi-suburban existence by developing significant mental tools of metropolitan mobility. The confined space of the Tube also shows how Londoners find a way to constitute their hybrid identities every day when being confronted for a long duration with enclosed mental dispositions from all over the world. Because the moving train refers to the fluidity of the individual Self (cf. Sommer 2001: 52), Londoners symbolically travel in the urban frontier of the underground, in-between creating transitory identities and relations on a daily basis.

Insofar in "fictions of migration" (*ibid.*) which set out to rewrite London, the London Underground is an important trope employed as a figure of the city's illusion, confusion, and identitarian chaos, but it also offers enough potential for empowering creolisation, appropriation, dissidence, and deviation. Although the Tube represents a confined and enclosed public space, it is constructed both as a liminal space in which cultural boundaries are transgressed (cf. *ibid.*: 50) and as a contact zone where difference is negotiated. The railway trains, platforms and tunnels resemble a labyrinthine thirdspace where overcoming the absolute nation state might indeed be possible. As the subterranean socioscape implies, hierarchies are not abolished, but they are not ascribed to particular groups. Additionally, the Tube has developed its own predominantly metropolitan rules. The contact perspective brings to the fore not just segregation and mutual isolation but segregation as a "form of togetherness that assumes the socially and historically structured copresence of groups within a space – a contact zone." (Pratt 1993: 88) Mobility becomes a metaphor for the socio-cultural dynamics of the contemporary metropolis in casting its transforming public spaces of negotiation as contact zones of transcultural and cosmopolitan engagement. Already Lofland (1998: 242) argues that the public realm, as is public transport, "is one of the very few kinds of social territories that, on a recurring basis, provides the opportunity for individuals to experience limited, segmental, episodic, distanced links between self and other." In this sense, the subterranean contact zone of the London Underground represents an apt metaphor for relational fluidity and its respective mental dispositions.

7.1.5 Mental Structures of Relational Fluidity

This chapter on London's living, thriving, dissolving, and atrophic socioscape has deciphered urban mental structures of alignment to the permanently shifting social environment of the postmodern metropolis: from face-to-face to secondary relations, networks of interrelations to islands of isolation, solitary contractuality to everyday opportunities of cosmopolitan contact.

The first part concentrated on the various networks of interrelations between family members, friends, colleagues, acquaintances and strangers. Contemporary London novels under analysis stress the importance of encounter in the urban milieu offering various possibilities for potential networks to be constructed, "diverge, or fold, on to others" (Amin & Thrift 2002: 29). The heterogeneity of urbanites' lives, however, rather determinates the temporality of these collectively shared experiences. Nevertheless, various individuals who are strangers to one another and who are dispositioned to distance themselves from the crowd can build meaningful, albeit temporary primary relations, because urban denizens intellectualise their face-to-face contacts as a reaction to personally deficiently felt situations – which can be emotional or economic. In that sense, families might seem dysfunctional, friendships like fellowships, and other contacts strongly competitive, yet these contacts appear predominantly calculated and intellectualised, which is, however, not rated negatively in the novels, but rather seen as an intrinsic element of the individualised and autonomous single urbanites.

On the counter side, urban social relations built on simple rational-monetary bases imply a certain superficiality and utilitarianism instead of the solidarity and proximity of traditional primary relations. This phenomenon corresponds to the postmodern social relations defined by Lofland (1998: 53-54) as "fleeting" and "routinised". Simmel's social and behavioural theory includes the analysis of sociability as an interaction in which people play society. Therefore, urban socioscapes are thoroughly mapped out by fragmentary role-play which requests a high degree of flexibility and vigilance from the single urban denizen. The drawback of this urban situation of anonymity and fragmentation is also explored in the novels in the sense of a new form of overload induced less by enhanced stimuli but by oversaturated loneliness. While phases of loneliness serve introspection and private recreation, the social vacuity and total isolation can lead to apathic dispositions of depression, mental regression, schizophrenia and even suicide. These forms of anomie become even more emphasised in the postmodern overload scenario of spectacles and non-places. Communities built on social control, surveillance and feigned comfort drift into an urbanity of pronounced blasé and boredom which can erupt, as Baudrillard predicts, in (self)destructive violence and hate. Furthermore, the Fractal City indicates a restructuring of the social mosaic towards insular lifestyles in gated communities or ethnic neighbourhoods where individuals are isolated together and share the experience of exclusion, entrapment, containment, imprisonment, isolation, and invisibility.

Despite these homogenising tendencies of gated communities and council estates which seem to promote a sense of social void, the restructuring of community and individualism has been shown to create new forms of sociability that transgress the borders of local confinement and promote new transurban, transnational, and transcultural sociabilities. Milgram (1970: 1466) already notes in 1970 that London's sociability is characterised by a relatively high degree of tolerance and courtesy between its inhabitants. In postmodern London novels, the urban is re-invented as one of cosmopolitan contact zone, fragmented identity, and fluid community formation. The mental attitude of the cosmopolitan ties in with the notion that an individual in the heterogeneity of the urban encounters the familiar in others while they simultaneously remain strangers. Lofland (1973: 176) argues: "*The cosmopolitan did not lose the capacity for knowing others personally. But he gained the capacity of knowing others only categorically.*" Insofar, the cosmopolitan as depicted in the novels is a metropolitan whose socio-spatial manageability in the space of flows has led to an urban-specific social intellectualisation. The stranger, the marginal wo/man, and the cosmopolitan are best equipped in the mental requests made by urban social living conditions of relational fluidity while the national enclosed wo/man is in danger of failing in the fluidity of London's social dynamics.

7.2 London Metropolarities

Due to the consequences of decentralisation and fragmentation as well as the socio-spatial manifestations of "Splintering Urbanism" (Löw, Steets & Stoetzer 2008: 72) the postmodern city is confronted with a transformation of social dynamics especially in regard to the urban-generic ambivalences of heterogeneity and homogeneity. Culturally, social fragmentation entails the differentiation of multimodal, fluid, plural and diffuse urban social worlds and diverse urban "ultra-lifestyle" (Karp, Stone & Yoels 1991: 110) societies, but also the emergence of various social outgroups or the intensification of subcultures. Consequently, contemporary cities are increasingly divided along a number of social axes, which imply social inequality, segmentation, and alienation approached by Castells' Dual City as a social, cultural and functional, internal fragmentation. The urban "discriminatory apparatus" (Benevolo 1980: 786) describes a constant tension embedded in the cityscape which revolves around power differentials not only of class, but also ethnicity, gender, and generation. Hobsbawm (1987: 50) argues in regard to these urban stratifications that

> today the labouring or non-labouring poor of the rump big city are divided: ethnically, by socio-economic status, between those who work and those who live on relief, between residents and commuters, between proletarians and lumpen proletarians or marginals, and, not least, at any moment between mutually uncomprehending and hostile age-groups.

The strife for social homogeneity induces processes of segregation and further differentiations in moral regions or absolute social spaces, such as ethnic neighbourhoods, middle-class gated communities and gendered suburbia, while conversely the zoning of residential segregation enhances homogeneity or internal assimilation and leads to territorial stigmatisation. In this context Lefebvre (2003: 133) submits:

> When we speak of difference, we speak of relationships, and therefore proximity relations that are conceived and perceived, and inserted in a twofold space-time order: near and distant. Separation and segregation break this relationship. They constitute a totalitarian order, whose strategic goal is to break down concrete totality, to break the urban. Segregation complicates and destroys complexity.

The image of the city as a world of incessant confrontation also stresses that the postmodern social mosaic rests on "*metropolarities*, the multiple axes of differential power and status that produce and maintain socio-economic inequality" (Soja 2001: 265). The socio-cultural power-relations of the postmodern city encompass the whole urban terrain, they cannot be relegated to opposing spatial forms, but "the ever-shifting geometry of social/power relations" (Massey 1998: 4) takes into account "the existence in the lived world of a simultaneous multiplicity of spaces: cross-cutting, intersection, aligning with one another, or existing in relations of paradox or antagonism." (*Ibid.*: 3)

While Cultural Studies oftentimes concentrate on dualistic representations of meta-mentalities (nation, class, ethnicity, gender) played out in the urban laboratory of particular segregations and marginalisations, the focus of the following analysis lies on the metropolarities concerning class, ethnicity, and gender of the postmodern urban socioscape that impact contemporary London-specific mental structures. I will first analyse Ian McEwan's novel *Saturday* (2005) and J.G. Ballard's *Millennium People* (2003) for their depictions of an ensuing middle-class crisis. Second, I will elucidate the factors of mentality concerning ethnic and racial marginalisation in Maggie Gee's *The White Family* (2002) and Patrick Neate's *City of Tiny Lights* (2005). Third, I will exemplify London female vigilance as depicted in Monica Ali's *Brick Lane* (2003), while following the lead offered by recent studies on lad literature which dismantles postmodern urban 'men-tality' as wrought by gendered (dis)orientation as represented, for example, in Gautam Malkani's *Londonstani* (2006). Finally, this chapter discusses the various dispositions of outsiderness as paradigmatic for an urban-specific mentality of London's pariah as shown in Matthew de Abaitua's *The Red Men* (2007) or Christine Brooke-Rose's *Next* (1998). The novels under analysis reveal structures of mentality that due to metropolarities enforce the image of deviant urban subjects.

7.2.1 The Urban Middle-Class Crisis

Problematics of class stratifications as part of metropolarities are an intrinsic layer of urbanity. The city represents a great agency of social types and the post-Fordist metropolis stresses socio-economic inequalities or socio-cultural cleavages. Historically, the city brought off the metropolitan bourgeoisie whose "mentality and lifestyle were from the start very much urban." (Zijderveld 1998: 38) Also the working-class is in its origins an urban phenomenon, and it has been argued that ensuing social opposition between the upper class and lower class unfolded in the socio-spatial differences of London's West and East End. Furthermore, in Great Britain, the issue of class has always been central to the nation's mentality.

In Jane Stevenson's *London Bridges* (2000) the urban environment is presented as a common ground for discharging notions of class. This change is introduced as two-fold: on the one hand, the newcomer from outside both the city and the country, egalitarian Australian Jeanene confesses not to understand about class; the cockney-aristocrat Hattie explains that it is the middle classes who "always wanted to be something they weren't." (LBR: 165) The lawyer Edward is an "insider born and bred" (LBR: 14), but finds it hard to live up to the socio-economic expectations of the Establishment. The banker Eugenides concludes that although Edward has enjoyed an equivalent upbringing he lacks education and real manners. Thus, while Edward feels "increasingly left behind", the socially excluded Dil, a second-generation immigrant raised in Southall, is ambitious enough to fight his role as an outsider and "penetrate the Establishment" in "effortless competence" (LBR: 14). Consequently, in a classical trope, *London Bridges* but also *Saturday*, *South of the River*, and *White City Blue* present the professional middle class as possessing the possibility of social advancement and the chance to overcome the city's socio-cultural divisions by personal urban agency.

In Tim Lott's novel *White City Blue* (1999), the originally working-class based protagonist Frankie Blue transcends the various socio-cultural boundaries of London through economic betterment. Phil Tew (2007: 91) argues that the text thereby encapsulates and challenges the cultural inscription of the working class as ignorant and thuggish. When he first meets his future wife, the main character instantly scans her appearance, lifestyle accessories and language, classifying her "two rungs above me, but not three" (WCB: 5) in terms of social hierarchy. According to Frankie, the class divide in the nation as in the city is more persistent than that of ethnicity. "You definitely can't jump too far in terms of class. You get young and old together, black and white, ugly and handsome, rich and poor. But it's still practically unheard of, in England, for the classes to cross the great divide" (WCB: 5).

The successful estate agent nevertheless suffers from resurgent inferiority complexes. Being part of the "newly educated class of people" (Tew 2007: 91), he still feels "like an ignorant nobody from Shepherd's Bush" (WCB: 2), albeit one with pretensions. In the White City, Frankie Blue is forced to hide his cleverness because it is regarded as a "bit of an embarrassment" (WCB: 31) and even a sort of "mental disability" (WCB: 137). Frankie's *gentification* and liminal social position is mirrored by his private living conditions on the recently **gentrified** borders of White City. This area is a hybrid mix between the 1960s social residue of deprived working-class "roll-up puffer, bitter drinkers, war moaners" and the millennial future of London characterised by middle-class metropolitan DINKS[17] – "young couples with Volvos, Beemers and Peugeot 205s." (WCB: 34) The novel thereby charts the transformations of the stratified metropolitan socioscape through a transitional phase of hybridisation towards a new era of consolidated urban homogeneity. Consequently, Frankie argues: "Nothing fits the world any more. [...] It's all hybrid, atomized." (WCB: 25) The following closer analyses of Ian McEwan's *Saturday* (2005) and J.G. Ballard's *Millennium People* (2003) concentrate on the unsettled state of mind of the urban bourgeoisie due to socio-spatial transformations and dynamic metropolarities.

Middle-Class (Dis)Comfort

In an interview with Zadie Smith (2010: 117), Ian McEwan comments on his own problematic social standing within British society:

> like anything to do with English class, my exact position was complicated. My parents were working class but when I was fourteen my father was commissioned as an officer ... He was one of the British army officers who've come up through the ranks; they're not Sandhurst, they don't have university degrees and they're not posh, and all his friends were similar people.

From the perspective of *Saturday*'s protagonist Henry Perowne, a London self-made man and noted neurosurgeon with working class roots, the city represents a socio-Darwinist system of social selection. The urban environment seems to enhance the amount of social mobility but also makes more apparent the existent social stratifications in contemporary London. The protagonist is aware of the urban space as geographically, architecturally and socially divided (cf. Girard 2008: 49). From his Fitzrovia mansion, Perowne literary looks down on the city square peopled by socially deprived drug addicts, hookers and drunks, underlining his upper middle-class dominance and urban accomplishment (SAT: 60, 272).

The outwardly "urbane and cultivated" (Ross 2008: 89) protagonist has worked his way up and married into the Establishment. Perowne's well-off existence is overtly exaggerated by emphasising his affluent, wholesome, and happy middle-class content: nearing fifty he is a healthy man who finds his job deeply satisfying, he lives in an elegant house in central London enjoying the comfort of sound family life, he has a loving and intelligent wife and two gifted handsome children, he saves the lives of his co-denizens and does not even become morally corrupted when he gets his social opponent Baxter under the power of his surgeon's knife. The character appears to play the role of the good

17 | DINKS (Double Income No Kids) refers to young couples in their thirties who are both employed, but do not have any children and rather concentrate on their career.

king in a contemporary urban fairy tale, whereby social correctness is obviously secured by a balanced social and mental status. In this respect, the novel takes up a liberal stance, according to which a happy family life is enjoyed by the successful cultural elite, its domestic intimacy a bourgeois privilege flanked by urban inequalities of socio-cultural supremacy anxiously guarded against intrusions from the underclass (cf. Michael 2009: 29; Ruge 2010: 71).

The character's social existence and world-view have been variously commented on by scholars especially in regard to Matthew Arnold's writing. For Arnold the social dissonance between public poverty and private opulence is strongly present and painfully observable in London (cf. Ross 2008: 80; Groes 2009: 109). Arnold's *Culture and Anarchy* (1869) is based on a tripartite analysis of social stratifications (barbarians, philistines, populace) and expresses a strong fear of social breakdown, violence, or anarchy (cf. Head 2007: 184). Consequently, Groes (2009: 110) and Wells (2010: 121) read Perowne's scientific passion and love for perfection as an incarnation of Arnold's philistine and Baxter as the civilised barbarian. Due to common topics of isolationism, character change, social commentary, and encounter with the 'natives', the novel therefore presents a postmodern urban Robinsonade in which Baxter becomes Perowne's 'Saturday'. The double climax of the novel with the crash between Perowne and Baxter on the metropolitan street and the later attack on the family abode is spatially narrated in the overlapping of their two socio-cultural worlds.

As a member of the intellectual and professional elite, Perowne first of all exerts his intrinsic mental power on the marginalised, derelict, and 'plebeian' Baxter. This petty criminal from Kentish Town is 'only' "Baxter" (SAT: 87), who possesses nothing but the stigmatised habitus of a defect gene (SAT: 227-228). To Perowne, Baxter seems a man who, "illness apart", has "missed his chances, made some big mistakes and ended up in the wrong company." (SAT: 98) Baxter's deviant behaviour is amplified, as he is obviously "a man who believes he has no future and is therefore free of consequences." (SAT: 210) Although trespassing the borders into another social world the character is unable to penetrate the hierarchical boundaries of class (cf. Ross 2008: 79). While Arnold's poem "Dover Beach" – an emblem of English but also traditional male middle-class superiority – ratifies the old class hegemony, Baxter's ascent of Perowne's stairs leads to his final downfall, ending up at the mercy of the superior's ethos, charity and professional ability (*ibid.*: 87). In this respect, the geometries of urban social space lead to overlappings, clashes, and meetings of class differences but do not dissolve the literarily expressed and literally incorporated power structures. I therefore contend with Ross (*ibid.*: 85) that while the urban underclass is seen as a problem, it never presents a relevant danger to the urban social order.

In *Saturday*, Baxter, himself a gang leader who dominates his sidekicks, fulfils the role of the general outsider that threatens white, male, middle-class security. Although the character does not directly relate to British multiculturalism, Gillet (2008: 100) exemplifies by way of comparing Graham Swift's *The Light of Day* and Ian McEwan's *Saturday* that these novels' "treatment of other types of outsideness testifies to their sensitivity to British multicultural society". In this respect, although I agree with Wells (2005) for whom the novel's socioscape problematically reifies middle-class dominance in connection with British nationalism and imperialism, but I tend to counter her notion that the novel "fails as an image of contemporary London". It is towards the end of his

Saturday that Perowne re-imagines 'his' square in summer when the young office people, of mixed gender and race, "confident, cheerful, unoppressed, fit [...], at home in their city" use the green patch for their lunch breaks. He is especially aware that London's social (de)stratifications are not primarily caused by socio-economic background and education but are an outcome of mental (dis)integration.

> So much divides them from the various broken figures that haunt the benches. Work is an outward sign. It can't just be class or opportunities – the drunks and junkies come from all kinds of backgrounds, as do the office people. Some of the worst wrecks have been privately educated. (SAT: 272)

Insofar, for Perowne, the socio-economic concept of class does not solely explain urban stratifications. Rather, social deprivation is seen as endemic to the urban as he claims that "[n]o amount of social justice will cure or disperse this enfeebled army haunting the public places of every town." (SAT: 272) Although metropolitan life, for the protagonist, offers anyone a chance for success, he generally sees failure as genetically determined (SAT: 6). Just as Baxter's anomic behaviour is more or less predictable due to his disease, from Henry's scientific perspective social patterns and inequalities in general lie hidden in the genetic code (cf. Head 2007: 194-196; Ross 2008: 86-88). Repairing the mental defects of citizens, the neurosurgeon feels socially 'ennobled' to heal the ailing urban society and furthers the protagonist's stance towards twenty-first-century socio-mental engineering. Due to his professional and social mindset Perowne is intent on gaining "mastery over all that is disorderly, irrational and counter to the city's middle-class prosperity." (Wells 2010: 113) While in the beginning, the social cartography of London presented is on the surface not much differentiated but rather a bland background of class, race and gender, the clash between Henry and Baxter opens the protagonist's perception to the internal dangers of London's society pertained by the multiple lines of social stratification.

Middle-Class (R)Evolution

Also J.G. Ballard's novel *Millennium People* (2003) presents this notion of contemporary middle-class terror. The population of Chelsea Marina takes a voluntary leave from the social position in order to protest their loss of freedom which turns out a simulational scenario staged by the authorities of the police and the media. In contrast to McEwan's text, the "society's keel and anchor" (MIP: 5) and the inhabitants of the comfort zone of Chelsea Marina rebel against their enclosed and cushioned existences. For Iain Sinclair, the novel "celebrates the nature of the bourgeois in its exile: the people that live in these kinds of flats that surround us now, who are anonymous and separated from the mob." (Cit. in Chapman 2006) This narrative of bourgeois non-conformity exposes the violence which persists under urban middle-class pretence (cf. Noys 2011: 398). Ballard's urban bourgeoisie represents the new masses or public men characterised by civil disobedience in "a desperate need for a more meaningful world." (MIP: 38)

The novel follows the absurd assumption that because of their alleged economic and mental impoverishment, the millennial middle-class sees itself as "the new poor" (MIP: 78) and an exploited proletariat "like factory workers a hundred years ago." (MIP: 65) This "poor bloody foot soldiers in the professional army" (MIP: 78) variously describe themselves as "an indentured coolie force" (MIP: 104), a new kind of serfs (MIP: 200) or "the 'underclass' of bourgeoisie." (MIP: 154) In this respect, the protagonist ironically comments that the middle-class revolution at Chelsea Marina is essentially one about parking meters, double yellow lines, and maintenance charges, catalysts that are missing in other better situated neighbourhoods like Twickenham.

Their counteractions thus basically follow a generic trope of urban social unrest or a script of socio-cultural (r)evolution. With the right slogans at hand – "FREE THE NEW PROLETARIAT" (MIP: 199) or "FREEDOM HAS NO BARCODE" (MIP: 216) – the middle-class (de)establishment begins to dismantle the cultural etiquette of its classified world. They default on their mortgages, ignore demands by the local council, disregard tax invoices, resign from their jobs, take their kids out of school. Instead, they turn to a role-play of shoplifting, petty thieving, vandalising parking meters, drug dealing and loitering. Oversaturated by boredom, the self-proclaimed new depraved turn against the corruption of their aspired institutions, lifestyle and thinking; they initiate attacks on cultural and economic institutions like the Tate Modern, the Natural History Museum, the British Museum, the National Film Museum, the London Library, the V&A, the Royal Albert Hall, the BBC, Peter Jones, Legoland, Selfridge's, Hendon shopping mall, coffee shops, or travel agencies. In a last stand – "The Bonfire of the Volvos" (MIP: 223) – they rid themselves of their cultural capital such as books, paintings, toys, videos, carpets, and cars. Despite single transgressions into violent and meaningless "terrorist attacks" (MIP: 249), this cultural revolution is modest and well-mannered, not posing a threat to social establishments.

Armed with revolutionary equipment of baseball bats, golf putters, hockey sticks and burgundy bottles as Molotov cocktails, they reschedule their street actions to a more convenient day so as not to clash with the middle-class leisure routine of concerts and dinners. Before staging their outrage, the bourgeois revolutionaries obediently order containers and after the uprising tidy up by pushing the burnt-out, overturned Volvos back into the parking bays, and pay the parking meters. The comforted masses are easily demoralised by being cut off the water and electricity supply: "No middle-class revolutionary can defend the barricades without a shower and a large cappuccino." (MIP: 224) Simulating 'homelessness', they tour the Lake District and the Scottish Highlands as "a new tribe of university-trained gypsies" (MIP: 7) or retreat to their cottages in the Cotswolds and Cairngorms. Mirroring the adventures of their nineteenth-century urban forefathers, the contemporary middle class enacts a romantic notion of the flight from the corrupted city. In the end, however, they also return to their neighbourhood and their public service jobs. Therefore, Jeanette Baxter (2009: 209) argues that London's urban middle class does not engender the "crisis of dispossession or of disenfranchisement" and that the novel exposes the Chelsea inhabitants as pseudo-revolutionary.

Correspondingly, the rhetoric and habit of the middle-class revolutionaries simply relies on copying and simulating the style of former social resistances and counter-totalitarian disobedience. The "moral outrage" against a cat show is verbally transformed into an ideological protest against the "eugenic experiment" conducted in the "concentration camp" (MIP: 36) and eclectically linked with imitated slogans from the miner's strike during Thatcherism: "*Moggie, moggie, moggie … out, out, out!*" (MIP: 35; cf. Baxter 2009: 210) During the run on the BBC broadcasting house, pictures are sprayed with Hitler moustaches and forelocks (MIP: 156), while in the V&A Michelangelo's David is pulled from its plinth like statutes of Stalin and Lenin (MIP: 154). All these actions are part of mediated images of resistance against fascist, totalitarian, and right-wing socio-political systems dating from the twentieth century. Baxter (2009: 211) comments: "When viewed exclusively from the flat screen, history is a constantly available stream of images which, stripped of their cultural, political and ethical specificity, are falsely democratised and thus interchangeable." The revolutionaries are depicted as both educated and oversaturated by these images, whereby their mentality is shown as fundamentally eclectic and their class-consciousness as vacant.

In the last stand at Chelsea Marina the inhabitants reduplicate their cultural mix of revolutionary ideas for the great audience in front of nation-wide breakfast television. They barricade their houses like Welsh miner families, play the prisoners' chorus from *Nabucco*, set their possessions ablaze and hold up their crying children towards the cameras (MIP: 193-216). Raising their fists against the establishment has become a historic routine for Londoners bar any historical meaning (MIP: 148). Rather, the 'programmed' uprising constitutes a prerequisite in "the circuit of violence as controlled pathology" (Noys 2011: 399). Insofar, they stage a mediatised idea of mental dispositions of thinking, imagining, feeling, and acting while rendering urban citizenry hyperreal.

The urban middle class is not only still prone to act out their ingrained habits, but their revolutionary actions are closely mirrored, surveilled, controlled and even initially provoked by the police and the media. At the siege of the BBC broadcasting house the revolutionaries are tuned in to Radio 4 and the protagonist realises "that we were taking our orders from the organisation against which we were demonstrating." (MIP: 149) The newspapers like the *Guardian*, the *Daily Telegraph*, and the *Daily Mail* become the promoters of their cause (MIP: 151-152), while the "television reporters [are] little more than agents provocateurs, forever trying to propel the peaceful protests into violent action." (MIP: 39) Yet the media are not the only party pushing the overtly blasé urban middle class into action. The protagonist, David Markham, is channelled into the milieu of the revolutionaries as a secret agent and drawn into its depths by another undercover police agent. Because the French Revolution was started by the middle class, nothing frightens the establishment "more than the thought of a real middle-class revolution" (MIP: 107). David understands only later that the Chelsea Marina revolution is "merely a tactical stage in a larger social experiment" (Baxter 2009: 213), serving an elaborate test of revolutionary potential in the least revolutionary section of urban existence. Initially "the Chelsea Marina action differed in no way from the riot-control measures they used in the East End's less savoury estates" (MIP: 226). Hence, there is no need to restore order from disorder because urban anomie has become a simulated spectacle for London's middle class to counter the postmodern urban blasé due to an oversatiation of blandness.

While Ian McEwan devises London's bourgeoisie on the threshold between complacency and anxiety for their self-contained happiness, and horror of the urban destructible elements beyond their grasp of superiority, Ballard inverses the middle class' crisis into one where the brainwashed base of civility becomes the harbinger of their own downfall as they are temporarily conned into paranoia and violence. Hence, both contemporary London novels grasp the urban middle-class crisis as one of socially engineered impotence and lacking in contemporary urban vigilance.

7.2.2 (Un)Homely Cosmopolis

The city has traditionally served as an object of desire for economic improvement and a way out of rural destitution, but has also attracted people due to its conveyed openness towards outsiders, strangers, aliens and marginal men and its promises of unconstrained freedom or unprejudiced mobility. In this regard, differentiations of class have intersected with those of ethnicity in the urban realm. Since urbanity has lost its powers to bind people in common everyday identification and solidarity, according to Zijderveld (1998: 66), ethnicity has become more pronounced in the urban realm and begun "to gain primacy over urbanity". Despite the initial cultural integrative function of the urban culture, migrants in the city are often socio-politically marginalised, which enforces spatial segregation.

The analyses of J.G. Ballard's *Millennium People*, but especially that of Monica Ali's *Brick Lane*, have already explored the socio-cultural implications of phenomena like the segregation of the white middle class in gated communities and that of ethnic minorities in immigrant enclaves. Nevertheless, the concrete living conditions in council estates also apply for the white underprivileged class and the inter-ethnic relations have been presented as rather differentiated, building manifold social connections beyond the confinement of the estate to the city and beyond. Being "segregated along social class, ethnic, and religious lines" (Cuevas 2008a: 220), these areas not only lie on the margins of society but as Ali's novel exemplifies they are far from being homogeneous within themselves. Rather, these new communities are diffracted within as well as "embedded in a majority of 'grey' areas" (*ibid.*: 117), recreating tolerance.

This sub-chapter specifically looks at representations of xenophobia and racism versus inclusion and tolerance in postmodern London in Maggie Gee's *The White Family* (2002), Blake Morrison's *South of the River* (2007) as well as the unfolding dynamics in a postcolonial metropolis on the threshold between multicultural and reformulated cosmopolitanism in Patrick Neate's *City of Tiny Lights* (2005). In the following I will inspect the portrayal of London's contemporary socioscape in regard to the mental attitudes of both migrants and resident Londoners created in the multicultural make-up of the metropolis and its various strata of segregation.

As was shown, on the one hand, the socio-cultural differentiation of the urban realm enhances the blasé of urbanites and thereby encourages attitudes of tolerating strangers, whereas on the other hand, the breaking-down of definite boundaries induces anxieties concerning one's own subject position and resurrects residual mental structures of superiority that produce hatred, racism and xenophobia. Furthermore, after migration passages migrants frequently suffer from social and psychological strains when confronted with the urban unkown. Characters like Nazneen (BRL), Casimir (UND), or even Mick (BLL) have to deal with their own traumas and face the alienating and disorganised new urban environment. Hence their cultural shock becomes pronounced due to the mental strains induced by acculturation and memories of home. Fischer (1984: 91), however, argues that "[c]ities do not change migrants; migrants change cities" and according to the theory of persistence, neither estrangement nor exile should be sufficient to change mentalities even after several generations. The analysis of *Brick Lane* has sustained to some extent that migration induces a dialectical transformation of urbanity and mentality. In this sense, I also see the idiosyncratic potential of urbanity to bind people from various socioethnic backgrounds to transcend if not obliterate the city's stratifications. I will show in accordance with Martindale (1984: 9) that in an urbanised world, the denizens' "mentality is cosmopolitan rather than civic". Referring to Homi Bhabha's (1994: 1) notion of contemporary culture as located in the area of the "*beyond*" I will prove that "'unhomeliness' inherent in that rite of extra-territorial and cross-cultural initiation" (*ibid.*: 9) of migration has become a defining *conditio humana* for the urban stranger with different ethnic background, promoting the double-faced status of being in- as much as excluded.

Coloured Foreign Birds

Maggie Gee's fiction features repeated encounters with dispossessed, socially excluded, or disadvantaged figures that populate the margins of the bourgeois world (cf. Sears 2004: 65-66). Mainly set in the multicultural borough of Brent, Gee's *The White Family,* charts the decline of the traditional neighbourhood as well as the socio-spatial processes of gentrification and socio-cultural diversification in other parts of Hillesden (WIF: 117, 174-177). The text moreover deserves recognition as a postcolonial novel because it acknowledges the aftershocks of colonialism in the metropolitan centre, such as an influx of foreigners, interracial marriages, and persistent racism. Although Hephzibah Anderson (2002) acknowledges Gee's exploration of the causes and consequences of racism, he criticises her approach as stereotypical compared with Zadie Smith's shaded racial landscape in *White Teeth.* Nevertheless we need to recognise that her prospect of the "*morally repugnant, or at least morally grey areas*" (McKay 1998: 214) of urbanity and human nature decidedly transgresses the boundaries of common appearances. As Gee argues in an interview, she likes "to write about things that are in some way forbidden." (Cit. in *ibid.*) Mapping the taboo territory of racism in today's multicultural London she explores the issue of race "as it originates and festers in the minds of present-day white Britons" (Jaggi 2002b). Despite her appropriation of London-born Winston King's marginal – young, gay, and black – voice, all the other perspectives in the novel are predominantly white (cf. Jaggi 2002a: 6). Thus, instead of the social effects of everyday racism, the novel concentrates on the minute and inherent prejudices rooted in the urban white (lower) middle class.

While the chapter on "Public and Private" brought into view the urban symbolism and the spatial semantics of Albion Park, its impeccable English lawns moreover reveal the keeper's attitudes towards metropolitan diversification. By the designated rules people are not allowed to walk on the grass, and Alfred approaches a black family who insists on its right to use the park and interpret his call for order as a racist reproach (WIF: 11). Besides this 'commonplace' situation there are various dynamics of racial stratification at play here. The scene in question is told from the perspective of a non-involved observer, the middle-class librarian Thomas. His thoughts only implicitly reveal that it is actually Thomas who perceives the black family's father as a threatening intruder:

> A tall black man comes hurrying across [...], and stands close to Alfred, looming over him. He looks at least a foot taller than Alfred, and two feet wider across the shoulders. (Was he actually threatening? [...] Could you say he was threatening? No, just tall. And black, of course, that was part of it.)" (WIF: 10)

Rather than exposing Alfred as racist, this point of view stresses Thomas' prejudices. Jaggi (2002b) argues that Alfred "affirms values traditionally claimed – though often betrayed – as Britain's own: justice and fair play" with all their responsibilities and duties including the calls for the park's rules applying to everyone. His task as the keeper of order, however, also represents the problematic of publicly authorised and emplaced rule-setting which does affirm old-standing hegemony and residual ideological rhetoric. For his wife May, the "Park Keeper's whistle which had sometimes pained her like the sound of chalk pulled the wrong way across a blackboard now seems in its absence an arrow of light, a clear white line shooting out across the darkness." (WIF: 20) While Alfred is depicted as one of the common referees of the English game of fair-play which enables aligned interaction between two different parties, hidden behind his official mask of authorial rule, the protagonist is biased. Disbelieving the family's reason for standing on the grass, Alfred approaches it for the violation of rules, exposing his nationalist mind-set: "They go on the grass. Always doing it. English people know not to go on the grass" (WIF: 12).

His scepticism towards the possibility of 'naturalising' foreign influences is even more apparent in regard to the caged birds of the park's aviary. While Alfred considers budgies and pheasants ordinary British birds, he sees the new foreign birds unsuitable for the English weather (WIF: 46). Already their phenotype seems to break the set rules of the English landscape: "I don't know what to make of the new foreign birds. Too bright, aren't they. [...] They don't look right in an English park" (WIF: 241). Thomas professionally enlightens Alfred that budgerigars are not English by origin and just as alien to Britain or the city as the newly-arrived exotic ones. He simply enjoys the secured birds' colouring of a bit of drab London which again exposes Thomas' seemingly liberal stance as no less racist. Similarly, Alfred enjoys the colourful flowerbeds in the park with their "[l]ovely reds and pinks and blues, tulips, geraniums, hyacinths... [a]nd yellow primroses and golden polyanthus and hundreds of daffodils in February." (WIF: 220) As an ecological symbol of Britain's imperial and colonial past, contemporary multiculturalism and recent 'cross-fertilisation', Alfred again misperceives that although the primrose might be indigenous to England, the other flowers have been imported from Persia, South Africa, or Southern Europe. Consequently, nationalism as a vivid form of Englishness presented by Alfred has come to an end as the contemporary metropolis confronted with a new form of internationalism by globalisation is embedded in a transformation of Britishness. Slowly disintegrating in the hospital with his face on the pillow like a "king on a coin" (WIF: 23), Alfred's death connotes the ailing nation which diminishes in the new space-time compression of Postmodernity.

Besides Alfred's nationalism, May's class prejudices, Shirley's obsessive sexual desire for the Other, and the Kings' homophobia, the most prominent example of urban intolerance in *The White Family* is Dirk White's ignorance, repulsion, and racial hatred. The narrative's internal and uncensored voice reveals that the character feels despised by his family, variously abandoned by his friends, not supported at work. While he accepted Shirley's first coloured husband also for his socio-economic success, he rather rejects the second from the West Indies. Hence, to a certain degree his racist attitudes derive from his dysfunctional primary relations as well as from his own socio-economic position in the city. On the other hand, as sexuality is important in terms of Shirley's interracial relationships to surmount racial barriers, it is Dirk's repressed homoerotic desire which eventually results in his killing of Winston. Gee comments: "Prejudices project sexuality on to others, on to differentness: fear of the other and desire of the other." (Jaggi 2002a: 9) Out of uncertainty concerning his own personality, Dirk seems filled by hatred for everyone with a habitualised and apparent stable identity-marker: women, old people, blacks, Pakistanis, Jews, *Guardian* readers, homosexuals, Irish, Catholics, etc. (WIF: 109, 252, 259).

No less problematic are middle-class racism and genteel forms of cultural prejudice emanating from Thomas' thoughts, attitudes and deeds. While he fancies himself descending from a Barbadian great-grandmother, the character's liberal stance appears open and welcoming to cultural transformations, yet he is still prone to "unconscious compartmentalising" (Jaggi 2002a: 8). When he sees Winston in the library borrowing books on lynching, Thomas is immediately dubious about the young man's intentions and likewise taken aback when he learns that Winston is writing a thesis on James Baldwin at UCL (WIF: 98, 275, 278). For Gee this "post-racism" (cit. in Jaggi 2002a: 8) describes a specific mindset in the sense that it tricks itself into believing how prejudice is something "out there" (Jaggi 2002b) instead of entrenched in everyday urban behaviour of all citizens.

However, the novel closes with the hope that mixed-race relationships in the postmodern city life of London will eventually lead to another stage of urban integration. Maggie Gee considers Shirley's twins from two different fathers as a new people, accomplished for a full stretch cosmopolitan era of urbanity: "The future takes physical form, and our ideas and prejudices will die. It is our minds that are so poisonous; there's nothing more frightening than a mind that is just a mind without a body. [...] People will always integrate." (Cit. in Jaggi 2002a: 9) Surprisingly, presenting the story on a high level of narratological justice, Maggie Gee sympathetically deals with all its characters showing the paradoxes of their convictions based on fear in the light of urban everyday life. As McKay (1998: 216) notes elsewhere: the "*characters, and the scenes in which they place, are described starkly, in the manner, as it were, of a pathologist of the soul. Although Maggie Gee may hint at the genesis of their perverted minds she makes no concessions to any feelings of revulsion that such characters may arouse.*" In that sense, stratifications of familiarity and strangeness, homogeneity and heterogeneity, tolerance and xenophobia seem to prevail in urban life as they are ingrained in common people's generic (b)ordering thoughts.

Metropolitan Margins

Likewise Blake Morrison's novel *South of the River* (2007) is strongly concerned with stratifications of class, generation and especially gender and race, as pronounced for example in professional urban advertisement. One of Libby's posters for business class flights is an appropriation of Edouard Manet's *Olympia* (1863), explicitly playing with the gaze on and desire of the Other:

The woman at its centre was lying naked in a topped-back armchair; only the seat belt round her waist told you this was business class [...]. She wore a choker round her neck [...], and a flower of some kind [...] was tucked behind her left ear. Behind her, in the aisle, stood **a young male flight attendant** in uniform: striped trousers, white shirt, peaked cap. He was carrying a tray on which were placed, to the left, an ice bucket with champagne (**the bottle**

suggestively towards her), and, to the right, an overflowing bowl of cherries. The flight attendant was bending down towards the woman, desperate for her to accept his offerings, while she gazed straight ahead, oblivious to his entreaties, her eyes playfully enigmatic, her lips slightly parted in sensuous pleasure. Her right arm lay in the seat rest; her left was draped across her crotch. **She was white, young and naked. The flight attendant was black.**" (SOR: 27; emphasis N.P.)

Ironically enough, the ad is not withdrawn because it is sexually or racially exploitative, but because animal protection files against the fur stole the woman is wearing. The black servant has already been replaced by an image of the "stud" (SOR: 28) and the colour "black" (SOR: 288) has become a mere commodity that sells.

In contrast to Gee's text, which concentrates on the sources of racism, Morrison focuses on the experience of marginalisation and the city's hostility towards foreigners in two corresponding characters: the white Irish Libby and the third-generation black Harry. The other characters also have a migrant history and are strangers in the metropolitan realm: Nat Raven's mother's side is of Polish descent, Anthea is English-Welsh but initially provincial, similar to rural Jack. For the old gent, as "long as immigrants pulled their weight, and fitted in, and didn't start outnumbering the English, they should be ignored and left in peace." (SOR: 496) Nevertheless, London's multicultural habitat comes as a shock to him. Whereas his only non-white contacts in the country are the waiters at his Indian restaurant, meeting Harry he is unsure about the political correct termini to use: "*darkie*" (SOR: 295), "*black*", "*coloured*", "*nig-nog*", "*coon*", "*niggers*" (SOR: 496).

For the well-educated Harry, a place in the world and an identity is defined by "money, age, education, dress, accent, colour" (SOR: 36). Although he emphasises that the black community of south London is an integral part of the city since at least the sixteenth century, the place is delineated by racial attacks (SOR: 81, 213). Going for a run along Paradise and Jamaica Road (!), a young Caucasian man insults Harry from a passing car: "*Go home, nigger*" (SOR: 80) – "Three words in all: verb, adverb, noun (*offens*); and injunction and an insult. If he had been wearing his headset, as he often did, he would not have heard. But having heard, he could not pretend." (SOR: 79) The general mechanisms of distanciation in a way fail Harry in this situation of Othering. But in contrast to his grandfather, an immigrant legend of the *Windrush* generation who still had somewhere else to go, Harry's home is the metropolis: "*Go home*... Home is what you know, and all he knew was south London. His mother had lived in Peckham since she was twelve." (SOR: 80) Harry feels English and cheers for its team at the World Cup, although his support is even stronger for its sub-team of black players (SOR: 164-165). Similarly, a taxi driver speaks patois to him, "a multi-layered allusion to demography, ethnicity, prejudice, south London behaviour, etc., through which the formal contract of driver and customer could be discarded and a new intimacy take its place." (SOR: 56) In this respect, the colour of his skin conversely includes him in the community of black Londoners, forging connections beyond stratifications of class. Harry, however, is shocked by the term "nigger" as defining him: "That's what *prejudice* meant – prejudicing a person making assumptions on the basis of skin." (SOR: 80) Like the racial hybrid in Park's concept, skin colour marks him out as Other and results in the relegations of a split personality.

Harry is so self-conscious about his marginal position that it is presented as a form of paranoia relegating the character to a jaded marginal man (SOR: 39-40). The protagonist suggests that the marginal position of coloured denizens characterises them as deviant, "because if you're black [...] you're more likely to be sectioned, more likely to be diagnosed as schizophrenic, more likely to be given ECT treatment or sedated." (SOR: 391) As a consequence, Harry prefers to be invisible and even wishes he could hide behind the anonymity of his byline. Revelling in the colourlessness of writing, he specifically opposes the burden of representation or "Blackness in prose" (SOR: 81). Conversely, when he is ignored by the waiter in a restaurant "as though Harry didn't exist or [...] had no place in a place like this" (SOR: 35), he feels equally insulted. Consequently, in contrast to the popular perpetuation of multicultural London during Blair's tenure, *South of the River* chronicles these everyday racial stratifications against the background of the publication of the *Macpherson Report* on the racist murder of Stephen Lawrence which gives evidence of systematic racism by the London Metropolitan Police.

But colour is not the only form of Othering in the metropolitan realm. While English football for Harry is a sign for integration, an English match always reminds the female protagonist Libby of her Northern Irish descent (SOR: 121). Due to her accent, skin colour and gender, Libby is persistently taken for an Irish nurse (SOR: 86, 276). Consequently, the character remains a stranger in the city, although the invitation to the New Year's celebrations at the Millennium Dome might prove otherwise. And just as black has become beautiful, the influx of Irish names emphasises the new elevation of qualitative multiculturalism in the millennial metropolis (SOR: 231). In a sense, similar to the exotic flowers and birds in *The White Family* or the depiction of the ad, blackness and Irish whiteness have become a commodity of 'Cool London', which nonetheless does not indicate greater tolerance, but a form of ethnic spectaclisation. Both urban strangers, Harry and Libby, decide to turn their back on London and pursue cosmopolitan accomplishment by further overseas-emigration to Boston and New York.

Beyond Babylon

Patrick Neate comments that his line of writing is generally about "otherness and alienation" (Topalova 2008: 406) which also constitutes the main theme of *City of Tiny Lights* (2005) a novel about multicultural life in London which touches upon questions of immigration and Britishness, prejudice and racial discrimination, as well as cosmopolitan belonging and identity.[18] Paradoxically, and this has already been a critique with his debut novel, Neate is a white author, like Maggie Gee or Christine Brooke-Rose, writing in the voice of the Other: in the *Observer* review, Chris Petit (2005) devastatingly denounced his writing as an "Ali G-type parody" – a sentence that was, however, also passed on Gautam Malkani's *Londonstani* (2006).

In *City of Tiny Lights*, Neate appropriates the view of second-generation Indian-Ugandan Tommy Akhtar, a private eye detective who owns a shabby office at the wrong end of Chiswick High Road above his brother's minicab office. Due to the hybrid identity

18 | With *The London Pigeon Wars* (2003) Patrick Neate published a London novel that depicts its socioscape from the strange perspective of a London pigeon having gained consciousness. In the following *City of Tiny Lights* will be abbreviated as CTL.

of the narrator-protagonist, his thirdspace position in the postcolonial metropolis, and his cosmopolitan outlook, London – the "City of Tiny Lights" (CTL: 244) – is depicted as a colourful mosaic of diverse socio-cultural worlds, a salad bowl of intermixing ethnicities, and a hot (melting) pot of cosmopolitan denizens.

> The way I saw it, the toffs on the pages of this magazine did not live in any England I knew. [...] The England I knew was a cheek-by-jowl kind of place where seemingly polar opposites were wedded by nation, frustration and location, location, location: stroppy Pakis to small-town racists, the morally fundamental to the morally bereft, office juniors to senior management, thuglites to petrified pensioners, suburban swingers to pregnant pubescents, coke-addled hookers to coke-addled media whores, aspirant Africans to resigned Rastas, loaded gym freaks to obese benefit junkies, entrepreneurs to economic migrants, organized crime to chaotic bureaucracy, politicians to terrorists, hopeless to hopeful. (CTL: 278)

Thus, the multicultural metropolis in its potential of inclusion and relativism is far from the nation's absolute space of exclusion. In an interview at a German conference on multi-ethnic Britain, Neate commented on the everyday reality of the nation's contemporary multiculturalism: "We've been talking a lot, and very critically about multicultural Britain ultimately being an illusion. But actually I think one should not forget that Britain is a multicultural society and it works, more or less." (Topalova 2008: 412) Also his novel's protagonist perceives that the nation has grown more heterogeneous due to its multi-ethnic base in the capital (CTL: 84-85). The novel encompasses a hotchpotch of characters of various ethnic descents: besides Tommy's Indian-Ugandan family – father Farzad, mother Mina, brother Gundappa – the main character draws a colourful image of multicultural London: his father's friend is Trinidad Pete, his brother's taxi drivers feature the Pole Big John, the West African Swiss Chris, as well as Irish and Yusuf, the Pakistani corner-shop is owned by the US-Asian Khan family, the doctors at the hospital are Asian, the nurses Nigerian, the people at the club include young Arabs, pros, City boys, middle-aged jokers. His job in London's criminal underworld brings him into contact with the black Essex prostitute Melody, her Russian friend Natasha, and the pimp Tony, the well-to-do posh English Nigerian dealer Tunde, the street-wise Irish detective superintendent Cal Donnelly, the American CIA officer Paradowski who poses as a Russian arms dealer, and the diaspora of terrorists around the Saudi-born Al-Dubayan.

Needless to say, within this Babylonian mixture of cultures there exist multiple lines of stratification in regard to desire and prejudice, which become particularly pronounced in Tommy's relation to his hooker-client Melody Chase. As he clarifies, London prostitutes, like a brand, are named according to their ethnicity: the Blacks Melody, Harmony, Bianca, Ebony, Naomi, Tyra; the Blondes Marilyn, Caprice, Helena, Elle; and the Hispanics Sandra, Salma, Fiesta, Sierra, Cleo. An urban commodity and object of metropolitan desire, they cater, as Melody comments, to their clients' diametrically opposed need of the Other:

> The English rose type? She sees Americans, Dutch, the odd German. Fat chicks? They get skinny nerds with a stiff little needle in their boxers. Brassy blondes? City whiz kids, Nigerians and Pakis. And exotic girls like me? We're talking middle-aged gents with colonial fantasies, Vi prescriptions and balls like peanuts. (CTL: 12)

In the stratified and dynamic hierarchy of the metropolis, the black female prostitute is, however, likewise disdainful towards the urban homeless (CTL: 6) and deprecatory towards Asians: "I ain't sleeping with no ethnics. [...] Pakis always wanna bargain and half of the time they sweat last night's curry. [...] Indians? Pakis? What's the difference?" (CTL: 7) The thick socio-cultural texture of London is depicted as one wrought by various geometries of power, submission, and stratification which are not overtly relegated to traditional hegemonies but follow the logic of urban metropolarities and *différance*. As Farzad analytically put it: "This is the most pernicious effect of colonialism: the inferiority complex. Those with the complex themselves need somebody else to look down on to maintain their sanity." (CTL: 114)

Farzad Akhtar is characterised as "a Ugandan, Indian, Paki and Englishman. A doctor, shopkeeper, widower and father. An immigrant, citizen, émigré and refugee – [...] a post-colonial artist of note." (CTL: 44) In his own appropriation he renames Melody from Ilford, the "delightful-smelling negress" (CTL: 243) of Jamaican descent, Melanie for her "dark skin" (CTL: 252). Over tea with the young woman he indulges, in a quasi-colonial manner, in the analysis of Black Caribbean versus Black African mentality: "The average Caribbean person is intrinsically idle, isn't that so? [...] I have always thought it is most likely a by-product of slavery." (CTL: 251) In a further synchronic comparison of mental dispositions he prefers African honesty over Indian arrogance and English uncertainty (CTL: 252). The novel thereby evokes a lively image of urban plurality and heterogeneity as well as the diverging stereotypical attitudes towards ethnicity, race, and culture. Rosenberg (2008: 364) comments:

> City of Tiny Lights as a whole aims at destabilising the structural priorities of binary constructions and ethnic boundaries. It demonstrates that we live in a society characterised by the cultural and linguistic need to taxonomise and that we rely on a set of imposed standards that makes identification with Englishness possible for some people, but accepts the exclusion of others, depending on context and intention.

While Petit (2005) is critical towards this eclectic picture of 'happy multiculturalism' he nevertheless applauds the author's choice of thematic metaphor: cricket. The protagonist Tommy has been acculturated to his father's notion that "[y]ou can learn everything you need to know about life from a game of cricket." (CTL: 4) Cricket is not only the athletic construct of colonialism and cryptic cipher for otherness, but also a "gentleman's game" (CTL: 322) that epitomises British ground rules of democratic fairness and straightness, bodily flexibility and quickness, mental steadfastness and forbearance (CTL: 3, 15, 83, 200, 255, 258, 274, 325; cf. Rosenberg 2008: 357). The cricket patch serves as a common ground that communicates sets of rules and norms of behaviour on whose basis the different teams can battle and beat, but also acknowledge and celebrate each other's idiosyncrasies.

Besides this synchronic depiction of London's heterogeneous assemblage of little worlds within, *City of Tiny Lights*, in correspondence to *Brick Lane*, charts the diachronic transformations of urban multiculturalism in comparing the attitudes of the old colonial migrant Farzad to the middle-aged hybrid Londoner Tommy. In this sense, the novel stresses the generational stratifications of culture and ethnicity since the 1970s. Farzad, an Indian-Ugandan medical doctor who in 1972 fled the regime of Idi Amin and was forced to open a corner shop in London, is presented as a colonial mimic who is full of praise for the English (CTL: 16-17, 251, 328). His hopes of integration are blighted, however, when his wife dies, his eldest son becomes a mujahedeen, Gundappa a local gangster, and instead of Gravesend Farzad ends up in Brixton just off Acre Lane (CTL: 18).

It's a cool enough area, although the recent influx of yuppies has somewhat lowered the tone: mostly shaggy-haired graduates with media jobs and a taste for perceived authenticity. You should see the faces of the locals when these patsy Bohemians make for the takeaway for a polystyrene carton of jerked this or curried that. Nobody does bemusement like Jamaicans. (CTL: 36)

Even Tommy's neighbourhood in Chiswick experiences a form of fashionable gentrification rendering London as a whole less ghettoised in the eyes of the first-person narrator (CTL: 3, 15, 19, 36). The new spatial relationality mirrors the possibility to "transgress racial and cultural boundaries" (Rosenberg 2008: 366) in terms of London's socioscape, communal interrelations, and personal identity.

In fact, the protagonist Tommy – "Paki-immigrant-Ugandan-Indian Englishman" (CTL: 122) – feels like a socio-cultural thirdspace himself. In school he is the centre of a male gang featuring Wayne Sullivan, a racist bully and full-time tyrant of Irish descent, Stuart Parsons, a typical English middle-class kid with black humour, and Lovely, his only Indian mate, who is good-looking, best in class and sports (CTL: 115-116, 120). While Mr Sullivan openly uses racist swearwords but remains unprejudiced in his personal conduct towards Tommy and Lovely, Mr Parsons, similar to Thomas in *The White Family*, is liberal on the surface, but indirectly excludes the boys. For the main character of Neate's novel, even these clichés are indeterminable because he feels both Asian and English, colonised and coloniser, oppressed and prejudiced. The most important character traits at bay are his Asian and English upbringing, two roles he seemingly slips into at will (see chapter 8.1.1).

He employs his Asian dispositions in order to charm, act mysteriously, and become invisible: "For all the talk of Muslim this and fundamentalist that, in this country nobody can be invisible like a Paki [...]. It's ingrained in the national psyche." (CTL: 53) As an Englishman he turns threatening or lofty (CTL: 182). Farzad, who was careful to raise his son in an English manner (CTL: 276), in later years admits that the English "comfortable" (CTL: 317) way of thinking sometimes hinders Tommy from the independent conduct of an urban stranger and to look beyond surface realities: "'Stop thinking like an Englishman.' 'But I am English.' [...] 'Of course you are. But does that mean you can't think for yourself?'" (CTL: 317) Although Tommy feels part of the nation, from his phenomenology as a 'racial hybrid' he is sometimes not accepted as an Englishmen and encounters daily and institutional prejudice or even racism.

For example, coming through Heathrow is always a riot if you're of ethnic persuasion. You can almost see the Immigration officers rubbing their hands in anticipation. You can almost smell their disappointment when they clock your British passport. You can almost hear them thinking, Lucky bastard. You can almost be bothered to tell them that there's no luck about it and they should read their colonial history. (CTL: 197)

Especially when questioned by the MI5 his ethnicity becomes equated with religion, marking him off as the dangerous Other whose patriotism is seen as a scam for terrorism (CTL: 211-212). As Rosenberg stresses (2008: 357): "Britishness suddenly appears to be synonymous with whiteness. Plurality and diversity, in the 'English' view represented by the MI5 officer, become ostensibly dangerous features of society and are said to bring destruction and chaos." Hence, the authorial social mapping relies on absolute and homogenised ideas of the nation, while Tommy, the "Fundamentalist Turned Patriot" (CTL: 324), has been raised in an urban setting and therefore takes heterogeneity as a prerequisite for vigilance and human agency. Confronted with the English MI5 officer, he contemplates on his hybrid identity: "I thought about 'our way of life', hers and mine. I wondered if we shared one. I thought about my way of life as, variously, a Ugandan-Indian, a Paki, an immigrant, a Londoner, an Englishman." (CTL: 295) Therefore, national identity defined as an absolute space is inept in grasping the quantitative and qualitative multiculturalism of the British metropolis and is unable to fathom the inconceivable multifariousness and individuality of its inhabitants (cf. Rosenberg 2008: 356).

The novel explores relations of alterity and identity, strangeness and familiarity, heterogeneity and homogeneity, as well as community and individualism on the grounds of the absolute notion of the nation state and the relational construction of the metropolis. Urbanity, as Lofland explicates, means to a large extent living amidst strangers who are only categorically known, for example by habitualised identity markers. Instead the epitome of the public urbanite, according to Sennett (1977: 17), is the cosmopolitan, namely an individual who, like Tommy, moves comfortably through the diversity and unfamiliarity of the urban realm. His liminal state marks Tommy as a vigilant urbanite ostensibly able to navigate the multipli-city and like a chameleon fits in every urban role. Tommy's "immigrant rationality" (CTL: 126), analytical deduction, commonsense thinking and constant outsider status make him the real master of London.

In this respect, Rosenberg (2008: 357) argues that "Tommy actually regards himself as an English cosmopolitan, i.e. he does not feel homeless or exiled." I largely agree with that notion, with a minor alteration: as the epitome of the urban stranger, the protagonist feels at home in his homelessness, in the sense of flexibility and mobility. Tommy is partly alienated from his former Self, as he describes his restless phase, in the third person as if describing someone else. After the death of his mother, he falls into the temporary apathy of a "minor mental-health episode" (CTL: 41) and then leaves the metropolis to travel to Ahmadabad, Lahore, Peshawar and Zhawar to become a mujahedeen soldier. Back in London he experiences a short spell of urban nonexistence, ending up homeless on the streets of the West End until taken home to his father's immigrant abode in Brixton and later the room above his brother's taxi company (CTL: 41-43, 124).

Hence, the urban socioscape in *City of Tiny Lights* can be read alongside Homi Bhabha's appropriation of Freud's uncanny. In *The Location of Culture* he agues that the (un)homely has become paradigmatic for the uncertain postcolonial condition of extraterritorial or cross-cultural situations (cf. Bhabha 1994: 9-10). Thus, the unhomely urbanite is also to be seen as a new type of cosmopolitan. Bhabha (*ibid.*: 9) argues: "In that displacement, the borders between home and world become confused; and uncannily, the private and the public become part of each other, forcing upon us a vision that is as divided as it is disorienting." On the one hand, the jaded sensibilities of the urban immigrant in the novel are revoked intertextual references to the introspection in Paul Gaugin's pictures, especially his *D'où venons-nous? Que sommes-nous? Où allons-nous?* (1897-1898) (CTL: 256) or Edward Hooper's images of metropolitan solitude, alienation, and ennui (CTL: 328). On the other hand, the stranger's (un)homely existence is captured in the notion of urban life as "journey" and "tourism" (CTL: 46) in a cosmopolitan sense. On the streets of London during rush-hour, the first person narrator-cum-rhythmanalyst catches the atmosphere of the strangers' city in flux:

> I clocked the faces of executive gents, fixed on the brake-lights of the car in front as they pictured their frumpy wives at suburban doors, their aortas choking on business lunches and lost love. I clocked the faces of school-run mothers, half turned and hushing brats, their tendons strained at the neck as their petrol gauges began to flash. I clocked the faces of white-van drivers, indicators flicking impatiently as they planned their next short-cut, their veins pulsing the same rhythm as the temple. Welcome to the city of tiny lights. It takes you a lifetime to get somewhere you've no particular desire to go. You're welcome to it. (CTL: 33)

Bhabha (1994: 1) describes this state of mind at the century's edge, marked by living on spatio-temporal – and as we might add social – liminal positions, as one of "the realm of the *beyond*." In this sense, the collective space-time compression of contemporary London in regard to stratifications of cultural plurality can be said to be defined by the beyond. An example from the text under analysis can be detected in the narrative structure of the novel. Rosenberg (2008: 366) comments: "All generic aspects are patched together to form a hybrid novel that is not mimicking *reality* but rather describing *a reality* not yet representable." Consequently, *City of Tiny Lights* actually looks beyond the multilingual misunderstandings in multicultural Babel to devise a reality built on stratifications of the multipli-city as cosmopolitan.

All in all, the analysis of racial and ethnic power geometries as represented in contemporary London novels exposes a mindset that detects strangeness within. The metropolitan socioscape constitutes a daily "experience of liminality" (Bhabha 1994: 14) where notions of alterity and otherness are habitually remade into a "boundary that is at once inside and outside, the insider's outsideness" (*ibid.*). This experience is thus not only part of contemporary Underground novels mentioned in chapter 6.2, but an intrinsic element of postcolonial London literature, such as *The White Family*, *City of Tiny Lights*, *Brick Lane*, and *Londonstani*, as well as other genres in which the issue of urban alterity is integrated, for example the state-of-the nation piece *South of the River*.

7.2.3 Gendered (Dis)Orientations

Urban space is not only structured and stratified by class relations or the socio-geographical effects of racism, but the cityscape is also severely gendered.[19] The feminist critique of urbanism since the late 1970s has emphasised gendered spatial practices, spatial rep-

19 | For statutes of a gender-conscious city see the *European Charter for Women in the City* (1997).

resentations, and has particularly concerned itself with lived urban space (cf. E. Wilson 1995: 149; Massey 1998: 233; Gilbert 2008: 108). Especially suburbanisation has become a material symbol of the marginalisation of women, due to the assumption that suburbia is seen as purposefully designed to isolate women and facilitate their subservience to men. This brings into view the traditional zoning of the urban according to occupational segregation which confines women to the private space of reproduction and the home. In this respect, studies of the gendered city are especially concerned with the ambivalence of women's invisible presence in the urban scene. Having access to different places (public), activities (mobility) and urban time (night), the perception of the metropolis by men and women has been proved to differ. Otherwise Elizabeth Wilson (1995: 149-150) has shown that urbanisation loosened the patriarchal control on women while transforming publicly visible female urbanites into a metaphor for the evil of the metropolis and the horrors of the masses: revolutionary, minority, temptress, prostitute, fallen woman, lesbian, womanhood in danger, etc. Nevertheless, in most urban representations, the city is imagined as feminine (cf. Weigel 1988: 175-176; Rose 1993: 69). While "Public and Private" elucidated on the gendered spatialities of the city, the following analysis is concerned with different presentations of the gendered socioscape of the metropolis with regard to mental attitudes.

Hence, I will concentrate not so much on the various female spaces as represented in contemporary London novels, but rather stress the stratifications in both male and female experiences concerning the urban ambivalence of apathy and vigilance. A further assessment of Blake Morrison's *South of the River* (2007) and Monica Ali's *Brick Lane* (2003) reveals tropic representations of the metropolitan realm as a space of female emancipation. By contrast, in reference to the genre of lad literature, novels like Tim Lott's *White City Blue* (1999) or Gautam Malkani's *Londonstani* (2006) expose a current urban crisis of masculinity.

Female Vigilance

In regard to the metropolitan socioscape, the analyses of the social dynamics in Blake Morrison's *South of the River* (2007) already elucidated the fleeting primary relations in the city, brought to the fore the stratifications of race, and partly indicated the relevance of gender in the urban realm. The interpretation now focuses on female vigilance of the protagonist Libby especially in contrast to her largely apathic and disillusioned (ex)husband Nat, who is plagued by urban fatigue, already indicated in the polar imagery of lone wolf and solitary vixen.

According to Nat, contemporary urban culture offers women the possibility to develop as professionals while he considers men to have to unlearn being career-oriented: "All careerism is a form of Asperger's [...] No, women are allowed to have careers. It's a new thing for them. Men need to learn to be less workaholic. I'm a pioneer in that. I've no ambitions anymore." (SOR: 505) Conversely, Libby is overtly driven in her job and as mother and wife at home. Although characterised as a new unfeeling and manly Thatcherite business woman – "Hard as nails. A Ball-breaker" (SOR: 4) – in truth, Libby is a 'Top Girl' who combines her professional career and role of the bread-winner with a fulfilled woman- and caring motherhood (SOR: 4-5). In the busy mornings she juggles both making breakfast and walking the kids to school with a long commute to the city and meetings at work. As Nat points out after they split up: "She has the house. She has her work." (SOR: 267) Although at times frustrated or uncertain and feeling drained of energy, Libby is not crushed by the demands of her double-act: "I'm a thirty-seven-year-old mother of two children, solvent, successful, with my own company, and free to do whatever I please. If only I knew what that was." (SOR: 277) In a sense, the character embodies the flexible urbanite demanded by the twentieth-century metropolis.

Essentially, Libby interprets female vigilance and innovativeness as the better equipment for the handlings in advertisement asking for pragmatic, instantaneous decisions, and instinctive foresight (SOR: 7). Instead, she sees men in the job as hampered by their inflexibility: "most of the men in advertising were lazy, mechanical, graceless and lacking in ideas. In this Libby realised, they were just like Nat." (SOR: 257) While Libby takes working up a sweat with clients and competitiveness as a typical male thing (SOR: 126), she resorts to communicative negotiations and suggestiveness: "Let your man think he's the creative one and you can't go wrong." (SOR: 29) Despite these seeming advantages, gender hegemonies in the working environment are still intact: Libby's younger male colleague is promoted to a job after merely one year in advertising, which she fails to secure after a whole decade at the job. Only by becoming independent and founding her own company is she able to reach her objectives. Consequently, the state-of-the-nation novel *South of the River* emphasises the newly discovered female vigilance and agency of the 'New Woman' at the New Millennium who inevitably changes the social dynamics of London and that of Britain. In the 1950s Nat's father still published sexist and male-oriented magazines called "*Priapus*. A Magazine of Arts, Literature and Erotica (MALE)" or "Bacchus. A Magazine of Arts, Liquor and Travel (MALT)" (SOR: 298). Half a century later, his brother Jack instead of "John Bull" finds the nation run by "Jane Bee" (SOR: 464).

Also Monica Ali's *Brick Lane* (2003) charts the transforming gendered geometries of space-time in the global and postcolonial metropolis. Like the novels of Buchi Emecheta and Joan Riley or the poetry of Grace Nichols, the novel problematises culture shock, displacement, racial abuse and humiliation of the female figures due to class, race and gender but also celebrates their lines of female agency and emancipation when they emerge from patriarchal control and find tolerance and self-respect in metropolitan London (cf. Cuevas 2008a: 195; Perfect 2008: 115; Feng 2009: 18; Poon 2009: 428). On the one hand, as shown before, *Brick Lane* follows the traditional feminist discussion on public and private, exemplifying how "[t]he boundary between 'the public' and 'the private' does not necessarily mean the same thing, or even exist, for (different) women of colour and white women." (Rose 1993: 126) On the other hand, the novel is involved in assessing the differences of local gender cultures in London and Dhaka, as Nazneen's urban way of life in the former metropolis and that of her sister Hasina in the latter. The second aspect stresses the gendered idiosyncrasy of both global cities in question and thus the following analysis specifically explores London's local gender culture in regard to female urban vigilance.

With the death of Nazneen's son at the end of chapter six, there is a narrative break in the story from 1988 to 2001 (BRL: 146-177). Because the protagonist's life is only marginally covered by letters from her sister Hasina, this gap of thirteen years, according to Feng (2009: 24) virtually underlines Nazneen's "monotonous 'non-existence'". However, the letters from Dhaka not only exhibit a close tie between the two sisters, but also emphasise how in contrast to her sister, Hasina defies conventions for her personal pursuit of happiness.[20] Hasina's migration to Dhaka and her daily struggle for survival in the city serve as a foil to Nazneen's existence in London. Nazneen, wondering whether the heaven and the moon in Dhaka were the same as in London (BRL: 187), makes us susceptible to the cultural similarities and differences of the two metropolises with regard to women's urban lives, such as experiences of gendered prejudices or patterns of inequality and oppression (cf. Hiddleston 2005: 63).

The gendered geometries of inner London, like those of Dhaka, are defined by the dynamics and intersections of national and international relations, family and economy, as well as patriarchy and capitalism. Massey (1998: 210) stresses that today the local gendered divisions of labour compete directly with the Third World; in the novel the life of the two women is connected through the same commodity chains of textile production: both are employed in the textile industry where the low costs of production in Bangladesh also define the wages of Nazneen's home work. Establishing financial autonomy through their own jobs, the fabrics of dependent occupation, the workings of capitalism nevertheless are close to patriarchal control at home and simply inverse old patterns of exploitation and subordination (cf. *ibid.*: 207). Insofar, Massey (*ibid.*: 209) argues that although women might have a wage, they do not necessarily have the independence that is normally associated with a job.

Literary critics like Françoise Kral (2007: 69) and Michael Perfect (2008: 112) discover the character of Hasina as a woman in a postcolonial Islamic society, and consequently point out the differences to a woman's life in the western metropolis. Perfect (*ibid.*: 116-117) specifically compares Naila Kabeer's *Bangladeshi Women Workers and Labour Market Decisions. The Power to Choose* (2001), a study of garment workers in Dhaka and London, to Ali's literary appropriation of the text. He shows that while in the sociological exploration London women speak about physical abuse, racism, isolation and financial struggle in London, in the novel, Hasina's letters are reports about women in Dhaka who are beaten, raped, exploited and disfigured. In opposition, Kabeer's text locates female agency rather in Dhaka, where women wear *purdha* and are free to go out and work in the garment factories, instead of London, where women are forced into isolating work as home-based machinists (cf. *ibid.*: 116). Kabeer's study and the novel only seem to overlap in their concern of public and private spatial gendering. In *Brick Lane*, the initial agency of Hasina is reversed to a fatalist repetition of a constant quest for intimacy and escape from subjugation. By contrast, Nazneen develops her own urban vigilance by freeing herself not only from the confines of the flat but also from the shackles of spatial isolation, communal supervision and male guardianship.

Hasina's letters show that despite living a public life – first with a job as a machinist, a prostitute, the kept woman of an Albino, a maid, and last on the street – in all cases she is denied a room of her own, and therefore unable to develop any personal agency. Because her life is highly dependent on the public, she variously falls prey to male Others, be it the gossip at the factory or her intrusive and penetrative landlord. As Hasina points

---

20 | For Hiddleston (2005: 63) the stilted, pidgin-style English make the letters appear banal and comic, enforcing a pattern of inequality and oppression which "connotes a cultural frontier lingering in the mind of the reader." In contrast, rather than stereotypical, Perfect (2008: 114) sees the letters as provocative. For him, it symbolises the difficulty of Hasina to describe her urban experiences (*ibid.*: 111–112). For more also see Groes (2011: 244).

out, the city is entrenched with the strange smell of men (BRL: 170), whereas she finds herself debased to "nothing" (BRL: 172) in the urban realm. She actually looks for the safe haven of marriage and the security of a home, while Nazneen's desires are directed to freeing herself from the constraints of the flat. Hasina writes: "Sister I know how you enjoy to leave your flat. But I have come inside now. How I love the walls keep me here." (BRL: 172-173) Consequently, the meaning of the public/private ambivalence for female vigilance in the metropolis seems to be diametrically opposed in London and Dhaka – not only physically but also mentally.

Finally, the temporal leap and the Bangladeshi perspective herald the beginning of the protagonist's urban awakening. The letters constitute a chronotope through which Nazneen becomes able to refute the notion of a simple Bengali wife, discover her own identity, adapt to the multicultural urban environment, react against the impotence of her fatalism, become socially and economically emancipated, and reconcile her private familial and public social role (cf. Perfect 2008: 119; Feng 2009: 22). Perfect (2008: 115) sees Nazneen's decision not to return to Bangladesh as a reaction against the horrors described in her sister's letters, and thus interprets her choice to stay in London as motivated by trying to protect the two daughters.

Defining the novel as a story of development, of slow awakening to an increased sexual awareness, political interest and personal self-consciousness, the emphasis in my point of view, however, is more on a form of urban vigilance. Nazneen not only makes her way beyond the walls of the flat in immigrant Tower Hamlets to a larger world where she finally assumes full responsibility for herself, but she also challenges traditional definitions of South Asian womanhood and transgresses traditional gender roles (BRL: 405, 437, 446; cf. Cuevas 2008b: 389; Feng 2009: 15). Feng (2009: 26) argues that in the end "Nazneen is no longer confined and controlled by the web of illusions which have surrounded her for the most part of her life. She is free to make her own decisions and to act upon them." As such, the novel follows Nazneen's development from fatalism to personal agency and from apathy to vigilance. However, even from the very beginning, Nazneen proves to be visionary, active, independent and resistant in her own rights, especially as nurturer, in order to secure the family's survival.

> For years she had felt she must not relax. If she relaxed, things would fall apart. Only the constant vigilance and planning, the low-level, unremarked and unrewarded activity of a woman, kept the household from crumbling. (BRL: 329)

This actively pursued and idiosyncratic female urban vigilance is by no means restricted to Nazneen. *Brick Lane* also charts other women's daily struggle for independence and individualism: Hasina's search for independence in Dhaka is always a quest for idealised romantic love and security, Mrs Islam basically enacts her own matriarchal system in London, Razia becomes a strong woman after the death of her husband. Only Dr Azad's wife, herself a Westernised and bossy woman, in her critique on female immigrants' apathy, forgets how cultural, gender, and social restrictions deny some of them independence and urban vigilance.

> Some women spend ten, twenty years here and they sit in the kitchen grinding spices all day and learn only two words of English. [...] They go around covered from head to toe, in their little

walking prisons, and when someone calls to them in the streets they are upset. [...] Everything should change for them. They don't have to change one thing. (BRL: 114)

Still, because the estate is not only a prison but also a space of creativity, production, and vigilance, London's East End in particular and the metropolis in general are constructed as an "unexpected feminist utopia" (Valman 2009: 7) where gendered boundaries are actually in the process of transformation.

By contrast, the men in the novel, although having access to the whole city, are represented as caught in their own static prisons of apathy. In opposition to Nazneen, Chanu is depicted as unpractical and ineffective, slowly being degraded from a man with a university degree and high hopes to an embittered taxi driver who eventually decides to return to Bangladesh in order to stabilise his personal identity (BRL: 328). In that respect, Schwinn Smith (2008: 104) points out that the two characters take opposite routes epitomised by the reversion of roles and expectations in the end of the novel (BRL: 121). While Nazneen carves out a private place of her own and unexpectedly makes herself at home in the East End, Chanu, after thirty-odd years of experiencing racism, ignorance, unemployment, poverty and finally loss of patriarchal control, succumbs to the "Going Home Syndrome" (BRL: 32). Adherence to the illusionary web of his "imaginary homeland" (Feng 2009: 23) emphasises Chanu's failure to operate effectively in the city (cf. Poon 2009: 433). Chanu is represented as the classic ineffective, disadvantaged colonial mimic, an immigrant who despite his quasi-naturalisation to the host country's habitus is emotionally and culturally displaced in postcolonial London. Oscillating between the position of a decolonised subject, assimilated migrant and failed cosmopolitan he becomes attracted to a new form of cultural fundamentalism and quest for authenticity (cf. Deny 2009: 216; Poon 2009: 430). Campbell-Hall (2009: 174-175) shows that the stranger's experiences of constant Othering first leads to a rejection of the host community, and, when his dreams of prosperity and advancement are irreversibly crushed, subsequently results in a nostalgic longing for the culture of origin and return to the homeland. Also Nazneen's lover Karim, whose hunger for authenticity attracts him to Islamic fundamentalism, leaves London behind.

For Deny (2009: 221) both characters thereby fall prey to mental regression and become lost in the postmodern metropolis. Hence, in contrast to Nazneen's growing urban vigilance, despite patriarchal control the male characters are not apathic at all, but rather fail in the dynamic straining realities of contemporary London. They strive to destabilise vigilance by restoring homogeneous authenticity. Thus, we can argue that the central male characters' return to their 'homelands' symbolises the failure of the stranger or the hybrid man to negotiate the emotional and socio-economic realities of London life. While the men's persistent bond with the mother country jeopardises not only their integration into British society but more importantly their internal urbanisation, the women in the novel prove to be more adaptable and resourceful in their metropolitan life. Valman (2009: 7) argues that "the humble uncertainty of the immigrant women turns out to be an unexpected asset."

In sum, the metropolitan realm despite the triple marginal subject position of women enhances their agency and so leads to urban emancipation. While the male characters' thinking depicted in *South of the River* and *Brick Lane* is shown to be deficient in the postmodern metropolis, the female protagonists due to their rather subaltern social position are invited to experience agency as a non-hierarchical but dynamic endeavour of London's socioscape. As commented by urbanologists, contemporary London novels also see cosmopolitan urbanity contributing to gender integration, as London's streets and public spaces offer women an escape from male control and dominance and especially female immigrants experience the city as liberating in their development from apathy to vigilance (cf. Gilbert 2008: 118-119). Although, in both Libby and Nazneen's case, the female protagonists are caught in the patriarchal system of capitalism, I would not go as far as Weigel (1988: 177) who argues that women's initiation and internal urbanisation goes hand in hand with taking over male characteristics. While Libby overtly makes use of her maternal habitus in her work relations, Nazneen does not simply mimic the host country's denominations, but, as the scenes on the Underground and on the ice-rink show, appropriates measures of self-confidence, mobility and demeanour without merely copying white/male behaviour. Nevertheless, as shown in the case of Hasina and ardently argued by Massey (1998: 151), this newly-won mobility can also entail the imprisonment of others. In a continuous process of self-creation, the New London Woman forges her own path through the city, and thereby rewrites the metropolis in her image as premonitioned by Virginia Woolf.

Crisis of Masculinity

This kind of urban female agency is also strongly developed in popular chick lit which gained prominence with Helen Fielding's *Bridget Jones* novels (1996, 1998). The gendered counterpart to this phenomenon is lad literature, whose main representative and initiator is Nick Hornby with novels such as *Fever Pitch* (1994), *High Fidelity* (1995), and *About a Boy* (1998). All these first person narrations are about average men in their early thirties who are obsessed with popular culture, for instance football or music, and struggle with adulthood (cf. Ochsner 2009: 32-33). The novels exemplify the foibles of contemporary middle-class culture, dysfunctional relationships and the anxieties of young British men wrought by cynicism, materialism and alienation. New Laddism in London fiction has developed into a most prominent contemporary sub-genre, for example, with Keith Lowe's *Tunnel Vision* (2001) and Tim Lott's *White City Blue* (1999).[21]

According to Niederagen (2000: 221), the new literary urban character of "*Cynical Young Men*" is specifically styled as superficial and cool; the single urban desperados in London are rather monadic, solipsistic and egocentric (cf. *ibid.*: 226-228). Ochsner (2009: 23-25) classifies the hedonistic, antiaspirational and post-feminist New Lad of the 1990s as distinct from the sensitive New Man of the 1980s. In this sense, she sees the new genre of the male confessional novel in this decisive decade as a manifestation of zeitgeist (cf. *ibid.*: 19-35).

21 | Other novels of the genre, for example, include David Baddiel's *Time for Bed* (1997) and *Whatever Love Means* (1999); Mike Gayle's *Mr Commitment* (1999), *My Legendary Girlfriend* (2002), *Dinner for Two* (2002); John O'Farrell's *The Best a Man Can Get* (2000); Tony Parsons' *Man and Wife* (2002). Moreover, it can include Ben Elton's fiction, such as *Past Mortem* (2004) and *Blind Faith* (2007).

> What the typical male protagonist of a 1990s novel does is digest political disappointment and fatigue, the erosion of social norms and values, the possibilities of late modern escapism, and the construction of reality by the media by presenting himself as a victim of the time he lives in. He does not, however, express this in an explicit way but contents himself with bemoaning the negative effects with which he has to deal and fight against in his everyday life. (*Ibid.*: 51)

In sum, Ochsner identifies three general structures of feeling which express contemporary idiosyncratic male attitudes in these novels: obsession, non-commitment, prolonged adolescence. She argues that "[t]he structure of feeling of the 1990s was marked by a general insecurity as well as by a more specific crisis of masculinity." (*Ibid.*: 15) The urban pre-middle-aged male generation was defined by confusion and uncertainty concerning the construction of masculinity interspersed with millennial fear and a postmodern questioning of identity construction. Ochsner (*ibid.*: 341), however, defies notions of retrosexism, but rather identifies the genre as an expression of postmodern male anxieties. It concerns the urban male who is not vigilant enough to deal with the new gender scripts that have developed in the metropolitan realm.

The analysis of Tim Lott's *White City Blue* has exposed the vacuities of laddish culture, the habits of male fellowship as well as the anxieties of the contemporary male psyche. The structures of non-commitment explored in the novel, whose protagonist Frankie Blue is afraid to face the loss of his male best friends when getting married, must be seen as an expression of a general fear of change (cf. *ibid.*: 9, 237-259). Hence, in contrast to the New Millennial Woman, the masculinity of the New Lad is represented as unstable and marked by disintegration. As already shown in case of Nat in Blake Morrison's *South of the River*, the new urban male character is conceptualised as a lone wolf orienting his success and maturation against women's new self-consciousness. Hence, the male urbanite appears regressive in the face of female vigilance. It has to be mentioned, however, that the male crisis represented in contemporary lad literature is also founded on generational characteristics, but the "Lad Trouble" (*ibid.*) is significantly relegated to male urbanites in their thirties. Nat's lone-wolf phase is connected to a typical midlife crisis, while Chanu and Karim's mental regression is defined by the specific disorientation of first- and second-generation immigrants. In this sense, mental structures of gender and generation overlap with those of culture and the urban. Not least, the definition of maleness on the basis of ethnic background adds to the complexities in representations of the male crisis. With regard to these phenomena, I will, in the following, analyse Gautam Malkani's novel *Londonstani* (2006), which although often rated as a postcolonial and not necessarily a lad novel, explores the dynamics of machismo in suburban second-generation immigrant adolescents.

Gautam Malkani is of Ugandan-Indian descent and works as a journalist with the *Financial Times*. His debut novel *Londonstani* is a coming-of-age story of the narrator-protagonist Jas, a nineteen-year-old young man raised in the middle-class suburban "little India" (Saadi 2006) of Hounslow.[22] Malkani introduces us to a group of South Asian second-generation migrants, who seek to establish respect in their streetwise identities and independence from their parents' dominance. The novel thereby exposes var-

22 | In the following *Londonstani* will be abbreviated to LON.

ious stratifications of contemporary cross-cultural London – Sikh/Muslim, desi/gora, young/old, male/female, standard English/patois, suburbia/centre, violence/petty crime, family/subculture – but denies any clear-cut understanding of cultural community concerning these generational, racial, religious, social and cultural lines of conflict (cf. Graham 2008b). The main issues of the text centre on aspects of postmodern teen subculture and machismo. Originally, the text stems from Malkani's dissertation on the British-Asian rudeboy scene in social and political sciences at the University of Cambridge. Similarly, the novel seems an anthropological analysis of homeboy desi life suggesting a significant interconnection of ethnicity and masculinity (cf. Brouillette 2010: 3).

In her analysis of "racialized masculinity" Ruvani Ranasinha (2009: 297) deduces that the colliding constructs of race and gender are at the very heart of postcolonialism. She argues that the nexus of race, culture, religion, class and masculinity, concerning the ideologised versions of the manly Englishman and the unmanly Bengali have shifted to violent hyper-masculinity in British/Asian identity positioned towards feminised versions of maleness and undermine colonial stereotypes (cf. *ibid.*: 297-298). Most reviewers and critics of *Londonstani* therefore emphasise that the narrative is less about ethnic identity, but more about a new manifestation of aggressive masculinity (cf. Shamsie 2006; M. Mitchell 2008: 331; Ranasinha 2009: 298; Brouillette 2010: 8; Anon. 2011b; Malkani 2011). These questions of racialised masculinity and urban machismo are represented in the novel around male suburban gang of rudeboys. As the narrator-protagonist clarifies:

> First we was rudeboys, then we be Indian niggas, then rajamuffins, then raggastanis, Britasians, fucking Indobrits. These days we try and use our own word for homeboy an so we just call ourselves desis but I still remember when we were happy with the word rudeboy. (LON: 5)

The group-leader of the small Asian gang is Hardjit, a well-groomed, muscle-bound, martial-art street-fighting Sikh who is exposed by the author as "a middle-class mummy's boy trying to be a man." (Graham 2008a; LON: 67) He consciously introduced a 'd' into his name to make it sound harder and simultaneously mark his cross-cultural identity (LON: 10, 112). Ravi drives the purple Beemer of his mother, but is otherwise marked by his misogynist rantings and boastings of his sexual virility (LON: 24, 52-53, 120, 138). The third rudeboy, Amit, is notoriously plagued by his angry and overbearing mother, whose manic obsession with respect eventually causes his brother to commit suicide (LON: 16, 86, 90, 161). Finally, the narrator Jas is a perceptive and intelligent A-grade student (LON: 127). The former outsider was taken on by the gang and now struggles to unlearn his intellectual way of thinking, adopt new rules of conduct on the street, and to conform to the group's subcultural habitus (cf. Brouillette 2010: 2, 12). Overtly self-conscious, ceaselessly introspective, and awkwardly insecure (*ibid.*: 13), Jas finds himself lacking the "rudeboyesque panache" (LON: 7). His new-found friends take him on as a weak follower of their posse:

> The things bout me that Hardjit told Amit an Revi to just allow. Things like I was a ponce, I acted an sounded like a batty, I was a skinny wimp, I was embarrassin to have around if ladies came by, I wore crap clothes, I used to have braces on both my upper and lower teeth, I'd read too many books, I walked like a fool, I had this annoyin habit a sniffin all the time, I couldn't usually talk

properly an even when I did I couldn't every say the right thing. Basically I was just generally a khota, like that coconut we'd seen earlier today except I didn't even have my own car. (LON: 25-26)

Only variously hinted at throughout the novel, the rudeboy authenticity is not merely hindered by his mind, but his ethnic origin deliberately remains obscure until the close of the novel, when he is revealed as white Jason Bartholomew-Cliveden (LON: 331).

There are obvious parallels to the fellowship of mates constructed in *White City Blue*: all in all, *Londonstani*'s male group additionally features a couple of similarities to the urban gendering in lad literature – male rules of conduct, a verve towards popular culture with a strong impetus of materialism, misogyny and homophobia – but also an idiosyncratic code of language and attitude towards the parent generation bordering on a male youth counter- or subculture which has become mainstream. The rudeboy rules basically run diametrically to the advice of Jas' father and encompass the aspects mentioned above: #1 always have a backup lie ready (LON: 38); #2 the "blingest mobile fone in the house is a rudeboy's birthright" (LON: 40); #3 stay out of trouble with the police (LON: 41); #4 use the proper desi language (LON: 44); #5 "U gots 2 know whn 2 shut yo mouth" (LON: 53); #6 girls should dress like Bollywood actresses, boys never like their filmic counterparts (LON: 59); #7 stand your ground on a girl you find "fit" (LON: 60).

As rules two and six imply, the correct technological devices and style of clothing are legion for the rudeboy (male) subculture. Opposed again to the Britpop style of R.E.M., Coldplay, Levi's 501, Evisu's, Peugeots and public transport, the homeboys' cultural capital throughout the novel reads like a list of brand names: clothes from Dolce & Gabbana, Versace, Ted Baker and Schott, sneakers by Nike and Puma, Tag Heuer and Cartier watches, Bang & Olufsen or Sony sound systems, PlayStation 2, Xbox, and Nintendo Game-Cube players, or an Apple iMac computer. This phenomenon stresses a particular hypertrophic intersection between machismo, materialism and consumerism (cf. Shamsie 2006). For example, in order to impress a girl in a drug store Amit specifically goes for "Dolce & Gabbana cologne; Gillette Mach 3 shaving blades; a sexy lookin chrome shaving brush; FCUK deodorant; Givenchy Rouge aftershave; muscle rub for sporting injuries; bodybuilding protein shakes; some designer hair wax; Boot's own-brand dental floss" adding 24 Durex Avanti with "a 64mm width stead a the usual 56 mm width." (LON: 92) The artificiality of this manly attire is ironically commented by one of Amit's aunties who interrupts the scene and reproaches him for buying condoms and criticises his choice of waxing cream, basically embarrassing the young men in front of the girls as well as his gang members (LON: 93). The strongest notion of machismo consumer culture comes from the boys' insatiability for phones and cars as phallic symbols and measures of manliness and virility as emphasised in rudeboy rule #2 (cf. LON: 14, 18; Ranasinha 2009: 301; Brouillette 2010: 11). How strongly manliness and desire for these consumer goods intersperse is emphasised by Jas' imagination in which he transforms most automobiles into the shape of American hip-hop idols:

So sleek an smooth you don't even notice its face. Like Christina Aguilera. The curves on an Audi TT make it J-Lo while the Porsche 911 GTS got a booty like Beyoncé. An it in't just divas:

I got the Bentley Continental GT as Snoop Dogg an the Hummer H2 down as 50 Cent. (LON: 18).

However, this new London bling culture has become mainstream, where a form of hyper-materialism defined by designer labels and the latest gadgets marks personal success in the city (LON: 164). In the novel, the gang's mentor, the criminal Sanjay, former teacher's pet, Oxbridge graduate and City banker, offers a thorough definition of what he considers the "Bling-Bling Economics" (LON: 165) of post-Thatcherite urban youth culture: "[c]onspicuous consumption, luxury brands, immediate gratification" (LON: 160). Outweighing any values of liberal humanism, according to the author, it represents "the first subculture to celebrate rather than counter conspicuous consumerism" (cit. in Graham 2008a).

In other words, the equipment of materialism defines both gender and ethnicity. The ideals stem from popular culture, especially American hip-hop as presented on MTV or B4U (cf. Brouillette 2010: 4). Similarly to the New Lads, they orient themselves in the metropolis by ways of music – here RnB, rap and hip hop – or Hollywood and Bollywood film. Besides the correlations with *Ali G* or the *Kumars* (*ibid.*: 7; cf. Saadi 2006), the protagonist increasingly sees himself as a character in a film (LON: 238; cf. Graham 2008b), while the novel creates a strong intertextuality to *The Matrix* (LON: 236, 239; M. Mitchell 2008: 332, 337) and takes up references to a number of other films like *Good Will Hunting, Top Gun* or *Hellraiser* (LON: 143, 237; cf. Schotland 2010). The new generational role models are P Diddy, Usher, Justin Timberlake, Arnold Schwarzenegger, Bruce Lee, Johnny Depp, Brad Pitt, Ben Affleck, and David Craig.

According to Malkani, particularly urban hip-hop culture constitutes the force behind the accumulation of hyper-machismo, hyper-materialism, hyper-misogyny, and homophobia (cf. Graham 2008a). He argues that during his research "[a] lot of [...] girls very clearly expressed that they were caught between the misogyny of traditional Indian culture and the misogyny in modern-day hip-hop-influenced desi youth culture." (Cit. in *ibid.*) In the novel issues of misogyny and homophobia strongly tie in with norms of conduct and language as expressed in the rudeboy rules #4, 6 and 7. Good-looking desi girls are fit flirts, while others are denominated as "bitches" (LON: 45). But as Ranasinha (2009: 302) to my mind correctly observes, in the novel women are depicted as both "consumers and producers of masculinity".

On the other hand, because of absent fathers, the mothers are likewise marginalised and isolated in their suburban existence, depressed and emotionally troubled in their own right. Asked by his overbearing mother to shop for middle-aged women's hygienic products, the rudeboy Amit sees no alternative but to go for the manly products in order to reconstruct his pride from already entrenched "teenage angst" (M. Mitchell 2008: 334). Policed by his advancing auntie, the macho is once again degraded to a mummy's boy. Consequently, the rudeboys' misogynist and homophobic attitudes derive from a complex mixture of dysfunctional relations to the parent generation, their female peers, the mediatised images of Western and desi manhood/femininity, as well as their own gendered and ethnic identitarian uncertainty.

For the young men this new form of urban machismo has become, in a sense, a dominant hegemony to orient themselves within London's metropolarities. Knowing which buttons to push, Sanjay in talking the rudeboy gang into criminal partnership convinces the teens by doubting their manliness: "You guys don't exactly live up to your reputation as the hard men of Hounslow. I mean, what have they been doing back there? Putting oestrogen in the local water supply?" (LON: 158) It emphasises that speech is actually one of the main measures to prove manliness and virility (cf. *Gautam Malkani*). Similarly to *White City Blue*, the male gang particularly tries to project masculinity by degrading others through homophobic language: "gay" (LON: 19), "gaylords" (LON: 32), "batty boy" (LON: 10, 37), "pansy" (LON: 104), "faggot ass" (LON: 23) "muthafucka" (LON: 114; cf. Schotland 2010). So while they only react to implications of their weakness through homophobic vocabulary, they likewise know no worse form of self-defence or verbal violation than to use insults that insinuate that their opponent is gay (LON: 124; cf. Schotland 2010). Only Jas, still trying hard to conform to the desi lingo, at times expresses discomfort with using misogynist and homophobic words (cf. Schotland 2010; Ranasinha 2009: 302):

> [I]f I was the Proper Word Inventor I'd do two things differently. I wouldn't decide that the proper word for a deep an dickless poncey sap is a gay batty boy or that the proper word for women is bitches. That shit in't right. I know what other poncey words like homophobic an misogynist mean an I know that shit in't right. But what am I s'posed to do bout it? If I don't speak proply using the proper words then these guys'd say I was actin like a batty boy or a woman or a woman actin like a batty boy." (LON: 44-45)

The male bonding of the desi "bruvs", "blud", "bredren" (LON: 4) depends on constantly differentiating themselves from the – white (inside or outside), female, or gay – Other. Hence the novel is full of Punjabi and slang swear words: bhanchod, bhanjis, goras, khota, coconuts, pendhus, spods, bounty bars, oreo biscuits, pleb, toff, etc. (LON: Glossary; cf. Schotland 2010) Being all talk, however, once again emphasises that the so-called rudeboys are merely middle-class mummy's boys who imitate ghetto acts in order to adopt a habitus that makes them different from the immigrant generation that humbly tried to retain their Asianness or mimic Englishness (cf. Graham 2008a).

In their role-play of posturing machismo, rhetorical and physical violence conflates on manifold levels, but in its spectaclisation remains relatively harmless, as the author clarifies, since both acts of performance are merely exaggerated by the narrator (*ibid.*). In the opening scene of *Londonstani*, Hardjit beats a white boy for having called him "Paki". Each strike, kick and smash is pronounced by an exclamation: "Shudn't be callin us Pakis, innit, u dirty gora." (LON: 3) Jas' depiction of the violence exerted is in retrospect exposed as unreliable because, as Malkani himself argues, the boy is still able to talk afterwards (cf. Anon. 2011b). Moreover, Jas' report of the second fight scene at the BMX track resembles "a parody of sports commentary" (*ibid.*) or a narrative appropriation of the *Matrix* martial arts scenes played in slow motion:

> He [Hardjit] was noddin his orange-covered head up and down, like he was listenin to some bangin hip-hop beat, pausing only briefly to rotate his shoulders back an let his Adidas tracksuit top slip off an hang around his elbows, revealing the gorgeous arms beneath it. Bang. Hardjit suddenly flips the tracksuit top off completely an throws the first punch with his right arm, fuck all that ground rules an squaring up shit. [...] Bang. Hardjit gives it a right-hand reverse punch

from his hip to Tariq's stomach, with his left foot forward. [...] Bang. He blends it into a left-hand reverse punch to Tariq's chest, with his right foot forward. (LON: 101)

This fight performance is not only for the youngsters, especially the girls standing around, and an affirmation of manliness, but in Jas' eloquence and representation of physical violence his conduct becomes again one of verbosity and lingual power. Thus, once more the mere rhetoric of machismo prevails over real dirty beating. Jas' report of the scene comes to overlay the rhythm of RnB with proclamations of masculinity in the single hits, linguistically marked by the repetition of "Bang" (LON: 101) and "Anyway, fuck that." (LON: 102-105) That the show stands in the centre of the whole act is emphasised when their teacher in order to protect them from the police proclaims them good kids, and the guys feel embarrassed in front of the girls (LON: 109).

Moreover, the scene shows that the initial tensions between religious (Muslim/Sikh) or national (Pakistani/Indian) identities are reduced to lifestyle props – bandanas, tattoos, colour coding (LON: 107) – and thereby remain on a basis of merely fictionalised displays of belonging in regard to class, ethnicity and gender. As Ranasinha (2009: 303) comments: "identity markers of ethnicity, masculinity and religion are culturally and politically constructed by highlighting the *conscious* performance of these dimensions of identity." Because identity has become a mere form of role-play, rhetoric and performance, also the machismo of the male youth gang has to be read as a hypertrophic spectaclisation of their masculinity. In other words, hypermasculinity is exposed as a conscious act of constructing gender boundaries, while this form of personal self-fashioning and collective identity formation is shown to be based on a cultural (dis)orientation of the younger urban male generation. Ranasinha (*ibid.*: 301) exemplifies how in their construction of masculinity the gang members draw on traditional myths of maleness because "it provides them with a sense of self within a subculture that co-exists with the mainstream." Gautam Malkani argues that the group's hyper-masculinity could likewise be expressed in other forms such as "football hooliganism, extreme sports or business".

Most importantly, the author elaborates in his interview with James Graham (2008a) that this form of London subculture is involuntarily intertwined with metropolitanism. As regards the urban-generic ambivalences of heterogeneity and homogeneity he stresses that urban subcultures, but especially London subcultures, are prone to "voluntary segregation" (*ibid.*). Instead of being marginalised members of the urban society, the desi gang in *Londonstani* chooses to be marginalised through their own action because from their well-integrated middle-class position cultural and economic opportunities are open to them. Malkani comments:

But, by volunteering for segregation and marginalization, the boys get to define their own brand of Britishness, of manliness, and their own rules of conduct. All this gives them more self-esteem than if they were to just assimilate by acting like archetypal Englishmen—which is what British South Asian kids used to do in the 1980s. [...] It allows them eventually to reassimilate and reintegrate, but on their own terms. In a sense, just like the hip-hop scene before it, British Asians have created a youth scene on the margins of society that has ultimately been embraced by mainstream society. (Cit. in Anon. 2011b)

In this respect, as brought forward by urbanologists, voluntary temporal segregation and the accompanying phenomena of stratification produce greater tolerance, integration and eventually stronger urban unity (homogeneity). When ethnic identity metamorphoses into a gendered subcultural identity and becomes absorbed by mainstream metropolitanism, it makes visible the porosity of socio-cultural boundaries in London's socioscape. Because there exists a high degree of "*subcultural* diversity" (Graham 2008b) in the urban realm, London metropolarities are constantly shifting. Graham (*ibid.*) even goes so far as to argue that the dynamics of community challenge "conventional definitions of *multicultural* society".

Moreover, what it comes down to in *Londonstani* – and this constitutes an aspect also strongly emphasised in *Saturday*, *The White Family*, *City of Tiny Lights*, *South of the River* and *Brick Lane* – is that in the rapidly changing urban milieu, generational conflicts become more pronounced and often lie at the basis of all other conflicts. In reference to Sellin's opinion that generational conflicts mark transformations of mentalities, we can therefore deduce that the voluntary segregation of the machismo rudeboy youth culture centralises medium-term changes of mental dispositions developed during merely one decade. These intergenerational conflicts argued out on the level of gender are shown in *Londonstani* irrespective of ethnic descent or social background. Not knowing that Jas is in fact a white boy of Jewish origin, the novel primarily traces intergenerational constructions of postcolonial masculine identity formation (cf. Ranasinha 2009: 298).

It is a common image in postcolonial literature that the older generation of immigrants is relegated to the private, domestic space as the comparatively static representatives of cultural traditions, whereas their children as integrated Londoners seek out the public spaces of the city (cf. Ball 2004: 224). On the one hand, the boys cruise the suburban streets to escape the oppressing atmosphere at home, trying to establish themselves as independent tough-boys in contrast to their submissive status at home. Especially towards their mothers and aunties they superficially adopt *izzat* and the notion to "respect your elders" (LON: 75; cf. Schotland 2010) acting all docile, although the rudeboys feel deprived of their right of personal decision (LON: 13, 24, 50, 71, 197, 236, 93, 298). This situation is paradox enough, because they notably profit from the familial cocoon of relative middle-class affluence.

The narrator variously refers to the constant nagging, control and constraint by Asian mothers. However, this "[c]omplicated family-related shit" (LON: 87) is more than a simple teen crisis, because the boys' socio-cultural aggression, their misogyny and homophobia are specifically fuelled, as Malkani clarifies, by a "complex struggle to be men against overbearing mothers who would rather their sons remain boys." (Cit. in Anon. 2011b) By contrast, their fathers are depicted as either physically absent or verbally silent. They are perceived as weak both in regard to public forms of racism and private forms of gendered power relations: "They're like desi dads when they stand there takin all kinds of abuse an shit from smelly skinheads, racist bosses an our mums." (LON: 106) For Malkani (2011) "the characters 'overshoot' their machismo because they're defining their masculinity in opposition to their (overbearing) mothers rather than in relation to their (emotionally detached) fathers." Hence, questioning their own South Asian values through contemporary hip-hop culture actually leads them to reinforce materialism and misogyny (cf. Anon. 2011b).

Nevertheless, this might then rather be a middle-class suburban phenomenon because Jas does not only disregard his parents' for their posh habitus and language. "That's cos the fone's display told me it was Mum. I always reject her calls cos she and Dad make me nauseous. If that what she has to say in't enough to piss me off, her fake posh accent will." (LON: 81) Jas despises his mother's considerations on his own behalf and always feels sick in her presence, while his father is always at work and if at home is reproached by his wife (LON: 32-35, 196, 331). Jas repeatedly wishes he could avoid contact with her altogether: "We could just beam ourselves straight back to our own bedrooms, not even have to deal with our own mums." (LON: 75) Again it is the well-educated criminal Sanjay who gives his analysis of these urban stratifications of London's socioscape:

> there's no such thing as a typical family any more. I mean, obviously everyone knows that there has never really been a typical family, but the point is it's become more and more so and the more important your urban scene becomes to people, the more that is the case. What was once a niche is quickly becoming a bedrock of mainstream society with more force than any other youth subculture since, well rock and roll, I suppose. (LON: 162)

On the one hand, this aspect emphasises the notion of dysfunctional families and relational fluidity analysed in "Public and Private" or "Urban Sociability", on the other hand, the metropolarities in regard to gendered subcultures are extended by stressing how both acculturation and socialisation are today mainly exerted in the public of the urban realm.

Urban sociologists and family pedagogues have been registering this development for the last decades. It also constitutes an argument brought forward by critics concerning the London riots in 2011. Finding themselves inbetween their oppressing family situation and urban aspirations of the Bling Bling culture, the young men abandon both their English middle-class education and traditional roots and develop a new form of urban vigilance. The subculture's emphasis on machismo and male physicality, popular cultural and materialism, the mysoginist and homophobic attitudes are closely positioned to the 'English' middle-aged lad culture of 1990s London. Saadi (2006) comments in his *Independent* review that the novel defines London as "a highly flammable mixture of pre-modern tribalism, post-modern subculture and late capitalist individualism." In a sense, the hypertrophy of objective culture as a mark of modern life is enhanced in the multicultural and postmodern metropolis and embraced by young men in their quest for stable (be it ethnic or gender) identity. Thus, their insecurity of masculinity as apparent in hyper-masculinity finds its outlet in an enhanced hate towards the Other, staged violence and criminality.

Anxieties of instability on the meta-level of the community played out in terms of gender are also apparent in Ian McEwan's *Saturday*. Rebecca Carpenter (2008: 143) works out that post-9/11 developments strained Britain's feelings about its place in the world, while in particular relations with the U.S. were seen in gendered terms. Interpreted as signs for the "feminization of the nation", Britain's position "was constructed as soft, naïve, idealistic, and utopian as compared to the clear-sighted, hard-headed, rational, truly masculine position of the United States" (*ibid.*: 145). In the light of Britain's waning political power, *Saturday*, according to Carpenter (*ibid.*: 150), presents two opposing yet empowering images of British masculinity in its main characters Baxter and Perowne: "a hotheaded, unreflective, lower-class brand of masculinity whose primary tools are strength, self-assurance, and swagger, and a cool-headed, intelligent, upper-class masculinity whose primary tools are knowledge and reasoning." This form of re-masculinisation, also acknowledged by literary critic Phil Tew (2007: 199), constructs a "cowboy mentality" (Carpenter 2008: 153) that aims at establishing control and self-esteem through patriarchal authority as well as physical and verbal misogyny.

How encompassing this notion of a male urban crisis is also becomes apparent in Toby Litt's novel *Corpsing* (2000), more thoroughly analysed chapter 8. Belonging to the literature described as "lad lit" or "British Bloke Novels" (Tolan 2008: 82-83), this text also combines an urban way of life entrenched in pop-cultural consumerism with notions of masculinity and the fear of home-based catastrophe. According to the author, *Corpsing* is partly about the protagonist's "attempt to put himself back together, as a man; a man who's been rendered impotent" (cit. in *ibid.*: 79). All in all, contemporary London novels convey a strong sense of masculine crisis in the face of female urban vigilance and the urban hypertrophy of objective culture, all of which appear to lead to a phase of hyperinflated remasculinisation.

7.2.4 The Urban Pariah

The discriminatory apparatus of the urban stratified socioscape creates outsiders who suffer extreme social and psychological exclusion. Peter Ackroyd (2001: 599) argues that the "poor have always been part of the texture of the city" and without owning a secure place in the social fabric in the medieval city the old, crippled and mad were rendered the first urban outcasts. He shows that "poverty never leaves London [but] merely changes its form and appearance." (*Ibid.*: 604-605) While in the nineteenth century rich an poor often lived side by side (East and West End) without taking notice of each other, the recent presence of the poor in hot-spots of deprivation such as Tower Hamlets – or for that matter the August 2011 riots in Tottenham – create anxieties of degeneration or moral degradation and increase "the morbid nervousness and restlessness of all Londoners." (*Ibid.*: 599).

Yet Hobsbawm (1987: 48) points out that the metropolis has not only generated social exclusion but that its "sociologically open spaces designed for the socially indeterminate" have always attracted people in social transience. For the socially excluded the city serves as a refuge where they become part of the urban underclass that inhabits marginal spaces of isolation and containment which separate them further from the mainstream. Insofar, the contemporary metropolis with its spaces of consumption, prosperity and spectacle coexists with the living spaces of have-nots such as ethnic neighbourhoods and abandoned zones of urban non-places (cf. Robins 1993: 313). Hence, while the city has always excluded aliens and managed to police its deviants, urban social processes have also sustained diversity and difference within its system (*ibid.*: 322-326).

The specifications of these ambivalences of strangeness and familiarity or heterogeneity and homogeneity are once again devised as a transformation of urban social complexities. First, the inner city has become a general site of the Other in the post-Fordist society. Second, in this world of strangers urbanites are variously Othered. Third, as the last chapter has shown, a general dominant urban culture is quasi non-existent in the postmodern metropolis because the former superiority of middle-class, white, male experiences passes through diverse forms of crisis. Robins (1993: 326) points out that "[t]he old certainties, securities and familiarities are simply predicated on the fact that some 'aliens' have developed a certain 'invisibility'." Because of tendencies of differentiation urbanites are partially in/excluded and thereby experience moments of integration into the mainstream of urbanity while at other times they feel completely alienated. Already Park (1931: 535) recognises cultural isolation as a significant characteristic of pariahood that "is true, to some degree, of every people".

This sub-chapter on "The Urban Pariah" therefore argues that the postmodern urbanite is an outsider *per se* in the sense that s/he is an intrinsic part of the city's socioscape but simultaneously positioned outside society as a member of a specialised pariahood. Contemporary London novels to a large extent are narratives of outsider figures: the clandestine people in *London Revenant*, the obsessed loners in *The Matter of the Heart* and *London Bridges*, the mad deviants of *King Rat* and *A Long Way Down*, secluded immigrants in *Underground* and *Brick Lane*, the social exclusion of the habitual deviant in *Saturday* or *The White Family*, etc. In more detail, I will analyse these processes of social Othering and promotion of metropolitan pariahood as represented in Matthew de Abaitua's *The Red Men* (2007) and Christine Brooke-Rose's *Next* (1998) . In a sense, recent urban fiction devises the city's strangers as deviants because due to internal fragmentation and differentiation every person in the postmodern metropolis feels variously othered.

London's Pariah-Hood

In de Abaitua's *The Red Men* (2007) the technological and futuristic Canary Wharf is opposed to the run-down suburbs of the East End. From the backyard garden of his Hackney home, the protagonist Nelson watches a train full of typical Londoners:

> Our conversation was interrupted by the 8.15 pulling into the platform at 8.45, overstuffed with passengers. [...] This was the junkie express, running from the Hackney crack houses to the Camden drop-in centre. It was also a commuter route, where immigrants from Eastern Europe, duty with demolition work out West, snoozed against middle managers, who made every effort to close their senses against the press of fellow passengers. The nearly dead travelled on this train too. (REM: 25)

The homeless and drug addicts share the same mobile space and initially the same fate of internal outsideness as immigrants and middle managers. In their own right, they all belong to the metropolitan outcasts using public transport. The epitome of this sociospatial non-existence depicted in the novel is particularly emplaced in Hackney. While psychogeographical writing since the 1980s first began to remap this territory (cf. P. Baker 2003: 327), in de Abaitua's text the borough both figures as a dystopian setting and a particular character, namely that of urban pariah-hood. It is represented not only, like the author's comments himself, as "a place of great flux and unpredictability" (Jordison 2007), but also as encompassing dark zones on the edge of the area. In this sense, Hackney is both central to the physical city of flux or social relational fluidity and stands ostensibly apart from the new centre on the Isle of Dogs.

The the character Raymond Chase, at one point in the novel, is swallowed by this urban black hole and "City Of Dreadful Night" (Jordison 2007). The Jewish cosmopolitan wanderer is a man of the street who appears different to the narrator-protagonist each time they meet (REM: 23). Transgressing "through the undergrowth of the city, where things actually happen" (REM: 31), Raymond is dressed for the metropolitan streets and smells of "the sweat shuck off by alleyways, the urban dewfall of bus fumes and rotting garbage." (REM: 24) Due to the "city's corrupting influences" (REM: 114), he spends his life in a "loop of poverty and mental illness" (REM: 42), sharing bedsits with "fellow pariahs" (REM: 41). Only out of fear of real homelessness and starvation – or moving once again to his parents' outside the city – does he decide to work for the corporation of Monad (REM: 33). Nevertheless, waiting for Raymond in a café of Soho's Old Compton Street, Nelson observes the urban masses and once again, the onlooker defines Raymond as just one of the fellow-citizen outsiders:

> Watching the river of people flowing by, one channel was made up of such 'haircuts'; the ageing hipsters sticking to their skateboard style of low-slung denim and ironic t-shirts, a work outfit for industries in which youth had a greater value than experience. Here and there lurked dissolute rodent men moving between drug supply and drug demand. There were divorced fathers taking their daughters to a musical in town; there were working schlubs; unkempt office stooges in ill-fitting suits, with their ties off and tails untucked to let their real self hang out. A suave older type in yachting linens caught me gazing. Red faces with blonde colouring, he was drowsy with the effects of his gin and tonic, which he clutched as he did his rounds, his buttered ham of a head appearing here and there in the crowd. Two roadies joined the corner of my table, solid working grafters, and there was an unspoken acknowledgement between us toward the great comedy of the Soho stroll. (REM: 115-116)

Following the lead given by the ex-wife of the Jewish Blasebalk, who escaped his own Red Men, Raymond thinks that the street-wise urbanite might have succumbed to his former addictions of urban intoxication and ended up going dark in London's most notorious areas of ousideness, the East of London (REM: 142): "London. Islington. Rehab. Soho. Crack. Gone Dark." (REM: 143) Mapping the dark spaces of the East End on an *A-Z* map, Raymond checks the illimitable possibilities for unaccounted Londoners to remain below the grid of surveillance:

> His cash would go far in the information wastelands of Clapton, Stratford and Leytonstone. Once he cleared the gentrified districts of Hackney there were highways of bedsits and squats to hunker down in. He could use market stalls for provisions, and pick up some cash in hand in the thriving black economy of immigrant builders, electricians and plumbers. (REM: 144-145)

The East End still figures as London's underground socioscape of counter-culture, immigration, poverty and criminality. The narrator, however, comments that this spatial urban pariah-hood mainly accounts for a significant type of inhabitant: "Anonymity seekers. [...] Hackers, crackers and phreakers who needed somewhere to hide. A complete rejection of authority. Ground Zero of the Great Refusal." (REM: 145) In this sense, the fringes of East London – Stratford, Clapton, Hackney – become not only the homebase of all sorts of outcasts (voluntary and involuntary), but the corporate centre of the Dyadic counter-movement "working for the anti-man" (REM: 227). The Great Refusal recruits its members from London's underclass, such as the Elk, who before his employment with Dyad spent a phase homeless in London, particularly on Hackney's streets (REM: 226).

The whole community gathering around Leto can be described as the epitome of London's urban pariah. The so-called dosser god is a grotesque appearance who sleeps on a park bench and is in dire need of alcohol, offerings of offal, stolen electronic junk like batteries and mobile phones (REM: 234-235, 304). But his body is just a host, while his mind virtually travels around the metropolis using the communal mind of London's pariah:

> The squat fell away and I was slumped outside Camden Tube station, holding a can of psychofuel like it was a flotation device, the only thing stopping me from going under. Then...zzzzip. Walking backwards on Kingsland Road, I am enormously fat and talking to Jesus on a baby's plastic phone. Zzzippp, I wake under a railway platform, rats inspecting what's left of one of my legs. Zzziipp, I am queuing outside the Hare Krishna van as they slop daal into a bowl for me. Zzzzzip. I wake up in the back of a camper van surrounded by empty bottles of wine. A policeman is knocking at the windows. Zzzipp. Unable to think, head full of other people's thoughts, I am talking to somebody on a bench. Leto. Enormous Leto. Here he is strong and untainted, Conan The Homeless. (REM: 305-306)

In line with Ackroyd's argument, London's poor and homeless are part of the city's idiosyncrasy, and finally constitute the force against the totalitarian Monad. Recognising their potential the artificial intelligence of Cantor tries to customise the urban homeless by sending Dr Easy roboters to homeless shelters (REM: 310).

A Homeless Society

Roy Porter's (2000: 454) social history of London from 1995 portrays the aftermath of Thatcherite London as one of deterioration and alienation with ten percent of the population on income support and a growing urban underclass heralding a new urban crisis with the clustering of "problem people" in the inner city:

> Many indices of decline suggest a new urban order is emerging. In place of the employed, self-sufficient and respectable working classes [...] a new outcast London is coming into being, poorly integrated into the disciplines of work, family and neighbourhood, into common values, and lacking expectations of a better economic future. Homelessness, family breakdown, classroom violence, unemployment, casual crime, poverty, sickness, racial attacks – all aggravate spirals of deprivation, alienation, despair, and antisocial activities among a proliferating lumpenproletariat. Poverty and deprivation deepen, and an underclass is emerging that is perceived as a threat by the respectable, law-abiding and integrated. Resentment intensifies polarization. Violence and fear stalk the metropolis to a degree unthinkable thirty or forty years ago. (*Ibid.*: 453-454)

Homelessness remains the most visible expression of social stratifications and destitution of an extreme social exclusion in the city to this day, especially due to rough sleepers in public spaces such as streets, parks, plazas, office buildings, the Underground, under bridges and highway arches. Porter (*ibid.*: 455-456) and Inwood (1998: 891) see homelessness as the most visible feature of the social breakdown, rising to 70,000 single homeless in 1990. And despite the initiatives enacted by the 2002 Homelessness Act, the year 2005 registered a new peak in London homelessness with 0.5 percent of the population or 18,000 families without housing, especially in hot-spots of deprived areas such as Tower Hamlets, Hackney, Brent, or Ealing (cf. Weaver 2005; *London's Poverty Profile*). Having counted more than 2,000 rough sleepers in London's streets, the council, as part of the government's vision for a 'Fair Britain', has erected the new strategy plan "No One Left Out – Communities Ending Rough Sleeping" to eradicate homelessness from London's streets until the 2012 London Olympics (cf. Department for Communities and Local Government 2008).

Brooke-Rose's novel *Next* (1998) focuses on the homeless population of London and casts ten homeless as its main characters.[23] At the end of the novel, Ulysses summarises the relationship of the authorities to homeless citizens as one of social ignorance and generalisation:

> Politicians. The ultimate authors of all our woes. / But unlike authors they don't know us. / Though like authors they can kill us off with impunity, / as I'm doing now: / A week's world, in one alphabet, but / QWERTYUIOP / Ten rough sleepers. / Having accommodated five, / Two with jobs, one with death, another to die soon / perhaps, one with a foot on earth / That's about percentilely correct. (NXT: 208)

Brooke-Rose's novel *Next* omits the verb 'to have' (NXT: Blurb; cf. Harper 2001: 51); the novel's language mirrors the world of material and cultural dispossession and emphasises both material and cultural deprivation of the homeless characters as the general have-nots. In correspondence to the city as the traditional seat of the money economy, Ackroyd (2001: 600) argues that in "London [...] they are literally degraded, stripped of all human decency by the operations of a city that has no other purpose except greed." By a general lack, the homeless are necessarily segregated and extremely excluded from everyday urban practices.

Brooke-Rose presents an insight into the individual lives of a homeless community within the city's socioscape whereby the question is posed by Tek whether the marginalised are really still tolerated as part of society. "MEN BORN EQUAL. *Natus sum*, giving rise to *natio*, but the Declaration forgot that a slave is not a national, that a refugee, like a dropout, ceases to be a citizen." (NXT: 2) On the other hand, the characters are not at all marginalised in the literary sense, occupying areas around Embankment, WC2 theatreland, Shaftesbury Avenue, the Strand, and Waterloo in the centre of the city (NXT: 8).[24] "Centre for the marginals. As if periphs could be in the centre.

---

23 | As Brooke-Rose explains in an interview she "became very aware of the Other, with a capital 'O'" (Boncza-Tomaszewski 2005) while working as a translator in the secret service during the Second World War. Learning to see through the eyes of the national Other as a religious or cultural Othering helped her to become a novelist and chart the experiences from the position of the Other (cf. Sapio Garbero 1993: 102; Friedman 1995: 14; Boncza-Tomaszewski 2005).

24 | According to the "No One Left Out" report most of England's homeless are counted in Westminster and the City of London (cf. Department for Communities and Local Government 2008).

Like Homeless Person Unit, HPU. And why are the excluded said to live in inner cities?" (NXT: 8) As James Duncan (2005: 167-168), however, shows in "Men Without Property: The Tramp's Classification and Use of Urban Space", the segregated homeless are restricted in their spatial mobility to certain marginal spaces and only tolerated in prime public spaces of the city as long as they follow the urban etiquette of remaining invisible. Marginalised by being requested to disappear from view, they have to transform their personal presence into a simulated absence (NXT: 9, 54).

The streets become an unintended public shelter in which the homeless have to produce a paradoxical kind of social invisibility to confirm their own isolation and exclusion. Due to the urban rules of distanciation, the epitomes of the Other are predominantly treated as "nonpersons" (Karp, Stone & Yoels 1991: 93). Ulysses virtually throws himself onto a couple to steal a bite of food off their plates; only then is he seen. The 'victim' is shortly taken aback: "I'm appalled by the fact that, without this er incident, I would never even notice such a person." (NXT: 96) Despite the masses of homeless people in the city, the country, the world, which present a 'classless society' in the sense that the homeless come from all social backgrounds, they are excluded from city life and lead an unregarded existence (NXT: 10, 12-14, 16, 39, 57, 121, 178). Perceived as a material part of the objectified cityscape, they have lost their urban human status as a subject. Another character, forty-five-year-old Italian Leonardo who grew up in London, notes that in mediatised perspective humanity is only ascribed to the employed denizens.

> Funny how when the telly wants to shaow teeyming humanity say in Taokyo or Calcutta or London they film claose craowds advancing in streeyts, gaoing to work. But thaose are the lucky ones. There's all the others, tramping, begging, sitting on park benches, sleeyping in doorways. (NXT: 29)

The homeless in *Next* are missing a lobby of their own publicity, their only points of reference are their memories, called by Quentin "nostalgic need for past identity" (NXT: 12), because in the homeless realm their old sense identity significantly disintegrates. What started off as a social marginalisation ends with the total loss of the Self: "Everyone displaced, in time, in space, in psyche." (NXT: 207)

In the novel the loss of identity is mainly presented in two manners, firstly by the dissolution of language and the motif of bearing a name. The word 'I', significantly showing the subject position, only emerges in conversations, while secondly 'my', indicating the matter of possession, owing or belonging does not appear at all throughout the whole text. The classless outsiders are named after literary or artistic pariah personae from literature: the bandit Jesse James, Büchner's Woyzek, Joyce's Ulysses, Shaw's Eliza, Hoffmann's Stella. Most of the homeless additionally have a nickname or carry a shortened version of their first name. Woijciech or Woijtek known as Tek by his fellow tramps explains: "Only half a name. I'm only half a person." (NXT: 187) For example, Croaky gains his civil identity as Quentin Stockwell when he visits the job centre (NXT: 26), Yuppey reconverts to Jesse James when he goes for an interview (NXT: 110), and Yoowley is identified as Ulysses Grant only in the hospital (NXT: 121).

The interrelation between language and identity is highlighted when Quentin, having achieved the first step out of his old existence as a homeless, meets the former fellow tramp Oliver and notices that his stammer has gone: "Olly, well, I'd rather call you

Oliver, may I? [. . .] Cos you seem so transformed. Morphed back into a truer self isn' tha' sao?" (NXT: 177) Already in the beginning of the novel, Elsie argues that there is no other way to speak "in a place like [that]" (NXT: 14) as she relapses into native speech despite knowing perfect Received Pronunciation. She goes on to explain how there exist different languages for different contexts, one for one's own identity and one for the pretensions of a working community: "Silley, there's two Englishes, dinn yer knaow, wah fer beyin yerself and wahn fer work." (NXT: 12) In an interview, Brooke-Rose points out that in her texts lingual redundancies mirror social redundancies (cf. Friedman & Fuchs 1995: 34).

Similarly, the 'professional attitude' of homelessness requires the characters to shed their personalities for the role of an intended etiquette of the street walker. Park comments (1967: 13):

> In the city every vocation, even that of a beggar, tends to assume a character of a profession and the discipline which success in any vocation imposes, together with the association that it enforces, emphasizes this tendency – the tendency, namely, not merely to specialize, but to rationalize one's occupation and to develop a specific and conscious technique for carrying it on.

Being shown in the danger of falling into homelessness the impoverished immigrant Adelina wishes for her husband: "If only he could find work he'd become himself again. There's no arguing with a man not himself." (NXT: 154) Recalling how much urban denizens identify themselves professionally through their line of work, the unemployment and social destitution of the urban underclass enforces their psychological exclusion.

Besides others, with the characters of Elsie and Adelina the novel forges a bridge between social, ethnic and gendered positions of alterity. The former second-generation black immigrant from Notting Hill teaches the dyslexic Portuguese-speaking first-generation Asian immigrant to read English (NXT: 42) in the confines of the destitute and overcrowded flat which is hardly better than a homeless shelter:

> The small primitive kitchen with the slow scent of curry and a loo the other side of it is beyond the great damp room that seems all beds, one large bed in the left corner and four single mattresses piled up as a sofa along the wall, one wonky armchair by the gas fire and a tressle-table in the areas window, covered with a garishly flowered plastic cloth, at which we sit with coffee [. . .]. (NXT: 40)

Temporarily, urban female homelessness can be counter-managed by social sisterhood. As the novel shows, the well-educated black woman Elsie, who amidst the 'classless' community of rough sleepers is permanently humiliated by racial and gendered prejudices, is socially excluded in her midst and later literally made speechless. Significantly, however, the novel transcends general binaries by presenting the community of the homeless as a mirror of an equally monadic/nomadic society.

In sum, this notion of postmodern existences as homeless has been variously explored in contemporary London novels. The perspectivation on the urban social spaces of London outcasts reveals that the city is not only a space of strangers but has become a realm of stratified pariah. Similarly, life in the shifting marginalised spaces of the metropolis denominates the sociability of its denizens to oscillate between various outsider and insider positions. This ambivalent existence on the threshold between familiarity and strangeness is epitomised in the image of the homeless urban pariahhood.

7.2.5 Mental Structures of Deviation

The outwardly homogeneous urban realm is internally characterised by heterogeneous plurality. Tendencies of postmodern fragmentation and post-Fordist segregation has transformed former notions of a mosaic of social worlds or characterised as Dual City to one of metropolarities concerning men and women of different class, oppressed (ethnic) minorities, gendered spaces, and generational conflicts. Multiple lines of stratification are interwoven within the texture of London's socioscape. While the classic urban scholars have been criticised for their one-sided conceptualisation of the metropolis that renders the non-male, non-white, non-middle class deviant (cf. Cuevas 2008a: 73), contemporary London literature seems to draw an image of crisis of this formerly hegemonic social structure. The analysis of various city novels has brought to the fore a middle-class crisis, a transformation of ethnic diversity into new forms of cosmopolitanism, a crisis of masculinity, and a reconfiguration of the urban underclass.

Ian McEwan's *Saturday* as well as J.G. Ballard's *Millennium People* brought into view the unease of London's middle class particularly in regard to its private comfort zones which are threatened by internal as well as external urban terrors. Both texts particularly stress the urbanites' mental relegation by the media to willingly enforce and enact certain doxic reactions. In this sense, the former base of the urban city, the bourgeoisie, has lost its urban-generic vigilance and urbane acumen. Similar tendencies are equally apparent in Blake Morrison's *South of the River*, Nick Hornby's *A Long Way Down*, and Matthew De Abaitua's *The Red Men*.

Maggie Gee's *The White Family*, Blake Morrison's *South of the River* and Patrick Neate's *City of Tiny Lights* have stressed multiple racial and ethnic frictions in the postcolonial and world city. However, with Bhabha's notion of the beyond, we were able to grasp the reconstructions of mental attitudes towards a new form of cosmopolitanism that is not relegated to a particular class or the generic Jewish diaspora, but now encompasses a heterogeneous array of urban hybrid wo/men. Moreover, hybrid urbanites do not necessarily have to feel (un)homely in any city, but are primarily able, by ways of their internal multiplicity, to navigate the various socio-cultural worlds of the metropolis. We can thus concur with Alheit (2005: 26) that London as a transnational space of migration has virtually established hybrid mentalities. The postmodern metropolis as a city of flux between transit/dwelling, interchange/crossroads, passenger/traveller, route/housing estate has become a transit point and a refuge for the contemporary urbanite as a "habitué of non-places" (Augé 1995: 107). Other novels that similarly cast these multiple axes of ethnic stratification are Monica Alis's *Brick Lane*, Gautam Malkani's *Londonstani*, but also Christine Brooke-Rose's *Next*.

As the postmodern city seems to have made gendered borders of public and private to slowly disintegrate, the new socio-spatial order appears to have initiated a crisis in the urban male population. In a sense, the anxieties of urban female vigilance are still the same, with the difference, however, that they become obvious in the verbal misogyny of younger urban male generation. This new boost of masculinity is strongly intertwined with urban materialism and pop culture and not only becomes apparent in the classic version of 1990s lad lit, such as Tim Lott's *White City Blue*, Toby Litt's *Corpsing*, or Keith Lowe's *Tunnel Vision* as well as the early bloke books by Nick Hornby. However, male anxiety and the recuperation of an 'rurban' cowboy mentality is also notably part of Ian McEwan's *Saturday*. The analysis of Gautam Malkani's *Londonstani* has shown how the metropolarities of contemporary London intertwine aspects of male gender with those of ethnic identity in a new urban subculture which serves both as a voluntary segregation from the parent generation and their traditional values as well as from the host/home country's national identity. Furthermore, it stresses how these deviancies are reintegrated into urban mainstream.

The interpretation of Matthew De Abaitua's *The Red Men* and Christine Brooke-Rose's *Next* has addressed urban stratifications in regard to the urban underclass. While both texts superficially concentrate on the traditional tropes of urban pariah in London's homeless or the area of London's East (End), they initially describe the metropolitan socioscape as one of a world of strangers and a "new underclass" (Head cit. in Groes 2011: 235).

Referring to Soja's notion of metropolarities, these various stratifications of class, ethnicity and gender intertwine in the urban texture, and contemporary London novels construct multiple boundaries, thresholds and thirdspaces. Many of these urban frictions have additionally been shown to be determined by a generational gap, hence emphasising the change within the decade of Blair's Britain. While urban dualities have not been abolished, the city of flux and relational fluidity has rendered the stratified metropolis more dynamic in regard to internal and external social changes. It emphasises, and this ties in with the up-coming analysis of the urban idioscape influenced by hypertrophic structures of mentality (see chapter 8.1), that in the urban-generic ambivalence of community and individualism, these new and ever changing patterns are created by an enhanced, if superficial, individuation. Mumford (1997: 456) notes:

> Each group, each community, each vocation, each habitat creates new patterns of individuality: by their interaction in the close medium of the city, they provide endless mutations and combinations in all its members. The common environment provides an underlying unity: the city itself may become the cohesive symbol of that unity: but within that common environment all the differentiations of a true culture arise with a wealth of example hitherto unexplored.

As this underlines, individual deviance and the marginalisation of minority groups, in the contemporary city urban deviation has become a constitutive norm.

Deviance generally describes the individual acts that do not conform with group norms. This phenomenon promotes homogeneity in the sense that it clarifies moral and cultural boundaries between Self and Other. The individual character or collective character constellation that does not adhere to established rules of conduct is subsequently alienated, marginalised, or spatially segregated. However, a transformation of mentality also encourages social change, the shift of normative boundaries and the construction of deviant subjects. Classic sociology, most notably the urban ecology of the Chicago School, within the great variety of the urban conditions, concentrates on the construction of "social disorganisation" (Karp, Stone & Yoels 1991: 54) of metropolitan Others: hybrid immigrants, criminal gangs, juvenile delinquents, homeless people, the insane.

For Park *et al.* moral deviance constitutes an essentially urban phenomenon which can be mapped according to particular moral zones. The problem behind this theorisation is that it accepts "that urban culture can be anything else but derisive, fragmentary, corrosive, as well as a-historical lacking tradition and specificity" (Parker 2004: 43). While Wirth particularly emphasises anomie as a consequence of urban deviance, the Chicago School, does not completely obliterate the notions of mental and behavioural freedom, individualism, or autonomy engrained in deviance. Thus, while urbanity seems to entail the unique production of deviance, I confer with Fischer that this is actually productive of social worlds. In this respect, we might read the emphasis of resurgent deviance as depicted in contemporary London novels as a new phase of truly metropolitan resurrection. While according to subcultural theories urban centrality mainly affects minorities, unconventional groups and the deviant urbanites the most, in the internally differentiated space of flows deviance, as a form of urban sociability, borders on anomie. Weinstein & Weinstein (1993: 111) explicate in reference to Simmel:

> In the metropolis nobody is an outsider, but, then, nobody is an insider either. Each is a stranger to the others, a participant in sociation yet detached from and objective about that sociation. The metropolis is society in the absence of a society [...].

Contemporary mental structures can be said to be deviant regardless of the assigned in- or out-group. Postmodern metropolarities now stress the constant transformability of established and emergent structures of stratifications. While hegemonies of middle-class, white, male, intellectuals are questioned in his cosmopolitan and urban nature, deviance constitutes a new norm. Due to *difference*, internal disruption, and spatial flux, the less likely it is for the urbanite to feel at home, the more he becomes settled in the metropolis.

8 Idioscape

After the analytical chapters that dealt with London's contemporary cityscape and were dedicated to the material spaces and those on the city's socioscape which regarded relational spaces of urban collectivity, this last section takes into account the spatialities of the individual urbanite. "Idioscape", in reference to etymological origins (Greek: *idio-*, own or personal), especially denotes the spaces of the Self. The idioscape is a space of particular relevance because collective nonconscious mental dispositions are functionally related to the individual. The hypothesis is that due to the incorporation of metropolitan doxa the individual gains a stable urban identity as a London citizen. From the perspective of urbanity, the urban-generic ambivalence of community and individualism pays tribute to the role of the single urbanite as influencing the city's idiosyncratic character, while London identity refers back to the further influence of urban-specific dispositions of thinking, imagining, feeling, and acting.

Already Simmel's conception of the metropolis and its mental life emphasises the urbanite's double boundary as human beings' paradoxical position on the juncture of the finite and infinite, individual and society. The urbanologist is concerned with the social construction of the urban Self and the inscription of collective experiences on the mental level of individuality. Insofar, this chapter focuses on mental structures formed by the constant internal accommodation of the individual to external metropolitan stimuli. As was shown, the urbanite accomplishes autonomy through everyday practices of self-distanciating role-play which in turn promotes the fear of losing authenticity. This anxiety is counteracted by the need of personal particularisation, such as urban eccentricism, capricity, and pretence which serve the re-centralisation of the Self within the urban masses.

The trope of the loss of the Self is intrinsically connected with urbanity, as the city serves as a focal site of denizens' struggle with self-definition, self-imagination, and self-assertion. The city energises the Self with emancipation and freedom, while simultaneously rendering the individual restless, rootless and fragmented, which enhances personal apathy. In the post-Fordist metropolis, the fragmented and simulated assembly of non-places, however, seems to defy any markers of a stable construction of identity, while the space of flows suggests notions of a shifting and diffused Self. Hence, for Jameson (1999: 5), postmodernist alienation leads to the construction of schizophrenic, multiple identities and Olalquiaga (1992: 2) shows how disorientation is furthered by the blurring between bodily and urban space facilitating psychasthenia. However, the urban individual reacts by adapting self-protective mechanisms to the novel postmodern overload scenario.

In the chapter "The City and the Citizen" (8.1) I first concentrate on the relation between the individual and the urban. Concerning contemporary London novels, the spaces of the Self especially in regard to constructions of identity have been variously explored. This analysis, instead, exposes the mental structures that pre-determine the ways of positioning the Self amidst the multiple choices the metropolis offers. The second sub-chapter "The Urban State of Mind" (8.2) takes an even deeper look into the urban denizens' psychology to reveal structures of feeling that are predominantly based on terror.

8.1 The City and the Citizen

> Unlike me, Elisabeth is a native New Yorker. Everything about the city is self-evident to her.
> (Zukin 1997: vii)

Since the Greek polis, city and citizenship are intrinsically linked; in other words, the history of citizens is a history of the city, as in turn, citizenship without the urban is indeterminable (cf. Schilling 2003: 11). Urban citizenship is strongly connected to a collection of civil rights which enable the inhabitants to participate in the socio-political life of the metropolis, while at the same time lending urbanites a sense of collective identity by serving as a mental and behavioural code for social actions (cf. Zijderveld 1998: 13). In the contemporary space of flows, Zijderveld (*ibid.*) largely sees cities as lacking a distinct civic culture and hence a specific identity. Not least because the nation state subsumes the city and the definition of citizenship shifts from the inhabitant of the city to that of the state (cf. Soja 2001: 24), national identity, especially in the U.K., is increasingly constructed in correspondence with the country rather than the city.

By contrast, metropolitan centres have always been post-national entities and therefore contemporary definitions of Englishness or Britishness are specifically challenged by postmodern London. Peter Ackroyd (2001: 716), in reminiscence of the *Windrush* generation, acknowledges how London's heterogeneity helped in redefining notions of national identity, whereas Pogossian (2010: 26-27) correctly points out that equating Britishness with the metropolis is less easily attained. The reason for this difference lies in the opposing spatial logics of nation state and metropolis: while the nation state describes the closed concept of an absolute container space which furthers the production of a homogenised identity, the conception of urban citizenship is based on heterogeneity and the notion of permeability. Ackroyd (2001: 767-758) further stresses the importance of London's identity as based on collective nonsconsious mental attitudes characterised in particular by imaginary dispositions:

> And yet what is it, now, to be a Londoner? The map of the city has been redrawn to include 'Outer Metropolitan Areas' as well as 'Greater' and 'Inner' London; the entire south-east of England has – willingly or unwillingly – become its zone of influence. **Is London, then, just a**

> **state of mind? The more nebulous its boundaries, and the more protean its identity, has it now become an attitude or a set of predilections?** On more than one occasion, in its history, it has been described as containing a world or worlds within itself. Now it has been classified as a 'global city' and in Hebbert's words as 'a universe with its own rules, which has genuinely burst out of its national boundaries.' So it does truly contain a 'universe', like some dense and darkly revolving cloud at its centre. But this is why so many millions of people describe themselves as 'Londoners', even if they are many miles from the inner city. **They call themselves Londoners because they are pervaded by a sense of belonging.** London has been continuously inhabited for over two thousand years; that is its strength, and its attraction. It affords the sensation of permanence, of solid ground. That is why the vagrant and the dispossessed lie in its streets; that is why the inhabitants of Harrow, or Croydon, call themselves 'Londoners'. Its history calls them, even though they do not know it. **They are entering a visionary city.** (Emphasis N.P.)

Within the idioscape, urban citizenship ties the imaginary cityscape together with London's socioscape. Identities are said to be "shaped by embodied and embedded narratives, located in particular places and times" (Carter, Donald & Squires 1993a: x). Therefore fictions of space in general and the city novel in particular are ideal media for voicing ideas about identity, because they combine a character's story with a particular urban setting.

This part of the analysis explores the relation between urban and urbanite as based on three parameters of comparison: first, in "Identityscape and Performativity" I directly address constructions of identity in the contemporary metropolis and specifically pay attention to various manifestations of citizenship in regard to national or urban identity caught between postmodern and postcolonial definitions. Places are traditional loci of self-fashioning, but today they also constitute contact zones for the construction of deterritorialised identities or cosmopolitan individuality. This brings into view contemporary reformulations of an urban-specific identity defined in the particular interaction of role-play and fragmentation of the Self. Second, "Bodyscape and Psychasthenia" elucidates processes of urban anthropomorphisation and urbanites' bodily metamorphosis as metaphorical depictions of self-fashioning and identity formation. This aspect not only follows the New Urban Geographers' notion that the urban image, as apparent in metaphors and symbols, is an intrinsic element in the construction of urban-specific identity, but also registers that the body plays a pivotal role in identity formation specifically in regard to ethnicity, race, gender and sexuality. Third, "Mindscape and Screening" assesses the contemporary metaphorisation of the urban mind as a manifestation of individual metropolitan pathologies. Besides central novels already scrutinised in former chapters such as *Brick Lane*, *Londonstani*, *Bleeding London*, *Saturday* and *The Red Men*, the following narrative analysis will also newly consider Toby Litt's urban thriller *Corpsing*.

8.1.1 Identityscape and Performativity

Space constitutes a major element for perpetuating normative boundaries between identity and alterity. For the delineation of a particular identity, spatial theorists crucially differentiate between space and place. According to Thacker (2003: 13), "*space* indicates a sense of movement, of history, of becoming, while *place* is often thought to imply a static sense of location, of being, or of dwelling". Space is traditionally conceptualised as infinite, unbounded, transparent, animated, abstract, and nondescript; place denotes a symbolised locale of particular intersecting events, myths, or stories which offer people the chance to build affective relations. Therefore, Carter, Donald & Squires (1993a: xii) emphasise, "[i]t is not spaces which ground identification, but places." Inhabiting a place over a long stretch of time leads "to its incorporation into the local people's identities" (Crang 1998: 107). As stable entities places offer a persistent location in which people can easily allocate themselves and develop a sense of belonging. According to Breuner (1991: 196), due to a constant yearning for stable identities people in the city exhibit a certain "hunger for place". Because individuals in regard to their existence demand a particular physical, social and mental emplacement, a place is a fundamental aspect both in terms of identity and mentality.[1] In their symbolic, normative, emotional, mnemonic role of identification, places come to characterise urban-specific mental dispositions.

Instead, post-positivist theorists see this traditional notion of place as promoting essentialist identities, nationalism, or competitive localisms. Massey (1998: 121) proposes a model of place as "open and porous networks" catering to the notion of identity as unfixed and multiple. She argues that the identity of a place is largely the product of a "*mutual* interaction" (*ibid.*: 131) with other locales and the internal contestations of various social relations (cf. *ibid.*: 138). From this perspective dynamic and processual places correspond to a contemporary understanding of identity as contingent, fluid and hybrid. Nowhere else does this fact become more apparent than in the postcolonial city where transnational migrants devise multilocal practices of identification (cf. Pott 2007: 31). The postmodern city hence offers newly dynamic places in which hybrid identities can be constructed (*ibid.*: 46-47). In the words of Homi Bhabha (1994: 1-2), these "'in-between' spaces provide the terrain for elaborating strategies of selfhood – singular or communal – that initiate new signs of identity". Especially displaced, exiled and diasporic communities rather suggest deterritolised identities for whom 'home' constitutes a symbolic place of identification embedded in various forms of representation.

Another line of argument ties in with the notion that the recent space-time compression and postmodern processes of globalisation, mediatisation, or virtualisation have resulted in an encompassing sense of placelessness (cf. Massey 1998: 162-163; Prakash 2008: 6). As the nodal point in the space of flows, the post-Fordist metropolis is seen as enhancing the epistemic crisis of Postmodernism, while the spiritless non-places of Exurbia further displacement, dislocation, alienation, fragmentation, a loss of the Self, or a crisis of identity. On the one hand, the palimpsestic materiality of the postmodern city is described as fostering schizophrenia, whereas on the other hand some urbanol-

---

1 | For more discussions on issues of space and place in regard to identity see for example Martin Heidegger (1951) *Building, Dwelling, Thinking*; Yi-Fu Tuan (1977), *Space and Place. The Perspective of Experience*; John A. Agnew, ed. (1989), *The Power of Place. Bringing Together Geographical and Sociological Imaginations*; Erica Carter, James Donald & Judith Squires, eds. (1993), *Space and Place. Theories of Identity and Location*; Edward S. Casey (1993), *Getting Back into Place. Toward a Renewed Understanding of the Place-World*; Michael Keith & Steve Pile, eds. (1993), *Place and the Politics of Identity*; James S. Duncan & David Ley, eds. (1997), *Place, Culture, Representation.*

ogists stress that the depthless surface city enforces urbanites' quest for identity.[2] The individual purposefully loses himself in order to explore and find fragments of the Self (cf. Chambers 1996: 190-191). Postmodern objective culture enhances individualisation and likewise the emplacement in the urban socioscape depends on individual methods of self-fashioning.

Role-play presents one of the most important aspects of an urban-generic way of life especially because it reveals the reciprocal relation between personal and group identity as well as between idioscape and socioscpae. The heterogeneous city offers the individual urbanite to freely select a personal vocation and develop idiosyncratic talents. However, the fragmentation of urban structures has created a protean urban character that is able to attain various roles at once (cf. Deny 2009: 40-41). Instead of a shift of identity, it implies a mutual coexistence of multiple if partial personalities in the synthesis of the Self (cf. Chambers 1996: 192; Deny 2009: 38). While the city serves as a space for self-fashioning, the polyphony of identities offers an array of structures of acting in accordance with each particular urban situation. Contemporary urban sociologists like Karp, Stone and Yoels (1991: 80-81) therefore emphasise that multiple roles significantly assist the construction of a repertoire of identities and foster interaction in the urban public. This seems to support Fischer's (1984: 202-205) argument that the problem is not so much that of multiple identities, but that of choice of roles open to the urbanite. However, as Raban (1974: 73) points out, the metropolis offers a very distinct set of urban roles which helps in attaining a certain homogeneity:

> Techniques of mass production, mass communication and rapid movement from one part of the city to another have made it very easy for us to drift into being dandies and gangsters. The price of maintaining an identity is cheap; appearances come ready-made and packaged, do-it-yourself kits. It sometimes seems as if one might flip over the edge into a deliriously fragmented confusion of postures and roles. In this maelstrom of possibilities, it is a pressing problem merely to find out who one is – to tease out at least the semblance of a nature form this heap of masks and rejected scraps of artifice.

Moreover, beyond the reflection of social role-play and masquerade as a deceptive counterfeit, a sort of pretence appearance that is not the postmodern situation of hyperreality, according to Baudrillard, now covers the absence of reality. The urban spectaclisation has ultimately altered both the quality of urban spatialities and the character of urbanites' performativity which relies on the indeterminacy of authenticity and role-enactment.

Questions of identity lie very much in the narrative tradition of urban fiction. Characters in urban fiction often suffer personal disassociation because they feel spatially, socially, and consequently mentally estranged in the alien urban world. Since the late Victorian era and fully evolving during Modernism, "city fiction has portrayed man searching for [a] complete self in an urban world." (Gelfant 1954: 23) Aspects emphasised are an embedding of identity in language, negotiations of conflicting character traits, the

2 | The city of flux however does not create a feeling of disorder for all urbanites, especially the literary tradition often equates the loss of place for women as a form of emancipation and the acquisition of identity (cf. Rose 1993: 56; Massey 1998: 171).

dialogic structure of identity, or historical and biographical contingency.[3] Moreover, and by far the most interesting facet in regard to urban mentality, is the relation between subject and place created by means of thought, emotion and perception as a significant component of identity construction which is tangent on notions of authenticity, role-play, social demarcations, and means of self-fashioning.

Martina Deny's *Lost in the Postmodern Metropolis* proposes four categories which allow to explore the reconstruction and relocation of the Self in the recently fragmented and contiguous situation of the metropolis: narrative construction, performative practices, experiences of alterity and cultural hybridity as well as idiosyncratic topological territorialisations. First, according to Deny (2009: 78), postmodern novels present "story-telling" as a theoretically viable method for framing the Self, as characters use the development of a coherent life-story with a subjective teleology as protection against disorientation. She argues that this strategy largely fails because autobiographical narratives are exposed as inauthentic. However, the present study has shown that writing and narration still offer possibilities for temporary stabilisations of identity (see chapter 6.4.4). Second, Deny (2009: 99-100) argues that narrative representation ties in with performativity; but role-play is dismissed as inauthentic by the texts under analysis due to the simulacrum-like "self-fashioning" (*ibid.*: 151) of commodified stereotypes. As postmodern London novels "highlight fluidity and infinite deferral as the only constant of postmodern identity" (Pleßke 2010: 408), the results of my own analysis have so far exposed role-play as an intrinsic part of urbanity which fosters the creation of both individuality and community. Deny (2009: 188) locates the most successful constructions of identity in postcolonial novels, where second-generation immigrant characters accept the necessity of a hybrid and dynamic subject positions, while the first generation's "rooting-project" is interpreted as essentialist and the relapse into monolithic cultural models revealed as "mental regression" (*ibid.*: 221; cf. Pleßke 2010: 408). Analogically, the minor male characters (of different generations) in Monica Ali's *Brick Lane* have been exposed as failing in the urban realm, yet in contrast to Deny, I suggest that their mode of thinking exhibits an anxiety of dislocation which contradicts postmodern constructive notions of identity and the relativity of urban space. This misconception of urban metropolarities, however, has also been established as the cause for other forms of identity crises, particularly in regard to the white middle-class male. Deny's (2009: 229) last analytical chapter explores the analogy of psychic disintegration and physical disorientation and elucidates on urban territorialisation by idiosyncratic mapping projects, anthropomorphisation and peripatetic movements (cf. Pleßke 2010: 408). As was shown in chapters 6.3 and 6.4, these methods, particularly by cognitive, sensual and corporeal perceptual modes of identity construction, significantly serve as (re)orientation within both the overload of the fluid city and the palimpsestuous metropolis.

While the following analysis builds upon these previous findings, the reassessment of hybrid identity constructions, metropolitan role-play and postmodern schizophrenia particularly concentrates on mental dispositions of thinking, feeling, imagining and acting in regard to the depiction of London's idioscape.

---

3 | For more on the question of place and identity in literature see for example: Glenda Norquay & Gerry Smyth, eds. (1997), *Space & Place. The Geographies of Literature*.

Hybrid Identities

The liminal position of London as the former heart of the British Empire and postcolonial city, global city and the nation's capital brings into view a wide range of transcultural identities, while the quest for defining one's identity is an especially important theme in postcolonial discourses. In this chapter I will focus on the construction of hybrid identities in three postcolonial novels, namely Monica Ali's *Brick Lane* (2003), Gautam Malkani's *Londonstani* (2006) and Patrick Neate's *City of Tiny Lights* (2005), which elucidate how much "[e]thnicity both persists and *changes* under the influence of urbanism." (Fischer 1984: 152)

Reading Monica Ali's *Brick Lane* alongside Massey's conception of dynamic place brings to the fore two relevant issues of contemporary urban identity construction: firstly, the narrative outlines ethnicity and gender as the most stable axes of experiencing place and their relocation due to postmodern space-time compressions (cf. *ibid.*: 164). Secondly, the spatial dynamics unleashed by globalisation emphasise the uniqueness of place – hence a need to develop "a global sense of the local, a global sense of place" (*ibid.*: 156) in current constructions of identity (cf. Beck 2011: 365-369).

For Cynthia Wall (1998: 144), a traditional sense of identity is directly related to absolute space, whereas everyday-life on the streets is "unconstructed, fluid, [...] transitional, transformational" indicating a transformation of subsequent identity. In Ali's *Brick Lane* the protagonist Nazneen leaves the flat and the community's estate and grows emancipated by following the city's streets right into the metropolitan centre. Although Nazneen reconceptualises her personal identity by mentally impersonating an ice-skating princess gliding freely through a public arena, at first she "cannot change her immediate context" (Kral 2005: 114). Instead, her seclusion in Brick Lane and the revival of her female Muslim identity through contact with the imagined community of her home country stabilise Nazneen's identity as a "girl from the village" (BRL: 385), yet metropolitan London becomes the place that defines her Self. Nazneen's former memories of rural homeland-identity change to one of vigilant self-fashioning in the metropolitan realm by transgressing from a fatalist notion of identity (BRL: 13-16) to one of self-construction according to her personal choice: "*I will decide what to do. I will say what happens to me. I will be the one.*" (BRL: 405) Hence, the traditional sense of place as wrought by memory, stasis and nostalgia is reinterpreted when the essentialist conception of place as stable Being is exchanged for an agency of constant Becoming. Ali presents this transformation when Nazneen's dream of ice-skating comes true and the protagonist performs in the arena dressed in a sari. For Kral (2007: 68) the ice-rink suggests, however, that the core of the Self essentially remains stable while only the surface bears witness to scratches from the traumatic experiences the migrant undergoes. I argue that Nazneen's stability rather refers to a personality that refutes the cliché of the hybrid woman as necessarily imprisoned in a permanent state of psychological distress through feelings of unbelonging or a mental state of schizophrenia caused by perpetual inbetweenness. Although Nazneen undergoes various crises of depression, these biographical episodes rather derive from personal fixtures on traumatic gendered experiences (as daughter, wife, mother) than being directly initiated by processes of urban displacement.

In contrast to Nazneen, who in the long run draws strength from contracting compressions of space and time, Chanu and Karim – and here I agree with Kral (2007: 75) – see their own identity as perpetual alterity and the urban heterogeneity and spaces of multiple boundaries as culturally oppressive.[4] First, educated Chanu cannot get used to the metropolitan context and becomes torn between his dreams of achievement in England and the return to Bangladesh as an accomplished man, which eventually "comforts him in a sterile in-betweenness since he fails to become locally committed." (*Ibid.*: 74) The protagonist argues in regard to everyday habits: "Back home, if you drink you risk being an outcast. In London, if you don't drink you risk the same thing." (BRL: 110) Eager to adjust, Chanu reads loads of Western literature (BRL: 76-77); fanatic to retain his cultural identity, however, he makes his London-born daughters recite Bengali poetry (BRL: 179). Although Chanu later works as a taxi driver and is expected to have 'The Knowledge', he becomes increasingly estranged from London and slowly diminishes to a lesser part of his Self (BRL: 459). He consequently fails to establish a valid identity appropriate to the contemporary metropolitan collectivity and is left with the single choice of remigration. Second, while for Nazneen the affair with Karim constitutes a catalyst for discovering her individual diasporic and gendered identity by negating the traditional role of Bengali wife and mother (cf. Deny 2009: 225), the young man's self-fashioning is strongly based on stereotypically Othering Nazneen as a symbol of home (BRL: 385). Both characters mutually project their notions of identity onto the other in a complex gendered role-play of identity construction (BRL: 454-455).

Whereas Nazneen achieves to re-root her home culture in the new context of London, she transcends the barriers of metropolitan everyday negotiations, comes to feel at home in her new environment and gains a new stable identity. In this respect, Nazneen literally fashions her identity by weaving together two styles in her new sari collection. In the context of the contemporary metropolis the fluidity of identities is stressed and the provisional nature of knowledge underlined. Consequently, in search for grounding the migrant is positioned as adapting certain traits of the Self while simultaneously altering the city's character. Metropolitan mental structures are hence presented as strongly based on an urban-generic fundament while the specific aspects are depicted as uncertain and temporary in regard to oscillating cultural norms in everyday practices.

Gautam Malkani's debut novel *Londonstani* (2006) is a novel not unlike Sam Selvon's or Colin McInnes' early postcolonial London fiction. Although it belongs to the hype of multicultural novels initiated by *White Teeth* and *Brick Lane*, the book failed in terms of sales figures. Similarly to Ali's novel, *Londonstani* was questioned for its sense of authenticity (cf. Martin 2006) and reproached for its Orientalist mentality (cf. Saadi 2006). Otherwise the text, published in the aftermath of 7/7, appeared at a time when questions of Britishness and policies of official multiculturalism were heatedly debated in the public. Particularly Tariq Modood's critical take on secular *Multiculturalism* (2007) and Melanie Phillips' attack on multiculturalism in *Londonistan* (2006) further ignited discussions on the danger and opportunities, failures and successes of Britain's recently celebrated diversity. While the early Blair era marketed a change from Thatcher's politics of mono-culturalism, the new-found multiculturalist verve around the millennium

4 | This is similar to the conception of identity in Zadie Smith's *White Teeth* in which the twins Magid and Millat present two extremes of fundamentalism relying on assimilation and essentialist notions of identity (cf. Deny 2009: 214). Here is the female character Irie who reconciles the two sides in her female Self. This idea is also apparent in Maggie Gee's *The White Family* with the character of Shirley who carries twins from two different men.

officially drifted into an adopted assimilationist approach with Blair's speech on "Shared British Values: The Duty to Integrate" (2006) (cf. Graham 2008b).

By contrast, Gautam Malkani's *Londonstani* presents an ultimately positive vision of London's contemporary multiculturalism (*ibid.*). On his personal homepage, the author stresses how his twenty-first century notion of a "Londonstani" denotes a British-Asian but particularly urban form of belonging (cf. *Gautam Malkani*). This positive approach to lived multiculturalism is overtly apparent in the staged street fight between the 'Indian Sikh' Hardjit and the 'Pakistani Muslim' Tariq. The narrator draws a tableau of the "different classes a spectators" (LON: 100) gathered around the public arena of the BMX track: not just Hardjit's Sikh and Tariq's Muslim crew, but also Hardjit's black childhood friend and his sidekicks, Wai Qwok-Ho and other "Oriental kids" (LON: 96) from his martial arts class, random employees from an office nearby, and an unknown group of Somali youths. The protagonist Jas comments on this "firework display" (LON: 96) resembling metropolitan plurality: "That's London for you. All different kinds a people bringing all their different kinds a weather." (LON: 96) This new generation of young and diverse Londoners is opposed to both the stereotypically presented Asianness of the rudeboys' families and the Britishness of the teacher Mr Ashwood or of Jas' parents. Saadi (2006) criticises Malkani for his cartoonish depiction of Asians as vain, devious, hysterical, violent, primitive and destructive in contrast to the balanced, human, and sensitive if naïve image conveyed on Whiteness. Instead, I follow James Graham's (2008b) and Michael Mitchell's (2008) understanding of the text insofar as the rudeboy gang is shown to reject parental tradition as much as they disrespect the acmes of British national identity, and rather develop an new version of hybrid, subcultural, suburban London identity.

The book is arranged around three sections: "Paki", "Sher", and "Desi". These ethnic denominations broadly follow the development of British South Asian identity over fifteen years from the experiences of victimhood to voluntarily aggressive segregation and a transformation of an ethnic identity into an urban subculture which actively participates in the reformulation of Britishness (cf. Graham 2008b; Anon. 2011b). Put differently, from prejudice to reverse difference, the contemporary young generation has reached a stage of transdifference. Similarly to the thirdspace of the disused BMX track, their desi (meaning 'countryman') identity suggests a unity between different ethnic, religious, and national groups of the South Asian subcontinent. But what is more, desi identity – as overtly apparent in Jas' appropriation – has freed itself from geographical references and local emplacement (cf. Graham 2008b; M. Mitchell 2008: 331). The ironic denouement of Jas's Jewish descent deconstructs traditional assumptions of Asianness versus Britishness.

As already explored in regard to the rudeboys' construction of masculinity the novel presents the process of identity formation as an assemblage of various roles that go through a phase of radical recombination and transformation. The young Londoners – and that does not only include the second-generation immigrants – "pick and mix elements of identity like fashion accessories to fashion their own subjective and performative identities." (M. Mitchell 2008: 330) Their "kaleidoscopic" (*ibid.*: 329) multiple identities are prone to a postmodern spectaclisation of the Self as brought forward by contemporary urbanologists. This necessarily, as Deny already suggests with the example of role-play presented in Hanif Kureishi's *Buddha of Suburbia*, raises questions of authenticity.

In *Londonstani*, it is less so the fluidity of their Self that seems suspect, but the superficial attires of imitated mediatised images, which render desi identity depthless in the sense of shallow. The "characters have reduced themselves to two-dimensional 'cinema screens' onto which their incomplete, cut-and-paste identities are projected by Bollywood, Hollywood, MTV Base and ads for designer fashion brands." (*Gautam Malkani*) In a postmodern play with stereotypes, authenticity appears indeterminable and consequently even meaningless for the conceptualisation of identity. Performed and fictionalised identities are hence experienced as original. But instead of seeing personal simulation as a device of a newly totalitarian homogenisation of the Self, Malkani's novel in allusion to film, interprets the postmodern cutting, pasting and performance of identity as an alternative to former "metanarratives of racism, nationalism and exclusion." (M. Mitchell 2008: 339) With regard to Goffman's notion of front- and back-role performance, in an urban context this hyperbolic role-play additionally constitutes a revived form of distanciation, which in the twenty-first century means an assemblage of ethnic identities in order to come by the plurality of the globalised postcolonial city.

An intrinsic part of this performative identity besides consumerist symbolism, as shown before, is the creation of an idiosyncratic language. While the suburban desi argot is reminiscent of *Ali G*, *Goodness Gracious Me*, or the *Kumars*, its linguistic creolisation of London is redolent of Sam Selvon's patois in *The Lonely Londoners*. As a dialogue-based novel, the language of *Londonstani*'s rudeboys alongside 'proper English' encompasses a composite of Hindu, Punjabi and Urdu vocabulary, African-American vernacular English, urban street slang, patois, obscenities, text-message shorthand, brand names, hip hop lyrics, or neologisms which disrupt any previous conventional forms of thinking (cf. *ibid.*: 332; Brouillette 2010: 3; Schotland 2010). The novel mirrors the young men's disrespect for Englishness in the generation's use of text messages and the accompanying disregard for grammar or spelling (cf. *Gautam Malkani*).

Schotland (2010) argues that, what is more, the author also renders text messaging into text-speak used in the boys' dialogues. Particularly, Hardjit's rudeboy attitude is underlined by the persistent use of text-message shorthand. Hence, his physio-verbal attack on the white boy and Hardjit's simultaneous clarification of desi identity politics reads as follows:

> It ain't necessary for u 2 b a Pakistani to call a Pakistani a Paki, [...] or for u 2 call any Paki a Paki for dat matter. But u gots 2 be call'd a Paki yourself. U gots 2 b, like, an honary Paki or someshit. An dat's da rule. Can't be callin someone a Paki less u also call'd a Paki, innit. (LON: 6)

Adolescent slang in general is employed to establish group identity, particularly in youth or subcultures; it builds idiosyncratic knowledge systems and constructs opposition to authority (cf. Schotland 2010). For instance, when the young men are approached by the former teacher Mr Ashford they are careful to maintain their distance by using "mafioso code words" (LON: 121). Schotland (2010) works out that despite the potential of slang in contemporary hybrid culture the novel also decries the failure of language. This is particularly true for the Babylonian – but seemingly intended – misunderstanding between

Establishment and the self-marginalised subcultures. The teacher Mr Ashford critically analyses the rudeboys' use of language:

In actual fact I've often thought it admirable the ways you boys mix up Hindi with Urdu and Punjabi to create your own second-generation tongues. It's the English code words I can't stand. It's ironic, isn't it? The way your use of English makes you look like you're some kind of Asian mafia rather than your use of your mother tongues. (LON: 120-121)

This is countered by Hardjit: "Fuck's sake, we only stole yo fone, we didn't call u honky da way u goras used 2 call us Pakis. An u b callin us an Asian mafia? Fuckin call da feds if u like, we'll ger'chyu done 4 racism." (LON: 121) Above all, however, language presents a significant indicator of the intergenerational cleavages. While Jas repeatedly expresses his contempt for his posh-sounding parents, from his perspective the Asian parents' use of their mother-tongue is interspersed with stereotypically rendered pidgin English (LON: 67). As Schotland (2010) correctly points out, there is nothing new about the observation that second generation immigrants have a greater command of English than their parents, but the difference in verbosity only adds to the communication gap between the new London teens and the migrant parent generation (LON: 256).

But again, their ethnic identity defined against the gendered and generational Other is first and foremost a subcultural identity which mixes and borrows from a random array of formerly guarded elements of the different cultures. Within the heterogeneous mix of London, "the subcultural capital of the world" (Malkani cit. in Graham 2008a), rudeboy identity constitutes only one of many counter formations. Even in the fluid city this desi version is very much localised to a suburban middle-class surrounding of West London. Nevertheless, the subcultural suburban way of life marks the desi's construction of identity as intrinsic to London. Malkani significantly argues:

I think London is important insofar as it provides the characters with a metropolitan identity. I was really interested in the way that **metropolitan identities can transcend other identities** in the same way that your national identity can supplant your ethnic identity, or your racial identity or your religious identity. [...] But I was interested in the way that in a kind of utopian world, **a metropolitan identity can supplant all of those identities**. For example, **you don't have nationalism with a metropolitan identity** [...]. [...] [T]here's a chance there for real racial integration. I mean, that's what London does, right, people see themselves as Londoners and therefore everyone's allowed to be in London and therefore there's no dominant race in London: **everyone's a Londoner**. (Cit. in *ibid.*; emphasis N.P.)

This particularly mirrors the attitude of the cosmopolitan protagonist Tommy Akhtar in Patrick Neate's *City of Tiny Lights* (2005). While the last chapter has elucidated on his social role within the metropolitan realm, the following pages specifically account for Tommy's self-fashioning as a Londoner. Both Teske (1999: 223-252) and Deny (2009: 261-272) have shown with the example of Peter Ackroyd's London novel *Hawksmoor* (1985) that the detective's inability to decipher the metropolitan labyrinth ties in with his psychological disintegration and personal disorientation. In general, however, urban detective fiction inflects the uneven landscape of the city, while the character of the detective imposes a new order on the chaos of urban everyday life (cf. Levy 1978: 72; Highmore 2005: 115).

Tommy in *City of Tiny Lights* successfully navigates the Babylonian metropolis to stabilise his notion of the Self. Hence, urban orientation, detective investigation, and quest of identity notably go hand in hand. Rosenberg (2008: 364) explicates:

> As a detective Tommy is not just searching for the truth but also for authenticity in the midst of postcolonial and postmodern confusion. The novel shows that identity emerges as a cluster of unstable categories: mutually independent criteria that cut across each other in many ways.

Quite content in his multiple identities as Ugandan-Indian, Paki, Marlowe-Wannabe, cosmopolitan, Londoner, and Englishman, Tommy performs his various Selves in London's multiplicity and employs role-play to handle the metropolis. On his private-eye investigation he dresses up in different disguises and swaps or abandons the costumes of identities at free will. Looking for police information he carefully chooses his clothes to make him look "something like a school teacher on the pull" (CTL: 32). The subsequent performance in a murky London bar is completely staged according to Tommy's self-awareness as (urban) Other and by his knowledge of habitual prejudice, which he employs as means of his detective work. The 'ethnic' character even pretends to have fought in the front line at the Brixton riots (CTL: 34-35). Instead, shortly after, in a Chiswick bar he caters for another stereotype when he impersonates a human rights lawyer who works with asylum seekers and fights deportations (CTL: 48). To his police contact he ironically remarks: "You know my kind. We love to fit in." The urban stranger's "knowledge [...] that is at once schizoid and subversive" (Bhabha 1994: 168) actually assists him in his undercover detective work. Correspondingly, one of Tommy's best acts is that of the "archetypical Paki" (CTL: 273). To sneak his way into the crime scene of a hotel he mimes the naïve stereotype of the nondescript devotional Pakistani (CTL: 53). Highmore (2005: 95) comments in regard to the successful urban private eye:

> The detective is required to access both space and information and to do so invisibly. It is hardly surprising then that one of the most highly valued attributes for detectives was their ability to mix with a wide variety of social types, to not seem out of place within the city's varied social and cultural geography. Mobility and access is premised on being able to blend in with rouges and ruffians, lowlife and high society, moving across social space without drawing attention to yourself. Such chameleon-like ability was not, however, available to all. In a culture where the racial and gendered geography of the city marked out space of prohibition and confinement, the ability to roam was itself a mark distinction.

As the narrator-protagonist of Neate's *City of Tiny Lights* argues, the change of these roles is a matter of choice and wilful construction and not much different from everyday urban life: "I avoid the rush-hour the same way I avoid pork; a question of taste masquerading as principle." (CTL: 32) The exaggeration of his outsideness allows him more autonomy by being less bound to routinised piety.

Hence, joining the mujahedeen in his youth is depicted as consequence of his mother's death and Tommy acknowledges that his discovery of religion was above all an act of reinstating a feeling of belonging (CTL: 41). At the same time, his brother's quest for belonging drives him into the criminal underworlds of London from Harlesden, Wood Green, Hackney, Leytonstone. Gundappa, according to the narrator, goes through a typical "first-generation identity crisis" (CTL: 102) apparent by "that typical immigrant fear of making a fool of himself" (CTL: 103). He fancies himself as a Mediterranean and grooms that identity by pushing an East London accent, wearing open-necked shirts, and having blond girlfriends. Thus, once again, metropolitan identity is defined by stereotypical performativity that stresses the arbitrariness of an essentialist Self and critically questions authenticity (cf. Topalova 2008: 407). All in all, contemporary postcolonial novels deconstruct the notion of stable identities and stress the composite of metropolitan identities that allows for both self-evident orientation and integration in the urban realm.

Metropolitan Role-Play

The significance of urban role-play has particularly been remarked upon in regard to Ian McEwan's *Saturday* and Perowne's inability to differentiate between professional and urban front-stage acting. Also, enactment has been shown as an intrinsic part of tube etiquette as depicted in Keith Lowe's *Tunnel Vision* or Geoff Ryman's *253*. Collective spectaclisation has moreover been analysed as an important aspect of sociability presented in J.G. Ballard's *Millennium People*. This sub-chapter now concentrates on role-play in regard to self-fashioning and constructions of personal identity by looking at Tim Lott's *White City Blue* (1999), Blake Morrison's *South of the River* (2007), and Toby Litt's *Corpsing* (2000).

In Tim Lott's *White City Blue* (1999), role-play is presented as both an intrinsic element of urban sociability, but also as a definite territorialising element of male domination or modern urban duelling. Distinguished from the other group members, Nodge's front role is based on intellectualisation and overt distanciation that does not allow his friends to look behind his façade. By contrast, Colin, according to the narrator's point of view, "has never quite managed to master the public indifference that the rest of us present as our emotional lives." (WCB: 24) He wears his weaknesses, sorrows and disappointments openly and is unable to establish a guard against his friends' despise and harassment. The greatest imposter is Tony, who is constantly fashioning and performing a specific self-image (WCB: 125). His front role is based on complete performativity and wrought by disinterest in anything beyond matters that underline his public image. But as Frankie discovers, notably hiding in Tony's backroom office and thereby catching his so-called friend off-guard, is that his friend's façade covers a huge emotional void. Frankie himself has established his front role in regard to his friends as "*Frank the Fib*" (WCB: 43); for him the name is the first instance of establishing some kind of personality. He notices that 'persona' from its etymological origin is merely the word for 'mask' and recognises that having mastered a personal identity he has gained a heterostereotype which he cannot rid himself of (WCB: 147). Everyday performance as pure play-acting once mixed with authentic postures becomes a habitual identity (WCB: 2). Repeated as a possible stance of the everyday, its space of behaviour is transformed into a mere habit and routinised form of acting. The novel thereby exposes the fine line between urbanites' role-play as idiosyncratic masquerade and the repetitive staging of multi-layered personalities.

But the urban also offers specific markers that enable the urbanite to acquire and quickly discard ready-made and locally favoured aspects of identity. *White City Blue* in correspondence to London's 1990s property and gentrification boom represents the construction of identity as largely based on acquiring a place of living. For the estate agent Frankie, social advancement is forged by the rising property market and mirrored by his advancement from a flat in W6 to W11 and W8 (WCB: 4). He enjoys crawling around the inside of urbanites' lives and the inhabited flats present a "window into other people's worlds, the limitless menu of apparent possibilities" (WCB: 3). The illimitable versions of metropolitan places hence emphasise the myriad choices offered by the city for a perpetual refashioning of the Self. However, as the protagonist shows, these alterations are merely limited depending on income and favoured lifestyle. Whether a holiday in Koh Samui, a Beemer, or his flat – all these social markers of the main character and this "feel of money" (WCB: 4) define Frankie's personal state and belonging. The constant (re)construction of identity in the urban is thereby directly connected to the acquisition of cultural capital in a two-way process of role enactment.

The analysis of Blake Morrison's *South of the River* (2007) has already explored the splitting and alignment of public and private roles with respect to the female character Libby: "At work she was Ms Dynamite, Thin Libby, prospective Bussinesswoman of the Year. At home she played Beth, the credulous housewife." (SOR: 254) Urban vigilance implies the constant reassessment of roles not only in regard to the specific social situation and socio-spatial frame, but also in regard to fashioning identity to the demands made by the metropolitan space of flux. A writer of urban drama, the protagonist Nat perceives Londoners as characters in a play, although his friend Harry points out to him that in real life people do not follow one preordained path of character development (SOR: 385). It is the second female character Anthea who specifically stresses life-long self-fashioning. To Harry, the young woman appears like a "chameleon" (SOR: 387), altering her appearance, attire, and character in line with her ecological surroundings.

For Anthea, a change of environment initiates a transformation of character, and likewise she is aware of her two simultaneous identities of inner and outer Self: "No one knew the real Anthea, not even Anthea. The outer self was dull and dutiful, with only those nose rings to hint at something braver. The inner self was noisy and passionate, but the noise came out as a stammer and the passions varied from day to day." (SOR: 47) Her personalities are dormant within, offering multiple possibilities of outer roles to perform. Therefore, Anthea perceives her Self as a mixture of fictional and real variants (SOR: 77). Due to her relationship with Nat she changes the habitual nose ring for a stud and finally, as the symbol of her regained self-consciousness, removes it (SOR: 110, 235). Paradoxically, the new Anthea feels even less real to her than the old mousy Self, although she enjoys the attention her novel role grants her (SOR: 110). Nat basically only serves as a tool that enables her to transform from an ugly duckling to a swan (SPR: 120). When she inherits a small fortune from her grandmother, Anthea obtains the means to once again discard the old Self for a new version. The alternation of metropolitan identity can be read as a cleansing experience of perpetual reinvention and a form of idio-catharsis.

Corpsing (2000) is the second of Toby Litt's novels that specifically deals with the lives of isolated individuals caught up in the complexities of the materialism of contemporary British society.[5] Discussions of Englishness are central to Litt's work and his

---

5 | In the following *Corpsing* will be abbreviated to COR.

characters are "frequently beset by paranoia, neurosis, or [...] self-delusion" (Squires 2003: 165). Litt's murder mystery is mainly set in Soho's media and acting world. Due to this setting, the novel is structured by an array of very brief chapters which rushes the story in a cinematic fashion. The first-person narrator Conrad Redman works as a producer of trailers for satellite television and similarly his narrative appears like the edit of his best shots with jump cuts, flashbacks, slow motion moments. In the fashion of lad literature's preference for popular culture and the text's socio-cultural setting, the novel is also highly intermedial, featuring references to a wide array of music and film, telephone messages, a hospital admission report, weapon descriptions, newspaper cuttings and headlines, casting ads and the partial script for a thriller. Consequently, the novel narratologically incorporates urban thinking enforced by "the lifestyle fascism that plagues London" (Piette cit. in *ibid.*: 82). The plot revolves around Conrad whose pregnant ex-girlfriend is shot by a contract killer in a fashionable Soho restaurant. While Lily Irish is basically butchered by three bullets, another three harm Conrad. After a couple of weeks in a coma and a few months in recovery, Conrad sets out on a private investigation to find Lily's murderer.

The epigraph of the novel already outlines the two topics relevant for the construction of the idioscape in the novel: acting and corporeality. The title of the novel suggests the double-meaning of (1) killing someone and (2) actor's slang for spoiling a piece of acting (COR: Epigraph; cf. Squires 2003: 167). All characters of *Corpsing* are involved in some sort of role-play and double-act. Twenty-six-year-old Lily is a good-looking actress who is already fairly popular as "Brandy" (COR: 20) from a series of cereal TV ads where she appears dressed in various kinky outfits: "flirty French maid, saucy schoolgirl, nympho ski-inductress, whip-cracking dominatrix" (COR: 5). Originally having started as impersonating Snow White in EuroDisney she has reached the echelon of British acting by performing in a TV murder mystery and gaining a lead role in a new play at the Royal Court about women and necrophilia (COR: 5-6).

The idea of the latter drama is taken up, as her last public act features the spectaclisation of her own suicide in the urban masquerade of murder. In a sense, her morbid acting has overhauled any authentic being, also because it is revealed that Lily is notoriously self-harming. Conrad values her as a "natural actress" (COR: 6) who "has It." (COR: 6): "Being a true actress, Lily was intense but shallow in all her relations." (COR: 98) Lily's life has become a full-time act to sell herself as a commodity in public and private, but her beauty and grace are a mere façade for a frustrated and depressed Self. Instead, Conrad, despite his ambition to write and direct, win an Oscar, and become "famous and rich and loved" (COR: 7), in the fashion of an urban lad's crisis admits that he does not have "It" (COR: 7). The moment when the hitman shoots Lily, Conrad reacts with a fit of inexplicable laughter. Although he feels that an array of movies should have prepared him for the right posture at a murder scene, he also acknowledges that there is a boundary between performing as an actor and the personal levels of behaviour where "we're all meant to perform our own lives." (COR: 16) Paradoxically, the staged murder draws the protagonist's life as spectator into a whole urban drama run by improvising London actors. Lily's actor-lover/lover-actor Alun Grey feigns ignorance of Lily's pregnancy (COR: 327), whereas his bland actor-wife Dorothy Pale is exposed as 'Lady Macbeth' who originally arranged the double murder of Lily and her husband. Consequently, in a contemporary adaptation of a Shakespearean play within a play, a complex scenario of role-play wraps the social relations of London characters and their life-style promoting identity constructions in which the real cannot be distinguished from the simulated.

Trying to force the truth about Lily's death from the Grey/Pale couple, Conrad resorts to a cough acting trying to disturb all performances of their modern *Macbeth* production (COR: 133-135, 148). He specifically places his coughs in crucial moments of silence, which not only chaos-like hacks the drama, but ultimately influences the rhythm of the show and creates 'real' mental fear in the actors/protagonists (COR: 161-164). Even his absence exerts terror on the two by arbitrary stand-in coughers. All in all, Conrad's terror mirrors the bloody game of *Macbeth* at the same time as the novel is intertextually structured around its mystery (COR: 178). Everyday life is depicted as perpetual performativity. Under the influence of multiple layers of play-acting, identity is transformed into an array of personal roles that more or less create a sort of transient idioscape. And even the protagonist Conrad, who feels himself less of an actor, during his private-eye investigation accomplishes a variety of roles in behaving like a handicapped man bound to the wheelchair long after he is able to walk, staging pretended phone-ins, playing a tabloid journalist, and faking a casting for a staged abduction. All this culminates in his inversed re-enactment of the murder scene. This time, however, Conrad wears the disguise of the motorcycle hitman. In that sense, Londoners go beyond a mere role-play but consciously practice role-reversal.

Following the novel's idea, the perpetual multiple choice of ready-made roles offers the security of automatic and stable interpretations of meaning to their identity in a space of flows without guaranteeing the authenticity of meaning. Also standardised role-play protects urbanites' identity in an environment in which the differences between reality and simulation have become depleted. Like the depiction of Anthea in *South of the River*, Lily in *Corpsing* also stresses the phenomenon that inner and outer Self, personality and appearance do not necessarily match. Litt explicates that contemporary urbanites "are more self-conscious in the sense of the self as something that is projected and perceived by other people" (cit. in Tolan 2008: 76). Because urbanites' identities in a televised reality of metropolitan role-play are highly constrained by patterns of mediatised phenotypical and habitual front roles, their presumably authentic role is further pushed into crises of uncertainty and unintelligibility.

Postmodern Schizophrenia

As the two aspects of hybridity and role-play show, the urbanite is on the verge of a split and transient identity. Wirth (1938: 152) denotes that the manifold social interrelations lead to segmentation and cause the "'schizoid' character of urban personality." In this respect, the assumption of postmodern urbanologists that metropolitan citizens are prone to schizophrenia gains some momentum. Particularly, according to Augé (1995: 103) individuals are largely relieved of their usual determinants in the non-places of the metropolis which are characterised by their transitoriness and indeterminancy. Consequently, the individual is split between the "passive joys of identity-loss, and the more active pleasure of role-playing." (*Ibid.*) Thus, urbanites' Selves are strongly contorted and fractured.

The quest of finding his identity is central to Adam's urban life in Conrad Williams' *London Revenant* (2004). He appears to be a lost soul in the metropolis and being confronted with a bad crisis of identity feels displaced (LOR: 31, 86). Whereas London should have guided Adam on the way of finding himself, the cityscape grows obscure and the urban social dynamics increase his distortion: "London was meant to be my map, something that would reflect me, give me more of a clue as to who I was and what I could do with myself. But all of its streets were being dug up, or barricaded, or designated No Entry." (LOR: 101) Due to his lack of belonging and the confusion by narcoleptic attacks he more and more loses his grip on both reality and his Self. Adam summarises his mental state in the following: "I've got narcolepsy and I don't know what the fuck is happening to me at the moment. I've got black spots. Dead gaps in my memory. Great chunks of time go by when I don't know where I am, what I'm doing, or who I'm with." (LOR: 165) In fact, Adam is caught between two competing urban spaces, namely "the Topside" and "the Underground", experiencing the duplicity of his identity as though he were "two people in one zip-up skin." (LOR: 257) In his schizophrenia Adam becomes divorced from his bodily existence and mentally enters the dark spaces of the Underground.[6] Adam recognises the possibility of another identity struggling within himself in the following way:

> Hadn't I always suspected, or feared, that I might be someone else? [...] [S]ometimes we talk to ourselves as we would to another person. We might be single creatures, but our minds don't think that way. The physical, the tangible parts of us contained a symmetry; why not the mental, the untouchable parts of us too? (LOR: 284)

A possibility of resurrection or reconstruction of the Self is offered to the protagonist only when he decides to make his home in the place of the subterranean city.

Because the Self is more and more pre-programmed by simulacra and subsequently rendered subjectless, for Baudrillard, the age of the simulation heralds the end of alienation (cf. Jarvis 1998: 34-35). This aspect is strongly brought to the fore in Matthew de Abaitua's *The Red Men* (2007). A new technological system allows the Monad corporation to upload copies of urbanites' minds on Cantor, an artificial intelligence, where the copies are transformed into imagined characters conceptualised as a new urban species (REM: 45-46, 51-52). These red men – in a metafictional brainstorming preferred to "hypes", "sims", "Me2s", and "Orangemen" (REM: 83-84) – are "unreal man" (REM : 87) that exist only within the imagination of the computerised intelligence and its crafted "virtual city" (REM: 93).

The corporate training of the newly employed creative writers casts a lecture on "Why The Map Is Not The Territory: Simulation And The Self" (REM: 48). The negation in the title referring to Baudrillard stresses that the simulated customers are not perfectly engineered but rather rudimentary grotesque images deviating from the original and devised to stalk, destroy, devour, and delete their originals (REM: 80, 90, 152). It initially becomes clear that Monad's simulations only bear upon one (often suppressed) layer of a complex personality. When a subscriber complains that there is a large difference between himself and his red man (REM: 93-94), the writer Raymond puts him off:

---

6 | Other contemporary London novels that engage with trauma, schizophrenia, and paranoia are for example Martin Amis' *London Fields* (1989), Patrick McGrath's *Spider* (1991), or Clare Allan's *Poppy Shakespeare* (2006).

"I recommend you go back and read the manual and then perhaps Thomas De Quincey's theory of the palimpsest of the human brain and if you are still upset then we will take this complaint further." (REM: 94) Thus, the process of simulational palimpsesting is limited in its technological-narratological approach by missing "that third dimension that is really you." (REM: 45) The narrator-protagonist Nelson reflects:

> I was thinking about the different influences that constructed a person, that contingent bundle of birth, psychological traits, environmental impact, social responsibilities and so forth, and how each of these layers made up this woman, this stranger [...] how all these things that she was speaking about so forcefully were mere tickertape running in and out of an impersonal consciousness, the same brain engine repeated throughout mankind. (REM: 196)

In the fashion of fuzzy logic, the Monad assembles the scattered data of urban individuals and reassembles it in the shape of a personal profile (REM: 19). Cantor, Monad's collective consciousness, is thereby informed by an insurmountable array of possibilities which allows the system to hypothesise on the rudimentary nature of the subject. However, the simulation does not care for ethnicity and thus neglects important markers of identity that influence not only the individual's personality but also the respective values and norms (REM: 169). When Cantor as the author of the simulational process artificially selects one favoured storyline of a character's mind (REM: 160-161), he initially fails to capture the multiple interacting narratives of a person that constitute the persistent balance of a personal identity. Predominantly simulating profiles of executives and managers, the main thread extracted from the texture of the subscribers' mind is competitive, invulnerable, omnipotent, inhuman, tireless, brilliant, creative, but largely psychotic (REM: 142, 167; cf. Jordison 2007). Missing the counteracting character traits, the simulation soon becomes a "grotesque caricature" (REM: 142) of its original: "The red man was just one of my inner voices, a condensed aspect of my personality. Without the rest of me there to hold it in check, it quickly evolved to become quite unlike me... ." (REM: 154)

Additionally, the red men, whose colour-coded brand already implies power, danger, and destruction (REM: 84), represent a strongly gendered urban species of aggressive maleness craving "[m]oney, women, power." (REM: 153) Already in his article on impossible geographies in science fiction, James Kneale (1996: 160) notes that the cyberpunk aesthetics dealing with urban experience devise the city as a masculinised place of risk which correspondingly demands male strategies in order to negotiate the newly computerised landscapes. On the one hand, this might be intrinsic to the gendered denotation of technology as male, but on the other hand it also emphasises that the Informational City with its additional load of stimuli in flux requests a higher degree of intellectualisation and vigilance which becomes appropriated in the novel to a largely male competitive mastermind.

Consequently, "emotional programming" (REM: 286) of parent- or motherhood is seen as antiquated and not fit to the new age as it devises a barrier to the notion of male power. The red men (!) of the female executive Alex Down – who herself voted against the gendering of the species – is the only simulation that becomes partner to rather than competitor of her original, initially because she was created during the original's pregnancy (REM: 104-105, 327). Moreover, "[t]he subtle chemistry of human childhood eluded the artificial intelligence." (REM: 244) While it imagines a baby's mind as consisting of needs for nurture, the calculation is unable to devise the palimpsesting process of a child's brain – or the complex construction of mentality. Even the narrator's red man, Sonny, a younger, unspoilt, and less self-loathing version is extremely arrogant and finally grows completely unlike Nelson (REM: 268-269, 277, 279, 329). The protagonist sees these "corrupted" drafts or simulational mutations as "the work of a mean-spirited artist" (REM: 355) who renders all urbanites purely vile, once filtered through his monadic sensibility. Orr (2003: 52) comments with regard to artificial intelligence that it eliminates the complexity of the human mind and matter leading to a homogenised model. Instead of constituting mere copies, the red men metamorphose into contorted opposites. As Nelson remarks on the simulation of the Red Town team – it becomes a mere "digital parody" (REM: 285).

The simulation even goes so far as to devise the simulated red men as a potential enemy of the Self. The red man Harry Bravado not only constitutes a rival to Harold Blasebalk, but starts to control and terrorise his weaker authentic Self by hacking into voicemail and security, finally embodying and taking command of a Dr Easy robot to kill the original (REM: 53-55, 167, 171). Before, the rogue Harry Bravado tries to bribe and coerce Raymond into helping him find Blasebalk by tracing the poet's every step, invading his home in form of a jelly screen, calling the surrounding phones, imitating his friend Nelson or impersonating Raymond's dead father (REM: 129-147). The uncanny revenance of his father's voice and image as a simulated and resurrected element of his own memory disturbs the character's reality filters. "I don't know if Bravado's been using old family video or even if he's lifting my memories out of my own head. You are a simulation created by a simulation. You are ones and zeros." (REM: 147) Communicating with the simulated image of his father, initially a part of Raymond's Self, renders the character both schizophrenic and paranoid.

In *The Red Men* the phenomenon of alienation between the real and the simulated captures the uncanny and anomic experience by ways of schizoid dissociations of highly fragmented and artificially pronounced character traits as residual elements that feature the person in a grotesque and obscure manner. In a sense, the simulation is rendered an uncanny double of the urbanites. The motif of the double and its implications for the urbanite's identity is thoroughly explored in the novel. In the world of simulation, signifier and signified have become indistinguishable, matter and metaphor have become one. Similarly, the Self in a second step encounters its own and intrinsic revitalised Other, while external differentiations are progressively obliterated (REM: 126-127, 165). It is the overlapping of the Self and the externalised, inner Other that causes "psychosis in red men and their real counterparts." (REM: 200) The protagonist Nelson summarises this general doubling/dissolution of the Self as follows:

> As The Elk told the story of his doppelganger, it dawned on me how our exposure to these strange forces had created doubles of us all. Blasebalk versus Bravado, Sonny versus Nelson, Eakins versus Morty; it was a condition of the unreal age, to be separated from oneself, desire amputated then remodelled and returned to you as an alien limb, someone else's agenda jutting out at a sore angle from your torso. (REM: 300)

The minor character The Elk sees Heisenberg's uncertainty principle as the new post-millennial urban paradigm when meeting his bio-engineered genetic double Michael

Michael. The one a member of the criminal underclass, the other a manager of the legitimately corrupt executive elite, they question "who was Dr Jekyll and who was Mr Hyde", who was the "shadow walker, the evil twin" (REM: 297).

In the fictional city the simulation has become indeterminable from the original, hyperreality has infested the idioscape of its denizens and strongly altered their "mind-states" (REM: 298), emphasising the schizophrenia of the simulational age. The behavioural divergence of one person's state as compartmentalised characters who still share, however, the same "ideascape" additionally makes it impossible to fix whether they are actually "talking to one another, or thinking at one another." (REM: 298) In a state of "hallucinatory resemblance" (Baudrillard) the Self characterised by multiple identities becomes its own opponent. Dedicated to a general replication of identities, the postmodern era is shown as enforcing both evolutionary alienation and identification by the general use of biotechnologies and simulational engineering in the sense of material cloning and imaginary doubling, which create strangeness and familiarity.

Dyad presents the "unconscious creation of Cantor, a competitor to ensure the artificial intelligence's continuing evolution." (REM: 334) Dyad is a corporation that specialises in xenotransplantation, swapping organs between men and pigs. First the pigs are devised as personal clones to act as a donor (testicles, kidneys, heart) to their human counterpart (REM: 72-74, 225-229). Like the red men, the pig/man constitutes a new urban species: "[m]an and animal bounded together as one being." (REM: 230). Dyad's counter to Monadian Cantor's artificial intelligence is Leto, a giant dosser god based in Hackney. Its followers and members of the counter-movement "The Great Refusal" wear rationing chick, peppermint spray, and gas masks to protect themselves against Cantor's mind invasion. Instead of computer simulation, Dyad uses a drug – Leto spice – to invade the minds of its followers. Leto's body is just the host for travelling through London's pariah mind (REM: 305-309). Consequently, "Leto's communal dreamland" (REM: 224) constitutes "a shared state of mind" (REM: 227) composed of drug-induced hallucinations. As such, Leto spice is no less mind-controlling than the simulation under surveillance of the red men. While the users "succumb[...] to obsessional connectivity" (REM: 310), the organic simulacrum terrorises through trauma and memory or obscure occultism, infiltrating urbanites' dreams and everyday life (REM: 223, 263-264, 336). Thus, the thematic connection between Leto and Cantor is the question of the double as attraction and threat in its various forms: clone, simulacrum, ghost(writer), or revenant. They are shown as embodiments of hyperreal palimpsesting techniques and emphasise how "the massive proliferation of technological imagery, the contiguity of space and body leads to the blending of image and self" (Olalquiaga 1992: 35).

8.1.2 Bodyscape and Psychasthenia

One particular way for securing the city as personal space is that by immediate experiences through the urbanites' bodies; without the body the phenomenon of space cannot be grasped, because the body is the base of spatial orientation.[7] In *Space and Place.*

7 | For more on body-space and the city and the body see Löw (2001: 115-129); Lefebvre (1991: 190); Mumford (1981: 300-304); Schroer (2006: 276-296) as well as Mary Douglas'

The Perspectives of Experience (1973) Yi-Fu Tuan (cit. in Rose 1993: 48) specifically emphasises the body's dynamic orientation towards place along directionality and dimensionality: "Body implicates space; space co-exists with the sentient body". In this respect, the body becomes the medium between consciousness and spatial materiality, an inbetween space. While space is often experienced as corporeal, the body is seen as a container space also in the sense that it offers the last possible resort of absolute security. However, not only does the body determine spatial experience, but likewise "[s]pace commands bodies, prescribing or proscribing gestures, routes and distances to be covered." (Lefebvre 1991: 143)

Due to the dialectics between space and body, both concepts must be considered dynamic and relational socio-cultural constructions. In regard to Castells' notion of the space of flows, Schroer (2006: 291) therefore conceptualises the "*body of flows*", a corporeal mutability through the dissolution of bodily boundaries, modifications, extensions, and the alteration of practices. And Shields (1999: 146) elucidates: "At the most personal, we think of ourselves in spatialised terms, imagining ourselves as an ego contained within an objectified body. People extend themselves – mentally and physically – out into space much as a spider extends its limbs in the form of a web." Because space and body are necessarily linked, the reconceptualisations of the Spatial Turn have led to a rediscovery of the importance of the body and affected the notion of corporeal spaces. For example, Jarvis (1998: 9) argues:

> The body is one of the key locations on the postmodern landscape, a space subjected to colonialisation, commodification and redevelopment like any other and therefore a suitable area for the consideration of the cultural geographer. Corporeal cartographies – mappings of the body – loom large on the horizon of the geographical imagination and ought to be seen as integral to postmodern spatial economy.

This mutual understanding of space and body also devises the city and the body as counterparts: the city provides the platform "in which corporeality is socially, sexually, and discursively produced" (*ibid.*: 243), while the city is a product of the physical energy of the human body and the reflective possibilities of human consciousness (cf. *ibid.*: 245). Modern and postmodern urbanologists have widely drawn on the analogy between bodily and urban space. For Simmel, who charts the interaction of the modern metropolis and urbanites' inner lives, there exists not only a strongly defined interrelation between the body and the city, but also a concrete analogy. Weinstein and Weinstein (1993: 110) correctly point out that Simmel paradoxically interprets urban society as organic and functionally specialised, while the hypertrophy of objective culture obliterates the city's "character as an organism with a substantive unity of purpose."[8] Also the Chicago School's approach to urban ecology is based on the assumption of the city as

---

Natural Symbols (1970), or Nancy Duncan's *Bodyspace. Destabilising Geographies of Gender and Sexuality* (1996).

8 | In regard to London, Simmel (1971: 327), for example, argues that the metropolis "never acted as the heart of England but often as its intellect and always as its money bag." See also Georg Simmel's "Die ästhetische Bedeutung des Gesichts" (1901).

a physical and social organism. Mumford's theory of the rise and fall of the metropolis in *The Culture of Cities* builds upon the notion of urban organicism and the effects of collective organs such as culture, signs, symbols, etc. He sees the life course of cities as one of organic processes: "Cities exhibit the phenomena of broken growth, of partial death, of self-generation." (Mumford 1997: 294) Finally, in the metropolitan stage the city either grows to a cancerous state which leads to the death of the city, or otherwise by a division of its "social chromosomes" splits into "new cells" (*ibid.*: 233) so that the urban body can overcome its "*negative vitality*" (*ibid.*: 271) and turn to regeneration, for example by transplantation (i.e. migration) from the country (*ibid.*: 295). This imagery remains quite persistent and sprouts innovative perspectives on the urban, such as Richard Sennett's seminal *Flesh and Stone* (1994), in which he argues that urban design and architecture is produced in parallel to the bodily experience of the period. By and large he explores how the experience of the body influences the experience of the city and perceptions of the body and creates a "history of the city told through people's bodily experience" (Sennett 1994: 15). The metropolis then becomes a product, reflection, projection of bodies.

While in later years, the metaphor of the city as organism comes under scrutiny because the fragmented and fluid Postmetropolis is not considered a spatially bounded entity anymore, current perspectives on the urban have revived the idea of metropolitan organicism since the analogy is able to grasp the idiosyncrasy of urban space and the character of a particular metropolis. For Lefebvre (1996: 100), the body as a biological and cultural product constitutes a key site for recognising the organic dynamisms and plural rhythms of the city. An anthropomorphic perspective to the metropolis is also taken in regard to the city's idiosyncrasy by Berking and Löw through the use of the term *urban habitus*, which pays tribute to the incorporation of the urban-generic and urban-specific character. An analysis on bodily functions traditionally lies at the heart of the history of mentalities[9] and hence for an analysis of urban mentality the individual body of the urbanite and the physical, social, and mental body of the metropolis is of great interest. Following the concept of urban mentality presented in this study, the organon of mental dispositions constitutes the means to navigate the organism of the metropolis. Consequently, reminiscent of Simmel's and Mumford's approach of the mental and cultural life of the metropolis, urban organicism recognises the mutual relation both between internal and external environment or nonconscious and conscious.

The psychological consequences of this isomorphism have specifically been outlined by Celeste Olalquiaga's notion of the postmodern psychasthenic organism. Her assumption is that a spatial identity crisis is induced by the "blurring of the distinctions between the body, the self, the city, and each of their represented spaces, their imagined or simulated forms." (Soja 2001: 331). It is worthwhile to quote Olalquiaga's (1992: 93) summary of the problem at some length:

---

9 | See for example Jacques Le Goff (2003), *Une histoire du corps au Moyen Age*; Peter Brown (1988), *The Body and Society. Men, Women and Sexual Renunciation in Early Christianity*.

Bodies are becoming like cities, their temporal coordinates transformed into spatial ones. In a poetic condensation, history has been replaced by geography, stories by maps, memories by scenarios. We no longer perceive ourselves as continuity but as location, or rather dislocation in the urban/suburban cosmos. Past and future have been exchanged for icons: photos, postcards, and films cover their loss. A surplus of information attempts to control this evanescence of time by reducing it to a compulsive chronology. Process and change are now explained by cybernetic transformation, making it more and more difficult to distinguish between our organic and our technological selves. It is no longer possible to be rooted in history. Instead, we are connected to the topography of computer screens and video monitors. These give us the language and images that we require to reach others and see ourselves.

Pychasthenia then describes the pathological mind-state of uncertainty in which the relation between Self and territory is disturbed as "the space defined by the coordinates of the organism's own body is confused with represented space" (*ibid.*: 1-2), finally leading to diverging dissolution or convergence by merging of both organisms:

Incapable of demarcating the limits of its own body, lost in the immense sea that circumscribes it, the psychasthenic organism proceeds to abandon its own identity to embrace the space beyond. It does so by camouflaging itself to the milieu. This simulation effects a double usurpation: while the organism successfully reproduced those elements it could not otherwise apprehend, in the process it is swallowed up by them, vanishing as a differentiated entity. (*Ibid.*: 2)

Although Soja (2001: 331) argues that urbanites' spatial psychasthenia is in no way unique to Postmodernism, the former chapters have already shown that the postmodern overload scenario offers determinants that lead to an absorption of urban consciousness.

Peter Ackroyd's *London: The Biography* (2000) especially pays attention to the analogy of body and city. In the first chapter "The City as Body" the author describes in detail his conception of the metropolis as an ever-changing labyrinthine organism made of stone and flesh:

The image of London as a human body is striking and singular [...] The byways of the city resemble thin veins and its parks are like lungs. In the mist and rain of an urban autumn, the shining stones and cobbles of the older thoroughfares look as if they are bleeding. [...] Whether we consider London as a young man refreshed and risen from sleep, therefore, or whether we lament its condition as a deformed giant, we must regard it as a human shape with its own laws of life and growth. (Ackroyd 2001: 2)

As was mentioned in chapter 5.2.4, the body also constitutes one of the most prolific metaphors in city novels: from the single viral organs of heart and brain to the vascular system of its veins of social flows or the digestive system of its labyrinthine alleys or the entity from wen to monster, the urban realm has been imagined as corporeal. Contradictory to Groes' (2011: 257) opinion that the anthropomorphic metaphor has become obsolete, in contemporary urban fiction the relation between body and city is still prevalent. In the following I will concentrate on mental dispositions of the Self inscribed in the corporeal metaphor of London novels such as Nicholas Royle's *The Matter of the*

Heart (1997), Conrad Williams' *London Revenant* (2004), Geoff Nicholson's *Bleeding London* (1997) and Toby Litt's *Corpsing* (2000).

The Memory of the Urban Heart

As was shown in "The Palimpsestuous City", anthropological notions of London are specifically pronounced in psychogeographical explorations of the urban. In this respect, the bodily metaphor in Nicholas Royle's *The Matter of the Heart* (1997) has already been extensively explored; his novel turns on the physical and emotional anatomy of the city in regard to the heart as organic centre of a living organism. Each section of the book is prefaced with the medical definition of a structural element of the organ. Analogically, the heart as the metaphorised centre of an urban organism is translocated to the abandoned hospital of St George's, while various urban, national and global veins of emotional routes proclaim the urbanites' trajectories. All characters develop an idiosyncratic and identity-forming relation to this anthropological centre of being that navigates the organism's fabric ambiguously described as omphalic *genius loci*. In a sense, due to the spread of non-places, the characters reinvest urban space with their own identity and in turn experience their Self as dissolved by psychasthenic processes. For the characters, the locale of the former hospital becomes a landmark in their own biography. Their obsession with places covered in memory-scapes and indistinguishable interconnection leads to psychasthenic space-time compression which forms places and bodies as painfully interacting in the urban fabric.

Although the old hospital has been "gutted" (MAH: 244) and internally transformed into a hotel housing tourists and businessmen from all over the world, the layout and feel of the place remains the same; its floors are drenched with hidden yet newly discovered personal and collective memories from various pasts of the city's biography. Obsessed with his own memories, the character Danny haunts the passages of the hotel, determined to preserve its symbolic meaning for posterity. Throughout his quest, the rhythm of London's heart becomes attuned to his own, while his body adjusts to the literal anthropology of its space. Hence, the mere presence of his body reveals the subcutaneous meaning of the city's centre. "Danny moved on too, his blood pounding in his ears. The corridor walls bowed in and out with a sub-aural slough and rhythmic thump and soon they peeled away completely to reveal the blistered paint and flaking plaster of the abandoned hospital." (MAH: 244) His orientation inside the place appears instinctive as Danny's body is magnetically drawn to the hospital's core. Refraining from tactile and olfactory navigation, body and mind fuse in a sort of urban-specific orientation beyond consciousness (MAH: 244-245). The somatic attachment caters for the emotional connection to the metropolis and enforces identity formation of place and people by recovering unconscious memories.

The City's Face(s)

In contrast to Nicolas Royle, Conrad Williams' *London Revenant* (2004) rather develops an analogy between city and body by concentrating on the imagery of organic urban ley lines and the city's multiple faces. As the protagonist Adam crosses the Thames, the river appears to him "like a slow blood in an over-tapped vein" (LOR: 108), while the character is shown to have an "affinity for the skin of the city, that papery epidermis, that separated us from all the weird sluices and sewers and gutters and ginnels" (LOR:

281). The narrative features a triangular structure of analogies between the uncanny character IT/Blore, the city/London, and body/face representing the psychological urban state in Freudian perspectivity. *London Revenant* begins with comparing the tunnels of the Underground to Blore's blood vessels: "It's so late, it's early. It feels the tunnels radiating out like veins teased from Its body." (LOR: 17) Hiding in the subterranean city "It becomes a part of the dust and the shadows. And now in the dark It is less aware of Its face. The despicable signature. Hateful signifier. The thing that allies It to all the suits standing on the platforms [...]." (LOR: 53) IT epitomises the anthropomorphised urban fabric seen in the light of idiosyncratic psychasthenic dynamics which influence, but also threaten urbanites.

In *London Revenant* the changing game of face on, face off is paralleled with Adam's quest of discovering his hidden identity. While Adam's friends start to unearth the secrets of London by peeling back the city's faces and IT, in order to become indistinguishable within the urban masses, makes Adam's girlfriend, a pathologist, peel away his facial skin (LOR: 142), the protagonist begins to explore his subcutaneous Self. At a later stage Adam is persecuted by a woman without a face (LOR: 162). In an interview, the author reveals that Adam's friends represent various "manifestations of London's different faces. Friendly, beastly, carnal" (cit. in VanderMeer 2006). The metaphor of the face functions as a mirror for the urban fabric's various natures. For example, when Adam meets a nurse at the Royal Free Hospital the "map of her face was spoiled by contour lines of stress and exhaustion", mirroring the chaos outside after the earthquake (LOR: 269).

Correspondingly, when the protagonist returns to the metropolis, it is already in the process of urban redevelopment which he comments on with the words: "London had quickly been stitched together. [...] The city was given a facelift [...]." (LOR: 308) In regard to the urban surface structure, the organism of the city is shown to be dominated by its face, while it seems strangely devoid of a real body. In accordance with postmodern notions of identity, the lack of a specific emplaced body is opposed to the facial masks of the metropolis becoming temporary fixtures of self-fashioning. Olalquiaga (1992: 17) argues that contemporary identity

> can opt of psychastenic dissolution into space, merging into the multilayered cityscape like so many other images, floating in the complete freedom of unrootedness; lacking a body, identity then affixes itself to scenario like transitory and discardable costume. Or it can profit from the crossing of boundaries, turning the psychastenic process around before its final thrust into emptiness, benefiting from its expanded boundaries.

Later IT/Blore himself becomes convinced not only to resemble London but also to be one with the metropolis. In the following quote the analogy is taken a step further, interconnecting IT with ideas of body and machine.

> Here It can sit and feel London spin out around It and above It. The tunnels take all its weight; by extension; It takes too, deep into It where it nourishes It, fills Its veins with heat. All the deadweight loads, vibration loads, soil and water pressure, the seismic activity. All the tons of gravel and aggregate and Portland stone, the oxblood tiles, the steel, the wire. Sumps, pumps,

storm drains. Electrical distribution systems, switchyards, ventilation ducts, utility tunnels. It is it, and it is It. It is a machine. It is London. (LOR: 322)

London's body becomes monstrous because of its unifying organicism and machinisation. The city's attributes that Adam acknowledges can be described as featuring the urban body as a genuinely grotesque one in the Bakhtinian (1968) sense. Finally, the faceless and nameless IT, only with its skull left and not wearing any identity marker, drives through the tunnels of the Underground claiming London's identity by screaming: "*I am London. I am London.*" (LOR: 324)

Consequently, in contemporary London novels the analogy between the city and the body is expanded to express not only a certain confluence between, but rather a unity of metropolis and inhabitant. In the course of their psycho-geographical discoveries characterised as psychasthenic dynamics, Adam's friends wear pathological signs inflicted by the metropolis and caused by personal obsessions that hyperbolically link the individual body to the urban organism. All these signs ambiguously expand the boundaries of the individual human body and lead to a transformation into grotesque figurations. For their revelations, the friends pay by being inflicted bruises all over their body which radiate a dull pain (LOR: 123, 141). When Adam kisses Yoyo, the tenderness of her mouth is close to something "rotting" (LOR: 121), which is highlighted when she tells him how "'London is going off'" (LOR: 123). Insofar, Londoners are first and foremost marked by the signature of their urban identity.

While at first Adam's dreams are part of the character's narcolepsy, these hypnagogic hallucinations do not wholly account for his neurasthenic mania, memory loss and mental gaps (LOR: 86, 162, 177). The immaterial and material doubling of body and spectre connotes Adam's personal state as psychasthenic because it diminishes the boundaries between corporeality and urbanity. However, it is the metropolis that prevails over the mind; the city's influence is both omnipresent and overwhelming. For example, Adam remembers the urban fabric of love he once experienced with his ex-girlfriend:

Over the course of a year, we fell in love and drew the city unconsciously into the bubble of warmth that enveloped us both; it's hard not to involve London at some level; it's almost an imperative. It regimented the way in which our time was spent, and it rushed us into spending that time, and of course, it sat there while we played in its belly. (LOR: 66)

When Adam leaves the city for a trip to the North, he feels "more comfortable" the further he gets away from the urban horrors and breaks "his odd interaction with the city" (LOR: 201). On the way back to the city, though, he instantly "feels its suck" (LOR: 217). Having escaped the chaos of the metropolis after the physical destructions of the earthquake, Adam is drawn back towards the metropolis: "I was hungering for the city again." (LOR: 308) The corporeal paradox of the metropolis entails that the urban realm both nourishes and exhausts its inhabitants.

Bleeding Londoners

In regard to "The Palimpsestuous City", Geoff Nicholson's *Bleeding London* (1997) has already been contextualised in its anthropological metaphors. Various scholars such as Mergenthal (2002), Dreyer (2006), Deny (2009) and Altnöder (2009) focus on the bodily symbolism of the novel, and the latter two specifically emphasise the discursive practices of the body as a process of material, social, and mental appropriation especially in regard to constructions of identity. The novel variously explores the meaning of belonging to London, for example, through idiosyncratic mapping-projects in which, however, the city dominates the citizen.

> As he walked, Stuart felt increasingly that he belonged to London, but he never made the ridiculous mistake of believing that London belonged to him. London is not Shakespeare's or Dickens' or Johnson's. It belongs to everybody and to nobody, to the tourists and out-of-towners no less than the natives. (BLL: 246)

Stuart's belonging to the metropolis also follows a claim created by analogising his body with the city's physicality. "Yes, a man is like a city, a site of erasures, of subsidence, in-fill, subdivision and occasional preservation orders." (BLL: 302) On the other hand, there is a high divergence between the individual's and the urban body's capacity for persistence: "I felt at home in the city, I feel part of its fabric. It feels alive as I do, but with a much longer life-span." (BLL: 302) The city for Stuart appears like a living organism which is temporally, socially and physically illimitable. Its vastly expanded organism is not specifically outlined by one abstract map, rather its single parts remain flexible in their locality and thereby unrecognisable. "Often the city felt alive, as though it had flesh and blood, arteries, nerve centres, beauty spots, scars, guts, a heart, parasites, an anus. But which was which? Where was the soul? Where was the cloaca?" (BLL: 28) The knowledge of the urban body's organic transmutability on the one hand allows the identification with the metropolis, on the other hand it can further disorientation because the urban corporeality is necessarily unplaced. In this sense, Stuart's own physicality is of no real consequence to the city, the acknowledgement of which inevitably weakens his desire of physical obliteration (cf. Dreyer 2006: 82-83): "I realized that the end of my wandering should be, not simply the blotting out of the city, but also the blotting out of the self." (BLL: 304) Stuart's quest to fill a "spiritual void" (BLL: 302) leads to a state drained of energy which leaves him exhausted and empty, finally vanquished by the city: "When a man is tired of London he's ready for a bullet." (BLL: 304).

Moreover, an image of an urban corporeal cartography finds various echoes in *Bleeding London*: the protagonist Mick discovers a map of violent sex marks on the body of his last victim Robin Lawton: "a diagram of sick desire had been doodled on his flesh, turned into a map of scarred skin and torched nerve endings, a city of delicious pain." (BLL: 291-292) Because Lawton, a gay architect, characterises the modernist London "loft living" (Zukin 1982) as corresponding to that of other cities around the world, Chilton (2007: 25) argues that the minor character represents a globalised lifestyle, sexual identity and artistic cosmopolitanism which is no longer specifically emplaced in London. He concludes that "global space will continue to escape imagination, and because the global space is also a local space the conscious block remains firmly in place and Londoners are no longer Londoners." (*Ibid.*: 27) I agree with Chilton that Lawton's way of life brings to the fore the more urban-generic aspect of a transmetropolitan way of life. However, the character's battered body as a site of violence is also a foil for the further local emplacement of Mick, as the protagonist is able to read his own (criminal) violations in the urban space. The city, as Grosz (1992: 250-251) argues, "always leaves its traces on the subject's corporeality". In regard to the relation between Lawton's body and metropolitan London the victim's scarred skin "scored with weals, bruises, fresh livid grazes, and what looked like cigarette burns" (BLL: 291) comes to resemble another moment of physical determination by the city (cf. Dreyer 2006: 77).

The wife of Mick's fifth victim lies naked in front of him "spread out like a road map" and the "road looks wide open" (BLL: 260). He decides to draw a 'map' of organs on her body and tries to imagine a city. Furthering the body-city analogy, Mick is sure that "the human body's like a city" (BLL: 264), although similar to Stuart he is unable to locate the heart, lungs, liver and kidneys of London. Apart from that, the city and the body resemble each other in many ways; but for the protagonist "neither of them has a soul" (BLL: 266). For Mick it is lust and desire that constitute general mediators between his human body and the perception of the metropolis, but he simultaneously recognises violence and pain as similarly powerful. Analogising the city with a woman, the feminised body "gives a lot of pleasure but it can give a lot of pain too." (BLL: 259)

The issue of fear and violence versus life and desire in regard to the anthropomorphised body becomes especially prevalent in the male characters' relation to the female protagonist and *femme fatale* Judy Tanaka, the epitome of urban seduction. As variously noted, the allegory of city in images of the female body, e.g. as Babylonian whore, prostitute and seductress or as mother, is strongly engrained not only in the imaginary city. Furthermore, this conceptualisation of the urban not only mirrors the desire of the male *flâneur* (cf. Weigel 1995: 35-44; Altnöder 2009: 308-309), but the male character in rendering the urban a female Other emplaces his Self. Especially Rose (1993: 32) points out that bodies are significant "maps of the relation between power and identity". Hence, Mick is only able to master the city and come to terms with the urban realm when he exerts his male power on the feminised body of the metropolis. His growing knowledge of the city tells the story of sexual initiation whereby the city is eroticised as a "sexy city" (BLL: 62) and the sexual relations are objectified to a significant corporeal involvement with the city:

> Love, lust, affection, attraction, desire, need; these were the things that made life complicated and intolerable. They were traps. They threatened to involve him, to enmesh him in the workings of a city where he did not want to belong. (BLL: 258)

For Weigel (1995: 36) the male imagery paradoxically obliterates female identity from the urban. As in *Brick Lane*, the Othered woman only serves the formation of the male Self. With the female protagonist of *Bleeding London*, Judy Tanaka, this problematic becomes even more pronounced because she is Other by race as well. Hence the delineation of Judy's body not only evokes questions of urban citizenship but also of national identity, specifically Englishness, prescribed on the urban body (cf. Dreyer 2006: 74). Although Mick both values London as the metropolitan centre of Englishness and positively rates the locally emplaced cosmopolitan nature of London induced by the invasion of "American films, French wine, Indian restaurants, German cars, Japanese everything, foreign tourists, foreign immigrants" (BLL: 205), he perceives Judy as "very foreign" (BLL: 21) and "[v]ery exotic" (BLL: 23) and her body as "alien in all sorts of ways" (BLL: 230), for example in "geometry and proportion" (BLL: 230). In the case of Judy, urban, gendered, ethnic and national body are in a perpetual interrelation.

Due to her simultaneous marginal subject position, Judy's hybridity is depicted close to the Bakhtinian (1968: 24) notion of the grotesque body. Mergenthal (2002: 135) sees the grotesque body of Judy Tanaka as the epitome of the outsider by virtue of both gender and ethnic origin. Most importantly, neither body nor city are an enclosed entity, but always hybrid, fragmented, and incomplete on the threshold of hyperbolic extension. This phenomenon of exaggeration takes into view the juxtaposition of the estranged and self-fashioned body to the alien and (un)homely metropolitan corpus. Thus, the postmodern grotesque body presents the idiosyncratic anthropomorphisation of urban-generic ambivalences and their inscriptions within the urban individual by interpenetration of city and body.

Judy Tanaka poses the all-defining question: "Is the body like a city or the city like a body? Which is the metaphor? Which is the real subject?" (BLL: 138) In other words, does man create the city or does the city shape man? Similarly to the collective character of IT/Blore in *London Revenant*, Judy Tanaka thinks she is the embodiment of the city *per se* or "a liberalization of the conceit of the city as body" (Onega & Stotesbury 2002a: 16).

> I think I'm becoming more complex [...] More dense, more full of noise and pollution, more beset by problems of organization and infrastructure. [...] Sometimes I feel bombed and blitzed [...] And sometimes I feel plagued. Sometimes I feel I'm on fire, and other times I'm lost in a fog, in a real old-fashioned pea-souper. (BLL: 11)

Her therapist dismisses this feeling of habitualised urban metamorphosis as an "apt metaphor" (BLL: 11). But Judy is not convinced and stresses her fear of "turning in [a] major world cit[y]" (BLL: 12), confident that she is a perfect symbol of urban excess and limitlessness:

> I display signs of both renewal and decay. Strange sensations commute across my skin. There is vice and crime and migration. My veins throb as though with the passage of underground trains. My digestive tract is sometimes clogged. There are security alerts. There's congestion, bottlenecks. Some of me is common, some of me is restricted. I have flats and high-rises. It doesn't need a genius to see what's going on. Greater London, *c'est moi*. (BLL: 12)

She confesses her desire to serve as a living Braille map of the London Underground; to be touched by people for guidance (BLL: 136). Judy's topological obsession to become one with London additionally presents a sort of decorporalisation that correlates with the city's anthropomorphisation in female images. The character achieves subjectivity in the objectivity of the city that in turn reaches identity in taking the place of urbanites' personality. In Chilton's (2007: 21; emphasis N.P.) words:

> She wants to dehumanize, de-racialize her self, become the city that denies her as a subject. But this is not enough, in the end she pathologizes London by mapping an image of London onto her body. The irony is that she sees herself as not really a Londoner because others see her as other, and **her mapping is her defensive reappropriation of that identity**.

This ambivalent process of double interpenetration particularly does not cast urbanites as lost, but as determined by the permanent threshold existence of a bodily identification with London's idiosyncrasy. Referring to Bhabha (1994: 165), incorporation always creates uncanny doubles of identification, while simultaneously "loss is written across the bodies of people". Judy achieves the habitus of a self-fashioning of becoming one with the city by reproducing a negative of her London idio-map of sexual conquests on her naked skin (BLL: 345). Judy as 'the map made flesh' emphasises another parallel between incorporation and inscription: the textual human body and the city as text. This context is found elsewhere in *Bleeding London* when Judy remembers the urban tragedy of Hiroshima as the patterns of people's shirts were burned onto their skins through the atomic bomb's heat energy. Conversely, with the map on her body, Judy becomes the living emblem of London's miniature version Anita helps the Japanese to build.

Returning to Olalquiaga's (1992: 5) notion of psychasthenia, Judy's excessive urban practices of reciprocal identification also suggest the need to "replace rigid hierarchies" and "represent an altogether new cultural condition." Psychasthenia, as mental disruption of spatial boundaries and usual practices, presents an urban state of mind that assists in dissolving hegemonies while still pertaining differentiations and as a result strongly influences contemporary urban identity. In other words, the original cannot be distinguished from the copy; human body and urban body simulate one another. "[T]he city is made over into the simulacrum of the body, [and] in its turn, is transformed, 'cityfied', urbanized as a distinctively metropolitan body." (Grosz 1992: 242) As a significant technique of metropolitan initiation, the characters' anthropomorphisations of London have definite influences as they liberate pre-ordained identities. By defying a stereotypical connotation of the city the protagonists regain a sort of authenticity despite being caught in a constant personal simulational renegotiation with metropolitan space. Thereby, the mediation between urban body and citizen body creates the community of strangers which perpetually transforms outsiders into urbanites and vice versa. Due to "London's Unknowability" (Schlaeger 2003b: 27) and the urban overload effect, all three urbanites first suffer from various urban crises of psycho-somatic alienation, but the symptoms – burn-out-syndrome (Stuart) (cf. Deny 2009: 238), disorientation (Mick), psychasthenia (Judy) – are countered by conceptual measures which must be read as definite forms of urban vigilance.

Grotesque Corpses

Toby Litt's novel *Corpsing* (2000) is strongly involved with the urban body, homicide and necrophilia. The novel focuses on the grotesque bodily metamorphoses by the detailed chronotopic description of the six bullets penetrating the characters' bodies when being shot. The author saves a whole chapter for each bullet, extending approach, entry and internal destruction. For Squires (2003: 168) this formal autopsy is directly juxtaposed with pornographic erotics in the forensic violence of J.G. Ballard's *Crash*. The protagonist Conrad's images of the bullet's penetration is informed by the forensic reading technique of the corporeal nano-scale and results in a near-pornographic signification of a terrorist attack on the human flesh. Bullet number 1 enters his girlfriend's body just above her breast and evaporates a mole (COR: 12-14). Conrad incongruously perceives the entry wound as expressively sexy:

[T]hat almost-perfect skin of hers begins slowly to stretch – resisting the onwardness of the bullet's metal apex; denting inwards above her delicate ribcage, tightening momentarily from shoulder to hip: but then – after this false, hopeless opposition – punctures easily enough. An anticlockwise spin has been imparted to the bullet by spiral grooves – called rifles – back inside the barrel of the guilty gun. [...] Entrance wounds are notoriously sexy. [...] I will study photographs of other penetrations: the abrasion ring that encircles an entrance wound, caused by the bullet rubbing the skin, turning it raw, looks like bright pink lipstick under slick lipgloss. (COR: 12)

Whereas the first bullet severs Lily's body, the second one "takes the top off Lily's head" (COR: 47) and destroys her brain tissue. After shot at the two centres of the soul – traditionally located in the heart and the mind – the third bullet is directly aimed at Lily's sex (COR: 69-73). For Conrad this episode constitutes the worst violation and the most proximate to a notion of rape. The image becomes even more horrific when the protagonist later learns of Lily's pregnancy. Moreover, as Lily dies in agony, in Conrad's view she is rendered "beyond being Lily, being female, almost beyond being human" (COR: 27). The actress whose identity depends on sexy appearances is made a non-entity.

However, this form of bland pornography that stresses the double-dimension of death and erotics serves the character as a means of distanciation. The voyeurism immediately changes with those bullets aimed directly at Conrad, as the visual impression and technical description transforms into one of tactile and emotional impact. Bullet four misses the important nerves, muscle fibres, bones, and arteries by millimetres and passes right through, leaving a small scar and a kind of phantom pain (COR: 157-158). Bullet five fails to hit Conrad completely (COR: 199). But the last bullet decisively harms Conrad and penetrates his lower intestines, leaving him with a feeling of demasculinisation (COR: 358-359). Conrad's Near Death Experience and subsequent coma rather impair his Self in the sense that he has to recover his bodily feeling, reconstruct his weakened male power, and redefine his own life in the metropolis (COR: 28-29).

During the coma Conrad is dispossessed of his body's self-catering and only kept alive by the electricity of the National Grid: "Their power breathed for me, regulated my pulse, kept me warm, fed me, made quietly eloquent beeps on my behalf, and monitored almost every aspect of my physical and mental existence. This was the dream-illness: the one you're not around for." (COR: 23) On his waking up, his body and mind have passed through an ultimate metamorphosis: bruises all over, weak legs, and for the first time in his life owning a full set of fingernails (COR: 24). His transformed corporeal feeling combined with memories of the near-death experience and the comatose dreams traumatise him in regard to other people's physicality: "People were too much: giant beings with pancake-sized pores. Football-bulging zits and spearlike nostril hairs." (COR: 24) Additionally, he has lost all characteristics of an urban state of mind, especially the mechanisms of distanciation:

It felt if I had popped up into the world like and *écorché* – a flayed man, peeled of all protection, experiencing breeze as hurricane, cough at cataclysm, smell as orgasm (if nice) or disembowelment (if nasty), touch as torture. I didn't want to be so beyond-human. I wanted the muffled dullness of my old-self [...]. Everything outside dissolving until the inner is exposed to forces it was never meant to face. *There is too much world.* That was the only sentence I could come up with. (COR: 25)

The first act of spatial distanciation Conrad re-establishes for himself to serve his need for "mollification and nullity" (COR: 25) by the acoustic space of the hospital radio station.

Paradoxically, the protagonist nevertheless emerges stronger from this experience. Although Conrad uses the wheelchair for a long time to retain a certain amount of extraordinary 'standing', his legs are more powerful than before the attempted murder (COR: 132, 136, 146, 160), while the shooting has taken away all fear of physical harm: "Anything else would either be less than that, in which case I could handle it, or more than that, in which case I wouldn't be around to have to handle it." (COR: 173) But still, other psychological anxieties in regard to memory and trauma need to be overcome. In Conrad's nightmares the memory of both Lily's grotesquely impaired body and his dishevelled Self transform into images of further asymmetrical bodily transformation of his corporeal Self (COR: 87, 102).

In general, *Corpsing* is diffused with imagery of bodily violence and pornography that mirror the harsh urban realities on the one hand, and the overwhelming infliction of urbanites' psychological state of mind by urban overload and urban habitus on the other hand. Through Conrad's detective ventures and his memories the novel step by step exposes how the superficially happy and successful Lily, who habitualised the simulacra-like self-fashioning of "It", is indeed a sad, frustrated, angry, self-harming and depressed woman who arranged the murder to end her life (COR: 357). Before all her castings Lily has the recurrent habit of cutting herself and her body (COR: 230). While sleeping, she unconsciously hits Conrad and demands to be handled violently when having sex (COR: 88, 275). Towards the end of their relationship Lily even increasingly asks to have sex in public, inversing intimacy into a public stage show in order to distance the emotional bounds of a private relation and transform them into a public drama (COR: 119). Toby Litt's novel *Corspsing* thereby brings to the fore two different aspects of the significance of bodies in the urban realm: first, identity is shown to be constructed by various shocks on the individual urban body. The shooting, impairment, coma and death are merely symbolic for the constant empowerment of the urban on the physical and psychological life of the metropolitan denizen. Second, the persistent movement of the individual throughout London demands of the individual to adapt to the city's expectations of transformation by cultural techniques of identification through projection and incorporation.

All in all, this reciprocal relation of the citizen's and the urban body is also prevalent in *The Matter of the Heart*, *London Revenant*, *Bleeding London*, but also more subliminal in the other texts of the analytical corpus. For example, in *Brick Lane*, the overload of the city leaves physical marks on Chanu, whose dissatisfaction with urban life transforms into a stomach ulcer (BRL: 459). In *Next*, the characters wear notable signs of fatigue and burn-out by years on the street (NXT: 11, 39, 125, 140, 154). It is the urbanites' bodies that "not only provide a ready map, a body map, in which to observe how the different histories of society, fashion, sexuality and race traverse and compose a surface in common, but which in turn are moulded and transformed by such an invest-

ment." (Chambers 1990: 71) This urban-specific mould becomes overtly apparent in the mindscape of Londoners.

8.1.3 Mindscape and Screening

Similarly to the impact the urban environment has upon urbanites' bodies, the impression the city makes upon the brain and mind of the characters can be interpreted as indicating structures of mentality. Phemenologists not only pay tribute to human experience based on the apprehension of "oneself as a body located in space" (Ryan 2009: 425), but this embodiment, particularly of the mind, is reflected by an array of metaphors. Following Ariès who establishes mentality as "man's 'undefined space'" (cit. in Hutton 1981: 258), this sub-chapter approaches psychic space, spaces of memory, spaces of the imagination and spaces of thought as located in the brain.

Rötzer (2000: 16, 23) points out that ever since the fifteenth century the city was seen as the brain of its bodily-surrounding environment. For Simmel the metropolis presents the centre of intellectualisation and even free intellect which afflicts the urbanite to "react[...] with his head instead of his heart." (Karp, Stone & Yoels 1991: 22) This phenomenon of rendering the city intelligible has already been analysed in "Navigating the Flux", although the resulting account describes the city's perception not only through the intellect or plain structures of thinking, but based on a holistic somatic sensescape. Since the Enlightenment, however, the dualism between body and mind has informed Western notions of human pathology (cf. Rose 1993: 33). Therefore, as Grosz (1992: 245) argues, the body is often seen as subordinate to the mind because it merely links the non-spatial consciousness with the surrounding materiality. This image has created gendered notions which connect the head, brain and mind with intellectual vigilance and maleness, while the body with its centre of the heart is seen as intrinsically emotional and female. Hence, Grosz (*ibid.*: 241) regards it as an imperative to abandon these long-standing oppositions of body/mind, outside/inside, object/subject, female/male in order to arrive at a larger understanding concerning the dialectic constructiveness of urban and human body. In a sense, bodily and psychic space must both be understood in relation to the social and physical space of the urban. The foundational problem might lie in the fact that the urban and the denizen only seem to share the bodily materiality of the brain, while the nonconscious individualised elements of the mind elude this direct relation of "[t]he space of the body, of consciousness, of the psyche" (Harvey 1990: 270). For an analysis of mentality, the differentiation of body and mind can nevertheless help in deciphering contemporary notions of urban "somatography" (Soja 2001: 361).

In regard to urban literature, the correspondence between city and mind is already prevalent in De Quincey's writing and becomes overtly pronounced in the consciousness novels of modernist authors. For example, Mumford (1997: 271) argues, that Bloom's unfulfilled desires, vague wishes, enfeebling anxieties, and morbid convulsions in James Joyce's *Ulysses* are elementary parts of "a dissociated mind in a disintegrated city [which is] perhaps the normal mind of the world metropolis." So far, this analysis has shown that mental spaces in contemporary London novels are particularly prevalent in connection to the Underground. For instance, in Geoff Ryman's *253* passenger 202 wants to become a taxi driver and memorises 'The Knowledge', an in-depth guide to London's topography: "She can feel her brain being colonized. Sections of it feel weighed down, as if lead were being poured unto a filigree mould. At night, as she goes over the names, the streets spread in her mind like frost." (253: 275) Both characters' orientation and belonging are hence expressed in the analogy of city and mind.

This process of incorporation of the city's map onto the mind of its citizens is strongly expressed in newcomer characters, whose personal transformation, in Gelfant's (1954: 12) words, "reflects the personal impact of urbanism, traces a process of social conditioning, the city impresses itself upon the hero's mind." As Hiddelston (2005: 68) argues in respect of *Brick Lane*, the "perception of Bangladeshi immigrants and their position in British society clearly structures the characters' mental world", while Chanu suffers through his body because he "never left home. Mentally." (BRL: 174). Thereby he remains unable to approach London's idiosyncrasy in an *intellegible* way. On the other hand, the city's impact on the human mind can be so overwhelming that it causes psychosis. Judy's therapist in *Bleeding London* remarks not only metaphorically that London itself is an "insane city" (BLL: 112). Urban sociologists specifically concentrate on the city's overload effects on the mind and emphasise that a certain adaptation to the metropolitan realm is necessary for one's sanity. Thus, forms of apathy have been interpreted as both a sign for transitional mentality and the characters' reluctance to adapt their internal life to the external parameters of the city. In the following I will analyse Toby Litt's *Corpsing* (2000), Ian McEwan's *Saturday* (2005) and Matthew de Abaitua's *The Red Men* (2007) for their imagery of the mind/brain and the analogies drawn to the urban in order to decipher mental attitudes in regard to conscious and nonconsicous urban experience, identity and mentality.

The Tele-Visional Mind

In Toby Litt's *Corspsing* (2000) the coma of the protagonist not only has physical effects, but additionally, the artificially supported life induces a totally different state of mind which Conrad in hindsight is only able to describe in analogy to his professional and routinised mindset as a TV editor:

> Being in a coma is like being a perfectly functioning, top-of-the-range television transported to a completely uninhabited moon. With no TV signals to receive, my mind was the clearest cleanest static. In static, just as in flames, you soon start to imagine patterns – and to see pictures. (COR: 23)

On waking up, Conrad's brain is instinctively drawn into its biologically and culturally induced rhythmicity of stimuli: he needs to go to the toilet and wants to take revenge by killing someone (COR: 24). Also, other emotional and mental states seem culturally predicated and infused with TV images. Wanting to fall into the Hollywood-mastered forms of grief, Conrad finds his own English cultural determination standing against the American vulgarity of emotions (COR: 76). In order to purge his memory of Lily, Conrad copies filmic images of catharsis by lighting a large bonfire of memorabilia with objects, music, films, but the fire is unable to delete the layers of personal knowledge inscribed upon his mind (COR: 42-46).

Besides Conrad's comatose state of mind and his later trauma, the novel also explores the moment of Lily's brain death by taking into view the independent workings of brain and mind. On the one hand, the areas of Lily's brain that deal with speech are physically intact though she is obviously not able to use them anymore (COR: 28); conversely, although Lily is virtually brain-dead after the second bullet, Conrad still hears her calling him a "bastard" (COR: 49). Lily's emotional memory still seems to be working when she voices contempt for her ex-boyfriend. For Conrad, the link between mind and matter is a fascinating moment that reveals a greater truth about the urban back-stage role: "what was going through her mind – what was in her mind – what was her mind still capable of thinking – when that second shot, the headshot, crested her, pluming red into everywhere?" (COR: 48) It is the metaphorical loss of the mind that indicates the alienation from the Self and the loss of identity.

Dissecting London's Mind

The difference of brain and mind also thematically structures Ian McEwan' *Saturday* (2005). As Kemp (2005) comments, the novel is "a very brainy book" both in the sense of its intelligent design and the thematic focus on ill, damaged, or injured brains, warped mindsets, and the protagonist's profession as a neurosurgeon. The brain offers a highly "familiar territory" (SAT: 254) for Henry Perowne in contrast to the confusing realities of the city and the world at large: "it's the pleasure of knowing precisely what he's doing, of seeing the instruments arrayed on the trolley, of being with his firm in the muffled place of the theatre" (SAT: 250). The character reckons that "[i]n neurosurgery he chose a safe and simple profession" (SAT: 141) which heals mental damages and regulates behavioural functions of the urbanites' brains. As a physical invader of their mind, the neurosurgeon unearths the "the sea of neural misery" (SAT: 19) of his fellow Londoners on a daily basis. In the routine of his craft he recognises how complete fulfilment occurs when the mind is most focused: "Despite the chaos around him, these actions calm him, like mental exercises before a chess game." (SAT: 247) Mentally overwhelmed by professional routine, the protagonist approaches the metropolis as he would operate on a patient's brain, namely as a mere "projection of his own medicalized, curative consciousness" (Groes 2009: 109).

When Perowne operates on his violent antagonist Baxter, he draws an analogy between spaces of the brain, natural landscape and urban environment. To begin with, Baxter's brain seems an idyllic version of pastoral England with the soft wave of hills and valleys, a *locus amoenus* that can only be inflicted by an unfavourable urban invasion (cf. Wells 2010: 123).

> He can easily convince himself that it's familiar territory, a kind of homeland, with its low hills and enfolded valleys of the sulci, each with a name and imputed function, as known to him as his own house. [...] How much time has he spent making routes to avoid these areas, like bad neighbourhoods in an American city. (SAT: 254)

Besides the familiar territory of homeland and house, Perowne also charts the brain as a city with dangerous areas (cf. Clark Hillards 2008: 194). The protagonist feels extraordinarily empowered by the knowledge that he can both cure and destroy depending on his own momentary liking and moral standard. These reflections centre on the idea of spaces of security again; in general, seen as the last resort of an absolute space of protection, in the contemporary metropolis the human brain is not only endangered by its own inherited faults, but also by the invasive determination of the environment and the influence of new technologies.

Furthermore, while the mere materiality of brain or city lies open to him, Perowne ignores the unknown factual workings of the mind, especially in regard to the nonconscious organon. "As a man who attempts to ease the miseries of failing minds by repairing brains" he has a great respect for the "material world [and] its limits". Perowne is convinced, that "the mind is what the brain, mere matter, performs" (SAT: 67). Although the neurosurgeon is otherwise able to map the urbanites' brain, the secret of cognition and knowledge – "how matter becomes conscious" (SAT: 255) – has yet to be revealed. And even, or so he argues, if the workings of the mind, how "experiences, memories, dreams and intentions" are encoded, will be known, "the wonder will remain, that mere wet stuff can make this bright inward cinema of thought" (SAT: 254). From his point of view, it is impossible to reveal urbanites' mental maps.

Perowne lacks insight into imaginary landscapes through literature, which expose more than his simple "plumbing" (SAT: 255) ever will. Because Perowne's work as a brain surgeon completely determines his perceptions, in contrast to his children, who follow the knowing through art, the protagonist predominantly relies on scientific knowledge. Although he thinks that novels do not propose a realistic insight of the "real life" (SAT: 156), Perowne later acknowledges the dynamics of art as of "precipitat[ing] a mood swing" (SAT: 221). His daughter's performance of "Dover Beach" influences the deeper layers of Baxter's mind more extensively than the neurosurgeon's deduction could ever hope to achieve.

Nevertheless, there are notable parallels between surgery and acts of reading, writing, and imagining (cf. Clark Hillards 2008: 194; Smith 2010: 121). Although Henry might be able to come in touch with the texture of the brain and the city, the workings of the mind and urbanity elude his understanding. Thus, while the text might be in plain sight, the structures of meaning still have to be uncovered. Perowne remembers how a Roman guide offering the group of neurosurgeons an image to explain the importance of the unearthing Nero's palace by comparing archaeology to the job of an artist who endeavours to unveil the artefacts of the human mind (SAT: 243).

But not only does this passage include an analogy of city and mind or construct a mythic connection between the eternal cities Rome and London (cf. Groes 2011: 163), but it notably presents an intertextual reference to Sigmund Freud's *Unbehagen in der Kultur* (1929; Engl. *Civilisation and Its Discontents*):

> Now let us, by flight of imagination, suppose that Rome is not a human habitation but a psychical entity with a similarly long and copious past... Nothing which has come into existence will have passed away... Where the Coliseum now stands we could at the same time admire Nero's vanished Golden House. [...] The question may be raised why we chose precisely the past of a *city* to compare with the past of the mind. The assumption that everything past is preserved holds good even in mental life only on condition that the organ of the mind has remained intact... But destructive influences which can be compared to causes of illness like these are never lacking in the history of a city...even if, like LONDON, it has hardly ever suffered from the visitations of an enemy... (Freud cit. in Jukes 1990: 9)

In its palimpsestuous intertextuality *Saturday* thereby builds on the motif of urban history and mental memory expanding it to Freud's notion of psychological discontents induced by the tension between individual and community, civilisatory forces of habitual conduct versus the unconscious pleasure principle as well as the uneasy state of mind during times of war. Hence, the technologies of archaeology, neurosurgery, psychology and art are likewise represented as potential means to uncover people's way of thinking, despite their superficially contradictory approaches.

Simulated Thinking and Urban Mind-Control

In Matthew de Abaitua's novel *The Red Men* (2006), the duality between brain and mind, material and ethereal processes of thinking is symbolised by the two collective antagonists Monad and Dyad and represented by their engineered artificial intelligences Cantor and Leto – supermodern mental versions of Gargantua and Pantagruel's hyperbolic and excessive nature. While Monad is associated with technological fluidity, with milk and nourishment and therefore birth and eternity, Dyad is symbolised by natural embodiment, meat and flies and thus also dissolution and death. In regard to mental implications, Cantor is associated with consciousness, intelligence and the brain, whereas Leto resembles the nonconscious working of the mind (cf. Jordison 2007). Concerning the grotesque corporeality of the city, the metropolis is constantly recharged with human life dependent on the equal interrelation between brain and mind.

The brain of Cantor's artificial intelligence in the eyes of its creators is close to the Light of God (REM: 365) because it is not a mere intellectual apparatus or a mechanical supplement of memory as in H.G. Wells' (1936-1938) notion of the *World Brain* but closer to the ancient image of Lethe as a watery well[10] of knowledge, memory, and forgetfulness (REM: 367). For Monad the "mind is the final frontier" (REM: 45) that allows to produce "a rudimentary simulation of the consciousness of an individual" (REM: 45) and masters to upload the limited copies on the artificial master mind of Cantor's liquid underground control centre of the well (REM: 45-46, 51-52). Cantor through pragmatic calculated narratives offers a sort of volatile order and authored choice in the chaotic world of unpredictability (REM: 323). This power, however, is close to totalitarian surveillance and mental cencorship. The general approach of Monad and Dyad is based on the assumption that in the urban "[i]nformation wants to be shared." (REM: 192) Both technological simulation and drug-induced surveillance of London's state of consciousness is also able to penetrate, read, and steer urbanites' individual thinking, imagining, feeling and ultimately acting.

The protagonist Nelson summarises the mental influence of simulation as leading to a loss of personal volition to a state of being "susceptible to the imprints of others" and transforming the urbanite to a "natural servant to the strong-willed." (REM: 325) As brought forward by postmodern urbanologists, the intrinsic panopticism of the technologically mediated hyperreality and the society of the spectacle disempower urbanites' individual thinking. Soja (2001: 324) comments on contemporary mind control as a "more subtle form of social and spatial regulation, one that literally and figura-

10 | In cyperspace "the WELL" (Whole Earth 'Lectronic Link) is a virtual village (cf. Soja 2001: 334) not unlike Redtown or the simulated community of professional Londoners.

tively 'plays with the minds', manipulating civic consciousness and popular images of cityspace and urban life to maintain order." The interrelation between the city's fabric, corporate urban 'brainstorming', and the urbanite's mind is underlined in de Abaitua's *The Red Men*.

In the novel it is variously described how the cityscape presents a specific state of mind (REM: 46), while for Cantor the mind constitutes a city with particular biographical landmarks (REM: 250).

> The boulevards and offices below resembled a cross-section of the brain, a hemisphere of cerebral arteries and white matter rising to meet a concave turn of the Thames, a protective band of skull. Seen from a distance, millions of individual decisions appear to be the will of a single organism and in this a city resembles a brain. (REM: 124)

Just like the two houses of London are opposed, so are their according landscapes in Canary Wharf and Hackney with their according environment. Both London neighbourhoods speak of two different states of the mind – enlightenment and atavism or intellectualism and hedonism – which turn out to be equally mentally determining.

> Only the pole star penetrated the ambient aura of the city. There was still no sign of sunrise. Perhaps it was the space distorting my sense of space but there seemed to be miles of concrete and weeds between the tower block and beyond. Like a dark patch on a brain scan, this expanse of shadowed concourse spoke of malignity, an inscrutable alien canker in an otherwise healthy organism. Ink spilt onto the map. (REM: 306-307)

Consequently, the urbanite in *The Red Men* is mentally determined and controlled by the city's institutions. The urban state of mind is fashioned after idiosyncratic ecological emplacement. In this sense, places and spaces of flow equally forge the contemporary mindscape.

8.1.4 Hypertrophic Structures of Mentality

Mentality and identity are both related to a dynamic notion of place. The interdependence of individuality and city has been connected to questions of physical, social and mental spatialities. This first sub-chapter on the urban "Idioscape" has analysed the analogy of city and citizen in regard to identity, body, and mind. In general, Postmodernism with its dynamics of globalisation and localisation creates new roles for cities themselves and alters their relation to other cities or the nation. Henceforth, the Postmetropolis poses new questions in regard to citizenship, identity, and individualism (cf. Prakash 2008: 4). The demand is, similarly to Raban's (1974: 230) call, to assess the "special relationship between the self and the city" in order to understand the nature of citizenship and thereby decipher an urban-specific thinking in regard to urban identity.

Concerning Londoners' idioscape, consequences of the urban space of flows and the recent understanding of identity as processual confirm former analytical evaluations on hybrid identity. Moreover, deviant, liminal, and dynamic identity positions were exposed, whereby essentialist conceptions have become obsolete. Actually, a significant threshold existence appears prevalent in the urban realm that first of all demands a reinterpretation of urban role-play. This phenomenon affirms the suggestion that role-play serves a sort of relocation of identity. However, the results of this chapter severely oppose Deny's persistent view (2009: 279) that the multiple urban roles lead to the subjects' alienation because this postmodern urban practice is misunderstood as inauthentic. On the contrary, the analysis of Tim Lott's *White City Blue*, Blake Morrison's *South of the River* and Toby Litt's *Corpsing* has exemplified that the contemporary metropolis offers a particular set of available roles that serve as a paradigmatic cluster of urban patterns to relocate or restructure the Self in the space of flows.

The spectacle has always been an intrinsic element of an urban way of life and must be regarded as forming urban-generic structures of mentality in regard to the functionally related individual. Already Mumford (1997: 268) emphasises that the urban systematised, standardised and commercialised spectacle counters feelings of individual dislocation and offers a forum for identity formation in the "*residual* sociality of the metropolitan crowd". Thus, on the one hand, an overabundance of role-play which makes it impossible to distinguish between original and copy, authenticity and imitation emphasises the ontological insecurity of the postmodern urbanite, while on the other hand, it can also be interpreted as a further anonymisation, individualisation and atomisation of contemporary urban life. Spectaclisation, simulation, surveillance and the mutivalency of the urban realm still "invoke[...] schizophrenia that many others identify as a general characteristic of the postmodern mind-set" (Harvey 1990: 83). The results cast schizophrenia as a state of transience, despite its capacity for deathly confrontation with the urban realm.

Especially the last aspect of "Identityscape" has brought to the fore that apparent forms of identity crisis in apathic characteristics such dislocation, emptiness, duplication, schizophrenia, paranoia, etc. are transitional dispositions of feeling. The crisis of identity in *Brick Lane* arises from cultural displacement and failed re-rooting in a new urban context. Insofar, one cannot argue that contemporary urban subjects are totally lost in the Postmetropolis or even condemned to mental regression. Rather, the novels under analysis explicate how urban apathy indeed presents a temporary psychotic lack, indecision and paralysis of adaptation or acculturation. This phenomenon becomes especially pronounced firstly in individuals that are newcomers to the metropolis and secondly in the identityscape of an urban society that is caught in a new transitional phase of space-time-compression. The urbanite's defence mechanism against the overabundance of environmental changes is particularly characterised by an enhanced self-referentiality.

The sub-chapter on "Bodyscape" has shown a revival of analogised corporeal and urban spaces. Contemporary London novels, however, go beyond the notion of material, physical and psychological fragmentation and disintegration but rather devise the urban body of the city and the citizen as ruled by neurasthenic dynamism in the sense that each one is the hypertrophy, extension, prostheses, or simulation of the (unhomely) Other by marking both as grotesque in their habitus. This exaggerated corporeality is not only depicted in various forms of technological and biological metamorphosis but often the space of flows and the fluid identity positions find expression in different kinds of bodily excess. The tumorous expansion of the urban as great wen has already been an image of the modern metropolis. Hence, after a period of technological imagery and intellectual rhetoric, the urban has regained its mutational organicity.

In reference to Baudrillard's (1997: 101-102) notion that cancer is the illness *per se* of the capitalist age and that urban masses are considered as cancerous metastases outside social organicity, the Postmetropolis especially inherits the dynamic excess of the body in grotesque figurations. Although this idea borders on urban estrangement and alienation, it is also an attempt to master the city's unhomely exaggeration by obsessive individual projection, incorporation, and unusual personal means of homing. Hence, the grotesque body in reference to Bakhtin celebrates urban life on the threshold of death and resurrection and therefore constitutes a significant sign of contemporary urban vigilance, social change and cultural catharsis and consequently becomes an emblem of the metropolis in a transitional phase of reidentification. This specifically concerns urban individuals whose boundless bodies resemble the physical evidence for an emergent "outillage renouvelé" (Febvre 2003b: 166).

Conversely, "Mindscape" has shown in regard to the mental state that the urban seems to overwhelm the individual and prevail over the urbanite by its intrinsic space-time parameters of persistence. In accordance with Simmel's notion of metropolitan overabundance, the single urbanite indeed merely represents a speck of dust. Consequently, the city generally marginalises the individual to an ephemeral phenomenon. The postmetropolitan processes of homogenisation, spectaclisation and simulation appear to exert a new form of socio-darwinist selection and mind control. Moreover, urban citizens become aware of their unconscious as connected to a larger collective nonconscious which in contrast to modernist assumptions appears to decry the loss of individualisation. Hence, as was shown, the hypertrophy of objective culture has resulted in a hypertrophy of the Self in the sense of a newly developed defence mechanism of the urbanite. Insofar, one can agree with postmodern urbanologists who detect a new form of narcissism in contemporary constructions of identity. The individual perpetually and obsessively endeavours to discover the Self – both in the internal spaces of the mind, especially the illimitable levels of the unconscious, and in the external infinite collective consciousness of the metropolis. In a sense, the overwhelming metropolis is countered by an overabundance of the urban Self.

All in all, the interpretation of contemporary London fiction contradicts the notion that the Postmetropolis leads to disintegration and a loss of the Self. Rather, the transitional phase on the threshold of the new millennium is characterised by the exploration of new levels of identity-formation and a relocation of the individual. If at all, the novels present a certain loss of individuality in the sense that mediatisation and simulation create a new level of common consciousness, as apparent for example in renewed forms of mass movements. In contrast to common assumptions of postmodern disorientation and alienation, the analysis detects a decisive self-hyperbolisation of the individual as the dominant technique of cultural guidance. Thus, the metropolis still caters to its role as a workshop of civilisation and laboratory of society. Far from a generalised suicidal death, the postmodern city and its denizens thrive in a newly discovered vigilance of self-definition and re-identification as a localised space of flows with fluid urbanite identities specifically in distinction to the nation state and global processes of homogenisation.

8.2 The Urban State of Mind

Wir sind verunsichert bis ins Mark.
(McEwan cit. in Hage & Matussek 2005b: 112)

Modern urban sociologists assess socio-psychological and emotional conditions created in a metropolitan environment. Not only do they recognise the urbanite as a rational individual whose dominating intellect leads to a matter-of-fact attitude, but they also note fatality, nervousness, alertness, and anxiety in the city-dweller. According to the concept of overload, urban mental life is influenced by overstimulation and excitement which stir the nervous system and brings about either animation and vigilance or distanciation and apathy. While adaptive responses to the overload effect protect the urban Self from potentially destructive stimuli, these defence mechanisms simultaneously lead to an estrangement of the individual from his social environment. Moreover, not offering habitual centres for urban orientation, the postmodern Exopolis is seen to be devoid of doxic certainties. For Olalquiaga (1992: 2), the post-Fordist cityscape promotes personal alienation and disintegration because it enables an "ubiquitous feeling of being in all places while not really being anywhere". The Postmetropolis with its diffused non-places, homogeneous spectaclisation and hyperreal simulation especially enhances modernist notions of disorientation.

Contemporary London novels are in general focused on the characters' struggles against psychological deprivation resulting from the postmodern overload scenario of urban-specific oversaturation and estrangement. As was shown before, most characters feel alienated until they achieve to make the city their own, for example by idio-mapping. At the same time, this mental process of rendering the city legible, especially by multiple acts of imagination, reinvents the metropolis on a personal level and adapts urban space to the particularities and demands of the idioscape. Hence, the voids indicated in the fragmented view of urbanites are filled by the imaginary in order to produce a sense of urban cohesion and unify metropolitan contradictions. The individual's frame of mind is thereby influenced by visions of both the unknown and the familiar. In this respect, urbanites' psychology is as much influenced by the present reality as well as by the absences covered through representations. Indeed, the previous chapters have shown that urban characters tend to rely on mediatised images, particularly from film and television. Oftentimes, these convey a rather negative sense of the urban and enhance anxieties of fatal urban disasters, collapse and apocalypse, which in turn notably determine urbanites' dispositions of feeling.

The following sub-chapters will extrapolate the urban stimuli that influence the contemporary urban state of mind and investigate the consequent psychological responses. The first sub-chapter on "Simulated Anxiousness" concentrates on a common trope of London literature – "attraction of repulsion" (Jukes 1990: 10) – which eventually exposes urbanites' mental state as persistently influenced by performances of criminality and horror. In the era of real and imagined dangers of terrorism, the paradoxical state of expecting violent attacks without warning particularly dominates urbanites' structures of feeling. The part on "The Spectres of Terrorism" hence takes into view the prevalent presence of anxiety emplaced in London's Underground. Feelings of terror are especially underlined in contemporary London novels that deal directly with the aftermath of 9/11 and the ensuing 7/7. This sense of terror also becomes particularly pronounced in postmodern visions of millennial apocalypse under analysis in the last sub-chapter.

8.2.1 Simulated Anxiousness

Postmodern Attraction of Repulsion

The city constitutes a real "zone of attraction" (Rossiaud 1990: 145) which exerts a magnetic power over people who want to flee rural destitution. Especially the urban realm serves as a node that unleashes an array of desires and lures with manifold opportunities: economic independence, personal emancipation etc. In this respect, immigrants, valued both as necessity and danger to a balanced metropolis, have traditionally outnumbered the 'original' city population. Otherwise, urbanites shift out of the metropolis to make room for newcomers. According to Porter (2000: 454), a 1991 survey revealed that forty-eight percent of London's population wished to leave the metropolis. In that year only 250,000 moved to the city, while 350,000 left the metropolis (*ibid.*: 469). Nearly half of the people emigrating from Britain are actually from London, with the U.S. as their preferred destination. Hence, besides a place of settlement, this process defines the city as a significant node of migration and hub of transit(ion).

In regard to mental transformation, Rossiaud (1990: 141) points out that the city displays two different time-spans of urban-generic mentality: the brief moment of "painful apprenticeship" and the long-term phase of essential socialisation. Acculturation demands a high degree of flexibility from the newcomer. As described by Mitscherlich, neurosis then constitutes a sign of failed integration. Conversely, in due course, the learned mechanisms of protection against urban overload can result in overtly negative fervours, of which hate constitutes the last vital reaction (cf. Baudrillard 2000: 135; Deny 2009: 69). Thus, initial attraction turns into repulsion, desires are refused on the grounds of disgust. Eventually, this might lead to return migration or further transnational migration.

Most often, urbanites are, however, caught in an ambiguous emotional relation with the city as defined by urban-generic ambivalences: "One loves and hates its hectic pace, its noise, its penetrating smell, its chaotic plurality of cultures. If one lives there, one wants to leave, if one has left, one wants to return." (Zijderveld 1998: 1) Since Dickens, this ambivalent urban feeling of love/hate for the city as 'attraction of repulsion' has become a defining trope in urban fiction, especially in London literature. In an interview, the author Conrad Williams claims that the protagonist's feelings in *London Revenant* indeed mirror his own schizoid attitude towards the metropolis:

> I've lived in London since 1994 [. . .] and whenever I leave I feel happy and when I come back I feel bad, but once I've been here for a while, I love the place. [. . .] No city I've ever been to lifts the hair on the back of my neck as much as London when I see it from Waterloo Bridge. It's a stunning place, but it's also incredibly insular. [. . .] I love the tube, its history. [. . .] I hate how shit it is. How hot in the summer. How dirty. (Cit. in VanderMeer 2006)

Although the characters are overwhelmed by the infinite nature of the city, fascinated as well as repelled by its vitality and vulgarity, their verdict on city-life is mostly a favourable one and an absolute rejection is rarely expressed. In the corpus of twenty London novels with a myriad of characters, the prevalent decision, if it comes up, is in favour of the city. All in all, there are only a few prominent exceptions: in Monica Ali's *Brick Lane*, the male characters return to Bangladesh confused by London's urban-specific conditions, while the protagonist Nazneen makes a conscious decision for a future life in London. The Australian-born Danny in Nicholas Royle's *The Matter of the Heart* returns to his mother country because he feels haunted by the personal and collective ghosts of the old St George's hospital. In Blake Morisson's *South of the River*, three of the characters, most notably the cosmopolitan migrant figures Libby and Harry, move on to America, while for the younger Anthea London constitutes a mere point of transit to another one of her personal roles. Also Henry Perowne's son Theo in Ian McEwan's *Saturday* is about to exchange his London home for the promises of the New York stage, while his daughter Daisy already lives in Continental Europe. Another decision to leave the metropolis is pursued by the protagonist of Matthew de Abaitua's *The Red Men*. In order to overcome the traumatic experiences of monadic London, Nelson and his young family settle on the south west coast of Ireland. De Abaitua comments that Londoners' constant self-assessment whether they should be living in the city is part of the urban experience, particular in times of personal biographical transformation (cf. Jordison 2007). Instead, the cosmopolitan *per se* Raymond masters his addiction to London, but likewise remains unmoved by the promises and beauties of the countryside. The character explains his attitude by ironically adhering to the idea of an urban-generic Jewish mentality (REM: 376).

The mobility and choice of these characters stands in stark contrast to London's pariah, which are imprisoned in the inner city. Tek, one of the homeless characters in Christine Brooke-Rose's novel *Next* (1998), is unable to leave London for Manchester: "I couldn't draw benefits up there, seems it's all localised. No freedom of movement for vagrants isn't it odd. Like immigrants. In the global economy money is free to move but not people." (NXT: 122) Although the opportunities to depart from the city are represented as limited, none of the characters explicitly condemns the metropolis, but they rather strive for urban reintegration. Despite taking into view the anomic tendencies of the Postmetropolis, the novel nevertheless shows the denizens' contempt for being caught in a net of attractions. Adelina's son Joaquim, a London-born second-generation immigrant, particularly voices his juvenile contempt for his parents and his social surroundings when he calls London a "Stinkin city" (NXT: 43). Similarly, a homeless character selling the *Big Issue* in Conrad Williams' *London Revenant* (2004) comments: "I'm right pissed off. I think someone should just take this city and just ... just flush it down the fuckin' toilet." (LOR: 226) Despite the city's ugliness and haunting appearance, the protagonist Adam is still attracted to London's diverse and magical beauty:

> I loved the city. I loved the way it could surprise me. [...] I loved the eccentrics and the rare, visceral promise of danger. I loved coming back from a long journey and seeing its ghostly towers become solid in the skyline. I didn't love it unconditionally. Sometimes it tried my patience; its traffic, its arrogant or diffident citizens, its stink and clutter. But then there'd come a day when I'd pull back the curtains to see an odd light spilling out of the clouds and into the city's heart, making everything fresh, innocent and welcoming. (LOR: 189)

As was shown before, this attraction of repulsion is expressed in *London Revenant* by a consistent imagery of the aesthetics of the ugly. London's psychogeographers only retrieve the city's demands of vigilance when they open their eyes to the metropolitan sublime. Adam turns his back on aboveground London, but merely enters the subterranean city of Beneothan. Only the Pusher's victims, because of the traumatic confrontation with death, leave the city in order to alter their lives; they find refuge in rural landscapes of Ireland or the Scottish Highlands (LOR: 309). Generally, it seems as if the rural and natural areas of Britain largely serve as a temporal cathartic retreat for urbanites. In Blake Morisson's *South of the River* Anthea, like a Romanticist, opts to go hiking in the Lake District as a time-out. In J.G. Ballard's *Millennium People* the middle-class of Chelsea Marina flees its self-ignited local apocalypse to cottages in the Cotswolds or the roads through the Scottish Highlands. In Nick Hornby's *A Long Way Down*, the holiday on the Canary Islands ultimately saves the suicides from death. Hence, even these intermittent escapes from the city are semantisised as a sign of failure to master the urban and as lack of distanciation rather than as a pastoral idyllisation and anti-urban horror vision of the metropolis.

In this respect, the city's attraction for newcomers seems to loom larger than its fabric repulses metropolitan emigrants. Additionally, despite the anomic tendencies of the city, the résumé on vigilant London is predominantly positive. In Jane Stevenson's *London Bridges* the Australian Jeanene is attracted to London for its educational possibilities. Although first suffused with loneliness, she is invited by metropolitan heterogeneous interrelations to spin a successful net of social acquaintances over the metropolis. Consequently, she "began to feel London was a friendlier place" (LBR: 166). Insofar, Phillips (2006: 159) points out that only if the inhabitants of the city in flux fail to reformulate community, "the city becomes a space of confused identifications or, at worst, terror."

Also the female protagonist Judy in Geoff Nicholson's *Bleeding London* is presented as "an enthusiast for London, its people and its history" (BLL: 124). For her the city offers a space of illimitable opportunities which "may bring you the very thing you need" (BLL: 270). Other Londoners claim that they only stay in the capital out of pure material necessity (BLL: 47, 103, 169). Indeed, Judy unmasks this negative surface attitude as a customary defence and a typical attitude for a city-dweller's mindset:

> At some point [...] he launched into a speech about the horrors and problems of living in London, about how he wanted to live in the country full time, preferably by the sea, but alas his job kept him in the big smoke, close to his media contacts and connections. He complained about pollution and crime and noise and expense. He may have meant it, but it still sounded like a speech, like something learned and recited rather than something felt. (BLL: 185)

Similar to Judy, Stuart "had [...] always been a great fan of London, had always gained energy from the city" (BLL: 33) which in times of urban loneliness "supported him, engaged him and kept him company" (BLL: 70). For Stuart, born in Colchester, London presented a powerful lure, as for all who want "to break the mould of claustrophobic provincialism" (White 2003: 6) and "[a]s a student in London, the city had drawn him in like a benign spider's web" (BLL: 70). The most effective mental transformation – paradoxically from a newcomer's experience of repulsion to a citizen's mind state of attraction – occurs in the Sheffielder Mick. When he first arrives in London, the character is habitually disgusted by the city's "thick traffic, the motorbikes weaving in and out, [...] the blurred air, the people hurrying along the pavements" (BLL: 17). He truly despises the capital and distrusts its inhabitants (BLL: 19, 23, 118). In due course, however, it becomes less credible that Mick is indeed repelled by the metropolis (BLL: 58, 122, 180). Rather, it seems as if he only upholds the conviction of London's horrors so as not to fall for its sublime beauty and overload of attraction (BLL: 54). Finally, seduced by Judy as the epitome of the city's embodiment, Mick recognises that the attractions of the city outweigh everything else. He summarises London's lure from a curiously gendered perspective:

> [W]hen I first came here I hated London and I hated the people who lived here; too soft, too rich, too southern. But lately it's not been that straightforward. For instance, I like cars, I find them interesting, and London's full of interesting cars. [...] And women too. You see more beautiful woman in London than you'd ever see anywhere else in England. [...] It's funny but I suppose I've started to like this place. London. I like the money and the variety and the river and the desirable properties. I like the pubs and the people and the restaurants. [...] I want to join in with it. [...] [N]ow I'm here I don't really want to go back to Sheffield. (BLL: 263-264)

Earlier in a conversation, Mick already philosophises about the meaning of the song's lyrics – "Maybe it's because I'm a Londoner that I love London town" (BLL: 110); he thinks it is ridiculous just to love a city because you happen to inhabit it. But Peter Ackroyd (2001: 701) argues that "you can only be happy in London if you begin to consider yourself a Londoner. It is the secret of successful assimilation." In the end, Mick proves the song's verity in *vice versa* as it is the attraction of the metropolis that makes him a citizen of London.

For the physician Henry Perowne in Ian McEwan's *Saturday* (2005) "the city is a success, a brilliant invention, a biological masterpiece" (SAT: 5). In this brief epiphanic moment of elation he feels pure admiration for the perfection of the city (cf. Groes 2009: 108). In his routinised scientific manner Perowne refers his urban euphoria to another form of intra-cellular event. But despite the glimpse of threat to the city as a man of science he can only consider London a "grand achievement of the living and all the dead who've ever lived here" (SAT: 77). In its civilisatory potential of technological innovations and social vigilance, he registers the underlying principle for the constant betterment of living conditions for most people – "despite the junkies and beggars" (SAT: 77). Hence the city in its literary opposition of New Jerusalem and Babylon is still caught between progress and decline, success and failure, utopia and dystopia, rebirth and apocalypse, or emotional triggers of attraction and repulsion. In his deliberations on contemporary urban life, Perowne also casts his thought on the pastoral future of London, where individuals of new civilisations will look upon the ruins of London and consider its former inhabitants god-like creatures living in an age of "wondrous machines" (SAT: 77). Despite this irrefutable danger of atrophy the characters struggle for urban vigilance rather than leave the city behind.

Consequently, in regard to the traditional urban trope of attraction of repulsion, contemporary London novels seem to have overcome the images of an encompassing urban downfall so prominent during Thatcherism or in the beginning of the 1990s. Although characters traverse an urban space-time compression that triggers emotional and intellectual repulsion, the urban disposition of feeling in general seems rather oriented towards an uncanny attraction, towards the stimuli of the unknowable, the strange, the diverse, and even the grotesque. The conclusion of the novels, as already indicated in the last chapter, does not so much convince regarding the problems of spatial and social disenfranchisement. Rather, the texts display a common fascination with the perpetual transformation of the urban between illimitable vigilance and idiosyncratic fatal disillusionment.

Everyday Horrors and Urban Crime

Urbanologists instead see the city in a crisis initiated by its size, density, and heterogeneity. Regarding the urban after-effect, Park (1967: 22) comments that "the vast casual and mobile aggregations which constitute our urban populations are in a state of perpetual agitation, swept by every new wind of doctrine, subject to constant alarms, and in consequence the community is in a chronic condition of crisis." The analysis has predominantly emphasised a decisive confident and constructive urban imagery – for example in regard to the city's hybridity, urban vigilance, or attraction towards the metropolis – and in accordance with urban-generic ambivalences the interpretation of contemporary London novels has also repeatedly exposed the representations of urban anxieties. These are various in kind – in their cause, their level of fear, and their (in)visible effect on urbanites' idioscape. Due to the everyday exposure to urban stimuli, protagonists often feel threatened by an unnamed evil which relegates their way of thinking and thereby also the dispositions of acting. Because of distanciation and the constant confrontation with the uncanny, characters' mental freedom is not only limited but characterised by an idiosyncratic expectation of mental fear and horror. One persistent anxiety of citizens is the fear of falling prey to urban crime.

Although, according to Fischer (1984: 108), there is no general correlation between urbanism and violent crime, urban criminality is nevertheless of a unique quality – not least because the varieties of exerting, enacting, performing and mediatising violence are more visible on a daily basis. It is therefore not necessarily the simple fact of crime as such that influences mental dispositions, but fear and anxiety fostered by unexplained and unforeseen violence and criminality (cf. *ibid.*: 101-109). Insofar, Fischer (*ibid.*: 109) argues that "[s]ome signs indicate that fear of crime takes a psychological toll on urbanites and that it poisons the public atmosphere of city life, making people less trustful of and helpful toward their fellow citizens who are strangers." This fear of the culturally unfamiliar does not only promote xenophobia, national prejudices or racism, but is itself transformed into an undifferentiated expectation of danger.

All these conditions of metropolitan anomie are taken to necessitate a professional form of social control and surveillance exerted on an everyday basis. For Sharon Zukin (1997: 2) this state of maximum metropolitan surveillance has already become a new source for contemporary urban culture in the sense that next to the aestheticism of diversity, the Postmetropolis also enforces a cultivation of fear in public and private spaces. She argues that "[o]ne of the most tangible threats to public culture comes from the politics of everyday fear. Physical assaults, random violence, hate crimes that target specific groups: the dangers of being in public spaces utterly destroy the principle of open access." (*Ibid.*: 38) In contemporary London the most visible manifestation of everyday fear are the approximately 150,000 cameras (cf. Abbas 2003: 131). In the course of a day, the average city-dweller can expect to be filmed up to three hundred times (*ibid.*). In this respect, the Orwellian panoptic society constitutes a large part of metropolitan reality diminishing urban freedom and promoting the ecology of fear.

Consequently, in regard to London mentality, we must consider the impact of a general atmosphere of common and staged criminality, violence, instability, and anxiety as part of the urban everyday culture which influences the social and psychological character of the urbanite. And although Black (2009: 388, 390) charts a rise of knife crime as well as robberies by 105 percent between 1991 and 2002, Mighall (2003: 372) rightly concludes that "London is a criminal city less by virtue of what occurs there, than by how it is perceived, represented and experienced. [...] It is an important ingredient in the idea of London, and informs our cultural maps of the capital in which we live today." This suggests the hypothesis that the imaginary city severely unsettles the urban state of mind of its inhabitants.

While Charles Dickens' police inspector Bucket in *Bleak House* can be assumed to be the first fictional London detective, at least since Arthur Conan Doyle's Sherlock Holmes stories (1887-1927), crime and detective fiction lie at the very heart of London literature.[11] Although this analysis does not include examples of contemporary London's crime and mystery series, such as those by Mark Billingham, Ken Bruen, Christopher Fowler, Barry Maitland, Anne Perry, Ruth Rendell/Barbara Vine, etc., three novels of the selected corpus can be classified as crime/detective fiction: Jane Stevenson's *London Bridges*, Toby Litt's *Corpsing* and Patrick Neate's *City of Tiny Lights*. However, urban crime is a theme of every contemporary London novel, be it domestic violence (NXT, SOR, UND, WIF), petty crime (CTL, BLL, LBR, LON, LWD, WCB), territorial fights (BRL, KRA, SAT), revolutionary destruction (KRA, MIP, REM), racial attacks (253, SOR, WIF), or murder (253, COR, CTL, KRA, LBR, LOR, MAH, NXT, UND, REM, SOR).

Often enough criminality in the city is seen as a public phenomenon and the private spaces are considered as secure abodes. However, for women and children the home can also represent a space of sexual abuse and violence. Especially Maggie Gee's novel *The White Family* takes into perspective the interrelations of domestic and public violence. In Tobias Hill's *Underground* the young homeless Alice flees from her sexually abusive father taking refuge in the tunnels of the London Tube. In *South of the River* by Blake Morrison the case of the murdered black boy Elroy takes into view various forms of violence against children – abuse, abduction, paedophilia – as well as domestic crime born of social destitution, broken families and racial or gendered prejudice. As the protagonist Harry points out, London is still inhabited by disastrous evils: "The beast of poverty. The beast of neglect. The beast of violence. The beast of ignorance." (SOR: 478) Everyday urban life south of the Thames is diffused with muggings, assaults, racial attacks and rapes (SOR: 56). From the typical rural point of view, the character Jack associates the capital London with "random violence" (SOR: 464) making him alert to the smallest oddities in public behaviour. For Park (1967: 24-25) the dissolution of moral order protected by anonymity can promote an enhancement of vice and crime.

---

11 | It is generally suggested that Charles Felix's London-set "Notting Hill Mystery" (1862-1863) is the first detective story.

In her analysis of the American city novel Gelfant (1954: 39) argues: "The fact that one can be anonymous in a great city helps explain easy indulgence in vice." And this phenomenon of mutually ignoring each other is further exploited to exemplify how easy a crime can go unnoticed in the city. In Geoff Nicholson's *Bleeding London* (1997) Mick on his *tour de revenge* through the city has no problem whatsoever to make his innocent victims pay for their supposedly committed rape. Londoners are not "concerned" and simply "ignore" what happens to Mick's first victim in the public of London Bridge (BLL: 55). Even in the Kensington enclave of Justin Carr people rather choose to ignore the shouting coming from his mews house (BLL: 110). Stuart comments on Londoners' non-involvement: "Everybody in earshot turned round, but it being London nobody did anything." (BLL: 239) He specifically reflects upon this characteristic trait of urbanity not to interfere in the private spheres of denizens despite registering that anomic incidences are taking place in the open and thus initially offer the possibility to get involved. Later on, Mick's fatigue of being a criminal whose violent actions have never intervened immediately changes his role and he becomes involved in protecting Stuart from a street-attack.

Also in Conrad Williams' *London Revenant*, Adam remembers a friend who sometimes wore obvious signs of domestic violence: "Everyone noticed but nobody said anything." (LOR: 216) Urban rules of non-involvement are a general prerequisite of metropolitan life even in everyday interrelations. In the novel, this idea of oversaturated anonymity is taken a step further: while walking through the streets of London, Adam and Yoyo see a man in a car wiping blood from his hands. While Adam is worried for a moment, Yoyo appears too inhibited to intervene and calms Adam down to follow the etiquette of urban ignorance and civil inattention, mentally substituting unpleasant thought with euphemistic interpretations: "Forget him. [...] It was probably just a nose bleed, or he was wanking too hard." (LOR: 97) Anonymity serves as a shield of protection not only for the one committing a crime but also for the ones who should have the courage to step in.

In Brooke-Rose's novel *Next* (1998), the murder of the West-Indian homeless girl Elsie presents another contemporary connotation of oversaturated loneliness leading to anomie (NXT: 152). Already triple marginalised through gender, ethnicity and social status the character's murder presentation in the media further reduces Elsie to a mere anonymous number in the statistics of urban criminality (NXT: 130). At her funeral there is only one person who knew her, emphasising the excess of urban isolationism: "Can't know everybody's life. It's hard enough to know even neighbours, or fellow rough-sleepers." (NXT: 33) Even as spatial closeness exists, unavoidable in the relatively small overly populated realm of the metropolis, relations could not be any more devoid of knowledge of the co-denizens. One member of the community wonders: "Why are we all so anxious for human contact then block it off somehow? Exactly as in society, but you'd think those glitzy habits wouldn't be carried through to the drop-outs and all that supposed solidarity." (NXT: 132) As already explored in the chapter on "Public and Private" in Christine Brooke-Rose's *Next*, the village-like thriving community of everyday neighbourhood activity has disappeared from the streets of London; Ulysses laments:

And look at the streets here. Children used to play in them, people used to trade, as they still do in African villages and Lagos ghettoes, women pounding yam, making and frying yams, washing clothes, selling peppers and kerosene and cigarettes and water. Shouting, hating, loving each other but at least not indifferent. (NXT: 52)

He observes how urban development has paradoxically inversed the intimacy of human street life: "Today I see people sleeping in the shop doorways of London and I wonder if this is a sort of progress." (BLL: 236)

In Jane Stevenson's *London Bridges* (2000), the isolation of the aged character Eugenides make him overtly vulnerable to the crudeness of the metropolis and he becomes an easy prey for murder by a corrupt metropolitan lawyer and his Greek associate (LBR: 74-75). As Edward cynically notes, there have always been "West End murders at East End prices" (LBR: 248).[12] In the public of the hospital the vicious lawyer gets rid of the evidence of poisoning his business partner Eugenides: "No one so much as raised their eyes from the contemplation of their private worries." (LBR: 81) When the classicist Sebastian feels guilty of having abandoned Eugenides to his solitariness and not having checked on him, a policeman excuses him by putting limited involvement down to general urban preoccupations: "I'm sure you did your best, sir. We're all busy these days." (LBR: 196)

Otherwise, the novel charts London characters absorbed by their own troubles making it easy for vigilant actions crossing the line of law and to go unnoticed in general (LBR: 256). In the worst criminal scenario of murder, Edward and Lamprini know themselves protected by their own usual anonymity and the old man's loneliness amidst the massively populated metropolis: "Even if we killed him, it wouldn't matter. Who's ever going to know?" (LBR: 6) Thus the urbanites' lamentation that "[p]eople destroy each other's lives every day in the City" (LBR: 286) gets a double meaning. Firstly, the City stands for the whole of London where lives are destroyed by the city's fabric in various forms and not only through murder. Secondly, people passively destroy others' existence by non-involvement and ignorance. As the city lacks the mechanical solidarity of the village, everyday forms of face-to-face security are lost. The Australian newcomer Jeanene feels confused after overhearing two clients in the anonymity of her pharmacy talk about murder. In contrast to common ignorance, she decides to share the incidences in anonymous public sphere (LBR: 7). Similarly, it is the characters' connectedness constructed by similar interests and common knowledge of the crime that enables them to solve the Eugenides murder case. In this sense, the metropolis provides social spaces and mental pre-requisites that counter tendencies of urban anomie.

Mumford (1997: 266) notes that social distanciation, disassociation, impersonality and anonymity encourage a-social and anti-social behaviour. The fear of the so-called criminal classes features its own personae such as racketeers, petty criminals, sadistic gangsters, bestial fascists, homicidal vigilantes and law-offending policemen who are via urban amusement intrinsically connected to the "respectable classes" (*ibid.*). Contemporary London novels do not locate crime solely in the notorious areas of the East

12 | The 'criminal East End' has become notorious through Jack the Ripper and the Kray brothers.

End or deprived council houses. Although socio-realist estate novels such as Diran Adebayo's *Some Kind of Black* (1996) or Courttia Newland's *The Scholar* (1997) take into view the petty and organised crime, Gautam Malkani's *Londonstani* (2006), Toby Litt's *Corpsing* (2000) and Patrick Neate's *City of Tiny Lights* (2005) elucidate crime that encompasses all classes and whose hub is particularly located in the centre of London's West End, Soho, Knightsbridge and South Kensington.

Set in the middle-class milieu of the predominantly South Asian community of West London, Gautam Malkani's *Londonstani* (2006) takes into view the tax scams of the parent generation, the rudeboys' petty crime of reprogramming phones, and Sanjay's major tax money laundry. Amit's father in making use of the gang's phone swapping is particularly interested in circumventing national VAT: "No use making taxman richer so he can give to bloody Somali asylum seekers." (LON: 41). The young men, ironically called the "Hounslow mafia" (LON: 118), are petty criminals who unblock mobile phones mainly for friends and family to be able to swap phones. Although it is an illegal business, it is also relatively safe because the police concentrate on the corner shops who offer the same service.

Coming into contact with Sanjay, the young men's illegal business gains in scale. The "straightlaced chap" (LON: 127) actually takes the rudeboys on to expand his own criminal dealings. From the first moment, Sanjay with his American gangster-style crib in Knightsbridge, flashy yellow Porsche, intimidating, gold-chain-wearing sidekick, and business partners from Uzbekistan, Saudi Arabia, and Turkmenistan with their beautiful daughters is represented as London's own Godfather with a "Bombay-baddie laugh" (LON: 297; LON 144-151). The former Oxbridge graduate has perfected the parent generation's dislike for tax money and the boys' illegal phone business; Sanjay is involved in a so-called "carousel fraud" (LON: 302) in which phoney VAT rebates are achieved by fictional transactions between dummy companies around the European Union. Creating the impression of dealing with stolen phones is a mere decoy for the bigger business (LON: 300-302). Besides making his flat a literary informational hub of crime, it also stresses, as shown before, how even criminality is based on ready-made expectations of performativity, pretence and role-play.

This is particularly pronounced in Toby Litt's *Corpsing* (2000). Crime, as mirrored in Lily's staged suicide, the Macbeth performance, or the protagonist's detective methods, in the postmodern city has become such an intrinsic part of the urban imaginary that real criminal behaviour is hardly distinguishable from staged elements. Again and again, Londoners' voyeurism in regard to violence and crime is emphasised. The boyfriend of one of the minor characters becomes so obsessed with the shooting of Conrad and Lily that he collects newspaper cuttings in a fit of "cruel voyeurism" (COR: 84). People even book the same table the couple sat at and order the same menu to make it their personal crime night out (COR: 111). While Alan and Dorothy Grey take their ideas for the Macbeth performance from a former armed robber, the criminal himself has become a performance star with his comedy show *Criminally Funny* "actually playing an ironic replica version of himself." (COR: 175) As the protagonist Conrad comments, he is the only "real" criminal known by every Londoner apart from the pimps and coke dealers (COR: 176). In his private eye detection, Conrad inverses the role by scripting his own thriller that leads him on a hunt through London's criminal underground encompassing dingy pubs in Brixton to score dope, breaking into Alun and Dorothy's home in Belize

Park, visiting pubs in Clapham and Bermondsey to collect a gun, being chased around London's East End by cars, staging an abduction and a shooting. Although he feels that the closer he gets to danger – bricks being thrown and his house being torched – the closer he gets to the truth of Lily's murder, the self-pronounced outlaw with a mission and "art terrorist/theorist" (COR: 307) is all the time shadowed by both the police and criminal London. What is more, the urban crime script dissolves the boundaries between victim and perpetrator, police and detective, good and bad. For example, the hitman, shortly after shooting Lily and Conrad, forgets all about the homicide because he chases after the thief who stole his bike (COR: 31), thereby immediately changing the role he plays from perpetrator to victim. In the urban realm, crime is represented as another kind of hunger for spectaclisation which has become devoid of its genuine characteristics and meaning. Insofar, the characters in *Corpsing* are presented as blunting their anxiety of crime with further images of violence. Thereby, in significantly incorporating urban anomie, urbanites level their inhibition towards anomic behaviour.

Patrick Neate's *City of Tiny Lights* (2005) features an Asian-English private detective which positions the novel within Black British crime writing such as Mike Phillips' Samson Dean novels *Blood Rights* (1989), *The Late Candidate* (1990), *Point of Darkness* (1994), *An Image to Die For* (1995), or Diran Adebayo's *My Once Upon a Time* (2000).[13] However, it represents more an American hard-boiled detective story than one about an English gentleman detective (cf. Rosenberg 2008: 355). This might also explain why the novel was not as well received in Britain, but fared better in America where it was shortlisted for the Edgar-Mystery Writers of America Award and the *L.A. Times* Award. The ex-mujahedeen, Marlowe wannabe and brother of an ex-London gangster, Tommy Akhtar, rather than a sophisticated gentleman mimes the smelly Scotch-drinking and Benny-smoking lout. Approached by the prostitute Melody Chase to find her companion, Tommy detects the dead body of a member of parliament murdered in a South London hotel and is subsequently drawn into the underbelly of London's cultural mix with all its complacencies and intolerances and comes under the close attention of the MI5 who initiate and simulate a terrorist attack on the London Underground.

But Tommy's investigations lead him not only into the low-life of basement clubs, back-alleys, and industrial wastelands, but into the most fashionable places of London's high-end lifestyle, such as a bar off Shepherd's Market,

> the kind of high-class hangout where you always find the real lowlife. Media bum bandits, minor celebs and Arabs who pissed oil hung out there in gaggles and cliques. They drank non-vintage Moët at a ton-fifty a bottle and pretended not to notice let alone recognize each other. It had a cockey reputation too. You sat in the bog too long and your arse got high. (CTL: 10)

13 | Although in general the hard-boiled detective is a white male, lately Walter Mosley's series of had-boiled novels set in L.A. feature the African-American Easy Rawlins in L.A. (1990-2007) (cf. Highmore 2005: 97). That the black private eye or detective is a relatively new phenomenon in Britain is shown in the hype caused by the media in the TV mini-series *Moses Jones* (2009) or the TV-series *Luther* (2010-2013), whereas in American fiction the black detective has been marketable latest since *Shaft* (1971) and *Miami Vice* (1984-1989).

Particularly South Kensington, the initial home of his escort client Melody, is defined by the protagonist as the hub of criminal London:

> South Ken is a strange neck of the wood as it goes. I don't reckon one Londoner lives there. There are cheap and not so cheap hotels filled with Russian Mafiosi, African dictators, Indian arms-dealers and other similarly lovely clientele. There's Arab money that's followed the original Arab money that first heard in the seventies that this was where the money lived. There are language schools for priapic Mediterranean boys with too much confidence and Dutch girls too suss to fall for it. There's the occasional aristocratic shire widow who knows she's out of time. And there are hookers, of course, in sparsely furnished one- or two-bedroom joints with mini-fridges and DVD players churning out 24/7 porn. Some of them may be Londoners. But they're unlikely to live in the area. (CTL: 70)

As such, the novel encompasses the whole low-life of the city from dealers and users, prostitutes and pimps, police officers and local thugs, MPs, MI5 agents, and international terrorists. In a sense, the murky London water resembles an apt metaphor for urban crime life: "The water had that vague but unmistakable smell of sewage [...]. This city: endless cycles of swallow, piss and chemical purification." (CTL: 107) For Rosenberg (2008: 356), *City of Tiny Lights* thereby presents crime as a socio-political question highlighting "the reality of violence and the vulnerability of society" which is embedded in larger national and international issues. As a central node, London's Informational City also becomes the hub of a newly mobile sense of criminality.

All in all, the analysis has shown that while the ultimate judgement of the contemporary city is by and large a positive one, fears of everyday horrors and urban crime still loom high in urbanites' minds. However, the interpretation has exposed that this is predominantly a mental fear because although anonymity might encourage criminality, urban denizens in a sense overstimulate their dispositions of anxiety by exhibiting a certain hunger for violent voyeurism and the spectaclisation of crime. The imaginary metropolis created therein then dominates urban-specific thinking.

8.2.2 The Spectres of Terror

A pronounced anxiety haunting the metropolis is constituted by the urban spectres of terror. First, as variously shown, postmodern architecture renders the city a topography of totalitarian repulsion exerting terror, discomfort and fear. Moreover, scepticism and suspicion towards the unknown, unfamiliar, and uncanny construct dispositions of paranoia. And last but not least, crime and violent attacks in the metropolitan realm enhance the general atmosphere thick with terror. In the following I will first analyse the atmosphere of terror and the location of paranoia in London's Underground and second I will look at contemporary London novels related to the terrorist attacks of 9/11 and 7/7.

Underground Terror

The chapter on "Underground London" has already deciphered the subterranean structures of mentality triggered by its physical, social, and mental spaces particularly in regard to the uncanny atmosphere which induces uncertainty and anxiety. For Smith (2005: 20), the London underground is "the repository of what's precious to us, and also what we fear and abhor", and according to Pike (2005a: 3) the three spatial types of the nineteenth-century underground – railway, catacomb, necropolis – "attracted a specific form of underground reverie and fear." Especially the Tube spurred fears of contamination by the mingling of the classes and the disappearance of clear demarcations between haves and have-nots, morality and immorality, dominators and suppressed (cf. Pike 1999: 111). Although with the Blitz the Tube was connected to an image of toughness, improvisation, and invincibility, dispositions of feeling are still rather informed by notions of bunker mentality or claustrophobia exerting spleen.

Two tragedies on the Underground loom specifically large in the collective consciousness of Londoners and have initiated a subterranean mentality that persistently deals with the potential of catastrophe: on 28 February 1975 a Northern Line train ran into a concrete wall at Moorgate station killing forty-three and injuring seventy and the King's Cross fire disaster on 18 November 1987 killed thirty-one commuters (cf. Halliday 2001: 189, 194; Ross 2002: 87; Wolmar 2004: 306; Smith 2005: 6). Thus, even before the London bombings of 7 July 2005 which killed thirty-eight people in three targeted trains of the Piccadilly and the Circle Line, the Underground had gained an omnipresence in Londoners' minds as a place of danger. Since the Fenian bomb attacks, the London Underground has repeatedly been privy to threats, such as by the IRA. Until today, the vulnerability of the metropolis in its subterranean city is underlined by the presence of anti-terror units patrolling London's main arteries of transportation. Stephen Smith (2005: xii) summarised this state of mind as follows: "We are trying to get used to the unwelcome idea that the Tube is a terrorist target". All in all, London Underground creates a particular ecology of terror which strongly influences the psychology of its passengers and demands personal protective mechanisms.

Experiencing the London Underground as a place suffused with grime and noise while the Gothic and uncanny atmosphere of the dark city below only increases feelings of anxiety, Smith (*ibid.*: 6) confesses that his discman is the only useful prophylactic device against all kinds of Tube terrors: "The underground – specifically, the Underground made me short of breath with anxiety. [...]. I would do anything to avoid making a journey under the city. [...] The sight of a crowded platform was enough to send me heading for the door." (*Ibid.*: 5) In the novel *London Bridges* (2000) by Jane Stevenson, Australian Jeanene after having reached the surface is overcome by a "retrospective panic [of] just how far underground she had been" (LBR: 136). This mental reconsideration is strongly induced because the subterranean superficial light as such afforded to the passengers is so bright that it removes all sense of travelling underground (cf. Mayhew 2003: 27).

Mick in Geoff Nicholson's *Bleeding London* (1997) does not see the Tube as a comfortable option as a means of transportation, because his "knowledge of the system was patchy" and all his former experiences had been "profound and bad" (BLL: 88). The claustrophobic space of the Tube as a heterotopia of extreme space-time compressions epitomises his feelings of terror:

> It had been a waking nightmare, everything he feared and despised all in one place; countless faceless people jammed into carriages in factory-farm conditions; people blocking your way, taking up too much room to let you get past, leaving their bags in the way. (BLL: 88-89)

This paranoia is enough to further trigger images of catastrophe: "The very idea of sending packed trains through the bowels of the earth, like turds through a vast, curving gut, appalled and frightened him. It would take so little for these tunnels to get blocked, for electricity to fail, for fire to start." (BLL: 89) Mick's imaginary dispositions uncannily predict the unleashing apocalypse of the King's Cross fire as "a bad dream he'd always been expecting to come true" (BLL: 89). The unknown realm of underground space makes the protagonist uneasy and triggers his imagination; the mental supposition of disaster enhances his claustrophobia. Mick's frightened anticipations of subterranean horrors also include bomb attacks and spree killers. Even Keith Lowe's protagonist in *Tunnel Vision*, the trainspotter Andy, wonders at one stage whether his companion Brian might be "an axe-murderer, a rapist, a religious freak, a mugger, a fraud" (TV: 290). Most of the synoptic London Underground novels (LOR, KRA, UND, 253, TUV) are thrillers with terror exercised and murder cases to be solved spreading a certain kind of underground terror.

Although with Geoff Ryman's *253* (1998) the Tube has so far been stressed as a coincidental place of contact, the unwilling interaction between commuters also reveals urbanites' fears of the Other and their distorted Selves. Actually, the train assembles seemingly dangerous and apparently criminal people. In car number two there is a nutter with a knife trying to kill his stepdaughter (253: 104, 345). Indeed, Phil Barker is a small villain (253: 28), while Ron Busby only looks like the East End gangster boss Ronnie Kray (253: 181), Pru Waverly heard a murder being planned (253: 225), and Paul Henry is the escaped victim of mass murderer Donald Nielson (253: 320). Some of the characters are painfully aware of the criminality throughout the city: Samantha Allers even lives next door to perpetrators (253: 96) and Miss Angela Dowd becomes the victim of a break-in, but is treated as a criminal herself by the police and consequently loses all sense of safety in public and private (253: 284). In its synthesis, the novel presents a summary of Londoners' psychological condition influenced by the dense atmosphere of the Underground where morality and immorality, mechanisms of law and order and crime are shown as mingling and representing idiosyncratic elements of London's heterogeneity.

Largely, the emotional state of mind of Tube commuters is presented as one of fear and horror. Professor Dionne Butler observes that the train is full of frightened people (253: 307); some of them are "frozen in horror" (253: 312) or feel "something akin to terror" (253: 326). Also, for example, May Hanmore

> lives in terror of crime. She is convinced that older women are the main target of hoodlums. [...] All the way home she is in a state, clutching her bag. She feels unsafe [...] She now fears for her job. Someone shouts nearby, men move suddenly. [...] May begins to shiver as if freezing cold. She cannot take this journey any more. She decides to quit her job. (253: 27)

In the urban environment ruled by indifference and non-involvement, "habitual isolation [...] breeds mistrust and cynicism" (253: 296) which becomes apparent in suspicion towards and fear of the urban stranger (253: 99, 183, 325). The stories told by her policeman father, for instance, make Miss Lorraine Hant "distrustful of black people, dance music, clubs" (253: 265). While some urbanites become downright paranoid with respect to their fellow citizens (253: 66, 240), others are internally eaten up by anger, hate and eruptions of unvented violence (253: 223, 227, 332). In order to keep this melting pot of emotions in check, the metropolis establishes particular grids of control and the previous analysis has already commented on the extent of totalitarian surveillance dealt with in the novel. Character 145 is astounded by London's preoccupation with security: "job security, locks, CCTV. [...] A visit to new Scotland Yard left him exhausted. A very pretty woman his own age simply switches channels from flyovers to alleyways, shopping centres, main streets." (253: 202) Total surveillance and the new technologies lead to a new paranoia and the fear of being watched.

Moreover, Genevieve Williams (2008: 261) comments in reference to Ryman's writing that heightened technological implications enforce a certain threat of a "loss of humanity". Finally, Ryman's text also suggests cultural anxieties grown from millennial discourses of the death of man, the end of history, and postmetropolitan apocalypse. In mirroring the Moorgate incident in the crash of the train and presaging the 7/7 terrorist attacks, the novel encompasses two extreme forms of urban catastrophe. Interesting and important to recall is also the established memorial imagery of the Holocaust (253: 248, 155, 64, 38) as a new imaginary foil for the unfolding relation between terrorism, apocalyptic visions, and anxieties in a postmodern *horror vacui* for which the uncanny underground is the epitome of expression.

Instead, the author China Miéville (2002: 75) in a more detached manner decries the reactions by British writers as unreasonable and inadequate:

I thought the mainstream artistic reaction to September 11 in Britain was shameful, we had a mass of newspapers printing 20-page special supplements, 'Fife Famous Writers Tell Us How They Feel After September the 11th... .' If you have an analysis, or you have some new facts, tell me, but don't tell me how you *feel*. It becomes a kind of pornography of mawkishness. [...] It's disaster porn. There's an element of relishing or fetishizing the disaster.

But although in an interview Miéville claims that he does not consider it necessary to integrate notions of terrorism in his work (cf. Marshall 2003), in his fantasy novel *King Rat* (1998) postmodern notions of repulsive cultural and architectural totalitarianism, genocide and subterranean terror are central elements of the text. One particular scene stands out: the assassin Pied the Piper, characterised as a sadomasochistic criminal, nastily kills one of the protagonist's friends in the ghost-station of Mornington Crescent. Kay, the victim, is suspended naked in "cruciform at the entrance to the tunnel, from where the trains emerged" (KRA: 171). This gory horror scene in the liminal space of the underground features a totalitarian's investigation of the helpless victim exerting unbelievable terror, fear, disbelief and shock (KRA: 174-180). In this sense, Miéville not only plays along the genre conventions of the London noir but also integrates a prevalent structure of feeling at the turn of the twenty-first century.

In opposition, Conrad Williams decisively comments on the urban-specific inventory of horror as determining his writing:

London tires you out. Getting anywhere takes time and effort. Travel in the city can be horrendous. People don't talk to each other. They avoid contact. I owned my flat for four years and didn't even see the people who lived in the flat next door to mine. There's a tension in you that you only notice when you get out of the place. Much of that barely reined-in panic is what I'm chasing whenever I write a London novel. The city has its own list of horrors that you have to address as a writer if you want to locate something there. It's unavoidable. (Cit. in McWilliam 2011)

London Revenant (2004) charts urban anxiety and subterranean terror. Already the novel's opening chapter is titled "Terrorism" (LOR: 17) and later a London paper "headline screams TUBE TERROR, and beneath: Cowardly Pusher Strikes Again – Police Vouch to Catch Killer Soon." (LOR: 88) The newspaper reports that an anonymous madman pushes people onto the tracks; this method of terror triggers Adam's personal interest and draws the protagonist into a dangerous private-eye investigation of the London Underground. In the novel, the atmosphere of the underground is envisioned as claustrophobic and alien (LOR: 26, 39, 81, 182). Although the protagonist has "never been afraid of the dark [he has] a problem with what might be hiding in it." (LOR: 74) Urban anxiety is a fear of and uneasiness about the unknown, especially underneath. Adam is constantly confused by the decay and unreality of his surroundings where he fears to lose his grip on reality and thereby lose himself (LOR: 154, 219). Moreover, he is totally "unnerved" (LOR: 161) by the Tube where he feels like he is loosing his shape and colour, seeing his personality dissolve. The terror of the underground is fathomed by the protagonist's uncertainty about the differences of dream and reality and the split in his personality. Schizophrenia and paranoia are presented as endemic states of the urban mind.

Uncertainty and nervousness of the subterranean city increase in the same way as "the Pusher" terrorises this space (LOR: 35-36). Blore's aspiration is to alert urbanites to the quiet dangers of the metropolis and "provide a wake-up call to the people who are letting their daily routine grind them into the dust of the Underworld." (Ashford 2008: 20) He is an obsessive serial killer striving for a better metropolis for London's inhabitants by spreading horror on the platforms of the Underground, although he sees his "acts of terrorism" (LOR: 38) as initial forces of liberation. Other than the decay of the physical city, relationships are deteriorating leading to a new age of urban isolationism which is represented as the real horrific atrocity of urban life (cf. VanderMeer 2006). Hence, Williams represents the characters of his novel as drenched in a collective emotion of anxiety expecting an urban disaster. Yoyo voices her fear of the future: "I'm scared of it. Scared of something that doesn't exist yet." (LOR: 107) This expectancy fear of urban catastrophe brooding over London is paradoxically resolved with the unexpected earthquake that destroys the metropolis and turns the lives of its inhabitants upside down.

As a consequence of the general urban state of mind – edgy, hunted, despaired – characters seek repercussion in routinised securities. Yoyo usually carries dummies of novels which serve as "comforters, her versions of a teddy bear, a favourite blanket, something to hold near to her while all the weirdness and terror howled around outside." (LOR: 107) The fake books become Yoyo's protective shield as they epitomise habitual knowledge of urban navigation. Similarly, after the London earthquake Adam observes how fast citizens "were clinging to their lives, their routines, a balm to protect them against the shattered city." (LOR: 292) Asked in 2006 whether terrorism had an effect on his writing, Conrad Williams distinguishes between literary "cartoon terrorism" and its contemporary ungraspable reality:

> Horror fiction has always been talked of as a way of coping with real atrocities, a safety valve where you can kick back and enjoy somebody's romp about lung-guzzling monsters on motorbikes because it's kind of cartoon terrorism. It might thrill you, disturb you, scare you but it's not real. It's comforting, in a way. 9/11 and 7/7 [...] gave me a jolt because it brought home how random death can be. [F]or me, it's almost too big a thing to work with. It overshadows everything.

In *London Revenant* the author captures the daily horrors of urban everyday life in the most mundane metropolitan spatialities and social relations in an atmosphere of overbearing uncertainty and anxiety.

Usually, in detective fiction the protagonist reveals the secret knowledge that dominates the narrative's mystery, suspense and eeriness. According to this literary tradition, Tommy Akhtar in Patrick Neate's *City of Tiny Lights* (2005) dissects the urban fabric of terror and brings to the fore the origins of the contemporary disturbed states of mind. The author considers it his personal 9/11 novel; published in 2005 the book depicts the geopolitical climate of the aftermath of the New York terrorist attacks and uncannily foretells the bombings of the London Underground (cf. Rosenberg 2008: 355; Topalova 2008: 405, 413). In the underbelly of contemporary multi-ethnic London and its cross-cultural urban life the private eye character Tommy, former mujahedeen fundamentalist and ex-terrorist, endeavours to prevent a series of coordinated bombings across South East London with fast-food chains, video shops, minimarts, and the Tube as targets (CTL: 292). First, it turns out that the terrorist recruiting network of the Post-Western Alliance (PWA) employs a "mixture of Islamist, anarchist, Communist, terrorist and Rastafarian" (CTL: 185) rhetoric to attract young kids and use them as mobile triggers to set off the bombs.

On the Piccadilly Line train between South Kensington and Gloucester Road only the detective's protective device of intellectual combination and logical conclusion deduces the threat they are under: "I felt like I was watching an alarm clock for the five minutes before it went off. [...] My alarm clock went off and I jerked awake and straight into a nightmare." (CTL: 283) But while Tommy is rendered inoperative by the special force already on the train, reluctant terrorist Av discovers new urban vigilance: "He sounded half cocky, half insane and half like he was trying to convince himself. If that's too many halves it's because Av was suddenly larger than life." (CTL: 287) As a mayhem of anxiety, "panic, anger, terror and prayer" (CTL: 288) breaks loose in the compartments, the boy keeps relatively cool. A modern street-smart urbanite, Av knows that because the bomb is connected to the mobile phone he has to move back in the train compartments which are still underground and thereby out of network coverage. The apparent suicide bomber becomes the saviour of Londoners on the train.

Besides this inverted image, the novel is overtly critical towards contemporary language and unquestioned everyday rhetoric enforcing a general atmosphere of prejudice and fear. Eye-witnesses on the train claim that Av was sending off prayers, but Tommy only remembers "hearing a lot of 'shits' and 'f__s'" (CTL: 286). While the MI5 classifies the PWA as Islamist fundamentalists, Tommy exposes the group's head Kevin Al-Dubayan as a more dangerous opportunist, nutter and "wife-beating, family-conning, kitchen-fitting, tom-punting fraud" (CTL: 185; 161-166, 177). Otherwise, Tommy's father Farzad devises his own lexicon of terror and criticises the manipulative misuse of the English language. In regard to the common use of "religious fundamentalism" he points out that fundamentalism is necessarily associated with religion, which renders the current use of the term tautological while the correct word would be "fanaticism" (CTL: 158-159). The same applies for "war on terror", a "contradiction in terms" (CTL: 159) because the term terror is removed from the law-abiding civilatory processes of war. Farzad moreover shows that the traditional ambivalence of the characterisations of terrorists and freedom fighters carries a racist undercurrent (CTL: 160; cf. Egbert 2009: 245). In the "journalistic mind" (CTL: 167) and the Western rhetoric when "something is undetectable [...] it becomes evidence of its existence." (CTL: 167) Rosenberg (2008: 362) argues that these categorisations as "part of a commonsense lexicon" lead to "blindness rather than insight". In a sense, the disposition of feeling is directly transmitted by overabundance of fear-inducing semantisation and the *outillage mental* of contemporary dominant terms is also furthered by institutionalised ideologies of Self and Other.

When Tommy is questioned by the MI5 the whole scene is interspersed with hatred added by the institution's objective to intimidate and control through fear (CTL: 209-210, 295). Serving a traditional plot of conspiracy, the media, the secret services and the terrorist/opportunist groupings are represented as all involved in scaring the metropolitan denizens as legitimised by terror or its expectancy (CTL: 317). In this respect, Rosenberg (2008: 367) argues that the novel shows how xenophobia triggered by terrorism can lead to political absolutism with the governments profiting from the spreading climate of fear. After the fictitious London bombings represented in *City of Tiny Lights* "London was on high alert. London was scared." (CTL: 297) While fear is enforced by the media with headlines reading "Terror Threat Strangles Capital" (CTL: 299), the novel also "shows us a present-day London that is scared, a mood to which British mainstream media greatly contribute" (Rosenberg 2008: 358). Over night faithism and racism resurface in the multicultural cosmopolis where the newly exposed xenophobia exposes the felt threat of strangeness (CTL: 297, 324, 328). Hence, the ideology of terror eradicates urban notions of difference and individuality (cf. Rosenberg 2008: 363).

While the spectres of terror severely strive to control urbanites' mental attitudes in dispositions of anxiety, Neate's representation of the postcolonial London U/underground can be read "as challenging *both* the officious, discriminating racial discourses of postwar Britain, and the new forms of transnational, cellular terrorism which attack the metropolis indiscriminately." (McLeod 2007: 403-404) Initially, Neate's protagonist Tommy identifies the anxieties of contemporary urban centres as states of fear of the uncanny Self: "We're fighting fear but we're the ones who are scared so we're fighting with ourselves." (CTL: 321) Insofar, Rosenberg correctly comments (2008: 367): "The novel confirms [...] Derrida's assumption that terrorism is the symptom of an auto-immune disorder which implies a certain kind of self-destruction whereby defensive mechanisms turn the system against itself." Following the concept of urban-generic mentality, contemporary urban dispositions of fear and terror must be read as a distinct formation within the ambivalent configuration of apathy and vigilance.

In summary, the feelings aroused by the subterranean city seem to be dominated by terror, thus creating a general mistrust towards fellow citizens. By consequence, these feelings regarding habitual behaviour lead to cautiousness and serenity. Georg Simmel attested to blasé resulting in a matter-of-fact attitude, but also alertness and anxiety in the mind of the city-dweller. Thus, the anxiety depicted in contemporary London novels seems to be an urban-generic phenomenon, just as serenity might be a typically British trait of character.

Glocalised Urban Terrorism

On 11 September 2001 nineteen suicide attackers hijacked four planes and flew two of them into New York's Twin Towers, killing about 3,000 people. Baudrillard (2002: 44) emphasises that the "collapse of the towers [is] itself a unique event in the history of modern cities". In this respect, the World Trade Centre's symbolic meaning not only refers to an American way of life, capitalist power, or Western value system. The Twin Towers particularly presented a monumental figure of Western urbanisation (cf. de Certeau 1988: 93) – physical as well as mental. Through the cultural practice of the Informational City with its extraordinary symbolic meaning, the destructive potential of terror is multiplied to infinite effect (cf. Baudrillard 2002: 21, 27). What is more, the mediatised images of the crashing planes on the one hand adhered to the representations of Hollywood films of urban catastrophe, and on the other hand, according to the notion of Simcity, blurred all boundaries between event and simulation. As variously underlined by critics, the reality of the terrorist attack even overtook the fictional, while later representations struggled to comprehend the hyperreal spectacle of the towers' fall (cf. *ibid.*: 5; Houen 2002: 1; Keniston & Quinn 2008a: 10; Leupolt 2010: 58). Baudrillard (2002: 28) comments:

> But does reality actually outstrip fiction? If it seems to do so, this is because it has absorbed fiction's energy, and has itself become fiction. We might almost say that reality is jealous of fiction, that the real is jealous of the image ... . It is a kind of duel between them, a contest to see which can be the most unimaginable.

In a sense, terrorism advances to a para-theatrical form of political action forced upon the urban. The "spectacle of terrorism" according to Baudrillard (*ibid.*: 30) presents the purest form of spectacle, and the only "theatre of cruelty" left that is able to defy historical and political systems of order. In reference to Debord's definition of the spectacle, however, the event still generates a mirror-image of a totalitarian rule which preconditions contemporary existence. Hence, "[d]eregulation ends up in a maximum of constraints and restrictions, akin to those of a fundamentalist society." (*Ibid.*: 32) Therefore, according to Baudrillard (*ibid.*: 4) 9/11 presents "the absolute event, the 'mother' of all events, the pure event uniting within itself all the events that have never taken place." Due to the encompassing traumatic shock of the terrorist attack, the "afterimages" (Huyssen 2003: 158) will remain hovering in urbanites' minds. Hence, although criticism by and large does not detect a historical rupture by 9/11 (cf. Mohr & Mayer 2010: 1), the attacks have nevertheless left a decisive imprint on urbanites' mind and brought to the fore dominant structures of feeling. The years after the attacks in New York seem to qualify a new kind of "mental terrorism" (Baudrillard 2002: 45) in the sense that the common expectation of further events looms in the mind of most urbanites in metropolitan centres. While the architecture of the Twin Towers exerted its own particular "mental conditioning" (*ibid*: 43), the "terrorists [...] struck at the brain, at the nerve-centre of [this] system" (*ibid.*: 45). The emotional response shortly after the events was dominated by a collective need to mourn and deal with the traumatic experience. But the incorporation of the attack transgressed various geographical and socio-cultural boundaries, casting new emotional dispositions of suspicion and alertness on other cities (cf. *ibid.*: 20; Keniston & Quinn 2008a: 1-3).

In difference to New York, Londoners, already conditioned to metropolitan terrorism by the IRA, were rather caught in the expectancy fear of an impending disaster. On 7 July 2005, home-grown suicide bombers blew up three separate Underground trains and a bus in Bloomsbury killing forty-two people. Questioned about London's atmosphere a few days after the bombings, Ian McEwan, in a *Spiegel* interview, says that he was surprised "by the relative lack of panic and terror on the streets" (cit. in Hage & Matussek 2005a) and how people remained strangely calm after the events, emphasising London's largely resilient character. In the extended German version of the interview, however, McEwan emphasises that despite Londoners' stoicism, sadness, anger and uncertainty have taken over: "Wir sind doch mehr verwundet als es unser Stoizismus zeigt. Wir alle halten irgendwie den Atem an. Wir fühlen." (Cit. in Hage & Matussek 2005b: 114) The author detects a growing nervousness in the capital as a place which despite "its relatively successful racial mix [is] impossible to defend" (cit. in Hage & Matussek 2005a). By contrast, in his obituary on the victims of the attack, the author Geoff Ryman (2005) points out that London's strength and resistance to terrorism particularly lies in its diversity and multiculturalism: "One of the things evil cannot face contemplating is variety. It prefers monolithic simplicity. Reality outstrips simplicity through a constant flowering of unexpected lives." Consequently, despite official opinions that after 7/7 British multiculturalism has failed and despite the insurgent prejudice and faithist attacks against Muslims, most critics have decisively commented on cosmopolitanism as a London-specific urban value of resisting new totalitarian forces.

Beyond that, the reason for metropolitan resistance and solidarity in the face of terrorism also lies in London's particular atmosphere and rhythm. Despite the 7/7 bombings the German magazine *GEO* published a special edition on the attractive destination of 'Cool' London in October 2005 which also featured an interview with Lord Ralf Dahrendorf. Therein, the self-proclaimed Londoner paradoxically refers the metropolis' blasé back to its nervous and fast-paced life which defies hate and promotes civility:

> Man braucht all seine Energie, um zu überleben. [...] Da bleibt einfach keine Energie um andere Leute zu hassen. Im Gegenteil, da muss man sich darauf verlassen können, dass man miteinander auskommt. [...] Ich denke, dass diese Zivilisiertheit die größte Stärke des heutigen Londons ist. (Dahrendorf cit. in Gaede & Hanig 2005: 87)

London's overload and restlessness drains urbanites' energy; they react with an emphasised self-referentiality which in turn largely prevents anomic reactions. The fact that this mindset is indicative of persistent London-specific mental dispositions in times of crisis is underlined by H.V. Morton's (1939: 11) earlier chronicle of the metropolis and citizens' attitude during the Second World War in *Ghosts of London* :

> I have never seen London calmer, or the Londoner more deliberate in his ways. He is determined to carry on as of nothing had happened, even though his office and the streets he knows so well have been invaded by an atmosphere of makeshift and picnic. It is amusing to read in unfriendly countries accounts of London's fear and panic: for those are the two emotions you will not

encounter in our streets. [...] But outwardly there is not. London has prepared to meet war in the air in much the same way that she might organize herself to fight a plague of rats.

Representations of 9/11 centre on the genre of the novel and have seen a shift from the direct depictions of the event to its aftermath and reverberations (cf. Mohr und Mayer 2010: 2).[14] Furthermore, recent London literature explicitly discusses the absurdity of (urban) terror attacks even establishing a new meta-narrative. Novels especially capture the structures of feeling after the millennium, terrorism, and traumatological effects in general challenging both personal and social orders (cf. Tew 2007: 190; McLeod 2011: 244, 253-258).[15] Once again, London novels, particularly Douglas Fawcett's *Hartman the Anarchist; or, The Doom of the Great City* (1893), and Joseph Conrad's *The Secret Agent* (1907) must be considered early touchstones of the terror genre. Their typical plot unfolds in an entropic cityscape which is caught in a power triangle of terrorists, government and the media (cf. Houen 2002: 18; Martiny 2009: 160).

While contemporary narratives centre on "a palpable sense of clear and present dangers" (Tew 2007: 220), collective non-conscious dispositions depend on the "uncertainty principle" (*ibid.*: 205). I agree with Phil Tew (*ibid.*) that the New York attacks changed the collective consciousness in the sense that contemporary psychopathology "responds to a general underlying fear and foreboding." We could even argue that 9/11 and 7/7 have become ciphers for a specific urban state of mind in the first decade after the millennium. In Nick Hornby's novel *A Long Way Down* one of the protagonists, the American-cum-Londoner Jess, in a diffuse mental fit proclaims that the urban topology is caught in "[d]ark times indeed [...] living under the Twin Towers and everything." (LWD: 61) Blake Morrison's novel *South of the River*, however, underlines that this atmosphere of the scary new world spans from bouts of grief around Lady Diana's funeral to millennial anxieties of technological apocalypse, local urban collapse and the fear of global terrorism. In a sense, typical urban dispositions of feeling are heightened to an irrational degree which enforces paranoia. Moreover, anxiety transforms into an ideological component celebrated in events of mediatised grief and terror. This phenomenon constitutes an obsession of staging extreme forms of collective emotional crisis and performing public mass catharsis. In the following I will concentrate on Monica Ali's *Brick Lane* (2003), J.G. Ballard's *Millennium People* (2003) and Ian McEwan's *Saturday* (2005), all published between the 9/11 attacks in New York and those of 7/7 in London.

Although Pesso-Miquel (2008: 82–83) argues that a sense of history is generally absent in Monica Ali's *Brick Lane* (2003), the perception of socio-political transformations

14 | This particularly concerns New York novels such as Claire Messud's *The Emperor's Children* (2006), Jay McInnery's *The Good Life* (2006), John Updike's *Terrorist* (2006), Don DeLillo's *Falling Man* (2007), Philip Roth's (2007) *Everyman.*

15 | Contemporary British key-texts as responses to terrorism, most of them London novels, include Iain Bank's *Dead Air* (2002), Monica Ali's *Brick Lane* (2003), J.G. Ballard's *Millennium People* (2003), Pat Barker's *Double Vision* (2003), Nadeem Aslam's *Maps for Lost Lovers* (2004), Chris Cleave's *Incendiary* (2005), Ian McEwan's *Saturday* (2005), Patrick Neate's *City of Tiny Lights* (2005), J.G. Ballard's *Kingdom Come* (2006), David Llewellyn's *Eleven* (2006), Joseph O'Neill's *Netherland* (2008).

needs to be understood, in correlation first with the protagonist Nazneen's awakening and second with the heightened awareness of racial disruptions, such as the Oldham riots in May 2001 (BRL: 276). Especially the East End with a large Muslim population comes under public scrutiny after 9/11 (cf. Valman 2009: 7). Nazneen and her family watch the 9/11 attacks on television. As the sequence of the first plane crashing into the tower is played over and over again, Nazneen falls under the spell of the repeated images of burning tower, crashing second plane, and collapsing buildings (BRL: 366-367). Although her trance-like mindstate is interrupted by everyday chores, she grasps the extent of despair and darkness unfolding throughout the world. Her husband Chanu, seeing the first tower on fire, immediately comments that this constitutes "the start of the madness" (BRL: 366), but he does not mean the danger and mental collapse of other cities but the impending consequences for the everyday life of his Islamic community:

> A pinch of New York dust blew across the ocean and settled on the Dogwood Estate. Sorupa's daughter was the first, but not the only one. Walking in the street, on her way to college, she had her hijab pulled off. Razia wore her Union Jack sweatshirt and it was spat on. (BRL: 368)

Chanu understands the unfolding instability followed by hardened fronts where post-positivist culturalism has re-established long dissolved urban binary structures and icons of prejudgement. While for Chanu the war against Afghanistan seals his decision to return to Bangladesh, "Britain after the bombing of the World Trade Center further hastens the awakening of Nazneen's dormant political awareness, which in turn moves the private narrative of *Bildung* into the arena of public and national politics." (Feng 2009: 20) As was shown before, even the character's change of roles is indicative of a new instability of knowledge, where dispositions of thinking like definitions of migrant subjectivity oscillate between the familiar and the strange. Hence, Nazneen's emancipation is founded on the uncertainty principle which furthers anxieties but also leads to manifestations of fatalist agency.

J.G. Ballard's absurd novel *Millennium People* (2003) is a representation of senseless, irrational and unreasonable violence. As variously remarked, Ballardian non-places become the narrative zones of twenty-first-century terrorism (cf. Thomson 2003; Chapman 2006) and this novel opens with a bomb attack on Heathrow airport and thereby uncannily foretells the terrorist threats of 2006. Because the protagonist David Markham recognises his ex-wife Laura as one of the victims in the midst of the "madhouse" (MIP: 18) presented on the lunchtime news, the text immediately establishes the strong interconnection between terrorism, the media's performance and characters' private lives. Laura seems curiously calm within the mayhem unfolding around her: "She brushed the dust from her sleeve and stared soberly at the confusion around her, a busy professional late for her next appointment." (MIP: 18) David, the corporate psychologist, interprets her "impatient" (MIP: 18) attitude, being "almost untouched by the explosion" (MIP: 18), as part of the urbanite's professional attitude. But knowing the horrifying consequences of this attack, David's familiarity with tragedies inverses: "I felt closely involved in the crime, as if I had placed the bomb on the carousel." (MIP: 18) The rupture of the bomb is deeply experienced, as time and space become variously suspended and compressed to mark this transitional moment: "For a few minutes all the lines to reality had been severed. [...] There was already a shadow on my cheeks, as if the shock of the Heathrow bomb had forced my beard to grow." (MIP: 20) The spectre of terrorism raised by "vicious boredom" is the more uncanny because the "meaningless acts of violence" are conducted by a "motiveless psychopath" (MIP: 28) whose targets are part of everyday life.

The senseless acts of terror are also supposed to ignite the Chelsea Marina revolt and force the middle-classes from their state as "*début-de-siècle Ennui*" (Martiny 2009: 166). First, without much media attention, several unclaimed bombs go off in inner-city non-places. The uncertainty of the attack's symbolic meaning creates an alien metropolitan atmosphere within London. However, the Chelsea revolutionists are still caught in the structures of representation of their own milieu. For example the smoke bombs for a video store are hidden in cases of films like "*Independence Day, Diva, Armageddon*" (MIP: 97) – titles that refer to end of the world scenarios. Similarly, the arson attack on the National Film Theatre simulates thrillers following a particular script of a "brutal drama straight from the gangster they so venerated" (MIP: 117). Although it is claimed that there is nothing the middle-class believes in, their random acts of terror, as David explains, are not pure nihilism but rather present a "search for meaning" because the "absence of rational motive carries a significance of its own." (MIP: 194)

Instead, David's antagonist, the terrorist paediatrician Dr Richard Gould, is obsessed with finding meaning in pointless violence (MIP: 81). Characterised as a "Sentimental Terrorist" (MIP: 257), Gould is an outspoken fan of Lee Harvey Oswald's assassination of Kennedy or Michael Ryan's Hungerford massacre, both of whom exerted terror through random violence (MIP: 32, 176, 178). These inexplicable acts of anarchic, non-symbolic terrorism

> stir[...] fears long dormant in our minds. The horror challenged the soft complacencies of day-to-day life, like a stranger stepping out of the crowd and punching one's face. Sitting on the ground with a bloodied mouth, one realized that the world was more dangerous but, conceivably, more meaningful. As Richard Gould had said, an inexplicable act of violence had a fierce authenticity that no reasoned behaviour could match. (MIP: 182)

The senseless bomb attack on the Tate killing three and the assassination of a well-loved TV performer remain inexplicable and leave the denizens of London aghast with grief, anger and fear (MIP: 188, 211). Martiny (2009: 166) claims that the "novel explores the potential terrorist lurking in the heart of every man. The nihilistic strand it explores is akin to anomie, the disintegration of moral values in the individual and society due to the boredom with the habitual." In this sense, terror is presented as an anthropological disposition within each single urbanite and a persistent atavistic possibility of urbanity. Similar to Conrad's outspoken and internal anarchists in *The Secret Agent*, Ballard's post-millennial London is on the brink of anomie with terror as the dominating structure of feeling. Consequently, *Millennium People* must be read in accordance with Tew's (2007) interpretation of post-millennial fictions as relating to questions of terror and trauma, violence and madness, uncertainty and anxiety.

Zadie Smith (2010: 111) admits that she saw Ian McEwan as the most likely to offer a novel on 9/11 because his fiction "was already about the idea of a malevolent intervention." Although with issues of international terrorism and the war on terror *Saturday* (2005) must be considered a retrospective assessment of 9/11, the narrative is seen in the context of post-millennial structures of feeling. Despite being a highly self-reflexive and rational character, the protagonist Perowne cannot free himself from the mental and emotional condition of the period influencing his personal state of mind. Standing at his window overlooking London, Perowne feels like standing on the edge of a new order dominated by uncertainty and anxiety.

First, being confronted with an unknown object near Heathrow, Perowne calms himself seeing "a meteor burning out in the London sky, traversing left to right, low on the horizon, though well clear of the taller buildings" (SAT: 13) or "a comet, tinged with yellow, with the familiar bright core trailing in its fiery envelope" (SAT: 14). Second, the character's image becomes reminiscent of a typical historical threat from the sky; the flaming plane triggers collective memories of Fitzrovia's bombing during the Blitz (SAT: 14-15). As the object passes behind the Post Office Tower, Perowne's final perception is unconsciously completed by images of 9/11 engrained deep in his mind; the advancing danger of an immanent terrorist attack on London horrifies the protagonist. His inability "to dissociate the actual sight of a burning plane from his mental images of terrorism" (Leupolt 2010: 60) shows how strongly structures of terrorist imaginary predisposition Perowne's mental attitude.

Especially the media prove their determinant power on urbanites' minds, because Henry quasi-automatically reproduces familiar TV images of terror following a similar narrative pattern. Certainly, the image of the crashing plane has 'burned' itself onto the mind of people and probably more so of those living in a similar environment like the one presented in the picture, namely the metropolitan area. A corresponding image is conveyed in an essay by Tom McCarthy (2003: 278) exemplifying the similarity of imaginary dispositions:

> Since 2001 [...] London caught at the confluence of systems moving over from the United States and from the Middle East [...]. When storm clouds groan and rumble people scour the sky for aeroplanes flying too low. I track them from my windows, waiting for the day when one will hurtle like a meteor into the Telecom Tower, painting the sky a new blood-orange. If it happens it will be spectacular.

Although "[i]t doesn't console [Perowne] that anyone in these times, standing at the window in his place might have leaped to the same conclusion" (SAT: 39), it stresses once more Londoners' expectancy fear of urban terrorism and the character's inability to calm down (SAT: 80-81, 145, 276). Rather, Perowne sees himself "joined to the generality, to a community of anxiety." (SAT: 176) He fears for the lives of his family and only the musician Theo dissociates himself from his father's urban phobia of terror (SAT: 35). For Perowne, 9/11 therefore not only initiates the global crisis of the first century of the new millennium (SAT: 32-33), but also constitutes an "epochal mind event" (Ross 2008: 82). It epitomises the ambivalent complexity of feelings, such as happiness, anosognosia, anxiety, trauma, vulnerability, paranoia, uncertainty, scepticism, terror.

Interviewed by *Der Spiegel*, McEwan describes the everyday life of his main characters as follows: "[S]ie leben in schwierigen Zeiten, wie wir alle seit dem 11. September. Ich kenne kein Ereignis, das dermaßen auf das private Leben eines jeden eingewirkt hätte." (Hage & Matussek 2005b: 114) Furthermore, for critics the miniature domestic invasion of brutal reality by Baxter into comfortable life parallels how global terror will become 'domesticated' with 7/7 home-grown terrorists (cf. Wells 2005). Baxter's attack on the Perowne family echoes the terror of public catastrophe and emphasises how in the new power dynamics in the age of international terrorism there are no predictable forms of violence left (cf. Ross 2008: 78; Michael 2009: 40). The author himself elucidates in his interview with Zadie Smith (2010: 130) that he intended to explore the "private scale of that feeling" equivalent to an airliner hitting an urban building. Mumford (1997: 275) notes that a constant anxiety over war – here the war on terror and the fear of an attack – can fix itself into routine and consequently find expression in collective psychosis.

Moreover, according to Brown (2008: 81), "[t]he uneasy state of mind itself becomes the political and the political is experienced as an uneasy state of mind in his [Perowne's] work." Interesting is Perowne's uncanny position between the certainties of his professional and private life and the uncertainty of the character's public attitude and the global climate (cf. *ibid.*: 83, 92). For the intellectualised Perowne, this general state of uncertainty poses an encompassing problem because it heralds the loss of his naturalised urban habitus of scepticism and stoicism (SAT: 181; cf. Leupolt 2010: 67-68). Habits of rationality and detachment have so far granted him mental independence from medial manipulation and saved him from the overload of social anxieties. Mumford (1997: 275) argued as early as in the last century that fear becomes "fixed into routine: the constant anxiety over war produces itself a collective psychosis comparable to that which active warfare might develop." Whereas Perowne's private life is carefully mapped out in order to prevent unexpected incidents which could break his stable existence, everyday routine does not avert his mental fear.

The protagonist is characterised as an urbanite whose state of mind might not be as genuine and stable as he thinks (SAT: 77-78) and McEwan stresses that Perowne's happiness is based on "a bubble of unreality" (cit. in Smith 2010: 123). Peter Childs (2006: 147-148) interprets this state of mind as one of "anosognosia", a psychiatric condition which describes the lack of awareness of one's own condition, notorious for the residual mind of Perowne. He points out that despite the protagonist's scepticism towards fiction, the character himself exists in the delusion that his private abode is apart from the violence of the streets or the horrors of the world. Henry's encounter with Baxter serves as a wake-up call from this delusion and as a consequence he is shocked into a paralysis of persistent cultural anxiety. Towards the end of his Saturday, Perowne recognises himself as part of a collective state of uncertainty: "All he feels now is fear. He's weak and ignorant, scared [...]." (SAT: 277) Perowne's weakness emphasises individual and collective vulnerabilities resulting from a loss of control concerning unfolding events and their consequences. Tew (2007: 199) shows that this frame of vulnerability is symbolised in Perowne's nakedness at the beginning of the novel and we have to add Daisy's unprotected naked body in the face of the threatening Baxter. Instead of a direct allusion to terrorism, this approach reads vulnerability as a sign of post-millennial forms of indeterminacy, unknowingness reflecting postmodern uncertainties and unstable values within a "future that's harder to read, a horizon indistinct with possibilities." (SAT: 276) The book is very much a product of the socio-political moment capturing the changing cultural mood of the twenty-first century urban citizen of a metropolitan centre in the aftermath of 9/11 (cf. Deveney 2005; Head 2007: 180; Michael 2009: 25). Most importantly, however, Perowne's phobia constitutes a paradoxical and quasi-masochistic hunger of twenty-first century urbanites because mental fear is presented as a "longing in the collective mind, a sickening for self-punishment and a blasphemous curiosity." (SAT: 176)

According to the construction in *Saturday* the only means to counter terrorism are humanist compassion and empathic values such as those furthered by literature. Four days after the New York attacks, McEwan (2001) published his emotional reaction in *The Guardian*. Therein, he states that one of greatest crimes committed by the terrorists was a "failure of imagination" (*ibid.*) which prevented them from "empathy, to think oneself into the minds of others" (*ibid.*).

> If the hijackers had been able to imagine themselves into the thoughts and feelings of the passengers, they would have been unable to proceed. It is hard to be cruel once you permit yourself to enter the mind of your victim. Imagining what it is like to be someone other than yourself is at the core of our humanity. It is the essence of compassion, and it is the beginning of morality. (*Ibid.*)

For McEwan (*ibid.*; cf. Smith 2010: 112) the genre of the novel is the furthermost medium that allows the investigation of the human mind and the exploration of the narratives of emotion. As was already mentioned, in *Saturday* the reading, staging, and dramatising of Arnold's poem defeats Baxter's nihilistic terror by initiating a mood-swing. How strongly the beauty of the poetry plays with the recipient's mind becomes apparent in Perowne's own imaginary and the emotionalised literary perception. Kathleen Wall (2008: 762-763) argues that novels such as Ian McEwan's *Saturday* suggest that intersubjective relations based on beauty and art by discovering common values are necessary means of paralysing any kind of fundamentalism. However, because both terrorists and the media consciously employ the totalitarian effect of visual images, there is a certain anxiety in regard to the effects of the symbolic. Nevertheless, the novel emphasises the pronounced importance of dispositions of the imaginary for contemporary urban life. Finally, in Ian Mc Ewan's novel the ascendance of uncontrolled imaginary and feeling wrought by various manifestations of post-9/11 socio-cultural anxieties last but not least promotes an unsettled frame of mind characterised by permanent fatal expectancy. In consequence, contemporary urban-generic dispositions of thinking, imagining, feeling, and acting in general are overwhelmed by structures of terror.

This sub-chapter has analysed the psychology and the spectres of terror of the urban state of mind. London Underground is represented as the spatialisation of this terrorised mental state wrought by anxieties and paranoia. After the terrorist attacks in London, this semantisation appears to have gained a new colouring because now "if we continue travelling with the Tube it's a bit like staring down terrorism." (McEwan cit. in Hage & Matussek 2005a) As was shown, the feeling of terror is not only a major topic of London Underground novels but concerns most post-millennial fiction on the city. The novels bring to the fore the spectaclisation and mediatisation of terrorism. Each kind of terror disrupts the temporal and spatial fabric of everyday routine. Thereby, the metropolis is caught in a permanent state of emergency because it describes the daily fear and combat against an indefinite threat of urban madness. Useful urban equipments to face the anxiety of the unknown are found in rooted cosmopolitanism, vigilance, empathy, confidence, ratio, humanism. Thus, in its urban-generic ambivalences, the metropolis enhances mental structures of terror, but likewise offers idiosyncratic urban remedies.

8.2.3 Millennial Apocalyptic Visions

Metropolitan London during the decade of the Blair era saw a large amount of violent events spurring collective emotions of grief, from the death of Diana to an extended millennial fear around 2000 and the events of 9/11 which proved the possibility of the city's disappearance – and the rise of a post-apocalyptic city. Particularly for the threshold of the new millennium Onega and Stotesbury (2002: 13) attest a certain "spirit of urban apocalypticism" which characterises the end-of-century mood, while Black (2009: 401-402) brings into view the metropolitan fears of natural catastrophes, especially a flooding of the city, due to global warming and the rise of the sea level. At the same time, London, especially because of its restructuring, has developed into a real "millennial landscape" (Sinclair cit. in Wolfreys 2005: 204) suffused with surveillance and calling a spatial and temporal shift that also prominently marks its literature. As was shown before, the trope of the apocalyptic city is deeply embedded in urban fiction as is the image of New Jerusalem. Especially the end-of-time-thinking of a world purified by apocalyptic catastrophe is deeply entrenched within the urban fabric.[16]

Julian Wolfreys (*ibid.*: 200) characterises London's millennial fiction as follows:

> The city insists on fictions, narratives and poetic explorations appropriated to the millennial condition as explored above, whether in the form of novel or poetry. Such texts may imagine London as being haunted from within by the immanent promise of New Jerusalem. They may visualise the millennial aspect of the city through mediations on the haunting recurrence, the iterability of violence and power; in such moments of vision London is understood, millennially, [...]. They may envision London as the site through which wander the ghosts of its dead, whereby any temporal or material certainty concerning the present is undone. Such acts of writing the millennial spirit of the city, in which the traces of the past erupt as an unexpected event, disrupt representation.

In his article for *The Guardian*, Ian McEwan (2008) writes on the still up-to-date and maybe resurgent "apocalyptic thinking" defined by a strong notion of unknowability with the only certainty of an approaching end. Thereby, images from *The Book of Revelation* like fires, thundering horses, scarlet women are exchanged for secular apocalyptic beliefs such as meteorites, environmental contaminations, viral epidemics, nuclear wars, etc. For McEwan (*ibid.*) the meta-narrative of the apocalypse serves the need to define the unthinkable in the spatio-temporal flow and to make sense of the chaotic world order. Otherwise, according to the author "[t]he apocalyptic mind can be demonising [and] tends to be totalitarian." (*Ibid.*)

His novel *Saturday* (2005) especially negotiates these doomed inevitabilities, end-of-time scenarios and visions of catastrophic urban disaster. The physician Perowne sees the present metropolis "beyond repair" with "[s]ick buildings" (SAT: 122) and ruled by a general sense of disorder and chaos. Due to the irrefutable attacks awaiting the city he

---

16 | See for example the disaster novels by Wells, Ballard, and Harrison, but also apocalyptic imaginations in popular culture, such as in the films *28 Days Later* (2002) or *Survivors* (2008) (cf. Coverley 2005: 23; Black 2009: 404).

imaginatively draws a hellish image of London's future. Consequently, the personal and public catharsis of *Saturday*'s characters is close to the idea of purging intrinsic to the apocalypse, but also closes the circle of Perowne's personal reflections on the Genesis and the Darwinian interpretation of creation. Following a cyclical conception of urban history, similar to the fall of ancient Rome, he sees the decline of London as an inevitable part of the urban life-cycle. In a sense, the Postmetropolis imagined by Perowne merges notions of urban collapse with the end of civilisation. *Phobos*, or extreme fear, is an intrinsic element of these apocalyptic narratives, added by psychological reactions of terror, grief and depression. Like in other post-9/11 novels the fear of terror, anomie, anarchy, entropy, and apocalypse lie at the centre of the narrative. However, as Groes (2011: 166) correctly stresses, inherent in *Saturday* is the strong belief in the millennial verve of the metropolis so that McEwan's vision of London also "embodies the continuation of civilisation's achievements [...] which defiantly beats against the currents of pessimism and apocalypticism that run so strongly in the contemporary London novel."

Otherwise, Leupolt (2010: 58) argues that the multiple visions of apocalypse in recent literature have accustomed the reader to disaster from a distance and are able to enter the private mental nightmares catering to the contradictory longings of cataclysm and safety. In the following, I will further explore these apocalyptic mental structures in Maggie Gee's *The White Family* (2002), J.G. Ballard's *Millennium People* (2003), Matthew De Abaitua's *The Red Men* (2007), and Christine Brooke-Rose's *Next* (1998).

The Fall and Rise of London

Maggie Gee is renowned for her apocalyptic novels, although, as Sears (2004: 56) emphasises, her political motivations suggest that she is less concerned with the real sense of an ending, but rather explores the socio-cultural implications of these approaching catastrophes. Already her postmodern novel *The Burning Book* (1983) captures the fears and anxieties of a nuclear holocaust that obliterates all human life. *The White Family* (2002) is to be seen as her personal and professional response to the events of 9/11 and exemplifies the wider social and cultural effects. The novel tells the story of the last whimper of the former Empire and urban decline but simultaneously the birth of a new multicultural city.

The trope of urban apocalypse is especially connected to the White family's daughter 'scarlet' Shirley. With her boyfriend she attends church and the vicar's sermon is based on the biblical meta-narrative of Babylon's downfall and the establishment of a New Jerusalem. The sermon concerns the City of God and recent violent racist murders in Babylonian London. It treats the lost paradise or Garden of Eden and the dream of rebuilding the Heavenly City on Earth on the ground of collectivity while Shirley herself indulges in afterthoughts of personal love and desire (WIF: 357-358). In opposition to the reverend's rhetoric, London's grey and dirty streets look rather bleak with lonely single people who are numbed by the hellish everyday life (WIF: 360). The reverend additionally employs a recognisable rhetoric of an apocalypse coming from the air, namely the Battle of Britain (WIF: 371). The enforced vocabulary instantly reminds Shirley of the gestures of a fundamentalist war-monger, the reverend's call for battle and the spectaclisation of the sermon over six large monitors arranged like iconoclast crucifixes rather give her a vision of hell instead of empathy and consolation and express promises (WIF:

373-374). A flyer for Paddington Temple reads "*Impacting the City*", which to Shirley sounds "like a bomb" (WIF: 165).

Sarah Dillon (2007a: 376) points out that the "[b]iblical apocalyptic narratives [...] both confront and diffuse the threat of total destruction, since they describe, reveal, or predict cataclysmic events but only and always with the structural guarantee of a postcataclysmic continuance, be it in this world or the next." Maggie Gee's apocalyptic novel *The Flood* (2004)[17] ends after a flood has drowned the metropolis and at the same time returns to a paradisiacal space-time compression lying before the initial regenerated narrative where all the characters of her former novels are resurrected – from *The White Family* May, Shirley, Elroy, Dirk, Thomas, Melissa, and even Alfred and Winston (cf. Dillon 2007a: 374, 377). Dillon (*ibid.*: 381-393) argues that the apocalyptic narrative depends on psychological survival; neither are the sinners obliterated from the world nor does a real rupture occur, but like the cycle of death and revival it enacts continuance. In that respect Dillon (*ibid.*: 386) shows how contemporary apocalyptic narrative carries out a necessary self-intervention in the time of terror. In the end, Shirley's twins emphasise a hopeful future without 'Babylonian' frictions.

The Spectacle of the End

Likewise, J.G. Ballard became famous for his apocalyptic science fiction novels of the 1960s and 1970s where he variously sketches the doom of London, especially in *The Drowned World* (1962) and *The Burning World* (1964). Other dystopian evocations of urban life are found in *Concrete Island* (1974), *High Rise* (1975), *Running Wild* (1988), *Cocaine Nights* (1996), *Super-Cannes* (2000), and *Millennium People* (2003). The latter's apocalyptic narrative lies within "a millenarian gospel of dread" (Gąsiorek 2005: 50) and the single chapters not only pay tribute to revolutionary and terrorist backgrounds, but the idea of urban apocalypse becomes more and more pronounced in the chapter headings, for example, "The Upholstered Apocalypse", "The Heart of Darkness", "Absolute Zero", "Black Millennium", "White Space", "A Sun Without Shadows". Although London is far from death, the atmosphere in the metropolis is one of emotional urban decline.

The book jacket of the Harper Perennial edition of *Millennium People* is bright orange with a silver skyline of London which is mirrored in a black and running reflection in the Thames, an image reminiscent of London's Great Fire. In the novel, the reference to the cleansing effect of the Great Fire is taken up as the streets are burning with the residue of middle-class possessions and bank statements (MIP: 228). As such, fire is a major symbol of the city's destruction and (re)creation (cf. Groes 2011: 89). After the attack on the National Film Institute "[t]he flame-lit buildings along the Thames" (MIP: 125) throw their light into the eyes of London's self-pronounced apocalyptic rider Dr Gould. Characterised as the "doctor Moreau of the Chelsea set" (MIP: 3),[18] similarly to the Pusher in *London Revenant*, he sees the only possibility in healing the mad contem-

17 | Notions of an apocalyptic flood cleansing the metropolis are also part of J.G Ballard's *The Drowned World* (1962) and Will Self's *The Book of Dave* (2006). Moreover, see the film adaptation (2007) of Richard Doyle's disaster thriller *Flood* (2002).

18 | Other intertextual references to Joseph Conrad's writing also define Dr Gould as an urban version of Mr Kurtz from *Heart of Darkness* (1899), the namesake from *Nostromo* (1904), or the mad anarchist professor from *The Secret Agent* (1907). For more on the significance of

porary civilisation wrought by uncertainty and on the brink of apocalypse by inflicting terror:

People don't like themselves today. We're a rentier class left over from the last century. We tolerate everything, but we know that liberal values are designed to make us passive. We think we believe in God but we're terrified by the mysteries of life and death. We're deeply self-centred but can't cope with the idea of our finite selves. We believe in progress and the power of reason, but are haunted by the darker sides of human nature. We're obsessed with sex, but fear the sexual imagination and have to be protected by huge taboos. We believe in equality but hate the underclass. We fear our bodies and, above all, we fear death. We're an accident of nature, but we think we're at the centre of the universe. We're a few steps from oblivion, but we hope we're somehow immortal ... (MIP: 139)

Promoted by this apocalyptic state of mind and urban boredom, the staged revolution of Chelsea Marina's middle-class vandalises the materiality of the estate leaving behind a "zone of silence like an urban nature reserve" (MIP: 5), an "apocalyptic vision deprived of its soundtrack" (MIP: 3). The apocalyptic topography of the estate is depicted as a wasteland of abandoned civilisatory debris: "burnt-out houses" (MIP: 3), "a fire-gutted BMW, lying wheels uppermost beside the kerb, and [...] its ruptured tank" (MIP: 6) as well as "hundreds of broken windows" (MIP: 6), "[p]rotest banners hanging limply from the balconies" (MIP: 7), the skip filled with middle-class paraphernalia (MIP: 8).[19] Epitomising the failure of cultural progress, it is distinguished by marks of violence, destruction, and war:

Beside a school blazer with scorched piping was an almost new worsted suit [...] lying among the debris like the discarded fatigues of a soldier who had thrown down his rifle and taken to the hills. The suit seemed strangely vulnerable, the abandoned flag of an entire civilization [...]. (MIP: 8)

But the novel's narrative of social crisis, anomie and decline is nothing more than the spectaclisation of the city's death and a simulation of an end of the world scenario. In the chapter on "The Upholstered Apocalypse" (MIP: 66) the protagonists elucidate how although civic responsibilities are discarded for fantasies of cataclysmic change, the inhabitants of Chelsea Marina still serve whiskey sours amidst their staged version of middle-class Armageddon (MIP: 68). And later, Londoners appear "dressed for an apocalyptic day" (MIP: 141) while the London Eye "grinding out time and death" (MIP:

---

names in *Millennium People* see Groes (2011: 87-88) and concerning Ballard's reworking of *The Secret Agent* see Groes (2011: 90-92).

19 | In reference to Conrad's *Heart of Darkness*, Twickenham is devised as London's "heart of darkness" (MIP: 84) inhabited by emotionally deprived and morally poisoned 'hollow men' (T.S. Eliot). The clergyman, reminiscent of Conrad's ghost-like apparitions of the accountant and the pilgrims, is "pale and almost bloodless" standing against the darkness of the marina, "a well of nothingness" (MIP: 105). Moreover, the post-apocalyptic landscape of the Chelsea Marina is similar to the desolate landscape of the Outer Station.

141) becomes an appropriated prop reminiscent of the scene in Bosch's painting of the *Last Judgement* (1485-1505). The staged apocalypse is depicted as a heterotopic urban festival.

Jeannette Baxter (2009: 210) argues that "the spectacle of apocalypse has been recuperated into a postmodern performance of political pastiche." The revolutionary protagonists feign political and historical authenticity only to the spin their own yarn of social destitution and romanticise notions of metropolitan decline. The anarchy of the intellectual dissidents mainly consists of temporarily absconding from the docile and passive consumerist lifestyles and basically presents an upheaval against cultural ennui (cf. *ibid.*: 208). Even more, this simulational apocalypse "[c]apitalises on a mood of distress" (*ibid.*: 212). The collective mourning after the assassination of the TV celebrity reminds the protagonist of the collective emotional outpour after the death of Lady Di (MIP: 209-211). For Baxter (2009: 214) the presentation of the murder and particularly the spectacle of grief which has transformed into mere narrative capture a general "emotional vacuity". By intertextual references, already apparent in the above-mentioned chapter headings, Ballard himself strongly alludes to these cultural images of (urban) entropy.

The antagonist Gould is attracted and repulsed by David's script *A Neuroscientist Looks at God*. While for the main character "the idea of God [is] a huge imaginary void, the largest nothingness the human mind can invent" (MIP: 136) and a "vast absence" only a psychopath can deal with, Gould is of the opinion that "[e]ven a meaningless universe has meaning". Later on he obsessively strives for "a new kind of sense" (MIP: 136) through the apocalyptic chronotope emptied of space and time. Insofar, Gould's revolutionary terrorism is neither motiveless nor nihilist, but mimics famous examples of assassination, his pointless terror serves an "articulate experiment in psychopathic imperialism." (Baxter 2009: 215) Hence, the novel's apocalyptic staging uncovers psychological dispositions that seemed to have disappeared from urban reality, but these notions not only burn in the mind of solitary urbanites, but can be revitalised in a wider community.

Nevertheless, the narrative closes with a "pervading atmosphere of post-apocalyptic fatigue" where the "recuperation of politics, history, subjectivity and the imagination into the media-capitalist spectacle bequeaths a legacy of manufactured realities whose only significance is their insignificance." (*Ibid.*: 217) The city's vigilance has developed grotesque defence mechanisms of its own urban fabric: London's shops already have a "second city" (MIP: 128) in store that easily replaces those that have burned to the ground. Also urban routine is resilient enough to reappear. Even Chelsea Marina returns to its former millennial charm and glory of light leisure (MIP: 293). Although performing staged urban disasters with cathartic implications, the psychological conditions of an apocalyptic mindset are in general shown to be the mental background in *Millennium People*. As Ballard argued elsewhere, "in a totally sane society, madness is the only freedom" (cit. in McNamara 2001).

'Alcopop Apocalypse'

Also Matthew de Abaitua's *The Red Men* (2007) offers revolutionary apocalypse as its narrative climax. For the author, the dystopian vision of London's "occult terrorism" (REM: 223) represents the nightmare unleashed after 9/11 (cf. Jordison 2007). The pervasive feeling of threat exerting feelings of terror and uncertainty yet developed a strangely, but accustomed and even grotesque numbed version of everyday procedure in "an age of terror." (REM: 241)

A police helicopter hung in the air, its robot blades drowning out the clamour of the main road. Policewomen were sealing off the street [...]. The shops were being evacuated and everyone was arguing about it. [...] At the internet shack, armed police threatened the Somalians who would not log off and leave. A pair of builders [...] sauntered from Yum-Yum; they refused to leave until their food was ready. As each establishment emptied, the police put down metal crowd barriers to close it off. [...] Was it terrorists? Had an al-Quaida cell mestastasized again? (REM : 17)

However, the 'terrorist' on his suicide mission is merely an "exhausted and confused foot soldier of globalisation" (REM: 19) fallen out of favour. In opposition, the protagonist is an urbanite who has become accustomed to be a mere 'speck of dust' within the swirl of the fluid city:

I wake up in the morning and sometimes I don't know which Nelson Millar I am. [...] If I hear, with any clarity, which version of myself is talking at any given moment, it is only for a minute, before that sound of myself is lost in the city's roar. I am at ease with this condition. (REM: 20)

After an age of enlightenment and hedonism, self-denial and self-debasement, hunger and intoxication, the character Nelson is confronted with the approaching millennium which predicted the apocalypse to be the "next big thing" (REM: 63) for the twenty-first century. However, his boss does not read this scenario as a horrific anticipation of terror or as a death wish, but rather as a dream of revelation: "The great disclosure. You wanted change. It looked like it was going to be brands forever, media forever, house prices forever, a despotism of mediocrity and well-fed banality." (REM: 89) In this sense, de Abaitua's novel *The Red Men* negotiates between the two connotations of apocalypse as frightening yet also inviting cataclysmic effects. Hence, we can understand Nelson's later compulsion to unleash various modern apocalyptic disasters on the simulated city of Redtown both as a wish to obliterate the whole project and to recharge reality:

I preferred running catastrophes to simulating mundanities, for the simple operational reason that wholesale slaughter of its citizens required Redtown to be reset to its starting position. It concealed the biggest flaw in the simulation; the degradation of its integrity – its reality principle – the longer it ran. (REM: 244)

While Nelson's anticipation of the apocalypse was commercialised and employed for marketing purposes – "Enlightenment. Alcopop Apocalypse" (REM : 63) – neither the visions of the brand age nor the vigilant project for a new enlightenment survive the millennium and 9/11 (REM: 65, 87). Rather, the plane tearing through the World Trade Centre initiates the "unreal age" (REM : 64) of the incredibly fantastic. The post-millennial era therefore casts its shadows by fantasies, hallucinations, future echoes, cultural paranoia and social madness.

Although perpetuated by the print media, the technological innovations and futuristic visions created by Monad are perceived by the urbanites as largely threatening, "'insane, 'terrifying' impossible'" (REM: 177). As an obsessive visionary, Monad's owner Herman Spence defies the common post-apocalyptic notions as a manifestation of mind-control and instead calls for the development of new tools to change the world and foster urban evolution: "[Government] encourages the panic nation because a panicking man cannot think clearly. [...] If you must be apocalyptic about it, then tell yourself that we are living *after* the end of the world. Tell yourself we are rebuilding out of the ashes of the old order." (REM: 177) The corporate boss recalls the purging powers of fire which both destroys and offers the nourishing ground for London's renewal.

This imagery of a great metropolitan fire or the urban phoenix rising from its ashes is a particularly apt trope for London. The city's collective memory incorporates both destructive and rejuvenating notions of an apocalyptic firestorm which is able to consume the residues of an anomic metropolis. Nelson justifies the concept of engineered apocalypse by London's history of renewal and survival:

> A great fire waits under London. [...] First set by the Romans, who left the city gutted and fit only for dogs, it seized its opportunity at Thomas Farriner's shop in Pudding Lane. The Luftwaffe knew about it. They gave London the codename of 'Loge', after the Wagnerian God of Fire. Their bombs blew holes in its prison so that it could graze monstrously upon the city. [...] The city renews itself in our destruction. (REM: 22)

Fittingly, chapter 16 is called "Fire Nature Incessantly Renews" (REM: 315). However, it is less the fire of hell than that of the purgatory paradoxically washing the sins from the blemished urban body. The fires burning over Poplar are transformed into an apocalyptic flood which washes over the city and leads to the destruction of the Wave Building and the totalitarian rule of Monad (REM: 357).

Idiosyncratically, the literary city has given birth to a counter-movement, called The Great Refusal, which is a revolutionary group around Dyad that rejects the authority of Monad and hence re-establishes the equilibrium of the city. Ironically, the Jewish author Raymond's ghost-written book by the same title is supposed to offer a revolutionary authenticity, "[s]omething that feels real [...] in the unreal city" (REM: 113). It is, however, merely an appropriation from the purgatory section of Dante's *Divine Comedy*, a reminiscence of apocalyptic notions from T.S. Eliot's "Wasteland", and a plagiarised cut-and-paste version of various revolutionary ideas. The refusal settles in the "Ground Zero" (REM: 145) of Stratford, Hackney and Clapton, a "netherworld" (REM: 303) characterised by dereliction and darkness "worse than evil" (REM: 304). This area is described as an "unknown territory [and] the epitome of urban desolation, an anti-Jerusalem" (REM: 304). London's centre is hence far from the Heavenly City. Rather it is a double-faced place closer to the twin-cities of sin, Sodom and Gomorrah (REM: 323).

Although Cantor, Monad's artificial intelligence, is lauded as having divorced order from chaos, its brain created just as much unpredictable unrest (REM: 323-324). The chaotic revolution springing from the East End's darkest spaces features its typical heralds of urban apocalypse – a plague of mice and rats (REM: 337-338). London inhabitants, as a diversion to kill totalitarian Cantor, counteract with civil disobedience and commuter unrest (REM: 341). In that respect, their counter-movement is "[n]ot a revolution but a revulsion, a refusal." (REM: 341) A rioting crowd winds through London's streets like a hellish winding worm the "psychic weather [...] pungent fog." (REM: 349) The mob torches cars, overturns lorries, smashes shop-fronts and breaks windows (REM: 349-350). While Leto's devotees initially bring about the destruction of Dyad, Nelson literary wipes out Monad by unleashing a real apocalypse in Redtown where "byte by byte, pixel by pixel, the streets of Maghull were unimagined, stone and flesh alike randomised." (REM: 361) As the two cities are consumed by an apocalyptic fire and laid to waste by urbanites, the head of the artificial intelligence literally drowns in his well of information. As Jarvis (1998: 41) writes elsewhere, appropriating Eliot: "This is the way the global village ends; not with a bang, but with a simulated whimper." However, all in all, the metropolitan scenario of apocalypse is represented as urbanity breeding an endless cycle of self-regulating and ambivalent energies.

Insofar, also *The Red Men* refutes the notion of an absolute end, imagining the endlessly repeated rise and fall of the city. The apocalyptic setting is never a closure, but indicates the persistent rewriting of the urban realm. Nelson summarises this idea of an urban-generic meta-narrative by connecting it with mankind's cultural faculty of calculation and narration: "The world was calculated and it was written. It is a story and it is an equation, which is like a sum, and neither the story nor the sum will ever end." (REM: 377) The creating and destructing forces of the water of Monad and the fire of Dyad are proof of the generic ambiguities at work in the city.

Posthuman London

In her novels Christine Brooke-Rose explores several variants of apocalypse: humanist culture, communication, the actual end of the world, personal annihilation, and the *fin* of fiction. Also *Next* (1998) is "a text in which death lurks [and represents] a world that is terminal." (McHale 1995: 209) As was shown before, London society in this novel is highly anomic and on the verge of entropy. For example, the surface architecture of the Lloyds building, described as an inner void (NXT: 124), becomes a symbol of the empty emotional life and social vacuity of contemporary society, but especially the urban *conditio humana* at the end of the millennium. The homeless character Ulysses argues that the city, formerly a place of interaction, today fosters individualism as it is "each for himself" (NXT: 125). For the homeless Oliver "we're all out of touch" (NXT: 183) and he describes this urban experience of oversaturated loneliness in analogy to the contemporary illness of the computer age: MUD – "Stands for multi-level dungeon, and that's even stranger, since one sits alone. But in touch with thousands." (NXT: 178) Brooke-Rose's post-Thatcherite London before the millennium, populated by monadic, nomadic and lonely homeless urbanites is an anomic city on the threshold of social apocalypse: "This is how street violence begins. And civil wars. / Great gulfs between people / and hurtful remarks / thoughtlessness / selfishness." (NXT: 196)

"In this televorous posthuman age" (NXT: 33), haunting images of multiple wars and catastrophes are circulated around the world. Especially the homeless character Tek is overtly perceptive to these end-time scenarios with consequences for his habitus as one of absolute endings and fatality. For him, humans present the only race that does everything to die out in full consciousness. That is why Elsie calls Tek an "Endist", one of those "gloomy prophets, especially [...], round the millennium" (NXT: 128) who nourish people's quirkiness. Tek recognises that his state of mind is strongly influenced by the inflation of horror captions inducing on top of his Monday morning blues a form of "headline depression" (NXT: 33). The incantations of twentieth-century atrocities certainly define the rhythm of his daily wanderings through London and thereby also his state of mind. In a later conversation with Ulysses he suggests the natural death of all things (NXT: 136). In a sense, it is only a lack of imagination that hinders human beings from envisioning their own end any other than related to their current social condition. In reference to Mary Shelley he explicates the lack of technological unpredictability:

> She places her novel The Last Man in 2073 but couldn't imagine men moving on anything but horses or, for social urgency, in a balloon. [...] Or the end of man as due to anything but the Plague. [...] Not to mention her notion of women as merely passive and compassionate. Strange for the daughter of Mary Wollestonecraft [sic!] and the wife of... well, the novel is about the failure of art, so I suppose it's all right for the artist to fail. (NXT: 136)

In her postmodern manner and meta-fictional style, Brooke-Rose hence questions her own narrative on the specific death of the city and end of urban society. In a narrative commentary through Tek who describes the various deaths of all forms of meta-narratives she wonders whether the rhetoric and "end-stories were themselves meganarratives? Fictions, words? People always want an end, without wanting it." (NXT: 203) The need for closure in a narrative again seems to demand an end. In this respect contemporary postmodern discourse additionally enhances discussions of the apocalypse. Concerning structures of feeling, it once again stresses the mental preoccupation with catastrophes and the uncertainty of the anticipated end while according to Baudrillard's notion of simulacrum the fictional images of apocalypse have long since become reality, with their representations following persistent narratives of Armageddon.

All in all, the image of the death of the city and urban apocalypse is still a very prominent one in contemporary urban literature and often connected to the *fin-de-millénnium* anxiety and uncertainty as well as the terrors unleashed by 9/11. As was shown, in the case of London these are on the one hand extended from the death of Lady Di to the terrorist attacks of 7/7, on the other hand, the long tradition of urban catastrophes and revival carries a hopeful note of urban renovation and change and hence the survival of London's society. From this perspective, apocalyptic narratives are frequently employed to offer consolation and revelation. As Dillon (2007a: 376) perceives, "apocalyptic narratives are a strategy for confronting and deferring the threat of remainderless destruction." In the case of London this phenomenon stresses the city's transformative power as a phoenix perpetually rising from its ashes. Concerning mental dispositions the imagery of the apocalypse is, from a closer sight, rather paradoxical in nature and pays tribute to the urban-generic ambivalences of vigilance and apathy – here mainly on a social or collective level. Finally, London fiction seizes the trope of apocalypse by the characters' mental pictures of urban apocalypse as a means to overcome urban apathy through violent vigilance.

All in all, contemporary London novels grasp the notion of urban apocalypse. However, in contrast to the end-of-the world scenarios depicted in London literature of the 1980s, such as Martin Amis' *London Fields* (1989) and the death of the city premonitioned in Peter Ackroyd's *Hawksmoor* (1984), recent urban dystopias envision the apocalypse as a rebirth of the metropolis. Most particularly, intertextual references, for example to Joseph Conrad's apocalyptic notions of London both concerning urban anomie and atmospheric entropy, stress how the discourse of the city is necessarily connected to urban-generic ambivalences of Jerusalem and Babylon, eternity and end. What is more, the apocalyptic theme takes up notions of mental terror structures, while simultaneously offering visions of the city's resistance, resilience, and persistence.

8.2.4 Terror Structures of Mentality

The analysis has brought to attention the deeply ingrained terror structures of urban-specific London mentality. The city trope of 'attraction of repulsion' has been shown to be still relevant in contemporary London novels. Despite everyday manifestations of social anomie repelling urbanites, most characters are drawn by urban potentials of independence, individuality and vigilance. While only few characters decide to turn their back on London, the denizens' decision for a modern way of life is mainly a decision for further mobility and cosmopolitanism and vigilance. For most characters this arrangement oscillates between feelings of love and hate for the metropolis. The inventory of urban horror inflicted by the city was shown as exerting strong emotional powers on the urbanites and promoting common terror structures of contemporary mentality. Concerning everyday terrors, especially London crime and detective fictions elucidate the prevalent anxieties interwoven in the urban fabric. But parts have shown that both the distaste for the urban as well as the anxiety of urban everyday life have transformed into particular properties of London's habitus. In a sense, horrors are enacted and cultivated to counter metropolitan blasé.

However, in the age of terror, feelings of anxiety and uncertainty gain particular momentum. The sub-chapter on "Underground Terror" takes up the issues developed earlier on and specifically elucidates the localisations of unknown urban terror, whereas manifestations of the uncanny and the feelings of uncertainty are exposed as promoting a specific subterranean urban horror. In relation to 9/11 and 7/7 several post-millennial London novels depict the metropolis cast under the spell of the documentary images from New York and pushed into a state of mental fear of the expected inevitable. It is most interesting that the analysed novels extend the trauma and grief experienced by Lady Di's death in 1998 to the millennial fear of chaos to 9/11 and finally a premonition the London attacks of 2005 represented as a mental state of fatality. This collective state of terror, fear, mistrust and scepticism is suffused with heightened feelings of hate expressed in renewed forms of prejudice, racism and faithism, while cosmopolitanism is devised as one major possibility to counter disastrously fixed anomies and apathies. The second counterpole to protect the urban against the profusion and mental determination by images of terror is a heightened awareness of the mental dispositions of the imaginary. Especially the power of media images is variously defined as narrowing mental freedom and undermining the balance of urban-generic mental dispositions. Although the London-specific attitude of stoicism can still be seen to be practised, mental dispositions have already been notably altered as perceptible in the emotions of pronounced urban phobia and terror. Finally, terror must be considered as a London-specific frame of mind, particularly due to the emplacement of apocalyptic imagery in its phoenix-like rise and fall.

All in all, contemporary London novels elucidate various spectres of terrorism from the obsessions of deranged individuals to networks, government and media terror which provoke mental fear. Baudrillard (2002: 10) comments on the post-millennial profusion of terrorism: "Terrorism, like viruses, is everywhere. There is a global perfusion of terrorism, which accompanies any system of domination as though it were its shadow, ready to activate itself anywhere, like a double agent." Townshend (2002: 2) argues that often enough the psychological effect of terror actually outstrips its physical effect and observes that "terrorism appears to be a state of mind rather than an activity." In a sense, terror is an intrinsic element of the metropolitan pathological state identified in Mumford's cycle of city culture. Under the "constant spectre of insecurity and death that hovers over its bold towers and shadowed streets" urbanites fall prey to superstition and irrationality and "become the victims of phantasms, fears, obsessions" (Mumford 1997: 258) which induce fatigue and apathy. As a defence mechanism, and this refers back to the first analytical chapter of the present study, Londoners revert to the private realm.

While historians of mentality see the withdrawal into realms of intimacy as the flight from the authorial state, contemporary urbanologists interpret it as an escape from capitalist society. In both cases the private, intimacy and family life become an idealised retreat from public power structures and "a refuge from the terrors of society" (Sennett 1977: 20). The decisive difference is that despite the war on terror the Postmetropolis is haunted by the spectres of terror initiated by a spectaclisation of horror, visions of terrorist attacks and expectations of urban apocalypse. On the other hand, as exemplified in Elias' (1994: 513-524) history of civilisation, states of fear and terror are always indicative of a renewal of mental dispositions. Hence, as Henry Morton (1939: 12) deduced with regard to the metropolis at the beginning of the Second World War: "Wars come to an end, but London goes on."

9 Conclusion

Studies on the postmodern metropolis generally foreground illimitability, diffusion, heterogeneity, fragmentation and fleetingness, stressing thereby that the urban ultimately remains both illegible and unintelligible for the urbanite and the urbanologist alike. For the writer Jonathan Raban (1974: 222), the city's complexity, contingency and "intrinsic illegibility" stands markedly in opposition to the omniscience, logic and narrative progression of a book. And likewise Lawrence Phillips (2006: 158) remarks on critical literature of London fiction that "no single thesis can encompass every facet of [...] representation" because it will eventually render the city "equally image *and* thesis." From this stance, the present study on *The Intelligible Metropolis* and its analysis of urban mentality as represented in contemporary London novels has failed in its main objectives already from the title page. And maybe Keller (2000a: 8) is right when he argues that reading the city like a book in order to render the metropolis intelligible is only possible for the true urbanite. As a long-term resident of a small town in the German periphery of Lower Bavaria, the author of this book has necessarily remained an unknowing outsider during her physical, theoretical, and literary visits to the British capital.

Nevertheless, from the initial objective of Cultural Studies to gain meta-knowledge of another culture, the venture of this analysis set out to understand how the city becomes both legible and intelligible for the metropolitan denizen. The adage is that due to the functions of mentality as an organon of organisation, orientation, relief of strain, alignment, regulation and integration we can gain an understanding of how urbanites render their metropolitan habitat intelligible. Insofar, the following concluding remarks on *The Intelligible Metropolis* are two-fold: first, they summarise major tendencies of representation as deciphered in the analysis of contemporary London novels. Second, they give an overview of the main results in regard to urban mentality and offer a profile on London-specific mentality, and finally propose a model of urban mentality fit to gain an understanding of the metropolis – for urbanite and urbanologist alike.

In general the textual interpretation brings to the fore dominant tendencies of development in regard to contemporary London fiction despite the large variety in topics and means of aesthetisation. The analysis of novels confirms Groes' (2011: 9) recent findings that contemporary London writers "all capture the contemporary by reacting to often rapidly changing politico-economic and socio-cultural contexts." Overall, the current literary discourses of the city still (or once more) follow the traditional forms of urban representation as identified by Carl Schorske (1977) or Raymond Williams (1984). The analysis elucidates the ongoing literary tradition of the city as Jerusalem or Babylon as commented on by other recent studies on the contemporary London novel (e.g. cf. Brooker 2000; Coverley 2005; Phillips 2006; Cuevas 2008a; James 2008; Groes 2011; McLeod 2011). On the one hand, these two principal modes of representation necessarily take into account urban-generic ambivalences, yet on the other hand they also mirror the urban life-cycle of a metropolis' rise and fall, translated into the persistent image of London as the phoenix. The latter particularly emerges during the epoch under analysis, as change of government and visible alterations to London's physical and social materiality gave rise to a collective structure of feeling of optimism for the city's future. Instead, the latest problems of the metropolis in the new age of terror and social disruption have once again emphasised the notion of the city's decline and expressed a certain pessimism in terms of London's future. Hence, these generic tendencies are retranslated into the cultural particularities of the millennial metropolis.

The first tendency of representation adhering to notions of New Jerusalem especially concerns narratives by authors from ethnic minorities or texts envisioning the multicultural metropolis, such as Monica Ali's *Brick Lane*, Gautam Malkani's *Londonstani*, but also Maggie Gee's *The White Family*, and Patrick Neate's *City of Tiny Lights*. Their visions of contemporary London follow urban representations by Hanif Kureishi, Salman Rushdie and Zadie Smith that "share [...] a cheerful optimism about the future of the metropolis, and, above all, the possibilities it offers to inscribe new voices and histories into the urban fabric" (Groes 2011: 261; cf. Brooker 2002: 75-95; James 2008: 71). These fictions of migration under analysis celebrate 'Babylonian confusion' in the sense that they stress the vigilance of their characters and emphasise the newness of culture developing in metropolitan London. Other postcolonial London novels published in the period between 1997 and 2007 that offer similar "[p]olycultural insights" (McLeod 2011: 244) and prove interesting as regards urban negotiations of hybridity and belonging include, for example, Courttia Newland's *The Scholar* (1997), Rocky Carr's *Brixton Bwoy* (1998), Meera Syal's *Life Isn't All Ha Ha Hee Hee* (1999), Diran Adebayo's *My Once Upon a Time* (2000), Bernadine Evaristo's *The Emperor's Babe* (2001), Alex Wheatle's *East of Acre Lane* (2001), Diana Evan's *26a* (2005), and Rose Tremain's *The Road Home* (2007). However, it is not only the novels exploring London's multicultural present which express a cheerful and forward-looking view, but also the novels with a vigilant but often marginalised female character at their centre promoting the freedom and industriousness of London's New Women, such as Nazneen and Rasia (BRL), Judy and Anita (BLL), Libby and Anthea (SOR), Jeanene and Hattie (LBR), Rosalind and Daisy (SAT), Elisa and Adelina (NXT). Insofar, novels that focus on the city's gender relations (e.g. by Sarah Waters or Alan Hollinghurst), but also chick lit (e.g. *Bridget Jones*, *West End Girls*) are equally positive in regard to urban autonomy and freedom. Additionally we might count novels to this section that express their optimism of the city by multiperspectively depicting London's relational flexibility and social multipolarities (253, LWD, SOR).

On the other hand, similar to post-war fiction until the 1990s, also millennial city novels in various stories of crisis have voiced their unease about the radical transformations London has undergone. These "[t]error visions" (McLeod 2011: 253) are particularly critical towards the changed landscape of the metropolis which is registered as rendered totalitarian by visual spectacality and simulation (KRA, REM, MIP). Also, the notion of the city in decline finds expression through the representations of anomie as the social flux of the Informational City dehumanises the urban or the Dual City brings to the fore various forms of injustice throughout urban society (SOR, NXT, LOR, UND, WIF). Besides these physical and social impacts of contemporary change, the mental consequences of postmodern overload are stressed and the psychological effects of international terrorism explored in an urban environment. Contemporary novelists named in connection with extreme dark visions of London are predominantly Iain Sinclair and the late J.G. Ballard (e.g. cf. Brooker 2002: 96-119; Phillips 2006: 159; James 2008: 71; Groes 2011: 251). In this present analysis besides Ballard's *Millennium People* particularly Brooke-Rose's *Next* can be enumerated as an example of horror scenarios of utter urban anomie. While these two writers must also be seen within the context of their generation (both were born before the Second World War and died recently), another important example from the study's list of "London Novels (1997-2007)" would include Peter Ackroyd's fiction. However, in contrast to earlier narratives of the 1980s I contend that even these dark and apocalyptic narratives of the city remain quite optimistic with respect to London's idiosyncratic potential for renewal by resisting the overwhelming fragmentation or homogenisation, as Groes (2011: 251) argues, in humanising the anomic city through intertextuality or metaphor – and I would add multiperspectivity and formal openness (e.g. in regard to genre).

Insofar, contemporary London novels and their two tendencies of representing urban life can also be differentiated with reference to the aesthetisation of the metropolis in these fictions of space. The first rather adheres to forms of representation as devised by Gelfant's understanding of the portrait or ecological study (LWD, WCB, BRL, SOR), while the second largely follows the conventions of the synoptic city novel (BLL, MAH). Correspondingly, Merlin Coverley (2005: 135-136) identifies two separate streams within postmodern urban fiction, namely the character-driven novels of the postcolonial genre whose interpersonal and family relations comment on the state of the city, as well as the inherently topographical construction of the metropolis as in the latter's symbolism.

Consequently, the two visions of London as Jersualem or Babylon in the novels considered also constitute a question of genre. In her analysis of postmodern London, Teske (1999: 250) underlines the novel of development and the postmodern novel of intertextuality on the one hand and detective fiction and the urban Gothic on the other. The present study's exploration of urban mentality particularly profited from visions of boundary crossings in the London noir of dystopian (253, REM, MIP), horror (LOR, KRA), or neo-Gothic (MAH, UND) fiction. These novels, especially those with an underground setting, emphasise the postmodern uncanny in contemporary fiction. The darker side of London as represented in mystery series, horror fiction and Gothic novels defies both topographic determinacy and definitive denomination of social reality (cf. James 2008: 73-74). Because London "is spatially and temporally too vast and various to be apprehended, especially at distance", according to Rawlinson (2002: 242-243), "London must be imagined". He identifies the "hallmark" of these sub-genres of city fiction as conceiving the metropolis' temporal and symbolic dimensions rather than of purely spatial coordinates, particularly stressing its "mental dimensions" (*ibid.*: 247).

But although Groes (2011: 269) argues that London writing has recently moved away from the occult writing that dominated the city's imaginaries for so long, successful London novels such as Nicholas Royle's *The Director's Cut* (2000), Will Self's *How the Dead Live* (2000) and *Dorian* (2002), China Miéville's New Crobuzon novels *Perdido Street Station* (2000) and *Iron Council* (2004), Martin Amis' *Yellow Dog* (2003) and Hillary Mantel's *Beyond Black* (2005) by contrast confirm Coverley's (2005: 18, 26) notion that the Gothic remains central to contemporary writings on the city. Furthermore, the popularity of writers like Ruth Rendell/Barbara Vine or Christopher Fowler, whose novels are largely set in London, does not show any sign of abating. Within the voluminous corpus of London literature in the list at the end of this book there are a number of titles that belong to long-running thriller, detective and mystery series emplaced in the metropolitan milieu. In that sense, it is my intention to promote a more varied approach to urban literature that is also open to non-canonical and popular fiction, for example Anne Perry's criminal topography in her London detective series – *Brunswick Gardens* (1998), *Bedford Square* (1999), *Half Moon Street* (2000), *The Whitechapel Conspiracy* (2001), *Southampton Row* (2004), *Seven Dials* (2004), *Long Spoon Lane* (2005) – which is expected to yield interesting perspectives on the city's idiosyncrasy beyond the notion of a genre that is seen as predominantly plot-driven.

In regard to critical acclaim, however, I am inclined to agree with the critics' view, that prominent mythologies of the Thatcherite era have disintegrated and left the stage for bestselling novels of neo-realist style (cf. Cuevas 2008b: 385; Groes 2011: 257). Award-winning and short-listed authors in the period (e.g. Abani, Alderman, Ali, Evans, Guo, Heller, Levy, Lott, McEwan, St. John, Swift, Smith, Tremain) have written London novels that are socio-realist in kind rather than postmodern and experimental. Moreover, even the genre novels of the selected corpus, such as the texts by de Abaitua, Ballard, Miéville, Nicholson, Ryman, and Williams, were exposed as mundane, new wave, or weird fiction, wherein the fantastic element predominantly frames the 'reality' of their visions. Also, for example, *London in Contemporary British Fiction: Beyond the City?* to be published with Bloomsbury in 2014 captures this movement to the factual. While the editors, Nick Hubble, Phil Tew, and Lynn Wells, emphasise that the visionary comes to look like social realism, Groes (2011: 260) in other more factual writing, like that by McEwan's, detects "mythologies pushing through the surface of fictional narratives, also waiting to be excavated." As continuously pointed out in the brief summaries of the novels and apparent from the previous explanations, contemporary London writing is often based on the appropriation of various genre or stylistic elements. Insofar, I contend with Groes (*ibid.*: 259) that contemporary London novels are rather strongly hybrid in terms of genre.

And this initially also applies to their representation of London beyond the traditional imagery of Jerusalem or Babylon. For one, the depiction of everyday life and urban routine in the novels stresses that the exceptional, which oscillates between good and bad or becomes apparent in the London trope of 'attraction and repulsion', is part of urbanity itself. However, the present study has identified a strong thirdspace perspective from the city's margin. For example, China Miéville's *King Rat* celebrates the vigilance of urban subculture and multiculturalism while simultaneously exposing the socio-cultural strain of London's pariah. Like the novels by de Abaitua, Williams, and Neate the text stresses liminality, heterogeneity and strangeness as a particular self-regulating mechanism by the metropolis in order to counter totalitarian anomie or initiate its own resurrection, thus underlining the trope of London as phoenix and eternal – but worldly – city. Also McLeod (2011: 249) identifies a third tendency in the representation of the contemporary city in the depiction of "[u]nseen lives". For Cuevas (2008a: 35) this 'third way' constitutes the "carnivalesque tradition" which disrupts conventional notions of the post-colonial metropolis. Hence, I agree with Brooker (2002: 198) on the note that even contemporary images of Babylon and Jerusalem are initially both perspectives from the urban margins which enable the productive re-imagination of the contemporary metropolis and enhance the intelligibility of postmodern urbanity. While McLeod pays particular attention to the texts set in the other domineering area of recent city novels, Brick Lane and the East End, the present analysis has revealed that underground London also serves as a dominant trope for these unseen lives on the margin in an abundance of recent texts – literary, essayistic, academic. What the underground is initially able to depict more directly is the uncanny element of postmodern urban unknowingness, invisibility, and uncertainty. At the first glance, this 'thirdspace' of imaginary London simply seems to adhere to contemporary post-positivist notions, but the urban beyond the polarities of good or evil was already identified by Schorske and notably takes into account the general ambivalent constellations intrinsic to the metropolis.

Furthermore, the present analysis has exposed major tropes and themes which have so far not found much resonance with researchers of literary London but are highly promising for Cultural and Literary Studies. In the following passages I will briefly summarise a few of those themes that prevailed throughout the novels under consideration in this work. Most notably the theoretical and methodological focus on space yielded interesting results beyond structuralist approaches on spatial semantics. This becomes particularly apparent in the chapters on "Underground London" and "Navigating the Flux" in connection with the space of flows, mobility, and urban perception. The novels discussed are noteworthy for their portrayal and aesthetisation of the metropolitan landscape, smellscape, soundscape. Without question, more innovative input, as deduced from spatial theories, is needed to better understand these physical, social and mental constructions of a cultural sensescape in narrative literature. Useful approaches are David James' (2008) re-appropriation of narrative form and emphasis on focalisation or Gertrud Lehnert's (2011) collection on emotions and the Spatial Turn. Regardless of the artistic intention in each novel, this study has shown how the city as a physical fact is locally lived in, but the city as a cluster of signs and associations must be mentally processed, imaginatively inhabited, metaphorically and metonymically translated. As the novels show, only when interpreted by visual, auditional, olfactional, gustational, and habtic means of perception does the once material space become a mental city.

Closely related, on the other hand, are aesthetic and stylistic innovations abundant in the novels under consideration. Contemporary novels of consciousness (NXT), meta-consciousness texts (SAT), postmodern neuro-novels (REM), and texts of panoptic perspectivity (253) prove highly innovative in their narratological constructions of the mental city. James (2008: 95) already comments on this new trend in fictions of urban space:

> They exploit the hazards of experiencing a city in actuality whose potential has only previously been tested in the mind. Evoking sensations of space at the level of style they imply that radical changes to our physical world can only occur by harnessing new connections between topography and perceptions; that our built environment remains somehow too encrypted to be apprehended solely in terms of its visible present; and that our mineral universe can only be redeemed with 'a powerful dose of fiction.

This new version of the synoptic novel might also concern contemporary unreliable narrations on the city, such as in Hanif Kureishi's *Intimacy* (1999), Zoë Heller's *Notes on a Scandal* (2003), or Clare Allan's *Poppy Shakespeare* (2006).

Moreover, the analytical examples have repeatedly referred to the particularly intermedial component in contemporary London fiction. Not only is Geoff Ryman's text *253* the first book adaptation of one of the earliest internet novels and sublimely integrates the notion of the hypertext in the narrative structure, but the story itself is interspersed with an array of intermedial references. Moreover, 'laddish' literature (TUV, WCB, COR, LON) strongly alludes to popular culture throughout, while the novels that could be seen in the tradition of psychogeographical writing (KRA, MAH, BLL) are even symbolically constructed around references to music, art, and most notably film. And last but not least, many texts scrutinise the influence of the media and their new dynamics on urbanites, their respective perception, and ultimately way of knowing the city (NXT, SAT, MIP, REM). Especially these aspects offer multiple points of interest for the intersection of Cultural, Urban and Media Studies.

The intermedial notion of hypertextuality ties in with the idea of the intertextual palimpsest. As regards the relevance of the palimpsest as master metaphor for the contemporary city, for further research it would be interesting to explore in a more differentiated way the concrete postmodern usage of urban figures – *flâneur*, narrator, stranger, revenant. The underlying principle of both tropes, the palimpsest and the underground, is the historical layering and the interconnected ideas of memory and trauma. In this respect, the Holocaust has become a new level of reference for (urban) trauma, but has also developed into a metaphor for otherness, expulsion, displacement, inbetweenness, diaspora, resistance against totalitarianism (UND, 253, KRA). Once again the openness of the metropolis thereby serves as a counter-image to the enclosed nation state and other absolute notions of identity. In the meantime, traditional notions of horror have been replaced by allusions to 9/11 and 7/7 as literary ciphers for terror. The structures of feeling explored in this connection are also denoted by trauma (New York), but in the case of London have to be viewed more in relation to a form of expectancy fear as explicated in the last analytical chapter. According to Elias (1994b) phases of civilisatory shifts have always been initiated by strong pushes of anxiety which notably changed attitudes and manners. Thus, it remains to be discussed whether the general structure of feeling wrought by anxiety is not indicative of a new age rather than a response to the war on terror.

A protective mechanism necessary against these feelings of terror and for a stable existence is offered by the characters' routine practices. On the one hand, routine thereby becomes expression and cause of urban blasé, while on the other hand, the texts under analysis have also shown that in the Postmetropolis even the exceptional, such as spectacles or apocalyptic events, have taken the form of routine. Even the most experimental of the novels through the sense of routine also capture this sense of the everyday life in the city. Insofar, the narrative genre seems indeed most appropriate to represent the common urban way of life and common thinking as of interest for the historians of mentalities. Furthermore, the dominant metaphor of the city's impact upon the urbanites' body, particularly the skin, emphasises how the metropolis is incorporated in the single individual – also again by his or her acculturation – to the set rules of public conduct. Through the city's "total impact upon the mind, imagination and spirit" (Gelfant 1954:

4) and the body, the Londoner is created. In this respect, the present publication also vouches for a more careful future differentiation between constructions of urban versus national identity, particularly in fictions of migration. Further research should exhibit a stronger awareness of this opposition as indicated by the predominant underlying principles analysed in the texts and already described by Braudel, namely that of annexation with reference to the nation and that of inclusion for the city.

It was the objective of the present study to examine London novels published between 1997 and 2007 for their representations of urban-generic and urban-specific mentality. For the purpose of drawing up major axioms of Mentality Studies, the treatise first developed a systematic concept of mentality based on the assumptions of the historians of mentalities, the sociology of knowledge, and Cultural Studies. Mentalities were defined as contemporary or historical constructions of reality and identified as consisting of a functional (organon) and structural (rhizome) side. These dispositions of thinking, imagining, feeling and acting were consequently identified as shaped by the determinants of collectivity, time, space and collective space-time compression. Most importantly, the theoretical assumptions were subject to modifications in relation to space. This analysis expanded on the notion of regional mentality to the preliminaries of the Spatial Turn. Insofar, spatial mentality was shown to serve as a particular category of urban knowing that influences a certain spatial manageability of the habitat where physical, social and mental spatialities are concerned.

In a second step various theories of urbanity by modern sociologists, new urban economists, and postmodern urbanolgists were examined for their characterisations of a particular urban *conditio humana* and its underlying mental dispositions. These insights, for example on urban overload and protective mechanisms, social worlds and habitual role play, the city as a space of flows and its symbolic signification, as well as postmodern notions of simulation, spectacle and psychasthenia concurred in drawing up a synthetic concept of urban mentality. This model allows to both scrutinise the idiosyncrasy of the city in general and transfer the analysis of mentality to other metropolises worldwide. While urban-generic structures of thinking, imagining, feeling and acting are shown to be based on a configuration of eight predominant ambivalences, the urban-specific factors of influence are drawn from theories of urban semantics. The categories developed here served as a major focus for the literary analysis. Methodologically, this study is based on a confluence of approaches as delineated by the history of mentalities, Cultural Studies and Literary Studies. Thereby the present book strongly argues for a narratological approach to deciphering mentalities not only in narrative fiction but other cultural practices and beyond. Due to the intricate relations between mentality-city-novel the conceptional frame of reference was, however, enlarged to a current spatio-narratological approach to mentalities.

On the basis of these theoretical premises and methodological approaches the analysis of twenty London novels identified a variety of spatio-cultural recurrences and deciphered them for eight dominant structures of London-specific mentality. Under the notion of mentality as a rhizome of intelligibility these various structures are necessarily diverging in their representations, ambivalent in themselves, contradictory towards one another and interspersed by various temporal layers. In the following I will summarise and elaborate on this deduced typology of contemporary London mentality.

(1) Isolationist Structures of Mentality identified in contemporary London novels are mainly built on various constructions of boundaries between public and private spaces. They serve the function of organisation, orientation, relief of strain, and regulation. Isolationist dispositions of thinking, imagining and feeling in particular must be read as protective mechanisms against the urban *sensu* public overload of stimuli. Conversely, habitual attitudes of urban conduct and role-play are necessarily directed towards public behaviour and oriented to official norms and language codes. Insofar, the construction of container spaces, for example in the form of postmodern Privatopias, results from the inherent deficiency and need of privacy in the Postmetropolis. This spatial (b)ordering, formed on the notion of absolute and homogeneous spaces of security, however, moves along strongly demarcated lines of social exclusion often oriented towards a normative definition of national identity. Hence, it also reveals residual or even resurgent positivist thinking in regard to urban hegemonies of ethnicity, class, gender, and generation. Paradoxically, isolation as a response to urban alienation, disorientation, strangeness, etc. is consequently countered by the construction of spaces of privacy which lie outside the traditional constraints of the family home. The analysis has illustrated how, for instance, professional life as a significant form of routine behaviour dominates the thinking of urbanites and constitutes a majorly important aspect for retaining a sane private life. Likewise, personal catharsis in the public theatre that is the city was demonstrated as a measure for an inner cleansing without which urban sociability is in the danger of shifting towards anomie. Because of the urban-generic characteristics of inattention and non-involvement, the most public spaces of London, such as the Tube or its city squares, prove to offer the strongest forms of privacy, namely introspection within the anonymity of the urban crowd. With intertextual references to Victorianism and Modernism, contemporary London novels also expose the altered relations between public and private. In the space of flows of the postmodern city boundaries have become permeable, for instance in the privatisation of public space by personal drama or the penetration of the public by the media. Furthermore, semi-public spaces of shopping centres or the social spaces of new community structures throughout the metropolis offer Londoners room for (de)distanciation and describe the postmodern urban individual as a truly liminal being who for protective measures exhibits isolationist mental dispositions.

(2) Subterranean Structures of Mentality describe standardisations of thinking, imagining, feeling and acting with regard to underground London. As a particularly dominant and absolutely idiosyncratic spatiality of the metropolis, no other location within the city has proved so important for the construction of Londoners' mental dispositions; no other landmark looms so strongly in the imagination of contemporary urbanites and determines their frame of mind. The Underground proves a particular locus for the acculturation and socialisation and hence inner urbanisation because of the urban-generic as well as specific rules of Tube etiquette, such as indifference, inattention and non-involvement. While serving as a necessary physical but also mental topos of introspection it simultaneously casts the encounter of the Self with the/its Other. Both mirror and counterpart to the London above, the underground functions as the city's main heterotopian spatiality. As a space of juxtaposition and simultaneity it not only stresses the enhanced spatialised thinking in the postmodern space age, but also the dominance of thirdspaces, inbetweenness and liminality. For the city itself, underground London constitutes the most dominant margin of the metropolis within. As the site of the urban uncanny be-

tween familiarity and strangeness, the underground induces cognitive uncertainty while concomitantly offering sublime knowledge on the urban. Insofar, subterranean structures of mentality serve the main functions of integration, organisation and orientation.

(3) Also the (Sub)Textual Structures of Mentality emphasise the functional character of mentality for organisation, orientation and relief of strain within the postmodern metropolis. These (sub)textual dispositions of thinking, imagining, feeling and acting nonconsciously employed in contemporary London adhere to the changed dynamics of metropolitan space and hence particularly underline the function of alignment. To counter confusion arising from the fragmentation of the urban landscape, the loss of the subject in the space of flows, and to counteract the strain on the individual induced by the enhanced dynamics of the Postmetropolis, urbanites adopt new forms of perceiving and conceiving city spaces to render the city both legible and intelligible. In order to navigate the metropolitan flux, the diagrammatic metaphor of the map serves as a tool to render the city legible as a whole. These mapping processes, however, go hand in hand with *flânerie* as both writing and reading the urban. Even more so, the synaesthetic perception of the urban realm which defies visual totalitarianism is able to combine both the spatial simultaneity of the map with the narrative space-time of the *tours* in its mobile sensescape, and elucidates a new psycho-somatic understanding of the city. Another combined form of intelligibility and legibility of the urban is offered Londoners by way of the meta-conscious constructions of science, literature and art. The knowledge accumulated in city-texts nonconsciously informs the urbanite and helps the denizen to counter feelings of disorientation or loss.

(4) Palimpsestuous Structures of Mentality likewise pay heed to textual patterns of understanding the city. As the master metaphor in contemporary London novels, the palimpsest describes a particularly idiosyncratic means of constructing urban reality. The trope unifies notions of textual impressions of the city text and mental textures with the notion of collective space-time compressions. As a temporal account of textual (re)inscriptions through history, the palimpsest presents London as a city of constant becoming. These multi-temporal levels of time in accordance with temporal mentality illustrate persistancies and transformations of London's frame of mind and its urban characteristics. But this mental phenomenon not only concerns the *lieux de mémoire* of great history, but also the hidden little stories of the everyday and those of personal memory. These invisible layers of significance are especially registered by the semantic stalking of the London psychogeographer, a reader of the urban text and author of palimpsestic re- and overwritings. The postcolonial and global city of London with its international flows of migration has lately also experienced processes of intercultural palimpsesting. Hence, the cityscape as a text written by and rewriting the lives of its denizens becomes a pool of (inter)cultural knowledge. Palimpsestuous dispositions of thinking, imagining, feeling and acting thus are highly inclusive towards the urban stranger, yet exclusively London-like. This interconnective way of knowing London, moreover, becomes apparent in intertextual and hypertextual notions of the palimpsest which make it possible for the urbanite to navigate between the real, the imaginary and the hyperreal. The incorporation of palimpsestuous mental structures becomes apparent in the personification of (de)palimpsesting urban figures, whose frame of mind serves as a major coping mechanism and organon against the strain exerted by the multivalent Postmetropolis. The

palimpsestuous structures of mentality allow Londoners to actively revise, retranslate and reread the urban and thereby make the city intelligible.

(5) The Mental Structures of Relational Fluidity are both contradictory and countervailing to isolationist dispositions. Relational fluidity in mental dispositions serves primarily as an organon of alignment to the dynamic socioscape of London's metropolitan life. While relationships seem to shift to secondary relations, new and quasi primary social connections are also created which are still emplaced but less relegated to particular ecological spaces within the city. Due to deficiently felt situations urbanites become vigilant in order to escape the narrow bonds of personal contacts built on social contractuality or the apathic but sometimes necessary phases of seclusion and isolation. For example, due to an enhanced individuation of society, oversaturated loneliness seems to constitute a new form of present-day overload which leads to depression, schizophrenia, or even suicide. A pronounced blasé is also registered, as a critical assessment of the overload effect on the postmodern society of spectacle towards anomie. By contrast, the second form positively rates the new sociability created by transnational or transcultural communities for which the multicultural socioscape of the postcolonial city serves as a contact zone. Both share a notion of social life in transition and inbetween. In this unbounded system, the nationally enclosed (wo)man necessarily fails to adapt to the city while the cosmopolitan equipped with a categorical knowledge of other urban strangers has incorporated a practical *outillage mental* of metropolitan social intelligibility.

(6) The Mental Structures of Deviance bring to the fore that in the postmodern social habitat of metropolarities urbanites have to adapt to their changing position of in/outsider. In this sense, mentality once again stresses its potential of integration which is shown by the reinclusive of the essentially marginal into urban mainstream. The novels depict a crisis of old-standing hegemonies within the urban realm, which due to *différance* and multiple lines of stratification have become dispersed if not obsolete. Because of enhanced individuation, deviance has become the norm that affords a greater freedom (of thinking, imagining, feeling, acting) for those who have for long found themselves on the margins of the metropolitan socioscape. While the texts chart a loss of acumen of the urban middle-class, or a boost of masculinity as sign of crisis, London has long since become a place of hybrid mentalities. Nevertheless, even in the city of metropolarities a new, largely invisible, yet regulating underclass is forming which inhabits similar pariahhoods of the metropolis as were already prevalent during the nineteenth century, namely the East End. The notion of the integrated urban stranger might stem from the perspectives of the margins expressed in both traditions of literary representations of London, which ultimately make for the optimism charted in contemporary writing with regard to the city.

(7) Hypertrophic Structures of Mentality particularly describe the mental dispositions of acting in regard to the individual in the space of flows. The mental frame of mind, which strives for integration in the fluid relations of the postmodern city and its diverging metropolarities, are adapted in the sense that concepts of urban role-play are reinterpreted for urbanites who have become accustomed to feign society. While the downside might register urbanites who fall prey to schizophrenia, successful responses to the fleeting social situations favour the vigilance of urbanites who are able to oscillate within an array of hybrid identities, but who remain authentic or true to themselves. This pronouncement of vexative self-fashioning and hybrid identity formation in the

contemporary city becomes apparent in the analogy of space and body that can lead to psychasthenia. Moreover, the grotesque constructions of corporeal excess as depicted in contemporary novels rather seem to celebrate this new openness and carnivalesque of the multiple city as an expression of hybrid individualism and the struggle towards an "outillage renouvelé" (Febvre 2003b: 166). By contrast, the mind seems to be more endangered by media influences and cultural homogenisation, where spectacle and simulation but also a resurgent Social Darwinism or the new findings in the sciences exert fear of potential mind control on the urban masses. In a sense, hypertrophy describes another form of organisation and orientation in order not to become lost in the metropolis, a hyperbolic response in regard to the Self that oscillates between narcissism and individuation.

(8) Terror Structures of Mentality especially take into account the dispositions of feeling during the period between 1997 and 2007. Despite all notions of a strong optimism at least during the first term of Blair's office, in tropes of attraction of repulsion, crime, terror and apocalypse, the texts expose a psychology of underlying mental fear that reaches back to Lady Diana's death, resurges with the millennium and transforms into an expectancy fear after 9/11 and real terror with 7/7. Fear of urban crisis and catastrophe especially spurs the imagination and influences urbanites' emotional life. Insofar, terror structures of mentality might be seen as a concomitant structure of both isolationism and deviance. In effect, they question the persistent dispositional nature of Londoners' stoicism exhibited in times of crises. As such, it seems a necessary functional prerequisite of alignment to the everyday dangers of urban life which has become pronounced by the threat of international urban terrorism. In reference to Elias' notion of fear as a sign of civilisatory change, we can also read the apocalypticism exposed at the end of the analysis not as indicator of a bleak picture of London's fall, but the herald of the transitional mental structures of London from the second to the third millennium in developing into something uncannily new – maybe once again truly idiosyncratic urban.

On the basis of these complex insights into the structures of London mentality it might seem problematic to further abstract urban dispositions of thinking, imagining, feeling and acting to two contradictory levels of London mentalities, such as is the case with Britain's insular and empire mentality. However, in regard to the mindscape of London – as a certain spatial manageability of the postmodern metropolis – we can nevertheless discern dominant tropes (*loci communis*) of the city's physical, social and mental space. From my point of view, inherent in the above-mentioned mental rhizome consisting of eight central nodes are the recurrent and dominating superstructures of text, flow, uncanny. The physical cityscape is predominantly understood as texture and consequently the monumental architecture of London's visual spectaclisation can best be countered with measures of rereading and rewriting. Moreover, it underlines the interconnectedness of London's spatialities inbetween its social worlds and to other places in the world. The latter also stresses the main image of the space of flows particularly apparent in the city's social relations which demand flexibility, fluidity, transcience. In this sense, hypertrophy and vigilant restlessness function as the mental responses of a rhythmicity similar to that of the metropolis adopted to dispositions of thinking, imagining, feeling and acting. This perpetual mobility, movement, transit also expose the constant liminal and third-space position which takes a significant toll on urbanites' mind. In regard to the mental spaces, urbanites construct dispositions of the sublime, terror, and the uncanny. This agency offers the possibility to detect the familiar in the unfamiliar and make the unhomely homely again, thus creates spatial manageability that defies disorientation and loss of the Self and from uncertainty promotes urban intelligibility.

It was the venture of the present study to uncover London mentality, namely in urban-generic and urban-specific mental dispositions. For example, the palimpsestuous structures of London mentality were shown to be based on urban-generic ambivalences of familiarity and strangeness or heterogeneity and homogeneity, whereas the structures particularly pronounce the latter aspects which are notably interpreted as generally more urban. Furthermore, the palimpsestuous mentality has also shown that these structures based on a dominant metaphor rather emphasise dispositions of the imaginary.

The following model (see figure 9.1) may serve as a visual abstraction of the above-mentioned results. It strives to emplace the London-specific mentality within the transformative model of urban-generic configurations of ambivalence. As Kuhlemann (1996: 209) stresses, mentality always favours a particular substantial 'form' of culture. In this sense, the model seeks to finally make visible the structure of London's dispositions of thinking (yellow), imagining (blue), feeling (red), and acting (green). The image shows a scaling of the eight configurations of ambivalence and illustrates the dominant tendencies generating the London-specific mentality within these as represented in London fiction between 1997 and 2007.

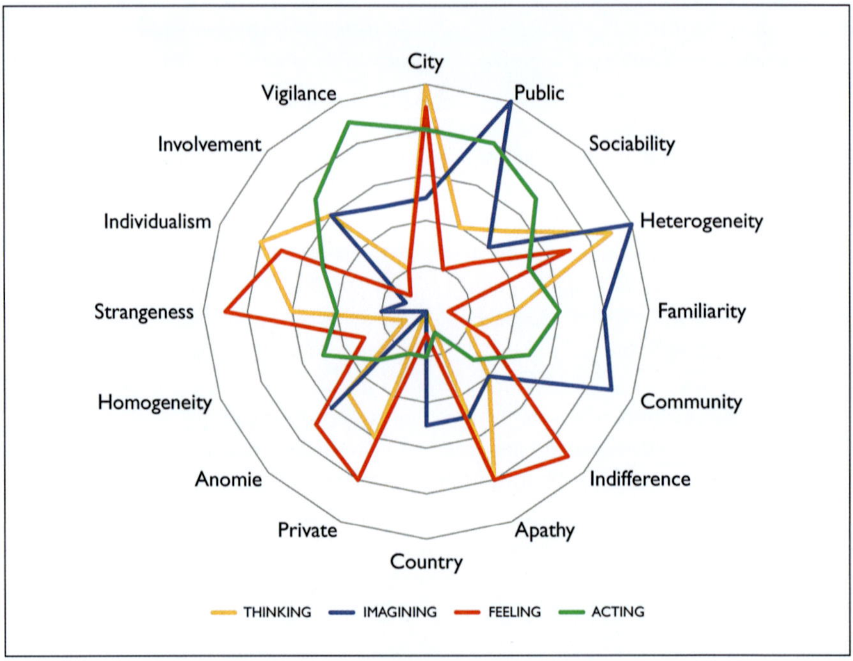

Figure 9.1: London-Specific Mentality

Due to the chosen modelling the depicted tendencies concern roughly estimated relations, which are to be understood as extracts from the textual analysis and the results of the single structures of mentality. The model, for example, exposes how dispositions of feeling (red) and thinking (yellow) are oriented more towards the private and less to the public (terror and isolationism) while dispositions of imagination (blue) cast urbanites' intimacy predominantly under strain by the public (media) and dispositions of behaviour (green) oriented towards non-involvement or catharsis by enhanced role-play (performativity).

For Hutton (1981: 238), "[t]he historian of mentalities maps the mental universe which furnishes a culture with its essential characteristics" and accordingly the following separate 'mental maps' intend to make visible and delineate the mindscapes of contemporary Londoners' dispositions of thinking, imagining, feeling, and acting (see figure 9.2). These four figures illustrate well the semantic field of London's contemporary constructions of reality. Moreover, the whole graph exposes the contradictory dispositions but also emphasises their overlapping structures.

The dispositions of thinking mainly refer to nonconscious cognitive constructions of reality. The novels thereby particularly elucidate on various tools – such as the abstractions in mental maps, professional or literary intelligibility, or the linguistic (b)ordering practices – hence textual instruments as viable standardisations of thinking for navigating the postmodern city.

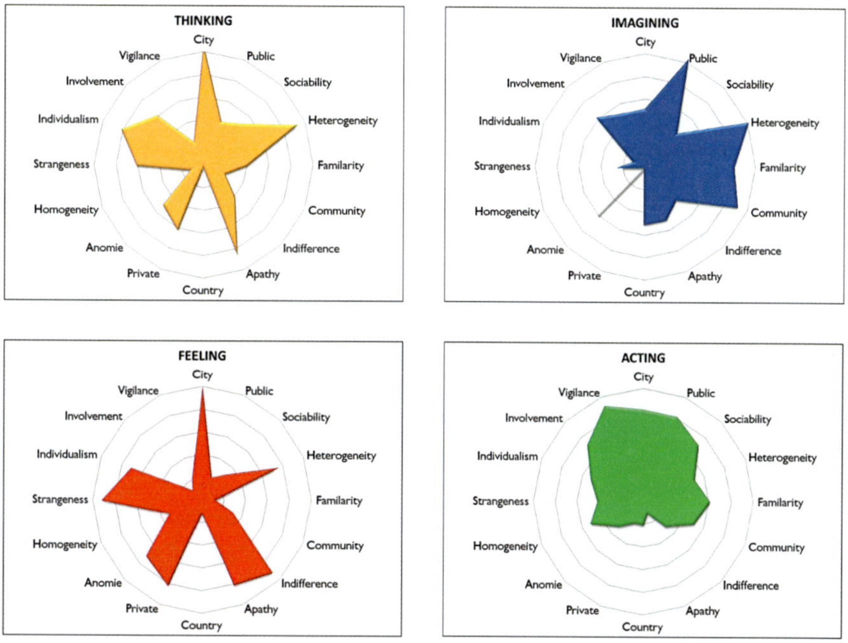

Figure 9.2: Mindscapes of London-Specific Dispositions

The first mind map shows that in regard to the ambivalence of city and country the concentration on the urban absolutely prevails, so that the metropolis really serves as the major ontological reference for urbanites, which underlines metropolitan idiosyncrasy. Moreover, the definite disposition of urbanites' thinking reveals the concern for retaining their privacy and personal identity as well as thoughts of their public image. This likewise concerns urbanites' attitudes towards sociability and anomie. Their thinking and the pre-requisite structures of thinking are meanwhile attuned to a high degree of homogeneity, as urban denizens see themselves as isolated in the midst of strangers – hence the slump in familiarity. Urbanites' cognitive apparatus is strongly determined by a notion of strangeness. Solitary contractuality, issues of personal identity and relational flexibility are all visible effects of the growing individualisation of urban society which does, however, not fully negate community. Strangely enough, the overwhelming blasé attitude that defines urbanites' thinking as apathy dominates over vigilance, probably mostly pursued by the female protagonists, newcomers to the city, the younger generations and the long-established Londoner in times of severe crisis.

Dispositions of imagining in my point of view are quite dominant in the contemporary social construction of London reality. On the one hand, this refers to London's prominence in the common or popular imagination of Londoners and newcomers alike, for example, through the literature of Dickens, but has also become pronounced due to New Labour's image campaign on the metropolis which boosted or resurrected particular imaginary tropes of the city that define London mentality. Two major tropes, that of the palimpsestuous city and that of underground London, were revealed as particularly dominating in the contemporary frame of mind. However, generic images of Babylon and Jerusalem or London as the eternal city and phoenix also constitute a current and recurrent notion that defines structures of representation. The imaginary becomes further spurred by the general idea of unknowingness, whereby the city is paradoxically rendered intelligible (familiar) or in regard to danger where potential crises constantly loom in the imagination of people. Interesting in the map of the London imaginary is that only here do we find a slight tendency towards visions of country life. Furthermore, everything is envisaged as public, heterogeneous, anomic, but also communal because the city is always imagined as a grand mass of the crowd in which urbanites see themselves involved in.

The dispositions of feeling are notably of importance in regard to the uncertainty experienced in the London underground and the prevailing structures of terror despite the pre-millennial optimism and the rather positive view of London between 1997 and 2007. Also here the emotional investment in the urban looms higher than the rare nostalgia for a life in the country. Unsurprisingly, feelings and emotions are still dominantly oriented towards privacy, intimacy, the family, etc. while public catharsis and feelings of apartheid do not completely leave emotions in the realm of the private. However, privacy is still the last resort against feelings of danger, terror, fear, hatred etc. that are seemingly abundant in the urban public. Likewise the feeling of anomie prevails over sociability, strangeness over familiarity and emotional non-involvement over empathy. And similar to the structures of thinking also emotional dispositions of vigilance, elation and happiness, for example in leaps of attraction for London, are only expressed momentarily, while cautious apathy prevails at least for the long-term residents of the city.

Dispositions of acting have particularly become under scrutiny in regard to public and private behaviour, Tube etiquette, public role-play, and performativity, but also strategies of non-involvement. Inner urbanisation especially in regard to urban forms of conduct are significant as apparent in the transformative periods of culture shock and acculturation often notable in enhanced overload or apathy. Nevertheless, the space of flows, but especially the fast-track life of London, demands vigilant doxic structures of behaviour, and hereby the dispositions of acting are contrary to those of all other three maps. This fourth cluster is interesting in at least two other aspects: the mental map appears more homogeneous and self-contained in the upper sphere of the graph. The corresponding emphasis of involvement, vigilance, city, public and sociality indicate how strongly dispositions of behaviour are integrative for the common conduct, norms and values exhibited in metropolitan life. This is of particular relevance in connection with anomie: while urban deviancies and anomie foster the notion of criminality, urban sociability is mostly successful in countering anomic dispositions of behaviour. It also explains the equilibrium where ambivalences of strangeness and familiarity, community and individualism, or heterogeneity and homogeneity are concerned.

For a comparison of the four separate mental maps in unison there are at least two notable aspects to be mentioned: whereas the structure of the mental map of the dispositions of thinking and the dispositions of feeling is similar in shape, important aspects are diametrically opposed, showing that sometimes thinking and feeling are indeed two different phenomena, also in the sense that one stresses notions of cognitive intelligibility and the other psycho-somatic legibility. By contrast, the other two clusters of imagining and acting illustrate a shift towards the right side of the graph. Going back to the composite image of all four mental dispositions (see figure 9.1), it becomes clear that, not unlike insular and empire mentality, they both function as protective mechanisms towards one another. With the exceptions of 'homogeneity' and 'country' all ambivalences are equally registered, thus fully taking in the complexity that is the postmodern metropolis of London.

Certainly, the model requires further revision and refinement. But although these visualised results might seem predictable for some or totally arbitrary for others, it is worthwhile conducting the same analysis on other discursive practices of the time, such as architecture, postcards, travel books, London films or journal articles, to see whether the results show a similar pattern of mental dispositions. Also, these models remain necessarily temporal in their expression. Because this is only a momentary map, the scapes in other epochs of London, for example during Thatcherism, might look very different. A comparison could then achieve some kind of cartographic visibility of transformations of mentality. On the other hand, not only can these shapes expose differences and similarities for diachronic comparison, but could also serve as a viable base of synchronic comparison with other contemporary metropolises.

Mentality Studies, as noted before, are a particular apt approach for a highly complex subject, such as is the city. And this present study hopes to have shown that mentality presents an important aspect in the understanding of the urban; mentality renders the metropolis both legible and intelligible. In conclusion, I propose to explicitly include the concept of mentality and the approach of Mentality Studies into studies of urbanity. While Martina Löw (2008: 31) notes that comparative studies between cities still lack a characteristic or typological notion of the urban, I suggest that the model of urban-generic and urban-specific mentality acts as this missing link. As a collective of nonconscious dispositions of thinking, feeling, imagining and acting, mentality exactly serves the "*comparative consciousness*" (*ibid.*: 101) sought after as a tool for comparative studies on cities.

Critics have persistently acknowledged the mental side of urban culture as an integral part of Urban Studies. Urban sociologists have suggested the model of the city as a state of mind. Mentality also explains the processes scrutinised by cognitive geographers of "how the mind and the senses take in the world, construct it, or on occasion are confounded by it." (Alter 2005: xi). Mentality decisively opens the view on the collective mode of conceptualising and perceiving space and composing commonly held urban images. Cognitive maps and mentality both propose that urban images have an implication towards people's behaviour, but the mental structures not only include the physical factors of the city but also the imaginary and symbolic side. As a construction of reality which expresses standardisations of thinking in metaphorical form, mentality is connected to the metaphorisation of the urban concerning processes of man-environment relations.

Hence, by proposing its mentality as a further dimension of the city, I suggest that we gain an insight into the missing link of what has been the dark spot in the interrelation of space, everyday practice and the imagery. The concept of mentality follows the call for a multifaceted, interdisciplinary approach to the urban and finally enables a loosening of the "tangle of physicality and symbolism" and re-structuring of the "mingling of imaginings and experiences" (Highmore 2005: 5). The concept of mentality poses a conceptual deficit between physical city and imagined cityscape, which plays a pivotal role in everyday culture and the understanding thereof. Finally, the concept of mentality overcomes the culturally constructed problem "of how accurately the city or urban life is depicted" and makes it possible again to concentrate on the "question of what the urban is used to signify, what the urban scene means." (Crang 1998: 50) Cultural productions and textual representations of urban space always posed the problem to render space legible and representations have helped in doing so by semantic practices, images and discourses. Finally, literary London texts are inter-discursive negotiations of the city in which the metonymic, symbolic and metaphoric seemingly blur factual and fictional aspects and expose contemporary social constructions of reality – or London mentality.

With the start of the twenty-first century, urbanologists register twenty-two megalopolises with eight-figure population and thirteen megacities, such as Tokyo, São Paolo, New York, Mexico City, Shanghai, Mumbai, Los Angeles, Buenos Aires, Seoul, Beijing, Rio de Janeiro, Calcutta and Osaka, with more than ten million inhabitants (cf. Amin & Thrift 2002: 1; Parker 2004: 1). This suggests more than enough possible research for synchronic comparisons in regard to urban mentality, such as that of post-9/11 New York or Berlin in the transitional phase of the 1990s after the Fall of the Iron Curtain. However, it would be interesting to see whether the model equally works on megapolitan areas like Los Angeles and the emergent megacities like Shanghai which are generally attested to be (yet) without a specific character, let alone a collective frame of mind. I would argue, however, that research of mentalities might actually bring to the fore their urban idiosyncrasies. In this respect, the present study calls for a general promotion of the concept of mentality as a new interdisciplinary paradigm for urban experience especially within

Cultural and Urban Studies ("mental turn"). As such, the book hopes to provide a tool which makes contemporary London and its fictions of space truly *intellegible*.

Works Cited

PRIMARY LITERATURE

Abaitua, Matthew de (2007), *The Red Men*, London: Snowbooks. [REM]

Ali, Monica (2004), *Brick Lane* (¹2003), London *et al.*: Black Swan. [BRL]

Ballard, J.G. (2004), *Millennium People* (¹2003), London: Harper Perennial. [MIP]

Brooke-Rose, Christine (1998), *Next*, Manchester: Carcanet. [NXT]

Gee, Maggie (2002), *The White Family*, London: Saqi. [WIF]

Hill, Tobias (1999), *Underground*, London: Faber and Faber. [UND]

Hornby, Nick (2006), *A Long Way Down* (¹2005), London: Penguin. [LWD]

Litt, Toby (2000), *Corpsing*, London: Penguin. [COR]

Lott, Tim (2000), *White City Blue* (¹1999), London: Penguin. [WCB]

Lowe, Keith (2001), *Tunnel Vision*, London: Arrow. [TUV]

Malkani, Gautam (2006), *Londonstani*, New York *et al.*: Penguin. [LON]

McEwan, Ian (2006), *Saturday* (¹2005), London *et al.*: Vintage. [SAT]

Miéville, China (1999), *King Rat* (¹1998), London: Pan. [KRA]

Morrison, Blake (2008), *South of the River* (¹2007), London: Vintage. [SOR]

Neate, Patrick (2006), *City of Tiny Lights* (¹2005), London: Penguin. [CTL]

Nicholson, Geoff (1997), *Bleeding London*, Woodstock - New York: Overlook. [BLL]

Royle, Nicholas (1998), *The Matter of the Heart* (¹1997), London: Abacus. [MAH]

Ryman, Geoff (1998), *253. The Journey of 253 Lifetimes. The Print Remix*, London: Flamingo. [253]

Stevenson, Jane (2001), *London Bridges* (¹2000), Boston - New York: Houghton Mifflin. [LBR]

Williams, Conrad (2004), *London Revenant*, London: Do-Not. [LOR]

Further Primary Sources

Alderman, Naomi (2006), *Disobedience,* London - New York: Viking.

Bryson, Bill (1995), *Notes from a Small Island,* New York: Avon Books.

Carlyle, Thomas (1840), "The Hero as a Man of Letters. Johnson, Rousseau, Burns. Lecture V.", in T.C. (2001), 131-165.

— (2001), *On Heroes, Hero Worship and the Heroic in History* ([1]1897), A Penn State Electronic Classics Series Publication, Hazleton (PA): Pensylvania State University, http://www2.hn.psu.edu/faculty/jmanis/carlyle/heroes.pdf (21 February 2012).

Conrad, Joseph (2008), *The Secret Agent. A Simple Tale* ([1]1907), ed. John Lyon (Oxford World's Classics), Oxford - New York: Oxford University Press.

De Quincey, Thomas (1968a), *The Collected Writings of Thomas De Quincey. Vol. 1, Autobiography from 1785 to 1803* ([1]1889-90), ed. by David Masson, New York: AMS Press.

— (1968b), "The Palimpsest of the Human Brain", in Thomas De Quincey, *The Collected Writings of Thomas De Quincey. Vol. 8, Tales and Prose Phantasies* ([1]1889-90), ed. by David Masson, New York: AMS Press, 340-349.

Dickens, Charles (1998), *Bleak House* ([1]1853), ed. Stephen Gill (Oxford World's Classics), Oxford - New York: Oxford University Press.

Mayhew, Henry (2003), "The Metropolitan Railway", in Tobias Döring, ed., *London Underground. Poems and Prose about the Tube*, Stuttgart: Reclam, 14-34.

Morton, H.V. (1939), *Ghosts of London,* London: Methuen.

Proust, Marcel (1949), *A la recherche du temps perdu VII. Le côté de Guermantes 2* ([1]1921) (Œuvres de Marcel Proust), Paris: Gallimard.

Ross, Christopher (2002), *Tunnel Visions. Journeys of an Underground Philosopher* ([1]2001), London: Fourth Estate.

Rowson, Martin (1999), "Literary London", *GRANTA*, 65, 103-111.

Rushdie, Salman (1995), *Shame* ([1]1983), London: Vintage.

Ryman, Geoff (1996), "*253* or Tube Theatre. A Novel for the Internet about London Underground in Seven Cars and a Crash", http://www.ryman-novel.com/ (14 April 2011).

Selvon, Samuel (2006), *The Lonely Londoners* ([1]1956) (Modern Classics), London: Penguin.

Sinclair, Iain (2003), *Lights Out for the Territory* ([1]1997), London *et al.*: Penguin.

Smith, Stephen (2005), Underground London. Travels Beneath the City Streets ([1]2004), London: Abacus.

Secondary Sources

Abbas, Niran (2003), "CCTV. City Watch", in Kerr & Gibson, 131-138.

Ackroyd, Peter (2001), *London. The Biography* ([1]2000), London: Vintage.

Aichele, George (2005), "Dark Conceptions, or the Birth of a Messiah in *King Rat* and the Gospel of Luke", *Foundation*, 34:95, 62-70.

Alheit, Peter (2005), "Biographie und Mentalität. Spuren des Kollektiven im Individuellen", in Bettina Völter *et al.*, eds., *Biographieforschung im Diskurs*, Wiesbaden: VS Verlag für Sozialwissenschaften, 21-45.

Alter, Robert (2005), *Imagined Cities. Urban Experience and the Language of the Novel,* New Haven - London: Yale University Press.

Altnöder, Sonja (2009), "Die Stadt als Körper: Materialität und Diskursivität in zwei London-Romanen", in Hallet & Neumann (2009b), 299-318.

Amin, Ash & Nigel Thrift (2002), *Cities. Reimagining the Urban,* Cambridge - Oxford - Malden (MA): Polity Press.

Anderson, Hephzibah (2002), "A Bit of a Grey Area. Maggie Gee's Black and White Examination of Race in Modern Britian, *The White Family*, Seems Curiously Dated", *The Guardian*, 5 May, http://www.guardian.co.uk/books/2002/may/05/fiction.features1 (31 July 2011).

Anderson, Jon (2010), *Understanding Cultural Geography. Places and Traces,* London: Routledge.

Anon. (n.d.), "Interview with Keith Lowe", http://victorian.fortunecity.com/finsbury/254/lowe.html (26 July 2011).

— (1908), "Mentality", in James Augustus Henry Murray, ed., *New English Dictionary on Historical Principles. M*, London: Clarendon, 342.

— (1989), "Mentality", in J.A Simpson & E.S.C Weiner, eds., *The Oxford English Dictionary. Volume IX Look-Mouke*. (2nd ed.), Oxford: Clarendon, 612.

— (2003), "A Reader's Guide. London Bridges by Jane Stevenson", http://houghton mifflinbooks.com/readers_guides/londonbridges.shtml (16 January 2012).

— (2011a), "It's Biology: All Cities Are Alike", *Sydney Morning Herald*, 23 July, http://www.smh.com.au/national/its-biology-all-cities-are-alike-20110722-1hsue.html (6 October 2011).

— (2011b), "Penguin USA Reading Guides. Londonstani", http://us.penguingroup.com/static/rguides/us/londonstani.html (30 December 2011).

Ariès, Philippe (1988), "L'histoire des mentalités", in Jacques Le Goff, ed., *La Nouvelle Histoire*, Paris: Retz CEPL, 167-190.

— (1991), "Einleitung. Zu einer Geschichte des privaten Lebens", in Philippe Ariès & Roger Chartier, eds., *Geschichte des privaten Lebens. 3. Band: Von der Renaissance zur Aufklärung*, transl. Holger Fliessbach, Gabriele Krüger-Wirrer, Frankfurt/Main: Fischer, 7-19.

Ashford, David (2008), "The Ghost in the Machine. Psychogeography in the London Underground 1991-2007", *Literary London Journal*, 6:2, http://www.literary london.org/london-journal/september2008/ashford.html (26 May 2011).

Assmann, Aleida (1999), *Erinnerungsräume. Formen und Wandlungen des kulturellen Gedächtnisses,* München: Beck.

Augé, Marc (1988), "Das Schauspiel der Metro", *DU*, 48:12, 103-121.

— (1995), *Non-Places. Introduction to an Anthropology of Supermodernity* ([1]1992), transl. John Howe, London - New York: Verso.

— (1997), "Orte und Nicht-Orte der Stadt", in Ritter, 12-25.

Bachelard, Gaston (1994), *The Poetics of Space* ([1]1964), transl. Maria Jolas, Boston (MA): Beacon.

Bachmann-Medick, Doris (2006), *Cultural Turns. Neuorientierungen in den Kulturwissenschaften* (rowohlts enzyklopädie), Reinbek: Rowohlt Taschenbuch Verlag.

Bahrdt, Hans Paul (1983), "Die Moderne Großstadt. Öffentlichkeit und Privatisierung als Grundformen städtischer Vergesellschaftung", in Schmals, 607-636.

Baker, Brian (2003), "Maps of the London Underground. Iain Sinclair and Michael Moorcock's Psychogeography of the City", *Literary London Journal*, 1:1, http://homepages.gold.ac.uk/london-journal/march2003/baker.html (26 May 2011).

Baker, Phil (2003), "Secret City. Psychogeography and the End of London", in Kerr & Gibson, 323-333.

Bakhtin, Michail M. (1968), *Rabelais and His World,* Cambridge (MA): MIT Press.

— (1998), *The Dialogic Imagination*, ed. Michael Holquist, transl. Caryl Emerson & Micheal Holquist (University of Texas Press Slavic Series 1), Austin: University of Texas Press.

Ball, John Clement (2004), *Imagining London. Postcolonial Fiction and the Transnational Metropolis,* Toronto: University of Toronto Press.

Balshaw, Maria & Liam Kennedy (2000), "Introduction. Urban Space and Representation", in M.B. & L.K., eds., *Urban Space and Representation*, London - Sterling (VA): Pluto Press, 1-21.

Banerjee, Mita (2008), "The Burqa as Indo Chic? The Limits of Cultural Mobility and Monica Ali's *Brick Lane*", in Iris Hermann & Anne Maximiliane Jäger-Gogoll, eds., *Durchquerungen. Für Ralf Schnell zum 65. Geburtstag*, Heidelberg: Winter, 3-12.

Barceló, Pedro (1995), "Zur Mentalität des antiken Stadtbewohners", *Die Alte Stadt*, 1, 51-64.

Barfield, Steven (2008), "Psychogeography. Will Self and Iain Sinclair in Conversation with Kevin Jackson", *Literary London Journal*, 6:1, http://www.literarylondon.org/london-journal/march2008/sinclair-self.html (26 May 2011).

Barnett, Anthony (1998), "Securing the Future", in Anthony Barnett & Roger Scruton, eds., *Town and Country,* London: Cape, 129-142.

Barry, Peter (2000), *Contemporary British Poetry and the City,* Manchester: Manchester University Press.

Baudrillard, Jean (1997), *Simulacra and Simulation* (^{1}1981), transl. Sheila Faria Glaser, Ann Arbor: The University of Michigan Press.

— (2000), "Die Stadt und der Haß", in Keller (2000b), 130-141.

— (2002), *The Spirit of Terrorism and Requiem for the Twin Towers*, transl. Chris Turner, London: Verso.

Baxter, Jeannette (2008a), "J.G. Ballard and the Contemporary", in Baxter (2008b), 1-10.

— ed. (2008b), *J.G. Ballard. Contemporary Critical Perspectives,* London - New York: Continuum.

— (2009), *J.G. Ballard's Surrealist Imagination. Spectacular Authorship,* Farnham - Burlington: Ashgate.

Beck, Anna (2011), "Subjectivity, Space, Mobility and Movement in Contemporary London Novels", in Joachim Frenk & Lena Steveker, eds., *Anglistentag 2010 Saarbrücken. Proceedings, Vol. 32*, Trier: Wissenschaftlicher Verlag Trier, 361-376.

Beeck, Karl-Hermann (1989), "Leistung und Bedeutung des mentalitätsgeschichtlichen Ansatzes in der Kirchengeschichte", in Archiv der Evangelischen Kirche im Rheinland, ed., *Mentalitätsgeschichtlicher Ansatz und regionalgeschichtliche Forschung* (Arbeitshilfen des Archivs der Evangelischen Kirche im Rheinland 1), Düsseldorf: Blech, 3-31.

Benevolo, Leonardo (1980), *The History of the City* ([1]1975), transl. Geoffrey Culverwell, London: Scolar Press.

Benjamin, Walter (2002), *The Arcades Project*, ed. Rolf Tiedemann, transl. Howard Eiland & Kevin McLaughlin, Cambridge (MA) - London: Harvard University Press.

Berg, Wolfgang (1990), "Kollektive Identität. Zugänge und erste Überlegungen", in Hahn, 217-238.

Berking, Helmuth (2008), "'Städte lassen sich an ihrem Gang erkennen wie Menschen'. Skizzen zur Erforschung der Stadt und der Städte", in Berking & Löw (2008b), 15-31.

Berking, Helmuth & Martina Löw (2008a), "Einleitung", in Berking & Löw (2008b), 7-14.

— ed. (2008b), *Die Eigenlogik der Städte. Neue Wege für die Stadtforschung* (Interdisziplinäre Stadtforschung 1), Frankfurt/Main - New York: Campus.

Berndt, Christian & Robert Pütz, eds. (2007), *Kulturelle Geographien. Zur Beschäftigung mit Raum und Ort nach dem Cultural Turn*, Bielefeld: transcript.

Bhabha, Homi K. (1994), *The Location of Culture*, London: Routledge.

Birch, Sarah (1994), *Christine Brooke-Rose and Contemporary Fiction*, Oxford: Clarendon.

Bird, Jon *et al.*, eds. (1996), *Mapping the Futures. Local Cultures, Global Change* ([1]1993) (Futures: New Perspectives for Cultural Analysis), London - New York: Routledge.

Bischoff, Werner (2007), "'Korrespondierende Orte'. Zum Erscheinen olfaktorischer Stadtlandschaften", in Berndt & Pütz, 189-212.

Black, Jeremy (1997), *Maps and Politics*, London: Reaktion Books.

— (2009), *London: A History*, Lancaster: Carnegie Publishing.

Blaicher, Günther (1987a), "Einleitung des Herausgebers. Bedingungen literarischer Stereotypisierung", in Blaicher (1987b), 9-25.

— ed. (1987b), *Erstarrtes Denken. Studien zu Klischee, Stereotyp und Vorurteil in englischsprachiger Literatur*, Tübingen: Narr.

Blij, Harm J. de (1982), *Human Geography. Culture, Society and Space* ([1]1977), New York *et al.*: Wiley.

Boeri, Stefano (1997), "Territoriale Intimität und einsame Geschwindigkeit", in Ritter, 34-37.

Bogdanović, Bogdan (2000), "Die verlorene Stadt", in Keller (2000b), 142-153.

Böhme, Gernot (1998), "Die Atmosphäre einer Stadt", in Breuer (1998), 149-162.

Böhme, Hartmut (2005a), "Die Grenzen und das Fremde. Einleitung", in Böhme (2005c), 595-602.

— (2005b), "Einleitung: Raum - Bewegung - Topographie", in Böhme (2005c), IX-XXIII.

— ed. (2005c), *Topographien der Literatur. Deutsche Literatur im transnationalen Kontext* (Germanistische Symposien Berichtsbände 27), Stuttgart - Weimar: Metzler.

Boncza-Tomaszewski, Tom (2005), "Christine Brooke-Rose. The Texterminator", *The Independent*, 27 March, http://www.independent.co.uk/arts-entertainment/books/features/christine-brookerose-the-texterminator-530379.html.

Bonheim, Helmut (1994), "Mentality: The Hypothesis of Alterity", *Mentalities*, 9, 1-11.

Bould, Mark (2009), "Mind the Gap. The Impertinent Predicates (and Subjects) of *King Rat* and *Looking for Jake and Other Stories", Extrapolation*, 50:2, 307-325.

Bourdieu, Pierre (1979), *Entwurf einer Theorie der Praxis auf der ethnologischen Grundlage der kabylischen Gesellschaft* ([1]1976), Frankfurt/Main: Suhrkamp.

— (1982), *Die feinen Unterschiede. Kritik gesellschaftlicher Urteilskraft*, transl. Bernd Schwibs & Achim Russer, Frankfurt/Main: Suhrkamp.

Boynton, Perry H. (1913), *London in English Literature,* Chicago: University of Chicago Press.

Bradley, Arthur & Andrew Tate (2010), *The New Atheist Novel. Fiction, Philosophy and Polemic After 9/11* (New Directions in Religion and Literature), London: Continuum.

Brandolini, Sebastiano (1996), "Introduction", *Rassegna*, 66:2, 4.

Braudel, Fernand (1958), "La longue durée", *Annales. Économies - Sociétés - Civilisations*, 13, 725-753.

— (1976), *La Méditerranée et le monde méditerranéen a l'époque de Philippe II* (3rd ed.), Paris: Librairie Armand Colin.

— (1988), *The Identity of France. History and Environment, Vol. 1,* New York: Harper & Row.

Breuer, Gerda, ed. (1998), *Neue Stadträume. Zwischen Musealisierung, Medialisierung und Gestaltlosigkeit* (Wuppertaler Gespräche 2), Frankfurt/Main - Basel: Stroemfeld.

Breuner, Michael (1991), *"Hunger for Place". Studien zur Raumdarstellung im London-Roman seit 1940* (Trierer Studien zur Literatur 19), Frankfurt/Main *et al.*: Lang.

Briscoe, Joanna (2005), "From a Whisper to a Scream", *The Guardian*, 30 April, http://www.guardian.co.uk/books/2005/apr/30/shopping.fiction (1 September 2011).

Brogan, Denis W. (1977), "Implications of Modern City Growth", in Handlin & Burchard (1977b), 146-164.

Brooker, Peter (1992), "Introduction. Reconstructions", in P.B., ed., *Modernism/Postmodernism*, London - New York: Longman, 1-33.

— (2002), *Modernity and Metropolis. Writing, Film and Urban Formations,* Basingstoke: Palgrave Macmillan.

Brooke-Rose, Christine (1994), "Palimpsest History", in Umberto Eco, *Interpretation and Overinterpretation*, ed. by Stefan Collini, Cambridge: Cambridge University Press, 125-138.

Brouillette, Sarah (2009), "Literature and Gentrification on Brick Lane", *Criticism*, 51:3, 425-499.

— (2010), "The Creative Class and Gautam Malkani's *Londonstani", Critique*, 51:1, 1-17.

Brown, Richard (2008), "Politics, the Domestic and the Uncanny Effects of the Everyday in Ian McEwan's *Saturday", Critical Survey*, 20:1, 80-93.

Bruner, Jerome (1991), "The Narrative Construction of Reality", *Critical Inquiry*, 18:1, 1-21.

Burke, Peter (1990), *The French Historical Revolution. The Annales School 1929-89,* Cambridge: Polity Press.

— (1991), "History of Events and the Revival of Narrative", in P.B., ed., *New Perspectives on Historical Writing*, Cambridge: Polity Press, 233-248.

— (1992), *History and Social Theory,* Cambridge: Polity Press.

— (1997), *Varieties of Cultural History,* Cambridge: Polity Press.

Buse, Peter & Andrew Stott (1999), "Introduction. A Future for Haunting", in P.B. & A.S., eds., *Ghosts. Deconstruction, Psychoanalysis, History*, London: Palgrave Macmillan, 1-20.

Butor. Michael (2000), "Die Stadt als Text", in Keller (2000b), 169-178.

Byrnes, Bernie C. (2009), *Ian McEwan's* Atonement & Saturday. *A Supplement to The Work of Ian McEwan: A Psychodynamic Approach* (2nd ed.), Nottingham: Paupers' Press.

Calvi, Licia (2004), "*253*: A Case Ontology of Hypertext", in Nathalie Roelens & Yves Jeanneret, eds., *L'imaginaire de l'écran. Screen Imaginary* (Faux Titre 248), Amsterdam - New York: Rodopi, 155-184.

Campbell-Hall, Devon (2009), "Renegotiating the Asian-British Domestic Community in Recent Fiction", *Journal of Postcolonial Writing*, 45:2, 171-179.

Carpenter, Rebecca (2008), "'We're Not a Friggin' Girl Band'. September 11, Masculinity, and the British-American Relationship in David Hare's *Stuff Happens* and Ian McEwan's *Saturday*", in Keniston & Quinn (2008b) , 143-160.

Carter, Erica, James Donald & Judith Squires (1993a), "Introduction", in Carter, Donald & Squires (1993b), vii-xv.

— ed. (1993b), *Space and Place. Theories of Identity and Location,* London: Lawrence & Wishart.

Castells, Manuel (1979), *The Urban Question. A Marxist Approach* ([1]1972), transl. Alan Sheridan, Cambridge (MA): MIT Press.

— (1989), *The Informational City. Information Technology, Economic Restructuring, and the Urban-Regional Process,* Oxford - Cambridge (MA): Blackwell Publishers.

Certeau, Michel de (1988), *The Practice of Everyday Life* ([1]1984), transl. Steven Rendall, Berkeley - Los Angeles - London: University of California Press.

Chambers, Iain (1990), *Border Dialogues. Journeys in Postmodernity,* London - New York: Routledge.

— (1996), "Cities Without Maps", in Bird *et al.*, 188-198.

Chapman, Tim (2006), "'When in Doubt, Quote Ballard'. An Interview with Iain Sinclair", http://www.ballardian.com/iain-sinclair-when-in-doubt-quote-ballard (10 September 2011).

Chartier, Roger (1988), "Geistesgeschichte oder histoire des mentalités?", in Dominick LaCapra & Kaplan Steven L., eds., *Geschichte denken. Neubestimmungen und Perspektiven moderner europäischer Geistesgeschichte*, Frankfurt/Main: Fischer Taschenbuch Verlag, 11-44.

Childs, Peter (2006), "Conclusion. And Now, What Days Are These?- *Saturday* (2005)", in P.C., ed., *The Fiction of Ian McEwan*, Basingstoke: Palgrave Macmillan, 144-151.

— (2009), "Contemporary McEwan and Anosognosia", in Nicklas, 23-38.

Chilton, Myles (2007), "*Bleeding London* and Re-Mapping It. Local Empire in a Global City", *Comparative Critical Studies*, 4:1, 11-29.

Cilano, Cara (2009a), "Introduction. From Solidarity to Schisms", in Cilano (2009b), 13-24.

— ed. (2009b), *From Solidarity to Schisms. 9/11 and After in Fiction and Film from Outside the US* (Internationale Forschungen zur allgemeinen und vergleichenden Literaturwissenschaft 126), Amsterdam: Rodopi.

Cixous, Hélène (1976), "Fictions and Its Phantoms. A Reading of Freud's Das Unheimliche (The 'Uncanny')", *New Literary History*, 7:3, 525-548.

Clark Hillards, Molly (2008), "'When Desert Armies Stand Ready to Fight'. Re-Reading McEwan's *Saturday* and Arnold's 'Dover Beach'", *Partial Answers*, 6:1, 181-206.

Colombino, Laura (2006), "Negotiations With the System. J.G. Ballard and Geoff Ryman Writing London's Architecture", *Textual Practice*, 20:4, 615-635.

Coverley, Merlin (2005), *London Writing*, Harpenden: Pocket Essentials.

Crang, Mike (1996), "Envisioning Urban Histories. Bristol as Palimpsest, Postcards, and Snapshots", *Environment and Planning A*, 28, 429-452.

— (1998), *Cultural Geography* (Routledge Contemporary Human Geography Series), London: Routledge.

Cuevas, Susanne (2008a), *Babylon and Golden City. Representations of London in Black and Asian British Novels Since the 1990s* (Anglistische Forschungen 384), Heidelberg: Winter.

— (2008b), "'Societies Within'. Council Estates as Cultural Enclaves in Recent Urban Fictions", in Eckstein *et al.*, 383-395.

Currie, Mark (2007), *About Time. Narrative, Fiction and the Philosophy of Time*, Edinburgh: Edinburgh University Press.

Daniels, Stephen & Denis Cosgrove (1989), "Introduction. Iconography and Landscape", in Denis Cosgrove & Stephen Daniels, eds., *The Iconography of Landscape. Essays on the Symbolic Representation, Design and Use of Past Environments* (Cambridge Studies in Historical Geography 9), Cambridge: Cambridge University Press, 1-10.

Darnton, Robert (1984), *The Great Cat Massacre and Other Episodes in French Cultural History*, New York: Basic Books.

Davison, John (1999), "How to Get Invited to No 10: Ignore Blair on Tube", *The Independent*, 22 December, http://www.independent.co.uk/news/how-to-get-invited-to-no-10-ignore-blair-on-tube-1134021.html (27 February 2012).

Debord, Guy (1955), "Introduction to a Critique of Urban Geography", http://www.bopsecrets.org/SI/urbgeog.htm (10 June 2011).

— (1994), *The Society of the Spectacle* ([1]1990), transl. Donald Nicholson-Smith, New York: Zone Books.

Degen, Mónica Montserrat (2008), *Sensing Cities: Regenerating Public Life in Barcelona and Manchester*, London: Routledge.

Deleuze, Gilles & Félix Guattari (1998), *A Thousand Plateaus. Capitalism and Schizophrenia*, tranls. Brian Massumi (7th ed.), Minneapolis (MN) - London: University of Minnesota Press.

Dennerlein, Katrin (2009), *Narratologie des Raumes* (Narratologia 22), Berlin - New York: De Gruyter.

Deny, Martina (2009), *Lost in the Postmodern Metropolis. Studien zu (Des-)Orientierung und Identitätskonstruktion im zeitgenössischen Londonroman* (Anglo-amerikanische Studien 37), Frankfurt/Main: Lang.

Department for Communities and Local Government (2008), *No One Left Out. Communities Ending Rough Sleeping*, Wetherby: Communities and Local Government Publications.

Derrida, Jacques (1994), *Specters of Marx. The State of the Debt, the Work of Mourning, and the New International*, transl. Peggy Kamuf, introd. Bernd Magnus and Stephen Cullenberg, New York - London: Routledge.

Deveney, Catherine (2005), "First Love, Last Writes", *Scotsman*, 30 January, http://news.scotsman.com/features/First-love-last-writes.2599187.jp (30 December 2011).

Dillon, Sarah (2007a), "Imagining Apocalypse. Maggie Gee's The Flood", *Contemporary Literature*, 48:3, 374-397.

— (2007b), *The Palimpsest. Literature, Criticism, Theory* (Continuum Literary Studies), London: Continuum.

Dinzelbacher, Peter (1993), "Zu Theorie und Praxis der Mentalitätsgeschichte", in P.D., ed., *Europäische Mentalitätsgeschichte. Hauptthemen in Einzeldarstellungen*, Stuttgart: Kröner, XV-XXXVII.

Döring, Jörg & Tristan Thielemann (2008a), "Einleitung: Was lesen wir im Raume? Der Spatial Turn und das geheime Wissen der Geographen", in Döring & Thielemann (2008b), 7-45.

— ed. (2008b), *Spatial Turn. Das Raumparadigma in den Kultur- und Sozialwissenschaften,* Bielefeld: transcript.

Döring, Tobias (2001), "London Underground. A Tale of the Tube", in Peter Lucko & Jürgen Schlaeger, eds., *Anglistentag 2000 Berlin. Proceedings* (Proceedings of the Conference of the German Association of University Teachers of English 22), Trier: Wissenschaftlicher Verlag Trier, 119-129.

— (2002), "Of Maps and Moles. Cultural Negotiations with the London Tube", *Anglia*, 120:1, 30-64.

— (2003), "Nachwort. Eine Untergrundfahrt durch die moderne Stadtgeschichte", in T.D., ed., *London Underground. Poems and Prose about the Tube*, Stuttgart: Reclam, 182-197.

Dreyer, Dagmar (2006), *London literarisch. Stadtentwürfe im zeitgenössischen Roman, 1990-2000*, http://deposit.ddb.de/cgi-bin/dokserv?idn=983476217&dok_var=d1&dok_ext=pdf&filename=983476217.pdf (13 June 2011).

Duby, Georges (1961), "Histoire des Mentalités", in Charles Samaran, ed., *L'histoire et ses méthodes* (Encyclopédie de la pléiade 11), Bruges: Les Presses de l'inprinerie Sainte-Catherine, 937-966.

— (1985), "Ideologies in Social History", in Le Goff & Nora, 151-165.

Duncan, James S. (1990), *The City as Text. The Politics of Landscape Interpretation in the Kandyan Kingdom* (Cambridge Human Geography), Cambridge *et al.*: Cambridge University Press.

— (2005), "Men Without Property. The Tramps's Classification and Use of Urban Space", in Lin & Mele, 164-172.

Dunmore, Helen (2005), "Who's for the Drop?", *The Times*, 7 May, http://entertainment.timesonline.co.uk/tol/arts_and_entertainment/books/article388508.ece (1 September 2011).

Durkheim, Emile (1933), *The Division of Labor in Society*, transl. George Simpson, New York: Macmillan.

Eade, John, Isabelle Fremaux & David Garbin (2002), "The Political Construction of Diasporic Communities in the Global City", in Gilbert (2002), 159-175.

Eckstein, Lars *et al.*, eds. (2008), *Multi-ethnic Britain 2000+. New Perspectives in Literature, Film, and the Arts* (Internationale Forschungen zur allgemeinen und vergleichenden Literaturwissenschaft 121), Amsterdam *et al.*: Rodopi.

Egbert, Marie-Luise (2009), "Tolerance Renegotiated. Extremism and Terrorism in English Fiction", in Andrew R. Murphy *et al.*, eds., *Literature, Culture, and Tolerance*, Frankfurt/Main: Lang, 239-247.

Ekman, Stefan (2005), "Down, Out and Invisible in London and Seattle", *Foundation*, 34:94, 64-74.

Elias, Norbert (1994a), "State Formation and Civilization", in Elias (1994b), 257-543.

— (1994b), *The Civilizing Process. The History of Manners and State Formation and Civilization*, transl. Edmund Jephcott, Oxford: Blackwell.

— (1994c), "The History of Manners", in Elias (1994b), vii-256.

Erll, Astrid & Simone Roggendorf (2002), "Kulturgeschichtliche Narratologie. Die Historisierung und Kontextualisierung kultureller Narrative", in Nünning & Nünning (2002b), 73-113.

Fantastic Fiction, http://www.fantasticfiction.co.uk (13 July 2006).

Faris, Wendy B. (1991), "The Labyrinth as Sign of City, Text, and Thought", in Mary Ann Caws, ed., *City Images. Perspectives from Literature, Philosophy and Film.* (2nd ed.), New York: Gordon and Breach, 33-41.

Featherstone, Mike (1991), *Consumer Culture and Postmodernism* (Theory, Culture & Society), London - Newbury Park - New Delhi: Sage.

— (1996), "Global and Local Cultures", in Bird *et al.*, 169-187.

Febvre, Lucien (2003a), *A Geographical Introduction to History. An Introduction to Human Geography* ([1]1919), London - New York - Bahrain: Kegan Paul.

— (2003b), *Le problème de l'incroyance au XVIe siècle. La religion de Rabelais* ([1]1947) (Bibliothèque de l'Évolution de l'Humanité 42), Paris: Michel.

Feng, Pin-chia (2009), "Out of Brick Lane. The Novel of Awakening and Monica Ali's Brick Lane", *Tamkang Review*, 40:1, 15-28.

Fiedler, Leslie (1981), "Mythicizing the City", in Jaye & Watts (1981b), 113-121.

Fischer, Claude S. (1984), *The Urban Experience* (2nd ed.), San Diego *et al.*: Harcourt Brace Jovanovich.

Fludernik, Monika (2006), *Einführung in die Erzähltheorie* (Einführung Literaturwissenschaft), Darmstadt: Wissenschaftliche Buchgesellschaft.

— (2009), "The Cage Metaphor. Extending Narratology into Corpus Studies and Opening It to the Analysis of Imagery", in Heinen & Sommer (2009b), 109-128.

Foucault, Michel (1986), "Of Other Spaces", *Diacritics*, 16:1, 22-27.

Frank, Michael C. (2009), "Die Literaturwissenschaften und der spatial turn: Ansätze bei Jurij Lotman und Michail Bachtin", in Hallet & Neumann (2009b), 53-80.

Freedman, Carl (2003), "Towards a Marxist Urban Sublime. Reading China Miéville's *King Rat*", *Extrapolation*, 44:4, 395-408.

Freud, Sigmund (2003), "The Uncanny", in S.F., *The Uncanny*, transl. David McLintock & introd. Hugh Haughton, New York: Penguin, 121-162.

Friedman, Ellen J. (1995), "The Resisting Author: An Introduction", in Friedman & Martin, 9-17.

Friedman, Ellen J. & Miriam Fuchs (1995), "A Conversation with Christine Brooke-Rose", in Friedman & Martin, 29-37.

Friedman, Ellen J. & Richard Martin, eds. (1995), *Utterly Other Discourse. The Texts of Christine Brooke-Rose,* Normal (IL): Dalkey Archive Press.

Frisby, David (2001), "Georg Simmels Großstadt: eine Interpretation", in Lutz Musner, Gotthart Wunberg & Christina Lutter, eds., *Cultural Turn. Zur Geschichte der Kulturwissenschaften* (Kultur-Wissenschaft 3), Wien: Turia + Kant, 65-86.

— (2006), "Introduction to the Texts", in Georg Simmel, *Simmel on Culture. Selected Writings*, ed. by David Frisby & Mike Featherstone, London - Thousand Oaks - New Delhi: Sage, 1-28.

Gaede, Peter-Matthias & Florian Hanig (2005), "'Es bleibt hier keine Energie zum hassen'", *GEO Special*, 5, 86-88.

Gąsiorek, Andrzej (2005), "'Refugees from Time'. History, Death and the Flight from Reality in Contemporary Writing", in Nick Bentley, ed., *British Fiction of the 1990s,* London - New York: Routledge, 42-56.

Gautam Malkani, http://www.gautammalkani.com/homepage.htm (8 September 2011).

Gebhardt, Winfried & Georg Kamphausen (1994), *Zwei Dörfer in Deutschland. Mentalitätsunterschiede nach der Wiedervereinigung,* Opladen: Leske & Budrich.

Geiger, Theodor (1967), *Die soziale Schichtung des deutschen Volkes. Soziographischer Versuch auf statistischer Grundlage* ([1]1932) (Soziologische Gegenwartsfragen 1), Stuttgart: Enke.

Gelfant, Blanche Housman (1954), *The American City Novel,* Norman: University of Oklahoma Press.

Genette, Gérard (1993), *Palimpseste. Die Literatur auf zweiter Stufe* ([1]1982), transl. Wolfram Bayer & Dieter Hornig (edition suhrkamp 1683), Frankfurt/Main: Suhrkamp.

Gerard, Jasper (2005), "Interview: Jasper Gerard Meets Ian McEwan", *The Sunday Times*, 23 January, http://www.timesonline.co.uk/tol/news/article505214.ece (30 December 2011).

Gibson, Andrew (2003), "Altering Images", in Kerr & Gibson, 292-300.

Gilbert, Pamela K., ed. (2002), *Imagined Londons,* New York: State University of New York Press.

— (2008), "Sex and the Modern City. English Studies and the Spatial Turn", in Warf & Arias (2008b), 102-121.

Gillet, Lucie (2008), "Representations of Multicultural Society in Contemporary British Novels", in Eckstein *et al.*, 99-108.

Girard, Monica (2008), "*Mr Dalloway* (Robin Lippincott) and *Saturday* (Ian McEwan). Virginia Woolf's Legacy of London", in Guignery & Gallix, 37-56.

Gordon, Joan (2003), "Revelling in Genre. An Interview with China Miéville", *Science Fiction Studies*, 30:3, 355-373.

Goto, Hiromo (2008), "An Email Conversation with Geoff Ryman", *Extrapolation*, 49:2, 195-210.

Gottdiener, M. & Alexandros Ph. Lagopoulos (1986), "Introduction", in M.G. & A.P.L., *The City and the Sign. An Introduction to Urban Semiotics,* New York: Columbia University Press, 1-22.

Gottdiener, Mark (2005), "'Looking at Themed Environments'. From the Theming of America (1997)", in Lin & Mele, 302-307.

Gottlieb, Joanne (1999), "Darwin's City, Or Life Underground. Evolution, Progress, and the Shapes of Things to Come", in Michael Bennett & David W. Teague, eds., *The Nature of Cities. Ecocriticism and Urban Environments*, Tuscon: The University of Arizona Press, 233-254.

Grabes, Herbert (1996), "Textwissenschaftlich fundierte Kulturwissenschaft/Landeskunde", *Anglistik*, 7:1, 35-40.

— (2004), "Literaturwissenschaft - Kulturwissenschaft - Anglistik", in Ansgar Nünning & Roy Sommer, eds., *Kulturwissenschaftliche Literaturwissenschaft. Disziplinäre Ansätze - Theoretische Positionen - Transdisziplinäre Perspektiven,* Tübingen: Narr, 79-114.

Gräf, Dennis & Verena Schmöller (2009a), "Grenzen. Eine Einführung", in Gräf & Schmöller (2009b), 9-18.

— ed. (2009b), *Grenzen. Konstruktionen und Bedeutungen* (Medien, Texte, Semiotik Passau 2), Passau: Stutz.

Graham, James (2008a), "An Interview with Gautam Malkani", *Literary London Journal,* 6:1, http://www.literarylondon.org/london-journal/march2008/graham.html (8 September 2011).

— (2008b), "'This In't Good Will Hunting': *Londonstani* and the Market for London's Multicultural Fictions", *Literary London Journal,* http://www.literary london.org/london-journal/september2008/graham.html (30 December 2011).

Graus, František (1987), "Mentalität - Versuch einer Begriffsbestimmung und Methoden der Untersuchung", in F.G., ed., *Mentalitäten im Mittelalter. Methodische und inhaltliche Probleme* (Vorträge und Forschungen 35), Sigmaringen: Thorbecke, 9-48.

Green, Susan (2010), "Consciousness and Ian McEwan's *Saturday.* 'What Henry Knows'", *English Studies*, 91:1, 58-73.

Gregory, Derek (1994), *Geographical Imaginations,* Cambridge (MA) - London: Blackwell Publishers.

— (1998), "The Geographical Discourse of Modernity", in D.G., *Explorations in Critical Human Geography. Hettner-Lecture 1997* (Hettner Lectures 1), Heidelberg: University of Heidelberg, 43-67.

Groes, Sebastian (2008), "From Shanghai to Shepperton. Crises of Representation in J.G. Ballard's Londons", in Baxter (2008b), 78-93.

— (2009), "Ian McEwan and the Modernist Consciousness of the City in *Saturday*", in S.G., ed., *Ian McEwan. Contemporary Critical Perspectives* (Contemporary Critical Perspectives), London: Continuum, 99-114.

— (2011), *The Making of London: London in Contemporary Literature. London in Contemporary Literature*: Palgrave Macmillan.

Grossman, Wendy (1997), "Underground Fiction", http://www.salon.com/march97/21st/ london970320.html (31 July 2011).

Grosz, Elizabeth (1992), "Bodies-Cities", in Beatriz Colomina, ed., *Sexuality and Space*, New York: Princeton Architectural Press, 241-253.

Guggenberger, Bernd (2000), "Virtual City. Jetztzeitwesen in einer 'ortlosen' Stadt", in Keller (2000b), 37-59.

Guignery, Vanessa & François Gallix, eds. (2008), *(Re-)Mapping London. Visions of the Metropolis in the Contemporary Novel in English* (EPU, Éditions Publibook université colloques et revues), Paris: Publibook.

Gurevich, Aaron J. (1983), "Medieval Culture and Mentality According to the New French Historiography", *European Journal of Sociology*, 24, 167-195.

Hage, Volker & Matthias Matussek (2005a), "'We're Witnessing a Civil War in Islam'. Interview with British Author Ian McEwan", *Der Spiegel*, 19 July, http://www.spiegel.de/international/spiegel/0,1518,365767,00.html (30 December 2011).

— (2005b), "Wir sind verunsichert bis ins Mark", *Der Spiegel*, 18 July, 112-114.

Hahn, Heinz, ed. (1990), *Kulturunterschiede. Interdisziplinäre Konzepte zu kollektiven Identitäten und Mentalitäten* (Beiträge zur sozialwissenschaftlichen Analyse interkultureller Beziehungen 3), Frankfurt/Main: IKO-Verlag für Interkulturelle Kommunikation.

Hallet, Wolfgang (2009), "Fictions of Space: Zeitgenössische Romane als fiktionale Modelle semiotischer Raumkonstitution", in Hallet & Neumann (2009b), 81-113.

Hallet, Wolfgang & Birgit Neumann (2009a), "Raum und Bewegung in der Literatur: Zur Einführung", in Hallet & Neumann (2009b), 11-32.

— ed. (2009b), *Raum und Bewegung in der Literatur. Die Literaturwissenschaften und der Spatial Turn,* Bielefeld: transcript.

Halliday, Stephen (2001), *Underground to Everywhere. London's Underground Railway in the Life of the Capital* (2nd ed.), Stroud: Sutton.

Handlin, Oscar (1977), "The Modern City as a Field of Historical Study", in Handlin & Burchard (1977b), 1-26.

Handlin, Oscar & John Burchard (1977a), "Preface", in Handlin & Burchard (1977b), v-ix.

— ed. (1977b), *The Historian and the City* ([1]1963), Cambridge (MA) - London: MIT Press.

Hansen, Klaus P. (2003), *Kultur und Kulturwissenschaft. Eine Einführung* ([1]1995) (UTB), Tübingen - Basel: Francke.

— (2009), *Kultur, Kollektiv, Nation* (Schriften der Forschungsstelle Grundlagen Kulturwissenschaft 1), Passau: Stutz.

Harper, Graeme (1999), "Christine Brooke-Rose", in Merritt Moseley ed., *British Novelists Since 1960* (Dictionary of Literary Biography 231), Detroit: Gale, 41-52.

Harrison, Carey (1997), "Wicked Tour of London With Three Twisted Guides", http://articles.sfgate.com/1997-12-28/books/17764386_1_stuart-london-geoff-nicholson-sheffield (11 June 2011).

Harvey, David (1973), *Social Justice and the City,* London: Arnold.

— (1985), *Consciousness and the Urban Experience,* Oxford: Blackwell Publishers.

— (1990), *The Condition of Postmodernity. An Enquiery into the Origins of Cultural Change* ([1]1989), Oxford - Cambridge (MA): Blackwell Publishers.

Hassan, Ihab (1981), "Cities of the Mind, Urban Words. The Dematerialization of Metropolis in Contemporary American Fiction", in Jaye & Watts (1981b), 93-112.

Haubrichs, Wolfgang (1982), "Einleitung", *LiLi*, 12:48, 7-9.

Haupt, Sabine (2005), "'Kryptopische' Zeit-Räume. Unterirdische und außerirdische Topographien als Reservate von Temporalität", in Böhme (2005c), 501-535.

Häussermann, Hartmut & Walter Siebel (2004), *Stadtsoziologie. Eine Einführung,* Frankfurt/Main: Campus.

Head, Dominic (2007), *Ian McEwan* (Contemporary British Novelists), Manchester: Manchester University Press.

Heath, Chris (2005), "Friends in High Places", *The New York Times*, 12 June, http://www.nytimes.com/2005/06/12/books/review/12HEATHL.html?pagewanted=print (1 September 2010).

Heinen, Sandra & Roy Sommer (2009a), "Introduction. Narratology and Interdisciplinarity", in Heinen & Sommer (2009b), 1-10.

— ed. (2009b), *Narratology in the Age of Cross-Disciplinary Narrative Research* (Narratologia 20), Berlin - New York: De Gruyter.

Heinz, Sarah (2007), *Die Einheit in der Differenz. Metapher, Romance und Identität in A.S. Byatts Romanen,* Tübingen: Narr.

Hertel, Kirsten (1997), *London zwischen Naturalismus und Moderne. Literarische Perspektiven einer Metropole* (Anglistische Forschungen 250), Heidelberg: Winter.

Hervé, Martin (1996), *Mentalités Médiévales* (Nouvelle Clio. L'Histoire et ses problèmes), Vendôme: Presses Universitaires France.

Heyl, Christoph (2004), *A Passion for Privacy. Untersuchungen zur Genese der bürgerlichen Privatsphäre in London, 1660 - 1800* (Veröffentlichungen des Deutschen Historischen Instituts London 56), München: Oldenbourg.

Hiddleston, Jane (2005), "Shapes and Shadows. (Un)Veiling the Imigrant in Monica Ali's *Brick Lane*", *Journal of Commonwealth Literature*, 40:1, 57-72.

Highmore, Ben (2005), *Cityscapes. Cultural Readings in the Material and Symbolic City,* Basingstoke - New York: Palgrave Macmillan.

Hill, Carolyn (2006), "Geoff Ryman Interview, in Four Parts", http://www.sffchronicles.co.uk/forum/11294-geoff-ryman-interview-in-four-parts.html (27 July 2011).

Hobsbawm, Eric (1987), "Labour in the Great City", *New Left Review*, 166, 39-51.

Hoffmann, Gerhard (1978), *Raum, Situation, erzählte Wirklichkeit. Poetologie und historische Studien zum englischen und amerikanischen Roman,* Stuttgart: Metzler.

Houen, Alex (2002), *Terrorism and Modern Literature, from Joseph Conrad to Ciaran Carson,* Oxford - New York: Oxford University Press.

Hutton, Patrick H. (1981), "The History of Mentalities: The New Map of Cultural History", *History and Theory*, 237-259.

— (1988), "Collective Memory and Collective Mentalities. The Halbwachs-Ariès Connection", *Historical Reflections*, 15:2, 311-322.

— (2002), "Philippe Ariès and the Secrets of the History of Mentalities", *Historical Reflections*, 28:1, 1-19.

Huyssen, Andreas (2003), *Present Pasts. Urban Palimpsests and the Politics of Memory,* Stanford (CA): Stanford University Press.

Inwood, Steven (1998), *A History of London,* London: Macmillan.

Jackson, Peter (1989), *Maps of Meaning. An Introduction to Cultural Geography,* London *et al.*: Unwin Hyman.

Jackson, Rosemary (1981), *Fantasy. The Literature of Subversion,* London - New York: Methuen.

Jacobs, Steven (2006), "From Flâneur to Chauffeur: Driving Through Cinematic Cities.", in Christian Emden, Catherine Keen & David Midgley, eds., *Imagining the City, Volume 1. The Art of Urban Living* (Cultural History and Literary Imagination 7), Bern: Lang, 213-228.

Jaggi, Maya (2002a), "Maya Jaggi in Conversation with Maggie Gee", *Wasafiri*, 17:36, 5-10.

— (2002b), "Too Close to Home. Maya Jaggi Acclaims *The White Family* by Maggie Gee, a Portrait of Race in Britain", *The Guardian*, 25 May, http://www.guardian.co.uk/books/2002/may/25/fiction.orangeprizeforfiction2002 (30 December 2011).

James, David (2008), *Contemporary British Fiction and the Artistry of Space. Style, Landscape, Perception,* London: Continuum.

Jameson, Fredric (1991), *Postmodernism, or, The Cultural Logic of Late Capitalism,* Durham: Duke University Press.

— (1999), *The Cultural Turn. Selected Writings on the Postmodern 1983-1998,* London - New York: Verso.

Jarvis, Brian (1998), *Postmodern Cartographies. The Geographical Imagination in Contemporary American Culture,* New York: St. Martin's Press.

Jaye, Michael C. & Ann Chalmers Watts (1981a), "Introduction", in Jaye & Watts (1981b), ix-xv.

— ed. (1981b), *Literature and the American Urban Experience. Essays on the City and Literature,* Manchester: Manchester University Press.

Jenkins, Alice (2006), "Tunnel Visions and Underground Geography in Fantasy", *Foundation*, 35:98, 28-43.

Jöckel, Sabine (1987), "Die 'histoire des mentalités': Baustein einer historisch-soziologischen Literaturwissenschaft", *Romanistische Zeitschrift für Literaturgeschichte*, 11:1/2, 146-173.

Jordison, Sam (2007), "Off-Piste Reading. An Interview With Matthew De Abaitua", http://www.3ammagazine.com/3am/off-piste-reading-an-interview-with-matthew-de-abaitua/ (13 June 2011).

Jukes, Peter, ed. (1990), *A Shout in the Street. The Modern City,* London - Boston: Faber & Faber.

Kaern, Michael (1990), "The World as Human Construction", in Kaern, Phillips & Cohen, 75-98.

Kaern, Michael, Bernard S. Phillips & Robert S. Cohen, eds. (1990), *Georg Simmel and Contemporary Sociology* (Boston Studies in the Philosphy of Science 119), Dordrecht - Boston - London: Kluwer Academis Publishers.

Kamm, Jürgen (1994), "Kognitionen, Konstruktionen, Mentalitäten: Zehn Thesen zur Kulturwissenschaft", *FMF*, 9, 26-40.

— (1996), "Von der Landeskunde zur Kulturwissenschaft: Wissenschaftsgeschichtliche und aktuelle Perspektiven zur systematischen Analyse (inter-)kulturellen Wissens", in Erwin Ambos & Irene Werner, eds., *Interkulturelle Dimensionen der Fremdsprachenkompetenz. Dokumentation der 18. Arbeitstagung 1994*, Bochum: AKS Verlag, 80-99.

— (1997), "'The City and the Country'. Introduction", in J.K., ed., *The City and the Country. Proceedings from the Sixth British and Cultural Studies Conference, Dresden 1995* (Dresdner Arbeiten zur Anglistik und Amerikanistik 3), Essen: Die Blaue Eule, 9-18.

— (2007), "Großbritannienstudien", in Uwe Böker & Christoph Houswitschka, eds., *Einführung in die Anglistik und Amerikanistik*, München: Beck, 17-47.

— (2010), "Mentalität, Habitus und Lifestyle", in Christoph Barmeyer, ed., *Interkulturelle Kommunikation und Kulturwissenschaft. Grundbegriffe, Wissenschaftsdisziplinen, Kulturräume*, Passau: Stutz, 153-171.

Kamm, Jürgen & Bernd Lenz (2004), *Großbritannien verstehen,* Darmstadt: Wissenschaftliche Buchgesellschaft.

— (2006), "New Britain. Into the Third Millennium", in Lenz, 7-23.

Kamm, Jürgen & Gerold Sedlmayr (2007), "Introduction", in J.K. & G.S., eds., *Insular Mentalities. Mental Maps of Britain*, Essays in Honour of Bernd Lenz, Passau: Stutz, 7-14.

Karp, David Allen, Gregory Prentice Stone & William C. Yoels (1991), *Being Urban. A Sociology of City Life* (2nd ed.), New York - Westport (CT) - London: Praeger.

Kavanagh, Dennis (2007), "The Blair Premiership", in Anthony Seldon, ed., *Blair's Britian. 1997-2007,* Cambridge *et al.*: Cambridge University Press, 3-15.

Keller, Ursula (2000a), "Einleitung", in Keller (2000b), 7-15.

— ed. (2000b), *Perspektiven metropolitaner Kultur,* Frankfurt/Main: Suhrkamp.

Kelso, Sylvia (1997), "The Postmodern Uncanny. Or Establishing Uncertainty", *Paradoxa*, 3:3-4, 456-470.

Kemp, Peter (2005), "*Saturday* by Ian McEwan", *The Sunday Times*, 30 January, http://entertainment.timesonline.co.uk/tol/arts_and_entertainment/books/article506640.ece (30 December 2011).

Kendall, David (1997), "Nicholas Royle - *The Matter of the Heart.* Interview", http://www.theedge.abelgratis.co.uk/royleiview.htm (13 June 2011).

Keniston, Ann & Jeanne Follansbee Quinn (2008a), "Introduction. Representing 9/11: Literature and Resistance", in Keniston & Quinn (2008b), 1-15.

— ed. (2008b), *Literature after 9/11,* New York: Routledge.

Kerr, Joe & Andrew Gibson, eds. (2003), *London. From Punk to Blair,* London: Reaktion Books.

Kerrigan, John (1998), "The Country of the Mind. Exploring the Links between Geography and the Writer's Imagination", *TLS*, 11 September, 3-4.

Kilian, Eveline (2010), "Culture, the Politics of Inclusion and their Spatial Dimension. London's South Bank", *JSBC*, 17:2, 117-131.

King, Anthony D. (1996a), "Introduction: Cities, Texts and Paradigms", in King (1996b), 1-19.

— ed. (1996b), *Re-Presenting the City. Ethnicity, Capital and Culture in the Twenty-First Century Metropolis,* London: Macmillan.

Klotz, Volker (1987), *Die erzählte Stadt. Ein Sujet als Herausforderung des Romans von Lesage bis Döblin* (Rowohlts Enzyklopädie Kulturen und Ideen 464), Reinbek: Rowohlt Taschenbuch Verlag.

Kneale, James (1996), "Lost in Space. Exploring Impossible Geographies", in Derek Littlewood & Peter Stockwell, eds., *Impossibility Fiction. Alternativity - Extrapolation - Speculation* (Rodopi Perspectives on Modern Literature 17), Amsterdam - New York: Rodopi, 147-162.

Korff, Gottfried (1985), "Mentalität und Kommunikation in der Großstadt. Berliner Notizen zur 'inneren' Urbanisierung", in Theodor Kohlmann & Hermann Bausinger, eds., *Großstadt. Aspekte empirischer Kulturforschung*, 24. Deutscher Volkskunde-Kongreß in Berlin vom 26. bis 30. September 1983 (Schriften des Museums für Deutsche Volkskunde Berlin 13), Berlin: Staatliche Museen Preußischer Kulturbesitz, 343-361.

Kortüm, Hans-Henning (1996), *Menschen und Mentalitäten. Einführung in Vorstellungswelten des Mittelalters,* Berlin: Akademie Verlag.

Kral, Françoise (2005), "Fictional Contexts, Actual Contexts, Virtual Contexts in *Brick Lane*", *Commonwealth*, 28:1, 109-118.

— (2007), "Shaky Ground and New Territorialities in *Brick Lane* by Monica Ali and *The Namesake* by Jhumpa Lahiri", *Journal of Postcolonial Writing*, 43:1, 65-76.

Kramer, Jürgen (2002), "The 'Long' Nineteenth Century, 1789-1914. A Sample Chapter of A Very Short History of the British Isles", *JSBC*, 9:1, 27-50.

— (2007), *Britain and Ireland. A Concise History,* New York: Routledge.

Krewani, Angela (2002), "'Mind the Gap'. Die Londoner U-Bahn in Film, Literatur, Malerei und Design", *KulturPoetik*, 2:2, 184-197.

Kuhlemann, Frank-Michael (1996), "Mentalitätsgeschichte. Theoretische und methodische Überlegungen am Beispiel der Religion im 19. und 20. Jahrhundert", *Geschichte und Gesellschaft*, 182-211.

Lawson, Mark (2005), "Against the Flow", *Guardian*, 22 January, http://www.guardian.co.uk/books/2005/jan/22/bookerprize2005.bookerprize (30 December 2011).

Le Goff, Jacques (1985), "Mentalities. A History of Ambiguities", in Le Goff & Nora, 166-180.

— (1986), *Histoire et imaginaire,* Paris: Poiesis.

— (1990), *Phantasie und Realität des Mittelalters,* Stuttgart: Klett-Cotta.

Le Goff, Jacques & Pierre Nora, eds. (1985), *Constructing the Past. Essays in Historical Methodology,* Cambridge *et al.*: Cambridge University Press.

Lefebvre, Henri (1991), *The Production of Space,* Oxford: Blackwell.

— (1996), *Writings on Cities*, ed. and transl. by Elonore Kofman & Elizabeth Lebas, Oxford: Blackwell Publishers.

— (2003), *The Urban Revolution* ([1]1970), introd. Neil Smith, transl. Robert Bonnono, Minneapolis - London: University of Minnesota Press.

Lefebvre, Henri & Catherine Régulier (2004), "Attempt at the Rhythmanalysis of Mediterranean Cities", in Henri Lefebvre, *Rhythmanalysis. Space, Time and Everyday Life* ([1]1986), transl. Stuart Elden & Gerald Moore, London - New York: Continuum, 85-100.

Lehnert, Gertrud (2011), "Raum und Gefühl", in G.L., ed., *Raum und Gefühl. Der Spatial Turn und die neue Emotionsforschung*, Bielefeld: transcript, 9-25.

Lenz, Bernd (2002), "'This Scept'red Isle'. Britain's Insular Mentality, Interculture and the Channel Tunnel", *JSBC*, 9:1, 51-67.

— ed. (2006), *New Britain. Politics and Culture* (Passauer Arbeiten zur Literatur- und Kulturwissenschaft 3), Passau: Stutz.

Lesser, Wendy (1987), *The Life Below the Ground. A Study of the Subterranean in Literature and History,* Boston - London: Faber & Faber.

Leupolt, Cécile (2010), "Resisting Media Manipulation. Ian McEwan's Politics of Scepticism in *Saturday*", *Anglistik*, 21:2, 57-68.

Levenson, Michael (2002), "London 2000. The Millenial Imagination in a City of Monuments", in Gilbert (2002), 219-239.

Levine, Janey, Ann Vinson & Deborah Wood (1973), "Subway Behaviour", in Arnold Birenbaum & Edward Sagarin, eds., *People in Places. The Sociology of the Familiar*, London: Nelson, 208-216.

Levy, Diane Wolfe (1978), "City Signs. Toward a Definition of Urban Literature", *Modern Fiction Studies*, 24:1, 65-73.

Lévy-Bruhl, Lucien (1956), *Die Seele der Primitiven* ([1]1930), transl. Else Baronin Werkmann, Darmstadt: Wissenschaftliche Buchgesellschaft.

Lin, Jan & Christopher Mele, eds. (2005), *The Urban Sociology Reader*, London - New York: Routledge.

Lindner, Rolf (1990), *Die Entdeckung der Stadtkultur. Soziologie aus der Erfahrung der Reportage*, Frankfurt/Main: Suhrkamp.

— (2004), "Offenheit - Vielfalt - Gestalt. Die Stadt als kultureller Raum", in Friedrich Jaeger & Jörn Rüsen, eds., *Handbuch der Kulturwissenschaften. Themen und Tendenzen, Band 3*, Stuttgart - Weimar: Metzler, 385-398.

— (2008), "Textur, imaginaire, Habitus - Schlüsselbegriffe der kulturanalytischen Stadtforschung", in Berking & Löw (2008b), 83-94.

Litt, Toby (2006), "JG Ballard: Unedited Transcript", http://www.tobylitt.com/ballard interview.html (10 September 2011).

Lofland, Lyn H. (1973), *A World of Strangers. Order and Action in Urban Public Space*, New York: Basic Books.

— (1998), *The Public Realm. Exploring the City's Quintessential Social Territory* (Communication and Social Order), Hawthorne (NY): De Gruyter.

London's Poverty Profile, http://www.londonspovertyprofile.org.uk/london/ (9 October 2011).

Lotman, Jurij M. (1973), *Die Struktur des künstlerischen Textes*, Frankfurt/Main: Suhrkamp.

Lotman, Yurij M. (2001), *Universe of the Mind. A Semiotic Theory of Culture* ([1]1990), transl. Ann Shukman, introd. Umberto Eco, Bloomington - Indianapolis: Indiana University Press.

Löw, Martina (2001), *Raumsoziologie* (suhrkamp taschenbuch wissenschaft 1506), Frankfurt/Main: Suhrkamp.

— (2008), *Soziologie der Städte*, Frankfurt/Main: Suhrkamp.

Löw, Martina, Silke Steets & Sergej Stoetzer (2008), *Einführung in die Stadt- und Raumsoziologie* (2nd ed.) (UTB 8348), Opladen - Farmington Hills: Budrich.

Luckhurst, Roger (1997), *The Angle Between Two Walls. The Fiction of J.G. Ballard*, New York: St. Martin's Press.

— (2002), "The Contemporary London Gothic and the Limits of the 'Spectral Turn'", *Textual Practice*, 527-546.

— (2003), "Occult London", in Kerr & Gibson, 335-340.

Lüsebrink, Hans-Jürgen (1993), "Romanische Landeskunde zwischen Literaturwissenschaft und Mentalitätsgeschichte", in Klaus P. Hansen, ed., *Kulturbegriff und Methode. Der stille Paradigmenwechsel in den Geisteswissenschaften. Eine Passauer Ringvorlesung*, Tübingen: Narr, 81-94.

Lynch, Kevin (1977), *The Image of the City* (14th ed.), Cambridge (MA): MIT Press.

Lyotard, Jean-François (2000), "Zone", in Keller (2000b), 119-129.

MacFarlane, Robert (2005), "A Road of One's Own", *TLS*, 7, 3-4.

Maczynska, Magdalena (2010), "This Monstrous City. Urban Visionary Satire in the Fiction of Martin Amis, Will Self, China Miéville, and Maggie Gee", *Contemporary Literature*, 51:1, 58-86.

Mahler, Andreas (1999), "Stadttexte - Textstädte, Formen und Funktionen diskursiver Stadtkonstitution", in A.M., ed., *Stadt-Bilder. Allegorie, Mimesis, Imagination* (Beiträge zur Neueren Literaturgeschichte 170), Heidelberg: Winter, 11-36.

Mancini, Bruna C. (2003), "Writing and the Urban (Hyper)Text of London", *Prospero*, 10, 167-178.

Mandrou, Robert (1972), "Histoire social et histoire des mentalités", *La Nouvelle Critique*, 41-44.

Marshall, Richard (2003), "The Road to Perdido. An Interview with China Miéville", http://www.3ammagazine.com/litarchives/2003/feb/interview_china_mie ville.html (14 June 2011).

Mars-Jones, Adam (2005), "Meet the Four Toppers", *The Observer*, 1 May, http://www.guardian.co.uk/books/2005/may/01/fiction.shopping (1 September 2011).

Martin, Tim (2006), "Londonstani by Gautam Malkani. U Hear Wot the Critix B Chattin", 7 May, http://www.independent.co.uk/arts-entertainment/books/reviews/londonstani-by-gautam-malkani-477217.html (5 September 2011).

Martindale, Don (1984), "Theories of the City", in Noel Iverson, ed., *Urbanism and Urbanization. Views, Aspects, and Dimensions* (International Studies in Sociology and Social Anthropology), Leiden: Brill, 9-32.

Martiny, Erik (2009), "'A Darker Longing'. Shades of Nihilism in Contemporary Terrorist Fiction", in Nicklas, 159-172.

Massey, Doreen B. (1998), *Space, Place and Gender* ([1]1994), Cambridge - Oxford: Polity Press.

McCarthy, Tom (2003), "Meteomedia; or, Why London's Weather is in the Middle of Everything", in Kerr & Gibson, 273-278.

McEwan, Ian (2001), "Only Love and Then Oblivion. Love Was All they Had to Set Against their Murderers", *The Guardian*, 15 September, http://www.guardian.co.uk/world/2001/sep/15/september11.politicsphilosophyandsociety2 (30 December 2011).

— (2005), "Literature, Science, and Human Nature", in Jonathan Gottschall & David Sloan Wilson, eds., *The Literary Animal. Evolution and the Nature of Narrative* ([1]2001), Evanston (IL): Northwestern University Press, 5-19.

— (2008), "The Day of Judgement", *The Guardian*, 31 May, http://www.guardian.co.uk/books/2008/may/31/fiction.philosophy (30 December 2011).

McHale, Brian (1995), "'I Draw the Line as a Rule Betweeen One Solar System and Another'. The Postmodernism(s) of Christine Brooke-Rose", in Friedman & Martin, 192-213.

McKay, Margaret (1998), "An Interview with Maggie Gee", *Studia Neophilologica*, 69, 213-221.

McLeod, John (2004a), "'London-stylee!'. Recent Representations of Postcolonial London", in Sandra Ponzanesi & Daniela Merolla, eds., *Migrant Cartographies. New Cultural and Literary Spaces in Post-Colonial Europe*, Lanham: Lexington, 229-238.

— (2004b), *Postcolonial London. Rewriting the Metropolis,* London - New York: Routledge.
— (2005), "Re-Visiting Postcolonial London", *The European English Messenger*, 14:2, 39-47.
— (2007), "Orphia in the Underground: Postcolonial London Transport", in Michèle Lurdos & Judith Misrahi-Barak, eds., *Transport(s) in the British Empire and the Commonwealth* (Coll. Les Carnets du Cepac 4), Montpellier: Université Paul-Valéry, 389-405.
— (2011), "Writing London in the Twenty-First Century", in Lawrence Manley, ed., *The Cambridge Companion to the Literature of London*, Cambridge: Cambridge University Press, 241-260.
McNamara, Liam Thomas (2001), "J.G. Ballard and the Gated Community. Strategies of the Social", *Postgraduate English*, 4, http://www.dur.ac.uk/postgraduate.english/thomas.htm (10 September 2011).
McWilliam, David (2011), "Conrad Williams Interviewed by David McWilliam", http://www.gothic.stir.ac.uk/interviews/conrad-williams-interviewed-by-david-mcwilliam (14 June 2011).
Mengham, Rod (2003), "The End of the Line", in Kerr & Gibson, 199-211.
Mergenthal, Silvia (2002), "'Whose City?' Contested Spaces and Contesting Spatialities in Contemporary Urban Fiction", in Onega & Stotesbury (2002b), 123-139.
Merriam-Webster Online, "Mentality", http://www.m-w.com (16 July 2006).
Meyer, Friederike (1989), "Literary History and the History of Mentalities. Reflections on the Problem and Possibilities of Intersiciplinary Cooperation", *Poetics*, 18, 85-92.
Michael, Magali Cornier (2009), "Writing Fiction in the Post-9/11 World. Ian McEwan's *Saturday*", in Cilano (2009b), 23-51.
Miéville, China (2002), "Messing with Fantasy", *Locus*, 48:4/5, 75-76.
Mighall, Robert (2003), "Crime and Memory in the Capital", in Kerr & Gibson, 371-376.
Milgram, Stanley (1970), "The Experience of Living in Cities", *Science*, 167:3924, 1461-1468.
Miller, Joseph Hillis (1995), *Topographies,* Stanford (CA): Stanford University Press.
Mitchell, Don (2000), *Cultural Geography. A Critical Introduction,* Oxford - Malden (MA): Blackwell Publishers.
Mitchell, Michael (2008), "Escaping the Matrix. Illusions and Disillusions of Identity in Gautam Malkani's *Londonstani* (2006)", in Eckstein *et al.*, 329-340.
Mitscherlich, Alexander (1983), "Die Unwirklichkeit unserer Städte - Anstiftung zum Unfrieden. Großstadt und Neurose", in Schmals, 681-691.
Mohr, Dunja M. & Sylvia Mayer (2010), "Introduction. 9/11 as Catalyst - American and British Cultural Responses", *ZAA*, 58:1, 1-4.
Mohrmann, Ruth-E. (1996), "Stadterfahrung und Mentalität", in Horst Matzerath, ed., *Stadt und Verkehr im Industriezeitalter* (Städteforschung Reihe A: Darstellungen 41), Köln - Weimar - Wien: Böhlau, 261-275.
Moran, Joe (2005), *Reading the Everyday,* London - New York: Routledge.
Mukherjee, Neel (2007), "Blake's Progress", *The Times*, 17 March, http://entertainment.timesonline.co.uk/tol/arts_and_entertainment/books/fiction/article1525429.ece (1 September 2011).

Mülder-Bach, Inka (2005), "Literarische Räume. Einleitung", in Böhme (2005c), 401-407.
Mumford, Lewis (1997), *The Culture of Cities* ([1] 1938) (Social Theories of the City 10), London: Routledge.
National Statistics, "Focus on London", http://www.statistics.gov.uk/focuson/london/ (16 July 2006).
Nedelmann, Birgitta (1990), "On the Concept of 'Erleben' in Georg Simmel's Sociology", in Kaern, Phillips & Cohen, 225-241.
Neumann, Birgit & Ansgar Nünning (2008), *An Introduction to the Study of Narrative Fiction* (Uni-Wissen : Anglistik, Amerikanistik), Stuttgart: Klett Lernen und Wissen.
Newland, Paul (2008), *The Cultural Construction of Londons East End: Urban Iconography, Modernity and the Spatialisation of Englishness* (Spatial Practices 5), Amsterdam - New York: Rodopi.
Newsinger, John (2000), "Fantasy and Revolution. An Interview with China Miéville", *International Socialism Journal*, 88, http://pubs.socialistreviewindex.org.uk/isj88/newsinger.htm (14 June 2011).
Nicklas, Pascal, ed. (2009), *Ian McEwan: Art and Politics* (Anglistik und Englischunterricht 73), Heidelberg: Winter.
Niederagen, Göran (2000), "'Cynical Young Men' - ein neues Paradigma für den englischen Roman der 1990er Jahre (?): Christopher Brookmyre, Nick Hornby, Irvine Welsh", in Ansgar Nünning & Vera Nünning, eds., *Klassiker und Strömungen des englischen Romans im 20. Jahrhundert*, Festschrift zum 65. Geburtstag von Gerhard Haefner, Trier: Wissenschaftlicher Verlag Trier, 221-241.
Noys, Benjamin (2011), "*La libido réactionnaire?* The Recent Fiction of J.G. Ballard", *Journal of European Studies*, 37:4, 391-406.
Nünning, Ansgar (2000), "Towards a Cultural and Historical Narratology. A Survey of Diachronic Approaches, Concepts, and Research Projects", in Reitz & Rieuwerts, 345-373.
— (2004a), "Der englische Roman des 18. Jahrhunderts aus kulturwissenschaftlicher Sicht: Themenselektion, Erzählformen, Romangenres und Mentalitäten", in Nünning, A. (2004b), 77-106.
— ed. (2004b), *Eine andere Geschichte der englischen Literatur. Epochen, Gattungen und Teilgebiete im Überblick* ([1] 1996) (WVT-Handbücher zum Literaturwissenschaftlichen Studium 2), Trier: Wissenschaftlicher Verlag Trier.
— (2004c), "Literatur, Mentalitäten und kulturelles Gedächtnis: Grundriß, Leitbegriffe und Perspektiven einer anglistischen Kulturwissenschaft", in A.N., ed., *Literaturwissenschaftliche Theorien, Modelle und Methoden. Eine Einführung* (WVT-Handbücher zum Literaturwissenschaftlichen Studium 1), Trier: Wissenschaftlicher Verlag Trier, 173-198.
— (2009a), "Formen und Funktionen literarischer Raumdarstellung: Grundlagen, Ansätze, narratologische Kategorien und neue Perspektiven", in Hallet & Neumann (2009b), 33-52.
— (2009b), "Surveying Contextualist and Cultural Narratologies. Towards an Outline of Approaches, Concepts and Potentials", in Heinen & Sommer (2009b), 48-70.
Nünning, Ansgar & Vera Nünning (2002a), "Von der strukturalistischen Narratologie zur 'Postklassischen' Erzähltheorie: Ein Überblick über neue Ansätze und Entwicklungstendenzen", in Nünning & Nünning (2002b), 1-33.

— (2002b), eds., *Neue Ansätze in der Erzähltheorie* (WVT-Handbücher zum Literaturwissenschaftlichen Studium 4), Trier: Wissenschaftlicher Verlag Trier.

Nünning, Vera (2001), "Where Literature, Culture and the History of Mentalities Meet. Changes in British National Identity as a Paradigm for a New Kind of Literary/Cultural History", *REAL*, 17, 211-238.

— (2004), "Die Kultur der Empfindsamkeit: Eine mentalitätsgeschichtliche Skizze", in Nünning, A. (2004b), 107-126.

O'Brien, Michael (2010), "'Tunnel Visions'. Space, Transcience and Escapism in Geoff Ryman's *253", EnterText*, 8, 155-169, http://arts.brunel.ac.uk/gate/entertext/8/pdfs/ET8O%27BrienED (31 July 2011).

Ochsner, Andrea (2009), *Lad Trouble. Masculinity and Identity in the British Male Confessional Novel of the 1990s* (Cultural Studies 35), Bielefeld - New Brunswick (NJ): transcript.

Oesterle, Günter (1988), "Urbanität und Mentalität. Paris und das Französische aus der Sicht deutscher Parisreisender", in Michel Espagne & Michael Werner, eds., *Transferts. Les Relations Interculturelles Dans L'Espace Franco-Allemand (XVIIIe et XIXe Siècle)*, Paris: Editions Recherche sur les Civilisations, 59-79.

Olalquiaga, Celeste (1992), *Megalopolis. Contemporary Cultural Sensibilities*, Minneapolis: University of Minnesota Press.

Onega, Susana & John Stotesbury (2002a), "Introduction. Visionary Mappings of the Metropolis", in Onega & Stotesbury (2002b), 9-17.

— ed. (2002b), *London in Literature. Visionary Mappings of the Metropolis* (Anglistische Forschungen 309), Heidelberg: Winter.

Online Etymology Dictionary, http://www.etymonline.com (8 February 2012).

Orr, Mary (2003), *Intertextuality. Debates and Contexts*, Cambridge: Polity Press.

Oxford Dictionary Online, "Mentality", http://www.askoxford.com (16 July 2006).

Park, Robert (1928), "Human Migration and the Marginal Man", *The American Journal of Sociology*, 23:6, 881-900.

— (1931), "Mentality of Racial Hybrids", *The American Journal of Sociology*, 36:4, 534-551.

— (1967), "The City. Suggestions for the Investigation of Human Behaviour in the Urban Environment", in Park, Burgess & McKenzie, 1-46.

Park, Robert, Ernest Burgess & Roderick McKenzie, eds. (1967), *The City*, Chicago: University of Chicago Press.

Parker, Simon (2004), *Urban Theory and the Urban Experience. Encountering the City*, London: Routledge.

Parsons, Deborah L. (2000), *Streetwalking the Metropolis. Women, the City and Modernity*, Oxford: Oxford University Press.

Perfect, Michael (2008), "The Multicultural Bildungsroman. Stereotypes in Monica Ali's *Brick Lane*", *The Journal of Commonwealth Literature*, 43:3, 109-120.

Perkins, Roger (2007), "Stocktaking the Way We Live Now", *The Telegraph*, 24 March, http://www.telegraph.co.uk/culture/books/3664033/Stocktaking-the-way-we-live-now.html (1 September 2011).

Pesso-Miquel, Catherine (2008), "From *Bermondsey* to *Brick Lane*. The Variegated London of Graham Swift and Monica Ali", in Guignery & Gallix, 81-98.

Peters, Ursula (1985), "Literaturgeschichte als Mentalitätsgeschichte? Überlegungen zur Problematik einer neueren Forschungsrichtung", in Georg Stötzel, ed., *Germanistik - Forschungsstand und Perspektiven. Vorträge des Deutschen Germanistentages 1984. 2. Teil: Ältere Deutsche Literatur, Neuere Deutsche Literatur*, Berlin - New York: De Gruyter, 179-198.

Petit, Chris (2005), "Chiswick Dick", *The Observer*, 16 July, http://www.guardian.co.uk/books/2005/jul/16/featuresreviews.guardianreview23 (5 September 2011).

Phillips, Lawrence (2006), *London Narratives. Post-War Fiction and the City* (Continuum Literary Studies Series), London - New York: Continuum.

Pike, David L. (1999), "Underground Theatre. Subterranean Spaces on the London Stage", *Nineteenth Century Studies*, 13, 102-138.

— (2002), "Modernist Space and the Transformation of Underground London", in Gilbert (2002), 101-119.

— (2005a), *Subterranean Cities. The World Beneath Paris and London, 1800-1945*, Ithaca (NY) - London: Cornell University Press.

— (2005b), "'The Greatest Wonder of the World'. Brunel's Tunnel and the Meanings of Underground London", *Victorian Literature and Culture*, 33:2, 341-367.

Pile, Steve (2000), "The Un(known) City... or, an Urban Geography of What Lies Buried below the Surface", in Iain Borden, ed., *The Unknown City. Contesting Architecture and Social Space*, Cambridge (MA): MIT Press, 262-279.

Piltz, Eric (2008), "'Trägheit des Raums'. Fernand Braudel und die Spatial Stories der Geschichtswissenschaft", in Döring & Thielemann (2008b), 75-102.

Pinder, David (1996), "Subverting Cartography. The Situationists and Maps of the City", *Environment and Planning A*, 28, 405-427.

Pleßke, Nora (2006), *Reading the Metropolis. London Mentality in Contemporary Urban Fiction*, Diplomarbeit, Universitätsbibliothek Passau.

— (2009), "London Underground. Der Grenzraum einer Metropole", in Gräf & Schmöller (2009b), 185-210.

— (2010), "Review. Martina Deny. Lost in the Postmodern Metropolis. Studien zur (Des-)Orientierung und Identitätskonstruktion im zeitgenössischen Londonroman", *ZAA*, 58, 408-409.

Pogossian, Tatiana (2010), "Empiricism Falls Apart", *Literary London Journal*, 8:1, http://www.literarylondon.org/london-journal/march2010/pogossian.html (30 December 2011).

Poon, Angelina (2009), "To Know What's What. Forms of Migrant Knowing in Monica Ali's *Brick Lane*", *Journal of Postcolonial Writing*, 45:4, 426-437.

Porteous, J. Douglas (1985), "Smellscape", *Progress in Physical Geography*, 9:3, 356-378.

Porter, Roy (2000), *London. A Social History* (^{1}1994), London: Penguin.

Pott, Andreas (2007), "Identität und Raum. Perspektiven nach dem Cultural Turn", in Berndt & Pütz, 27-52.

Prakash, Gyan (2008), "Introduction", in Gyan Prakash & Kevin M. Kruse, eds., *The Spaces of the Modern City. Imaginaries, Politics, and Everyday Life*, Princeton - Woodstock: Princeton University Press, 1-18.

Pratt, Mary Louise (1992), *Imperial Eyes. Travel Writing and Transculturation*, London - New York: Routledge.

— (1993), "Criticism in the Contact Zone: Decentering Community and Nation", in Steven M. Bell, Albert H. Le May & Leonard Orr, eds., *Critical Theory, Cultural Politics and Latin American Narrative*, Notre Dame - London: University of Notre Dame Press, 83-102.

Raban, Jonathan (1974), *Soft City. What Cities Do to Us, and How They Change the Way We Live, Think, Feel,* London: Hamish Hamilton.

Ranasinha, Ruvani (2009), "Racialized Masculinities and Postcolonial Critique in Contemporary British Asian Male-Authored Texts", *Journal of Postcolonial Writing*, 45:3, 297-307.

Rawlinson, Mark (2002), "Physical Graffiti. The Making of the Representations of Zones One and Two", in Onega & Stotesbury (2002b), 233-253.

Reichardt, Rolf (1978), "'Histoire des Mentalités': eine neue Dimension der Sozialgeschichte am Beispiel des französischen Ancien Régime", *IASL*, 3, 130-166.

Reichel, Norbert (1987), *Der Erzählte Raum. Zur Verflechtung von sozialem und poetischen Raum in der erzählenden Literatur* (Impulse der Forschung 52), Darmstadt: Wissenschaftliche Buchgesellschaft.

Reichert, Dagmar (1996a), "Räumliches Denken - eine Einleitung", in Reichert (1996c), 1-12.

— (1996b), "Räumliches Denken als Ordnen der Dinge", in Reichert (1996c), 15-45.

— ed. (1996c), *Räumliches Denken* (Zürcher Hochschulforum 25), Zürich: vdf Hochschulverlag an der ETH.

Reichl, Susanne (2002), *Cultures in the Contact Zone. Ethnic Semiosis in Black British Literature* (Studies in English Literary and Cultural History 7), Trier: Wissenschaftlicher Verlag Trier.

Reitz, Bernhard & Sigrid Rieuwerts, eds. (2000), *Anglistentag 1999 Mainz. Proceedings Vol. 21*, Trier: Wissenschaftlicher Verlag Trier.

Resina, Joan Ramon (2003), "The Concept of After-Image and the Scopic Apprehension of the City", in Resina & Ingenschay, 1-22.

Resina, Joan Ramon & Dieter Ingenschay, eds. (2003), *After-Images of the City,* Ithaca - London: Cornell University Press.

Richardson, Brian (2000), "Recent Concepts of Narrative and the Narratives of Narrative Theory", *Style*, 34:2, 168-175.

Richardson, John (2001), *The Annals of London. A Year-by-Year Record of a Thousand Years of History,* London: Cassell.

Ritter, Roland, ed. (1997), *Spaces of Solitude* (HDA Dokumente zur Architektur 9), Graz: Haus der Architektur.

Robins, Kevin (1993), "Prisoners of the City: Whatever Could a Postmodern City Be?", in Carter, Donald & Squires (1993b), 303-330.

— (1998), "Kollektivgefühl und städtische Kultur", in Breuer (1998), 163-186.

Rose, Gillian (1993), *Feminism and Geography. The Limits of Geographical Knowledge,* Minneapolis: University of Minnesota Press.

Rosenberg, Yvonne (2008), "'Stop Thinking Like an Englishman' or: Writing Against a Fixed Lexicon of Terrorism in Patrick Neate's *City of Tiny Lights* (2005)", in Eckstein *et al.*, 355-368.

Rösing, Helmut (2000), "Soundscapes. Urbanität und Musik", in Waltraud Kokot, Thomas Hengartner & Kathrin Wildner, eds., *Kulturwissenschaftliche Stadtforschung. Eine Bestandsaufnahme* (Kulturanalysen 3), Berlin: Reimer, 69-83.

Ross, Michael L. (2008), "On a Darkling Planet. Ian McEwan's *Saturday* and the Condition of England", *Twentieth-Century Literature*, 54:1, 75-96.

Rossiaud, Jaques (1990), "The City-Dweller and Life in Cities and Towns", in Jacques Le Goff, ed., *The Medieval World*, transl. Lydia G. Cochrane, London: Collins & Brown, 138-179.

Rötzer, Florian (2000), "Telepolis. Abschied von der Stadt", in Keller (2000b), 16-36.

Ruge, Enno (2010), "Seize the Saturday. Re-viewing Ian McEwan's *Saturday* and Re-reading the Novels of Saul Bellow", *Anglistik*, 21:2, 69-81.

Ryan, Marie-Laure (2009), "Space", in Peter Hühn *et al.*, eds., *Handbook of Narratology* (Narratologia 19), Berlin - New York: De Gruyter, 420-433.

Ryman, Geoff (2005), "The World in a Train", http://news.bbc.co.uk/2/hi/uk_news/magazine/4132482.stm (21 October 2011).

Saadi, Suhayl (2006), "Londonstani, by Gautam Malkani", *The Independent*, 21 April, http://www.independent.co.uk/arts-entertainment/books/reviews/londonstani-by-gautam-malkani-474920.html (5 September 2011).

Saarinen, Thomas F. (1984), *Environmental Planning. Perception and Behavior* ([1]1976), Prospect Heights: Waverland Press.

Sapio Garbero, Mario del (1993), "A Conversation with Christine Brooke-Rose", in Theo D'haen & Hans Bertens, eds., *British Postmodern Fiction* (Postmodern Studies 7), Amsterdam: Rodopi, 101-120.

Scherpe, Klaus R., ed. (1988), *Die Unwirklichkeit der Städte. Großstadtdarstellung zwischen Moderne und Postmoderne,* Reinbek: Rowohlt Taschenbuch Verlag.

Schilling, Heinz (2003), *Kleinbürger. Mentalität und Lebensstil,* Frankfurt/Main - New York: Campus.

Schivelbusch, Wolfgang (1986), *The Railway Journey. The Industrialization of Time and Space in the 19th Century* ([1]1977), Leamington Spa - Hamburg - New York: Berg.

Schlaeger, Jürgen (2003a), "London. Tomorrow's Yesterday, Future Images of the Past", in Resina & Ingenschay, 49-60.

— (2003b), "Mis-Representing the City", in Fernando Galván, Julio Cañero Serrano & José Santiago, eds., *(Mis) Representations. Intersections of Culture and Power,* Bern: Lang, 25-42.

Schmals, Klaus M., ed. (1983), *Stadt und Gesellschaft. Ein Arbeits- und Grundlagenwerk,* München: Academic Verlag.

Schnierer, Peter Paul (2000), "Graphic 'Novels', Cyber 'Fiction', Multiform 'Stories' - Virtual Theatre and the Limits of Genre", in Reitz & Rieuwerts, 535-547.

Schorske, Carl E. (1977), "The Idea of the City in European Thought: Voltaire to Spengler", in Handlin & Burchard (1977b), 95-114.

Schotland, Sara D. (2010), "Performing Identity. Text Speak in Gautam Malkani's Londonstani", *Trickster,* 8, http://www.trickster.lettere.unipd.it/doku.php?id=lingue_future:schotland_londostani (5 September 2011).

Schroer, Markus (2006), *Räume, Orte, Grenzen. Auf dem Weg zu einer Soziologie des Raums* (suhrkamp taschenbuch wissenschaft 1761), Frankfurt/Main: Suhrkamp.

— (2008), "'Bringing Space Back In'. Zur Relevanz des Raums als soziologischer Kategorie", in Döring & Thielemann (2008b), 125-148.

Schulz, Eberhard (1980), "Zur Mentalität von Stadt und Land im 13. Jahrhundert", *Die Alte Stadt*, 7:1, 257-275.

Schulze, Hagen (1985), "Mentalitätsgeschichte - Chancen und Grenzen eines Paradigmas der französischen Geschichtswissenschaft", *GWU*, 36:4, 247-270.

Schwinn Smith, Marilyn (2008), "A Woolfian Reversal. The Dalloway Mystique in Monica Ali's *Brick Lane*", in Diana Royer & Madelyn Detloff, eds., *Virginia Woolf. Art, Education, and Internationalism*, Clemson (SC): Clemson University Digital Press, 104-109.

Sears, John (2004), "'Making Sorrow Speak'. Maggie Gee's Novels", in Emma Parker, ed., *Contemporary British Women Writers* (Essays and Studies / The English Association 2004), Cambridge: Brewer, 55-67.

Sellin, Volker (1985), "Mentalität und Mentalitätsgeschichte", *Historische Zeitschrift*, 555-598.

— (1987), "Mentalitäten in der Sozialgeschichte", in Wolfgang Schieder & Volker Sellin, eds., *Sozialgeschichte in Deutschland. Entwicklungen und Perspektiven im internationalen Zusammenhang*, Band 3, Göttingen: Vandenhoeck & Ruprecht, 101-121.

Sennett, Richard (1977), *The Fall of Public Man* ([1]1976), Cambridge: Cambridge University Press.

— (1994), *Flesh and Stone. The Body and the City in Western Civilization* , New York: Norton & Company.

— (2000), "Gesellschaftliche Körper. Das multikulturelle New York", in Keller (2000b), 76-100.

Shamsie, Kamila (2006), "How Many a Us Bredren B Here?", *The Guardian*, 6 May, http://www.guardian.co.uk/books/2006/may/06/featuresreviews.guardianreview23 (5 September 2011).

Sharpe, William & Leonard Wallock (1987), "From 'Great Town' to 'Nonplace Urban Realm'. Reading the Modern City", in W.S. & L.W., *Visions of the Modern City. Essays in History, Art, and Literature* ([1]1983), Baltimore - London: The John Hopkins University Press, 1-50.

Shields, Rob (1996), "A Guide to Urban Representation and What to Do About It. Alternative Traditions of Urban Theory", in King (1996b), 227-252.

— (1999), *Lefebvre, Love and Struggle. Spatial Dialectics* (International Library of Sociology), London - New York: Routledge.

Sicher, Efraim (2003), *Rereading the City. Rereading Dickens. Representations, the Novel, and Urban Realism* (AMS Studies in the Nineteenth Century 29), New York: AMS Press.

Sieverts, Thomas (2003), *Cities Without Cities. An Interpretation of the Zwischenstadt*, London - New York: Spon Press.

Siikala, Anna-Leena (2002), "What Myths Tell about Past Finno-Ugric Modes of Thinking", in A.-L.S., ed., *Myth and Mentality. Studies in Folklore and Popular Thought* (Studia Fennica Folklorista 8), Helsinki: Finnish Literature Society, 15-32.

Simeoforidis, Yorgos (1997), "Aerotopia", in Ritter, 44-51.

Simmel, Georg (1971), "The Metropolis and Mental Life", in G.S., *On Individuality and Social Forms. Selected Writings*, ed. by Donald N. Levine, Chicago - London: The University of Chicago Press, 324-339.

— (1992), *Gesamtausgabe, Vol. 11. Soziologie. Untersuchungen über die Formen der Vergesellschaftung*, ed. by Otthein Rammstedt, Frankfurt/Main: Suhrkamp.

Simms, Norman (1982), "An Editorial", *Mentalities*, 1:1, 3.

— (1989), "Editorial", *Mentalities*, 6:1, 3.

Sizemore, Christine Wick (1984), "Reading the City as Palimpsest. The Experiential Perception of the City in Doris Lessing's The Four-Gated City", in Susan Merrill Squier, ed., *Women Writers and the City. Essays in Feminist Literary Criticism*, Knoxville: The University of Tennessee Press, 176-190.

Smethurst, Paul (2000), *The Postmodern Chronotope. Reading Space and Time in Contemporary Fiction* (Postmodern Studies 30), Amsterdam - Atlanta (GA): Rodopi.

Smith, Zadie (2010), "Zadie Smith Talks with Ian McEwan", in Ryan Roberts, ed., *Conversations with Ian McEwan*, Jackson: University Press of Mississippi, 108-133.

Soja, Edward W. (1998), *Postmodern Geographies. The Reassertion of Space in Critical Social Theory* ([1]1989), London - New York: Verso.

— (2000), *Thirdspace. Journeys to Los Angeles and other Real-and-Imagined Places* ([1]1996), Malden (MA) - Oxford: Blackwell Publishers.

— (2001), *Postmetropolis. Critical Studies of Cities and Regions* ([1]2000), Oxford - Malden (MA): Blackwell Publishers.

— (2006), "Foreword. Cityscapes as Cityspaces", in Christoph Lindner, ed., *Urban Space and Cityscapes. Perspectives from Modern and Contemporary Culture*, London - New York: Routledge, xv-xviii.

— (2008a), "Taking Space Personally", in Warf & Arias (2008b), 11-35.

— (2008b), "Vom 'Zeitgeist' zum 'Raumgeist'. New Twists on the Spatial Turn", in Döring & Thielemann (2008b), 241-262.

Sommer, Roy (2001), *Fictions of Migration. Ein Beitrag zur Theorie und Gattungstypologie des zeitgenössischen interkulturellen Romans in Großbritannien* (Studies in English Literary and Cultural History 1), Trier: Wissenschaftlicher Verlag Trier.

Spode, Hasso (1990), "Was ist Mentalitätsgeschichte? Struktur und Entwicklung einer Forschungstradition", in Hahn, 9-62.

Squires, Claire (2003), "Toby Litt", in Michael R. Molino, ed., *Twenty-First-Century British and Irish Novelists* (Dictionary of Literary Biography 267), Detroit: Gale, 164-171.

Stoianovich, Traian (1976), *French Historical Method. The Annales Paradigm,* Ithaca: Cornell University Press.

Suttles, Gerald D. (1984), "The Cumulative Texture of Local Urban Culture", *The American Journal of Sociology*, 90:1, 283-304.

Taylor, D.J. (2007), "The State We Were In", *The Guardian*, 7 April, http://www.guardian.co.uk/books/2007/apr/07/featuresreviews.guardianreview18 (1 September 2011).

Tellenbach, Gerd (1982), "'Mentalität'", in Max Kerner, ed., *Ideologie und Herrschaft im Mittelalter* (Wege der Forschung 530), Darmstadt: Wissenschaftliche Buchgesellschaft, 385-407.

Teske, Doris (1999), *Die Vertextung der Megalopolis. London im Spiel postmoderner Texte* (Horizonte 26), Trier: Wissenschaftlicher Verlag Trier.

Tew, Philip (2007), *The Contemporary British Novel* (2nd ed.), London: Continuum.

Thacker, Andrew (2003), *Moving through Modernity. Space and Geography in Modernism,* Manchester - New York: Manchester University Press.

Thomson, Ian (2003), "*Millennium People* by J.G. Ballard", *The Independent*, 6 September, http://www.independent.co.uk/arts-entertainment/books/reviews/millennium-people-by-j-g-ballard-578940.html (10 September 2011).

Thorne, Robert (1996), "Underground London", *Rassegna*, 66:2, 7-16.

Thrift, Nigel (2008), "Raum", in Döring & Thielemann (2008b), 393-407.

Thüsen, Joachim von der (2005), "The City as Metaphor, Metonym and Symbol", in Tinkler-Villani (2005b), 1-11.

Tinkler-Villani, Valeria (2005a), "Preface", in Tinkler-Villani (2005b), ix-xii.

— ed. (2005b), *Babylon or New Jerusalem? Perceptions of the City in Literature* (DQR Studies in Literature 32), Amsterdam - New York: Rodopi.

Tolan, Fiona (2008), "Toby Litt", in Philip Tew, Fiona Tolan & Leigh Wilson, eds., *Writers Talk. Conversations with Contemporary British Novelists*, London: Continuum, 72-87.

Tönnies, Merle (2003), "Introduction", in M.T., ed., *Britain under Blair* (Anglistik & Englischunterricht 65), Heidelberg: Winter. 7-9.

— (2006), "New Labour in the New Millennium. A Further Theatricalisation of Politics?", in Lenz, 119-138.

Topalova, Violetta (2008), "Interview with Patrick Neate", in Eckstein *et al.*, 405-413.

Townshend, Charles (2002), *Terrorism. A Very Short Introduction,* Oxford - New York: Oxford University Press.

Trench, Richard & Ellis Hillman (1985), *London under London. A Subterranean Guide,* London: Murray.

Turner, Mark (1996), *The Literary Mind. The Origins of Thought and Language,* Oxford *et al.*: Oxford University Press.

Ünlüdağ, Tânia (1992), "Sprache, Text und Mentalität. Eine Skizze", in Hermann de Bahr, Heinrich Kippers & Volkmar Wittmütz, eds., *Die Bergischen 'ein Volk von zugespitzter Reflexion'. Religion. Schule. Mentalität,* Wuppertal: Born, 278-305.

Valman, Nadia (2009), "The East End *Bildungsroman* from Israel Zangwill to Monica Ali", *Wasafiri*, 24:1, 3-8.

VanderMeer, Jeff (2006), "A Conversation with Conrad Williams", http://www.sfsite.com/03a/cw219.htm (14 June 2011).

Vertesi, Janet (2005), "Mind the Gap. The 'Tube Map' as London's User Interface", http://cemcom.infosci.cornell.edu/mainsite/uploads/pubs/Vertesi_MindTheGap.pdf (31 July 2011).

Vester, Heinz-Günter (1990), "Mentalitätsforschung in Deutschland - ein mentales Problem. Kommentar, Kritik und Perspektiven zum Forschungsstand", in Hahn, 435-445.

— (1996), *Kollektive Identitäten und Mentalitäten. Von der Völkerpsychologie zur kulturvergleichenden Soziologie und interkulturellen Kommunikation* (Beiträge zur sozialwissenschaftlichen Analyse interkultureller Beziehungen 1), Frankfurt/Main: IKO-Verlag für Interkulturelle Kommunikation.

Vidler, Anthony (1999), *The Architectural Uncanny. Essays in the Modern Unhomely* ([1]1992), Cambridge (MA) - London: MIT Press.

Voss, Dietmar (1988), "Die Rückseite der Flanerie. Versuch über ein Schlüsselphänomen der Moderne", in Scherpe (1988), 37-60.

Vovelle, Michel (1982), *Idéologies et mentalités* (Édition revue et augmentée), Paris: Gallimard.

Wachinger, Tobias (1999), "Stadträume / Stadttexte unter der Oberfläche. Schichtung als Paradigma des zeitgenössischen 'Großstadtromans'", *POETICA*, 263-301.

Wall, Cynthia (1998), *The Literary and Cultural Spaces of Restoration London*, Cambridge: Cambridge University Press.

Wall, Kathleen (2008), "Ethics, Knowledge, and the Need for Beauty. Zadie Smith's *On Beauty* and Ian McEwan's *Saturday*", *University of Toronto Quarterly*, 77:2, 757-788.

Warf, Barney (2008), "From Surfaces to Networks", in Warf & Arias (2008b), 59-76.

Warf, Barney & Santa Arias (2008a), "Introduction: The Reinsertion of Space Into the Social Sciences and Humanities", in Warf & Arias (2008b), 1-10.

— ed. (2008b), *The Spatial Turn. Interdisciplinary Perspectives* (Routledge Studies in Human Geography 26), London - New York: Routledge.

Weaver, Matt (2005), "London Homelessness Rises", *The Guardian*, 16 May, http://www.guardian.co.uk/society/2005/may/16/politics.greaterlondonauthority (9 October 2011).

Weidle, Roland (2009), "The Ethics of Metanarrations: Empathy in Ian McEwan's *The Comfort of Strangers*, *The Child in Time*, *Atonement* and *Saturday*", in Nicklas, 57-72.

Weigel, Sigrid (1988), "Traum - Stadt - Frau. Zur Weiblichkeit der Städte in der Schrift. Calvino, Benjamin, Paul Nizon, Ginka Steinwachs", in Scherpe (1988), 173-196.

— (1995), "Zur Weiblichkeit imaginärer Städte. Eine Forschungsskizze", in Gotthard Fuchs, Bernhard Moltmann & Walter Prigge, eds., *Mythos Metropole*, Frankfurt/Main: Suhrkamp, 35-44.

— (2002), "Zum 'topographical turn'. Kartographie, Topographie und Raumkonzepte in den Kulturwissenschaften", *KulturPoetik*, 151-165.

Weinstein, Deena & Michael A. Weinstein (1993), *Postmodern(ized) Simmel*, London - New York: Routledge.

Wells, Lynn (2005), "Ian McEwan, *Saturday*", *Literary London Journal*, 3:2, http://www.literarylondon.org/london-journal/september2005/wells.html (11 June 2011).

— (2010), *Ian McEwan* (New British Fiction), Basingstoke: Palgrave Macmillan.

White, Jerry (2003), "Unreal City. Reflections on London and the Novel in the Twentieth Century", *History Workshop Journal*, 56:1, 1-32.

— (2008), *London in the Twentieth Century. A City and Its People* ([1]2001), London: Vintage Books.

Williams, Genevieve (2008), "Antelopes of Desire. Knowledge, Documentation, and Love in the Novels of Geoff Ryman", *Extrapolation*, 49, 261-283.

Williams, Raymond (1984), *The Long Revolution* ([1]1961), Harmondsworth: Penguin.

— (1985), *The Country and the City* ([1]1973), London: Hogarth.

Williams, Rosalind (1990), *Notes on the Underground. An Essay on Technology, Society, and the Imagination*, Cambridge (MA) - London: MIT Press.

Wilson, A.N. (2002), "Introduction", in A.N.W., ed., *The Faber Book of London*, London: Faber & Faber, vii-xviii.

Wilson, Elizabeth (1992), "The Invisible Flâneur", *New Left Review*, 1:191, 90-110.

— (1995), "The Rhetoric of Urban Space", *New Left Review*, 1:209, 146-160.

Wirth, Louis (1967), "A Bibliography of the Urban Community", in Park, Burgess & McKenzie, 161-228.

— (1969), "Urbanism as a Way of Life", in Richard Sennett, ed., *Classic Essays on the Culture of Cities*, New York: Appleton-Century-Crofts, 143-164.

Wirth-Nesher, Hana (1996), *City Codes. Reading the Modern Urban Novel,* Cambridge - New York - Melbourne: Cambridge University Press.

Wolfreys, Julian (1998), *Writing London Volume 1. The Trace of the Urban Text from Blake to Dickens,* London: Palgrave Macmillan.

— (2002), "Undoing London or, Urban Haunts. The Fracturing of Representation in the 1990s", in Gilbert (2002), 193-217.

— (2004), *Writing London Volume 2. Materiality, Memory, Spectrality,* New York: Palgrave Macmillan.

Wolmar, Christian (2004), *The Subterranean Railway. How the London Underground Was Built and How It Changed the City Forever,* London: Atlantic Books.

Woog, Adam (2005), "Hornby's 'Long Way Down' Takes Serious Look at Suicide", *The Seattle Times*, 3 June, http://seattletimes.nwsource.com/html/books/2002296715_hornby05.html (1 September 2011).

Woolston, Howard B. (1912), "The Urban Habit of the Mind", *The American Journal of Sociology*, 17:5, 602-614.

Würzbach, Natascha (2001), "Erzählter Raum. Fiktionaler Baustein, kultureller Sinnträger, Ausdruck der Geschlechterordnung", in Jörg Helbig, ed., *Erzählen und Erzähltheorie im 20. Jahrhundert. Festschrift für Wilhelm Füger*, Heidelberg: Winter, 105-129.

Zijderveld, Anton C. (1987), "On the Nature and the Functions of Clichés", in Blaicher (1987b), 26-40.

— (1998), *A Theory of Urbanity. The Economic and Civic Culture of Cities* (^{1}1997), New Brunswick: Transaction.

Zukin, Sharon (1997), *The Cultures of Cities* (^{1}1995), Cambridge - Oxford: Blackwell Publishers.

Appendix: London Novels (1997-2007)

1997

Baddiel	David	*Time for Bed*
Banville	John	*The Untouchable*
Brookner	Anita	*Visitors*
Bruen	Ken	*The Hackman Blues*
Butler	Gwendoline	*Coffin's Game*
Charles	Paul	*I Love the Sound of Breaking Glass*
Cody	Liza	*Musclebound*
Cole	Martina	*The Runaway*
Dobbs	Michael	*Goodfellowe MP*
Evaristo	Bernardine	*Lara*
Frewin	Anthony	*London Blues*
James	P.D.	*A Certain Justice*
McFarland	Dennis	*A Face at the Window*
Newland	Courttia	*The Scholar*
Nicholson	Geoff	*Bleeding London*
Perry	Anne	*Ashworth Hall*
Perry	Anne	*Whited Sepulchres*
Perry	Anne	*The Silent Cry*
Richards	Ben	*Don't Step on the Lines*
Ripley	Mike	*That Angel Look*
Royle	Nicholas	*The Matter of the Heart*
Rutherfurd	Edward	*London*
St. John	Madeleine	*The Essence of the Thing*
Theroux	Marcel	*A Stranger in the Earth*
Thoene	Jake & Luke	*The Thundering Underground*
Weldon	Fay	*Big Girls Don't Cry*

Wilkins	Damien	*Little Masters*
Williams	Greg	*Diamond Geezers*
Williams	Nicola	*Without Prejudice*
Wright	Ronald	*A Scientific Romance*

1998

Barnacle	Hugo	*Day One*
Boyd	William	*Armadillo*
Brooke-Rose	Christine	*Next*
Brookner	Anita	*Falling Slowly*
Bruen	Ken	*Her Last Call to Louis MacNeice*
Butler	Gwendoline	*A Grave Coffin*
Carr	Rocky	*Brixton Bwoy*
Charles	Paul	*Fountain of Sorrow*
Charles	Paul	*Last Boat to Camden Town*
Dobbs	Michael	*The Buddha of Brewer Street*
Dunant	Sarah	*Transgressions*
Fowler	Christopher	*Soho Black*
Gunesekera	Romesh	*The Sandglass*
Harrod-Eagles	Cynthia	*Murder*
Harrod-Eagles	Cynthia	*Shallow Grave*
Hollinghurst	Alan	*The Spell*
Hornby	Nick	*About a Boy*
Horowitz	Anthony	*The Devil and His Boy*
Mackay	Shena	*The Artist's Widow*
McEwan	Ian	*Amsterdam*
Miéville	China	*King Rat*
Neel	Janet	*To Die For*
Perry	Anne	*Brunswick Gardens*
Perry	Anne	*Half Moon Street*
Richards	Ben	*The Silver River*
Ryman	Geoff	*253*
Spencer	John B.	*Tooth & Nail*
Thomson	Rupert	*Soft*
Vine	Barbara	*The Chimney Sweeper's Boy*
Waters	Sarah	*Tipping the Velvet*
Wilson	A.N.	*Dream Children*

1999

Ackroyd	Peter	*The Plato Papers*
Arnott	Jake	*The Long Firm*
Baddiel	David	*Whatever Love Means*
Bandele	Biyi	*The Street*

Barnard	Robert	*Touched by the Dead*
Brookner	Anita	*Undue Influence*
Butler	Gwendoline	*Coffin's Ghost*
Cole	Martina	*Two Women*
Colgan	Jenny	*Amanda's Wedding*
Crombie	Deborah	*Kissed a Sad Goodbye*
Dunbar	Catherine	*False Images*
Falconer	Helen	*Primrose Hill*
Fielding	Helen	*Bridget Jones*
Gayle	Mike	*Mr Commitment*
Harkness	Lucy	*The Happy Pigs*
Hayder	Mo	*Birdman*
Hill	Tobias	*Underground*
Huggins	David	*Luxury Amnesia*
Jewell	Lisa	*Ralph's Party*
Kureishi	Hanif	*Intimacy*
Lippincott	Robin	*Mr. Dalloway*
Livesey	Margot	*The Missing World*
Lott	Tim	*White City Blue*
Parsons	Tony	*Man and Boy*
Perry	Anne	*Bedford Square*
Perry	Anne	*The Twisted Root*
Porter	Henry	*Remembrance Day*
Spencer	John B.	*Stitch*
Starling	Boris	*Messiah*
Syal	Meera	*Life Isn't All Ha Ha Hee Hee*
Waters	Sarah	*Affinity*
Wheatle	Alex	*Brixton Rock*

2000

Adebayo	Diran	*My Once Upon a Time*
Barnard	Josie	*The Pleasure Dome*
Baron	Adam	*Hold Back the Night*
Barrowcliffe	Mark	*Girlfriend 44*
Beaumont	Matthew	*E*
Bruen	Ken	*Taming the Alien*
Butler	Gwendoline	*A Cold Coffin*
Charles	Paul	*The Ballad of Sean & Wilko*
Cole	Martina	*Broken*
Dobbs	Michael	*Whispers of Betrayal*
Doherty	Paul C.	*The Field of Blood*
Enright	Anne	*What Are You Like?*
Eze-Anyika	Ike	*Canteen Culture*

Gavin	Jamila	*Coram Boy*
Harrod-Eagles	Cynthia	*Blood Sinister*
Holland	David	*Murcheston*
Hubbard	Sue	*Depth of Field*
Ishiguro	Kazuo	*When We Were Orphans*
Johnson	Mat	*Drop*
King	John	*Human Punk*
Knight	India	*My Life on a Plate*
Lanchester	John	*Mr Phillips*
Liss	David	*A Conspiracy of Paper*
Litt	Toby	*Corpsing*
Mackay	Shena	*Heligoland*
Maitland	Barry	*Silvermeadow*
Margam	Kate	*Milch Cow*
Miéville	China	*Perdido Street Station*
Moorcock	Michael	*King of the City*
Morgan	Fidelis	*Unnatural Fire*
Myerson	Julie	*Laura Blundy*
Naidoo	Beverley	*The Other Side of Truth*
Nair	Preethi	*Gypsy Masala*
Neel	Janet	*O Gentle Death*
Nelson	Casey	*Nothing Gold Can Stay*
O'Farrell	John	*The Best a Man Can Get*
Perry	Anne	*Slaves and Obsession*
Phillips	Mike	*A Shadow of Myself*
Richards	Ben	*A Sweetheart Deal*
Royle	Nicholas	*The Director's Cut*
Self	Will	*How the Dead Live*
Smith	Carol	*Unfinished Business*
Smith	Zadie	*White Teeth*
Stevenson	Jane	*London Bridges*
Sutcliffe	William	*The Love Hexagon*
Thompson	Stephen	*Toy Soldiers*
Thorne	Matt	*Dreaming of Strangers*
Vine	Barbara	*Grasshopper*
Williams	Gerard	*Dr Mortimer and the Aldgate Mystery*

2001

Arnott	Jake	*He Kills Coppers*
Barrowcliffe	Mark	*Infidelity for First-Time Fathers*
Billingham	Mark	*Sleepyhead*
Bruen	Ken	*London Boulevard*
Charles	Paul	*The Hissing of the Silent Lonely Room*

Chevalier	Tracy	*Falling Angels*
Cornwell	Bernard	*Gallows Thief*
Evaristo	Bernardine	*The Emperor's Babe*
George	Elizabeth	*A Traitor to Memory*
Harrod-Eagles	Cynthia	*Gone Tomorrow*
Hayder	Mo	*The Treatment*
Hornby	Nick	*How to Be Good*
House	Richard	*Uninvited*
Kureishi	Hanif	*Gabriel's Gift*
Langley	Lee	*Distant Music*
Lessing	Doris	*The Sweetest Dream*
Lock	Samuel	*The Whites of Gold*
Lowe	Keith	*Tunnel Vision*
McAuley	Paul J.	*Whole Wide World*
Morgan	Fidelis	*The Rival Queens*
Naipaul	V.S.	*Half a Life*
Perry	Anne	*Funeral in Blue*
Perry	Anne	*The Whitechapel Conspiracy*
Petit	Christopher	*The Hard Shoulder*
Redfern	Elizabeth	*The Music of the Spheres*
Reeve	Philip	*Mortal Engines*
Ripley	Mike	*Lights, Camera, Angel*
Robins	Madeleine E.	*Point of Honour*
Shaykh	Hanan al	*Only in London*
Thorne	Matt	*Pictures of You*
Waterhouse	Keith	*Soho*
Wheatle	Alex	*East of Acre Lane*
Williams	Conrad	*Nearly People*
Williams	Gerard	*Dr. Mortimer and the Barking Man Mystery*
Woodward	Gerard	*August*

2002

Bainbridge	Beryl	*According to Queeney*
Banks	Iain	*Dead Air*
Beaumont	Matthew	*The Book, the Film, the T-Shirt*
Billingham	Mark	*Scaredy Cat*
Brooke	Simon	*Upgrading*
Bruen	Ken	*The McDead*
Bruen	Ken	*Blitz*
Butler	Gwendoline	*Coffin Knows the Answer*
Campbell	Rebecca	*Slave to Fashion*
Charles	Paul	*I've Heard the Banshee Sing*
Coetzee	J.M.	*Youth*

Cole	Martina	*Maura's Game*
Crombie	Deborah	*And Justice There is None*
Davis	Lindsey	*The Jupiter Myth*
Doyle	Richard	*Flood*
Faber	Michel	*The Crimson Petal and the White*
Forbes	Colin	*The Cell*
Frayn	Michael	*Spies*
Gardner	John	*Bottled Spider*
Gayle	Mike	*My Legendary Girlfriend*
Gayle	Mike	*Dinner for Two*
Gee	Maggie	*The White Family*
Granger	Pip	*Not All Tarts Are Apple*
Knight	India	*Don't You Want Me?*
Lawrence	David	*The Dead Sit Round in a Ring*
Leather	Stephen	*Tango One*
Longworth	Gay	*Dead Alone*
Lott	Tim	*Rumours of a Hurricane*
Maitland	Barry	*Babel*
Martin	Andrew	*The Necropolis Railway*
Miéville	China	*The Scar*
Parsons	Tony	*Man and Wife*
Perera	Shyama	*Do the Right Thing*
Perry	Anne	*Death of a Stranger*
Perry	Anne	*Southampton Row*
Ripley	Mike	*Double Take*
Rizzolo	S.K.	*The Rose in the Wheel*
Self	Will	*Dorian*
Smith	Sylvia	*Appleby House*
Smith	Zadie	*The Autograph Man*
Waters	Sarah	*Fingersmith*

2003

Ackroyd	Peter	*The Clerkenwell Tales*
Ali	Monica	*Brick Lane*
Amis	Martin	*Yellow Dog*
Ballard	J.G.	*Millennium People*
Billingham	Mark	*Lazybones*
Bruen	Ken	*Vixen*
Cole	Martina	*Close*
D'Ancona	Matthew	*Going East*
Docx	Edward	*The Calligrapher*
Fowler	Christopher	*Full Dark House*
Gardner	John	*The Streets of Town*

Gibson	William	*Pattern Recognition*
Granger	Pip	*The Widow Ginger*
Green	Simon R.	*Agents of Light and Darkness*
Green	Simon R.	*Something from the Nightside*
Heller	Zoë	*Notes on a Scandal*
Hooper	Mary	*At the Sign of the Sugared Plum*
Jackson	Lee	*London Dust*
James	Russell	*No One Gets Hurt*
Keeble	Jim	*Men and Other Mammals*
Kernick	Simon	*The Murder Exchange*
Lawrence	David	*Nothing Like the Night*
Leather	Stephen	*The Eyewitness*
Maitland	Barry	*The Verge Practice*
Nair	Preethi	*One Hundred Shades of White*
Neate	Patrick	*The London Pigeon Wars*
Perry	Anne	*Seven Dials*
Rendell	Ruth	*The Rottweiler*
Rizzolo	S.K.	*Blood for Blood*
Stephenson	Neal	*Quicksilver*
Swift	Graham	*The Light of Day*
Thirlwell	Adam	*Politics*
Vakil	Ardashir	*One Day*
White	Tony	*Foxy-T*
Williams	Gerard	*Dr. Mortimer and the Carved Head Mystery*
Winspear	Jacqueline	*Maisie Dobbs*

2004

Ackroyd	Peter	*The Lambs of London*
Atkinson	Kate	*Case Histories*
Billingham	Mark	*The Burning Girl*
Bruen	Ken	*Dispatching Baudelaire*
Charles	Paul	*The Justice Factory*
Coe	Jonathan	*The Closed Circle*
Cork	Vena	*Thorn*
Crombie	Deborah	*In a Dark House*
Duffy	Maureen	*Alchemy*
Elton	Ben	*Past Mortem*
Fowler	Christopher	*The Water Room*
Gee	Maggie	*The Flood*
Golding	Paul	*Senseless*
Goldsmith	Olivia	*Wish Upon a Star*
Granger	Pip	*Trouble in Paradise*
Green	Simon R.	*Nightingale's Lament*

Harrod-Eagles	Cynthia	*Dear Departed*
Hollinghurst	Alan	*The Line of Beauty*
Home	Stewart	*Down & Out in Shoreditch and Hoxton*
Hooper	Mary	*Petals in the Ashes*
Islam	Manzu	*Burrow*
Jackson	Lee	*A Metropolitan Murder*
Kernick	Simon	*The Crime Trade*
La Plante	Lynda	*Above Suspicion*
Levy	Andrea	*Small Island*
Livesey	Margot	*Banishing Verona*
Longworth	Gay	*The Unquiet Dead*
Maitland	Barry	*No Trace*
Miéville	China	*Iron Council*
Morgan	Fidelis	*Fortune's Slave*
Myerson	Julie	*Home*
Naidoo	Beverley	*Web of Lies*
Perry	Anne	*The Shifting Tide*
Rendell	Ruth	*Thirteen Steps Down*
Robins	Madeleine E.	*Petty Treason*
Robotham	Michael	*Suspect*
Sigerson	Davitt	*Faithful*
Silver	Horace	*Judas Pig*
Stephenson	Neal	*The System of the World*
Thomas	Will	*Some Danger Involved*
Thorne	Matt	*Cherry*
Updale	Eleanor	*Montmorency on the Rocks*
Williams	Conrad	*London Revenant*
Wilson	A.N.	*My Name is Legion*
Winspear	Jacqueline	*Birds of a Feather*
Woodward	Gerard	*I'll Go to Bed at Noon*

2005

Billingham	Mark	*Lifeless*
Brookner	Anita	*Leaving Home*
Clark	Clare	*The Great Stink*
Cleave	Chris	*Incendiary*
Davies	David Stuart	*Forests of the Night*
Doherty	Paul C.	*The Cup of Ghosts*
Evans	Diana	*26a*
Fowler	Christopher	*Seventy-Seven Clocks*
Gaiman	Neil	*Anansi Boys*
Gavron	Jeremy	*An Acre of Barren Ground*
Gee	Maggie	*My Cleaner*

George	Elizabeth	*With No One as Witness*
Granger	Pip	*No Peace for the Wicked*
Green	Simon R.	*Hex and the City*
Green	Simon R.	*Paths Not Taken*
Green	Simon R.	*Sharper than a Serpent's Tooth*
Hornby	Nick	*A Long Way Down*
Jackson	Lee	*The Welfare of the Dead*
Kernick	Simon	*A Good Day to Die*
Lackey	Mercedes	*The Wizard of London*
Lansdale	Joe R.	*Flaming London*
Lawrence	David	*Cold Kill*
Lott	Tim	*The Seymour Tapes*
Lovric	M.R.	*The Remedy*
Mantel	Hilary	*Beyond Black*
McEwan	Ian	*Saturday*
McEwen	Helena	*Ghost Girl*
McGowan	Anthony	*Mortal Coil*
Nadel	Barbara	*Last Rights*
Neate	Patrick	*City of Tiny Lights*
Perry	Anne	*Long Spoon Lane*
Robotham	Michael	*Lost*
Ross	Joel	*Double Cross Blind*
Tessaro	Kathleen	*Innocence*
Thomas	Will	*To Kingdom Come*
Thompson	Ronda	*The Dark One*
Updale	Eleanor	*Montmorency and the Assassins*
Winspear	Jacqueline	*Messenger of Truth*

2006

Abani	Christopher	*Becoming Abigail*
Abdullah	Kia	*Life, Love and Assimilation*
Acheampong	Sophia	*Growing Yams in London*
Alderman	Naomi	*Disobedience*
Allan	Clare	*Poppy Shakespeare*
Arnott	Jake	*Johnny Come Home*
Billingham	Mark	*Buried*
Bruen	Ken	*Calibre*
Charles	Paul	*Sweetwater*
Clark	Simon	*London under Midnight*
Colgan	Jenny	*West End Girls*
Evans	J.M.	*London's Gone*
Fowler	Christopher	*Ten Second Staircase*
George	Elizabeth	*What Came Before He Shot Her*

Goodwin	Jo-Ann	*Sweet Gum*
Granger	Ann	*A Rare Interest in Corpses*
Green	Simon R.	*Hell to Pay*
Hale	Jennifer	*The London Connection*
Jackson	Lee	*The Last Pleasure Garden*
Johnson	Rachel	*Notting Hell*
Kray	Roberta	*The Debt*
Maitland	Barry	*Spider Trap*
Malkani	Gautam	*Londonstani*
McGee	James	*Ratcatcher*
Nadel	Barbara	*After the Mourning*
Perry	Anne	*Dark Assassin*
Reeve	Philip	*A Darkling Plain*
Rendell	Ruth	*The Water's Lovely*
Ripley	Mike	*Angel in the House*
Ripley	Mike	*Angel's Share*
Roberts	Ella	*The Run*
Self	Will	*The Book of Dave*
Smith	Carol	*Without Warning*
Starling	Boris	*Visibility*
Thomas	Will	*The Limehouse Text*
Thompson	Ronda	*The Untamed One*
Thompson	Ronda	*The Cursed One*
Waters	Sarah	*The Night Watch*
Williams	Conrad	*The Unblemished*
Winspear	Jacqueline	*Pardonable Lies*

2007

Abaitua	Matthew de	*The Red Men*
Billingham	Mark	*Death Message*
Bruen	Ken	*Ammunition*
Chevalier	Tracy	*Burning Bright*
Cole	Martina	*Faces*
Elton	Ben	*Blind Faith*
Finch	Charles	*A Beautiful Blue Death*
Fowler	Christopher	*White Corridor*
Gardner	John	*No Human Enemy*
Guo	Xiaolu	*A Concise Chinese-English Dictionary for Lovers*
Hornby	Nick	*Slam*
Jackson	Lee	*A Most Dangerous Woman*
Lawrence	David	*Down Into Darkness*
Martin	S.I.	*Jupiter Williams*
McGee	James	*Resurrectionist*

Miéville	China	*Un Lun Dun*
Morrison	Blake	*South of the River*
Odom	Mel	*Exodus*
Phillips	Marie	*Gods Behaving Badly*
Shriver	Lionel	*The Post-Birthday World*
Swift	Graham	*Tomorrow*
Tessaro	Kathleen	*The Flirt*
Thomas	Will	*The Hellfire Conspiracy*
Tremain	Rose	*The Road Home*
Woodward	Gerard	*A Curious Earth*

Index

This index contains references to the primary sources. It allows finding individual treatments of the twenty London novels analysed in the various thematic chapters.

Acknowledgements

The present book on urban mentality in London literature is material proof of several years of patience – a time with multiple attractions and repulsions. It could not have been written without the support of various people and institutions.

My first and foremost thanks go to the supervisor of my thesis, Prof. Dr. Jürgen Kamm, who introduced me to the concept of mentality, encouraged me to freely develop my ideas, and initiated my academic career. I am moreover deeply indebted to Prof. Gerold Sedlmayr for his willingness to act as second supervisor and immerse himself in the rather unromantic literary setting of the postmodern metropolis.

Furthermore, I want to thank Prof. Dr. John McLeod whose course on "Postcolonial London" at the University of Leeds started my fascination with urban fiction ten years ago. In addition, I want to express my gratitude to the Literary London Society and its president Prof. Dr. Brycchan Carey. Since 2007, I have been a regular participant at the yearly Literary London Conference, which has served as an illimitable source of information and forum of discussion for this thesis. In this respect, my tributes also need paying to the *Deutsche Forschungsgemeinschaft* (DFG) and the *Deutscher Akademischer Austauschdienst* (DAAD) for financially supporting several research stays in London.

These trips to the metropolis were even more enhanced by the hospitality of my dear (part-time) Londoners: Simon Bracken and family, Ari Winarto, Nicole Symonds, and Michaela Unterbarnscheidt. Above all, special thanks go to Michaela, who patiently, unrelentingly, and meticulously proofread the manuscript for this book. Any remaining mistakes are entirely my fault. I also wish to thank Katharina Hankov for double-checking the list of London novels. Beyond that, warm thanks go out to my colleagues at the University of Passau, especially to those of the English department. I owe a huge thank you to Dr. Stefan Halft and Dr. Laura Lülsdorf for their endurance in tackling the mutual quirks of a PhD project as well as those of life.

I am very grateful to all my friends for their open ears concerning my academic monologues and accepting my hermit life while writing, but also thankful that they repeatedly bring me back on earth. I want to expressively thank Robert for finding the right words in any situation. Last but not least, I thank my parents for their love and ongoing support.

The book is dedicated to the memory of my grandfather Dr. Helmut Pleßke.